western reports on the
TAIPING

This book is published with the assistance of a grant from the Prescott Clarke Memorial Fund of Monash University

western reports on the

TAIPING

a selection of documents

Prescott Clarke and JS Gregory

The University Press of Hawaii
Honolulu 1982

First published in The United States of America 1982
Printed in Australia for The University Press of Hawaii
Simultaneously published by the Australian National
University Press, Canberra

© M. E. Clarke and J. S. Gregory 1982

ISBN 0–8248–0807–X Cloth
ISBN 0–8248–0809–6 Paper
National Library of Australia

Library of Congress No. 81–68942

In Memory of
PRESCOTT 'PETE' CLARKE
(1935–80)

Scholar and Friend of China

Preface

This documentary collection was put together by myself and Prescott Clarke, who died of cancer in March this year. A native of Boston, a graduate of Harvard's East Asia Centre and subsequently of the School of Oriental and African Studies in London, Prescott Clarke came to Australia in 1967 to teach Chinese history at Monash University in Melbourne. 'Pete', as he was known to his many friends in Australia, had for some years been working on missionary connections with the Taiping, while in 1969 my own study of British policy and attitudes towards this important movement of revolt was published. Since we were in the same city, even if not at the same university, and had both worked on aspects of Western relations with the Taiping it was natural that we should begin, in 1971, to collaborate on a collection to supplement the then just published two volume collection of translations of Taiping documents edited by Franz Michael.

It must be admitted that we began too grandiosely, thinking to put together a two volume collection which would match the Michael volumes physically as well as in other ways. Also, we proved far from perfect collaborators. Apart from some substantial, though academically healthy, differences of view about the nature and significance of the Taiping movement, and therefore to some extent about the best selection of Western documents on it, both of us at times turned away to do other things, and occasionally hinted at abandoning the project. But we never did quite abandon it, because it always seemed worth doing and reflected some long standing concerns of both of us, though more especially of Pete's.

I do not think the shade of Pete Clarke will object to my writing thus about our less than perfect collaboration toward the book he did not live to see fully completed. He was an honest man, with a wry sense of humour and with much courage to the last, courage both of his own convictions and of the more general kind. I write this with great respect for him and for his work, and with great sorrow that it was not given to him to see this collection take final shape.

vii

His contribution to that shape was, of course, substantial. Before his death the selection of documents was, with a few exceptions, agreed upon by us and he had written many of the footnotes and some of the introductory comments. In the last few months of his life, after his return from the May 1979 Nanking conference on the Taiping—which fired him in his last year of life to plan new work on his beloved Taiping—he put together the glossaries as the best way of overcoming the awkward problem of providing both Pinyin and Wade-Giles forms for the sometimes obscure romanisations used by the writers of these documents. After his death an extensive bibliography of Western writing on the Taiping and on Western missionary activity in China down to the end of the Taiping period was found among his papers, and part of this has been used to provide a bibliography to this selection. Thus, apart from the final arrangement and selection and the final version of the introductory comments, the book stands as he helped conceive and form it, and as testimony to his long continuing interest in the study of the Taiping.

Acknowledgments of assistance and encouragement are due to a number of people and institutions. Since this is not something we ever discussed I can only guess who Pete would have wished to include, and ask pardon for any inadvertently omitted. I know he was grateful both to Monash University for granting periods of study leave, during part of which he sought out additional material, and to The Australian National University at which, in 1973, he was a Research Fellow in its Department of Far Eastern History. Both he and I have particular reason to thank the head of that department, Professor Wang Gungwu, for his unfailing interest, support—and patience! We must also thank the Australian Research Grants Committee which, at an early stage in the project, gave financial support which enabled us to acquire xerox and microfilm copies of relevant materials. I also received some aid from the La Trobe University's School of Humanities Research Grant Committee, aid which was particularly helpful in speeding the tedious task of checking final typescript against copies of original documents. We owe thanks to Dr Charles Curwen, of the School of Oriental and African Studies, University of London, for drawing our attention to documents 90 and 91. Mr J. Gershevitch of Sydney advised us about Russian materials, including K. A. Skachkov's Memoirs, although in the final selection none of this was included since no Russian ever got very close to the Taiping. Some French observers did, however, and thanks are due to Dr Anthea Hyslop for making our translations of some of their reports more accurate and readable. I am sure

Pete would have wished to thank the several typists in the Department of History at Monash University who prepared early drafts of the selection, as I myself wish to thank their counterparts, particularly Mrs Louise Bennie, at La Trobe University who patiently worked over those drafts to produce the final typescript. I also wish to thank the staff of the ANU Press for the editing and production of the book.

Finally, it remains to thank the many friends of Pete's who contributed so generously to the memorial fund set up by his colleagues of the History department at Monash University. A grant from the fund has helped make possible the publication of this work.

J. S. Gregory
La Trobe University
November 1980

Table of Contents

General Introduction

The Taiping movement, whether seen as 'rebellion' or 'revolution', has long been recognised as one of the seminal events in modern Chinese history. Probably more than any other single theme in that history before the rise to power of the Chinese Communist Party it has engaged the attention of contemporary historians, and the list of scholarly studies devoted to or substantially concerned with it grows steadily. No one can study modern Chinese history without becoming in some measure engaged with the Taiping.

So important a movement has naturally stimulated varying interpretations of its essential nature and of its significance. Apart from the question whether it was simply another of the rebellions endemic within the dynastic cycle of traditional China, albeit larger than most, or whether it was a genuinely revolutionary movement promising to break that cycle and to recast Chinese society and institutions into a new mould, many other issues about it are debated by serious students of the movement. Should it be seen as a genuinely peasant movement? Did the internal rivalries which so weakened it in its middle years reflect a struggle between conflicting class interests in the movement? Was it essentially a millenarian religious movement throughout its course, or did it develop a coherent political and economic program capable of regenerating China along the 'rational' modernising lines so beloved of many Western scholars? What was the balance of forces and factors that in the end defeated it? Did its defeat seriously delay the emergence of a new, nationally conscious and integrated China capable of standing up independently in the world of the twentieth century? Was it truly 'the beginning of the end of Confucian China', the starting point of the modern Chinese revolution? These are the kinds of questions asked about the movement today. Inevitably the answers given vary widely.

Whatever their answers to such questions, one problem facing all serious students of the Taiping is the paucity, relative to the scale and undoubted significance of the movement, of the primary sources available. Although it may be true, as Jen Yu-wen has written, that compared to the dearth of material available to that eminent scholar when he began his studies of the movement over fifty years ago there is now a multiplicity of sources before the historian, the student of the Taiping is still likely 'to look with envy upon the resources available (to take a roughly comparable example) to the historian of the French Revolution'.[1] Certainly, almost alone among the great popular uprisings of Chinese history, the Taiping did leave a sizeable body of records of their own making, but the historian concerned to study their movement in depth finds many issues and events within it obscure and poorly documented, and he necessarily remains heavily dependent upon what may be called second layer primary material, that is on records produced at the time of the movement but not by those actually in it. Thus, for example, the eight volume collection of Taiping records published in Shanghai in 1952 devoted only 900 of its total 3400 pages to first hand Taiping records, the rest being reports about the movement from official Ch'ing or other sources.[2] The two volume collection of Taiping records edited by Franz Michael and published in 1971 set out to provide as complete a collection of Taiping documents as could then be obtained; to present, as its editor put it, 'the legacy of the Taipings, the basic source material for the study of the Taiping rebellion'.[3] It contains 391 documents in all, covering some 1600 pages in English translation. Although some other 'first layer' Taiping documents can now be added to that collection it does contain, within only two volumes, the great bulk of the available sources of Taiping origin. Short of a Tun-Huang or Dead Sea Scroll type discovery of further material, the historian of the Taiping must continue to rely a great deal more than he might ideally wish to do upon sources coming from outside rather than from within the movement itself.

Such is one justification for the collection of Western reports which follows. Clearly these are not basic records in the way that those in the Michael volumes are. They were written by outsiders who were certainly not cameras, recording dispassionately

1   See Jen Yu-wen, *The Taiping Revolutionary Movement* (Yale, 1973), p. xxi, and C. A. Curwen, *Taiping Rebel: the Deposition of Li Hsiu-cheng* (Cambridge, 1977), p. 13.

2   *T'ai-p'ing T'ien-kuo*, ed. Hsiang Ta *et al.* (Shanghai, 1952) 8 vols., 3405 pp.; reviewed in *Journal of Asian Studies*, vol. XVIII (1957–8), pp. 67–76.

3   F. Michael, *The Taiping Rebellion* (Seattle and London, 1966, 1971), vol. II, p. vii; note also p. ix: 'It has been our aim to make available for the historian an English version of the Taiping documentary legacy.'

whatever they saw. But making due allowance for their prejudices, hopes and preconceptions, many of these Western writers were able to report from a measure of direct observation and experience of a kind that few literate non-Taiping Chinese observers could match. Also they enjoyed a relatively privileged vantage point from which to observe and write accounts which, however limited in certain respects, remain of distinctive value to the historian, asking questions and reporting details of a kind and in a manner which adds much to the Chinese record. A study of these Western reports can, therefore, help significantly towards a fuller understanding of this major movement in modern Chinese history.

Of course not all aspects of Taiping life and history are well represented in the Western sources, any more than they are in the Chinese. The religious and political aspects of the movement received the most attention from Western observers, the former naturally in the many missionary reports, the latter especially in the diplomatic-consular records. But economic and social aspects were also frequently reported on, even if only in passing, and most observers tended to make comments beyond the range of their own predominant interest. Thus, despite the limitations and preoccupations of individual observers, the Western accounts taken over all provide a fairly wide range of significant information, albeit information often heavily larded with comment and judgment. In a sense the documents presented here are as revealing of mid-nineteenth century Western assumptions and hopes about China as they are of the Taiping; certainly they may be read on at least two levels.

In selecting them we have made it our primary aim to reproduce firsthand eye witness reports, based on actual visits to Taiping held areas. There were, however, long periods during the history of the movement—before 1853 and from late 1854 to late 1858 especially—when there was little or no direct contact between Westerners and Taiping. Wishing to put together a collection which would, at least in some measure, provide a summary of Western responses over the whole history of the movement, we have therefore drawn on some secondhand reports during these years—from China coast journals and newspapers, from intelligence reports of British consular officers and from reports by missionaries stationed in the interior—to maintain a degree of continuity. The great bulk of the selection is nevertheless direct reportage, presented chronologically according to the time of the contact rather than according to the date of actual publication, though these were usually closely linked. The

Summary of the Documents provides information about author-
ship and date of writing; details of source and date of publication
are provided at the head of each document.

Westerners of the time wrote a great deal about the Taiping—
quite as much, one suspects, as did the Chinese of the time. This
was the age when the reporting of major events wherever they
occurred was becoming a major industry in the West (the second
Special 'Our Own' Correspondent of *The Times* went to China for
the war of 1856–8), and the printing presses, not least the
missionary presses, poured forth a rising flood of reports,
comment and opinion to inform and instruct their readers about
developments in the world at large. The Taiping movement, as a
major revolt in one of the world's major societies, inevitably
attracted interest and attention, all the more so of course because
of its quasi-Christian ideology. Most of this attention, and the
writing it occasioned, came from people remote from the scene.
But there was also a very substantial body of writing occasioned
by actual observation and experience of the Taiping. Very often
this observation was of a rather false and fleeting kind. But some
Westerners saw a good deal over a fair length of time, and most
who went wrote something about what they saw and came to
think of the movement. In a piecemeal sort of way—in reports to
governments or to missionary society headquarters; in personal
journals and diaries; in letters to friends, or to official superiors,
or to newspapers; in pamphlets and in books—there built up
during the course of the Taiping movement a sizeable body of
Western writing about it which was not merely opinion or
second-third hand reporting. To recapture all or even the greater
part of that writing is hardly possible, certainly not in one
volume, and we cannot pretend to do more than bring together a
part of it. But it is a sizeable part containing, we believe, extracts
from nearly all the major accounts of Western visits to the
Taiping.[4]

We have tried to make the selection represent as wide a range
of types of Western observers as possible. Consular officials and
missionaries are, of course, the commonest, but also represented
are merchants, mercenaries and the rare special traveller,
explorer or geographer. It must be admitted that the selection is
heavily Anglo-Saxon, although one of the longest documents

4 One well known Western account and analysis by an eye witness not represented here is T. T. Meadows' book *The Chinese and their Rebellions* (London,
1856). Since this is so well known to students of the subject and is now
generally available in a reprint version we have represented Meadows by
some of his other writings on the Taiping.

presented (in full) is an account by a French missionary of a visit to Nanking in 1853. The fact of the matter is, however, that most of the Westerners who actually visited Taiping territory were British or American, in the case of the latter nearly always missionaries. The French made some direct contact, represented here in ten or more of the documents, but it may well be that there is more French material which might have been included. However, an examination of the records of the French Ministère des Affaires Étrangères indicated that they contain little or nothing comparable to the kind of reports that the British were producing and printing so abundantly. The British were very much the vanguard of all Western contact with China during these years.

As far as possible we have allowed the documents to speak for themselves, with a minimum of comment and footnoting. Spelling throughout is as in the originals, including of course the romanisation of Chinese names and terms. Certain identification and transliteration into modern Wade-Giles and Pinyin forms has not always been easy, but in most cases the informed reader should have little difficulty. Rather than interrupt the flow of the original document by providing either or both Wade-Giles and Pinyin forms in brackets every time a Chinese name or term occurred it seemed best to concentrate all into separate glossaries. Three maps are included; for more detailed maps the reader is referred to those presented in the standard works of Franz Michael and Jen Yu-wen.[5]

As already indicated this collection was originally conceived as a supplement to the basic Michael volumes of Taiping documents. That still seems a valid basis on which to present it to the serious student of the Taiping movement. Used in conjunction these two documentary collections provide a substantial body of primary material, both Taiping and Western, from which to analyse and assess this movement of major importance in modern Chinese history.

5   See Michael, op. cit., vol. I, appendix I, and Jen Yu-wen, op. cit., pp. 565–74.

Summary of the Documents

1
The Early Years 1850–4
Section 1 The First Reports (1850–3)

1 A report, dated 16 August 1850, on the presence of rebels or robbers in Kwangsi, by Thomas Taylor Meadows, Interpreter in the British Consulate at Canton; from Foreign Office Correspondence PRO, London.

2 A report, dated August 1850, indicating growing alarm in Canton; from the *Chinese Repository*.

3 A report, dated March 1851, on the growing strength of the rebel movement in Kwangsi; from the *Chinese Repository*.

4 A report, dated May 1851, presenting the new 'Emperor' as a scion of the Ming dynasty and a Christian convert of some sort; from the *Overland Friend of China*.

5 A report, dated 13 June 1851, arguing the virtues and serious nature of the rebel movement, by T. T. Meadows; from Foreign Office Correspondence PRO, London.

6 A report, dated July 1851, discussing the origins of the movement and quoting a memorial by the governor of Kwangsi; from the *Chinese Repository*.

7 A report, dated 25 September 1851, indicating 'Strange Doctrines' within the movement, by T. T. Meadows; from Foreign Office Correspondence PRO, London.

8 A report, dated 30 January 1852, on the attempts of Imperial forces to recapture the city of Yungan, and including a Taiping proclamation to the inhabitants; from the *Overland Friend of China*.

9 A report, dated 25 March 1852, on the situation at Yungan, by Harry S. Parkes, Interpreter in the British Consulate at Canton; from Foreign Office Correspondence PRO, London.

10 A report, dated 24 May 1852, on the evacuation of Yungan, by 'our Chinese correspondents' of the *Overland Friend of China*.

11 A letter, dated 6 October 1852, suggesting that in 1846 Hung Hsiu-ch'üan, the Taiping leader, had received instruction in Christianity in Canton, by the American Baptist missionary Rev. I. J. Roberts; from the *Chinese and General Missionary Gleaner*.

12 A letter, dated 6 November 1852, reporting on the progress of the Taiping through Hunan towards the Yangtze river, from the Catholic Lazarist missionary Dr L. G. Delaplace, Vicar Apostolic of Kiangsi, to members of the Councils of the Propagation of the Faith at Lyons and Paris; from *Annals of the Propagation of the Faith*.

13 A report, dated 15 January 1853, of the Taiping capture of Hankow and anticipating their capture of Nanking; from the *North China Herald*.

14 A letter, dated 28 January 1853, reporting the rapid Taiping advance towards Nanking and discussing their religious affiliations, by the Italian Franciscan missionary Mgr Rizzolati, Vicar Apostolic of Hukuang, to members of the Councils of the Propagation of the Faith at Lyons and Paris; from *Annals of the Propagation of the Faith*.

15 A memorandum, dated March 1853, on 'the Origin and Progress of the Kwangse Rebellion', by W. H. Medhurst, Chinese Secretary to the British Superintendency of Trade at Hong Kong; from Foreign Office Correspondence PRO, London.

16 A newspaper report, dated 23 April 1853, on the Taiping capture of Nanking; from the *North China Herald*.

17 A letter, dated 8 June 1853, reporting the fate of Chinese Christians in the capture of Nanking, from the Catholic Bishop of Nanking, Mgr F. X. Maresca, to the central councils of the Propagation of the Faith; from N. Brouillon's *Mémoire sur l'état actuel de la mission du Kiang-nan 1842–55*.

Section 2 The First Contacts (1853)

18 A report, dated 11 May 1853, on the first British official visit to Nanking, in HMS *Hermes*, by Sir George Bonham, Governor of Hong Kong and Superintendent of British Trade in China, to the British Foreign Secretary, Earl Clarendon; from *British Parliamentary Papers*.

19 Reports, dated April–May 1853, on conversations with Taiping chiefs at Chinkiang and Nanking, by T. T. Meadows, Interpreter on the British expedition to Nanking; from *British Parliamentary Papers*.

20 A report, dated 7 May 1853, in praise of the Taiping; from the *North China Herald*.

21   An account, published in 1855, reporting very favourable impressions of the Taiping, formed in 1853, by the commander of HMS *Hermes*, Capt. E. G. Fishbourne; from his book *Impressions of China and the Present Revolution: its Progress and Prospects.*

22   Journal entries, dated June–August 1853, recording unsuccessful missionary efforts to reach the Taiping, by the American Baptist missionary Nathan Wardner; from the archives of the American Baptist Foreign Missionary Society, Valley Forge, USA.

23   An account of a visit to the Taiping at Chinkiang made in mid 1853, by the American Methodist Episcopalian missionary Dr Charles Taylor; from his book *Five Years in China.*

24   A letter, dated 30 June 1853, recounting a visit to Canton by some Taiping in search of Rev. I. J. Roberts, by the American Presbyterian missionary Rev. A. P. Happer; from the *Overland China Mail.*

25   A diary, dated June–July 1853, recounting a journey to Chinkiang in search of British naval deserters, by Mr Williams, mate on HMS *Hermes*; from the *Illustrated London News.*

26   A letter, dated 4 August 1853, passing on reports from Chinese Christian converts in the interior condemning the Taiping, by Mgr Rizzolati to Councils of the Propagation of the Faith at Lyons and Paris; from the *Annals of the Propagation of the Faith.*

27   A letter, dated 26 November 1853, passing on reports by 'a Canton man' on conditions at Nanking, by Rev. W. H. Medhurst of the London Missionary Society; from the *North China Herald.*

28   The conclusion of a report, dated 28 December 1853, predicting the probable success of the Taiping, after an official visit to Nanking in the *Cassini*, by M. Alphonse de Bourboulon, French minister to China, to the French Foreign Minister, Baron Lhuys; from the Archives des Affaires Étrangères, Paris.

29   A letter, dated 6 January 1854, reporting the French visit to Nanking, by the French Jesuit missionary Fr Stanislas Clavelin, Interpreter on the *Cassini*; from N. Brouillon's *Mémoire sur l'état actuel de la mission du Kiang-nan 1842–55.*

Section 3 The First Books (1853–4)

30   An account, published in 1853, of the beginnings of the Taiping revolt and of the early leaders of the movement, by the French writers J. Callery and M. Yvan; from their book *History of the Insurrection in China.*

31 An account, published in 1854, of Hung Hsiu-ch'üan's early years and of the visions which were to become the basis of his claim to be the T'ien Wang, by the Swedish missionary Theodore Hamberg; from his book *The Visions of Hung-siu-tshuen and the Origin of the Kwang-si Insurrection.*

2
The Middle Years 1854–9
Section 1 The West Looks More Closely (1854)

32 A report, dated 14 June 1854, on the visit of a US mission to Nanking in the *Susquehanna*, by Robert M. McLane, US Minister to China, to the Secretary of State, W. L. Marcy; from *U.S. Congressional Papers.*

33 A letter, dated 5 June 1854, giving another account of the *Susquehanna* visit, by the American Presbyterian missionary Rev. M. S. Culbertson; from *Home and Foreign Record.*

34 A letter, dated 4 July 1854, reporting certain conclusions on Taiping political and religious principles subsequent to the *Susquehanna* visit, by the American missionary Rev. E. C. Bridgman; from the *North China Herald.*

35 A report, dated 4 July 1854, offering various general conclusions on the Taiping after the second official British expedition to Nanking, in HMS *Rattler* and HMS *Styx*, by the consular official W. H. Medhurst and Lewin Bowring, to Sir John Bowring, Governor of Hong Kong and Superintendent of British Trade in China; from Foreign Office Correspondence PRO, London.

36 A later account of the *Rattler–Styx* expedition by Lewin Bowring; from his book *Eastern Experiences.*

Section 2 Loss of Contact (1855–8)

37 A letter, dated 19 April 1855, reporting on a journey up the Yangtze, by the French Jesuit missionary Fr S. Clavelin, to M. Edan, French consul at Shanghai; from *Annals of the Propagation of the Faith.*

38 A letter, dated 8 October 1855, reporting critically on the Taiping and on the presence of some foreigners among them, by the French missionary Mgr E. Danicourt, Vicar Apostolic to Chekiang and Kiangsi, to his brother; from the book *Vie de Mgr. Danicourt.*

39 An intelligence report, dated 12 April 1856, on the chronic state of the struggle, by T. F. Wade, Chinese Secretary at Hong Kong; from Foreign Office Correspondence PRO, London.

40 A letter, dated 4 November 1856, reporting a meeting with 'a Nanking man recently escaped', by H. N. Lay, Inspector in the Chinese Customs Service at Shanghai, to Sir John Bowring; from the Bowring Papers in the John Rylands Library, Manchester.

41 A narrative, published in January 1857, describing serious internal dissensions among the Taiping during 1856, by 'two Europeans who for several months have been living at Nanking'; from the *Overland Friend of China*.

42 A letter, dated 17 February 1857, reporting on the parlous state of the interior in both Taiping and Imperial held areas, by Mgr Danicourt, Vicar Apostolic of Kiangsi, to the Procurator General of the Lazarists in Paris; from *Annals of the Propagation of the Faith*.

43 A letter, dated 9 October 1857, reporting on the Taiping as seen from Foochow, by the American Episcopalian missionary Rev. R. S. McLay ('M.S.R.'); from the *Overland Register and Prices Current*.

44 An intelligence report, dated 29 November 1857, reviewing the political and military situation within China, by T. F. Wade, Chinese Secretary at Hong Kong; from Foreign Office Correspondence PRO, London.

Section 3 Contact Renewed (1858–9)

45 A report, dated 5 January 1859, reviewing the Taiping as observed during the British Expedition to Hankow, November–December 1858, by Lord Elgin, British High Commissioner and Plenipotentiary in China; from *British Parliamentary Papers*.

46 An account, privately printed in January 1859, of the British visit to Nanking during the Elgin expedition, by T. F. Wade; from Foreign Office Correspondence PRO, London.

47 A report, dated January 1859, giving some further general impressions of the Taiping formed during the Elgin expedition, by Rev. A. Wylie of the London Missionary Society; from Foreign Office Correspondence PRO, London.

48 A report, probably January 1859, mainly on the religious condition of the Taiping, also by Rev. A. Wylie of the London Missionary Society; from the *Missionary Magazine and Chronicle*.

3
The Later Years 1860–4
Section 1 The Missionaries Make Close Contact (1860–1)

49 A letter, dated 29 June 1860, reporting on a visit to the recently captured Soochow, by the American Baptist missionary Rev. J. L. Holmes; from the missionary journal *The Commission*.

50 A letter, dated 16 July 1860, reporting a visit to Soochow by five missionaries, including an interview with the Kan Wang, by Rev. Griffith John of the London Missionary Society; from the *Missionary Magazine and Chronicle*.

51 A letter, dated 3 September 1860, reporting a visit to Soochow by six missionaries and their interview with the Kan Wang, by Rev. J. S. Burdon of the Church Missionary Society; from the *Church Missionary Intelligencer*.

52 A report, dated 11 August 1860, on questions put to the Kan Wang and his answers, by Rev. Joseph Edkins of the London Missionary Society; from the *North China Herald*.

53 A letter, published 1 September 1860, reporting unfavourable impressions after a visit to Nanking, by Rev. J. L. Holmes; from the *North China Herald*.

54 A letter, dated 3 September 1860, reporting the Taiping advance on Shanghai and their seizure of the Catholic mission at Zikawei, by Fr M. Lemaitre SJ, to the Directors of the Work of Propagation; from *Annals of the Propagation of the Faith*.

55 A letter, dated 9 October 1860, reporting a meeting with the Chung Wang, by Rev. I. J. Roberts; from the *Overland China Mail*.

56 A letter, dated 13 November 1860, reporting an audience with the T'ien Wang, by Rev. I. J. Roberts; from the *Overland China Mail*.

57 A letter, dated 9 February 1861, reporting a meeting with the Kan Wang in Nanking and some conclusions on the prospects of the Taiping and of missionary work among them, by Rev. W. Muirhead of the London Missionary Society; from the *Missionary Magazine and Chronicle*.

58 A letter, dated 24 February 1861, answering certain questions on the Taiping system, by Rev. I. J. Roberts; from the *North China Herald*.

59 A pamphlet, published February 1861, presenting some general conclusions after a month in Taiping territory, by Rev. Griffith John of the London Missionary Society; from *The Chinese Rebellion*.

Section 2 The Missionaries Withdraw (1861-2)

60 A letter, undated but written January–February 1861, describing Nanking as a ruin and the T'ien Wang as an impostor, by the English Methodist missionary Rev. W. N. Hall; from the *Missionary Herald*.

61 A narrative of a visit made early in 1861 to Nanking, Soochow and the countryside between, by Rev. Joseph Edkins of the London Missionary Society; from his wife's book *Chinese Scenes and People*.

62 Letters, dated 9 and 16 March 1861, reporting bleak conditions and poor missionary prospects among the Taiping, by the American Episcopalian missionary, Rev. S. Schereschewsky; from the journal *Spirit of Missions*.

63 A letter, dated 22 April 1861, reporting his disappointment after a further visit to Nanking, by Rev. Griffith John; from the archives of the London Missionary Society.

64 A letter, dated 18 May 1861, reporting unfavourable impressions after a three-week journey up the Yangtze, by Rev. John Hobson of the Church Missionary Society; from the archives of the Church Missionary Society, London.

65 A letter, dated 30 May 1861, reporting on visits to Hangchow, Nanking and other Taiping held areas, by the American Methodist missionary Rev. Young J. Allen; from the book *Young J. Allen; "The Man who seeded China"*.

66 A letter, dated 13 June 1861, reporting favourable impressions after a meeting with the Chung Wang at Soochow, by Rev. R. Dawson of the London Missionary Society; from the archives of the London Missionary Society.

67 A letter, dated 27 June 1861, reporting unfavourably after a visit to Chinkiang and Nanking, by the American Presbyterian missionary Dr D. B. McCartee; from the missionary journal *Home and Foreign Record*.

68 A journal, dated December 1861, reporting unfavourable impressions after a visit to Nanking, by the English Methodist missionary Rev. Josiah Cox; from *Wesleyan Missionary Notices*.

69 A letter, dated 22 January 1862, reporting his withdrawal, after fifteen months residence in Nanking, by the American Baptist Rev. I. J. Roberts; from the *North China Herald*.

Section 3 Other Close Encounters (1861–2)

70   A report of impressions of Nanking and of a meeting, held on 1 March 1861, with Taiping chiefs there, by H. S. Parkes, Interpreter for Admiral Sir James Hope's expedition up the Yangtze; from *British Parliamentary Papers*.

71   An account of visits to Nanking, Wuhu and Anking in March 1861, by Capt. T. W. Blakiston of the British army, who accompanied Hope to Hankow and went on to explore the Yangtze; from his book *Five Months on the Yang-tze*.

72   A letter, dated 8 March 1861, reporting impressions of Nanking and of trade prospects there, by Alexander Michie, one of a deputation representing the Shanghai Chamber of Commerce, who went in the Hope expedition; from *British Parliamentary Papers*.

73   An account of a short stay in Nanking during March 1861 by Lt Col. G. J. Wolseley of the British army, who went in the Hope expedition; from his book *Narrative of the War with China in 1860*.

74   A report of a meeting, with the Ying Wang, held on 22 March 1861 near Hankow, and of impressions of a Taiping army on the march, by H. S. Parkes; from *British Parliamentary Papers*.

75   A report, dated 28 March 1861, of a journey from Shanghai to Nanking via Soochow, giving impressions of the state of the countryside between, by the British consular official R. J. Forrest; from *British Parliamentary Papers*.

76   Diary extracts, dated April 1861, reporting impressions of Nanking and Wuhu and of trading prospects in Taiping territory, by the American merchant John Heard; from the archives of Augustus Heard & Co., Boston.

77   A report, dated 2 May 1861, indicating no trade prospects at Nanking, by R. J. Forrest; from *British Parliamentary Papers*.

78   An account, first published 29 June 1861, of conditions in and near Nanking, and of visits to the Kan Wang and to the brother of the Chung Wang, by R. J. Forrest; from T. W. Blakiston's *Five Months on the Yang-tze* and the *North China Herald*.

79   A journal, dated March–June 1862, of travels through the silk districts between Ningpo and Shanghai and giving some impressions of trading activities and of the countryside, by the unidentified merchant 'A.Z.'; from the pamphlet by W. H. Sykes, *The Taiping Rebellion in China*.

Section 4 The Ningpo Encounter (1861–2)

80 A memorandum of interviews, held May–June 1861, with leaders of Taiping forces approaching Ningpo, by the British consular official C. Alabaster; from *British Parliamentary Papers*.

81 A report, written December 1861, of contact with Taiping leaders preparing to attack Ningpo, by the British consular official A. R. Hewlett; from *British Parliamentary Papers*.

82 A report, dated 31 December 1861, giving his first impressions of the Taiping occupation of Ningpo, by the British Consul there, F. W. Harvey; from *British Parliamentary Papers*.

83 A letter, dated 15 January 1862, describing the capture of Ningpo and giving his judgment on the Taiping, by Rev. W. H. Russell of the Church Missionary Society; from the archives of the Church Missionary Society, London.

84 Reports, dated November 1861 to April 1862, on the Taiping capture of Ningpo and its effect on trade there, by Capt. F. S. Green, agent for Jardine, Matheson & Co.; from the archives of Jardine Matheson & Co., Cambridge.

85 Journal entries, dated January 1862, describing the Taiping occupation in and near Ningpo by the English Methodist missionary Rev. Josiah Cox; from *Wesleyan Missionary Notices*.

86 A report, dated 20 March 1862, giving his judgment on the Taiping after three months of occupation, by the British Consul F. W. Harvey; from *British Parliamentary Papers*.

Section 5 The Mercenary Experience (1861–4)

87 A report, dated 20 April 1861, on the capture of twenty-six British mercenaries on the Taiping side, and their condition, by the British consular official, R. J. Forrest; from *British Parliamentary Papers*.

88 Letters, dated August–December 1862, describing operations with Gordon's force against the Taiping near Shanghai, by Lt T. Lyster; from the book *With Gordon in China*.

89 A letter, written October 1863, justifying his desertion to the Taiping and comparing them favourably to the Imperialists, sent to Gordon by the former commander of the Ever Victorious Army, the American adventurer, H. A. Burgevine; from the Gordon Papers, London.

90 Draft of a letter, written 4 November 1863, asserting loyalty to the Taiping cause and praising the Mo Wang, by an officer in the Anglo-American-Taiping force at Soochow, George Smith; in the Taiping Museum, Nanking.

91 A diary, kept October–November 1863, indicating conditions during the Taiping defence of Soochow, by George Smith; in the Taiping Museum, Nanking.

92 A statement, published 12 November 1864, recounting eight months' service with the Taiping during 1864, by Patrick Nellis; from Foreign Office Correspondence PRO, London.

93 Extracts from his book, published 1866, illustrating his experience and very favourable impressions of the Taiping under the Chung Wang, by A. F. Lindley; from his book *Ti-Ping Tien-Kwoh*.

5
The Aftermath

94 A letter, written February 1865, reporting the capture, by retreating Taiping forces, of Changchou, near Amoy in Fukien, by the English Presbyterian missionary Rev. Carstairs Douglas; from the *English Presbyterian Messenger*.

95 A letter, dated 22 May 1866, reporting on a visit to Soochow and other nearby cities and the extent of their recovery, by Rev. W. Muirhead of the London Missionary Society; from archives of the London Missionary Society.

96 Some comments, published December 1867, criticising existing Western ideas about and judgments on the Taiping, by the British consular official, R. J. Forrest; from his article in the *Journal of the North China Branch of the Royal Asiatic Society*.

97 Letters, dated July–August 1871, describing the condition of former Taiping territory by the German geographer, Baron Richtofen; from his *Letters 1870–72*.

Note on the Sources

The richest repository of Western reports on the Taiping is in the
Public Record Office, London, mainly the Foreign Office General
Correspondence (China) Series, listed as FO 17. During the
period of the Taiping a number of printed parliamentary papers
relating to the movement and British policy towards it were
produced from these records. These are now conveniently
brought together in vols. 32–3 of the Area Studies Series (China)
of the Irish University Press reprint of British Parliamentary
Papers (*BPP*). The papers drawn on for this selection, and
referred to in the text only by year and number are:

1852–3	C 1667	Papers Respecting the Civil War in China.
1859	C 2571	Correspondence Relative to the Earl of Elgin's Special Mission to China and Japan 1857–9.
1861	C 2840	Correspondence Respecting the Opening of the Yangtzekiang River to Foreign Trade.
1862	C 2976	Papers Relating to the Rebellion in China and Trade in the Yangtze Keang River.
1862	C 2992	Further Papers Relating to the Rebellion in China.

Apart from British consular officials the other main Western
group to report at length on the Taiping were the missionaries.
Their accounts are of course scattered in a wide range of
archives, but fortunately many of their reports also were repro-
duced in printed form in various missionary publications. These
publications have been drawn on heavily in the selection below,
as indicated in the source given with each document. In addition
material from the following missionary archives has been used.
Acknowledgment is made to these societies for providing access
to their manuscript material and permission to reprint from it.

American Baptist Foreign Missionary Society, Valley Forge,
Pennsylvania, USA.

Church Missionary Society (CMS), Waterloo Road, London, UK.
London Missionary Society (LMS), in the library of the School of
Oriental and African Studies, London, UK.

Other manuscript collections which have been drawn on are:

Bowring Papers, John Rylands Library, Manchester, UK.
Gordon Papers, British Library, London, UK.
Heard Collection, Baker Library, Harvard University Graduate
School of Business Administration, Boston, USA.
Jardine Matheson Collection, in the University Library,
Cambridge, UK.
Ministère des Affaires Étrangères, Quai d'Orsay, Paris

A further major source of Western reports and opinion on the
Taiping is the *North China Herald* (*NCH*). An extensive list of
material relative to the Taiping published in this paper is to be
found in H. Cordier's *Bibliotheca Sinica* (Paris 1905–6), vol. I, pp.
654–62. Jen Yu-wen's *The Taiping Revolutionary Movement* (New
Haven and London: Yale University Press, 1973), pp. 592–5 also
contains a list.

1
The Early Years 1850–4

The Taiping formally declared their challenge to the ruling Ch'ing dynasty of China in January 1851, when their founder Hung Hsiu-ch'üan proclaimed his new dynasty, the Taiping Tienkuo, or Heavenly Kingdom of Great Peace. Already a very troublesome movement for the provincial officials of Kwangsi and Kwangtung, their challenge to the Ch'ing became formidable when, in the middle months of 1852, they exploded northward from their original, relatively remote base in southern China into the central Yangtze basin, capturing Nanking, China's 'southern capital' and the second city of the empire, in March 1853. Nanking was re-named T'ien-ching or 'heavenly capital', and became the centre of the new Taiping base area in the lower Yangtze region. The Taipings at this stage advanced only a little further down the Yangtze to capture Chinkiang, at the junction of the river with the Grand Canal, but did not immediately push on to the coast. A number of other sizeable cities above Nanking along the Yangtze river remained in Taiping hands, so that by mid 1853 what had been a serious but contained rebellious movement in the rural hinterland of southern China now straddled the main waterways and the rich heartland of central China. The ruling dynasty remained in control of most of the country still, but there was now a feasible alternative government. Throughout 1853 the political future of China seemed very uncertain.

For most of these early years of growing Taiping challenge Westerners in China could only observe developments from a distance. Awareness of the presence of some kind of serious rebellious movement in south China came fairly early; certain knowledge of its development, character and program much more slowly. Not until April 1853 was the first direct contact made, briefly and warily, when a British party under the leadership of the then Governor of Hong Kong and Superintendent of British trade in China, Sir George Bonham, sailed to Nanking. No other substantial contact was made that year until, in December, a French party under its minister to China, Alphonse de Bour-boulon, also visited Nanking. The French, like the British, left

1

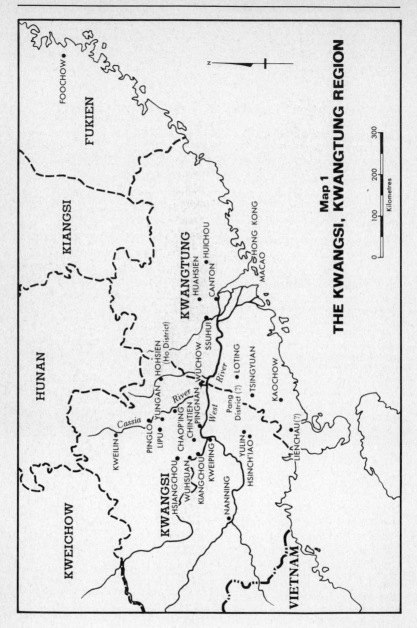

Map 1
THE KWANGSI, KWANGTUNG REGION

2

Nanking unsure of the long term prospects of the Taiping movement, but were strongly impressed by its evident zeal, power and successes. By the end of 1853 it seemed that the West would soon have to somehow come to terms with a new power within China.

Section 1 The First Reports (1850–3)

In April 1849 the British consul at Canton, Dr John Bowring, who was subsequently to be knighted and to succeed (1854–9) to Bonham's posts at Hong Kong, forwarded a translation of a memorial by the Governor General of the Kwangtung-Kwangsi provinces reporting to the Emperor on the troubles in the region. Bowring commented in his covering despatch to Bonham that 'as far as our imperfect sources of information throw light on the matter I am disposed to believe that the position of the insurgents is far more menacing to the public tranquillity than would appear from these official statements'.[1] Future events were, of course, abundantly to confirm Bowring's impression.

For some time not much more appears to have been learnt by Westerners. Bowring's own source of information was the brilliant young interpreter in the Canton consulate, Thomas Taylor Meadows, a keen student of Chinese government and a most enterprising intelligence officer. In August 1850 Meadows began a series of reports to his superior at Canton, who sent them on to Hong Kong where, in turn, Bonham sent copies on to the Foreign Office in London. Meadows' reports were usually of about five hundred words, occasionally much longer, written every few weeks but sometimes more frequently, as news and rumours poured in to Canton to be sieved through in the consulate. About fifty in all were written before Meadows moved, at the beginning of 1852, to become interpreter at the Shanghai consulate. From there he was later to make more direct contact with the Taiping than was ever possible for him at Canton. His successor at Canton, the twenty-two year old Harry S. Parkes, continued the series, though rather less frequently, and occasionally the Chinese secretary to the Superintendency at Hong Kong, W. H. Medhurst (Jr) also prepared summary reports. From a very early stage therefore British officials stationed in South China endeavoured to keep themselves informed about the movement they were to come to know as the Taiping (see Docs. 1, 5, 7, 9, 15).

In addition to British consular officials some other Westerners showed an early interest in the movement. There were fairly

1 FO 228/100, no. 88, Bowring to Bonham, 20 April 1849.

frequent references to developments—or alleged developments—in the Hong Kong published *Friend of China*, which was to be the most consistently sympathetic to the Taiping cause among the English language China coast newspapers (Docs. 4, 8, 10) and in the scholarly *Chinese Repository*, then in its last years of publication from Canton under the editorship of the American missionary S. Wells Williams (Docs. 2, 3, 6). As the Taiping moved northward the Shanghai published *North China Herald* also became interested, and was to become thereafter a major repository of Western reports and opinion on the movement (Docs. 13, 16).

As reports of the peculiar religious character of the Taiping movement also came in missionaries, both Catholic and Protestant, naturally sought information, and speculated about its origin. Roman Catholic missionaries stationed in the interior of some of the central China provinces were the only Westerners in any kind of a position to report at all closely upon the Taiping advance northward and to provide, through their converts, some account of the capture of Nanking (see Docs. 11, 12, 14, 17).

At this stage no Westerners, not even the Catholic missionaries in the interior, could provide eye witness accounts of the movement. As these early reports make abundantly plain, reliable information was difficult to sort out from the very mixed sources available—Chinese official reports printed in the Peking gazette; the verbal reports of Chinese travellers from the interior and of a few Chinese Christians; 'the common newsman', and the rumours circulating in the streets of Canton. Some Westerners were disposed from the start to dismiss the Taiping as just another bandit movement, perhaps larger and potentially more damaging to trade than most, but lacking in any real political organisation or program. Others, notably Meadows, quickly saw it as a serious challenge to the ruling dynasty and began to pin their hopes, whether for the political or the religious transformation of China, upon it. Not before the early months of 1853 were Westerners to gain anything like an informed picture of the movement—and it was to remain always a picture marred by uncertainties and distortions.

1
A Report by T T Meadows
FO 17/169, no. 85, enc. in Bonham to Palmerston, 23 August 1850

REPORT FOR HER MAJESTY'S CONSUL

The rebels or robbers who have openly defied the authorities of Kwangse during the last twelve months have recently been making considerable advances. During the time mentioned they have killed one Civilian—the Chief Magistrate of the Pang district—and about 20 military officers of different ranks, a Major General being among the number. Within the last few days certain intelligence has reached Canton of their having taken the chief city of the Ho district, the Chief Magistrate committing suicide on their making good an entrance. The Ho district borders on the North West of Kwangtung, and the chief city is situated on a navigable branch of the Canton River, about four days journey off. A well confirmed Report states that advanced parties of the Rebels have penetrated into Kwangtung as far as Sze Hwuy district, within 100 miles of this city, which is said to contain many of their agents; but no one seems as yet to apprehend their appearing openly here in arms. The family of a member of the former Cohong, known as Hing-tai, which had retired from business to the west of the Province, has arrived here during the past week, and many others have been obliged to fly in the same way before the rebels.

The leader of the latter is named Li-ting-pang. He has assumed the title of Tseang-keuen, that of the highest Tartar Generals, and carries banners with the inscription 'Commissioned by Heaven to exterminate the Tsing (the present) and re-establish the Ming (the former) dynasty.' The aggregate number of the different bodies under him are said to comprise about 50,000 men.

About three weeks ago it was rumoured that Chin—the Governor of Kwangse—had committed suicide in despair on the rebels cutting off his retreat when heading an expedition against them, but this still wants confirmation.

The Imperial Commissioner, Seu, has been degraded four steps, but allowed to retain his post. One reporter states this is in consequence of the steps lately taken by H.M.'s Plenipotentiary at Shanghai and at the mouth of the Peiho, another that the punishment has been awarded to him in his capacity of Governor General of the two Kwang, on account of the success of the rebels in Kwangse....

(Signed) Thos. Taylor Meadows
Interpreter
A true copy
A R Johnston

2
A Report from the Chinese Repository
Chinese Repository, vol. XIX, p. 462[2]

Disturbances in Kwangsi have lately risen to such a height, and the insurgents have become so numerous and so well organised as seriously to alarm the authorities of Canton. The governor-general is the only one of the rulers here who can officially notice them, and it is reported that he is not at all inclined to proceed to the scene of trouble, and the troops under his command are still more unwilling to leave their garrisons and face their refractory countrymen. What particular grievances have aroused the people of Kwangsi to take up arms, we can not clearly ascertain, nor who are their leaders, though we have little doubt that more are induced to join the original movers from hope of plunder or expectation of bettering their position, than from any well concerted plan of asserting acknowledged rights. Rumor states that a body of fifty thousand has laid siege to the large town of Wu-chau fu on the borders of this province, and put an embargo on all trade on the West river on which it is situated. It shows how little sympathy exists between the various parts of this large empire, and how little information transpires of what is going on elsewhere in it, when we state that one of the most tangible consequences in Canton of a sedition involving the peace of a neighbouring province containing nearly ten millions of people, is the rise in price of cassia of six or eight dollars per pecul, and the collection of a large fleet of boats, whose crews are afraid to proceed westward.

3
A Report from the Chinese Repository
Chinese Repository, vol. XX, p. 165

The insurgents in Kwangsi are evidently gaining serious advantages over the imperialists, and the reports of battles fought, towns taken, villagers slaughtered, and armies routed, come so frequently to the provincial city, that one's curiosity is greatly excited to learn something more definite. In China, rumor not only so greatly exaggerates as to make it difficult to distinguish between the truth and its appendages, but so often manufactures the whole story itself, that those at a distance are totally unable to get at the facts. The imperial commissioner Li and his coadjutor

2 For a description of this publication see E. L. Malcolm 'The *Chinese Repository* and Western Literature on China 1800 to 1850' in *Modern Asian Studies*, 8.2, April 1973.

Chau Tien-tsioh have been obliged to retire from the country south of the West River, leaving the departments of Sinchau, Yuhlin and Nanning in possession of the enemy; the contiguous departments of Kauchau and Lienchau in Kwangtung have also been attacked. Another report mentions that the district towns of Ho and Kaikien, lying coterminous in the two provinces east of Pingloh fu have been ravaged, and thirteen officers of government have lost their lives. Demonstrations are making [sic] by the insurgents to proceed up the Cassia River to Kweilin, and if the provincial capital falls into their hands, their position to control and collect the resources of the whole province will present a formidable obstacle to the imperialists. H.E. Gov.-gen. Su has been ordered by his master to proceed to the scene of action, and the fuyuen Yeh is soon to return to Canton from Tsingyuen where the 'thieves' are reported to be exterminated—most of them having probably dispersed to join their luckier comrades in Kwangsi.

4

A Report from the *Overland Friend of China*
Overland Friend of China, 23 May 1851[3]

The linguists and others in Canton still speak of the rebels as mere robbers, whose sole object is plunder; that they are seriously frightened, however, there is no denying, and we hear that measures have been taken for barricading the river in the San-shwui district, so that the City of Rams may not be reached by that route. In some of the daily papers statements are given of the amounts of money ordered to be sent on to the commissioners, which are recorded as exceeding a hundred thousand taels, and the great merchants have been required to make up a further sum of five lacs of dollars without a moment's delay. A report has got into circulation that the new Emperor, a scion of the Ming dynasty, is a Roman Catholic, and that he is destroying idols and temples with all the fury of a zealot—Others speak of him as a

3 For details on this and other China coast newspapers, such as the *China Mail* and the *North China Herald*, see F. H. King and P. Clarke *A Research Guide to China Coast Newspapers 1822–1911* (Harvard, 1965). The 'overland' editions of such papers were normally published monthly, to coincide with the departure of the mail for England, and contained the main news items from the local editions.

Shang-te[4] man, (the name generally given to converts of protestant missionaries) but that is more unlikely to be true than the other report, which, in connection with past events, has some possibility of truth in it; by those, however, who are carefully watching the turn affairs are about to take, the report of the new Emperor's profession of Christianity, (we may not call him an usurper, for if he succeeds he has but recovered his own again) is only got up by the Ta'tsing adherents, for the purpose of creating disaffection towards him—it is also rendered improbable by the assumption of the purely heathen designation Tien-teh[5] (heaven's virtue).

5
A Report by T T Meadows
FO 17/178, no. 72, enc. in Bonham to Palmerston, 21 June 1851

REPORT ON THE INSURRECTION IN THE TWO KWANG

... They levy contributions according to established rules, and pay for their supplies where the contributions in kind are not sufficient; they are at some care not to make themselves obnoxious to the lower classes, and even occasionally share with the poor what they take from the rich; their object is to go on in this manner gradually increasing their funds and recruiting their numbers from the disaffected until they deem themselves sufficiently numerous for permanent occupation of the cities they take; they never hesitate to engage (and almost always signally

4   *Shang-ti*—this was the term that the Taipings used to render 'God' in Chinese. There was considerable argument among Protestant missionaries in China as to the proper term to employ. Some urged the use of the generic *Shang-ti*; others, including most of the American missionaries, wished to use the more neutral *Shen* or spirit.

5   T'ien-te, or T'ien-te Wang. There was confusion concerning the leadership of the Taiping movement and the titles which the leaders held in these early reports. Hung Hsiu-ch'üan was often referred to as T'ai-p'ing Wang rather than by his correct title of T'ien Wang. Several of the early reports refer to T'ien-te as the leader of the movement, or as one of the more powerful figures. The question as to who he actually was has never been wholly clarified, and there have been several theories put forward: a) that he was Hung Ta-chuan, a follower of the Taipings who was captured in 1852 and confessed to his captors that he had borne the title and had been one of the leaders; b) Chu Chiu-t'ao, a leading figure in the Triad secret society; c) Chiao Liang, another Triad figure from Hunan; d) that it was a reign title which different people held at different times, including Feng Yün-shan, the major organiser of the God Worshipper's Society in Kwangsi who was later made Southern King (Nan Wang). Feng died from wounds in June 1852. See Teng Ssu-yu, *New Light on the History of the Taiping Rebellion* (New York, 1966), pp. 20–4.

defeat) any bodies of the Imperialists that interfere seriously with the prosecution of these immediate objects, but for the present they do not seek to fight; lastly, while they give no quarter to volunteers or to mandarins that go out of the strict line of their duty to act against them, they are far from sanguinary in their treatment of regulars who fall into their hands while merely obeying orders.

I conceive that men who seem to have on the whole consistently kept in view these objects and rules for a whole year, and whose aggregate numbers are never given at *less* than 20,000 cannot, without plain perversion of language, be termed 'robbers' ... I deem it advisable to make these remarks because the periodicals of Canton and Hong Kong, with the exception of one of the latter which has prematurely rushed into extreme opposite views, appear to concur in representing the present disturbances as one might regard the proceedings of a few bands of burglars and robbers in the Scottish Highlands. That the Imperial Government considers the affair nothing less than what we would call a rebellion, and a very serious rebellion, is made sufficiently plain by the measures it is taking. . . .

Thos. Taylor Meadows
Interpreter
A True Copy
A R Johnston

6
A Report from the *Chinese Repository*
Chinese Repository, vol. XX, pp. 497–500

. . . We have made many inquiries as to the probable origin of the sedition, and where the chief strength of the insurgents lies, but have received little satisfaction in the answers. Some of the Chinese have told us that the insurgents are composed of the riff-raff of the Two Kwang, aided by discontented persons near the frontiers of Cochinchina and Laos; while others have the impression that they are banded together in a league like the old Pih-lien kiau, or White-lotus sect, whose intrigues and struggles gave so much trouble to Kienlung. Both these suppositions may be partly true, but they are hardly sufficient to account for the support the outlaws have received from the inhabitants of the province. There is a very general impression in Canton and its vicinity, that they are somehow connected with foreigners and with Christianity, and the term *Shanti hwui* is often applied to them. This rumor is so prevalent that it can hardly be referred altogether (as some are inclined to do) to a ruse on the part of the authorities at Canton to increase a dread of the insurgents among the people hereabouts, by associating them with foreigners, but it seems to have come from Kwangsi. Some have asserted that the self-styled emperor Tienteh was baptised at Macao some years ago, but to this we attach little credit; yet the people here generally believe that he and his party worship none of the gods of the country, nor pay the least reverence to their images, but clear their temples of all idols, and appropriate the buildings to other use; they agree too in saying that he keeps a seventh day of rest, but are ignorant of any ceremonies peculiar to it. The following memorial of Chau Tientsioh, dated in May last, gives some countenance to the supposition of a league against the authorities, and the expressions in it respecting the 'books of Jesus' may be the principal source of the rumor in question elsewhere, for we have seen no such remark in any other document emanating from officials on the spot. The paper furnishes, too, the only attempt we have seen to explain the origin of the rising and is on that account worthy of perusal:

Chau Tientsioh, specially appointed to superintend the military operations in Kwangsi, with the powers of governor-general, kneels and memorializes, showing how he has degraded a prefect, district-magistrates, justices, and secretaries who have sided with or overlooked the seditious acts in their jurisdiction, requesting the imperial will upon these degradations and arrests, that strict severity may be visited on them, and humbly begging His Majesty to bestow his glance upon it.

I was staying at the time in Wu-siuen, the better to repress the seditious bands, when Wang Tsohsin, a graduate of Wusiuen then living in Kweiping district, came to my encampment and informed me of the compact formerly sworn to, and the club formed by Fung Yun-shan with Tsang Yuhchin and Lu Luh: 'It was in 1849, when this Wang seized Fung and Lu, and some books belonging to the club, and handed them all over to the head of the township of Kiang-kau, who forwarded them to the Kweiping hien for examination. Lu Luh died in confinement, but Tsang Yuhchin heavily bribed the justice of the township, so that he with the gentry of the place falsely represented the case to the district-magistrate, and his underlings surreptitiously set Fung at liberty. Fung then went to the authorities of the district and department, and falsely accused the graduate Wang of having wrongfully charged him.' On hearing this, I instantly sent a special order to bring all the papers connected with this case, that I might closely examine them.

It appears that Fung is from the district of Hwa[6] in Kwangtung, and came to Kweiping hien in Kwangsi in 1844; he lived in Lu Luh's house teaching youth in 1845, and during the next two years in the house of Tsang Yuhchin in the same occupation. In Dec. 1847, this graduate Wang, aided by the constables and headmen arrested Fung on the 28th of December, because that he and Tsang had been propagating magical arts to seduce the people, and forming bands and cabals, to destroy altars and images in the temples, and handed him over to the head elder Tsang Tsukwang; but his accomplices, Tsang Asun and others, rescued him by force. Wang and his friends then informed the justice of Kiangkau of all these particulars, and gave him the documents of the league; but Fung, on his part, also accused Wang of planning to extort money under false pretenses and implicate him in crime, and requested the magistrate to examine him. He also, at the same time, brought the affair to the notice of Wang Lieh, the district magistrate, who on his part judged that the graduate was making a great bluster out of nothing in his paper, and accordingly replied 'When the parties are brought up, I will examine and judge the case equitably.' The township justice, named Wang Ki, thereupon brought Fung and Lu Luh to the Kweiping hien's office, where they were both questioned and detained in the lockup, in which place Lu sickened and died. Wang Lieh at this time vacated his office, and Tsang Chu became acting *chihien*. Fung now once more petitioned Ku Yuen-kai, the prefect of Sinchau, stating the false accusations and wiles of Wang Sintsoh; a reply was given, 'Let the parties be brought up for examination.' But the district-magistrate had already examined Fung, and acquitted him of being a seditious person and of all illegality, and sent him back to his own place in Hwa hien in Kwangtung, with request that he might be detained there. These facts are in the records of the case.

On examining the whole matter, it seemed to me that these circumstances did not altogether agree with the paper given in by the graduate Wang. I examined Ku, the prefect, and Wang Lieh who had before been the district magistrate, to learn why they had not extirpated seditious, and sup-

6 A *hsien* north of Canton, the home district of Hung Hsiu-ch'üan.

11

ported loyal persons, a duty which they could not shift onto others; and also, when this villain Fung was forming cabals during a number of years, and swearing persons into it within a few miles of the city in the house of Lu Luh and Tsang Yuhchin, why they had heard nothing of it? When the graduate Wang had informed them of it, what hindered them from going to the village and personally examining, so as to be perfectly sure whether the altars and temples with their images had been destroyed or not, and whether the vagabonds possessed heretical books in which Jesus, a false god (*sie shin*) of the Europeans was spoken of, and had themselves seditiously worshiped and honored him? And whether, too, Fung had himself written or taught these books in a guileful way, and had planned sedition in so doing, could, with every other of his acts, have been ascertained. Why did this prefect and magistrate act so, like statues as they were, unable to distinguish between black and white? Not to speak further of their vacillating conduct, the manner in which their official secretaries issued the replies was like that of fools.

I find that the rule of the officers in this whole province of Kwangsi has been very negligent; indeed I have seldom heard or seen a place where matters have come to such a pass. It has thence resulted that this Fung Yunshan in his perverse heart has not had the least fear of them, but privately returning to the province has stirred up the rustic people, some of whom have suddenly come out in their seditious conduct, and we know not how many have secretly joined them. The people having experienced this calamitous misfortune, the service and outlay for the troops have been greatly increased, and all owing to these officers having so given in to this disobedience; they have injured the people and impeded the government; their crimes are unpardonable. [End of Memorial]

The degradation of these officers was of course decided on, but so far as regards quelling the rising, with as little effect as if they had been so many corporals in Kirin. The chief scene of conflict has been near the department of Sinchau lying on the southern banks of the Pearl River, and along the Yuh River, especially in the districts of Kweiping, Wusiuen, and Siang, where the imperialists have also centered their forces. This Fung Yunshan mentioned in Chau's memorial is he who has assumed the imperial style of Tienteh. His father's name is Fung Shautsun and that of his chief adviser Yang Shau-tsing of Pingnan hien. A

12

reward of twenty thousand dollars has been offered for the head of each of them. An officer was also deputed not long since by Su and Yeh to proceed to Hwa hien, and completely destroy the ancestral tombs of the Fung family, in order to vitiate the *fung-shwui* of Tienteh. This was done in former times by Litsing, the rebel who destroyed the last emperor of the Ming dynasty, and if one can judge from the formality with which it has been done, it is probably regarded as a powerful remedy against such maladies in the body politic. The officers of Tienteh, except his father, are all men from Sinchau fu.

The emissaries of government in Canton evidently try to repress all rumors relating to the insurgents, and this accounts in some measure for the discrepancy in those we hear. Governor-general Su is now at some point in Kau-chau fu in the southwest of this province, to oversee the frontier. A large body of troops from Hwuichau fu left in September for Loting chau to assist in repressing a rising there; but we agree with those natives who think H.E. is not likely to reap any laurels in warring against the 'thieves'.

One result of the troubles in Kwangsi is that they are likely to derange the trade of Canton for a long time. We think that the inhabitants of all the southern departments of Kwangsi more or less sympathise with the outlaws, and that the hopes intimated by Wurantai of reducing them by starvation are not likely soon to be realised. A large proportion of the towns in this region are governed by local and hereditary chieftans whose authority over their retainers is stronger by far than the sway of the government. Long continued oppression on the part of the prefects and generals stationed there, may have made them ready to listen to the suggestions of a schemer; for Tienteh, like all his race of reformers, promises largely, telling the people that if he gets the power, their wrongs shall all be righted, and peace and plenty will fill the land. It may be added too, that persons apparently well informed, say that he is fair in his dealings, restrains his soldiers from rapine, and levies no more than the legal demands of the usual rulers. He has coined money, instituted literary examinations, and appointed his six Boards; but, with all this, we can hardly ascertain where his headquarters are; they are most likely, however, to be still in Kweiping district.

7
A Report by T T Meadows
FO 17/180, no. 116, enc. in Bonham to Palmerston,
29 September 1851[7]

REPORT ON THE REBELLION IN THE TWO KWANG

No news of any importance direct from the disturbed district has become public in Canton during the past month. The party of rebels which entered Lo Ting in the West of this Province about 5 weeks ago were, by the latest accounts, still in that department, and a force of 400 regulars and 1000 Volunteers which passed up the river on the 19th Inst was said to be despatched against them
. . .

In another edict just received, the Emperor (after referring to a memorial of the Governor General of the Two Kwang of December last, reporting the spread of 'Vicious Doctrines'— especially Romanism in China and even in Tartary) states that he has received memorials, from whom is not mentioned, to the effect that the disturbances in the Two Kwang are in a great degree owing to the spread of 'Strange Doctrines', for which reason he now gives orders that all the proper Officers take steps for diffusing knowledge of the national ethics among the people. No mention is made of the Christian religion, but it is evidently included in the term 'Strange Doctrines'. . . .

Thos. Taylor Meadows
Interpreter
A True Copy
A R Johnston

8
A Report from the *Overland Friend of China*
Overland Friend of China, 30 January 1852

FROM OUR CHINESE CORRESPONDENTS

. . . We have received a letter from Kwangse, stating that the great Tartar General Sae shang ah received an Imperial rescript insisting that the city of Yung gan-chow be again brought under royal authority within the space of fifteen days, and that in case of failure the General Heang ying, Lieut.-General Woo lan-tai and Colonel Ting sam, were to be beheaded. On the receipt of this

---

7   For further examples of Meadows' reports from Canton see his book *The Chinese and their Rebellions* (London, 1856), pp. 160–4.

news, on the 17th day of the 10th moon,[8] all the officers collected their troops, and from various points proceeded to attack the city of Yung gan-chow, but did not pitch their encampment within 70 le of the city. The rebels however, pretending to be defeated, gradually led them on to where they had a large body of troops in ambush, and then suddenly turning upon them, poured forth a complete shower of cannon balls, killing upwards of 10,000[9] soldiers, and more than 60 officers of various ranks.

It is reported that Seu, the Governor General, is at present in the city of Kaou-chow-foo and that the rebels have attacked it on all sides, having erected a powerful battery before each of the city gates so as to be ready to attack the soldiers whenever they venture to come out. The Tartar troops are afraid to go out and fight, and have now been besieged for more than 10 days. A most urgent message has been sent by Seu to Woo chow (in Kwangse) for the 2000 troops lately sent there under Hen tseang-kwang, to return immediately for the relief of the city. We have not yet heard which side has gained the victory—12th moon, 9th day. *F. of C.* Jan. 7.

PROCLAMATION OF THE SHANG-TE SOCIETY* TO THE INHABITANTS OF WING-ON-CHOW

The Teaou-ching-sz,[10] Chief Officer in the left wing of the army, has received the royal commands to publish this, that the hearts of the people may be changed.

Know ye people that the middle ground (China proper) belongs to those of the former dynasty. Be not afraid ye scholars, farmers, workmen, and merchants, but hold stedfastly, every one to his work. The fortune of the Han dynasty is about to flourish, and the foreign Dynasty of the Mantchoos will soon end. This is the decree of heaven in which there can be no mistake. After a long union, division must ensue, in order that affairs may be arranged

---

* Can this society have had any connection or origin in the 'Christian Union', many of whose members became followers of Teen-tih?

8 Probably meaning 17 October; the equivalent date on the Chinese lunar calendar would be 9 December 1851.

9 Simply meaning a very large number.

10 Tso-fu Cheng-chun-shih, chief officer of the left, the title used by Yang Hsiu-ch'ing (d. 1856), the Tung Wang or Eastern King of the Taipings, and one of their best military commanders in the early period.

again. Our Kings* publishing laws, exhibited their benevolence and before ever they bowed the knee to Shang-te (God), they assisted the distressed, and after they had learned to worship God, they exerted all their strength to save the people from ruin;—they supported the weak, resisted the strong, and assisted each other in opposing thieves and guarding against robbers, with united strength and unanimity of mind. They were not like Tai-tow yeong, Tai-lee-yu, Cheong ka-chen, and others, who stopped the vessels on the rivers, plundered everywhere, and killed the inhabitants of the towns and villages. On the arrival of officers and troops these men were afraid—they only cared to sell passports of safe conduct, as a protection to the people, but their assurance of peace was in vain, for the inferiors depending upon their superiors, also went abroad to sell these passports and collect a tax, so that the inhabitants had no peace till they had yielded to all these demands. In this way the merchants and Traders suffered great and indescribable injury. 'The cats and mice slept in the same place,' hence numbers of inferior persons, assumed unusual effrontery, and formed all kinds of schemes to do as much harm as they possibly could:— they also raised troops from amongst the inhabitants and even called upon our kings to submit to them. On the day that Wingon city was settled, there were three contending parties, but he who walked according to the wishes of heaven obtained possession. Our kings have spread their benevolence to the utmost, and regarding the people as their children, they have commanded the army to abstain from murder, and to take nothing without permission; they are just and impartial as the balance, and the trade in the markets now goes on quietly as before. If any one refuses to obey the laws, let him be reported to the law officer of the army. Our kings invite the inhabitants of all districts and departments to surrender, and will reward those who establish their merits by exerting their strength. They are now waiting to be joined by the kings of the other provinces in order to unite their troops for an attack on the capital city Peking; after which they will proceed to divide the

---

* The word King here signifies a prince, or one of noble family, and not a King as understood by Europeans. These kingly titles are merely assumed, the common names of the parties being given underneath, one of them King-tai-ping, commonly called Hung-sow-tsei, was a *member of* Gutzlaff's Christian Union.[11]

11 Karl Gutzlaff (1803–51), a German missionary, had founded a society of Chinese preachers known as the Chinese Union. He sent them into the interior to preach and distribute tracts, and several of them joined the Taiping. It is likely that the Taiping received at least some of their knowledge of Christianity from this source. See P. Clarke, 'The Coming of God to Kwangsi', *Papers on Far Eastern History*, 7 (March 1973).

empire. *Kings* Taie-ping, Heuen-teen, Ping-teen, Yin-tik, Teen-tik, Shun-tik.[12] *Commanders in Chief.* Yeong sew-tsing, Generalissimo.—Hoo-e-kwang, Chief Assistant General—Sew-chaou kwei, Second Assistant General. *Teen keo*, first year, 8th moon, *Friend of China, January 29.*

9
A Report by H S Parkes
FO 17/188, no. 42, enc. in Bonham to Palmerston, 29 March 1852

REPORT ON THE INSURRECTION IN THE TWO KWANG

The chief efforts of the Government continue to be directed to the reduction of the two main bodies of the Insurgents, who for several months past have successfully maintained their ground at Yunggan, in Kwanse, the other at Loting in this Province . . .

The Reports direct from Yunggan confirm those of the Gazettes as to the city being invested, but add that it is prepared for a siege, whether as regards the strength of its defences, or, what is of more importance, the supply of provisions. It is also stated that the Government troops have not yet deprived the Rebels of communication with the hills which flank the city on its western side from whence they are able to derive supplies. The number of Insurgents thus enclosed is said, by common report, to be four or five thousand. There is a rumour (not a novel one I believe) that the rebel chief called Tien tih, who had hitherto been at the head of this body, is dead and that the command has been divided between two parties surnamed *Seaou* and *Seay.*

Harry S Parkes
Interpreter
A True Copy
A R Johnston

10
A Report from the *Overland Friend of China*
Overland Friend of China, 24 May 1852

We hear that the band of Kwang si rebels, styled the Shang te (God) Society have determined to quit the city of Wing on (Yung gan) partly on account of their scanty supplies, and partly because they consider the moat round the city too narrow and

12 Apart from T'ai-p'ing and T'ien-te (Teen tik) these titles are obscure.

shallow to enable them to hold out long, in case of attack. They moved out during the night about the middle of the second moon, and have taken up a position in the district of Ping low foo, as if they wished to see whether that city would afford them a secure residence. The city of Wing on is now entirely deserted, and Woo lan tai the Lieut. General having ascertained that the rebels have moved to a good distance has entered with his troops and published a proclamation calling on the inhabitants to return—3rd moon, 4th day.

It is reported that the rebels of Yung-Gan (Wing on) chow, having despatched a part of their force to attack the city of Chaon-ping succeeded in taking possession on the 23rd day of last month, but finding it too small, and the city wall not high enough to afford proper protection, they gave it up after plundering the granaries and treasury. On leaving the city they encamped on the north side of the Tsz king hill intending to attack the district cities of Seaou jin and Le-poo, but suddenly turned about in the opposite direction, and made an assault on the capital city of Kwei-lin foo. They continued the attack for 3 days but without success, and finding their labour in vain, they set fire to a part of the city, destroying the Wan chang gate, and a great many shops in the adjoining suburbs. By the combined exertions of the inhabitants and the Tartar troops, the rebels were driven away, but the city is still closely guarded and the gates kept shut—3rd moon, 13th day.

Some vanquished soldiers who have returned to Canton, report that about the middle of last month, the rebels of the 'Shang-te hwuy' pretended to evacuate the city of Yung-gan (Wing-on) and moved their encampment into the district of Pan-lo. As soon as the Tartar troops saw that the city was empty they thought that the rebels had really forsaken it, and had taken up their abode in another part of the country, so they immediately entered, and issued proclamations for the guidance of the inhabitants, and sent a report to the Commander-in-chief that the city of Yung-gan had been taken back from the rebels. There was no suspicion that the pretended desertion of the city by the rebels, was only a trick to induce the Tartar troops to enter it. Without any delay the rebels immediately returned, and made an attack on the city, setting fire to it in many places both within and without the walls, by which upwards of 30 civil and military officers, besides an immense number of soldiers were burnt to death. Large quantities of provisions and ammunition were captured by the rebels, who thus again took possession of the city.—3rd moon, 13th day.

11
A Letter from the American Baptist Missionary Rev. I J Roberts
The Chinese and General Missionary Gleaner, vol. II.9 (February 1853), pp. 67–9

... Some time in 1846, or the year following, two Chinese gentlemen came to my house in Canton professing a desire to be taught the Christian religion. One of them soon returned home, but the other continued with us two months or more, during which time he studied the scriptures and received instruction, and maintained a blameless deportment. That one seems to be this *HUNG SAWCHUEN* the chief; and the narrator was perhaps the gentleman who came with him, but soon returned home. When the chief first came to us he presented a paper written by himself, giving a minute account of having received the book of which his friend speaks in his narrative; of his being taken sick, during which he professed to see a vision, and gave the details of what he saw, which he said confirmed him in the belief of what he read in the book. And he told some things in the account of his vision which I confess I was then at a loss, and still am, to know whence he got them without a more extensive knowledge of the scriptures. He requested to be baptized, but left for Kwangsi before we were fully satisfied of his fitness; but what had come of him I knew not until now.[13]

Description of the Man: He is a man of ordinary appearance, about five feet four or five inches high; well built, round faced, regular featured, rather handsome, about middle age, and gentlemanly in his manners.

Reports: It has been reported that a part of the rebel army was composed of a party calling themselves the *Seongti* society, i.e., '*The God Society*'. And some said that one of Mr Gutzlaff's disciples had joined the rebels; but I had little thought of it being this man, and least of all that had become a leader in the matter! Nor had I before any adequate idea of the nature of the struggle. It has been supposed that the object was to upset the present dynasty, and that may be the design of some of the rebels yet for aught I know; for, like David's army, it is made up of a mixed multitude. (1 Sam. xxii, 2) I presume this consists of all the malcontents in the country, on whatever account, who are uniting with them; but at least that part of the rebel army composing the Seongti Society, must have not only a different

13   T. Hamberg in *The Visions of Hung-siu-tshuen* (1854), pp. 31–2, gives a different version of this incident, suggesting that Hung left because of the intrigues of two of Robert's assistants who feared they might be displaced in Robert's confidence by Hung.

object in view, but a much more important one. Instead of rebelling against the government, with a design of upsetting the dynasty, they seem rather struggling for religious liberty, and *are really upsetting idolatry*! I now begin to sympathise with them in their struggle, and to look for important results. How wonderful was the providence, and how unexpected was the opening into China effected by means of the foreign war; and now no less wonderful will be the results should the present be the means of casting down their idolatry, and opening the way for the universal spread of the gospel among them! The followers of HUNG SAWCHUEN, I presume, look upon him not only as a chief commander, but also something in the capacity of a prophet or teacher of religion. And he himself, I presume, is somewhat imbued with superstition; yet, he is represented as strict in his morality, and as a destroyer of idolatry, even forbidding his followers to write *pi*, 'to worship', on their visiting cards, because, said he, 'I was taught at Canton that it was wrong.' Now if he is really thus acting conscientiously, and doing the best he knows according to the scriptural instructions which he has received, doubtless good will result, though, like Apollos, he may still need some one to 'expound to him the way of God more perfectly.' (Acts xviii, 26)

A few days ago I was conversing with a Chinese gentleman here who is personally acquainted with the chief HUNG, and seems well informed as to his movements. But he says it would not be well for the Mandarins to know that one is even personally acquainted with him; and to write to him, or to have any communication with him, would lead to execution if caught in it. This gentleman says, that about 100,000 of the people are now numbered on the side of the chief, that he is popular among the people, treating them with respect, generosity, and kindness, much more so than the soldiers of the government; and hence he is more popular among the common people than they! That he is abstemious, self-denying, and fast gaining ground. Said he, 'If the Lord assists him—is on his side, he will succeed, if not he will be overcome; nor will it be long until the matter is determined.' How much this is like the sentiment of Gamaliel expressed in the Jewish council: 'Now I say unto you, refrain from these men and let them alone; for if this counsel or this work be of men it will come to nought: but if it be of God ye cannot overthrow it, lest haply ye be found even to fight against God.' (Acts v, 38, 39) How deeply I should now regret to see any foreign power aid the Chinese government against these men! This thing has been somewhat canvassed, and before I was better informed I felt but little on the subject; but now, with the information received, the knowledge I have myself of the facts in the case, and the view I take of the whole matter as under the direction of Providence, I should feel much, and exceedingly regret to see any foreign power fight against TIEN-TEH and his party, 'Lest haply they should be found even to fight against God.' The idolatry of this nation must come to an end, and who knows but this is the Lord's set time? While I am not prepared fully to commend nor to condemn what HUNG is doing, yet I would say, let the matter, under the wise dispensations of Providence, be left in the hands of the Lord who will do right. Though the very thing the chief is doing may not in itself be altogether commendable, any more than the former foreign war, yet in its results, as to the spread of the gospel in China, the tendencies may prove equally propitious.

The still small voice in which the Lord spoke to Elijah, was preceded by a 'great and strong wind that rent the mountains and brake in pieces the rocks by an earthquake and fire', in which the Lord was not; but by these Elijah was prepared to listen to the voice of the Lord. Now one thing is certain, that nothing less than a mighty shaking and rending of the old customs of the Chinese, both internally and externally, could ever have moved them from their regular routine of doing things, both in political and religious matters. That breaking and rending of external barriers was realised in the 'great and strong wind' of foreign war in 1842, when the mountain of obstacles to national intercourse was broken, rent and brought to a plain; and now in 1852 a like mighty shaking and internal fiery renovation is going on, which I sincerely hope and pray may result in the prostration of idolatry and the preparation of the people, for listening to the 'still small' peace speaking voice of Christ in the gospel.

This is China's crisis. How earnestly ought Christians to pray and strive for the furtherance of the gospel among this people under present circumstances; and to make the most of every opportunity of usefulness that may soon offer! Behold, what God hath wrought! Not only opened China externally for the reception of the teachers of the gospel, but now one has risen up among themselves, who presents the true God for their adoration, and casts down idols with a mighty hand, to whom thousands and tens of thousands of the people are collecting! Shall we say that this is by chance or of the devil? Such things do not come by chance. A sparrow, said Jesus, 'shall not fall on the ground without your father.' (Matt. x, 29) And the people in their idolatry have doubt-lessly been doing for many ages, just as the devil would have them do; and hence we could hardly conclude that he would war

21

against himself, and set one of the people to battering down his own fortresses! May we not therefore humbly trust, though with fear and trembling, that this struggle is going on under the wisdom and guidance of the deep counsels of Almighty God, and designed by Him to bring about His own purposes and glory in the renovation and salvation of this numerous people.

I J Roberts[14]
Canton, Oct. 6th, 1852

12
A Letter by the French Lazarist Missionary Dr L G Delaplace
Annals of the Propagation of the Faith, vol. XIV (1853), pp. 215–18

PROPAGATION OF THE FAITH AT LYONS AND PARIS

Choui-Tcheou-Fou, Nov. 6th 1852

Gentlemen,

I have had the honour of addressing you several times during the last few years on the Mission of Hou-nan. On the present occasion, and henceforth, you will permit me to speak to you of Kiang-si, since I am now occupied with the administration of this province. I will lay before you our wants and our hopes, the joys and sorrows of the Missioners, the blessings and evils of our Christians; all this I will communicate to you with the greatest confidence feeling convinced that your charity will not be less benevolently disposed towards us than it was formerly towards the Right Rev. Dr Rameaux and the Right Rev. Dr Laribe, my predecessors.

The general aspect of the Mission is not this year very satisfactory, civil war being at our gates.

You are doubtless aware, Gentlemen, of the unsettled state of the Chinese empire, the insurrections of Kouang-si, the invasion of two or three large provinces, the audacity of the rebels, excited by an almost uninterrupted success, and the rapidity of their victorious march. They have now laid siege to *Tchang-Cha*, the capital of Hou-nan. They have but just surrounded it, and already the report is spread that it has been carried by storm. Now, *Tchang-cha* is only fifty leagues from the place where I write this letter. Will Kiang-si, in its turn, be invaded? Some people think not, judging from the experience of past invasions. From the period of the remotest dynasties, whatever may have been the

14   For a further elaboration of Robert's early views on the movement see *Putnam's Monthly*, October 1856; for his later experiences and views see documents in Part III.1, 2.

nature of the war, Kiang-si was never the scene of combat. In fine, when once *Kiang-nan* has been taken, and the insurgents have made themselves masters of Hou-nan, Kiang-si, as a necessary consequence, is included in the conquest without a blow being struck. This is what is expected by some to take place in the present instance. Others, on the contrary, maintain that the taking of Nan-Tchang-Fou, our capital, is included in the plan of the insurgents, and that they may be expected to appear very shortly under its walls. Whatever may be the value of these rumors, the fact is, that our mandarins are on the alert, as if they considered themselves in imminent danger. Bands of soldiers are defiling on every road; the secret police are multiplying their vigilance; terror reigns in all places; arrests, ransoms, and executions, are made on the slightest pretext. The enemies of our holy religion know how to avail themselves of this public terror to our disadvantage. Hence our neophytes are in great trepidation, our Chinese priests more than reserved, the European Mission-ers less free than ever, and the visits of the stations more perilous and less fruitful.

This state of things is too violent to last long; but what will be the result? If poor people, little skilled in diplomacy, may be allowed to express their presentiments, it appears to us that the Chinese empire is about to be dismembered, and some catas-trophe is perhaps at hand. It has of late been accumulating all the causes that, according to the Holy Scriptures, contribute to the ruin of states: 'This nation has corrupted its ways. Men of all ages have walked in *the ways of Sodom and Samaria.* Their iniquities are monstrous enough to have reached unto heaven. *As for the ministers* of the prince, the rage of crime has troubled them *as a man in his drunkenness.* The *prince himself has lost his majesty, and contempt has fallen upon him.*'

These Chinese people, whose respect, veneration, and filial piety towards their sovereign and their magistrates have been so much talked of, are now treating their *son of heaven* with supreme contempt, and murdering his mandarins. Now, what do these prognostics portend? We Europeans can easily foresee. Even in China it is anticipated; for I have seen old men, on being informed in my presence, that in such a place a mandarin had been killed by the people, that in some other locality a mandarin had been expelled by them, shake their heads, remain astounded with fear, and cry out: 'We never before heard of such things; what will become of the country?'

It must also be admitted that the emperor, Hien-Fong, and his ministers appear to be really infatuated. At the very time when it is of the utmost importance to gain popularity, they appear to do everything to alienate public feeling from them. The nation is weighed down with taxes; it is exhausted with statute-labour. For the equipment of a few soldiers, it is incredible what a number of families have to be troubled; for it must not be imagined that the Chinese foot soldier will go on foot: no, no; he must be provided with a car. The cavalry-man, likewise, would be too much fatigued were he to go on horseback; he also must have a car. In fine, the war-steed himself cannot carry his saddle. To transport his harness, cars must also be employed; so that last week, in the town of Choui-Tcheou-Fou, two leagues hence, a thousand men were required to transport the equipments of three hundred soldiers.

Nor is this all: the pretended defenders of the country are almost so many brigands, who pillage the honest citizen even in his own house. And hence, let it only be announced in the market-place that the troops are about to pass through, and in an instant every stall will have disappeared. To crown the disaffection, it is said that the mandarins are proposing to levy an extraordinary tax: they select a wonderfully propitious time, especially during a season of drought! Hence, complaints are beginning to break out into open sedition; no secret is made of the desire to witness the arrival of the insurgents; there is not a village that is not anxious to place itself under their government. It is also said that the Chinese mandarins are equally anxious as the people to free themselves from the Tartarian dominion; it is even supposed that, if at a crisis the mandarins should redouble their vexations—if they aggravate instead of softening the yoke—it will be for the purpose of securing the victory to the rebels, whose friends they will thus multiply by increasing the dissatisfied and malcontents.

These rebels, on the contrary, adopt the most prudent measures. No pillage among them; no disorder; this has been announced in their proclamation from the very outset. 'Our hostilities are directed against the Tartars alone—we only seek to exterminate the Tartars;' and the facts correspond to the words. Whenever a town is taken, the Tartar soldiers are put to the sword without exception; no quarter is given to the Mandchoorian mandarins; the Chinese mandarins, if they have not previously made their submission, are likewise massacred. But the people are respected; the merchant can continue at his business, and the traveller pursue his road in tranquillity.

The information which I obtained on these matters, during my recent journey from Hou-nan to Kiang-si, enables me to enter into details. Through every district that I passed, whether travelling along the western portion of Ngan-Hoey, or traversing Han-pe from north to south, all the observations that I heard lead me to this conclusion:—that the inhabitants of the north are prepared to make common cause with the rebels of the south.

I enter into these details, Gentlemen, because this affair very probably involves for us a question of life or death. No, I am wrong; it is a question of life. I meant to say: 'It involves for us a question of liberty or atrocious persecution.'

If, as it now appears very probable, the insurgents are victorious, we may perhaps expect some emancipation for our holy religion. If, on the contrary, the Tartar dynasty triumph, we may expect to witness a terrible re-action against every thing bearing the character or semblance of an association; and as the Church in China is to the government one of the most prominent and odious of associations, the Christian community will be assailed with the utmost fury, and we may have to suffer a persecution unto fire and blood.

Liberty or persecution—either will be acceptable in the Lord Jesus Christ. Liberty will be attended with labour; persecution with suffering and death. To labour for the Lord, to suffer for the Lord, to die under torture, or fall by the sword, would be a glorious consummation. Respected members of the Propagation of the Faith—they who labour and they who suffer are always consoled by your charity, and sustained by your prayers. They also feel towards you all that gratitude and devotedness which are so eminently due to you.

Penetrated with these sentiments, I have the honor to be, with the most profound respect,

Gentlemen,

Your very humble and obedient Servant,

L G Delaplace,

Bishop of Andrianople, Vic.–Apost. of Kiang-si.

13
A Report from the *North China Herald*
North China Herald, 15 January 1853

... The rebels finding that as at Kwei-lin it would cost more time and trouble to effect the capture of Chang-sha than the place was worth, seem to have directed their progress to the north-east; and about ten days ago news reached this place, brought by merchants to Soochow, that a portion of the rebel forces advancing to the Yang-tsze-kiang had seized upon Wu-chang the capital of Hupeh—that business was there at a stand—the Shan-see merchants and others who could, flying from the place. More unfavorable news from foreigners interested in the trade of China, should this prove true, it has never been our lot to record. If the reader will again refer to the Map, he will observe that Wu-chang-foo is situated in the very heart of the country, on the south bank of the Yang-tsze-kiang, where the great river receives one of its chief tributaries, the river Han, from the north-west. At the mouth of the latter lies on one side the town of Han-yang opposite to Wu-chang, and on the other extensive suburbs, the name of the whole place being called by traders Han-khow (mouth of the Han), well known to every Chinese as the seat of the most extensive commerce in the interior of the country. Not only is an immense native trade carried on there, but to Han-khow is also sent a very large portion of the British and American Manufactures and Opium imported through Shanghai. Its distance from the sea is perhaps over 600 miles, but as there is no doubt that the Yang-tsze-kiang is navigable thus far up for the largest ships, it is destined when the great river is opened to steam communication, to become hereafter an important seat of Foreign trade. The Moning Tea Districts in Kiang-see are but a short distance to the south-east, and for these as well as for the Hoo-nan (Oo-nam) and Hoo-peh (Wo-pak) Teas it will be the natural outlet.

This then is the place which if not already seized upon, or laid under contribution, there is too much reason to fear will soon be so. Further down the river at the entrance to the Poyang-lake lies Kew-kiang, the next place to be attacked; it is of less value as a trading place, than an important military post. We believe we do not exaggerate when we say that the Government functionaries in every town and place along the river down to Chin-kiang-foo, are in a state of complete consternation. At many places houses are being pulled down, and the City walls repaired for defence. Nanking the ancient Capital of China, is now the goal to which the insurgents avow their intention to push on; and viewing dispassionately the numbers of the brigand host, of which every recent estimate given us far exceeds 500,000 men; their resolute courage amounting to ferocity; the determined character of the Kwang-tung and Kwang-see men who form the nucleus of the rebel army; and their superiority in skill as well as numbers to the Government troops, we confess our hopes of their progress being arrested now begin to disappear.

The imminence of the danger is thoroughly felt by the Government; all the disposable troops from the north and south-east are ordered to hasten to the defence of Nan-king and Kew-kiang, but the paucity of soldiers in such a densely populated country must excite surprise. The Government of this enormous country seems positively unable to bring together at any one point a force of 30,000 or 40,000 men—in fact anything deserving the name of an army, and the reason assigned is the want of money. During the past week the military Commandant of this place, of the rank of Colonel, departed for the wars at the head of *one hundred* regulars, and as many more volunteers, a contemptible force surely from a wealthy and populous district.

But the question is 'have the rebels the sympathy of the people and is the prospect of a change of masters welcome to the nation at large?' Taking the opinion of many natives we have consulted as our guide, we conclude that although the men with whom the insurrection originated are neither esteemed nor liked by their northern brethren, yet any change it is believed must be for the better, and throughout the country the feeling seems to be growing deeper, that the exactions and oppressions of the Mandarins are no longer to be borne. True, these Mandarins in nine cases out of ten are Chinese, yet the responsibility for their misdeeds is laid to account of the Supreme Government.

This deep feeling of dissatisfaction has been adroitly turned to account by the rebel leaders, and while they exact contributions from the rich, they ostentatiously hold out protection to the poor. Their discipline it is said is severe. The reign of Tien-teh is to usher in the dawn of official virtue! and in short the Radical Reform by all felt to be so necessary, is then to be effected!

As foreigners resident in this country, the spectacle of a great nation convulsed to its centre in the struggle for empire, not only challenges our earnest attention as a grand political problem, but as concerned in its trade it also behoves us to look to the future, and endeavour to discover how our interests are thereby affected. Ere many months* have elapsed, the rebels will have commenced their descent to Nanking—so say the natives, and the possession of Chin-kiang-foo will give them the command of the most valuable provinces on the south of the Yang-tsze-kiang. But we know that great changes are of slow operation in this country; the Chinese cannot like the French commence and conclude a revolution in a week's time.

Surprising as the conquest of China by the Manchows must ever be regarded, yet they fought for an age ere they won the Empire; and the standard of rebellion against the Mongols had

---

* We say months, although many China prone to exaggerate [sic] speaks of weeks, or even days.

been borne by various leaders for a series of years, ere Hung-wu the founder of the Ming Dynasty commenced the liberation of his country. We cannot then believe that the present Dynasty boasting in its annals the illustrious names of Kang-hi and Kienlung, can yield dominion without a prolonged contest; neither the history of the past, nor the appearance of current events permits us to do so. This indeed we conceive to be the most gloomy view of the subject; for as the Government seems powerless to crush the rebels, so on the other hand it appears to us that years must go by ere they can expel the Manchows, or the nation be restored to a state of tranquillity, during which period the material interests of the country must greatly suffer.

It is altogether a mistake to suppose that men of rank or wealth have declared for the insurgents. Men of rank will hold by the Government that bestowed their honours—their adhesion is not courted by the rebels; and wealthy men, when they cannot escape it, will contribute their quota of ransom money for their towns. All will propitiate the favour of the conquerors, like the people of the town in Che-keang, who sent a portion of earth to the British Invaders at Ningpo, to signify their submission, and all will perhaps without reluctance accept the change of masters when imposed. When a whole nation becomes involved in such a struggle, the adhesion or defection of men of rank or wealth will little affect the course of events; genius and force of individual character overcoming all obstacles will then rise to the surface. Thus Hung-wu from a menial in a Monastery became master of China; thus rose the great warrior of the west, Napoleon; and thus perhaps the 'coming man'* is about to emerge in China from the mystery and obscurity in which he is as yet enveloped.

We have not space to treat of the present crisis in commercial affairs at this Port, but we may observe that while various other causes, as the deficiency of water in the interior, and the great

* The Pretender's Title as our readers will remember is King Tien-teh. There is also another King, the Tai-ping Wang. Whether the original Tien-teh was captured or not as stated last year, is not yet very clear. A person who recently returned to the neighbourhood witnessed the entry of the rebels into one of the towns in Hoo-nan. Tien-teh he describes as a youth of about 23 years of age. He was borne in a Yellow Chair by sixteen bearers, followed by his chief adviser an elderly man in a green chair. After them came the King's ladies, thirty-six in number, carried in as many chairs. The number although in Chinese eyes sufficient for a King (Wang), would form a very inadequate 'establishment' for an Emperor (Hwang-tee); but on Tien-teh's arrival at Nanking, when he assumes the latter title, more liberal arrangements will doubtless be made. The proximity of Soo-chow and Yang-chow will afford every desirable facility in this respect.

increase in the export trade have combined to render money scarce, one by retarding arrivals from the inland provinces, and the other by the large sums taken into the country, we are only expressing the Chinese Public Opinion when we say that the paramount cause of the present depression, is the progress of the rebellion. Trade is at a stand at Han-khow, capitalists at Soo-chow are withdrawing their money from business, when they see sure signs of approaching troubles in the preparations going on to put the neighbouring city of Chang-chow, and also Hang-chow, into a state of defence, and when they know full well the alarm which reigns at Nanking.

... In conclusion we have only to add for the information of those at a distance that everything connected with the movement induces the belief that its ultimate success will be the signal for hostile measures against foreigners in China; we have thus much to lose and nothing to gain by the subversion of the Ta-tsing Dynasty, unless Foreign interference be hereafter solicited, which is not very probable.

14
A Letter by the Italian Franciscan Missionary Mgr Rizzolati
Annals of the Propagation of the Faith, vol. XIV (1853),
pp. 219–22

Hong Kong, Jan. 28, 1853

Gentlemen,

I cannot refrain from relating to you the grave events of which my Vicariate-Apostolic is at present the scene, and which have thrown my Missioners, but more especially the Europeans, into the greatest tribulation. It is not alone the prospect of persecution that troubles them; they are even more alarmed at the Chinese insurrection, at the present time so terrible that the emperor himself begins to be seriously alarmed for the safety of his throne, and has already, according to report, taken measures for translating the seat of his government to Leao-Tong, in Tartary. The rebels, after having opened the breach at Cham-Cha-Fou, the capital of Hou-nan, have taken possession of Jouo-chou-Fou and other neighbouring towns, and have increased their army by these conquests to 40,000 men.

Having made this conquest, they embarked without opposition on the great river Kiang; and without meeting with the slightest resistance from the imperial troops, entered the large and illustrious city of Han-Keou, the commercial centre of the eighteen provinces of the empire. The imperial troops made a disgraceful flight, and hastened to shut themselves up in the fortresses of Ou-Cham-Fou, the capital of Hou-pe, situated opposite Han-Keou, from which it is only separated by the river, in this place about a gun-shot in breadth. Here, under the eyes of the imperial army, the insurgents freighted the thousands of barques or junks with which the Kiang is covered to transport to Nankin their soldiers and ammunition.

The revolutionists appear to be well disciplined, and are by far superior to the imperial army in point of military tactics. They everywhere announce themselves as the deliverers of their country from the yoke of the Tartars, whose vices and whose tyranny they hold up in their proclamations. Those who are desirous of seeing established the Chinese dynasty, applaud these pamphlets vilifying the foreigners. This enables the rebels to obtain voluntary subsidies, in enormous sums, and affords them the means of increasing their army daily. The imperial troops, on the contrary, are gradually falling into degradation; alarmed in the highest degree at the valour, audacity, and superior forces of the rebels, they appear studiously to avoid any engagement with them, contenting themselves, instead of fighting, with giving up to them their positions, and introducing them into the abandoned towns. In fact, they only fight when driven to the necessity of so doing by an unavoidable rencontre, or when they consider themselves certain of the victory, which is a case of rare occurrence.

For my part, I know not what opinion to form of the rebels of China. They have nothing in common with idolatry, which extends throughout the whole empire and the adjacent kingdoms. Wherever they come, they overthrow and destroy to their very foundations the temples of the idols; they break up, trample under foot, and reduce to dust the so-much venerated gods of the people. The monasteries of the Bonzes and Bonzesses are no less summarily dealt with. After having sacked and demolished their convents, the insurgents parade their divinities in a sort of masquerade, and make a complete carnival of their idols and other objects of their superstition.

This extraordinary conduct on the part of the rebels renders it impossible to say to what religion they belong, or what form of worship they are thinking of establishing in China. Their designs in this respect are an impenetrable enigma, which has become the subject of conjecture and the general theme of conversation among the Chinese. Now, as the destruction of the temples and the idols is an act opposed to the principles of all the pagan sects, not excepting that of Confucius, the government of the celestial empire is beginning to believe, that the leaders and instigators of the rebellion are Christians, and supports this suspicion on the fact that, of all the religions in China, the Gospel is the only one professing the hatred of idols and the worship of them. My couriers assure me, that lately, in consequence of this suspicion, the imperial government has made a prisoner of an old man of upwards of sixty years of age, who is well known to me, and whom all the Christians hold in great veneration, as being the principal catechist in the province of Hou-nan. On his premises were found a few treatises against idolatry, and this circumstance has aggravated his fault in the eyes of the authorities, who have declared the doctrine of these books conformable to that of the insurgents. I have just motives to fear that these arrests will go on increasing.

But nothing could be further from the truth than what has been stated in the Hong-Kong papers, viz.: that some of the French Missioners are at the head of the rebels. Almost the entire revolt at the present time is concentrated in the two provinces of Hou-Kouang, where all the Missioners are Italians or religious of the Reformed Franciscan order. It is, moreover, clearly shown that the rebel chiefs are very different men from the Catholics, from these three words inscribed on their banners: Xam-ti-houoei (*religion of the supreme emperor*). Who is not aware that Benedict XIV, forbade the Missioners to make use of these two first words to represent the name of God, because these words, expressing only the great and supreme emperor, were inadequate to express the name of the omnipotent God. The same pope ordained that the expression *Tien-chou*, which means master of heaven, should be used; and, at the present time, there is not a Catholic in China who makes use of the term *Xam-ti* in reference to God, whilst the term *Tien-chou* has become popular throughout the whole empire.

The *Coum-tou*, the viceroy of Canton, however, having been appointed general-in-chief of the imperial army in the south, and seeing these letters inscribed on the banner of the insurgents amid their destruction of the temples, concluded that the Christians must be at the head of the revolt; he said so openly and unhesitatingly to the emperor. This false and calumnious allegation has produced among the Christians fears so serious, that many of them have concealed themselves in strange houses, and others are already thrown into prison. Those from whom no profit can be expected are treated by the mandarins without the least consideration. Two Chinese priests, Paul *Chang* and Andrew *Coung*, are at the present time in the same dungeon, unless they have already been delivered by the victorious insurgents. The latter case is very probable, for the rebels refrain from persecuting the Christians. Another priest recently ordained, Paul *Ouang*, taking advantage of the permission which I had given him to absent himself for a fortnight, was in the bosom of his family—he was instructing his parents and compatriots, still Gentiles—when the mandarin arrived with a troop of satellites, who plundered the house of all the provisions it contained, of the linen, books and sacerdotal ornaments, and made prisoners of all present; but, as the rebels were approaching, the mandarin contented himself with the booty he had made, and sent all the captives home with the exception of the young priest's father, who is still sighing out his existence in chains.

February 7th, 1853

The whole of the southern part of China is in a terrible state of disorder; the rebels are everywhere triumphant, and gain the most brilliant victories, especially in Hou-Kouang. The internal commerce of the empire is completely suspended; all the shops are closed; whole communities have fled or emigrated. Besides the conquests they have made in Hou-Kouang, the insurgents have taken up anew in Kouang-si their old positions, and have even entered Kiang-si. After having considerably reinforced their army, they took some towns in the province of Kiang-Nan, and have flown, as it were, to within a four-days' march of Nankin. From this position, their chief, Tien-te, has summoned the mandarins of that capital to surrender, and come out with all possible parade, and acknowledge him as the legitimate emperor, a descendant of the last princes of the Dynasty of the Mings to the ninth generation. At the time I am writing, I presume that Tien-te has already made into Nankin the solemn entry, so long in view, so ardently desired, and that he is already proclaimed emperor. May Heaven grant that this new dynasty may be more favourable to the Catholics than that of the Tartars, and that Jesus Christ, henceforward announced throughout the empire, may send down upon it the most abundant blessings.

I am, with affection and respect,
Your devoted Servant,
Fr. Joseph
Bishop of Arade and Vic.-Apost. of Hou-Kouang.

15
A Memorandum by W H Medhurst
FO 17/200, no. 16, enc. in Bonham to Malmesbury, 10 March
1853

Owing to the entire absence in China of any medium save passing
rumour, or epistolary correspondence, through which general
intelligence can be circulated, it has been found almost impossible to collect detailed and credible information regarding the rise
and progress of the disturbances, commonly known under the
name of the Kwang-se Rebellion. The Peking Gazettes have of
course been fully at disposal, but, not to mention the mis-
statements with which the mass of these papers is known to
abound, the amount of pertinent information contained in them
is so limited, and withal so vague and defective, that little can be
gathered from them beyond a general idea of the numbers of the
banditti and the localities they disturb, together with a slight
insight into the extent of alarm which their proceedings occasion
to the Supreme Government. No light is thrown upon the true
object of the marauders, nor is it made clear what amount of
combination exists among their various bands, every memorialist
upon the subject affecting to look upon them all, no matter
whence sprung and by whom led, as thievish vagabonds, who
cannot hold their ground against the slightest show of force. With
such imperfect data at our disposal it may easily be conceived
how conjectural must every conclusion be to which foreigners
can as yet arrive with regard to their ultimate designs. Thus I am
able only to note the localities in which the insurgents first
appeared and to trace their subsequent progress up to the date of
the latest events of which we have any tidings.

The first reference to the banditti of Kwang-se to be found in
the Gazettes, occurs in a number published towards the close of
1849, in the shape of a memorial from the Governor of that
province, denouncing the Magistrate of Yung-fuh hien for neglect
of duty in having failed to bring to justice a daring band of
robbers who had come down the stream from some other parts of
the country and had committed several depredations in that
vicinity. In this paper the writer speaks of this species of
brigandage as being then very prevalent in the province, and
strongly urges the necessity of punishing the instance of remissness complained of, as the only means of checking the evil.
Another memorial, however, obtained by Mr Wade, through
private sources, in detailing the proceedings of these outlaws as
related by certain literary graduates, states that they commenced
to disturb the Department of Non-ning Too and Lew Chow Fow as

early as April-May 1849, plundering in bands of several hundred men, under chiefs whose names had already become a terror to the whole surrounding country. All accounts seem to agree in the fact that *plunder* was the principal if not the sole object of these marauders, at this stage of the insurrection, although some of their bands marched under banners bearing treasonable mottoes, and an extensive correspondence seems to have been carried on between the various chiefs as co-members of the same fraternity, called the 'Brotherhood of Heaven and Earth'.

During the course of nearly three years that elapsed between the summer of 1849, when the insurrectionists thus first attracted attention as mere predatory bands, and the month of April 1852, when their main division left the city of Yung-an Chow, a formidable army, their ravages were principally confined to the province of Kwang-se, every one of the eleven Departments of which they more or less disturbed, occasional forays being made across its border into Kwang-tung, Hoonan, and Kwei Chow. The Districts and towns visited by them during this interval, and the movements of the Imperialists in consequence, will appear from the following summary of the principal incidents of this part of the campaign, as derived from the Peking Gazettes.

In April to August 1849 the outlaws disturbed the Departments of Non-ning Foo and Low-Chow Foo, and the district of Shang-sze in Nan-ning Foo, whence a party crossed the border into the district of Ling-shan in Kwang-tung province; in the same month, the District city of Sin-ning in Hoonan province was captured, and several other District towns in that vicinity plundered. The division which crossed into Sin-ning was exterminated in May, 1850.

In February, 1850, they disturbed the District of Seang in Low-chow Foo, and in May ensuing they captured the District city of Ho in Ping-lo Foo.

In August 1850 appeared the first Imperial Decree commanding troops to be detached from other provinces to co-operate with the provincial forces of Kwang-se against the insurgents. Huang Yung (a Chinese) Commander in Chief in Hoonan, passed accordingly into Kwang-se, with 2,000 men and the expenditure on account of the army of extermination commenced. In November following Lin-Tsih-seu was appointed Commissioner to pacificate Kwang-se; he died on the 21st of the same month, and in December Li sing-yuen, ex Viceroy of Keang-nan and Keang-se was nominated his successor.

In December 1850, a division of the insurrectionists crossed the border into the District of Ung-yuen, Kwang-tung; another sacked the district city of Lung in Tae-ping Foo, and others ravaged the districts of Kwei-ping and Woo-seun in Tsin-chow Foo, as well as the Departmental city itself, and also the Department of King-yuen Foo . . .

The above details are derived from Gazettes which have reached this place, and which date only the 12th of January last. Mr Meadows of Shanghai, however, reports the receipt of a file of Gazettes dating up to the 26th of January. From that it appears that Woo-Chang Foo was by last accounts still in a state of siege; that a body of the rebels had advanced to the neighbourhood of Kwang-Chow, about 60 miles further down the Yang-Tsze Keang river; that Seu Kwang-tsin was yet in charge of the Commissioner's seals, though in disgrace; that Luh Keen-ying,[15] Viceroy of Keangnan and Keangse, has been ordered to Kew Keang Foo on the Po-yang Lake, to intercept the eastward progress of the enemy towards Nan King; that to Keshen in Hoonan has been entrusted the occupation of the routes and approaches to Peking, with an army of 15,000 men, in addition to the local troops; and a corps of 1,000 banner-men under his own command; and that 2,000 Manchow horsemen have been drafted down to join the army of extermination.

Independently of the special expenditure on account of the war, extended in December last as above mentioned, at some $5\frac{1}{2}$ millions sterling, the Government has no doubt been subjected, in consequence of the insurrection, to a serious deficit in its annual revenue for the past three years; though in what proportion to the total receipts it is next to impossible to determine.

(Signed) W H Medhurst
Chinese Secretary

16
A Report from the *North China Herald*
North China Herald, 23 April, 1853

We were unable to find room last week for the latest accounts we had received from the interior, what we now state and which we give on good authority, are quite confirmatory of our previous statements, viz., that Nanking had been completely invested by the Insurgents on the 8th of March, and was taken by assault on the 21st ulto.[16] We learn further that the Governor Luh Kien-ying

15 Luh Chien-ying, Imperial Commissioner and Governor-General of Kiangnan, who was to be killed by the Taiping at Nanking in March.
16 Actually 19 March.

had been met at one of the city gates by the enemy, was abandoned by his bearers, and the Insurgents observing the large green chair and the emblems of official dignity, on enquiring who he was—the unfortunate governor replied Luh: Luh are you, said his ruthless murderers, then we will cut you into six pieces! Whether this be true or not, we have some doubt—at any rate it gave the narrator the opportunity of a cruel pun on the word *Luh*, signifying in Chinese *six*. The Manchow General of Nanking is said to have been slain manfully fighting at the head of his men.[17]

Subsequently the Insurrectionists attacked Chin-keang which they took on the 2d of April. Yang-chow has also been invested. All the male Manchows are said to have been destroyed—three thousand are believed to have perished at Nanking, and the females are reported to have been invited into straw-houses outside the city and there destroyed by fire. However revolting this may appear to Europeans it is not believed to be too vindictive for Chinese, when their passions are aroused; their modes of punishment being known to be brutal in the extreme.

The Officers of the nascent dynasty are dressed in red uniform (regular bricks), the soldiers black, and any who join them assume sky blue.

Tien-tih is reported to be dead, and the chief command to have devolved on T'hae-ping-wang, a relation of his, who is expected to be made the next Emperor of the *After Mings*.

As we have already reported, the T'hae-ping-wang is assisted by four other kings, princes or commanders, severally called the Pih-wang, Tung-wang, Nan-wang and Se-wang. Considerable organization exists in their army; their immediate force consists of thirty or forty thousand men at Nanking, and a further force of twenty or thirty thousand men at Chin-keang and Yang-chow. The officers are generally mounted, but their followers are mostly infantry.

It is not known what has become of the successor of Luh Kien-ying.

The Insurgents' forces had moved back to Nanking from Chinkeang, on hearing accounts of the approach of the Imperialists under Ke-shen and Heang-yung—but their whereabout was not exactly known.

Rumour says that the treasure destined for the ransom of Suchau, is still retained there by order of the Insurgents for security; its amount is stated to be 200,000 taels of silver.

---

17   Hsiang-hou, commander of the Banner troops garrisoned at Nanking.

17
A Letter by Mgr F X Maresca, Catholic Bishop of Nanking
N. Brouillon, *Mémoire sur l'état actuel de la mission du Kiang-nan 1842–55* (Paris, 1855), pp. 274–81

Shanghai, June 8, 1853

Since the beginning of 1853, the Christians of Nanking and the surrounding districts have been extremely anxious, and unfortunately their fears have been only too well based. Meanwhile, as the rebels approached, Nanking prepared itself to repel them: the city's fortifications had been repaired, the means of defence augmented and abundant provisions amassed in the warehouses. The peasants hastened into the city, where they hoped to find more security: the Christians gathered together in the city chapel, to which they brought provisions.

On March 6th, the mandarins had the gates of the city closed, and forbade movement in or out.

On March 8th, the insurgents arrived under the walls of the city and established their camp there, divided into 28 divisions.

On March 19th, they set fire to the mines which they had dug and filled with powder. At dawn, the wall as well as the East Gate were blasted. Instantly the signal was given and they rushed forward, some to the breach, others to the wall, with a vehemence which terrified the defenders. From the first attack, they were masters of the city. The mandarins who had not escaped quickly enough were captured and put to death.

On March 20th, the insurgents spread quickly through the city without finding any resistance, carrying with them terror and death on all sides. A venerable old man, head of the Christians, and his elder son were killed in their house; his second son was grievously wounded, the third captured and taken away, the youngest fled. On the same day, four other Christians fell in the confusion.

On March 21st, the Tseu family, the richest and most distinguished of our Christian families, was expelled from their house which the rebels wanted for their leaders, and thirty-one members of this family were shut up in a neighbouring house, where they were all quickly burnt alive. Two young men of this family, aged seventeen and eighteen, who had been absent when their parents were burnt, have just arrived in Chang-hai, after having covered seventy or eighty leagues as beggars. Five other members of the same family were also absent during the execution of the thirty-one, but no one knows where they have gone or what has become of them. Everything which pertained to Christianity at Nanking, church ornaments, silver, papers, all

37

were deposited with the Tseu family. Consequently everything is lost without recourse. The same day several insurgents entered the city chapel, where the Christians were gathered and were reciting the prayers of Holy week; the rebels forbade them to kneel for prayers and ordered them to be seated while reciting the new prayer to Tien-fou.[18] The Christians answered that they were Catholics and did not know any other religion. It was pointed out that if, within three days, they still would not obey, they all would be decapitated.

On March 23rd, several wretches entered the chapel and threatened violence against the young Christian women; but they soon had to leave, and since then they have made no more such attempts of that kind. In the afternoon, there was a new summons to worship Tien-fou: another refusal on the part of the Christians, and more threats from the other side.

On March 25th, the Christians were engaged in the adoration of the Cross according to the custom of Good Friday. Suddenly the insurgents entered, shouting and threatening: they smashed the Crucifix and overturned the altar, then ordered the Christians to recite their prayer; they gave them books in which it was written. Then one of the catechists took up one of the religious books, an explanation of the Commandments of God, and presented it to one of the leaders. He perused the book quickly, then gave it back saying: 'Your religion is good, ours cannot be compared to it, but the new Emperor has given his orders, it is necessary to obey or die.' After the demands were repeated in vain, the soldiers seized the Christians and tied their hands behind their backs: the women and children exhorted the men to suffer in good heart for the purity of their faith; they were tied and maltreated in their turn. When all were thus bound, the men were told that they would be taken to the tribunal of the Emperor to receive their final judgment, and they were all taken out onto the street; the women and children followed them, and they all proceeded cheerfully towards the tribunal. When they arrived, they were made to wait in the outer rooms until one of the officers came on behalf of the Emperor to tell them that, seeing that they would not obey, they would all be condemned to death and would be sent to their execution at the West Gate. Then they resumed the procession across a section of the city to the place of punishment. But at the very door of the tribunal, an old man who could no longer walk, was beheaded. The others arrived together at the designated place, numbering one hundred and forty; there,

18 T'ien-fu, Heavenly Father, a term frequently used by the Taiping to refer to God.

38

the Christians were again called upon to comply, to which they continued to answer: 'We are Christians'. Many threats were made, but no one was executed. Towards evening, all of them were taken back to the city and shut up in a large warehouse, which had once been the church at Nanking. There they passed the night, with their hands tied, and some of them bound to the columns. Only one succeeded in freeing himself and escaping. The next day, more threats and several blows.

On Easter Day, everyone awaited death. Soon the rebels came into the warehouse and asked if the Christians wished to recite the prayer. Some of the rebels said: 'We must kill them all, they will not obey'. Another answered: 'No, because they would go to heaven and have what they desire, while we would only have sin'. In the meantime, all the Christians remained firm and would not yield. In particular, the women and some of the children defied the soldiers and cried out to them: 'Kill us all, that we may become martyrs and go to heaven'. The soldiers who despaired of conquering the women's courage, and who no doubt did not have orders to kill them, opened the doors of the store and forced the women and children to leave. They all went to the chapel, some seventy or eighty persons, and have since remained there. The men remained in the store, having their hands tied more tightly than in the first days.

On March 28th, several young men, tired of suffering and fearing more torments, convinced themselves that they could recite the famous prayer, since it contained nothing contrary to the dogmas of our Holy religion. After having protested that they intended to remain Catholic, twenty-two of them recited the prayer and were shortly afterwards unbound; but the others declared that they preferred to die rather than recite the prayer before knowing if it was proper: therefore several of them were cruelly beaten. Since that day, those who had weakened have shown great contrition and regretted that they had not imitated the firmness of their brethren and the courage of the women and children.

While the women and children stayed in the chapel without a single man to assist or protect them, the men were assigned to work for the insurgents, some as soldiers, others as workers. Ten of them who had been brought into the battle for Tchen-Kiang, took advantage of a dark night to desert their ranks and escape. They have come here and narrated to us what they have witnessed. It was April 14th when they succeeded in escaping.

Since their departure from Nanking, they have heard it said that the insurgents have forced many women and children out of

39

the city. The bridge over the canal crumbled under the crowd, and more than a thousand persons were drowned. We do not know whether any of the Christians took the opportunity to leave at that time.

We have also received news of Yang-tcheou. On April 1st, the rebels entered the city without finding any resistance. There they also committed the same horrors that occurred at Nanking: the Christians were not spared. The administrators of the chapel were taken, bound and led away with their families. Again they were all asked to recite the prayer to Tien-fou. Then two catechists got up to speak, clearly stating before the masses our dogmas and customs. The response was that one catechist was condemned to three hundred blows of the cane, and the other to five hundred. It is not yet known if they managed to survive that cruel whipping and other harsh treatments.

So, out of six hundred Christians which we calculate were in the cities of Nanking, Yang-tcheou and Tchen-Kiang, fifty have been killed or burnt, many others have been bound and beaten. Most of them have been totally lost and remain captives, exposed to all kinds of dangers to their souls and bodies.

Sincerely, sirs, etc.

Fr-Xavier Maresca,
Apostolic Administrator of the Diocese of Nanking.

Section 2 The First Contacts (1853)

Since, despite their capture of Nanking and Chinkiang, the Taiping themselves did not advance to the mouth of the Yangtze nor, despite the influence of Christianity upon their ideology and leadership, show any disposition to make contact with Westerners, Western moves to travel from Shanghai through the Imperial lines into Taiping held territory quickly developed.

Early in April the Chinese speaking Meadows, with a few fearful Chinese boatmen, made a risky but unsuccessful attempt in a sampan, while an American effort to sail up to Nanking in the large war sloop *Susquehanna* ran aground in the uncertain waters of the Yangtze. Bonham had by this time hurried up from Hong Kong and on 22 April set out in the shallow draught steam sloop *Hermes*, taking Meadows with him as his chief interpreter. Bonham's reports of that voyage summarise the first face to face encounter between the Taiping and the West, conducted by Meadows in conversations with various Taiping chiefs. (Docs. 18, 19). On his return to Shanghai Meadows wrote the first substantial public Western reports based on direct observation of the

Taiping for the *North China Herald*, while the commander of the *Hermes*, the evangelical Capt. E. G. Fishbourne, subsequently published his own impressions. These illustrate the very high hopes in the movement held by some Westerners at this stage (Docs. 20, 21). Bonham was rather less impressed than either Fishbourne or Meadows, but recommended to his government a policy of neutrality, one expression of which was to prevent Westerners, such as naval deserters, engaging themselves as mercenaries in the struggle (Doc. 25).

Given the now more certainly known religious nature of the movement, the Western missionaries in China were naturally also eager to make contact. However, unless engaged as interpreters for the diplomatic missions—which the French and Americans but not the British found necessary—the missionaries found it by no means easy to reach the Taiping. Several unsuccessful attempts were made, but Dr Charles Taylor of the American Methodist South mission persevered and managed to spend a few days at the rebel camp in devastated Chinkiang (Docs. 22, 23). Others could only pass on reports from Chinese contacts (Docs. 24, 26, 27), but at the end of the year the French Jesuit Stanislas Clavelin had the opportunity, as a member of the *Cassini* expedition, to see the Taiping in Nanking—the first Western missionary to do so. His account, while by no means minimising the probable difficulties inherent in future relations with the Taiping, and recognising the 'protestant' elements in their version of Christianity, was not unsympathetic to them, and both he and the French minister, de Bourboulon, were clearly impressed by many aspects of the movement (Docs. 28, 29).

By the end of 1853 therefore the West had achieved intermittent contact with the Taiping and was far better informed than it had been at the beginning of the year about many aspects of the movement. Anticipation of its ultimate success was widespread, though by no means universal, and opinion as to whether this would be to the advantage of the West in China divided. Many questions remained. From here on the Western answers proffered tended more and more to be negative.

18
A Report by Sir George Bonham
BPP, 1852–3, C. 1667, pp. 23–6, Bonham to Clarendon, 11 May
1853

My Lord,

In continuation of my despatch of the 6th instant,[19] reporting my
visit to Nanking in Her Majesty's steam-sloop 'Hermes', I have
now the honour to lay before your Lordship, in a more detailed
manner, a narrative of the events which took place from the time
of her departure from, till her return to, this port, on the day of
my last report.

As I had stated in my despatch of 22nd April last, announcing
my departure for the seat of the rebellion, it was at first my
intention to allow Mr Meadows to proceed in a China boat in
advance of the 'Hermes', so as to announce our approach and
make the necessary preliminary arrangements for our reception
—and to this end Mr Meadows was landed at a place called
Tantoo, some twelve miles below Chin-keang-foo, whence he
might despatch a messenger overland to the latter city. But having
failed in procuring anybody willing to undertake the commission,
he returned to the ship, which proceeded slowly as far as Silver
Island and in sight of Chin Keang. Mr Meadows again landed,
visited Silver Island, which he found almost deserted by its usual
occupants, priests and bonzes, and having got on board his own
boat, made sail for some small junks anchored opposite to the
city, from the crew of one of which he was to have obtained the
hire of a man to convey his message to the Insurgent Chiefs. The
'Hermes' followed close on Mr Meadows' steps, but the moment
she appeared in front of the city heights several shots were fired
at her from the forts. These not being returned, the firing ceased,
and on the Interpreter's coming back to the ship, a letter was
prepared in Commander Fishbourne's name, in which the arrival
of the 'Hermes' and the object of her visit were briefly stated.
During the preparation of this document, the Taoutae's lorchas
and schooners were seen to advance between Silver Island and
the mainland, and on their nearing the forts, an engagement took
place between the whole fleet and the Insurgent forces, which
lasted as long as we lay to, some three-quarters of an hour. In the
meantime the note had been finished and given in charge of a man
who promised its safe delivery—and this done, the 'Hermes'

19   For this preliminary despatch see the same source as for this document, pp.
      21–3. Save for Enclosure 1, which constitutes Document 19, the enclosures
      referred to by Bonham in this despatch are not reprinted here.

sailed out of sight of the engagement, which appeared to be carried on with much spirit by both parties. I am thus particular in these details, because I am anxious to show that though the 'Hermes' was fired at on her appearing in front of the batteries, thanks to the false reports spread by the Shanghae Taoutae, the firing ceased the moment it was noticed that she did not return the fire. It is true that a short distance beyond Chin Keang several shots were sent from some junks anchored within sight and hearing of the fight between the lorchas and the Chin Keang forts; but it can be easily understood that the men who commanded the junks, and who had no knowledge of our pacific intentions, took the steamer for an enemy, in the midst of all the confusion and excitement prevailing at the time. Her forbearance ought, however, to have opened their eyes to the true facts of the case; and with the view of setting right the matter, I made for Nanking at once, where I arrived on the morning of the 27th ultimo.

As already reported, her appearance was the signal for more firing, but this soon stopped when it was ascertained that we remained perfectly quiet. Between Chin Keang and Nanking the services of two Chinese were obtained for the purpose of proceeding up the river with us, and landing at the last mentioned city, with a letter similar in tenour to that despatched at Chin Keang. This was effected, and a reply was soon received from the Commandant of one of the forts, written in a courteous but somewhat unscholarlike manner. It is needless to trouble your Lordship with a perusal of this production; on its receipt, however, I felt justified in despatching Mr Meadows ashore, in order to seek the Chiefs and make arrangements for the interview. For a full and detailed account of Mr Meadows' proceedings, I beg leave to refer your Lordship to the inclosed report,[20] which, in addition to the narrative of his interview with the Northern King, contains a review of all the conversations which, in conjunction with Mr Harvey,[21] I directed him to hold. In none of these was I personally present.

During Mr Meadows' absence, two of the Chiefs, of the rank of Emperor's body-guardsmen, having come on board, Mr Harvey,

20　See Document 19. All the other enclosures referred to by Bonham may be found in the source for this document, pp. 30–5. Franz Michael, *The Taiping Rebellion*, vol. II, pp. 511–20 gives the Taiping documents.

21　Harvey was at this time assistant Chinese Secretary at Hong Kong; he was subsequently to be British consul at Ningpo and to report on the Taiping occupation of that city in 1861–2 (see Part III.4). Harvey's views on the Taiping were by then, and probably even as early as 1853, diametrically opposed to those of Meadows.

under my instructions, gave them the same explanations as I desired Mr Meadows to offer to those whom he might meet on shore, and it was arranged that next day a messenger would be sent from the city to state which of the four Princes would meet me on board, but up to a late hour next day no message was received. Towards the evening two Chiefs made their appearance, and after some conversation produced the accompanying paper, which, owing to the improper mode in which it was couched, was returned to them with a strong expression of dissatisfaction at the very objectionable manner in which that document was written. It was further stated to them in plain terms that productions of this nature could not for an instant be tolerated by the British authorities, and I now wished it to be conveyed to the Chiefs that the British Government had a treaty with the present dynasty, and that to enable them to learn the conditions of that treaty, and the true position of the English nation, I sent to the Chiefs a Chinese version of that treaty. After having thus conveyed my sentiments in a courteous but unmistakeable manner, these two Chiefs retired, and said we should hear from the shore next morning.

Accordingly, on the afternoon of the next day a message came on board, to the effect that one of their high Chiefs was on his way to visit me; and shortly after a large State boat was seen making for the steamer. On its coming alongside, it was ascertained that a Chief called Lae,[22] of the rank of Minister, or Secretary of State, was on board. In Mr Meadows' report will be found a minute of the interview, which passed off very satisfactorily, the previous day's message having evidently told well. Ample apology was made by this Minister for the objectionable document above alluded to; and under these favourable circumstances arrangements were made for my landing in a proper manner the following morning, to proceed to one of the Princes' official residences, in order to explain personally the object of the visit of the steamer to Nanking.

Next morning, the weather being exceedingly boisterous, I sent an excuse to the Princes. I had in the meantime thought over the matter, and I was apprehensive lest some difficulties in the way of ceremonial might interfere with the good feeling then apparently existing. The inclosed communication was therefore prepared and despatched by Mr Meadows, who went, accompanied by Commander Fishbourne, and several other officers. Mr Meadows' minutes will supply all the details of the interview on shore.

22   Lai Han-ying, brother-in-law of Hung Hsiu-ch'üan.

Early on the 1st of May, according to the notice given to the Chiefs in inclosure No. 3, the Hermes proceeded some twelve miles above Nanking, and then fell in with a few of the Imperialist war-junks and boats. On seeing the steamer approach, a few shots were fired at her from these boats, but after an explanation of our intentions, the Commandant of the force came on board and informed us that the Imperial General, Heang Yung, was at a town called Taeping-foo some distance from the spot. The amount of force under Heang was stated to be very considerable, but I imagine that the whole number of fighting men cannot exceed 20,000 or 25,000. On the northern bank again, Keshen was reported to be stationed with 7,000 to 10,000 men under his orders. It is difficult to obtain anything like an accurate statement on these points, as the Chinese are so prone to exaggerate the number to hundreds of thousands, but I think the numbers above stated are not very far from the truth. In the evening of that day we returned to Nanking, in order to receive a reply to the letter sent through Mr Meadows.

Early on the 2nd, Lae, the Secretary of State already mentioned, came on board, as will be seen from Mr Meadows' minutes, and brought an answer, a translation of which I inclose. To this very extraordinary document I returned the accompanying reply, which I deemed, under all the circumstances, necessary, as the sooner the minds of these men are disabused in regard to their universal supremacy, the better for all parties. After the despatch of inclosure No. 5, the 'Hermes' got under weigh and left Nanking for her return to Shanghae.

On passing Chin-keang-foo the following morning, the 3rd instant, some junks and stockades opened fire upon us, and, as already reported to your Lordship, the steamer did, on this occasion, return the fire, but not until seven or eight shots had passed over the ship. The forts and batteries of Chin-Keang, on the southern bank, followed the example of those on the northern shore, and were treated by us in the same manner. This firing, after the assurances given at Nanking, and the explanations and warnings conveyed at the very last interview with Lae, as will be seen from Mr Meadows' minutes, appeared to all exceedingly incomprehensible, and it was thought nothing but a mistaken notion of our intentions could have brought it about. These views were partially confirmed on reaching Silver Island, where the 'Hermes' anchored for the purpose of visiting the island. Signals were made from the shore, and a letter, the translation of which is annexed, arrived on board from the principal Chief at Chin-Keang. This communication appears to have been written previously to the appearance of the steamer, and has some reference to a letter sent from Tanyang by Mr Meadows when he proceeded into the country, as already reported in my despatch of April 22. Mr Meadows went ashore and spoke to a man, Lo, who seems to hold a high office in Chin-Keang. The particulars of what passed on this occasion will be found in the minutes; and in the meanwhile the accompanying communication having been prepared, it was sent on shore by one of the rebels who came off with Mr Meadows. An answer having been promised in a short time, I determined to wait two or three hours longer, within which time it came on board. Annexed is a translation of that answer, which is as satisfactory as could be expected under all the circumstances of the case.

During our stay in Nanking we found the insurgents, from the highest to the lowest, much inclined to dilate upon their present creed, and anxious to communicate every possible information upon the extraordinary tenets which they profess to follow. Several very interesting conversations were held on board, respecting their faith and its origin—as also upon the objects they have in view, and the means they propose to adopt to carry out those intentions. On the latter point, I think, I have in my despatch of May 6 stated all I could collect in the shape of information, and I repeat, speculations should not be indulged in, as so much depends upon circumstances with which we are not at all familiar. As regards the religious question, our views upon that point are as clear as they are ever likely to be, judging from the extraordinary nature of the books with which I was liberally furnished by the Princes. I have caused the annexed digest of the contents of the twelve pamphlets to be prepared under the able supervision of the Reverend Dr Medhurst, whose familiarity with these matters and just appreciation of the real meaning of the text I could depend upon. I have likewise requested him to prepare the inclosed summary of all these pamphlets, so as to place at one glance before your Lordship the whole nature of their contents. Few will be prepared for so extraordinary a sect, and for tenets so absurd, intermingled as they are with Christian principles, as those now under consideration. As I already expressed, I am loath to believe that the minds of the whole of the Insurgent body are influenced by the doctrines contained in these books, and I rather think the source of their existence may be traced to political motives on the part of the Chiefs, in the success of which they have not been greatly disappointed; but at the same time I think there must be in their ranks many who, having embraced the new faith, are determined, like all proselytes, to carry it out in all its integrity. These books are now being translated by Dr Medhurst, and I hope in a very short time to forward to your Lordship complete translations of them, printed here at the newspaper office.[23]

Since the date of my despatch of May 6, no intelligence respecting the movements of the rebels has reached Shanghae. I confess I do not think that they will visit this place, and I propose leaving this port for Hong-Kong this evening in the 'Hermes', the 'Salamander' remaining here to protect the port; and in the event of my presence being again required at Shanghae, I can in a few days reach the place, either in a ship of war or in one of the Peninsular and Oriental Steam Navigation Company's steamers.

In my despatch of the 22nd April, I acquainted your Lordship that Mr Interpreter Meadows had gone to Soochow, with a view of proceeding by land to Nanking and its vicinity, for the purpose of obtaining information relative to the intentions of the insurgents; and as, from the shallowness of the Grand Canal, he could not proceed on his journey, I thought it only fair to him that he should accompany me to Nanking.[24] On both occasions Mr Meadows acquitted himself to my entire satisfaction. On the first occasion he underwent a considerable degree of personal inconvenience, if not of risk, and I think it right therefore to bring his services to your Lordship's notice.

I was also accompanied by Mr Secretary Harvey, who, from his knowledge of the language and of the mode of thinking and acting of the Chinese, afforded me much valuable assistance.

I find that during my absence Dr Bowring has spoken highly of Mr Harvey's attainments in the Chinese language, as well as of his ability when discharging 'the serious and delicate duties of his mission' to Amoy, and I am much gratified in having this opportunity of assuring your Lordship that I fully concur in the sentiments expressed by Dr Bowring in regard to Mr Harvey.

I have, etc.

S G Bonham

23 Rev. W. H. Medhurst's translations appeared in the *North China Herald* from 14 May 1853 on, and his review of them on 3 September. Translations are also in Michael, op. cit., vol. II, pp. 86–167. Medhurst was a representative of the London Missionary Society and the father of the consular official of the same name.

24 For Meadows' own account of the *Hermes* voyage to Nanking, as well as of his earlier individual attempt to reach that city, see his book *The Chinese and their Rebellions*, chs. 16–17; also the *North China Herald*, 14 and 21 May 1853.

19
A Report by T T Meadows
BPP, 1852–3, C. 1667, pp. 26–30, enc. in Bonham to Clarendon,
11 May 1853

CONVERSATION WITH THE NORTHERN AND ASSISTANT PRINCES

About an hour or two after the 'Hermes' dropped anchor at
Nanking on the 27th April, 1853, I, in conformity with instructions, landed, accompanied by Lieutenant Spratt, and requested
to be conducted to the highest authority to whom immediate
access could be obtained. After about half an hour's walk, led by
one or two volunteer guides, and surrounded by numbers of the
Insurgent troops, we were stopped in front of a house in the
northern suburb. Our attendants here ranged themselves in two
rows, forming an avenue of ten or fifteen yards in length from the
door of the house to ourselves. Two persons clothed in yellow silk
gowns and hoods then appeared at the threshold, and the soldiers
about called on me to kneel. This I refused to do, but advanced
and, uncovering, told the two persons that I had been sent by Her
Majesty's Plenipotentiary to make inquiries and arrangements
respecting a meeting between him and chief authorities at
Nanking. As they retreated into the house without giving any
reply, while the summons to kneel was being continued, and Mr
Spratt was called on by words and gestures to lay aside his sword,
I, after recommending that gentleman to disregard the requisi-
tion, deemed it advisable to follow the Chiefs without awaiting
invitation. I accordingly entered the house, and, advancing to the
spot where they had seated themselves, on the only two chairs
within sight, again informed them of the purpose for which I had
come. Before I had well finished I heard scuffling and angry
shouting at the door behind me, and the Chiefs were crying out,
'Ta!' 'Beat!' two or three of their armed followers commenced
beating the man who had been most prominent in guiding us
there. One of the Chiefs, whom I subsequently ascertained to be
known as the Northern Prince, then asked if I worshipped 'God
the Heavenly Father'? I replied that the English had done so for
eight or nine hundred years. On this he exchanged a glance of
consultation with his companion (the Assistant Prince), and then
ordered seats to be brought. After I and my companion had seated
ourselves, a conversation of considerable length ensued between
myself and the Northern Prince, the first in rank of the two; the
other, the Assistant Prince, listening and observing attentively,
but saying nothing to me directly, and only making a short remark
when looked to or addressed by his superordinate. The con-

versation on my part was turned chiefly on the number and relative rank of the Insurgent Chiefs, and on the circumstances under which they would be prepared to meet Sir George Bonham; but I also explained, as authorised, the simple object of his visit, viz., to notify the desire of the British Government to remain perfectly neutral in the struggle between them and the Manchoos, and to learn their feelings towards us and their intentions in the event of their forces advancing on Shanghae. I explained to him that we had no concern with the square-rigged vessels, lorchas, and other craft that had followed the Hermes into Chin-Keang; also that the proclamations of the Manchoo officials, stating that they had engaged the services of a number of foreign steamers, were false in so far as British vessels were included; and that though we could not prevent the sale of English craft, private property, more than the sale of manufactures generally, such craft, after sale, were not entitled to the use of the national colours.

To all this the Northern Prince listened, but made little or no rejoinder; the conversation, in so far as directed by him, consisting mainly of inquiries as to our religious beliefs, and expositions of their own. He stated that as children and worshippers of one God we were all brethren; and after receiving my assurance that such had long been our view also, inquired if I knew the 'Heavenly Rules' (teen teaon). I replied that I was most likely acquainted with them, though unable to recognise them under that name, and, after a moment's thought, asked if they were ten in number. He answered eagerly in the affirmative. I then began repeating the substance of the first of the Ten Commandments, but had not proceeded far before he laid his hand on my shoulders in a friendly way, and exclaimed, 'The same as ourselves! the same as ourselves!' while the simply observant expression on the face of his companion disappeared before one of satisfaction as the two exchanged glances. He then stated, with reference to my previous inquiry as to their feelings and intentions towards the British, that not merely might peace exist between us, but that we might be intimate friends. He added, we might now, at Nanking, land and walk about where we pleased. He spoke repeatedly of a foreigner at Canton, whom he named Lo Ho Sun,[25] as being a 'good man'. He described this person as one

25 Lo Hsien-sheng, i.e. Mr Lo. It became generally accepted that this referred to Rev. I. J. Roberts, whose Chinese name was Lo Hsiao-ch'üan. However, it is possible that this Mr Lo was either Rev. Benjamin Hobson of the London Missionary Society based in Canton (whose Chinese name was Ho-hsin), or Rev. W. Lobscheid (Lo Ts'un-te) of the Rhenish Missionary Society.

who cured the sick without remuneration, and as having been recently home for a short period (Dr Hobson, Medical Missionary?). He recurred again and again, with an appearance of much gratitude, to the circumstance that he and his companions at arms had enjoyed the special protection and aid of God, without which they could never have been able to do what they had done against superior numbers and resources; and alluding to our declaration of neutrality and non-assistance to the Manchoos, said, with a quiet air of thorough conviction, 'It would be wrong for you to help them; and, what is more, it would be of no use. Our Heavenly Father helps us, and no one can fight with Him'.

With respect to the proposed meeting, he pointed to one of his officers standing near, and said the latter would come on the following day to guide any who might choose to come to an interview. I replied that such an arrangement might do very well for myself and others, but that Sir George Bonham was an officer of high rank in Her Britannic Majesty's service, and could certainly not proceed to any meeting unless it were previously settled where, by whom, and how he was to be received. 'However high his rank may be', was the reply, 'he cannot be so high as the persons in whose presence you are now sitting'. And I could obtain nothing more definite than that the reception would take place in a yamun in the city, and that we should have no cause to take objections to the station of the personages met. I said I should make my report to his Excellency accordingly, but could not answer for his landing. In reply to my inquiries respecting the Tae-ping Wang, the Prince of Peace, the Northern Prince explained in writing that he was the 'True Lord' or Sovereign; that 'the Lord of China is the Lord of the whole world; he is the second Son of God, and all people in the whole world must obey and follow him'. As I read this without remark, he said, looking at me interrogatively, 'The True Lord is not merely the Lord of China; he is not only our Lord, he is your Lord also'. As I still made no remark, but merely kept looking at him, he did not think fit to insist on an answer, and, after a while, turned his head and began talking of other matters. His conversation gave great reason to conclude that though his religious beliefs were derived from the writings, or it might even by the teachings, of foreigners, still he was quite ignorant of the relative positions of foreign countries, and had probably got most of his notions of international dealings from the Chinese records of periods when the territory of the present Empire was divided into several States.

CONVERSATION WITH TWO OFFICERS, THE BEARERS OF A MANDATE

On the 28th of April the official who was to have acted as guide did not appear, but late in the afternoon two others came, with an open and unsealed mandate, concerning the forms to be observed by those who wished to appear at Court. As this stated that the Lord of China had been sent down into the world as the true 'Lord of all Nations', and was otherwise objectionable, it was returned by the bearers, with an unequivocal message, fitted to disabuse the senders of their notions of universal supremacy.

CONVERSATION WITH LAE, THE KEEN-TEEN (OR SECOND MINISTER)

On the afternoon of the 29th of April, Lae, the second of the Insurgent Chiefs beneath those bearing the title of Prince, came on board the 'Hermes'. He at once apologised for the tone of the mandate of the preceding day, saying it had been drawn up by persons ignorant of the fact that 'Wae-heung-te', foreign brethren, could not be addressed in the same style as native brethren. It was distinctly explained to him that while the English had, for 900 years, adored the Great Being whom he called the Heavenly Father, they on earth acknowledged allegiance to but one Lord, the Sovereign of the British Empire; and that, under no circumstances whatsoever, would they for an instant admit fealty to any other, though they were quite prepared to recognise as the Sovereign of the Chinese whomsoever the Chinese themselves might choose or submit to as such. After this had been fully assented to by Lae, I stated to him, at considerable length, the circumstances of our desire to preserve neutrality, of our having no connexion with the vessels in the employ of the Manchoo Government, &c. &c., as had been done to the Northern and Assistant Princes two days before. After this it was settled that Lae, or a lesser officer, Leang, who accompanied him, should be in attendance at the landing-place on the following day, at 11 a.m., with a sufficient number of chairs and horses to convey Her Majesty's Plenipotentiary, his suite, and some naval officers to the residences of the Northern and Eastern Princes.

CONVERSATION WITH LAE AND OTHERS, IN THE CITY OF NANKING

On the 30th of April, the two officers, Lae and Leang, came to the landing-place with chairs and horses as had been arranged, but his Excellency sent to state that the tempestuous weather (which rendered it difficult to land dry) and indisposition prevented his carrying out the intention of yesterday, and that I should in an hour or two land as the bearer of a letter, communicating all that was to have been stated verbally. I landed accordingly at 1 p.m., Captain Fishbourne and Messrs. Woodgate and Burton accompanying me. Horses were furnished at the landing-place, and we were guided into the city, to a house occupied as a Yamun, by the four officers next in rank below those called Princes, Lae being of the number. We found that the latter had, after leaving the landing-place, gone to the Northern and Eastern Princes, and had not yet returned to his residence. As one of the other occupants was just then engaged in investigating a case of rape, we found the place crowded with spectators, whose curiosity subjected us to some annoyance until the house-steward procured us seats in an inner apartment. We waited here about an hour, during which tea and other refreshments were offered us, and an officer came from Lae to apologise for his delay in appearing, and to beg us to attribute it to nothing but to pressing business. Eventually we were received by the Ching-seang, his immediate superordinate and three others. I was explaining the nature of my errand, and endeavouring to get them to take me either to the Northern or Eastern Prince to deliver the letter, when Lae appeared. He and the others pressed us very much to dine and sleep there that night, engaging to take us to the Northern and Eastern Princes on the following morning; but as we were quite unprepared for this, I ultimately delivered the letter to Lae, and we reached the 'Hermes' again just before dark.

CONVERSATION WITH LAE ON BOARD THE 'HERMES'

Early on the morning of the 2nd of May, Lae followed on board the 'Hermes' the communication on yellow silk of the Eastern and Western Princes. Our intended departure at four p.m. of that day was formerly notified to him. Reference was made to the circumstances of the 'Hermes' having been fired on when passing Chin Keang inwards, and he was told that this had been overlooked, solely because the circumstances under which we appeared were certainly suspicious, but that as all parties had now been informed of our pacific intentions, any fire on the vessel would be at once returned. Lae replied that we need give ourselves no thought on that score, as communications had, since our arrival, been exchanged with Chin Keang, and the nature of our position to them was well known.

CONVERSATION WITH GENERAL LO AT CHIN KEANG

Notwithstanding this we were fired on by the shipping and stockades both at Kwa-chow and Chin-Keang. The 'Hermes' returned the fire as she slowly passed and then anchored off

Silver Island. A letter from Lo and Woo, the Commanders of the forces at Chin-Keang and Yang-chow, was here brought off by a fishing-boat, and shortly afterwards some of the Insurgent officers and troops came down to the water's edge on the right bank and made signs of a desire to communicate. I was accordingly sent on shore, and found it was the Insurgent General Lo, who explained that the fire had been opened at Kwa-chow by mistake by some new troops, who were not aware of our having been in peaceful communication with their Princes at Nanking. He stated that, on hearing the noise of the firing, he had hurried down from the City of Chin-Keang to the stockades to stop it. I told him, as instructed, that Her Majesty's Plenipotentiary was still willing to continue neutral, but that all acts of aggression would be repelled by force, and might compel the British Government to side with the Manchoos. He asked why we, who had an old enmity with the Manchoos, and were on the other hand brethren of his party, in as much as we acknowledged the same God and Christ, did not rather aid the latter. I replied that it was an established rule of the British Government not to interfere with the internal struggles of foreign States; moreover, that though we had been at war with the Manchoos, we had concluded a treaty of peace with them, and could not therefore take arms against them without breaking our plighted faith. He then introduced the subject of opium, saying we ought not to sell it. I replied that it was with the opium as with the vessels bought by the Manchoo officials, the British Government took no cognisance of it, but left it to the Chinese authorities to deal with those found engaged in the traffic as they thought fit. I invited him to accompany me on board, assuring him of a safe landing whenever he pleased, but he declined. I then asked for one of his people to come in order to bring back the reply to his letter. Three volunteered at once, one of whom I found to be a Meaou-tsze, or Independent Mountaineer, from Kwa-chow, who stated that about 3,000 of his people were in the ranks of the insurgents.

20
A Report from the *North China Herald*
North China Herald, 7 May 1853

The *Hermes* returned to this port on the afternoon of the 5th instant, with His Excellency Sir George Bonham on board. She has made an eventful trip up the Yang-tsze, during which she lay five days at Nanking, and brings back intelligence of a deeply interesting and even astounding character respecting the Insurgents; giving us much cause to thank H.M.'s Plenipotentiary for the steps taken to obtain some positive information regarding them. The following particulars we give on good authority; and hope to furnish from the same source more details in a future issue.

The Insurgents are Christians of the Protestant form of worship, and anti-idolaters of the strictest order. They acknowledge but One God, the Heavenly Father, the Allwise, Allpowerful, and Omnipresent Creator of the world; with him, Jesus Christ, as the Saviour of Mankind; and also the Holy Spirit, as the last of the Three Persons of the Trinity. Their Chief on earth is a person known as '*Tae-ping-wang*, the Prince of Peace', to whom a kind of divine origin and mission is ascribed. Far, however, from claiming adoration, he forbids, in an edict, the application to himself of the terms 'Supreme', 'Holy', and others, hitherto constantly assumed by the Emperors of China; but which he declines receiving on the ground that they are due to God alone. Their moral code, the Insurgents call the 'Heavenly Rules', which on examination proved to be the Ten Commandments. The observance of these is strictly enforced by the leaders of the movement, chiefly Kwang-tung and Kwang-se men, who are not merely formal professors of a religious system, but practical and spiritual Christians, deeply influenced by the belief that God is always with them. The hardships they have suffered, and the dangers they have incurred, are punishments and trials of their Heavenly Father; the successes they have achieved, are instances of His Grace. In conversation they 'bore' the more worldly minded by constant recurrence to that special attention of the Almighty of which they believe themselves to be the objects. With proud humility and with the glistening eyes of gratitude they point back to the fact that at the beginning of their enterprise some four years ago, they numbered but one or two hundred, and that except for the direct help of their Heavenly Father they never could have done what they have done.

'They', said one, speaking of the Imperialists, 'spread all kinds of lies about us. They say we employ magical arts: the only kind of magic we have used is prayer to God. In Kwang-se when we occupied Yung Gan we were sorely pressed; there was then only some two or three thousand of us. We were beset on all sides by much greater numbers; we had no powder left and our provisions were all done. But our Heavenly Father came down and showed us the way to break out. So we put our wives and children in the middle and not only forced a passage but completely beat our enemies.' After a short pause he added—'If it be the will of God that our Prince of Peace shall be the Sovereign of China, he will be the Sovereign of China. If not, then we will die here.'

The man who used this language of courageous fidelity to the cause in every extreme and of confidence in God was a shrivelled up, elderly, little individual, who made an odd figure in his yellow and red hood. But he could think the thoughts and speak the speech of a hero. He and others like him have succeeded in infusing their own sentiments of courage and morality to no slight extent, considering the materials operated upon, into the minds, of their adherents. One instance was of a youth of 19 who acted as one of the guides to a party that rode into Nanking, and who again and again, as he ran along on foot, begged and beseeched Mr Interpreter Meadows, if he came back from Shanghae, to bring him a double sword; but also exhorted that gentleman to refrain from smoking, from drunkenness and other vices with a simple earnestness at once amusing and admirable. This lad, the son of a literary graduate in Hoonan of the second degree, and himself no bad scholar, had left his father's house at the age of 17 and travelled some days to join the Insurgent camp before Kwei-lin, prompted by an adventurous spirit to share in 'conquering the rivers and mountains', the expression by which the 'holy warriors' of Tae-ping designate their enterprise.

That there are ambitious self-deceivers, shrewd impostors, and calculating hypocrites among them in plenty, we doubt not; we also doubt not that numbers join, and will continue in, their ranks influenced exclusively by motives as worldly and ignoble as those which guide the conduct of so many professing Christians of the West. But among the leaders and originators of the movement there are ummistakable signs of a good leaven, which we trust, and earnestly wish, may ultimately spread throughout the whole mass. One convincing proof of the sincerity of the ruling minds is that, while fighting to free their country from a foreign yoke and anxious to obtain adherents, they nevertheless throw great difficulties in the way of a rapid increase of numbers by insisting on the general adoption of a new and reviled religion learnt from the 'barbarians'.

While they have manifestly derived their religious beliefs from the writings, if not in some cases the direct teachings, of foreign protestant missionaries, they appeared to be extremely ignorant of foreign nations. Canton was known to them as the seat of a great foreign commerce; but Shanghae (which has indeed sprung into importance during the few years they have been fighting in the west) was found to be quite unknown to several of their leading men. It is gratifying to learn that under these circumstances the existence of a common religious belief disposed them to regard their 'foreign brethren' with a frank friendliness which past experience renders it difficult to comprehend in a Chinese; but which we earnestly trust every effort will be made to cultivate and establish in their minds. It would, to speak of nothing else, do more for our commercial interests, should the Insurgents succeed, than hundreds of ships and regiments. We understand that during a long ride of ten or twelve miles into the city of Nanking and back, along what may at present be called one of the streets of a large camp, Mr Meadows did not hear one of those abusive and derogatory epithets applied to himself or companions, which have always been so liberally bestowed on passing foreigners by the heathen Chinese. There was also the fullest evidence that the obscene expressions, with which the latter garnished all their conversations, are prohibited and almost banished from the language of the Christians. . . .

21

An Account by Capt. E G Fishbourne

E. G. Fishbourne, *Impressions of China and the Present Revolution: its Progress and Prospects* (London, 1855), ch. 5

It has been too generally believed that the insurgents were most sanguinary in their operations, and that like the followers of Mahomet, they propagated their faith (if this were possible) by the sword; this belief is in part founded upon the misrepresentations of the Imperialists, and partly, perhaps, upon their own proclamations, which stated that they would take the heads off the priests and Tartars.

As to propagating their faith by the sword, this is not correct; they do not compel any to join them: but they will not admit any to fellowship unless they profess the same religion, commit to memory the same form of prayer, and observe the same daily rules of worship. The mere superscription of the Chinese character *shun* 'obedient' over the door of a house, is held a sufficient token of the submission of its inmates, and they have refused numbers upon the grounds of their not making profession of the same faith.

Their code of morals, chosen evidently from the Old Testament, and not suited to our habits or dispensation, is sanguinary, but is no doubt administered with justice and mercy as compared with any administration of law amongst the Imperialists; and it is probable that a law of such a character is necessary for the low and depraved state in which China is at present.

Some of the statements of their conduct are evidently a little figurative: thus it was the impression that they destroyed all the priests. Now on visiting Silver Island—a celebrated shrine of idolatrous worship—we found the priests there, and they stated that they had not been injured; they were given books, and informed that they must allow their hair to grow—their practice being to shave their heads.

The idols, it is true, were all destroyed; some of these must have been magnificent, made of clay, and forty or even sixty feet high. Those of wood or stone were defaced, and many thrown into the water.

Golden Island was another celebrated place of idol worship, and there also the temples had been defaced. We observed the same in the suburbs of Nankin. The hostility was to the idols much less than to the temples; but idolatrous emblems are always woven into these buildings in such a way that it is next to impossible to remove the evidences of idolatry and not injure the temple. The celebrated porcelain tower shared in some degree general rage against idol-worship; for, though it does not appear to have been erected with reference to worship, but in commemoration of an individual, yet many of its ornaments were idolatrous; these, we were informed were all destroyed, and as far as we could see with the aid of our glasses, the tower had been slightly defaced, though it was still standing. Fire had been the agent used in Golden Island.

Nor is it to be wondered at, that on awakening to a sense of the degradation their nation had been brought to by these priests and their idolatrous worship, they should be carried beyond the line of conduct which indifferent spectators would deem proper.

The city of Nankin is a walled city, said to have contained half a million inhabitants. Its walls are high, and extend twenty-one miles; but not more than a quarter of the indirect space was occupied with houses; and these for the most part new in one corner—the remainder being gardens and fields.

It was said that the insurgents destroyed all the Tartars and their families to the number of twenty or twenty-five thousand. This I do not credit—not that I pretend to say what they would have done—but I think this is too much built upon the evidence of the boy-attendant of Lae's—intelligent though he was, and to be relied on, as far as his knowledge could enable him to speak. But the fact is, as I think, that the greater part were seized with the panic which appears to seize all on the approach of the insurgents, and had fled; for the houses gave conclusive proof that the city had not only been abandoned of its inhabitants, but that they had taken all their furniture and other removable property out with them; for had it been simply removed from the houses and thrown into the streets, we should have seen some remnants. It was quite remarkable how completely street after street and house after house were emptied, and with few exceptions. Again, we saw many people as we passed along, carrying back their furniture, as they did at Shanghae; confidence having returned. We saw a few houses sealed up, and from their appearance they were the houses of rich people; the silk looms also seem to have been left. These they would naturally suppose would not be injured by the insurgents; the more particularly as they had always studiously avoided any thing that affected trade; and it is owing to this care that our export trade has been so little interrupted.

Indeed, it is evident that the policy of Tae-ping, and his followers, is to protect the people, but make war, even 'to the knife', against the Tartar authorities.

A further reason for doubting the correctness of those statements, as to the wholesale destruction of the Manchoos in Nankin, is, that it was stated in the Pekin Gazette, that the Emperor had commanded pensions to be given to the wives of those Tartar soldiers that had lost their lives in Nankin; consequently, some must have escaped to ask for and obtain the pensions alluded to.

The insurgent army, as it appeared to us, was for the most part composed of young men. Many of these were mere boys, and yet they were doing the duty of men; they used to cross the river, a dozen at a time, to destroy junks floating down the stream, land, and drive hundreds of the peasantry before them, as if they were so many sheep.

They adopt the ten commandments, translated by themselves —perhaps from less perfect Chinese—to which they append annotations; thus they state, under the seventh commandment, that smoking opium is always associated with adultery, and must be discontinued. They behead for smoking or selling opium, and bamboo for smoking tobacco. They are Iconoclasts, and destroy every vestige of idol-worship. They circulate tracts, drawn from the Scriptures by themselves. They are generally called 'worshippers of Yesu'. Roman Catholics are called worshippers of Tien-chu; one or two told us that they were worshippers of Tien-chu, by which I understand them to say that they were different from others of the movement, and they appeared not to wish it to be generally known that they said so; it might be that they meant to say merely that they had been such, until they had joined the movement.

They have no priests—they stated that they needed none, as all were priests or teachers in their respective stations; yet they have people amongst them with ecclesiastical titles. They may not have understood the question; as I have no doubt there is a difficulty in putting such questions into Chinese, and when put, it requires time and circumlocution before they are understood. Some few spoke a very little English, learnt at Hong Kong and Canton; some said they had been at school at the former place. They said they had men amongst them who could translate the English edition of the Scriptures into Chinese. One said, on going down amongst our men, that he was a Protestant; several said they were of the same religion as us; others, that they were of the ten commandments' religion, the same as the schools at Hong Kong; and one said he was of the same religion as King Victoria.

They are very severe for any infraction of morals, and separate the sexes to prevent improprieties of any kind. It appears, that up to their arrival at Nankin, the wives fought side by side with their husbands; but that, on arriving at Nankin, they agreed to separate till they should have won the Empire, to effect which, they gave themselves twelve months. Hence it was that Dr Taylor did not see any females at Chiang-kiang-foo. The women were placed under instruction; this part was styled the women's quarter, and it was death to enter it, except such persons as were appointed for the purpose of instructing them.

They hold an open court, confronting litigants: not so in the old Chinese courts, where they nearly always have recourse to tortures. They style the army the holy army, and have changed the name of Nankin to Tien-king, or Holy city. Nankin, I fancy, means North city.[26] They style each other brethren, and us foreign brethren. They have removed the queues, as a badge of slavery imposed by the Tartars.

They quite look upon themselves as favourites of Heaven, and are proportionally sanguine of success; yet they did not neglect any precaution to ensure it, but were fortifying when we were there, with remarkable diligence and judgment. I saw them carrying some very good twenty-four pounders into exceedingly well-chosen positions, to cover where they had entered; and the breach in the walls which they themselves had established, they had had repaired.

They are men of their word; a Chinaman, describing this characteristic difference from other Chinamen, said, 'If they say

26   In fact it means Southern Capital.

they will give you twenty blows of a bamboo, make up your mind they will not stop short at nineteen, come what may of it'.

They are most frank in their manner, quite unlike what we are accustomed to in Chinese.

They hold the Imperialists cheap, and I think it more than probable that they know that the Imperialist's soldiers do not care to do more than make a shew of fighting. In fact, there is almost an understanding amongst them, and this will become more so, as their success increases.

I rode with an interpreter about twelve miles, and must have passed many thousand people carrying rice, furniture, clothes, guns, &c.; and the interpreter assured me that he only heard one expression that could offend the nicest ear, whereas one can hardly move as many paces elsewhere, without hearing many; indeed, I am told the very children use the grossest expressions, in their ordinary play.

It was obvious to the commonest observer that they were practically a different race. They had Gutzlaff's edition of the Scriptures, at least, they told us so; we know they had twenty-eight chapters of Genesis, for they had reprinted thus much, and gave us several copies; and some of them were practical Christians, and nearly all seemed to be under the influence of religious impressions, though limited in their amount. They believed in a special Providence, and believed that this truth had had a practical demonstration in their own case. That though they had had trials and had incurred dangers, these were to punish and to purify. They had also successes, such as they could have had only by God's special interference.

They referred with deep and heartfelt gratitude, to the difficulties they had encountered, and the deliverances which had been effected for them, when they were but a few, and attributed all their success to God . . .

They appeared to me to adhere strictly to the truth, regardless of how it affected their interests; thus they did not hesitate to say that their leader had no connexion with, and was not descended from the Ming dynasty, as had been said, and seemed to be quite indifferent to the influence which they would lose by this denial, for the idea was not without its weight. Thus the insurgents at Amoy declared for Tien-teh, stating that he was descended of the Ming dynasty and all the Triads were committed by their organization to support the claims of that dynasty.

The quiet self-possession and confidence of the leaders we came in contact with, was quite un-Chinese. When it was told them a second time that we should in future return their fire, they seemed to think that we wished to frighten them, and said, 'Well, do as you please; we are not afraid'. Another time they said, 'If you are come to assist us, we shall be glad; but do as you please! We are independent of your assistance; only if you are going to join the Mantchoos, be good enough to let us know'. And when told if they came to Shanghae and attacked any of our people there, they would be treated as the Mantchoos were in 1842, they said, 'But why should we fire upon you; we are brethren, and worship the same God?'

Their policy is only to be known by first knowing their religion; and this, because of imperfectly understanding their language, we are not clear about. On the interpreter's first visit he endeavoured to explain to one of the princes the power and resources of England; he said, 'We don't want to know that; we want to know your religion' . . .

22
Journal entries by the American Baptist Missionary Nathan Wardner

The Journal of Nathan Wardner in the archives of the American Baptist Foreign Missionary Society, Valley Forge, Pennsylvania, USA

13th [June 1853] Br. C. [Solomon Carpenter] started to see if he cannot get to Chinkeang with his teacher . . .

14th . . . The insurgents sent a letter by Mr Taylor requesting foreigners to keep away from them till they get the Empire, as the imperialists take advantage of their visits to attack them . . .

16th . . . Messrs Muirhead and Wylie, who attempted to go among the insurgents were discovered at Soo-chow, had their false tails pulled off and the mob were consulting about beheading them to get the bounty offered for rebels in disguise, when they applied to a mandarin who was passing who rescued them and sent an escort with them to their boats.

17th . . . Br C. returned. Only got to Lee-oo, as his boat man got frightened.

21st . . . Learn that Ta-ping-wang has written to Rev. Mr Roberts to go to Nanking to preach and baptize, and that the latter has applied to Mr Marshall[27] for permission, who refuses . . .

Aug. 1st . . . Saw Rev. Mr Roberts who has just arrived from Canton on his way to Nanking.

27 Humphrey Marshall was the US Minister to China until October 1853, when he was succeeded by Robert M. McLane. For his obstruction of Taylor and Roberts see his reports of 21 June and 10 July 1853 in *US House of Representatives Executive Documents*, 33rd Congress, 1st Session, 16, no. 20.

6th . . . Messrs Roberts and Taylor started for Chinkeang yesterday . . .
11th . . . Learn that Roberts and Taylor have returned, did not get to Silver Island because of the imperial fleets. They bring word that 3000 of the imperialists' best troops have gone over to the rebels . . . [28]

23
An Account by the American Methodist Episcopalian Missionary Dr Charles Taylor
Charles Taylor MD, *Five Years in China* (Nashville, 1860), pp. 339-60

CHAPTER 27 SECOND TRIP TO THE INSURGENT CAMP

Far from being satisfied with the result of this effort, I procured a set of boatmen on whose courage I thought I could rely more confidently, embarked a second time as already narrated, and proceeded once more to Silver Island.

To reach this spot I had again to run the blockade by the Imperial fleet, which consisted of near a hundred sail of war junks, Portuguese lorchas, and, to their shame be it said, five English and American vessels, with their crews, who had hired themselves to aid the Tartar usurpers in this unrighteous warfare, for sustaining their corrupt dynasty and perpetuating idolatry among an entire third of the human family. We passed directly under the guns of one of these foreign vessels, and stopped at Silver Island until nightfall, when we crossed over to the southern shore and anchored till morning, under a steep, rocky bluff. My boatmen this time also, proved to be very timid, and absolutely refused to go any nearer Chin-kiang-fu. For, besides the blockade by the fleet, the Imperial army besieging that city was encamped on some hills in sight. We had also learned that, seeing foreign vessels in the hostile fleet, the insurgents had supposed foreigners generally were enlisted against them, and had issued a proclamation offering a reward of five thousand dollars for the head of any 'outside-country man'. No inducement would prevail with my boatmen to advance any further, and they endeavored to dissuade me from the attempt, saying that if I persisted, they felt certain I would never come back alive. No alternative was then left me between returning, or

28   For examples of other unsuccessful attempts by missionaries at this time to reach the rebels see W. A. P. Martin, *A Cycle of Cathay* (Edinburgh, 1900), pp. 129–33, and Islay Burns, *Memoir of the Rev. W. C. Burns* (London, 1885), pp. 426–35.

going alone on foot to the stronghold of the insurgents. So, at daybreak the next morning I landed, against the earnest entreaties of my companions, taking with me a carpet-bag filled with copies of the Gospels and other Christian tracts, and finding a path leading along the bank of the river, now through dense thickets of reeds, and then on the top of a dike, which had been thrown up to prevent inundation, as related in a former chapter. I had visited this city by the inland route from Shanghai a year before, disguised in Chinese costume. With this exception, no foreigner had been here since its capture by the British, after the most sanguinary battle of the war, eleven years before. Nor was I insensible to the danger of thus approaching it alone and defenceless, since it was to be presumed the present occupants had conceived no very favourable feelings toward foreigners, from the fifty-three rounds of shell by the *Hermes*, which were supposed to have taken terrible effect. I knew all this, and thought much upon it, and upon the possibilities and probabilities of a rough, perhaps fatal reception. And yet I walked on with a cheerful hopefulness that amounted almost to an assurance of my safety. The city stands a third of a mile from the river, in an amphitheatre of hills on the east, south and west. A steep, narrow ridge runs from the northeastern gate to the river, where it terminates at the water's edge in a high, precipitous, rocky promontory. On the top of this bluff are a temple, an imperial pavilion, and a cast iron pagoda nine stories high—the octagonal piece forming the wall of each story is one casting, and its projecting roof with curved corners, is another. The interior is entirely filled with brick masonry, and as the stories are of diminutive size, the whole structure is not more than fifty feet high. Still, it is quite a curiosity as a work of ancient art, for it is said to be several hundred years old. The pavilion is simply a quadrangular pyramidal roof, with curved slopes, ornamented after the usual style of Chinese architecture, and supported by four granite pillars. This promontory, with its edifices, had been converted into a garrison by the insurgents. A stockade had been thrown up along on the top of the ridge, beginning at the wall of the city and running around the summit of the bluff. It consisted of a double row of stakes ten feet high, driven into the ground and walled, or rather boarded up, with the doors, shutters and floors of the shops and dwellings in the city, and the intervening space of five feet was filled in with earth. I found this hill, and indeed the whole city, fortified with great strength, and a degree of military skill that was quite surprising. For several hundred yards the approach to it at this point, which was a wide, smooth path, a year before, was rendered exceedingly difficult by means, first, of a deep ditch, which I jumped across; then the high bank, up and over which I climbed; then a fence of palisades, through which I succeeded, after some danger to my clothes, in finding my way. Next, a number of trees cut down and thrown in the way, with the boughs pointing outward, called by military men, *abattis*; then another row of palisades and more *abattis*. Next, a quantity of *coups de loups*, i.e., pitfalls, or round holes, a foot in diameter and two feet deep, dug so near each other as to give the spot the appearance of a piece of honey-comb. These holes had been covered with straw, but as some unsuspecting Imperialists had probably attempted to walk that way before myself, and had evidently walked into the holes, I profited by their experience and cautiously picked my path among them. Beyond these, were great numbers of strong, bamboo splints, driven firmly into the ground and sharpened. They projected about four inches, and stood so thickly together that, after taking a step, I had to stand on one foot and look about with the greatest care for a place in which to put the other. Then more palisades and *abattis*, and another ditch, deep and wide, with a long plank for crossing it; that is for the rebels to cross when they wished, but not for me, for it was pulled over on their side. So, after throwing my carpet-bag of books across, I jumped almost across; but, as the sides were nearly perpendicular, might as well have not jumped at all, that is, if the old adage, 'a miss is as good as a mile' be true, and it *was* true in that instance, for my experience convinced me that the properties of mud and water were the same near the bank of a ditch as in the middle. I clambered out according to the most approved method, and thus reached the foot of the steep hill. Discovering men on the summit, I made a signal to them, and they beckoned me to come on. I pointed to my carpet-bag and gave them to understand, by the language of signs, that I was fatigued and would like some assistance, particularly as there were more sharpened bamboo sticks, and another ditch half way up the hill. Whereupon one of them came down, replied briefly to my salutation, and taking the carpet-bag, led the way up the rough ascent. Just as the sun was rising we entered the stockade by a large port-hole, and in a moment more I was surrounded by a motley crowd of dark-visaged, 'long-haired' men and boys, armed with swords, matchlocks and long spears, with small, triangular, yellow flags, flying from the points. Many of them had their hair fastened up on the top of the head by small turbans of red and yellow silk. Their uniform was multiform, apparently from the want of a sufficient quantity of cloth or silk of the requisite colors, which appeared to be yellow for their close jackets, and red or blue for their loose pantaloons. As it was, their garments were as diversified in color as were the soldiers themselves in age, size, cast of countenance and dialect, for they had been gathered from the several provinces through which the patriot army had passed in its victorious march from Kwang-si northward, to the capture of Nanking, the ancient capital of the empire. I thus found myself a new and unexpected arrival in the midst of these fierce-looking 'long-haired men' who crowded about me in great numbers, and with eager curiosity to learn whence I came, who I was, and what brought me. To these inquiries I replied that I was from Shanghai, that I was an American, and my name was Taylor. With reference to my business there, I requested to be conducted to their highest officer in the city, to whom I would make known my object in visiting them. Being very anxious to have me tell them at once, they showed me the way into a well-furnished hall and had tea brought for me, having first desired me to be seated in one of the many cushioned chairs ranged along in two rows, facing each other, up and down the middle of the large apartment. Alternating with the chairs were what we call *teapoys*—small, square, or oblong stands, for holding cups of tea and refreshments. While I was sitting here sipping my tea, and the object of strange interest to these wild-looking men and boys, who had never before seen a foreigner, one who seemed to be a subordinate officer came, and seating himself by my side, again asked for what I had come. Fearing if I should tell him, that having once satisfied their own curiosity, they would not take me to the commandant, I resolutely refused to answer any questions on that subject till I was conducted to his presence. Seeing my determination, they furnished me with a guide and an escort of two or three soldiers, all armed with long spears and swords. The man who, in the first instance, came down the hill for my carpet-bag, still kept possession of it and followed on. Our path lay along the narrow ridge before described, within the stockades, which were being rapidly taken down and replaced by a substantial wall of brick and stone, three or four feet thick, furnished with embrasures and port-holes, through which cannon of various calibre were poking their ugly noses. The soldier-artisans were working like bees on the unfinished portions—some bringing brick, some laying them, and some making mortar. My guides were frequently asked, as we passed along, who was that stranger, and their invariable answer was, *Yang shoong dee*; i.e., 'Foreign brother'—a term of civility and affection never before applied to foreigners in China.

We soon came to the northeastern gate of the city, through which I had walked a year before. It had been completely filled up with heavy stone masonry, and now the only access was by a narrow flight of stone steps to the top of the wall. Through a narrow door in the parapet we entered, and here were again surrounded by multitudes of astonished spectators, who stared till their eyes seemed ready to leap at me from their sockets like so many bullets. Their curiosity being a little, and but a little, abated by the answers of my escort—for many of them spoke dialects which I did not understand—we proceeded on through the stone-paved streets, now entirely deserted, but which, when I was here a year ago, disguised as a native, were teeming with a busy, thriving population. The inhabitants had all fled at the approach of the patriot forces, leaving their shops and dwellings, and most of their furniture, goods, utensils, and effects of various kinds. The buildings were, for the most part, left standing, but without doors and shutters—these all having been taken, as before stated, to assist in the construction of stockades on the hill, and along the river bank fronting the city. Tables, chairs, trunks, boxes, bedsteads, cooking utensils, etc., lay strewn about in the houses or piled up together in confused masses, with straw, ashes, bits of paper, rags, and rubbish of every conceivable description. The contrast with the appearance of things here the year before, was truly painful, and I could but breathe a prayer that the former inhabitants of this once populous city might be restored to their homes again, in the possession of Christianity and its blessings, to such an extent as to far more than compensate for their present privations, losses and inconvenience in exile. As we passed along, I saw several very aged men and women, who were probably too old and infirm to flee, and perhaps, considering they had not long to live at any rate, thought they might as well die then, as to drag out a few more days of miserable, homeless existence. But, probably quite contrary to their expectations, their lives were not only spared but they were furnished with food, and allowed to retain their dwellings and property. Still, the poor creatures looked the pictures of sorrow, and my heart yearned over them as their sun seemed likely to set in clouds and darkness. Oh might even their dim eyes be permitted to see a dawning of a brighter day than has ever yet shone on the 'flowery land', and might their ears—but stay, had they not already caught some of the notes of praise to the one only living and true God? For morning and evening ascended from that beleagured city the doxology:

Praise the True God, who is the Imperial Supreme Ruler;
Praise Jesus the Saviour of the world;
Praise the Holy Divine Influence—the Holy Spirit—
Praise these three who compose one True God.

Indeed, these were the first sounds that saluted my ears when I entered the garrison, for it was about sunrise, and they were engaged in their morning devotions. What words to hear in the heart of the most populous pagan empire on the globe, and that, too, from lips that five years before were repeating the sensless mummeries of idolatrous superstition!

We soon reached some spacious premises that had lately been the residence of the chief mandarin of the city and surrounding country, but was now the headquarters of *Lo-ta-yun*, the commandant of the patriot forces at this place. My escort led the way through five successive buildings, and as many open courts, all in a line from the street, from which the innermost of all, the sixth, is visible. The buildings had large yellow curtains flaunting in the breeze, on each side of the passage through them. Having reached the interior building, which was in fact the dwelling, the others being occupied by attendants, soldiers, and servants, I was here directed to a seat in the large reception hall, which was quite similar in its general features to the one into which I had been ushererd on my first appearance in the garrison. It had ornamental lanterns of fantastic shapes, and rich embroidered hangings suspended from the roof and about the sides of the apartment. The courtyard in front of this, was filled with rare and beautiful flowers and plants, in unique pots of every size and shape. I soon inquired for *Lo-ta-yun*, and on being asked why I wished to see him, I replied that I should tell no one but himself in person. There was here, as before, a crowd of curious spectators, who examined my hat and dress, and hands, with much the same interest with which you would look at a strange animal of some heretofore unheard of species, in a menagerie. It was almost enough to make one doubt of himself whether he were indeed of the *genus homo*. Before many minutes a man of middle stature, apparently about forty-five years of age, came out from an adjoining room and took a seat near me. He was stoutly built, had a well-formed head, and a piercing black eye that looked out from under a pair of prominent, over-arching brows. One of the attendants, who afterward acted the part of interpreter for me, as he was a kind of secretary to the commandant, told me this was *Lo-ta-yun*. There was no appearance of an officer in his manner or dress. He had on a short blue silk jacket, and dark brown loose trowsers. I had formed such an idea of the princely appearance of Lo, whose reputation for military sagacity and skill had spread his name widely abroad, that when this personage made his appearance, so destitute was he of the pompous display so common to Chinese officials I did not believe he was the man, and began to think another attempt was being made to hinder me in my design of obtaining access to their chief. I frankly expressed my doubts, refusing, at the same time, to reply to his interrogatories, and requested again, to see the highest officer in the city, for I was resolved not to be thwarted in my intention to have an interview with Lo himself, if it was in the power of perseverance to compass it.

I have since wondered at his forbearance with my pertinacity, when he knew I was so completely in his hands. He could have had my head taken off at a word, and never have been called to account for the act. I could scarcely credit his repeated assurances that he was the man whom I sought to see, and it was not until his attendants attired him in his official uniform, and he took his seat in the large chair at a table in the middle of the hall, and began to issue his orders to the soldiers who placed themselves in array, and received his commands in the most deferential manner, that my doubts were quite removed. I then informed him fully of myself, my occupation, and my object in visiting his camp. At the same time I opened my carpet-bag and laid its contents on his table. The books were the four Gospels and Acts, the book of Genesis, and many other tracts and books on the Christian religion. He appeared quite pleased in looking at them, and said the doctrines, he believed, were the same with ours. Notice of my arrival had been sent to the second officer in command, and he soon came in a large handsome sedan, borne by four coolies, and with quite a train of soldiers and attendants going before and following. He came in, and a seat was placed for him at the right of Lo. The uniform of the two was nearly alike, being a yellow silk or satin cap, covering the whole head and extending in a short cape, half-way down the back, leaving only the face exposed. It had a binding of red satin an inch and a half wide all around the edge, and looked in shape somewhat like the representations of the caps or helmets of Egyptian heroes, or of the human heads on the monsters represented in Layard's Nineveh. Next was a long richly-figured, satin gown, reaching to the ankles, and over this a red, figured satin waistcoat, or jacket-like garment, with sleeves conveniently loose and short. You know they eschew 'shaving the head', that being one of the abominations introduced by the 'fiendish Tartars'. So they have their long hair all twisted or braided up, and fastened on the top of the head by a piece of yellow silk, answering the purpose of a turban, without being as full; the common soldiers wear red silk on the head. All the members and dependents of Lo's household assembled in the large hall, morning and evening, when he or one of his secretaries read a portion either from the book of Genesis—that being the only part of the Bible yet discovered among them—or from some of the religious tracts written by *Tai-ping-wong* himself. After reading, during which all present sit and listen attentively, they all join in chanting a hymn, always closing with the doxology above translated. Then each one takes the cushion from his chair, and putting it down before him on the brick floor, kneels on it in a very solemn manner, with his eyes closed, while Lo himself, or the secretary, prays audibly, the rest remaining perfectly silent. It was the most impressive scene I ever witnessed, from the reflections and associations to which it gave rise, and which I must leave for the imagination of my readers to supply. The only drawback to its solemnity, to my mind—but none in theirs—was the accompaniment to the chanting, consisting of all the discordant sounds of gongs, drums, cymbals, horns, and various other instruments, but ill-suited, in our estimation, to produce that devotional feeling so important in Christian worship. Breakfast was soon announced, and I was conducted into an adjoining room to a square table, with seats for two at each side. I was politely invited to sit down first, and then seven others, the secretaries and officers of Lo, also took their seats. I had heard the insurgents were in the habit of saying grace before eating, and I wanted to see how this would be done, but presently one of them took his chopsticks and requested me to do the same, for as a mark of civility, they would not eat till I had begun. I mentioned to them what information we foreigners had received about their practice of asking a blessing, and they immediately replied it was true, and that it had just been done in the room from which we came, at the conclusion of the prayer. I thereupon informed them that it was our custom to ask a blessing *at the table*, and if they had no objection I would do so at that time. They very cheerfully assented, and after I had finished they seemed quite gratified, saying that the spirit and design of the thing was the same, though the manner of performing it was different.

At every meal after this, during my stay, all at the table waited for me to ask a blessing.

In the middle of the room in which we ate was a table, on which were placed twelve bowls—three each of rice, of meat, of vegetables, and of tea. On inquiring the meaning of this, I was told it was designed as an offering to the Supreme Ruler—one of each kind respectively for the Father, Son and Holy Spirit. After being allowed to remain thus for some time they were removed, but whether eaten or not by others I did not learn. The fact of their presenting offerings of this kind is proof presumptive that they had as yet no knowledge of the *New* Testament—a want which I supplied as far as practicable on that visit, with what effect time only can reveal. I went about freely among the officers and soldiers and was allowed to visit any part of the city. In my walks through the different streets, I saw many blacksmiths and carpenters making warlike implements and gun-carriages. They were the only artisans seen pursuing their regular avocations. I also noticed great numbers of boys bearing spears and swords, and performing duty with the older soldiers.

Their stockades and batteries were well provided with guns of every size and description, from jinjalls to large cannon. Their flags of a triangular form were very numerous, inscribed with the name of their chief and the title of the new dynasty. On repeated inquiries of different individuals, at different times and places, as to their numbers, I was uniformly told that they were fifty or sixty thousand strong in that city. I observed no regularity or order in their movements, and yet a state of perfect discipline and subordination prevailed. I was struck with the calm and earnest enthusiasm that pervaded the entire body, and the perfect confidence evinced in the justice of their cause and its final success. To my frequent inquiries as to when and in what direction they would next move, and especially on asking the officers when they proposed to come towards Shanghai, they replied, that whenever they received an intimation from the Heavenly Father, as they never moved in any quarter without such direction.

The insurgents abounded in fresh provisions, which were brought in clandestinely and sold by the inhabitants of the surrounding country.

After some hours I returned to my boat to get the other bag of tracts, and at the request of General Lo, together with his assurance of perfect safety to my boatmen, to bring them along with me. I found them with the boat a few rods from the spot where I had landed, and hid from view on the land-side by the tall reeds on the river bank. They seemed almost as much surprised at seeing me, as if one had appeared from the dead; but they had so thoroughly imbibed the dread of the 'long-haired men'—so industriously cherished by the accounts of their cruelty, which the imperialist mandarins circulated in their proclamations far and wide—that no assurances of safety I could give them would induce them to go any nearer to the city. So, to accomplish my objects, I was under the necessity of making three several visits on foot to my boat, two miles distant, in doing which it was unavoidable to pass the imperialist lines, not very far from their camp, as their tents lay spread out on the hills to my left, and within gun-shot of the river bank, along which my path lay. The second time, I took as many more copies of the books as I could well carry, and as I was approaching the fortified hills by the same path as the first, the imperial fleet came up and attacked the city. At the commencement of the attack I heard a cannon-ball whistling through the air, some distance above my head, and strike on the earth beyond. I picked up one that I found lying on the bank, and taking it, clambered the hill, entered the fortress, and gave it to the gunners, with which to return the compliment. With General Lo at my side, using my spy-glass to watch the movements of the enemy, I witnessed the engagement from the top of the ramparts. The enemy kept at such a safe distance that most of their balls were spent before reaching the shore. I could not ascertain that the insurgents suffered the least injury from the cannonade of the imperialists; nor could I discover what amount of execution was done to the assailants.

Observing that I was carefully watched in all my movements, I soon divined that I was suspected of being a spy, who had communicated with the enemy since leaving the city in the morning, and that this attack was the result. It is a marvel that they did not take my life. They had promised me an escort to Nanking, but I knew this would not now be allowed, so to relieve them, I prepared to depart. I took my leave of Lo-ta-yun at night, and he, after having hospitably entertained me during my stay, gave me three live fowls and two hams, for my food on the way back to Shanghai. He also had my carpet-bag filled with the books that had been published by the order of *Tai-ping-wong*, and with the royal proclamations he had issued. Lo also wrote a friendly letter to his 'foreign brethren' at Shanghai, of which the following is a translation:

Lo, the fifth arranger of the forces, attached to the palace of the celestial dynasty of Tai-ping, who has received the command of Heaven to rule the empire, communicates the following information to all his English brethren. On the first day of the fifth moon (June 5th) a brother belonging to your honourable nation, named Charles Taylor, brought hither a number of books, which have been received in order. Seeing that the above named individual is a fellow-worshipper of the Supreme Ruler, he is, therefore, acknowledged as a brother: the books likewise which he has brought agree substantially with our own, so that it appears we follow one and the same road. Formerly, however, when a ship belonging to your honourable nation came hither (the *Hermes*), she was followed by a fleet of fiendish vessels belonging to the false Tartars: now also, when a boat from your honourable nation comes among us, the fiendish vessels of the Tartars again follow in its wake. Considering that your honourable nation is celebrated for its truth and fidelity, we, your younger brothers, do not harbour any suspicions. At present both Heaven and men favour our design, and this is just the time for setting up the Chinese and abolishing the Tartar rule. We suppose that you, gentlemen, are well acquainted with the signs of the times, so that we need not enlarge on that subject; while we, on our parts, do not prohibit commercial intercourse, we merely observe that since the two parties are now engaged in warfare, the going to and fro is accompanied with inconvenience; and judging from the present aspect of affairs, we should deem it better to wait a few months, until we have thoroughly destroyed the Tartars, when, perhaps, the subjects of your honourable nation could go and come without being involved in the tricks of these false Tartars. Would it not, in your estimation, also, be preferable? We take advantage of the opportunity to send you this communication for your intelligent inspection, and hope that every blessing may attend you. We also send a number of our own books—which please to circulate amongst you.

The provisions and my carpet bag were all given to a servant who followed me to the outer gate of his head-quarters, where was a horse saddled and bridled waiting for me, with a number of lieutenants and several hundred men, each one having a lantern, and variously armed with swords, matchlocks and long spears, whose polished blades gleamed in the light of the torches and lanterns. With this imposing procession I was escorted through many narrow, winding streets, all lined on each side with fully armed soldiers standing shoulder to shoulder. This left barely space for my *cortége* to pass in single file, and it brought me within arm's-length of these swarthy, stalwart warriors, who looked savagely at me, as if they longed to plunge their flashing steel into the foreign spy instead of allowing him thus to escape unharmed. I was in this manner conducted up one street and down another—it seemed to me for miles—between these double lines, evidently with the design of giving me a full impression of their numbers and equipments, to counteract any idea I might before have entertained of their weakness. We emerged at length through the west gate of the city, and proceeded to the bank of a river, where was a boat waiting to convey me down to my own. Three brave fellows, armed *cap-a-pie*, got in with me. One of them was the chief of the men from Kwei-chow, a district in Kwang-si province, and he boasted of his native tribe, the *Miau-tsz*, having never been subject to the Tartar rule, and having never adopted their custom of shaving the head. He was a noble looking young man, tall, straight and muscular, with prominent cheek bones, and an eye like an eagle. He reminded me of some fine specimens of our North American Indians. His hair was bound up with a piece of yellow silk, the long ends of which hung loosely down on his back. He told me his hair would reach the ground, its great length being evidently to him a source of much pride. This is a peculiarity, indeed, in which they all take great satisfaction, and it has given them one of their distinctive names—*chang-fah*, 'long-haired'. But as the tide was against us, the wind high, and the night dark, it was determined to take me on board the general's large war junk that lay there among many others, close to the shore. Here I was assigned to his stateroom, which was well furnished; but as the night was excessively warm, and the mosquitoes troublesome, I slept but a little. The tide changed about two o'clock in the morning, and with my escort I got into the small boat once more. We were proceeding slowly down the river near the shore, and had not yet passed beyond the stockades, when we were hailed by a sentinel. My long-haired friend replied that he and two comrades were just going down the river a little way to accompany the 'foreign brother' to his boat; but so strict were the orders of this sentry, and so faithful was he to them, that he said we must come to land and allow him to see for himself, or he should fire into us. My companions protested that he surely knew who they were, but all to no avail—to the shore we had to go, and undergo an examination by the trusty sentinel, who came up with his lantern as we landed, and when he had the evidence of his eyes to corroborate that of his ears, he was satisfied, and we passed on a few hundred yards, till we had got beyond all those difficult obstructions in the path before enumerated. Then I insisted on being put ashore, and walking to my boat; for I would not allow these brave, noble fellows to risk their lives on my account, as I knew there were Imperialist scouts out night and day. We parted, with many expressions of good feeling and urgent requests on their part, that I would soon visit them again. The carpet-bag, fowls and hams having been so adjusted on a stick as to balance across my shoulders, I started on, after hearing the splash of their oars far enough to satisfy me that my long-haired brethren were within hail of their own intrenchments. My load was so heavy and troublesome that after having carried it half a mile, an opportunity presented itself not only to relieve me, but to bless another. It was now daylight, and I had come near to one of the few mud and straw cottages by the path-side. A poor old man had just come out, and I, throwing my load down on the path, beckoned to him to come. At first he hesitated, but as I told him not to fear, and that I had something to give him, at the same time pointing to the hams and fowls at my feet, he mustered sufficient courage to approach. I told him to take those provisions into his house and make the best use of them he could. The poor old man, who appeared as if he had never possessed so much at one time in his whole life, seemed to misunderstand me, and offered to carry them for me to my boat. On being assured that they were his own, he poured out all his vocabulary of gratitude and blessings on my head. This little circumstance made me feel richer than could the possession of all the hams and chickens in China. Shouldering my carpet-bag I trudged along not only with a lighter load, but with such a light, glad, happy heart, that I noted not the remaining mile and a half of distance, but found myself at my boat as if by a few steps, and in a few moments. My boatmen were no less rejoiced than surprised to see me come back with my head on my shoulders. I was unwilling to leave the insurgents with the impression which they evidently entertained respecting myself, and therefore resolved to attempt removing it by still another visit. So on setting out the third time, I took the medicines and a small case of surgical instruments, which I had brought with me from Shanghai. My reappearance in the camp created more surprise than had my first. I explained to them my object and requested to be afforded an opportunity to benefit if possible the sick among them. At first they hesitated, but their confidence in me seemed gradually to return, and in a short time the demand for medical aid was greater than I had the means of supplying, but I afforded relief to many applicants, as far as within my power. Passing along a street I observed a man at an anvil in one of the shops, forging a spear head, and saw that he was suffering from a disease in one eye, which a simple surgical operation would remedy. After much persuasion both from his companions who crowded around, and from myself, he sat down and submitted to it. Thus did I flatter myself with the hope of becoming partially, at least, reinstated in their good opinion. Leaving them finally, and returning to my boat once more, we weighed anchor and in a few minutes we were on our way back to Shanghai, which we reached safely after running the blockade again, and three days' sail down the Yang-tsz-Kiang.

24
A Letter by the American Presbyterian Missionary
Rev. A Happer
Overland China Mail, 23 July 1853

WHO AND WHAT ARE THE REBELS?

To the Editor of the 'China Mail'

Canton, 30th June 1853

Dear Sir,

I have jotted down some intelligence about the Rebellion and its leader, which has accidentally come to my knowledge, and which you are at liberty to publish, if you consider it of sufficient importance and interest.

On the 11th of May, 1853, three men came into my residence in Canton, and without communicating with my servants, proceeded up-stairs to my study-room door. On my approaching them to inquire their business, one of them held out a large Chinese letter to me, stating that 'it was from the "brethren" at Nanking, and was sent to their brethren in Canton.' Having taken the letter, I found it was addressed in Chinese on one side to the 'Canton Chapel', which is occupied by the Rev. I. J. Roberts, and on the reverse side had written 'T'hai-p'ing T'ien-kwok', and the name of the sender. I of course did not receive the letter, and the men left me to go to Mr Roberts' to deliver it. When I next saw Mr R., I inquired if he had received such a letter, and was surprised that he had not received it. There were various surmises as to why it had not been delivered. After waiting several days, a small reward was offered for it. Soon after a letter was brought to him, but when the envelope was sent to me to be identified, it was easily seen not to be the same. A larger reward having been offered, on the 13th of June a second letter was brought to Mr Roberts. The envelope of this letter was also sent to me, but it had less resemblance to the original envelope than the other one. But the man who brought this second envelope to me was one of the men who had brought the original letter, on the 11th of May. He appeared much dissatisfied that I would not recognise this as the original envelope, and he would not, even after I had convinced him that it was not the same, give any account of the original letter.

As it now appeared hopeless to expect the true letter, I informed Mr Roberts that I did not wish any more envelopes referred to me, and advised him to withdraw the offer of a reward; which he did.

On the 27th of June, the man brought a letter from himself addressed to me. He said, on delivering it, he wished me to read it, and to give him a letter to carry back to Nanking, or to persuade Mr R. to write one, as he was to leave to return to Nanking on the 4th or 6th of July. He said he would call again for my answer. The purport of his letter is as follows—that he is an officer of the T'ai-ping T'ien-kwoh, and he was sent to convey this letter to Canton. He left Nanking on the 24th March (which was three days after it was taken) and arrived at Canton on the 11th of May. He took the letter first to the Foreign Commissioner at the Factories, but it was refused. He next came to my house, and I declined to receive it. He went to Mr Roberts' house, but they would not open the door. He afterwards returned to his 'brethren' at Wu-chao in Kwangsi: and there some of the 'brethren' opened the letter and destroyed the envelope; at which he was so frightened that he fainted away. But finding this smaller envelope which was inside the larger one, he brought it, and asseverates that it is a *true* letter, and wishes me to urge Mr R. to answer it; and if he will not, he requests me to write a letter for him to take to Nanking. He then says, 'If you have any doubts about my being a messenger from Nanking, they will be removed by the following signs.' The first sign is the Triad use of the word *Hung*, as given by the late Rev. Dr Milne[29] in his account of the Triad Society, reprinted from the Asiatic Society's Transactions in the *Chinese Repository*, vol. xiv, p. 63; and also the secret sign made of the character *Siu-tsiuen*. Then he transcribes some lines of poetry from 'The Book of Celestial Decrees', which has been translated by the Rev. Dr Medhurst, and which translation was published in the *North-China Herald* of May 28th. After perusing this letter, and obtaining this evidence that he was a member of the Triad Society, and a veritable rebel from Nanking, I was anxious to see him, and sent for him to call. In the meantime I had a letter prepared for him, stating why the letter had not been received at the Factories or by me—because it was addressed to Mr Roberts, and confirming his own statements in regard to having offered it, which might serve as his justification at Nanking; and also stating that I could not answer a letter addressed to another person.

In answer to my invitation, he called at my residence yesterday, 29th June. The following are the most important and interesting

29   An early representative of the London Missionary Society in China (d. 1822).

statements made by him to me during a conversation of two hours' duration.

He says Hung Siutsiuen is still alive. The report of his death originated from his having been sick. Siau Chaukwei the Western King and Fung Yunsan the Southern King are both dead, and their ranks and titles have been conferred upon a son of each respectively. The latter was killed at the attack on Chang-sha, the capital of Hu-nan, with many others, on which account the Insurgents have vowed vengeance against Chang-sha whenever they have the power and the leisure to execute it. He could repeat all the Prayers, Doxologies, Graces before meat, Hymns and Ten Commandments contained in 'The Book of Precepts' and many of the Hymns from 'The Book of Celestial Decrees'. On the day preceding, notice is given throughout the camp, by means of flags, that the next day is the Sabbath. All the host are required to rise early on the Sabbath, to prepare the offering made to Shang-ti, on that day. This ceremony which distinguishes the Sabbath, consists in spreading a table in each house with three bowls of rice, three dishes of greens, three plates with roast pork, and three cups of tea, all of which are offered to Shang-ti; a portion to each one of the Trinity. After it has been offered, it is eaten by the offerers. They do no work on the Sabbath. There is no public assembling for worship or explaining the doctrines. The men spend the day in memorizing the Hymns, Prayers, &c. Anyone found working on the Sabbath-day is whipped. They all daily repeat the morning and evening prayers. They chant the doxologies, and say grace before meat. Men and women occupy separate barracks, and all communication between the sexes is forbidden. Stealing, opium-smoking, and sexual intercourse even between husband and wife, when detected, are punished with death.

The money which they have obtained by plunder is beyond all count. It took several tens of large vessels to convey it from Wuchang in Hu-pih to Nanking. A miracle was wrought for their deliverance from the city of Yung-ngan-fu in Kwang-si; but of what nature there was no statement. The number of long-haired 'brethren' is Four or Five Thousand. His first remark to me, after he got seated in a private room, was—'We are your brethren: we wear our hair long as you do, and worship Shang-ti.' The number of fighting men is from Thirty to Forty Thousand, while the whole number of men, women, and children, in Nanking and vicinity, is about One Hundred Thousand. When the number of soldiers amount to sixty thousand, thirty thousand will remain in charge of Nanking, with the men, women, and children, T'ien-wang remaining in Nanking also, and thirty thousand will march on Peking.

Their creed is very concise and pertinent: All who follow and serve T'ien-wang will obtain heaven, while all who follow Hien-fung will be condemned to hell. His usual expression to denote the death of any of the 'brethren' was, that 'they had ascended to Heaven.' In speaking of Shang-ti, and the most sacred truths, and when repeating prayers, hymns, and doxologies, there was an utter want of any appearance of reverence.

Their watchword at first was, 'Overthrow the Tsing dynasty, and restore the Ming'. But after the resistance encountered at Tsiuen-chau in the N.E. of Kwangsi, where many of their members were killed, they changed it to a cry for the utter and complete extirpation of the Tartar race. In consequence of the people of that city aiding the Mandarins in the defence of their city, the inhabitants were given over to wholesale and indiscriminate slaughter of men, women, and children, after its capture.

He at first, as the Northern King did to Mr T. T. Meadows at Nanking, denied there ever was such a person or title as T'ien-tih; but when confronted with the evidence of its having been used in the proclamations from Nanking and Amoy, he admitted there had been such a leader; and that, while he did not know whether it was true or not, he had heard that, to escape being captured, he had jumped into a well in Kwangsi and was drowned. He did not know who composed their books, but supposed that they were approved conjointly by all the five leaders styled Kings.

He stated that Shangti hwui was used in common with T'ien-ti hwui, San-hoh hwui, Hung-kia,[30] as a designation of their fraternity. It was adapted to conceal that they were the San-ho hwui, and because Shang-ti was explained to be 'Three in one'. Hung Siu-tsiuen has been the acknowledged head of the Hung-kia for many years. He was formerly styled Yih-ko, or First Brother, Yang Siutsing was styled Rh-ko, or Second Brother, and Liau Ch'au-kwei was styled San-ko, or Third Brother. This agrees with the statement made by Dr Milne in his article on the Triad Society, in relation to the government of the fraternity, that it was committed to three Brethren, styled respectively First, Second, and Third Brother. See *Chinese Repository*, vol. xiv, p. 61. These designations were continued till 1850, when Hung Siu-tsiuen was entitled, in addition to the title T'ai-ping Wang, Chin-chü, or True Lord: which title is given to him in 'The Book of Celestial

30   All these are alternative names for the Triad Society.

Decrees', in a line of poetry, thus translated by the Rev. Dr Medhurst. 'Heaven has sent down your King to be a true Sovereign' or Lord. The others were respectively styled, Eastern King and Western King. They were driven to commence the insurrection, by the interference of the Mandarins, before they had secured as many adherents to the Shangti fraternity as they had desired.

Of himself he stated, that he is from Tung Kwan district, some twenty miles to the East of Canton. He went to Kwangsi several years ago, as a volunteer to fight against the Insurgents. But when the Insurgents threw into their camp evidence that they were Hung Kia men under another name, all the fraternity in the volunteer ranks refused to fight against them, and many of them, he being of the number, joined the ranks of the Insurgents. The fact that there were numerous desertions from the ranks of the Imperialists to join the Insurgents in Kwangsi, will be remembered by most of your readers. He immediately knew the Amoy seal,* when I shewed a copy of it to him, and all the other Triad literature I could shew him. He gave me the characters which are used on the Triad flags, and among them are 'the five mysterious' characters which are on the flags of the Insurgents in Wu-chau in Kwangsi.† He stated these insurgents were 'brethren' of the Hung family, and numbered some five thousand. The Amoy Insurgents are also brethren, and there are three thousand brethren gathered in the Lo-fau mountains, some twenty-five miles to the East of Canton. The Nanking army does not now use the Triad flags, but the Imperial yellow flags. He supposes that a majority of the male adult population in Canton are members of the Triad fraternity; and says there is no contemplation of an early rising in this city.

All these statements were made in answer to questions. The point on which he most hesitated was in reference to T'ien-tih. At first, he rather evaded the question about the identity of the Shang-ti hwui with the San hoh hwui. But when I pressed him with the Triad sign he had given me in his letter as proof of his true character, and the word Hung in the Amoy seal, he broke through his reserve; and was then as free in answering the questions in relation to it as any others. He had no fear of speaking his sentiments. He rejoices in his character as a rebel, and apparently has the most confident expectation of receiving the promised blessedness of heaven.

* *Friend of China*, 15 June.
† Ibid., 29 June.

There were many other points in relation to which I asked him, but which he said he did not know, and hence could not answer me. He admitted he could not explain the books. He could only tell me what he had seen and what was known to all. He appeared to have no intelligible idea of what was meant by repentance for sin and conversion, as used in the prayers, other than turning from following Hien-fung to serve T'ien-wang.

I am sir, yours very respectfully,

A.P.H.

P.S.—July 4—I have seen the rebel again today; I find, on more particular inquiry about the offerings of rice, tea, vegetables and roast pork to Shang-ti, that they are made before *every meal*, on week days, as well as the Sabbath.

The Northern King is lame with a stiff knee, having been wounded in the knee. The present style of this regime is, 'T'ien Wang of T'ien chiu of the T'ai-p'ing T'ien kwoh,' i.e. Heavenly King of the Heavenly dynasty of the Great Peace Heavenly country. He says it is not the wife of Fung Yunsan that is in confinement in the custody of the Nanhai Chi hien,[31] *but the wife of Hung Siu-tsiuen*; and the wife and family of Yih, the Governor-General of Kwangtung and Kwang-si, who were reported to have been killed at the taking of Wuchang, the capital of Hupih, were not killed, but were carried into captivity, and they are now in safe keeping at Nanking, where they are treated kindly.

China Mail, July 7.

25
A Diary kept by Mr Williams, Mate of the *Hermes*
Illustrated London News, 5 November 1853

At 5.30 p.m., Thursday, June 23rd, our small fleet of four sail shoved off from the Consulate jetty (Shanghae), and with a light breeze and strong ebb, stood down the river. Our party was thus divided; in the leading, or Commodore's boat, were Lieutenant Spratt and myself; this was a most ancient and leaky boat, whose appearance held forth little promise of comfort. In the second, were one corporal and private, of the Hermes, and two blue-jackets, and two Marines, of the Salamander, with two sets of irons. The third contained one of the inferior Mandarins of the Taoutae's suite (gold ball, 7th cl.) and his retinue; this was a most superior boat, not only in point of size, but being also fitted up

31   Nan-hai chih-hsien, i.e. the district magistrate of Nan-hai.

with most excellent furniture. The fourth boat carried Mr Thomas Taylor Meadows, Government interpreter . . .

Wednesday, 29th.—Daylight. Weighed. Crossed the river, and tracked, and poled the boats. 8.—Stopped to rest and breakfast. 9.—Weighed. Two p.m.—Passed Tam-too, where we saw a small fleet of war junks; and about three moored off the stairs of the Buddhist monastery of Silver Island. Found the Imperial fleet of Lorchas, junks, and one schooner, comprising nearly seventy sail lying the other side of the island. Found about twenty of the priests of the lowest class only on the island. Dined, and ascended the hill, from which we had a fine view of both parties. Below us lay the fleet, and at the distance of about six miles were the walls of Ching-Kiang foo, connecting which, and the extreme hill of Kan-loo-sze, were a long line of walls and stockades. At the distance of about a gunshot were the Imperial camps, of which we counted seven, and in which lay about 15,000 men. Towards sundown they occasionally fired at each other, but I should imagine without great damage on either side. In the evening smoked our cigars and took tea in the monastery. The priests said, when the rebels came over and destroyed the josses, all the higher priests fled; but as they were only poor wretches, they went down on their knees, and had their lives spared; they now subsisted by charity, daily sending a member over to the mainland to beg rice. Before turning in, we took a stroll through the cloisters, and sitting down on the steps of the principal entrance, between the two lions, watched the fire from the city walls. Had a yarn with Loynen-ew,[32] the mandarin's interpreter, on the Buddhist religion, and turned in. Plenty of mosquitoes.

Thursday, 30th.—Bathed, and ascended the hill. Camps and city keeping up a desultory fire. After breakfast went round to the fleet. Linqui, first-class mandarin, and controller of the whole forces, came into our boat, and had an interview. This man is a Manchoo, and by far the best specimen of a mandarin I ever saw—agreeable, affable, and courteous in his demeanour, with a handsome person. His dress consisted of a white linen tunic, over which he wore a purple crape jacket, silk gauze trousers, turned into black velvet knee boots, on his head a light mandarin hat of dark cloth, and the opaque red ball and peacock, with feathers. For permission to search the fleet he referred us to Lee-lan the Admiral, and having concluded his business, went off. . . .

---

32 Probably Lo Yuan-yu—see J. K. Fairbank, *Trade and Diplomacy on the China Coast* (Harvard, 1953), p. 442 n.

We commenced our search with the lorchas, of which there were about twenty: Mr Spratt taking the inner and I the outer. These vessels were all heavily armed and manned, by a mixture of Portuguese, Lascars, and Chinese. They were mostly commanded by the former, who, on our visit, were generally engaged either in drinking gin or playing cards. We were treated civilly throughout; but after a thorough search but one Englishman could be found, and he was too stupid-looking ever to have been in a ship of war. From the lorchas we went to the Imperial fleet of junks and Chinese jorchas. The crews of these vessels were all Chinese, and a more perfect set of cutthroats I never saw. They were armed with guns of all calibre, mounted on raised platforms. Their captains were all mandarins, and received us with great respect. All had bamboos, about three feet high (on which to trice boarding nettings) all round. After a most fatiguing search under a burning sun, and being unable to trace even a sign of the 'deserters', we returned to Tamtoo, whither Linqui had gone. To him we sent our cards, and were instantly admitted. Not having succeeded in tracing the 'deserters' in the fleet, we wished to ascertain whether they might be serving in the camp, and for this purpose sought the interview. After a variety of compliments, etc., he came to business; but, as it was in the Chinese style of prevaricating, it was hard to deduce any certainty from his expressions. He said, if we went he could not be answerable for our heads; and again, he could not give us leave—not having the immediate charge of the camp, and the mandarin who had that was away. After an hour's conference, we came to the conclusion —that a search was out of the question; so we told him that it would be necessary for us to go to Chin-Kiang to ask the insurgents if they had seen anything of the men; but, as they were blockading, we looked to him to see that the fleet did not fire on us, either going or returning. To this he answered that fire, or not fire, he could not help it, and that he did not know anything about it. Having assured him, that in case we were fired at, we should look to him as responsible, we took our leave . . .

Friday, July 1st.—Daylight.—Shifted berth without opposition to Silver Island. After breakfast Lieut. Spratt and Mr Meadows took a boat, and went over to inform the mandarins that we were about to start for Chin-Kiang. On their return they told us that the mandarins had begged them not to start till they had informed Lin-qui, which, they said, they would do immediately. I spent the day in the monastery. Saw the alligator pond, where they keep two alligators quite tame. An occasional fire kept up.

Saturday, July 2nd.—No answer having come from Lin-qui, we determined to start. The Chinese struck work, demanded their wages (which was a pretty sure sign they did not expect to see us again), and servants, boatmen, and all being put ashore, where we left them under the charge of two Marines, we took the remainder, and shoved off. One of the war junks fired a shot, but we took no notice, hoisted our colours, and set off, passing the junks. We had a friendly sign made that we should lose our heads, and, indeed, we heard that 5000 dollars were offered for each. By dint of tracking, managed to get the boat along. Soon after a slant wind setting in, we made sail, and keeping close in with the shore, both to avoid the fire of the lorchas and Imperial camps; in about an hour came within musket shot of Chin-Kiang. We had been for some time expecting to see the flash of a gun from Pakooshan or Kauloosye, but as I fancy they saw our colours, they desisted. When within 150 yards we had an admonitory musket shot, so we ran the boat in. Mr Spratt and Meadows landed, and walked away through the high grass. I remained in charge of the boat, keeping a good look out against an attack from the Imperial camp. Heard them fire several guns, saw the party led up the hill by the rebels, and then admitted into the fort. Remained there two hours; in the meantime, a boat, with six rebels, came down to look at us; treated them civilly. Tried to work the boat up higher, but tide proved to be stormy. Mr Spratt and Meadows returned. Treated well; and told that they had not seen the men; also, that they did not like us to come up, as the mandarins were very likely to kill us; and then say they did it. Moreover, they did not come to Shanghai, as they did not want to injure our trade. Were fired at by the camps, coming down the hill—one shot pitching into the mud, close to the party. We then returned to Silver Island and were looked upon as prodigies of valour by the Chinamen. Servants and crew re-embarked, squadron got under way, and ran down the river. Passed Tamtoo, and came to under Chooshan Hill. Took a stroll in the evening.

Wednesday, 6th.—Daylight, weighed. Beat out the tide; anchored; and, with the next ebb, made Woosung river.

26
A Letter by Mgr Rizzolati
Annals of the Propagation of the Faith, vol. XV (March 1854),
pp. 79–81, 84

TO THE MEMBERS OF THE CENTRAL COUNCILS OF LYONS AND
PARIS

Hong-Kong, August 4th, 1853

Gentleman,

I have at length received a large packet of letters, written by my Missioners and numerous catechists. This voluminous correspondence contains the most authentic details on the recent important events that have happened in Hou-Kouang. On this account, I have determined to resume the narrative of the most interesting portion of the news, that you may extract therefrom what may appear to you most likely to satisfy the curiosity of your readers.

After so many murders and scourges, and the state of anarchy which has been already described, it appears that the provinces of my Vicariate are beginning to experience a better state of things, with a prospect of further improvement; unless the rebels, after the taking of Pekin, if they should be successful in their attempt, create further disturbance in the district. The Missioner of this portion of my vicariate has not been able to enter the parish of *Siam-tan*, nor administer the sacraments to the Christians, who were so violently persecuted last year by the local mandarin. Father Paul Cham is still in prison for the faith at *Cham-xa-fou*, without an immediate prospect of deliverance. Six pupils, who were incarcerated at *Han-iam-fou*, have now returned to the seminary; one of our most distinguished scholars, was so cruelly flogged, that he has already departed for a better life.

All my priests, both European and Chinese, describe the rebels as the propagators of the most frightful communism. The pen could not depict, nor the imagination conceive, the cruelties and impostures that are perpetrated by these sectarians. The number of victims of their savage barbarity, in the village of *Ou-Cham-fou* alone, amounts, it is said, to two hundred thousand, exclusive of a great number of persons who have voluntarily destroyed themselves rather than fall into their hands. After having plundered the most opulent families and persons in easy circumstances, whom they have reduced to the most abject poverty, they set off in the direction of Nankin. There, as at Ou-Cham-fou, and in all the towns of my province, murder and pillage went hand in hand, and the insurgents finally left for Pekin, leaving after them piles, ruins, and heaps of dead bodies.

But let us say a few words of the scenes that occurred at the time of the siege. A report having been circulated that the rebels were Catholics, the mandarins decided that as soon as the revolt should have subsided, the neophytes should all be put to the sword. And yet, on perceiving their forlorn position, they placed their wives and children for safety in the houses of the Christians, in the hope that they would find therein protection amid the common ruin. Among the latter was a mandarin named Ly, my friend, the ex-prefect of the civil and military guards who form the garrison of the prison in which I was confined. This functionary, in dread of being murdered by the rebels, came in the most simple costume, together with forty other personages of the administration, and took refuge in the locality where the zealous Francis Fou and his fellow-labourer, the octogenarian Thaddeus-Ma reside. These two catechists were obliged to hire the neighbouring houses and connect them with their own, to accommodate this great mandarin, who would not for the world have been recognized, although the Chinese nobility are easily distinguished by the dignity of their bearing and features. No sooner had he taken up his abode in this retreat, than the ex-prefect informed Francis Fou that public report designated me as the principal instigator of the revolt; that my aim was to deliver the Christian religion from the tyrannical oppression of the imperial dynasty; but both he and his colleagues were soon undeceived, when they saw one of our young catechists fall dead before their place of concealment, and were still further convinced, when they were told that five others of the Christians had been killed in different parts of the city. Hence, all these mandarins in disguise were fully satisfied, that the Catholics were the victims, and not the partisans of the revolt. At length, these outlawed nobles, perceiving that they could not expect any greater security among the Christians than elsewhere, expressed their desire to put an end to their existence by poison, strangulation, or by shooting themselves; but our two good catechists prevented this act of despair from being carried into effect; and by their devotedness, succeeded in preserving the lives of all those who had taken refuge with them . . .

. . . my Missioners, one and all, describe the barbarity and cruelty of the sectaries in the most odious colors. Their sole aim would appear to be the entire depopulation of the towns which they take; and their atrocities have been severely felt in the large cities of *Ou-cham* and *Han-iam-fou*. During three consecutive days, their muskets and swords were so vigorously employed in the execution of their murderous designs, that the streets and the banks of the river were covered with dead bodies.

But the God of Israel constantly watches over his people. His intervention was manifested in an especial manner on this occasion, when, as I have already stated, the mandarins had resolved upon the destruction of all the Catholics, whom they were intending to put to the sword, without exception, so soon as rebels should have retreated from the town. They were laboring under the erroneous impression that we were making common cause with the insurgents; and this conviction appeared to be confirmed by the conduct of the rebels, who destroyed all the temples, but spared our church and *residence* of *Zao-pou-men*. Nothing could dissuade them to contrary, until they saw six of our principal Christians fall under the brigands, which proved that they were not their accomplices. Hence, the innocence of the Catholics and their submission to the legitimate authority is now an admitted fact, and they now enjoy perfect freedom, and are no longer looked upon by the mandarins as enemies to the state. . . .

Fr. Joseph, Bishop of Arade,
and Vicar-Apostolic of
Hou-Kouang

27
A Letter by Rev. W H Medhurst
North China Herald, 26 November 1853

To the Editor of the

'NORTH-CHINA HERALD'

Dear Sir,

I have just fallen in with a Canton man, who was for some time a follower of the Tae-ping-wang, and who left Nan-king in August last. His account may be considered trustworthy, because it corresponds in its main points with what we know of the state of things there; and it is important, inasmuch as it reveals certain facts with which we were not before acquainted. I do not conceive that the man had any motive for deceiving me, and his statements were delivered with an air of candour which carried with them a conviction of his sincerity. True or not, you have them, as nearly as possible as he delivered them, and you may take them for what they are worth.

When questioned as to the religion of the insurgents he answered with an air of reverence that they worshipped God (Shang-te). When asked when they did it? he replied, every day, and previous to every meal. He was then requested to repeat something of what they said; when he chanted the doxology, as it is found in the Book of Religious Precepts of Tae-ping-wang, in such a tone and manner as shewed that he was familiar with it. As he had referred to their daily meals, he was asked whether they had sufficient to eat? Abundance, he replied. And whether they had enough to wear? To which he answered, that they had plenty of clothing. He was then asked, how long he had been with them? he said, that he had followed them from Canton, and that his hair had grown three or four inches long. How came it, then, he was asked, as he had enough to eat and to wear; with good instruction, and a prospect of going to Heaven when he died, that he came to leave them. Oh, he replied, a man could not smoke common tobacco, and by no means opium; a man could not gamble, nor drink, nor indulge his lust, nor quarrel, nor steal; and if one did but rail at another he got a bambooing. It was suggested that by urging these as the reasons for leaving, he exposed himself to the suspicion that he was fond of all these bad practices, and thereby laid himself open to just ridicule and reproach. On hearing this, he appeared rather ashamed, and seemed willing, if he could, to retract his expressions. He was then asked, whether he got any pay? to which he replied, not a cash; no pay being dealt out to the troops from one month's end to the other. He was also asked whether he was allowed to enjoy the society of his wife? to which he replied in the negative; adding that the women in Nanking were all kept in a particular quarter of the city, where there were whole streets of them, but that no men were allowed to approach, under pain of death.

On a subsequent occasion, he was asked whether such a person as Tae-ping-wang actually existed, or whether he was dead, and his image carried about, as some had reported. He said, that he had no doubt that Tae-ping-wang was an actual living man: that he frequently went about in a chair, but so shrouded in deep folds of silk, that the common people could not get a glance at him. The highest officers, however, saw him every night, when they went to consult about affairs of state, and to receive his orders. He was asked whether he had ever heard that Tae-ping-wang had been up to heaven? to which he replied, Certainly—it was commonly reported, and fully believed among his followers. Recurring to the subject of the soldiers receiving no pay, he was asked whether any of them possessed any property of their own? to which he replied, None whatever; and if more than five dollars are found in the possession of any man, he is immediately bambooed, for not having given it up previously. All monies, immediately they were acquired, were instantly to be handed over to the general treasury, and any person secretly hoarding wealth is suspected of treasonable practices. Was there much, then, in the general treasury? Oh abundance; heaps upon heaps of untold silver, which was all reserved for the carrying out of the great cause. As no person was allowed to have any private resources, how did they manage, it was asked, when they wanted to buy anything nice for food? There was no need for that, he said, as the centurion for every company bought what was necessary for the mess, and when it was put on the tables they shared every one alike, the dish of the highest officer being in no way different from that of the meanest soldier. He was then asked, why the men were separated from the women, and when such separation took place? He said, that during all their progress from Kwang-se, the women fought by the side of the men, and conducted themselves as bravely; but when they arrived at Nan-king, they were separated, because there was no more need for them to engage in warfare. They were therefore kept apart, had their various duties to perform, and were engaged for a great part of the time in learning! Every band of twenty-five women, having an instructress over them. As for the men they were told, it was their business to fight and to work for the present; and when the empire was gained, they might enjoy their wives. But how, it was asked, is each one to find his own, when the war is over, among such a multitude. He replied, every man and woman is regularly registered, and there will not be the slightest difficulty in restoring to every man his rightful partner. He was asked whether there were any secret society men among Tae-ping-wang's followers, specifying the Teen-te-hwuy, San-ho-hwuy, Seaou-taou-hwuy and others? when he immediately and distinctly replied, that there were none, for Tae-ping-wang put them to death. How did he know that Tae-ping-wang acted thus by the secret society men? he replied, that in the month of May of the present year, he killed three hundred of them. (This accounts for the omission of all reference to the Teen-te-hwuy in the revised edition of Tae-ping-wang's books, which were brought down by Dr Taylor from Chin-keang. It is possible that he found them an unmanageable set, as their banding together was altogether independent of the religious views entertained by Tae-ping-wang, and so when he felt himself strong enough, he cast them off.) Speaking of learning, he was asked, what books they learned; to which he replied, none other than the books published by Tae-ping-wang; all others were burnt. He was then asked, whether the books of Confucius were burnt likewise? being no scholar he said he could not give a definite answer. He was then asked, whether he had ever been to school, and what books he had then learned. He said, he had only been to school for about a year, when a boy, and the school-master flogged him so grievously that he ran away. During that year what books did he learn? he said the Ta-hëoh and the Chung-yung. Had he ever seen these books in Nan-king? Yes, he said, he had seen them, but they were *altered*. Were books on history permitted? He did not know. What about the books of Buddha? Oh every thing belonging to Buddha and Taou, were indiscriminately destroyed: the temples and images were smashed all to pieces, and he supposed that the books of those religionists shared the same fate. As for the priests they dared not shew their faces, and together with gamblers, opium-smokers, and whoremongers were scattered to the four winds. There was no use talking about such, as they were utterly exterminated. He was then asked whether they kept the sabbath? to which he replied, that it was regularly observed; that no work was done on that day, except what was necessary. That they all assembled for public worship in large halls where they knelt down, to prayer, and that the chiefs exhorted them. On being asked, who the exhorters were? he mentioned, among others, Lae, at Nanking. He knew nothing about baptism or the Lord's supper. He was asked, if he had heard much of Jesus? he replied that he had heard his name frequently, but he was not competent to detail what he had heard. He was then asked, what was now his settled opinion—he had been for several months with Tae-ping-wang, and for several months with the Imperialists; which now, honestly speaking, did he prefer? He looked round, and asked if no one was near, and whether we would accuse him? We replied, there was no danger. Upon which he exclaimed, with emphasis, I am for Tae-ping-wang. Why, then, it was again asked, did he leave him? Because, said he, I had a brother among the imperialists, and I wanted to see him: in order to accomplish this I went out secretly; my brother then had my head shaved, and reported that I was a distressed subject of the emperor, who had been deceived into following the insurgents. I was then taken into the pay of the imperialists, and was afraid to go back, lest I should lose my head.

What an extraordinary view does the above present of the insurgent army! What a moral revolution! To induce 100,000 Chinamen, for months and years together, to give up tobacco, opium, lust and covetousness; to deny themselves in lawful gratifications, and, what is dearer to a Chinaman's heart than life itself, to consent to live without dollars, and all share and share alike, braving death in its worst form, and persevering therein without flinching. There may be defective teaching among them, there may be errors of greater or lesser magnitude—but if what is above-detailed be true—or the half of it—it is confessedly a moral revolution—it is the wonder of the age.

Yours truly,

W H Medhurst.

28
The Conclusion of a Report by A de Bourboulon, French Minister to China
Archives des Affaires Étrangères, Correspondance Politique de Chine, t. 144, ff. 325–6

In summary, although with regard to the special aim of protecting our religious interests and, if I may so express it, in the diplomatic aspect, my journey to Nanking has not had the immediate success that I should have liked to obtain, I believe nonetheless that, from a general point of view, we may congratulate ourselves upon its results. While confirming the principal data brought back from Nanking eight months ago by the *Hermes*, this journey has added thereto a substantial amount of new intelligence and, considering only this outcome of general information, France will have assisted greatly in throwing light upon a situation the understanding of which is vital to so many interests. What stands out most for me from all that I have seen is the strength of this revolutionary movement, which promises nothing less than to accomplish a complete transformation, at once religious, social and political in this immense Empire, by tradition a land of custom and immobility. Whatever doubts may exist about its ultimate success, whatever obstacles the indifference of the masses and the resources of the Tartar dynasty may yet oppose to the rebellion's triumph, it is clear to me that this revolt is one of formidable character and proportions; that it is led by men who, be they fanatical or ambitious, have faith in the success of their venture, and who, besides their audacity, have in their favour ideas, a strength of organisation, tactics, in short a moral force which gives them great superiority over their adversaries; finally, that if the ultimate triumph of the Thai-ping-wang cannot yet be considered as certain, it is at least probable and that, even supposing a decisive event, such as the capture of Peking, does not hasten its fall, the Government of the Tartar dynasty has received a blow too severe to permit of its ever recovering. As to what one may expect to be the attitudes of the new power, in the event of its becoming the Government of China, and should the foreign Powers be called upon to establish new relations with it, I leave it to your Excellency to evaluate the lesson emerging from the first analysis I made of these reports; it can be the measure of the various difficulties that would have to be overcome before one could enter into regular communication with people who are ignorant of the very names of the world's most powerful nations.

29
A Letter by the French Jesuit Missionary Fr Stanislas Clavelin
N. Brouillon, *Mémoire sur l'état actuel de la mission du Kiang-nan 1842-55* (Paris, 1855), pp. 337-89

ACCOUNT OF THE EXPEDITION TO NANKIN (NOVEMBER AND DECEMBER 1853)

In November 1853, the *Cassini* went up the Yang-tse-kiang as far as Nanking, to examine the respective situation and disposition of the two parties which disputed that important place. At the request of M. Edan, acting-consul, Fathers Gotteland and Clavelin were appointed to accompany the expedition. On returning to Zi-ka-wei, Father Clavelin sent to Father Languillat the following account:

Zi-ka-wei, January 6 1854

My Reverend Father,

It was on the feast day of St. Stanislas that you resolved to send me to Nankin. It was the last thing in the world that I expected, remote as I was, almost forty leagues, from Shanghai. Nevertheless, on the 30th of November we were on board the *Cassini*. There, as you know, we received from the Commander, the excellent M. de Plas, and from all the officers, the most friendly and cordial reception, which has not lessened for a moment. M. de Bourboulon, Madame and their suite, were not long in arriving; and I am yielding to a fitting sense of gratitude when I tell you that on their part equally we have been the object of the most eager and agreeable attentions. The anchor was raised at ten o'clock, and towards noon we were sailing upon the Yang-tse-kiang. We soon caught sight of the land of Tsom-ming and the upper bank of the Hai-men peninsula. I had left these parts more than five years ago; yet the memory that rose before me of the solaces so sustained and profound that I had experienced there during four consecutive years was so acute and so moving that I remained for a long time contemplating the line of the land that barely stood out from the midst of the waters. May it always be, as it is still, abundant in the fruits of salvation, and may it thus make

91

its missionaries forget whatever is hard to bear in the ministry they perform there.

Since we were favoured by continual good weather, and since the ship's draught, the shallows of the river and moving sand banks, little explored, allowed us to proceed only with the greatest caution and only by day, we could contemplate at leisure this great river, second in the world. Its mouth is close to thirty leagues wide. When we had gone up it a similar distance, the view could easily embrace the two banks.

On the 3rd of December, towards noon, we passed by Kiang-in, a town of the third order. Its situation on the river, its ring of hills, its ramparts, its towers, its suburbs half hidden among the trees, all helped to make it appear delightful to us. Since in this spot the bed of the Yang-tse-kiang is considerably narrower, batteries have been set up on either bank, commanding the river. Like the town, they are still under the control of the imperialists, but nonetheless very badly defended. Needless to say, they made no attempt to impede our progress.

Kiang-in was formerly a centre for numerous and flourishing Christian communities. There is still to be seen in the town, which no longer contains a single Christian family, a stone altar raised by our ancient Fathers and religiously preserved in a pagan residence. From the remains of these Christian communities, a single one has been formed at some distance from the walls, in the countryside; it may number some four or five hundred faithful. Their zeal, their assiduous care will, I am convinced, soon end in communicating a new life to these sad remants of a happier age.

Two days later, at sunrise, we were before Tchen-kiang-fou, a town of the second order. We had found the situation of Kiang-in delightful, but that of Tchen-kiang-fou soon made us forget it. It is, indeed, the best thing I have seen in China. The city is erected on a slightly elevated knoll, its walls forming a veritable crown around it; a fortified road, several hundred paces long, joins to the crenellated fort built on a sheer rock whose foot is washed by the waters of the river. An elbow of the river and two islands to the left and the right form a charming harbour. On the shore, between these two islands, one sees a vast suburb which hems in the river and stretches far out over the plain; one very high tower, further away from the river, stands out from all around it, and forms the background of this truly picturesque scene. The island on the right, called Silver Island, is worthy of its name. It may be a quarter of a league around and a little less in height. Its regular shape, a ring of pretty houses at its feet, pagodas a little higher up, amid bowers of greenery their curled-up roofs appearing here and there through the foliage, and the trees which cover it right up to the summit—something quite rare in this region—all making a singularly pleasing whole. Nevertheless, despite all its advantages, Silver Island must give precedence, and in fact does give it, to its sister, Gold Island. That is the name of the island situated to the left of Tchen-kiang-fou. To the charms of Silver Island, it adds that of a beautiful tower which seems made to serve it as a diadem. Close by, the imperial canal coming from Sou-tcheou crosses the Kiang, and then runs northward, passing by Yang-tcheou. Imagine this scene animated by a population such as only China can offer, and you will have an idea of what Tchen-kiang-fou was less than a year ago, but not at all of what it is now. How times have changed! What a sad scourge is civil war! Now the city is deserted; the population and the garrison, fearing for themselves the same fate as those at Nankin, took flight at the arrival of the Kuam-si-jen, who seized this strong position without firing a shot. Its suburbs have been ruined and burned, the harbour is entirely deserted. On all sides, the eye can rest only upon ruins and debris. We saw then, for the first time, though at a distance, those Kuam-si-jen who have made themselves so terrible to the imperial soldiers. We caught sight of some of them on the ramparts and at the batteries that they have established, one on the river's edge, in the burnt suburb, and the other on the opposite bank, at the entrance to the imperial canal. The *Cassini* continued on its way without entering into any negotiations with them and without being impeded. Moreover, we were ready for any eventuality. The day before, we had likewise passed through the imperial fleet lying at anchor near Silver Island and blockading the city from that side, two or three leagues to the south-east of Tchen-kiang-fou. On the top of a high hill, we were shown the camp of the ground force which, together with the fleet, was supposed to be besieging the city. But from the rate of their progress towards it, the imperialists appeared to make no pretence of ever seizing it by force. They waited.

In other times Tchen-kiang-fou also contained a numerous Christian community, which today has been reduced to some forty faithful; but they are no longer living there: they took flight at the arrival of the insurgents.

Several hours later we were opposite the town of Y-tchin, also under the control of the Kuam-si-jen. A fleet of two hundred vessels was anchored there. In the afternoon, we encountered yet another under sail, which amounted to at least three or four hundred junks. All these craft, although manned by a great number of men, appeared to us to be badly armed and intended for carrying provisions wherever the need would be felt rather than to combat the imperialists. Moreover, they showed no hostility. In this way, sailing by short stages, we arrived on the morning of the 6th in sight of Nankin. We were quietly at lunch when a cannon-shot, fired from the battery below the ramparts of the city, sent a ball whistling past our ears. The ship did not cease its progress because of it. But the extinguishing of all the fires and the preparation of all the guns was the work of a moment. We awaited a second shot in order to reply. The Kuam-si-jen had the good sense to hold off. Shortly after we dropped anchor and a small boat left our ship's side to go and demand an explanation. The answer came that they were under orders to fire on any foreign vessel that arrived, in order to warn it to anchor at a distance, and that their cannon were always loaded with ball and had long been so. In short, they appeared honest and polite. An interview was asked for the next day. In the evening, an affirmative answer was transmitted on behalf of the authorities in the capital.

While waiting, the *Cassini* had received a large number of Kuam-si-jen soldiers and officers as visitors. We could therefore examine their winter costume at close quarters. Basically, it is still the usual Chinese costume save that red and yellow are more dominant; all their hair is left to grow, and the hats and skull-caps are ruthlessly put aside. The former is replaced by a large hood, and the latter by a sort of turban, or else by a head-band of bag-shape which holds back the hair, and falls a little on to the neck. In general, those we saw were well dressed; good quality cloth, silk and even satin were all quite common.

On the morning of the 7th, M. de Courcy, secretary of the legation, accompanied by two ship's officers and by his interpreter, set off to attend the interview. He permitted me to accompany him, and my catechist followed us. Some horses were awaiting us on the shore. Kuam-si-jen officers led the way and brought up the rear, preceded and followed by standards and by deafening *yongs*. Soon we arrived at the ramparts, which we skirted for close to an hour and a half.

Arriving in front of a gate, we had to wait for quite some time, because the post had not received the order from inside to let us pass. It was not long before we were surrounded by a dense crowd of men and women. They showed much curiosity, but without any sign of malevolence. One of them I saw stare at me attentively, then, pushing through the crowd, he came up quite close to me. Opening one of his hands, he let me catch a glimpse of a rosary and a medallion. Seeing in my face that he was understood, he also made the sign of the cross. I knew then that he was the brother of a student of the little seminary of the mission. He told me that, by the grace of God, our Christian women had been able to stay in their house or their chapel, that they were in no way molested on account of their religion, and that they had what was necessary in the way of provisions and clothing. As to the men, there remain scarcely more than twelve or fifteen in the city. Almost all have escaped. I took advantage of the occasion to give him, and through him to our Christian women, advice appropriate to their position. I saw with pleasure that it had been understood and well received; for it was time to finish. Indeed, although I had spoken to him in a whisper and with a good deal of circumspection, a blow of a rod, which an overseer gave him on the shoulder, made us understand, both of us, that it was time to put an end to our conversation. Three other Christians whom Father Gotteland was able to see several days later, confirmed with him these details. Only it appears that several of our Christians, scattered or forced to serve the Kuam-si-jen, have had to suffer harassment at the hands of some of the rebel chiefs, the more rigid observers of the new religious prescriptions.

Eventually we were given permission to pass through the western gate; but before reaching the official residence where we were awaited, we had still to go for a good league on horseback through the city streets. These streets were wide, and paved, at least in the middle. The appearance of the houses has nothing to commend it. In general they are badly kept up; several have been burnt by their own occupants, who preferred death rather than submit themselves to the discretion of their new masters. Not a single store is open. The whole picture is thus very sad; it is less a city than a camp. How I felt my heart tighten as I thought of the former splendour of this ancient capital, and above all of those many ardent Christians for whom this was once the centre. It was at Nankin that Father Ricci laid the solid and lasting foundations of the first Christian community in China. His first and most illustrious disciple, Paul Siu, became its ornament, its support, and its apostle. Without doubt our fathers had trodden the very soil that I trod then. How envious their zeal makes me! In memory of their success, I would have liked to share the privations and difficulties of every kind that they endured, for these are always inherent in the apostolic ministry, and because the cross, and the cross alone, can make it abundant and productive. Instead of those thousands of earlier Christians, was I proud to encounter still a few dozen? I looked about for faces which might have understood me; but it was in vain.

To distract myself a little, and so as not to lose an opportunity of obtaining some information, I began to question, from my horse, the most intelligent of those who pressed closer to me; for we were followed by quite a dense crowd at times. Some thirty horsemen, children of the principal chiefs, scarcely twelve or fifteen years old, came and capered around us. They were all extremely well dressed and mounted on pretty little horses equally well harnessed. We also saw a large number of women carrying the rice ration assigned to each of them. At the gate of the city we had already seen piles of rice deposited on the shore and surmounted by banners which constituted it public property. Several overseers were there to share it out according to right. The appearance of these women did not at all reveal any poverty: I saw no beggars among them. Some of them wore rich clothing; but the majority, without showing much affluence, were nevertheless decent and passable. Their countenance expressed in general a calm resignation, a little sad no doubt, but nevertheless much less so than I would have expected, considering the sacrifices of all kinds that they have had to make. Many have lost that which they had held most dear in the world; all are deprived of the comfort of their family, separated from their husbands, their brothers, and their children. Gathered together in groups of twenty-five, they live truly communally, receiving from day to day the necessary provisions and clothing. Those who do not know how, do not wish, or are unable to do anything, have nevertheless the basic necessities. Those who are able to use their hands or their arms, find themselves correspondingly better off. I have not noticed any significant change in the dress of the women. Only we were told that unbound feet were more in favour, as being more serviceable for public usefulness.

Arriving at the official residence, we again had to wait for everything to be made ready to receive us. I took advantage of this forced leisure to make the acquaintance of a young chief with a most interesting countenance. There was soon sympathy between us. He was a scholar from Hou-kuam who, despite himself, had been caught up in the wake of the Kuam-si-jen invasion. Being endowed with talents, amiability and tact, he occupies a position of trust close to one of the ministers who were to receive us. The charm of this conversation made me find the wait less long. It was not altogether the same with M. de Courcy. Irritated, and not without reason, at such a lack of ceremony, he had already quite decided to return to advise that nothing could be done with such people, when someone came to inform us that we were awaited in the audience hall.

The scene which thereupon met our eyes struck us by its contrast with everything that we had seen up until then. With the aid of torches which lit up the room, we saw on each side a large number of onlookers; and at the end, in front of us, the two ministers who would receive us. Their splendid robes of blue satin, richly enhanced, on the chest mainly, by magnificent embroideries, their red boots, diadems wholly of carved gold on their heads, their grave and dignified bearing, and a large retinue forming a second rank behind them; all, in a word, contributed to giving to this interview a character of dignity and grandeur which, as I have said, contrasted markedly with the reception we had had at first. When M. de Courcy appeared, the ministers rose, the introduction was made through an interpreter, and then we took our places on seats placed at either side. After some explanations as to the object of the visit, others were sought from them concerning the articles of their religion. Then one of them, taking the floor, gave us, in the space of five or six minutes, a rapid exposition of their doctrine, doing so with an incomparable calm, assurance and dignity. He confined himself, however, to talking of the first principles of natural law, of the manner in which idolatry had had its birth in China, and then touched in a few words on the mission that the emperor Tai-ping believed he had received from Heaven to extirpate it from the surface of the earth. As we told them that we certainly had not come with any hostile intentions but rather as friends, the minister directly replied: Since you worship the same God as we and since we all have only a single Creator, you are not only friends, but brothers. In fact, they showed themselves to be so friendly and so attentive that M. de Courcy then asked for an interview for M. de Bourboulon. That was at once agreed to, and it was added that it would take place with the highest ministers of the emperor, or even with the emperor himself if there were serious interests to discuss. Whereupon the assembly arose, the ministers gravely came to conduct M. de Courcy to the doors of the room, and then we mounted our horses.

As it was night, we were given torches and guides; but there was no remedy against the rain which had started to fall. The streets were narrow and slippery, and often bordered by deep ditches full of water. It was necessary to pass along the ramparts guarded by sentinels. To their *Who goes there!* the reply was: *Brothers!* At the end of three dreary hours, we finally arrived on board, safe and sound, though not without a few tumbles from the horses. I was fortunate enough to have my inexperience spared this unpleasant occurrence.

Since the minister's interview would not take place until the next day, several officers on board took advantage of this break to go ashore for the pleasure of a walk or of hunting. Everywhere they encountered friendly faces. They could see the part of the wall that the Kuam-si-jen had knocked down during the taking of Nankin. It is now completely repaired. Quite close to that place one could also see the hill on which the English, in 1842, had established their batteries. They were about to blast the city, when the news of the combat which had taken place meanwhile at Tchen-kiang-fou, and of the disaster which had ensued, brought terror to the Chinese and determined them to make their surrender. The fortified enclosure of Nankin is truly immense; but I do not think that a third of it is inhabited. The wall encloses hills covered with trees, where one sees no habitation. The ramparts are at present unbreached, and quite well conserved. In some places they are even forty or fifty feet high. Nevertheless, if they are formidable for the Chinese they would not be so at all for Europeans. The gates are the best things we have seen. When we entered by the eastern gate, it was as if we were in a fine church nave. The vault was a good thirty to forty feet high, twenty to thirty wide, and sixty to eighty deep. In the middle there was a huge cannon trained on the outside avenue. And before passing into the streets of the city, we still had to pass through two more fortified gates. Outside, a large canal running from north to south skirts the ramparts, defends the approaches and serves at the same time as a shelter for part of the fleet of the Kuam-si-jen. Several batteries have been established on the banks. Between the canal and the ramparts there were, before the war, numerous dwellings. Almost all have been burnt or destroyed. We had to pass through the middle of these ruins.

The day after our first visit to Nankin, a Chinese came on board, quite ill clad. Once on the deck, he let fall his pigtail, which out of fear of the Kuam-si-jen he had until then hidden under his cap. He introduced himself as an envoy of the commander-in-chief of the imperial camp established at some distance from Nankin, and indeed delivered to the commander the visiting card of the imperial generalissimo Hiam-ta-jen and those of several of his principal lieutenants. These chiefs apologised, through the mouth of their envoy, for not having come themselves, since the place had little security, to present their respects to a very distinguished member of a nation united by treaties with the emperor Hien-foung; they added that they would be happy if, in consequence of this (alliance) they could receive aid and succour from the French. Commander de Plas gave them this answer: 'The French certainly have not come here either to defend or attack anybody. The object of their voyage is to ascertain whether the rumour of the harassment which the Christians had suffered from the Kuam-si-jen is well founded or not. In consequence the imperialists must well understand how important it is for them never to molest the Christians, for, sooner or later, France would certainly come and ask the reason why.' The envoy seemed satisfied with the answer and departed, putting his queue back under the protection of his cap.

On the 10th of December, first thing in the morning, the minister left with his suite to go to the interview that he had asked for. Instead of going on shore immediately, the cutter followed for more than an hour the canal that flowed beside the city ramparts. Arriving before one of the gates, the minister and the commander mounted horses; the officers, the European and Chinese interpreters, in all at least fifteen persons, did likewise. Then an entrance was made into the city. The ministers Houan and Lai, whom we had visited a few days before, wished to receive M. de Bourboulon in grand ceremony, likewise, before taking him to minister Tchen, whose rank was superior to theirs, and with whom the interview was to take place. After several moments, we set out again for the tribunal of this latter. When all was ready for the audience, the minister was taken into quite a large hall, whither we followed him. At the far end we saw a dàis, a table and an armchair; along the sides several seats, and, in front of the dais, but *in plano*, two rows of chairs.

Almost immediately the doors at the end of the room were opened and we saw approaching, in strict order, a crowd of chiefs, and of secretaries, then the two ministers Houan and Lai, though without their fine costume; then finally under a sumptuous parasol appeared Tiu-tien (the minister Tchen), in a magnificent costume in keeping with his high dignity. At a given signal, the whole audience bowed low to salute him. You would have thought it was a bishop approaching his throne, followed by a large number of clergy. Minister Tchen indeed took his place in the arm-chair, then motioned to M. de Bourboulon to sit on one of the chairs placed before the dais. The pompous and princely manners of the Chinese minister did not at all dazzle the French minister, and in no way made him forget what was due to his rank and to the dignity of the country that he represented. Through his interpreter, M. de Bourboulon told the minister Tchen that, being of a rank equal to his, he insisted that the latter immediately cause to be prepared a chair similar to his own on the platform; otherwise he would go at once and return whence he came. At first the Chinese objected that their customs forbade such an arrangement, but in the end he proposed their going, without ceremony and in an informal group, to continue the conversation in an adjoining room. This was accepted.

In all these proceedings, at least from what little I could see, M. de Bourboulon always seemed to me to have a double objective in view: (first) that of obtaining as much precise information as possible concerning the great revolution which is now taking place in China, and even more especially touching religious and Catholic interests; secondly that of conveying an accurate idea of France in keeping with her importance and dignity. In effect this double objective sums up in itself all that is truly serious and reasonably practical in the question at the present time. In view of the blazing controversy which has recently arisen among the chief Paris newspapers on the subject of events in China, and in particular about the persecutions that our Christians have had to endure at the hands of the Kuam-si-jen, the minister fully realised France was entitled to expect something of her representative. But before judging, he wished to see. Equally it is quite natural that, amid the eventualities that are brewing in the bosom of an empire which contains one third of the population of the globe, France seeks to be in a position to make her moral and civilising influence felt there opportunely. The minister has striven to attain these two ends, but, of course within the bounds of a wisdom which wishes neither to precipitate nor to prejudge definitely anything in the future. But this reserve did not at all satisfy the Chinese. I knew for certain that M. de Bourboulon would have enjoyed every facility for seeing the emperor himself if he had given the impression of intending to recognise his authority as legitimate and of uniting with him by means of treaties. Doubtless it was with this objective that, after having tried to give us an exalted idea of their strength and their splendour, if not their superiority, they tended to prolong the conversation with their politeness and with the oft repeated invitation to be so kind as to accept their hospitality at least for one night. It was then that the minister took advantage of their obliging offers to tell them that there had come with him two priests of his religion, one of whom was there, with the intention of having several conferences with them on the subject of the religion that they themselves professed and practised; in consequence of which, he asked them to consent to assigning a day on which these conferences might take place. The Kuam-si-jen acceded to this proposal with no less eagerness than I myself expressed in accepting that which they made to me, of staying amongst them from that very evening. Father Gotteland, we anticipated, would come and rejoin me the next day. This matter settled, the minister retired, leaving all the Chinese most intrigued as to the true object of his visit. They could not conceive that one could limit oneself to that after a voyage of six thousand leagues, as they put it. Hence conjectures and hence, for two days and nights, comings and goings among the ministers and the kings to consult with one another about what to make of such proceedings.

As for me, after M. de Bourboulon's departure I was taken into an adjacent apartment, along with my catechist, by an officer who was always full of kindness on our behalf. He never failed to introduce me to his colleagues under the name of *brother from the foreign kingdom*. We supped together, then we were led back to the official residence where we had first been received. First of all we were given as lodgings the house where what could be called the staff of the place gathered: that is to say where a large number of the secondary chiefs lived, or came to visit one another, to converse, and to seek and bring news. Everyone showed much consideration on our behalf; but after some time, by their reserve and by certain words, we understood that the nature of our relations with them was about to change. Very soon, indeed, we were called before the minister Houan, who received us with a severe and rather haughty countenance. Without being invited, I took a chair to seat myself by his side. The minister then began to enumerate all the wrongs of which the minister, according to him, had made himself guilty towards their persons and towards the cause which they espoused. Among other things, he could not stomach the fact that the treaties which had been concluded between the Tai-tsing dynasty and France had been mentioned before them, and especially that we had dared to give Hien-foung the title of emperor, a title so venerable in their eyes that they did not even dare to give it to their own foremost chief. They reserved it for Chan-ti alone. Then, in a voice full of anger he added: Since the leader of the imps (Hien-foung) is so venerable and so revered among you, you are therefore his friends; we are therefore rebels; hence you are our enemies; and the better to help your friend you have come to spy on us, and to acquaint yourselves with the strengths and weaknesses of our position? Is there not reason enough in that, he continued, turning towards me, for having you beheaded, or at least for having you reduced to slavery?

To which I replied, after that, what would be the result? As he made no reply, I told him again through my catechist: The French minister is a man of honour as much as anyone is. Besides he is not far from here; would it not be suitable to address to himself the observations which his actions may have occasioned rather than make them to us, who are in no way concerned? Then, I took the opportunity of explaining to him the peculiarity of my mission, which entitled me to decline all responsibility. The Chinese minister, seeing that his threats hardly moved me, softened remarkably. He believed, or pretended to believe, the sincerity of my words, and ended by inviting me to partake of his supper. After that, as it was already very late, we took leave of him in order to retire to our rest.

The next morning the minister Houan had us come again before him. I do not know if it was that he had repented of softening thus before us the previous evening, or if it was the outcome of his interview during the night with some of the kings; the fact is that once more he set about exposing in the conduct of the French everything that was irreverent and insulting to the Kuam-si-jen, and did so with an energy and an anger which caused his followers to tremble. Finally, turning towards me, who had shared none of his emotion, he asked me what I had to say in reply. I told him through my catechist: My reply of yesterday holds good for today in its entirety; that will suffice, I have nothing to add. The Heavenly Father, whose name and witness you so often invoke, knows that I have spoken only the truth; it is useless to insist further on this point. The minister saw clearly that he had nothing to gain from us, and we were allowed to retire. But we were well aware, from then on, that our entourage drew its inspiration from the thoughts of its chief.

Nevertheless it was only a short time later that we had the pleasure of being able to converse with the secretary of the minister Tchen, in a manner that was serious and very interesting for us. He presented himself to us as having been sent by his master to discuss the religious question. We began by clearing up the matter of the reproaches that had been made against the French. This Kuam-si-jen appeared to us to be a man of uncommon intelligence. He understood our reasons: they pleased him, or at least he pretended to yield to them completely; then we spoke of religion. We complained to him about the incoherence that we had remarked in what a good many of the chiefs had told us were the articles of their faith. This Kuam-si-jen then said to us: Be a little on your guard and do not take as gospel truth everything that you hear from the mouths of these men. Without doubt they are of good faith, but ill-informed; it is hardly a year since they came over to the banner of Tai-ping; moreover, they are almost always out on excursions; it is therefore not surprising that they are little acquainted with their religion. They know the principal dogmas of the natural law; they believe in one God in three persons, in the creation, the incarnation, the redemption, in heaven and in hell; then they know that they must pray to Chan-ti. But do not ask more of them about it for the moment.

And Houng-sieou-tsuien (the emperor of the Kuam-si-jen), we replied, do you believe as it is printed in your books, that he is really the son of God, younger brother of Jesus Christ?—No, our speaker replied. God being a pure spirit can have neither wife nor child in the manner of men; we believe only that just as it is true that God himself sent his Son Jesus Christ on earth to save mankind, likewise it is he who has given Houng-sieou-tsuien the mission of rooting out idolatry from the face of the earth. The common people, even some of the chiefs, I know, give this mission or connection a character much loftier and more extraordinary; but as the result for them is an increase of confidence in their cause, Houng-sieou-tsuien has not yet thought it necessary to explain himself more clearly. It is a fact that the words father and son have a much more varied meaning in China than in France.

And the revelations of which your books speak, what of them? Are we to believe that the Heavenly Father manifests himself so openly to Houng-sieou-tsuien? Here is the answer we received: Houng-sieou-tsuien is a most religious man, who is very fond of meditation and of consulting with Heaven, particularly when he finds himself in difficult positions. He then retires by himself to meditate on what he has to do. After his prayer he always says: 'Here is what Heaven inspires in me'. Or else: 'Here is what the Heavenly Father, or Jesus, has come to inspire in me'. And since, in essence, the course that he proposes has always been followed by complete success, it is not surprising that the mass of people, ill-educated as they are, have been able to believe in actual conversations between him and the Heavenly Father. Thus it is, for example, that when a number of the chiefs here had asked to attack the Tartars encamped below the walls, they went to consult Houng-sieou-tsuien. The latter made his prayer and gave this answer: 'Here is what Heaven has just inspired in me: Let the Tartars waste away here together in the repose in which they stagnate. Apart from the fact that our best troops are in the north, if we attacked our enemies now they would take flight as is their custom, dispersing themselves in all direction, and these agents of the devil would breathe their foul spirit everywhere in the north; we will hem them in, and the dominion of the devil will be destroyed'. Today everyone believes that this will surely come to pass.

We asked if the Kuam-si-jen *honoured the Holy Mother*, as the Holy Virgin is called here. We were not understood.—The mother of Jesus? we went on—Yes, was the reply; we call her the *venerable matron*. Neither was the Holy Virgin known at all under her name of Mary. We showed it to them in the Gospel according to Saint Matthew that they have had printed, and on the very next day noticed that she was known by that name by some chiefs in another office. We asked also how they explain and practise this passage from the same Gospel: Go, and *baptize* all the nations, etc. Our Kuam-si-jen told us that they set three cups full of water on a table, and lightly washed their forehead, chest and hands with it: Then, to cut short the other explanations we had asked of him, he added: We do not yet know well all the precepts and observances of our religion. Our chiefs have not yet revealed all their intentions nor said their last word. The books which will be successively printed will gradually bring the light and disperse the darkness. Many things have been printed in our first collections, which can be fully grasped only with the help of subsequent clarifications. Moreover these publications sometimes have been written by pagans who are only recent worshippers of the Heavenly Father, and still more sensitive to the cadence of the phrase than to the accuracy of its expression. Thus it is that after having spoken of a heavenly father and brother in a certain book, they have added, to make a complete sentence, *a heavenly mother and sister*: some even think that this heavenly mother and sister are the wives of the heavenly father and brother; whereas the true sense is that in Heaven we shall all be brothers and sisters.

This secretary had a truly remarkable mental range. The day before we had given him a summary of the Christian religion; he spent the night reading it, rendered an account of it to us and added that, according to it, eight tenths of our religion resembled his own. When we had explained to him what the Pope was, he answered: Houng-sieou-suien has the aim of destroying idolatry, first in China, then in the neighbouring kingdoms; then, after that, he will go to Europe to visit his brothers, worshippers of a single God like himself: it is then that he will categorically explain himself and settle all matters.

Here are some details which we have been able to gather about the origins of Houng-sieou-tsuien and the mission he had received from Heaven. Houng-sieou-tsuien is a true Kuam-si-jen. From his youth he devoted himself to the study of Chinese language and literature. At some time past the age of twenty, he suffered a very serious illness. Having lost consciousness, he was considered dead for some time. Even today, a large number of his subordinates still think that he really died and was later resurrected. Finally, coming out of his long coma, he recounted that he had just had a vision in which the Heavenly Father had appeared to him and ordered him to go everywhere to preach the true doctrine and to abolish idolatry and all the false religions from the face of the earth. Houng-sieou-tsuien said he had protested to the Heavenly Father that he felt himself incapable of such a mission, seeing that he knew little of the doctrine himself that he had to preach, that he had no books in which the doctrine was expounded in detail, and furthermore he had no means of making the truth of his mission believed. And the Heavenly Father answered him: 'Make enquiries in the vicinity, and thou wilt find books which contain all my doctrine. As for the rest, be calm, I am with thee to protect thee; obey, and nothing can resist thee'. On hearing these details, Houng-sieou-tsuien's family believed that the sickness had affected his brain, and that the mission that he claimed to have received had no other foundation than the hallucinations of his mind. Houng-sieou-tsuien's old teacher, today known under the name of King of the South, was less incredulous. Shortly he began making inquiries with his pupil which ended in the discovery of a case of books. For the most part, these books seemed to be very ancient, at least two hundred years old. Some, a small number, were evidently of much more recent date. Most of the old books were manuscripts. The master and pupil eagerly gave themselves up to the study of these books for several years, then sought to make proselytes among their following. Progress was still slow, when there occurred a conflict between the Miao-tse, of whom Houng-sieou-tsuien was a member, and the imperialists. The Miao-tse, directed by Houng-sieou-tsuien, who had promised them victory with the aid of the Heavenly Father, triumphed indeed, and the number of disciples of the new doctrine increased considerably. Such was the beginning of this conflagration which threatens altogether to consume the Tai-tsing dynasty and paganism in China.

Some twenty pamphlets, containing the religious doctrine of the Kuam-si-jen, their civil and military administration, etc., have already been printed by them. We have been given a great many copies of these. At the present time, more than five hundred men are still engaged in cutting out the characters to be used for the printing of numerous other works. Among those we have received from them, there is a Gospel according to St. Matthew. I have not yet noticed any obvious mistakes; I do not know whence this version comes. On the other hand, it seems certain that the section of the Old Testament that they have also printed, to wit: Genesis, Exodus, Leviticus and Numbers, is of protestant origin. It is Houng-sieou-tsuien, we are told, who, with the help of his old teacher, now his colleague, reserves the final inspection over the productions of the press. And, in fact, all the copies that we were given bore a kind of seal which might be called the *imprimatur* of censorship.

The King of the South—still according to our speaker, who made us known to him under the name of To-te (just as the former missionaries were called)—the king of the south gave us to understand that our presence was agreeable to him, and that consequently, we could remain amongst them, if we thought proper, to study the religious question. The secretary of whom I speak here twice had a long interview with us. It was the same with the secretary of the minister Houan. And it is particularly by conversing with them that we were able to gather what remains for me to say concerning the present state of things at Nankin and the regime to which the people are subjected by their new masters.

As I have said above, Houng-sieou-tsuien, principal leader of the Kuam-si-jen, by no means adopts the title that we ordinarily translate as emperor; he reserves that for Chan-ti and has taken for himself that of heavenly king. The name of the dynasty is Tai-ping (great peace), or else the heavenly dynasty; its court is the heavenly court; *Nan-kin*, which means *southern court*, has again just changed its name, but this time without losing anything by it, for that of *Tien-kin*, or heavenly court. *Pé-kin*, on the other hand, is now designated only by that of *Tsuei-ti-tchen*, city of the origin of sin, or new Babylon. Everything related to the present dynasty is invested with the qualities of the devil. It is the devil *Hien-foung*; it is the *diabolical dynasty, army,* etc. Immediately after the heavenly king come, as prime ministers, five persons who have also taken, as in other days, the title of king. Of one, it is said, it is purely an honorific title. The others, to distinguish themselves, have added to their title of king one of the four cardinal points (of the compass). The ministers that we have seen form the second class. All the inhabitants are divided into categories of ten thousand, women as well as men. The women are governed by women; only a body of three thousand women, for example, has a male chief to communicate with the ministers.

106

While we were with one of them, a chief came to give him a petition thus conceived: 'The sisters of such and such a division ask for a further issue of clothing, because of the cold which has become more intense'. The minister replied: 'Go and see, and do what is right'. The communal life is truly represented in Nankin in its most expressive aspect and in the widest sense of the word, but without the slightest detriment to morals; on the contrary moral outrage, like pillage, is irremissibly punished by death. In all women's quarters there is always some light during the night, and one of their number guard and strikes a small drum from time to time.

The principal chiefs are without doubt anxious to preserve a hierarchy and to have it respected. Cannon always announce their departure or their arrival. There is music during their meals. Nevertheless we have seen not only the secondary chiefs, but even the simple people approach them with complete freedom.

One cannot deny it, there is some thing in their relationships with one another which justifies the name of brothers which the Kuam-si-jen adopt among themselves. There is moreover a family likeness now. Thus all the dwelling places are communal property: provisions and clothing have been deposited in public stores; gold, silver and precious objects taken to the public treasury. One cannot sell anything nor buy anything; money, in fact, would be useless in the hands of individuals. It has been impossible for us to procure for ourselves costumes such as the Kuam-si-jen currently wear. It is for the chiefs to provide for the different needs of their subordinates. And it is truly something worthy of admiration, that a population which the invasion has raised to more than a million can be regularly nourished and clothed in this way, as we have seen with our own eyes; and that done in the midst of a civil war and in face of an encamped enemy besieging the city. Furthermore we have encountered several fleets full of provisions to supply the other towns which have fallen into the power of the Kuam-si-jen.

As for us, we were simply fed it is true, but abundantly, and as guests who were to be honoured. Several times, the secretaries, our friends, shared our meal. Before and after, they said their prayer to the Heavenly Father; while we ourselves said our *Benedicite* and our grace. Twice a day, gathered in a hall or a fairly large room, the Kuam-si-jen make their prayer to Chan-ti. Ten shots from the cannon announced when the Heavenly king is saying his own. For our part, in the midst of all of them, we performed our spiritual exercises with the greatest freedom. My catechist especially recited prayers like fifty Kuam-si-jen; and if I may be allowed to pay him here my tribute of a just admiration, truly this catechist is animated by the spirit of God. Although head of a large family, of which he is the principal provider, he has given his attention almost solely to the saving of souls, and to preaching to sinners, and certainly not without success. After the threats that had been made us by the minister *Houan*, he told me very calmly: 'When it is for God, I fear nothing, even having my throat cut'. And it is not because of him that we have not remained in Nankin.

To return to their prayer, we asked them how they would treat those who might refuse to pray with them. They answered: 'Those who will neither pray nor renounce the idols are put to death; those who believe in nothing and who do not pray on their own account, we leave them alone, often however at the price of a few strokes of the rod; but if they became a mob, they also would be put to death'. I made the observation that it would be much more brotherly, since they spoke so much of brotherhood, to exhort rather than kill; to draw closer the family bonds rather than to break them, as I saw to have been done; to spare at least the women and children of the Tartars, instead of enveloping them all in the same anathema. The Kuam-si-jen responded: 'He who persists in refusing to pray to the Heavenly Father is an unnatural child, unworthy of the name of brother; however, outside of battle, provided that he smashes his idols, in general we close our eyes to his conduct. As to the present regimen imposed on all the women, it is a momentary necessity. Indeed, how could we do otherwise? While we go into battle in the name of the Heavenly Father to destroy idolatry and to deliver our country, in whose case would we leave the honour of our mothers, our wives and our sisters? The Chinese, such the yoke of the *imps* has long since made him, can respect nothing. Besides, is it proper that those who remain in the camp should be better treated than we who go into battle? Moreover, in the great peace that will soon come about, everything will return to order, and members of the same family will be able to be reunited once again. Finally, concerning the Tartars, when one thinks of the evils that they have caused us, and the depth of abasement to which China has sunk under their government, one cannot dream of entering into an agreement with them; let them return to graze their flocks, or else prepare themselves for a war of extermination. And besides they are idolators, incorrigible idolators. Would the Heavenly Father forgive us for thus forgiving them? Similarly in order to destroy one of the principal stew pots of idolatry, we have changed the direction of studies and the means of obtaining degrees. Hereafter one will no longer study the ancient Chinese books, good though they may be in themselves; but their original doctrine has been distorted by the commentators, above all by the philosopher Tsu-tse, whose commentary has been for a long time the one most generally accepted. The subjects for questions (thèses) in the examinations will henceforth be taken from our religious books; and already this year more than four hundred Chinese have taken their degrees. It is also to work for the regeneration of our country that we cut off the heads of opium smokers without mercy. We do not even permit the use of ordinary tobacco'. In fact, they showed me, at a certain place, several heads fairly recently cut off and which, according to a placard posted beside them, had belonged to opium smokers. The cangue was the punishment for those who were caught smoking ordinary tobacco.

We should have very much liked to visit the part of the city which is enclosed within the third wall, and then the tower, the famous tower of Nankin; but as the third enclosure serves as the citadel and imperial residence, and as the tower is located close to the retrenchments built at the foot of the walls to protect the city against imperialist attacks, we believed that we would spare ourselves a refusal by concealing our desire. However, beyond the walls, from three to four li away, we glimpsed the tower, but could admire only its height.

In this way we spent two days and nights amongst the Kuam-si-jen, honourably detained as prisoners under the pretext of awaiting a communication to take to the minister, which never arrived. We were right in thinking that there was anxiety on our account on board the *Cassini*. Father Gotteland had tried in vain to rejoin me the evening before, and thus I found myself deprived of the assistance of his experience and wisdom. Then the commander wrote me a letter which opened the gates for me, and we arrived on board happily just in time to forestall the rigorous measures which might have been put into operation. They had been disposed to seize some of the chiefs to serve as hostages. However, to keep to the truth, we must say that, apart from the suspicions which weighed upon us because of the circumstances, and which were without doubt the cause of the reprimand that the minister Houan gave us, the attentions we received were respectful and sometimes even amicable. Once only, a young chief took it on himself to ask me, in a rather familiar tone, if I was for the Tai-pings or for Hien-foung. Neither for one nor the other, I answered.—And what country are you from then? he responded in rather the same tone. I am from the country where one treats foreigners with courtesy and as true brethren . . . The other officers repeated to him this answer for fear that he had not at all understood it. Whereupon I saw the young man blush, bite his lips, and then disappear.

Without doubt it would have been very consoling for us to visit our Christian women, to make a mission to them to encourage them to persevere; but when we saw how complete was the separation that existed between men and women, and how absolute the prohibition even for the chiefs against communicating with them, it was unanimously considered impossible. Indeed, would it not have been utterly improper to have two men who present themselves as doctors of their religion wishing to inaugurate their ministry in a foreign country by relations which are there considered, whether rightly or wrongly does not matter, as blameworthy not to say dishonourable. Moreover we took advantage of the obliging offers which had been made to us at different times, to recommend to the Kuam-si-jen to treat Christians well, wherever they encountered any. The Kuam-si-jen promised us to treat them as brethren, because they worshipped the Heavenly Father, and not to trouble them on the subject of the difference that may exist between our manner of prayer and theirs. They likewise accepted with pleasure our proposal that we should send them, on our return to our vessel, some books on our religion, some images, crosses, and medallions. Indeed we sent a few of these on the day of our departure from Nankin. My catechist enclosed with them a long letter, first thanking them for their good conduct towards us, then explaining the use of pious objects among Christians, and several other points of doctrine essential to us but still none too clear to them. He ended by adding that we would not forget the offer that they had been kind enough to make us for staying amongst them, and that we had the firm intention of taking advantage of it before long.

Now, summing up, what is to be thought, and what to be concluded about such a state of affairs? Will China change its masters and its religion? Those are the questions that everyone is asking, and which very few people, in my view, would be able to resolve. Here are the pros and cons as I understand them. The insurrection of the Kuam-si-jen is a fact of the gravest import, one can no longer deny it. Though we may call its instigators rebels, barbarians, brigands, as often as we please, it has travelled two to three hundred leagues, sweeping all before it. Three days were sufficient for it to take by assault this last city. It restored to

Nankin its ancient title of capital, raising high on its walls the national banner and installing itself in power there. Then, reclaiming all China for the Chinese, it launched an army of more than a hundred and fifty thousand men on Pekin. We know already for certain that this army has entered Pé-tché-li, that it has seized Tien-tsin, the main supply-route to the capital, and some even claim that it is under the walls of Pekin. An unlimited, even perhaps a fanatical, confidence, in the wisdom of its chief and the protection of the *Heavenly Father*; a faith in the success of its cause such as to multiply its strength tenfold; a firm and regular administration; a discipline which respects property and customs; then, in the opposing camp, the cowardice and incompetence of the imperial troops, the injustices, spoliations and ever increasing imposts; in a word the faults upon faults of the Tai-tsing government, which have alienated from it the spirit of the nation: such are the principal elements which work in favour of the insurrection.

Nonetheless, the present government maintains itself still in the greater part of the empire, which is thus expected to make common cause with it. The Tartars, with incontestable courage, will no doubt make, if only to avoid dying of hunger, a supreme effort to save a dynasty of their nation. Although Tartar in origin it has reigned for over two hundred years, and in other times has caused fortune to smile upon China. It has prescription and legal right, and this fact of legitimacy, here as elsewhere, always rallies many people to the party which claims it. Then the mandarins, who can expect no mercy of the Kuam-si-jen, the scholars who tremble for their buttons, the rich who fear for their wealth, the people who prefer to remain oppressed rather than to see themselves entirely stripped by war, the winter which can cause the enemy army to perish, the discord which could creep in amongst them, the impossibility of maintaining an administration so stretched as that which we observed at Nankin, these are likewise the principal chances of salvation remaining to the followers of the present regime.

Moreover, a solution of some kind cannot be long in coming. By spring, supposing that it will be necessary to wait until then, the question will be resolved in the north. If the Kuam-si-jen are beaten, they will return to the southern provinces to look for new reinforcements, and the civil war will drag on; if they take Pekin, then probably everything will be over. In that case, what will become of us? What kind of situation will face Christianity? Here again it is difficult, it seems to me, to form any definite opinion as yet; for, judging by all that I have seen, read and heard, the

111

religious inclinations of the Kuam-si-jen have still not been revealed in all their aspects, and their doctrinal system seems to me to be composed of rather diverse elements, although the Christian element is dominant therein. The Kuam-si-jen, from the outset, gave me the impression of being a people who in the past, perhaps even several generations ago, used to practise the Christian religion. Afterwards, deprived of pastors and of religious succour, they were unable to conserve their belief in all its purity. Subsequently, having found books which discussed it at length, they borrowed from the Old and New Testaments though without having the key to them, to add to their religious system: then the oriental style and customs came to give to the whole an original colour which baffles all supposition.

Indeed, some say to you: Houng-sieou-tsuien in truth presents himself as the leader, if not as the creator, of a new religion; he propagates it by fire and the sword; add to that the divine mission that he has set himself, his visions which he transforms into dogma, the prescribed absolutions, the prescribed prayer twice a day, announced by the sound of the cannon, the multiplicity of wives that he seems to permit himself, and does it not all seem to indicate the successor to Mahomet? There are within that some points of contact with the law of Mahomet; that cannot be denied, it seems to me. But does not Mahommedanism also bear certain marks of resemblance to Christianity? A man who would make religion a pedestal for his ambition can always, like Mahomet and his associates, make appeal to the passions. Now, it is not yet ascertained whether Houng-sieou-tsuein has several wives, something which the Old Testament, moreover, seems to permit him, whilst it is certain, for the moment, that he exacts from his subordinates the most painful sacrifice by strictly prohibiting, as he does, all relationships, however legitimate, between man and woman. The Chinese, without having any firm religious convictions, are nonetheless attached to the cult of certain pagan sects. They have a well-known aversion to the Christian religion for the sole reason that it did not have its birth amongst them. Well! Here is Houng-sieou-tsuien who comes to them saying: Burn that which you worship, accept that which you scorn, for my doctrine is foreign, it comes from the kingdom of the Messiah, Judea. The Chinese always insisted on shaving a part of his head, on wearing certain garments on protecting his queue; and now he must renounce all these customs. Ordinarily, it is not at all in this way that one humours the passions. And then the Bible, the Gospel, Saint Matthew, which he presents as the foundation of his doctrine, how is one to reconcile all that with the tendencies stated above and attributed, not without some reason, to Houng-sieou-tsuein? I confess that I do not know.

Would this new religion approximate more closely to protestantism? I know that several ministers have claimed on their own behalf, through the voice of the newspapers, the glory if not of having fomented the revolt, at least—which is very much the same thing—of having taught to its champions and caused to be acknowledged the religious principles which sustain it. Indeed, the protestant Bible (what has been translated of it) has been reprinted by the Kuam-si-jen. In a chapel at Nankin, a cross and some images have been smashed, and our Christians have been maltreated. However, if the protestant ministers are really the fathers of this new doctrine, the characteristics it has which resemble mohammedanism do them no great honour. Besides which, all the Kuam-si-jen that we have questioned have always rejected such an origin. They have taken the Old Testament, spoken of in their ancient religious books, just as they found it, without concerning themselves about the source whence it came. It must also be confessed that if their religion did come from some anglican ministers, the disciples showed little gratitude towards their teachers, for none of these has been able to establish himself amongst them; nor did they receive at all well the officers of the *Hermes*, which sailed up close under the walls of Nankin shortly after the taking of that city. Finally, the Kuam-si-jen cut the throats of opium smokers, which is certainly not an encouragement for the principal branch of English commerce in this country. Our Christians have not been maltreated in so far as they are Christians, and if a cross and images have been destroyed at the hands of some subordinates, the chiefs have received such things from ours—with much respect.

It seems to me that these few details suffice to show that it is difficult to express a decided opinion regarding the origin, progress, tendencies and peculiar character of the religious doctrine of the Kuam-si-jen. And if the insurrection should succumb in the struggle, what fate awaits us? Again I do not know, but I doubt that the Tai-tsing dynasty, if it escapes the danger which threatens it, could ever regard with a favourable eye a religion whose first principles must seem to it absolutely identical with those of its mortal enemy. The future has its roots in the past. [Le passé nous répond de l'avenir] Fear of the Europeans may make it [the dynasty] conceal its ill will, but that is all.

From whatever angle then that one views the events of which China is now the scene, one sees scarcely more than uncertainty so far. God alone knows what the future holds for us. Perhaps this is a reason for us always to be very cautious in our words as well as in our actions, in everything that touches on these serious questions. I know that that is your feeling, my reverend Father, and the course followed by the missionaries. May the Christians strive to imitate them, and we shall feel that, in default of human succour, we are only the more assured of it from divine protection: *Dominus regit me*. As you know, it is already a matter of admiration for us all, to see how God protects His own and how little our Christians have suffered thus far in regard to the scourge which has devastated our province. May the Father of mercies look with compassion on this vast empire! The Kuam-si-jen are in His hand, may He make of them an instrument of salvation for their unfortunate country. At the present time, they are clearing the ground, that is certain. Even more, it is a devastating torrent, truly, especially so for paganism, but one which brings in its flood, and raises to the surface a crowd of new ideas, more universal and more in harmony with those of the rest of the civilized world; and consequently tending to bring into the bosom of the great family of the human race this empire hitherto so careful to hold itself apart. It is now that these tendencies are showing themselves. They have not yet assumed a character of complete stability. Would it not be possible to give them a certain direction, in a word, to *catholicize* them? That is without doubt the dream of more than one missionary. You have had an excellent opportunity, you will tell me, why let it escape? Why not stay at Nankin? My reverend Father when the fear of ruining everything with such a resolution is held suspended over your head like another sword of Damocles, in what way do you wish that one should resolve to grasp it? According to most of the enlightened and well intentioned people that we have been able and obliged to consult, to stay amongst the Kuam-si-jen would be to go over to the insurrection, to break with the imperialists; it would be, in the hope of an uncertain success, to expose nine tenths of our Christians to obvious dangers; it would be to sacrifice all our other missions, who would not fail to attribute their misfortunes to our imprudence and recklessness. The fact is that these reasons are well founded, yet nevertheless they have made less impression on me, I confess, than the suspicion of espionage that I felt hovering over us. And then, arriving under the French flag as we did, would it not have imposed on France's representatives in China some sort of obligation to safeguard our persons? In the present circumstances was such an obligation possible? Was it proper? I would not dare to vouch for it.

Be that as it may, on the morning of the 14th of December, the *Cassini* left Nankin. The same day, towards six o'clock in the evening we were before Tchen-kiang-fou. On the 15th, at eleven in the morning, we saw Kiang-in again; and finally at noon on the 18th, we once again dropped anchor at Chang-hai, after an absence of some twenty days.

Our voyage from Nankin was therefore finished. Nevertheless, as you know, I had to prolong my stay on board for several days. It was because our good commander strongly desired to have a priest on the *Cassini* for the celebration of Christmas.

On Christmas eve we heard the roar of a cannon just before night fall; one ball even fell in our midst. However, at the moment of beginning the mass, which was attended by the whole crew, a complete silence fell; and this, combined with the meditation of the congregation, with the novelty of the spectacle, with the feelings inherent in such a festival, and finally with the sight of the commander, the four officers, and several lesser officers and sailors coming with that piety that distinguishes them, to receive Holy Communion in the presence of the whole assembly; all this, I say, made a profound impression on me, and the memory of this festival will always be preserved in my memory.

The day after Christmas I still could not respectably leave the ship; for it was a question of obtaining from the rebels who had taken possession of Chang-hai some reparation for the serious injury which they had done us in seizing two catechists from the mission and treating them as spies. One of them had been cruelly tortured. It was not known whether the rebels would agree to it; that was why there was an inclination to fire the cannon. Happily the reparation was made: the French forgave, and everything went off very well. Thus it is that, thanks to the representatives of France, we enjoy here a perfect tranquillity, that is quite extraordinary in the circumstances; may it last a long time.

If this were not to be, it will certainly not be the fault of our good and worthy consul, M. Edan. You know as well as I do, my reverend Father, how much integrity, firmness, and skill there are in that good soul. One cannot deny that the mission has many obligations towards him. He has therefore a very special right to our affection and our gratitude.

Stanislas Clavelin, SJ

Section 3 The First Books (1853–4)

From a very early stage, even before the influence of Christian ideas on the Taiping was known with certainty and, naturally, even more eagerly once that was known, Westerners began to seek out the origins of the movement. As early as the middle of 1851 the *Chinese Repository* had sought to throw light on this question (Doc. 7) but until the middle of 1852 little firm evidence was available. Even then the problems were formidable, as is illustrated by the first serious book on the Taiping in a Western language, Callery and Yvan's *L'Insurrection en Chine*, published in Paris in 1853. A few pages from this work, recounting the beginnings of the political revolt, constitute Doc. 30.

Earlier and unbeknownst to Callery and Yvan, more reliable information had reached the ears of some Protestant missionaries with the arrival in Hong Kong of the Taiping leader's cousin, Hung Jen-kan, in April 1852. Jen-kan had come into contact with the Swedish missionary Theodore Hamberg when seeking protection from Chinese authorities investigating the Hung family. Hamberg was impressed with his sincerity and eventually published, in Hong Kong in 1854, his account of Taiping beginnings under the title *The Visions of Hung-Siu-tshuen* (Doc. 31). Hung Jen-kan's version of Taiping origins was not accepted unquestioningly by the Western community in China. Many continued to feel that the movement had its origins in the missionary efforts of Karl Gützlaff, while the American Presbyterian A. P. Happer emphasised the connections with the Triad society (Doc. 24). Western scholarly debate on the Taiping was well launched by 1854.

30
Callery and Yvan's Account of the Beginnings of the Taiping Revolt
J. Callery and M. Yvan, *History of the Insurrection in China . . .* (Paris and London, 1853; tr. from the original French by J. Oxenford), pp. 55–9, 188–91

According to documents which we have ourselves inspected, it appears that the insurgents passed the first months of 1850 in the South-west of Kouang-Si, performing some strategic movements of no importance, and approaching the frontiers of the Kouang-Toung. The first towns which fell into their hands were the town of Ho—one of the most commercial in the province—and the capital of the district, Kiang-Men, where three mandarins of high degree persisted in opposing them. These manoeuvres gave great uneasiness to the Governor-General of the two Kouangs. The titulary head of this vice-royalty, whose name was Siu, was an irresolute man, prudent to a degree of cowardice. When he learned that the rebels were approaching him, he urgently solicited the honor of visiting the tomb of the late Emperor, and prostrated himself before it, hoping thus to escape the responsibility with which he was threatened. This request was not granted; and the viceroy, fearing that he would be accused of allowing the evil to increase, sent troops to reduce the rebels. The Imperial soldiers were, however, conquered and destroyed.

The tactics of the insurgents consisted in feigning flight, and thus drawing their enemies into ambuscades, where they slaughtered them without mercy. This stratagem answered on several successive occasions. Siu, hearing of these calamities, set off without delay to Pekin, where he spread the alarm. While he was proceeding towards the capital, the insurgents obtained new successes, and the Chinese journals gave a daily bulletin of the advantages gained by these guerillas. Two rebel chiefs, Tchang-kia-soung and Tchang-kia-fou, did wonders on two successive occasions, and the soldiers of the 'Son of Heaven' nearly all perished in the field.

Hitherto there was no notion of a pretender to the throne. There were merely generals appointed on the spur of the moment, who did not conceal their intention of overthrowing the reigning dynasty, but made no mention of any sovereign whom they intended to set up in its stead.

The insurgents, emboldened by success, now passed the limits of the Kouang-Si, and penetrated the Kouang-Toung. Between Tsing-Yuen and Ing-Te they met a detachment of the Imperial troops. The rebels retreated according to their ordinary tactics, but turning back almost immediately, they slaughtered the Imperialists to a man.

At this moment two political acts of great importance took place almost simultaneously—one at the Court of Pekin, the other in the insurgent camp. The young Emperor, faithful to his retrograde policy, ordered old Lin who was living in retirement in a charming habitation in the environs of Fou-Tcheou, to subdue the rebels of the Kouang-Si. Our readers will no doubt recollect this austere mandarin, this conscientious barbarian, who had opium destroyed to the value of 50,000,000 francs. Notwithstanding his advanced age, the old servant obeyed the orders of his young master, and set off for the province he was commissioned to reduce.

The insurgents answered the commissioner's envoy by the following proclamation, which makes the Chinese appear much less Chinese than they are generally supposed.

'The Mantchous, who, for two centuries, have been the hereditary occupants of the throne of China, were originally members of a small foreign tribe. With the aid of a powerful army they took possession of our treasure, our lands, and the government of our country, proving that superior strength is all that is required for the usurpation of an empire. There is, therefore, no difference between us, who levy contributions on the villages we have taken and the officials sent from Pekin, to collect the taxes. Taking and keeping are both fair alike. Why then, without any motive, are troops marched against us? This appears to us very unjust. How! have the Mantchous, who are foreigners, a right to collect the revenues of eighteen provinces, and to appoint the officers who oppress the people; while we, who are Chinese, are forbidden to take a little money from the public stock? Universal sovereignty does not belong to any individual to the exclusion of all the rest, and no one ever saw a dynasty which could count a hundred generations of emperors. Possession—and possession only— gives a right to govern.'

This proclamation was the first political act of the rebels. Hitherto the principle for which they fought had only been promulgated by those vague rumors which, when the moment of revolution has arrived, circulate among the masses, as if they had a presentiment of what was about to happen.

At the commencement of the insurrection, the Anglo-Chinese press was divided into two parties. One looked upon the insurgents as mere robbers, ready to lay down their arms as soon as they had filled their pockets, or perhaps their hands; the other, on the contrary, feigned to regard the rebel army as a troop roused to fanaticism by dexterous chiefs, and ready to shed every drop of their blood in the overthrow of the reigning dynasty. Neither of these exclusive opinions was correct.

Revolutionists cannot live in China any more than in Europe, on pure water and patriotic maxims; while, on the other hand, it must be confessed, to the honor of humanity, that the most detestable causes, to act on the masses, must appeal to elevated sentiments, and generous ideas, by which, as isolated individuals, the members of these obscure bodies would be but little moved. The proclamation of the insurgents of the Kouang-Si gave the insurrection its true significance. By openly proclaiming that they looked upon possession as the sole source of legitimacy, they avowed that their object was not only to expel the Mantchous, but to transfer the administration of the public revenues into the hands of the Chinese. Now, this latter consideration was not without value in the eyes of the politicians of the Celestial Empire.

This was the last act of the insurgents in 1850. It was simultaneous with the death of Lin, which took place in the month of November. The old mandarin died as he was proceeding to his post, at Tchao-Tcheou-Fou, in the province of Kouang-Toung. He was about sixty-nine years of age, and sank under the fatigue and cares of government. His death cast a gloom over the public mind, and seemed a bad omen for that cause which the courageous old man had supported to his last hour . . .

We have not yet given any details respecting the chiefs of the insurrection, and the organization of the rebel army. The Chinese documents which previously came under our inspection contained no precise information on the subject; but now the rebels have reached the richest provinces of the empire, namely the Kiang-Nan and the Kiang-Si, information pours upon us in abundance.

We shall not repeat here what we have already said respecting Tien-te, on the strength of popular rumor. Fame first enlightened us as to this personage; and though her voice is generally deceitful, her information perfectly accords with that which we have since received.

We are now, therefore, going to make the acquaintance of the General in chief and his four predatory colleagues. Houng-sieou-tsiuen, who takes the title of Tai-ping-wang, or King grand pacificator, is a man of tall stature, with a face bronzed by the sun, and of a bold, confident aspect. He is about forty years old; his beard and his hair are already gray; and he is said to be endowed with great courage. Although his accent betrays a Canton origin, no one knows his real name, or in what district he was born.

Hiang-tsiou-tsing, or Toung-wang, that is to say, the 'King of the East' is a man of five-and-thirty. He is short and pitted with the small-pox, and his scanty moustache stands bristling on his upper lip. Hiang-tsiou-tsing speaks with remarkable facility, and is very accessible to all his subordinates. No one knows from what country he comes; it is only known that he is married to the eldest sister of Tai-ping-wang.

Siao-tcha-kouei, or Si-wang, 'King of the West', is the Achilles of this pleiad of kings. In every engagement he shows himself regardless of personal safety, always fighting in the foremost ranks, and directing his troops with a precision which gives evidence of a superior knowledge. His figure is graceful, his countenance is animated, and there is nothing of the Mongol type in his oblong face, except the distension of the nostrils and the obliquity of the eyes; he does not wear moustaches. This man, who is one of the most gifted of the party, is not more than thirty years of age. They say he is married to the youngest sister of the 'King-pacificator'.

Foung-hien-san, or Nan-wang, that is, 'King of the South', is a man of letters, of the province of Canton. He has gone through several public examinations, and has gained degrees. He is thirty-two years old, and is said to be much beloved by his fellow students, who consider him endowed with great talents. He does not wear the moustache, and his features still have something youthful in their character. Even amid the agitated life of a camp he lives as much in retirement as possible, to pursue his literary studies.

Wei-tching, or Pe-wang, the 'King of the North', is the Ajax of the insurrectionary army. He is very tall, and has the dark complexion of a Malay, so that his black moustache forms but a slight contrast to his brown skin. He is only twenty-five years of age. His physical force and his intrepidity have given him a high position among the insurgents, and it is said that he is a native of the Kiang-Si.

Such are the five kings, whose united armies now act in concert. They are all young; and have all resolved to sell their lives dearly in case of defeat. A large number of functionaries and officers surround these sovereign chiefs. We shall only mention here the two prime ministers, who are assuredly destined to play an important part, if the insurgents gain their end. The prime minister, Foung-je-tchang, is thirty-seven years of age. In person he is short and thin, while his mind is subtle and fertile in resources. It is known that he was born in the province of Canton.

Tche-Ta-Kai, the second minister, is extremely ugly. He is very thin; his complexion is the color of soot, and his long neck supports a bony face, with a head rising to a point. He is a man of letters; and it is said that he is the author of most of the proclamations lately published—a circumstance which might lead to the supposition that he is a Chang-ti—perhaps a member of Gutzlaff's union. After the ministers, come the high officials of the army. It will be seen at a glance, that the kings have not been lavish of titles or decorations. They are soldiers in active service, and do not yet think of arraying themselves in empty names.

31
An Account by Theodore Hamberg of Hung Hsiu-ch'üan's Early Years

T. Hamberg, *The Visions of Hung-siu-tshuen and the Origin of the Kwang-si Insurrection* (Hong Kong, 1854), pp. 4–6, 8–13

The whole population of Hung's native village only amounts to about four hundred people, the most part of whom belong to the Hung family. There are only half-a-dozen houses in the front, but behind are two other rows of houses with narrow lanes leading to them, and in the third row on the west side we find the humble dwelling of Hung's parents. Before the village in front of the houses is a large pool of muddy water, where all the dirt and refuse of the village is carried down by the rain, and which forms a rich supply of water for manuring purposes, though the smell thereof is offensive to persons unaccustomed to Chinese agricultural economy. Upon the left hand from the village, and on the side of this pool, is situated the schoolhouse, where every boy may study the same Chinese classics as are studied everywhere and by every student in the whole country, with the hope ultimately of rising from his present humble station to the highest dignities in the Empire.

In this village, in the year 1813[33] Hung Siu-tshuen was born, and received upon his birth the name 'Brilliant fire'; afterwards upon attaining the age of manhood, another name was given him, marking his relation to the Hung family; and subsequently he himself adopted Siu-tshuen, 'Elegant and Perfect', as his literary name. The two elder brothers of Siu-tshuen assisted their father in cultivating their paddy-fields, and a few simple vegetables, which supplied their principle nourishment. The family was in a humble position, possessing only one or two buffaloes, besides some pigs, dogs, and poultry, which are generally included in a Chinese farming establishment. The young Siu-tshuen soon developed an extraordinary capacity for study, and was sent to school when seven years of age. In the course of five or six years, he had already committed to memory and studied the Four Books, the Five Classics, the Koo-wun and the Hau-king; afterwards he read for himself the History of China, and the more extraordinary books of Chinese literature, all of which he very easily understood at the first perusal. He soon gained the favour of his teacher as well as of his own family relations, who felt proud of his talents, and surely hoped that he would in course of time attain the degree of Tsin-tzu, or even become a member of the Han-lin

33   Actually 1 January 1814.

college, from which the highest officers are selected by the Emperor, and thus by his high station reflect a lustre upon his whole family. Several of his teachers would not receive any pay for instructing him, and though some of the schools he visited were at a great distance, and the circumstances of his family not very good, yet, in order that he might continue his studies, they rejoiced to bring him provisions, and several of his relatives shared their clothing with him, for the same purpose. His old father, in talking with his friends, was particularly fond of dwelling upon the subject of the talents of his youngest son. His face brightened whenever he heard any one speak in his son's praise, and this was inducement enough for him to invite the speaker to the family hall, to partake of a cup of tea or a bowl of rice, and quietly continue this his favourite topic of discourse.

When Siu-tshuen was about sixteen years of age, the poverty of his family did not permit him to continue his studies, but like the other youths of the village, who were no students, he assisted in the field labour, or led the oxen to graze upon the mountains, a common occupation in China for those who, either by their age or by their youth, are unable to perform heavy manual labour. Still it was regretted by all, that Siu-tshuen's studies should thus be discontinued; and in the following year a friend of the same age as himself invited him to become associated with him as a fellow-student for one year, hoping to derive benefit from a companion of so much talent. After the expiration of this period, his relatives and friends regretted that his talents should be wasted upon mere manual labour in the fields, and they therefore engaged him as teacher in their own village, whereby an opportunity was given him quietly to continue his literary pursuits, and develop his character. The yearly income of a Chinese schoolmaster depends upon the number of boys who attend his school. The usual number is between ten and twenty; a smaller number than ten would be insufficient for his support, and to more than twenty he could not give proper attention, as he has to teach every boy separately, and hear him repeat his lessons by heart, after he has committed them to memory. Every boy is bound to supply his teacher with the following articles annually: Rice 50lb., for extra provisions 300 cash, lamp-oil 1 catty (1 1/3lb.), lard 1 catty, salt 1 catty, tea 1 catty, and, besides a sum of from $1\frac{1}{2}$ to 4 dollars, according to the age and ability of the boy. In the district of Hwa-hien, the school studies are continued throughout the whole year, with only about one month's intermission at the New Year. At this time the teacher's engagement terminates, a new engagement must be made, and a change of teachers often follows . . .

Siu-tshuen's name was always among the first upon the board at the District Examinations, yet he never succeeded in attaining the degree of Siu-tshai. In the year 1836* when he was twenty-three years of age, he again visited Canton, to be present at the public examination. Just before the office of the Superintendent of Finances, he found a man dressed according to the custom of the Ming dynasty, in a coat with wide sleeves, and his hair tied in a knot upon his head. The man was unacquainted with the Chinese vernacular tongue, and employed a native as interpreter. A number of people kept gathering round the stranger, who used to tell them the fulfilment of their wishes, even without waiting for a question from their side. Siu-tshuen approached the man, intending to ask if he should attain a literary degree, but the man prevented him by saying,—'You will attain the highest rank, but do not be grieved, for grief will make you sick. I congratulate your virtuous father.' On the following day he again met with two men in the Liung-tsang street.† One of these men[34] had in his possession a parcel of books consisting of nine small volumes, being a complete set of work entitled 'Keuen shi leang yen', or 'Good words for exhorting the age'; the whole of which he gave Hung-Siu-tshuen, who, on his return from the examination, brought them home, and after a superficial glance at their contents, placed them in his book-case, without at the time considering them to be of any particular importance. The following year, 1837, he again attended the public examination at the provincial city of Kwang-tung. In the commencement his name was placed high upon the board, but afterwards it was again put lower. Deeply grieved and discontented, he was obliged once more to return home without his hopes being realized, and at the same time feeling very ill, he engaged a sedan-chair with two stout men, who carried him to his native village, where he arrived on the first day of the third Chinese month in a very feeble state, and was for some time confined to his bed. During this period he had a succession of dreams or visions. He first saw a great number of people, bidding him welcome to their number, and thought this

---

* It may also have been some time before that period.

† Siu-tshuen supposed these two men to have been the same whom he saw the previous day, and who had told him the future; but in all probability, his memory was here mistaken, which however was very excusable, as seven years had passed between his first getting the books and his studying their contents carefully.

34   It has been supposed that this was Liang A-fa (Liang Kung-fa, 1789–1855), the first Chinese converted by Protestant missionaries who, together with Revs. Robert Morrison and William Milne, composed the tracts referred to. However, Liang was in Malacca in 1836.

dream was to signify that he should soon die, and go into the presence of Yen-lo-wang, the Chinese King of Hades. He therefore called his parents and other relatives to assemble at his bedside, and he addressed them in the following terms: 'My days are counted, and my life will soon be closed. O my parents! How badly have I returned the favour of your love to me! I shall never attain a name that may reflect its lustre upon you.' After he had uttered these words, during which time his two elder brothers had supported him in a sitting posture upon his bed, he shut his eyes and lost all strength and command over his body. All present thought he was going to die, and his two brothers placed him quietly down upon the bed. Siu-tshuen became for some time unconscious of what was going on around him; his outward senses were inactive, and his body appeared as dead, lying upon the bed, but his soul was acted upon by a peculiar energy, so that he not only experienced things of a very extraordinary nature, but afterwards also retained in memory what had occurred to him. At first when his eyes were closed, he saw a dragon, a tiger, and a cock entering his room, and soon after he observed a great number of men, playing upon musical instruments, approaching with a beautiful sedan chair, in which they invited him to be seated, and then carried him away. Siu-tshuen felt greatly astonished at the honour and distinction bestowed upon him, and knew not what to think thereof. They soon arrived at a beautiful and luminous place, where on both sides were assembled a multitude of fine men and women, who saluted him with expressions of great joy. As he left the sedan, an old woman took him down to a river and said—'Thou dirty man, why hast thou kept company with yonder people, and defiled thyself? I must now wash thee clean.' After the washing was performed, Siu-tshuen, in company with a great number of old virtuous and venerable men, among whom he remarked many of the ancient sages, entered a large building where they opened his body with a knife, took out his heart and other parts, and put in their place others new and of a red colour. Instantly when this was done, the wound closed, and he could see no trace of the incision which had been made. Upon the walls surrounding this place, Siu-tshuen remarked a number of Tablets with inscriptions exhorting to virtue, which he one by one examined. Afterwards they entered another large hall the beauty and splendour of which were beyond description. A man, venerable in years, with golden beard and dressed in a black robe, was sitting in an imposing attitude upon the highest place. As soon as he observed Siu-tshuen, he began to shed tears, and said—'All human beings in the whole world are produced and sustained by me; they eat my food and wear my clothing, but not a single one among them has a heart to remember and venerate me; what is however still worse than that, they take of my gifts, and therewith worship demons; they purposely rebel against me, and arouse my anger. Do thou not imitate them.' Thereupon he gave Siu-tshuen a sword, commanding him to exterminate the demons, but to spare his brothers and sisters; a seal by which he would overcome the evil spirits; and also a yellow fruit to eat, which Siu-tshuen found sweet to the taste. When he had received the ensigns of royalty from the hand of the old men, he instantly commenced to exhort those collected in the hall to return to their duties toward the venerable old man upon the high seat. Some replied to his exhortations, saying, 'We have indeed forgotten our duties towards the venerable.' Others said, 'Why should we venerate him? Let us only be merry, and drink together with our friends.' Siu-tshuen then, because of the hardness of their hearts, continued his admonitions with tears. The old man said to him, 'Take courage and do the work; I will assist thee in every difficulty.' Shortly after this he turned to the assemblage of the old and virtuous saying, 'Siu-tshuen is competent to this charge;' and thereupon he led Siu-tshuen out, told him to look down from above, and said, 'Behold the people upon this earth! Hundredfold is the perverseness of their hearts.' Siu-tshuen looked and saw such a degree of depravity and vice, that his eyes could not endure the sight, nor his mouth express their deeds. He then awoke from his trance, but still being under its influence, he felt the very hairs of his head raise themselves, and suddenly, seized by a violent anger, forgetting his feeble state, put on his clothes, left his bedroom, went into the presence of his father, and making a low bow said, 'The venerable old man above has commanded that all men shall turn to me, and all treasures shall flow to me.' When his father saw him come out, and heard him speak in this manner, he did not know what to think, feeling at the same time both joy and fear. The sickness and visions of Siu-tshuen continued about forty days, and in these visions he often met with a man of middle age, whom he called his elder brother, who instructed him how to act, accompanied him upon his wanderings to the uttermost regions in search of evil spirits, and assisted him in slaying and exterminating them. Siu-tshuen also heard the venerable old man with the black robe reprove Confucius for having omitted in his books clearly to expound the true doctrine. Confucius seemed much ashamed, and confessed his guilt. Siu-tshuen, during his sickness, often, as his mind was wandering, used to run about his room, leaping and fighting like a soldier engaged in battle. His constant cry was, 'Tsan jau, tsan jau, tsan ah, tsan ah,'—'Slay the demons! Slay the demons! Slay, slay; there is one and there is another; many many cannot withstand one single blow of my sword.' His father felt very anxious about the state of his mind, and ascribed their present misfortune to the fault of the Geomancer in selecting an unlucky spot of ground for the burial of their forefathers. He invited therefore magicians, who by their secret art should drive away evil spirits; but Siu-tshuen said, 'How could these imps dare to oppose me?' I must slay them, I must slay them! Many many cannot resist me.' As in his imagination he pursued the Demons, they seemed to undergo various changes and transformations—one time flying as birds, and another time appearing as lions. In case he was not able to overcome them, he held out his seal against them, at the sight of which they immediately fled away. He imagined himself pursuing them to the most remote places under heaven, and every where he made war with and destroyed them. Whenever he succeeded, he laughed joyfully and said, 'They can't withstand me.' He also constantly used to sing one passage of an old song—'The virtuous swain he travels over rivers and seas; he saves many friends and he kills his enemies.' During his exhortations he often burst into tears, saying,—'You have no hearts to venerate the old father, but you are on good terms with the impish fiends; indeed, indeed, you have no hearts, no conscience more.' Siu-tshuen's two brothers constantly kept his door shut, and watched him, to prevent him from running out of the house. After he had fatigued himself by fighting, jumping about, singing, and exhorting, he lay down again upon his bed. When he was asleep, many persons used to come and look at him, and he was soon known in the whole district as the madman. He often said, that he was duly appointed Emperor of China, and was highly gratified when any one called him by that name; but if any one called him mad, he used to laugh at him and to reply, 'You are indeed mad yourself, and do you call me mad?' When men of bad character came to see him, he often rebuked them and called them demons. All the day long he used to sing, weep, exhort, reprove by turns, and in full earnest. During his sickness he composed the following piece of poetry:

> My hand now holds both in heaven and earth the power
> to punish and kill—
> To slay the depraved, and spare the upright; to
> relieve the people's distress.
> My eyes survey from the North to the South beyond
> the rivers and mountains;

My voice is heard from the East to the West to the
   tracts of the sun and the moon.
The Dragon expands his claws, as if the road in the
   clouds were too narrow;
And when he ascends, why should he fear the bent
   of the milky way?
Then tempest and thunder as music attend, and the
   foaming waves are excited,
The flying Dragon the Yik-king describes, dwells
   surely in Heaven above.

One morning very early when Siu-tshuen was about to leave his
bed, he heard the birds of the spring singing in the trees which
surrounded the village, and instantly he recited the following
ode:

The Birds in their flight all turn to the light,
   In this resembling me;
For I'm now a King, and every thing
   At will to do I'm free.
As the sun to the sight, my body shines bright—
   Calamities are gone;
The high Dragon and the Tiger band
   Are helping me each one.

Siu-tshuen's relatives asked the advice of several physicians;
who tried to cure his disease by the aid of medicines, but without
success. One day his father noticed a slip of paper put into a crack
of the doorpost, upon which were written the following characters in red—'The noble principles of the heavenly King, the
Sovereign King Tshuen.' He took the paper and shewed it to the
other members of the family, who however could not understand
the meaning of the seven characters. From this time Siu-tshuen
gradually regained his health. Many of his friends and relatives
now visited him, desirous to hear from his own mouth what he
had experienced during his disease, and Siu-tshuen related to
them without reserve all that he could remember of his extraordinary visions. His friends and relatives only replied, that the
whole was very strange indeed, without thinking at the time that
there was any reality in the matter.

2
The Middle Years 1854–9

Between 1854 and 1859 the fortunes of the Taiping movement declined significantly from the peak of 1853, but it remained a serious challenge to the Ch'ing rulers of China. The Taiping attempt during 1854–5 to capture Peking, the northern and primary capital of the empire, was defeated and they were themselves besieged, though not very closely, in their own capital by Imperial forces. A long stalemate ensued, marked mainly by the savage internal dissension which broke out in Nanking in mid 1856, resulting in the slaughter of several leading adherents and thousands of their followers. In May 1857 Shih Ta-k'ai, the Assistant King and one of the most capable of their military leaders, deserted Nanking with a large following and set out, unsuccessfully, to establish his own base elsewhere. The movement was later to find outstanding new commanders, but during these years it failed to extend the great victories of 1852–3 effectively.

Western contact in this period fluctuated between the relatively close observation of three further official expeditions, two made in 1854 and one at the end of 1858, and the almost total absence of direct contact and certain news during the years between. For a time the Taiping almost dropped out of Western calculations about future prospects in China, prospects immeasurably widened for the West by the second Opium War. But the treaty settlement of that war, made in the latter part of 1858, had perforce to recognise the continued presence of the Taiping in the lower Yangtze valley, at about the time when both the West and the Ch'ing government were to feel that presence very strongly once again.

Section 1 The West Looks More Closely (1854)

Apart from their northern campaign directed towards Peking the Taiping also launched in 1854 a westward campaign, back up the Yangtze towards Hankow. But they still showed no disposition to advance eastwards beyond Chinkiang, despite the seizure of

128

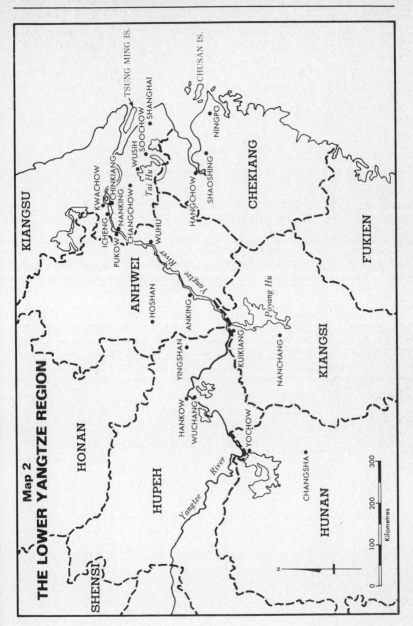

Map 2
THE LOWER YANGTZE REGION

Shanghai in September 1853 by the Small Sword Society (Hsiao Tao Hui) which claimed a connection, not recognised by the Taiping, with the Nanking based movement. The disorganisation and unruly behaviour of the Small Sword rebels in Shanghai led some Westerners to ask whether the Taiping were not of similar stamp, but an official policy of neutrality was maintained towards the Nanking regime by all the Western treaty powers, though in a somewhat erratic and selective fashion.

Two diplomatic missions, one American and the second British, went to Nanking in the spring of 1854, reflecting continued Western official concern and uncertainty about the nature and policies of the Taiping movement. The first was led by the newly arrived US minister to China, Robert McLane who, like Bonham before him, remained on board his ship, the *Susquehanna*, determined not to appear in any way as a tributary seeking favours. McLane left the handling of conversations with Taiping leaders to a consular official, Lewis Carr, and to naval officers, assisted by two missionary interpreters, E. C. Bridgman, who had edited the *Chinese Repository* from 1831 to 1848, and the Presbyterian N. S. Culbertson. McLane's own critical assessment constitutes Doc. 32; Culbertson's narrative is Doc. 33, and Bridgman's conclusions, which were incorporated into Carr's official report to McLane, is Doc. 34.

The ambitious new governor of Hong Kong and Superintendent of British trade in China, Bowring, sent a second British expedition to Nanking soon after the return of McLane. Sir John did not himself go into rebel territory at all, preferring to leave the conduct of this mission to his son Lewin, who was in China as his personal secretary, and the Chinese secretary to the superintendency, W. H. Medhurst (Jr). Lewin was not a consular official and knew no Chinese, so one may reasonably presume that Medhurst was the real leader of the expedition and the main author of its report. Although Medhurst was the son of a missionary, no missionary accompanied them. They journeyed in two small naval vessels, the *Rattler* and the *Styx*, and stayed off Nanking for ten days, longer than any previous Western visitors, but were able to communicate with Taiping leaders only by letter. Like McLane's their report (Doc. 35) was highly critical of the movement and sceptical of its potential, whether political, military, religious or economic. Indicative of the rapid decline of British hopes, and indeed of interest, by this time is the fact that this report was never published in any Parliamentary Paper, as was done with the reports of all four other official British expeditions to Nanking between 1853 and 1862. Even the *North China Herald* carried no very full account, though some years after the event Lewin Bowring's book of personal reminiscences provided contemporaries with a little information about it (Doc. 36).

By the end of 1854 the Taiping movement was entering its limbo years of stagnation, dissension and defection. For some years it was to be almost as cut off from direct Western observation, as it had been in its earliest years.

32
A Report by Robert M McLane, US Minister to China
US Congressional Papers, 35th Congress, 2nd Session, Senate Executive Document 22, vol. VIII, pp. 50-5

... Whatever may have been the hopes of the enlightened and civilized nations of the earth, in regard to this movement, it is now apparent that they neither profess or apprehend christianity, and whatever may be the true judgment to form of their political power, it can no longer be doubted that intercourse cannot be established or maintained on terms of equality. Unhappily, too, their civil policy is intimately blended with their religious profession, and any attempt to combat their monstrous misapprehension of scriptural truth, involves a conflict with the organisation of their civil system.

I propose to submit a brief summary of the case established by the documents herewith transmitted,[1] and the personal information obtained from intercourse with the principal chiefs of the revolution.

Tae-ping-Wang, the chief, represents to his followers by the immediate decree, herewith enclosed, of his principal minister of State, 'Yang', the Eastern King, that God created the world in six days, and the history of this creation he sets out in the decree in the terms of the book of Genesis, as translated by the christian missionaries. The first dispensation of the wrath of God is then set out as the deluge, in the terms of the same book of scripture, then follows the history of the second dispensation, which is the Mosaic narrative, expressed again in the literal terms of the Old Testament; following which is the history of the christian dispensation as related by the Apostle Matthew, and translated by the missionary, Dr Morrison; the decree then sets out the mission of Tae-ping-Wang, the younger brother of Jesus, as the fourth dispensation of the wrath of God, to exterminate unbelievers and

---

1   None of the enclosures referred to in McLane's report are included here. The Taiping communications to the Americans are to be found in Michael, op. cit., vol. II, pp. 520-31.

gather together the faithful throughout the world, reducing all to an earthly submission; in the manner of expression no less than in the sentiment expressed, the biblical history of the millennium is followed. This principal minister of State, Yang, who issues these decrees, represents himself in the very language of the New Testament to be the comforter or Holy Ghost[2], sent with this younger brother of Jesus, to comfort those who believe and are gathered together under the earthly sway of Tae-ping-Wang, relieving them from all calamities, and performing for them all the functions which appertain to the holy spirit; the identical language of scripture as translated by christian missionaries, being taken to express in the decree the functions and character of this principal minister of State. The truth would seem to be that the chief of this revolutionary movement, with his principal minister of State, who are both scholars, have taken those translations of the Bible which fell in their hands, and whether as uninstructed converts or as charlatans, have constructed upon the narrative of the revealed word, a system of religious and civil faith; the one a mixture of heathenism and mahometanism, the other a rude despotism.

Proclaiming these views, and day by day advancing in their pretensions, they arouse the political passions of the people in the interior provinces against the ruling dynasty. Commencing in the southern and middle parts of the empire as early as 1848, continued conflicts were had between the followers of Tae-ping-Wang and the imperial authorities. Little was clearly known concerning the progress of the revolution for several years; and until the latter part of 1852, and through the year 1853, when they reached Nanking, the capital of the old 'Ming dynasty', nothing was known of their true character or intentions; and even so late as last year, when that city was visited by the British and French ministers, the most unsatisfactory impressions prevailed concerning them.

They have now, to some extent, consolidated the form of their civil government; and, extending their political power along the

---

2   This is an error made by several translators of Taiping documents. The term often translated as 'the Holy Ghost' (sheng shen feng) was based on Morrison's version of the Bible, but in fact the Taiping used Gutzlaff's version, which gives Holy Ghost simply as 'sheng shen'. In Taiping documents the longer term 'sheng shen feng' should be translated as 'wind (or messenger) of the Holy Ghost'. Many contemporary observers, like McLane, concluded that Yang was referring to himself as the Holy Ghost, although the American Presbyterian M. S. Culbertson, who was on the *Susquehanna* with McLane, translated the term as 'the Holy Divine Breath' (see Doc. 33).

line of the Yang-tsze-kiang, they are directing their operations upon the capital of the empire. Nothing can be more shocking than the manner in which they have misapprehended and misapplied the scripture, and nothing more absurd than the pretensions with which they have inaugurated their civil government. When their operations are regarded in a more practical bearing, the case presented for your consideration is not less unsatisfactory than their civil and religious organisation itself. They are composed almost exclusively of the ignorant and unenlightened population of the interior; limited in numbers, not exceeding from fifty to one hundred thousand men, in the field and in the besieged cities throughout that portion of the empire, they hold in check or in actual possession; yet the imperialists are quite incapable of resisting them, and still less hopeless is their immediate prospect of recovering the main points that have fallen. Thus is presented the melancholy spectacle of an enfeebled and tottering imperial government, ignorant, conceited, and impracticable; assailed at all points by a handful of insurgents, whose origin was a band of robbers in the interior, whose present power is quite sufficient to drive before them the imperial authorities, and hold control over five or six principal provinces in the heart of the empire, possessing as they do some of the principal keys to the navigation of the Yang-tsze-kiang—a river draining an area of seven hundred thousand square miles of arable land, but who are, nevertheless, unworthy the respect of the civilized world, and perhaps incapable of consolidating civil government beyond the walls of the cities captured and pillaged by a multitude excited to the highest pitch of resentment against all who possess property or betray a partiality for the imperial authorities.

What then shall be the policy of foreign nations having treaty stipulations with China? To the present time it has been justly urged that a strict and impartial neutrality should be maintained until the one or the other of the contending parties should obtain an ascendency; and meanwhile so conduct our relations with the empire that we may be ready to take advantage of the present crisis to enlarge our commercial intercourse, and extend the lights and blessings of civilization, for which so many enlightened and enthusiastic men have so fondly looked as one of the legitimate results of a successful revolution. It cannot be doubted that such a policy of neutrality was imposed upon us by the highest obligations of honor, so long as the imperial government remained faithful to the treaty stipulations, by which our present intercourse with China is secured. For sometime past fidelity to these treaty stipulations by the imperial authorities has been vainly entreated, and whether the weakness and disorder which prevails in the civil organization of the empire, or the inveterate hostility of those charged with the administration of foreign affairs, be the immediate cause of our difficulties, the fact is undeniable that the treaty between China and the United States is practically abrogated at the port of Shanghai, and executed elsewhere in a manner most unsatisfactory to all concerned . . .

I would first invite your attention to the character of the revolutionary movement, and to the almost insuperable difficulty of any satisfactory intercourse with them at this time of a diplomatic character, for, independent altogether of those considerations, which are not now to be discussed, that would influence me in recognising the revolutionary government as a *de facto* government over a portion of the Chinese empire, and without for the moment any regard to the disposition of the revolutionary authorities touching trade and commerce with foreign nations, I am absolutely excluded for the time being from satisfactory intercourse with them, in consequence of their own peculiar civil organization, as is very clearly set forth in the official documents herewith transmitted, unless their extraordinary doctrine that China and the United States are one country, and all mankind one nation, to be governed by Tae-ping-Wang, be accepted, and the minister of the United States become the minister of Tae-ping-Wang, and the citizens of the United States his subjects, coming from afar as brethren, bringing precious gifts and tribute, as evidences of their submission to the heavenly king. The words used to express this idea of *tribute* are in the official communication herewith transmitted, the ordinary Chinese characters for tribute as used when applied to Siam, Cochin-China, and Corea, as tributaries of the Chinese empire; but in conversation with one of the chiefs, he made use of the Scriptural character used by Gutzlaff to express '*precious gifts*', when he spoke of foreign brethren bringing tribute to indicate submission to Tae-ping-Wang. In either case the idea was the same, and however friendly they might be induced to be, our people would be obliged to hold intercourse with them as brethren coming from afar to accept their faith and their sovereign, a man sent by the Almighty to reign over all on earth; so that, whatever might be the actual political power of the revolutionary government, or my conclusions concerning the morality or spiritual character of its organization, I should be quite unable to deal with it in any mode by which intercourse is conducted between foreign nations.

The next point to which I ask your attention is, that the imperial government is unable, and when able still unwilling, to perform with efficiency those functions which pertain to it under the treaty. I have thought it proper to persist in every reasonable undertaking to engage their attention, and I shall represent to the viceroy of the Liang Kiang, and perhaps to the higher authorities of the empire at Peking, should this local functionary fail to apply an efficient remedy, that the Government of the United States must with its own means enforce the treaty stipulations under which American citizens have resorted to China for the purposes of commerce.

Could this government be made to understand and acknowledge the true state of its relations with foreign nations, it would not be difficult, even at this time and in face of the prevailing disorder, to adjust existing difficulties and greatly enlarge our commercial intercourse. To accomplish this result, whether the empire be governed in whole or in part by the ruling dynasty, or by those who are now conducting the revolutionary movement, it is necessary to enlarge the powers and duties which devolve on the United States by the terms of the treaty, both to enforce the stipulations of the same and to prevent the abuse of their flag, when used as a cover to the violation of the laws of the Chinese empire. Without such an exercise of power on our part, it will be quite impossible to maintain the honor and integrity of our flag, or avoid those collisions which the weakness and corruption of the Chinese authorities render inevitable. As a consideration for such enlargement of the *protectorate* character of the existing treaty, the interior should be opened to us, where we would extend the moral power of our civilization and the material power necessary to protect the lives and property of our people. At this port commerce is now maintained, and the lives and property of our people protected, by the exercise of this material power. It cannot be extended or even maintained where it now is without an enlargement of our right to exercise this protective power, or a continuation of the unauthorized extension which has been recently given to it under the presence of what seemed to be conceived an imminent necessity.

It is not necessary to vindicate the propriety of dealing with the imperial authorities as long as they possess the sovereignty of the country, and effecting with the measures which may insure a faithful and honorable discharge of our respective duties under the treaty between the two countries; but it becomes a much more difficult question to determine what shall be our policy when regular and satisfactory intercourse is difficult, if not impossible, with either the one or the other of the contending parties. Shall we await a determination of this contest, or shall we impose upon each and either a respect for those rights already secured by treaty, with such enlargement as circumstances will permit? These are the questions to be determined, and foreign governments must shape their policy accordingly, without regard to the opinions of those who cherish respect for the existing order of things in China, or the expectations of those who anticipate the civilization of the empire from the progress and ultimate ascendency of the revolutionary principle. Should we determine to await the result of domestic strife disorganizing the empire, no foresight can anticipate when the period would arrive for the establishment of new relations with the government, which may in the future give peace and tranquillity to the country. Meanwhile, the foreign import trade which is well nigh arrested at Shanghai will entirely disappear, and the same causes which induce that result here must extend to the other ports, and instead of an enlargement of our commerce that which we possess will be involved in the desolation which is now so widely diffused through the interior.

On the other hand, should we enforce our treaty rights, we would at least maintain our presence in China, and whether the one power or the other should prevail, we could not fail greatly to extend our intercourse with the people, and to dispose of that property on which we have paid duties, and which we have by treaty the right to sell to all persons, without distinction, from whom, without restraint, we have the privilege to purchase return cargoes on the payment of certain stipulated duties. No practical difficulty would attend the exercise of this right, though the imperial authorities and the revolutionary chiefs might alike oppose it, for they are equally incapable of offering effective resistance, and the millions who inhabit the great valley of the Yang-tze-kiang would regard such a determination on our part as a boon to themselves, not less than a vindication of our rights and privileges as fixed by the treaty.

Should Tae-ping-Wang prevail, and succeed in establishing his empire over China, our presence at the five treaty ports, with the connexions we should form in the interior, could not fail to exert a powerful influence in correcting the errors he has embraced, and tend greatly to give a truly Christian direction to that movement, which though now shrouded in heathen darkness, is yet founded on the text of the Bible, which has been widely diffused throughout the empire, but not understood or even read by the mass of those who profess to be the followers of the revolutionary chief.

Should the imperial government maintain its ascendency, we would have overcome by our presence in the interior the only obstacle that has heretofore restrained a development of that trade and commerce, which if freely opened would offer to the American manufacturers a market more valuable than all the other markets of the world to which they have yet had access . . .

I remain, with great respect, your obedient servant.

Rob't M McLane
Hon. W L Marcy,
Secretary of State, Washington City.

33
A Letter from the Rev. M S Culbertson
Home and Foreign Record, vol. v (November 1854), pp. 337–40

CHINA: SHANGHAI MISSION
NARRATIVE OF A VISIT TO THE INSURGENTS AT NANKING, BY THE REV. M S CULBERTSON

Shanghai, June 5th, 1854

Having been invited by His Excellency, R. M. McLane, United States Minister to China, to accompany him to Nanking in the steam frigate Susquehanna, I gladly embraced the opportunity of visiting that famous city, and of seeing something of the new party now rising to power, in their own headquarters. We returned to this place yesterday, and I purpose now to give you some account of our voyage, and the results of our observations.

The Susquehanna left Wusung on Monday the 22nd May, accompanied by the steam tug 'Confucius'. Proceeding slowly, in consequence of the difficulty of navigating so large a vessel in an unknown channel, we arrived at Chinkiang-fu on Thursday the 25th.

As the vessel was about to come to anchor, a shot was fired across her bows from one of the batteries on shore. A communication from Capt. Buchanan was immediately sent on shore, for the commandant of the place. Dr Bridgman and myself accompanied the officers in charge of it. Landing at the battery, we found ourselves surrounded by a motley crowd of men and boys, whose unshorn and unshaven heads, not generally dressed in the neatest manner, gave them a rather unprepossessing appearance. We were requested to wait until word could be sent into the city. After waiting a long time, sheltered under a shed from the drenching rain, horses were brought, and we were conducted into the city, and to the residence of Wu, the present commandant. On hearing of our intention to visit Nanking, he very earnestly pressed upon us a request to wait until he could send word thither and receive a reply. In explanation of the shot fired, he merely said that it was not known to them whether we came as friends or enemies. In his written reply to Capt. Buchanan, an ample apology was made. Having finished our business, we returned as we went, on horseback.

The city is a scene of desolation and ruin. Within the walls, the houses have been in a great measure broken up, leaving nothing but the dilapidated shell. Many rooms were seen filled with broken tables, chairs, and cupboards. Indeed, the place is no longer anything more than a fort, valuable only as commanding the Imperial Canal. No labour was seen going on, except the manufacture of gunpowder and implements of war. Not a female was seen; the women and children who did not flee when the place was taken, having been sent to Nanking. The men and boys were taken into the army. The large suburbs without the walls have been totally destroyed by fire. The town of Kwachau, on the opposite side of the river, is now but a heap of ruins; not a house having escaped destruction.

Just below Chinkiang is Silver Island, a place devoted to the service of Buddha. It is a round peak, rising very abruptly to the height of several hundred feet from the surface of the water. There are here a number of large and highly ornamented temples, which have not been injured, although the idols have been broken to pieces. Near to this island a large Imperial fleet lies at anchor. On the right bank of the river, on the tops of the distant hills south-west of the city, we could discern several Imperialist camps.

Just above the city is another island hill, called Golden Island. Its summit is crowned with a tower of seven stories, and its sides and base were once covered with temples. The temples are now in ruins, and the materials are used for fortifications, which the insurgents are now constructing.

NANKING

On Saturday morning we weighed anchor, and reached Nanking in the afternoon. A communication was immediately sent ashore, and delivered to an officer of rank, who promised to forward it to the authorities in the city. Large numbers of the insurgents soon crowded the decks of the steamers. They were from many different provinces, but chiefly those bordering on the Yang-tsz river. With many of them I was able to converse intelligibly, though with more or less difficulty. A considerable number were able to repeat the ten commandments, as given in their own books. Further than this, they seemed to have received but little instruction. They were frank, open, and friendly, and all seemed very cheerful and happy. The day was their Sabbath, and they seemed to observe it so far as to abstain from labour. In a long walk on shore, I saw no work going on where it was carried on next day. On our own vessel, it was thought best to pass the day quietly, and very few of the people from shore were allowed to come on board. When the reason was explained to them, they seemed fully to appreciate it, and went away with the greatest cheerfulness. They seemed greatly interested to know whether we worshipped T'ien-fu, the Heavenly Father, as they did, and were much pleased when told that we did. We inquired, then and afterwards, with equal interest, whether worship was rendered by them to any other than the Heavenly Father and Jesus, and invariably received a decided negative. The term T'ien-fu was the one used in conversation to designate the Deity, to the almost entire exclusion of every other term.

The situation of Nanking renders it in every way worthy of being the site of royal palaces, and the capital of the world's most populous empire. Standing on the bank of one of the noblest rivers, which gives it direct communication with the sea, and access to a vast and densely peopled region of the greatest fertility, and rich in mineral resources, this cannot but become a splendid city, when the appliances of modern science shall be brought to bear upon the development of the mineral, commercial, and agricultural wealth of the country. The spot itself is one of great natural beauty. The city stands in a basin, surrounded on all sides by hills, around the base of which the walls are built. The walls are about twenty miles in circumference, and are some forty or fifty feet high. Only a small part of the space within the walls is occupied by the city proper, the remainder being cultivated fields.

That this is indeed destined to be the capital of China, there can scarcely be a doubt. Having established their headquarters here, the insurgents are now sending out their armies in various directions to subdue the country, and everywhere these armies are successful. Peking, it is true, has not been taken, and may long hold out, but it is cut off from all communication with the southern provinces, except by sea, and the insurgents have command of the whole Yang-tsz river, from Chinkiang-fu to the province of Hupeh, if not further. They appoint officers, collect revenue, and make laws, for all the region bordering on the river, and the Imperialist armies are so far held in check, that they cannot molest them in the exercise of their authority.

Nanking is itself at present strictly a military camp. The insurgents appear to have appropriated for the public use the entire property of the place, and even the inhabitants themselves. The men and boys were enrolled in the army, while the women and children were quartered in companies in a separate part of the city. All are under military rule, and are compelled to do the work assigned them. They are therefore fed and clothed from the public stores, but they do not, it would seem, receive any wages. Some of the women, evidently belonging originally to the working class, were seen carrying rice into the city. A few well-dressed ladies were seen on horse-back, riding like men. This segregation of the females is not to be regarded in any other light than as a temporary expedient to facilitate the enforcement of military discipline, and it is restricted to the army.

Nanking does not present the desolate, deserted appearance which was observed at Chinkiang-fu, yet many of the houses are empty, and their interior broken up. Many of the streets are wide, and they seem to be kept in a state of cleanliness not common in Chinese cities. I observed indeed generally signs of attention to personal cleanliness, and to the decencies of life, so commonly disregarded by their countrymen.

We did not obtain the privilege of free access to the city; our stay being very short, and the official communications not very satisfactory. The answer to Capt. Buchanan's communication was not received until Tuesday morning. Its character was such as to give some ground for apprehension that the new party will be brought into serious collision with foreign governments, if they succeed in obtaining the throne. There is nothing in it exhibiting hostility to foreigners, or inconsistent with a purpose to throw open the whole country to foreign commerce, but there are claims of universal supremacy, which will, if persisted in, prevent any foreign power from entering into treaty with them. They are the same claims which have always been made by the Tartar Emperors—claims which would prevent the exchange of ambassadors, and admit a minister from a foreign court only as a tribute bearer, coming to pay homage to the Lord of the World. The chief difference between the old and the new doctrine appears to be this, that the old Emperor claimed supremacy as the 'Son of Heaven'; the new Ruler, as the 'Brother of Jesus'. In consequence of the language employed in this letter, Mr McLane determined to leave the next day, and run some distance up the river. He requested me, however, to enter the city if possible, and in a

140

friendly way, explain to any officer of rank I might fall in with, the object of our visit.

Having the address of an officer named Hu, from whom an informal note had been received, I set out to find his residence. The gate nearest the anchorage having been closed, I proceeded along the western face of the wall by a good paved road to the West gate. Here the guards said thay had received no orders to admit me. The gateways are very high. The entrance is through an archway or tunnel, some forty or fifty feet long. Of these arches there are three in a direct line, separated by a considerable intervening space, and closed by heavy doors of great strength.

About half a mile further on is the 'Water West gate', at which I was allowed to pass in. Walking through a very wide street about two miles, I reached another wall, probably that which separates the former Tartar quarter from the Chinese city. On inquiring for Hu, I was taken at once to his residence. Passing through several wide doors and open courts, I found myself in the reception hall. At the head of it sat Hu, dressed in his official robes of yellow silk, with a high cap covered with gilt ornaments. The attendants who conducted me in, kneeled before him. He seemed reserved and distant in his manner, and made but a single inquiry, asking for what object the steamers had come to Nanking. I explained at some length who we were. He listened in silence to what I had to say. I also handed to him some copies of Genesis, Exodus, and some of the Gospels and Acts, with a few tracts printed at Ningpo. These he received and laid aside. He then addressed himself to me with a rather haughty air, and an authoritative tone. He said that the 'foreign brethren' did indeed worship the 'Heavenly Father, and the Heavenly Elder Brother Jesus', but were ignorant of the fact that their 'Celestial King' was the brother of Jesus. He laid much stress upon this, and urged, on this ground, the necessity of our coming with suitable presents and tribute. He intimated, that having enlightened me on this point, he would expect compliance with the 'ceremonials' of the 'Celestial Dynasty'. Having said a good deal on this subject, making sure as he went on that I understood what he said, though I assured him that I did not understand his doctrine, he held an earnest consultation with an officer who sat by him, and two or three of his attendants. The two officers then called for horses, and left the room, without offering any explanation. I of course proposed to leave at once, but the attendants very decidedly objected; and, hoping to see more of my host, and perhaps obtain some books which the attendants said he would bring, I waited for his return. After waiting a long time in vain, the lateness of the hour reminded me that it was time to return to the ship, which was some seven miles distant. Under all the circumstances, I thought it best to return. I was satisfied too, that Hu had gone to receive the orders of his superiors, and after so much had been said about 'ceremonials', I would not have been surprised to have been called on to do homage, by kneeling or prostration, before the Eastern King, or perhaps the 'Brother of Jesus' himself.

On making known my intention to leave, one of the attendants deliberately closed the door, placed himself before it, and gave me to understand that I could not depart until his master returned. Another, however, shortly offered to conduct me to another part of the building, and I then went to the street, and proceeded toward the city gate. The attendants opposed this very strenuously, and with a good deal of anger on the part of some of them, but they dared not use force. So far as their conduct might be regarded as an index to the feelings of their superiors, it certainly did not impress me very favourably. On reaching the city gate, no opposition was made to my leaving. A boat was there furnished me, and I returned to the ship.

On Tuesday morning we proceeded up the river. The day was pleasant, and we had a delightful sail through a rich and populous country. The right bank of the river is hilly, the left rather low and flat, with occasional hills some distance back from the river. The people were getting in their harvest, and could often be seen leaving their work, and running down to the bank of the river to see so strange a sight as two vessels running without sails, and at so rapid a rate, against a strong current. It was perhaps not less interesting to us than to them, for we were in waters never before disturbed by a foreign vessel, and we could not but anticipate as near at hand the day when this noble river shall be traversed by many steamers, richly freighted with the products of foreign lands, and of the fertile region through which it flows. The river is free from the difficulties which obstruct most of the rivers of our own land, and there are probably few streams in which the navigation is easier or less dangerous.

We lay at anchor during the night, and about noon arrived at the city of Wu-hu. This city is situated on the right bank of the right bank of the river, about three hundred miles from its mouth, and sixty-five miles above Nanking, in the province of Ngan-hwui. It was visited by Lord Amherst's embassy in 1816, and is described as having at that time a population of over half a million, and carrying on an immense inland trade. It is beautifully situated on a wide bay formed by a bend of the river, and on the banks of a navigable branch river, which here flows into the

Yang-tsz. Even before the steamer came to anchor, boats pulled alongside, with persons wishing to board her. The first boat brought some officers dressed in yellow satin. One of these was on his way to Hupeh, to attend to the collection of the revenue; another was going in the same direction for charcoal for the use of the 'Celestial King'; and a third had charge of a raft of timber, which he was taking to Nanking, to be used in the erection of palaces for the parents of the five subordinate kings. While they were surveying the steamer, their boat, which was towed along-side, was swamped by the motion of the wheels, and three men in it narrowly escaped being drowned. All were eventually rescued.

Wu-hu is now in possession of the insurgents, and is guarded by a naval force anchored before it. Here, therefore, we had a specimen of the character of their rule in districts where it is not strictly military. The admiral received us in the most friendly manner, and furnished guides to accompany us wherever we wished to go. The people gathered in crowds to see the strangers, but stood in considerable awe of the police, who were armed with long bamboo whips, which they used very freely. In several instances respectable men, having some special object in view, fell on their knees in the streets before us and our guides. Here the great effort of the new rulers seems to be to induce the people to go on quietly with their business as before, only yielding obedience to the new regulations imposed. The titles of the officers are changed, but their functions are much the same, and the new regime, while stronger than the old, is equally arbitrary and despotic. During the contests between the two parties, a large portion of the city, both within and without the walls, was destroyed by fire. It was sad to pass through streets which had evidently been occupied by many buildings of the largest and most substantial class, but which now present nothing to view but tottering walls and heaps of rubbish. Even the countenances of the people passing through these desolate ruins seems to wear an expression of sadness in harmony with the rest of the scene. Trade, however, is beginning to revive, and the people engage in their ordinary avocations. Here there is no separation of the males and females as at Nanking.

On Friday morning we left Wu-hu on our return to Shanghai, which we reached without difficulty or accident on Sabbath evening, passing Nanking and Chinkiang-fu without stopping.

It is to be regretted that the shortness of our stay rendered it impossible to obtain satisfactory and reliable information on many points of great public interest. It would not be just to infer from the character of our reception an intention to return to the former exclusive policy of the Tartar Emperors. It is not surprising that the chiefs are averse at present to the visits of foreign vessels, since they do not well understand their object, and cannot certainly know that they will not turn to the advantage of their enemies. Their independent tone is conclusive evidence, however, that their profession of Christianity has not been made with any view to concilate foreign governments.

The opium trade, however, they are evidently resolved to destroy. Its use is prohibited, and there is every reason to believe that the prohibition is rigidly enforced. The use of tobacco, even, is not allowed, either to soldiers or people. Both these prohibitions seemed to be as effectually enforced at Wu-hu as at Nanking. The use of wine is not absolutely prohibited, and betel-nut seems to be freely allowed.

As to the religious features of this movement, we are still left in a great measure ignorant of the facts necessary for forming a reliable judgment. The spirit of fanticism seems to be increasing with the success of their arms, and also the pride and arrogance of the chiefs. Since Hung Siu-tsiuen founds a claim to universal supremacy upon his assumption that he is the 'Brother of Jesus', he must mean something more by that expression than the Scriptures authorize. However he may have been self-deluded, and however sincere he may have been in his adhesion to Christianity, this claim thus made gives ground to fear that he has not been taught of God.

His chief minister, Yang Siu-tsing, the Eastern King, has also assumed a title, which, if he knew what it meant, would stamp him with the guilt of the most horrid blasphemy. He calls himself 'the Comforter, the Holy Divine Breath'. The latter is the term used by Morrison to designate the Holy Ghost. I cannot see how any of the chiefs could have correct views of the doctrine of the Trinity, but their ignorance cannot excuse so gross a misappropriation of sacred terms.

All of the other kings have also thought it necessary to add to their dignity by the assumption of high-sounding titles. The following is part of an ode given out by the favour of 'the Heavenly Father, the Heavenly Elder Brother, and the Heavenly King' and ordered to be used by 'all soldiers and people under heaven'.

Praise the Supreme Ruler, who is the Holy Heavenly
    Father, the only true God.
Praise the Heavenly Elder Brother, the Saviour of the
    world, who laid down his life for men.
Praise the Eastern King, the Holy Divine Breath, who
    atones for faults and saves men.

Praise the Western King, the rain teacher, an as high
as heaven honourable man.
Praise the Southern King, the cloud teacher, an as
high as heaven upright man.
Praise the Northern King, the thunder teacher, an as
high as heaven benevolent man.
Praise the Assistant King, the lightning teacher,
an as high as heaven righteous man.

The rest of the ode is in praise of the true doctrines, and is taken from a former publication, entitled 'The Book of Religious Precepts'. These titles are not to be understood as implying a claim to any control over the elements. They are intended merely for effect, and probably do not strike the Chinese as absurd, however we may regard them. Some officers of rank, of whom I inquired the meaning of the title 'Brother of Jesus', as applied to Hung Siu-tsiuen, seemed as much puzzled by it as myself, and I therefore infer that he does not lay much stress upon it among his followers. They seemed not only to not understand it, but not to have even heard of it.

The worship enjoined is attended to three times daily, that is, before each meal. It consists of the chanting of a hymn, in which all join, remaining seated, and a short prayer, all kneeling. This is done with solemnity and reverence. I could see, however, little or no evidence of any just views of true religion. With so little opportunity of judging, it would be folly to affirm that none such exists; but I fear the number of spiritually enlightened men is small. I was told that there was occasional preaching, and was shown a large stage in the open field used for this purpose. The printing of the Scriptures is still carried on, and that of the Old Testament extends to Joshua, if not further.

The above facts tend to increase the fears, rather than the hopes which have been entertained with regard to the immediate effect of this revolutionary movement. As to the eventual result, we cannot doubt for a moment. Whatever the character of the insurgent chiefs, and whatever errors they may have imbibed, the Lord will make use of them in answer to the prayers of his people, to prepare the way for the triumph of the truth in this land. We may well hope, too, that the publication of the Bible, even though the motives be purely selfish, will accomplish good. It is still God's word, and will not return unto Him void. If the chiefs are indeed mere imposters, they have made a great mistake. What imposture ever yet succeeded by encouraging the people to read the word of God? Impostors have ever been afraid of the Bible. I do not think, however, that the way is yet open for missionary efforts at Nanking.

34
A Letter from Rev. E C Bridgman
North China Herald, 22 July 1854

To the Editor of the *NORTH-CHINA HERALD*

Dear Sir,—In reply to many inquiries, which have been made about the Insurgents—as seen at Chinkiang fu, Nanking and Wuhu, on the recent visit of the American Minister, and his suit,—I submit for your Readers, the following brief paragraphs, embracing such particulars, as seem most worthy of notice at this juncture. The character and conduct and principles of the men, who are turning this country upside down, claim the most considerate attention of the politician and the merchant, while to the missionary, and in view of the vast population of the empire, they have a thousand times more interest than words can express. The particulars given in detail, with few exceptions, are restricted to such facts as have been gathered up from personal observation and intercourse with the Insurgents—*facts*, too, for the most part, abundantly substantiated by Books, which they themselves have written and published.

Yours, &c.,

E C Bridgman.[3]

Shanghai, July 4th, 1854.

1 Their government is a *theocracy*, the development, apparently, of what is believed, by them, to be a new dispensation. As in the case of the Israelites, under Moses, they regard themselves as directed by one who has been raised up, by the Almighty, to be the executor of his will on earth. They believe their body-politic to be under the immediate direction of the Deity. Sometimes their leaders, they say, are taken up to heaven; and sometimes the Heavenly Father comes down to them.*

2 Their government is a *mixed form*, half political and half religious. It would seem also to have both an earthly and a

---

* One of the new books, brought from Nanking by our party and which I had not seen when I wrote the above paragraph, gives an account of a more recent descent of the Heavenly Father.[4] More on this topic in the sequel, suffice it here to remark, that, in this more recent one, the Heavenly Father commanded *Hung Siu-tsiun* to receive *forty blows of the bamboo*! Prefaced to this Book is a list of one-and-twenty works published with the sanction of the Royal Will.

3 Rev. E. C. Bridgman, a former editor of the *Chinese Repository*, had been one of the interpreters on the *Susquehanna*. Another version of this report is included in Section B of McLane's report (Doc. 32) pp. 70–6.

4 The *T'ien-fu hsia-fan chao-shu*, translated in Michael, op. cit., vol. II, pp. 197–220.

heavenly magistracy, or rather perhaps a visible and an invisible machinery. They most distinctly avow a personal intercourse between their principal actors (men and women) on the one side, and the Heavenly Father and the Heavenly Elder Brother on the other. All their affairs of state—things, temporal—are strangely blended with things divine: I say not *spiritual*, because, I do not know what ideas they have of Spirit and things spiritual.

3 Their government is, moreover, a *royal despotism*. In their new organization there is no emperor, but a Fraternity of kings, (A) viz: a Heavenly king, an Eastern king, a Western king, a Southern king, a Northern king, and an Assistant king. These six royal personages, we were told, were all residing in their new capital, which they call *Tien king*, 'Heavenly Capital.' Under their sway there is no more to be, as of old, a *Nanking*, 'Southern capital,' or *Peking*, 'Northern capital,' or aught of this kind. (B)

4 This royal Fraternity claims, also *universal sovereignty*. Of what the kingdoms and nations of the Earth really are, in numbers and in power, these kings and their brethren, are doubtless almost wholly ignorant; but their claim to universal dominion, on earth, is put forth in language most unequivocal. As the Heavenly Father, the Supreme Lord, the August High Ruler, is the Only One True God, the Father of the souls of all nations under heaven; so their Heavenly king is the peaceful and true Sovereign of all nations under heaven. These, and words like these, are common both in their conversation and in their writings; and from these—partly true and partly false—premises, they draw the conclusion, that as all nations ought to obey and worship the only one True God, so ought they to bow submissively and respectfully *bring tribute* (C)—rare and precious gifts—to their Heavenly king, even to Hung Siu-tsiuen. Some of the great men of the realm were specially concerned lest their 'Brethren, from a foreign land,' should not at once and fully comprehend the oneness of the true doctrine, but should imagine that there really were such distinctions that we might speak of this kingdom or of that kingdom, and of my Sovereign and your Sovereign! The address—on a despatch from the ministers of the court—was, in courtesy, almost equal to that, in other revolutionary times, once conveyed 'to Mr George Washington.' (D)

5 Their government is administered with *remarkable energy*. It is now only four or five years since it struggled into existence in some obscure place, called 'Golden Fields,'[5] in the province of Kwangsi. There they fought their first battles; and from thence,

5 Chin t'ien, the village where the Taiping revolt began.

147

vanquishing or rendering submissive all the imperial hosts that went out against them, the Insurgents moved northwards through the Lake provinces, and then, like the waters of the Great River, eastward, carrying all before them and taking possession of the old southern capital and Chingkiang fu, the Guardian city of the Grand Canal. Far in the distance, hovering over the hill-tops— southward from Chinkiang fu and northward from Nanking—we saw encamped small bands of the Imperialists, while all the armed multitudes in and immediately around these two cities, wrought up almost to frenzy, seemed eager to rush forth and take vengeance on them as their deadly foes—'fat victims,' said they, 'fit only for slaughter.' They exulted as they exhibited to us the scars and the wounds they had received in bloody conflicts with the Manchu troops—always called, by them, 'monster-demons.'

6 Their *order and discipline* are no less remarkable than their energy. Under their new *regime* both tobacco and opium are prohibited. Every kind of strong drink, too, would seem to come into the same category, and if any is used, it is only by special permission. No woman or child was seen within the walls of Chinkiang fu. For the time being, that city is made one vast camp. Its entire suburbs are in ruins; and all the houses within the walls, not required for public service, are sealed up.

At Wuhu there were few or no troops, but a vigilant police and a few cruisers. No inconsiderable portions of both the city and suburbs had been burnt in the storming of the place, only last year; but to those remaining undemolished the people had returned: whole families,—men, women, and children—were seen in their own houses, merchants in their shops, and market-people going and coming with provisions—all most submissive to the officers and police, as they passed along the streets.

It was in their 'Holy City,' however, as they frequently called their new capital, that their order and discipline were observed in the greatest perfection. Parts of the city were appropriated exclusively for the use of the wives and daughters of those men who were abroad in their armies or elsewhere employed in the public service: these I did not see, nor was it ascertained, by those who traversed the city, how far this separation of the sexes is maintained.

On two occasions I was at the North gate, and had much conversation with the officers there in command. They called themselves the relatives of the Assistant King. No one was allowed to pass out of that gate without leaving a ticket, with a registry of the name, &c., of the person; and no one could enter without permission. For those returning, it was sufficient to report their names and receive back their tickets; but when a stranger arrived, a long and minute examination had to be gone through with, and the case duly reported and a permit received, before an entrance could be had. A case of this sort occurred while I was there. Several women had passed in on horse-back, and now came one attended by her aged mother and servant. As they approached the outer gate (for there are two, an outer and an inner, the wall being some sixty feet thick,) they all dismounted. The aged woman and her servant were newcomers, brought in from some remote place by the daughter. Accordingly an examination must be had. This was at once commenced, and when I came away the whole party was still kept outside of the outer gate.

Everywhere else—as well as in the 'Holy City',—extreme watchfulness was observed in the maintenance of order; and all irregularities, and infractions of the laws were rebuked or punished with a promptitude seldom seen among the Chinese. All persons, without exception, had their appointed places and appropriate duties assigned, and all moved like clockwork. In short, martial law, throughout all their lines—in their streets, in their boats, and wherever else they were seen—was the order of the day.

7 Their *religious creed*, though it may recognize, in some sort, all or most of the doctrines of the Bible, is, through ignorance or perverseness, or *both*, grievously marred with error. While their government,—as already remarked—is of a mixed form, being partly religious—having in it a very strong religious element— still they have no Church. There is no community separate from their one body-politic—at least none appears, and no traces of any could we find.

Christians they may be, in name; and they are, in very deed, iconoclasts of the strictest order. They have in their possession probably the entire Bible, both the Old and the New Testaments, and are publishing what is usually known as 'Gutzlaff's version' of the same; I have said, therefore, that, 'In some sort,' they may recognize its doctrines. How far their errors are to be attributed to errors or defects in that version, is a question which I must not here discuss. Their ideas of the Deity are exceedingly imperfect. Though they declare plainly that there is 'Only One True God,' yet the inspiration of the Holy Scriptures; the equality of the Son with the Father; and many other doctrines, generally received by Protestant Christians as being clearly revealed in the Bible, are by them wholly ignored. True, they have formulas in which some of these doctrines are taught; but, then, these are borrowed formulas, and they have used them without comprehending their true import. So I believe; and I think this is made manifestly plain in the new version of their Doxology, or Hymn of Praise, where *Yang Siu-tsing*, the Eastern King, is proclaimed the *Paraclete*, the Holy Spirit! (E)

Our Saturday we found observed, by them, as a Sabbath day; but they appeared not to have any houses for public worship, nor any Christian teachers, ministers of the Gospel, properly so called. Forms of domestic worship, forms of prayer, of thanksgiving, &c., &c., they have, and all their people, even such as cannot read, are required to learn and use these. We saw them repeatedly at their devotions; some of them were exceedingly reverent and devout, while others were quite the reverse. Most, who were asked to do it, promptly recited that form of the Decalogue which is given in their tracts. *T'ien Fu*, 'Heavenly Father,' was the appellative used almost invariably, by them, when speaking of the Deity.

A form of Baptism was spoken of by them; but no allusion was made by them to the ordinance of the Lord's Supper. We found them, according to their reformed calendar, discarding the old notion of lucky places, times, &c. May 27th, A.D. 1854—the day the *Susquehanna* and the *Confucius* arrived off the 'Heavenly Capital,'—was marked, in their chronology, 'the 21st day, of the 4th month, of the 4th year of the Great Peaceful Heavenly Kingdom'.

They have a list of Books which are published by royal authority. (F) It, and their Books, usually bound together, bear the impress of a seal of State. On this list they have the names of more than twenty different works, two of which are the Old and New Testaments, noticed above. Whether other Books, not on that list, will be accepted or not, by their government, or even tolerated, remains to be seen. In the shops and stalls at Wuhu, I saw a few popular books and ballads of the old sort, but none elsewhere except those published by the Insurgents themselves.

8 To the inquiries, What is their *literary* character, and What their general intelligence,—their books and state-papers afford almost the only sure data we have for answers. Great numbers of proclamations were seen on the gates and walls of the cities visited, and most of them were from Yang, the eastern King. These included a much greater circle of topics than is found in their books, and as to style, were like their books, not above mediocrity. The distribution of food, of clothes, and of medicines; the payment of taxes; the preservation of property; the observance of etiquette and decorum; an injunction to repair to certain quarters for vaccination;—these were among the topics dis-

cussed in them. One document announced the names of sundry candidates, who had been successful in winning honors at a recent literary examination in the 'Heavenly Capital.'

The commandant at Chinkiang may perhaps be taken as a fair specimen of their officers, both as to literary attainments and general knowledge. He has been chief in command since the departure of *Lo*, some three months back, to join the northern army. He is a native of one of the eastern departments of the province of Canton, and has traveled over half of the Empire. This man, *Wu* by name, hardly knew that there were any foreign kingdoms. The national ensign borne on our ships—'the Stars and Stripes'—was a new thing to him! 'It had never before,' he said, 'been seen on the waters of the Great River.' The use of the white flag was equally strange to him. He was, however, in his general bearing more courteous than any one of his fellow officers, and nothing could well have been more dignified than his language, and especially his note. It was a manly apology for the shot which had been fired, and couched in terms wholly unexceptionable. Taking them all in all, however, as we saw them, both officers and people, the Insurgents cannot be ranked high for their literary character or their general intelligence. Certainly, 'much learning hath not made them mad.'

9 Of their *social* condition very little is known. To a certain extent, at least, they have a community of interests. The old dogma, that all the land and water, and all people under heaven, belong to the Sovereign, 'Heaven's Son,' does not seem to have been discarded by them. By what tenure all these are held, I do not know. But as under all the old dynasties, so now, with the 'long-haired gentry,' those wanted for soldiers must be soldiers; those needed for the river-service,—must serve on the rivers. The same rule obtained in each department of the state. With very few exceptions, no one seemed to say that aught of the things he possessed was his own. Whether this results from the necessities of the case, or is an established principle with them, I could not ascertain. Certain it is, however, that immense stores and treasures had been accumulated by them, and that these were being daily augmented.

10 Their *numerical strength* and the *extent of territory under their control*, are by no means inconsiderable. They said they had undisputed control from Chinkiang-fu four hundred miles up the Great River; and that, besides the large numbers of troops garrisoned and entrenched about Chinkiang, Kwachau, and the 'Heavenly Capital,' they had *four armies* in the field, carrying on active aggressive operations: two of these had gone northward,

one along the Grand Canal and one farther westward; they were designed to co-operate, and, after storming and destroying Peking, to turn westward and march through Shansi, Shensi, Kansuh, into Sz'chuen, where they are expected to meet their other two armies, which from Kiangsi and the Lake provinces are to move up the Great River and along through the regions on its southern bank.

11 The *personal appearance* of their men in arms and of their women on horse-back was novel. They formed a very heterogeneous mass,—having been brought together from several different provinces, principally from Nganhwui, Kiangsi, Hupeh, Hunan, Kwangsi and Kwangtung. The finest men, we saw, were from the hills of Kiangsi; and those from Hunan were the meanest and least warlike. Their arms and accoutrements were quite after the old fashion of the Chinese; but their red and yellow turbans, their long hair, and their silk and satin robes—so unlike the ordinary costume of the black-haired troops,—made the Insurgents appear like a new race of warriors. All the people we saw were well clad, well fed, and well provided for in every way. They all seemed content, and in high spirits, as if sure of success.

12 Their *farther progress*, judging from their past career, is almost certain. In all probability they are destined, under the inscrutable providence of God, to overrun the whole eighteen provinces, to break down the principal cities, to slaughter the Manchus, and to sweep away every vestige of their authority. At their approach the people and the retainers of the old administration are everywhere appalled, and fly like chaff before the stormy wind. Their *ultimate success*, in establishing and consolidating a new empire, wide and prosperous as that of the ancestors of Hien-fung, is less, far less probable.

13 In the present attitude of affairs their *bearing towards foreigners* is becoming every month and every day more and more a matter of grave and exciting interest. Their officers, at Chinkiang and Nanking, told us, again and again, that their troops would not approach Shanghai, and that, for the present, they would have nothing to do with the city of Canton. They remarked also, what is here well known, that the Insurgents in Shanghai are anxious to join them, and that many thousands of the people in the city and province of Canton are their true friends, their Brethren. (G) Still, in everything that was said by their high officials in the Celestial Capital, a tone and a spirit of high assumption were too extraordinary—too far from the simple dictates of all reason—to be passed by unheeded as idle vaunting.

Will that royal Fraternity, and their Ministers of State,—if they become Masters of the Middle Kingdom—recognise the existing treaties between the Chinese empire on the one side, and the governments of England, France, and the United States on the other? Most assuredly they will not, except on compulsion, or unless they willingly descend from their high position. They, the 'Second Son' of the most High God and his royal associates, they, and *they alone*, are to be *the dispensers of all authority and all instruction*, in that their Heavenly Kingdom, truly ordained of Heaven, and of which they are to be *the Head and the Chief Supports!*

ADDENDA

A few points, touched upon in the preceding paragraphs, require additional illustration, and references have been made to the following notes.

Note A
These six Kings are all southern men, from the provinces of Kwang-tung and Kwang-si: their names are—

> Hung Siu-tsiuen, the Heavenly King;
> Yang Siu-tsing, the Eastern King;
> Siau Chau-kwei, the Western King;
> Fung Yun-shan, the Southern King;
> Wei Ching, the Northern King; and
> Shih Tah-kai, the Assistant King.

About the *personality* of the first, Hung Siu-tsiuen, obscurity and doubt still predominate. I am not aware that any foreigner has seen him since the outbreak of the Insurrection,—or more recently than 1847, when, for a short season, he is believed to have been a resident in the house of the Rev. I. J. Roberts at Canton. No one among the people or officers, whom we saw at Nanking, would tell us that he *had seen* him, though they all spoke of him as then present in that city, and as the greatest on earth, being 'the *second son* of the Heavenly Father.' No one ever spoke of him as *Tae-ping-wang*, but always as *T'ien-wang*, 'Heavenly King.' Formerly, at the commencement of their enterprise, they said that he also bore the title of *T'ien-teh*, 'Heavenly Virtue,' but had laid it aside, for the time being, on account of the warlike character he had to sustain. In some of their more recent books, he is called *Urh Hiung*, 'second brother,' (Jesus being the first), and by the Heavenly Father he is only addressed by his common name, Siu-tsiuen.

The second on the list, Yang Siu-tsing, is quite a different character. No doubt exists as to his personality. To the Heavenly

King he is more than Aaron was to Moses. By the officers of the court, he is regarded as almost, if not altogether, divine. With them it is a fearful matter to approach his 'Golden Person.' Thus high in dignity and great in influence,—alike with the Royal Fraternity and the popular mind—his name is continually before the public, and prefixed to it, in all his state proclamations, are the following titles in broad capitals:

'OF THE TRULY HEAVEN-ORDAINED, THE GREAT PEACE-FUL HEAVENLY KINGDOM, THE COMFORTER, THE HOLY SPIRIT, THE UNIVERSAL PROVIDER, THE REDEEMER FROM MALADIES, PRIME MINISTER OF STATE, COMMANDER-IN-CHIEF OF THE ARMY, THE EASTERN KING, YANG.'

The use of some of the terms, in this long list of titles, is as extraordinary as it is unintelligible; *blasphemous* I do not say, only because I do not know, and am unwilling to believe, that these terms, applied to the Godhead by inspired penmen and here assumed to himself by a sinful mortal, have been, or are, understood by him. Indeed, I fear exceedingly that 'the Golden Intelligence' does not yet know—nay, that he has not even begun to know,—that there is any Holy Ghost. I was anxious, beyond measure, to test this point, by a personal interview; and it was chiefly for this one object, that I desired to remain at Nanking, while the two Steamers proceeded on to Wuhu and back. I wanted to have an opportunity, if it were possible, to correct or rebuke such ignorance—and to bear testimony against the use of the terms *Kieuen-wei-sz*, and *Shing-shin-fung* in a manner so shocking.—*Kieuen-wei-sz* is Gutzlaff's translation of *ho parakletos*, and *Shing-shin-fung* is Morrison's of *to penuma to bagion*.

The title *Ho-nai-sz*,[6] 'Universal Provider,'—as I have ventured to translate it,—is not only new, but if literally rendered would be utterly unintelligible, to all but the initiated. It is an enigma, and would seem to be employed as a sort of watch-word. P.S.—Since writing the foregoing, a paper has reached me, purporting to be an historical sketch of *Hung Siu-tsiuen*. In it are these sixteen words, forming a stanza of four lines, thus:

San pah 'urh yih
Ho nai yuh shih
Jin tso yih tu
Tsoh 'urh min keih

6 Ho-nai-shih, 'the Honai teacher'. The meaning of the term Honai is obscure—see for example Hamberg, op. cit., p. 46.

This stanza has been regarded as prophetic, foreshowing that the persons referred to, in it, were to become, one the Sovereign and the other the prime-minister of a universal kingdom. The four words of the first line, rightly placed together, make the family name *Hung*; the first and second, of the second line make the word *Siu*=grain is *Yuh-shih*, i.e., grain is precious food; the first, third, and fourth, of the third line, make the word *tsiuen*=complete *Tso*, i.e., grain is completely provided; then comes the conclusion, in the fourth line, *Tsoh 'urh min keih*, i.e. Hung Siu-tsiuen shall be the people's Regulator, and Yang Siu-tsing shall be his prime-minister, providing the Staff of Life for all people,—*Nai-mai*, 'drawing together,' as one family, all the nations of the earth!

Other explanations have been given,—all, with the one above, more or less arbitrary, and alike false. The instances are numerous, where the Insurgents have changed the form or meaning of the characters of the language. For instance, when writing the word *Kwoh*, to denote their own country, Judea, and Heaven, these kings do it by delineating royal personages within an enclosure, but in all other cases by describing, therein, what is common, uncertain, or of doubtful character! The two words, or two forms of the same word, differ in sense but not in sound, differ, I mean, only in the Insurgents' Vocabulary.

Note B
Two of the books, on the new list alluded to above, bear directly on this point. One is 'A Discourse on building the Heavenly Capital at the Golden mounds,' i.e. Nanking; the other is 'A Discourse on degrading the monsters' den into a prison-house for sinners;' i.e. on making Peking a Botany Bay.[7]

Note C
'Bring tribute' is a well established phrase, and one of no doubtful meaning, in Chinese; it is written *Tsin kung*; and it does not mean taxes on land, nor duties on merchandize; but offerings, gifts; with reference to ourselves, and all others from afar, the language used was this,—you, or they, 'must prepare (and bring) extraordinarily fine and precious things,'—such presents as the kings of Corea, Cochin-China, and Siam, are now accustomed to bring to the Court of the Great Pure Dynasty.

Note D
It is proper to remark, here, that the original of these paragraphs was prepared at the suggestion of H. E. Mr McLane, for his

7 The *Chien T'ien-ching yü Chin-ling lun* and the *Pien yao-hsüeh wei Tsui-li lun*, both translated in Michael, op. cit., vol. II, pp. 251–94.

government at Washington; in that case, this allusion was wholly apposite; and it so well illustrates the matter in hand, that its insertion here will I hope, be pardoned. As the mother country did not know any authorities 'in the Colonies,' except those of her own appointing, so, and much more, would it be heresy for Ministers in the 'Heavenly Capital' to recognize, as office-bearers, any but those appointed by the Heavenly King!

Note E
From the original Doxology, as it appeared in the books brought down by the *Hermes*, it was believed that the Insurgent kings had gained some correct knowledge of the 'Holy Father,' 'Holy Son,' and 'Holy Spirit,'—for which latter they used the terms *Shing-shin-fung* and *Shing-ling*,—and used them interchangeably. But from their new version, as given in the *North-China Herald*, No. 204, June 24th, it is quite certain that its authors—the author of that new version—can have no knowledge of the Holy Spirit.

Note F
In the new list of Books—twice alluded to above—only one-and-twenty are enumerated; but we are told, by some, that they had already published four-and-twenty, and by others, five-and-twenty. Copies of all these and in any quantity we wished, were promised to be in readiness for us on our return from Wuhu,—but the determination, subsequently and prudently formed, to pass by the Heavenly Capital, and to leave to themselves its rulers, for a season, prevented our obtaining the promised supply.
P.S.—Of that new one brought by our party, containing a new Revelation, I had purposed here to give a synopsis, but as this has been promised from another quarter, it is now omitted. One thing only will I note, which is that, in it, the words of Jesus, that a Comforter should come into the world after him, are applied by Hung Siu-tsiuen to Yang Siu-tsing,—like one of old, quoting Scripture to support his wicked perversion of its true import.

Note G
The notions of a Brotherhood, a universal Brotherhood, often expressed by the Insurgents, clearly militates against the opinion that there are any subordinate associations, like the Triad, existing within their new kingdom. All under heaven, they said, were Brethren, but there were different classes; whenever they made any distinction between themselves and us, we were called 'Foreign Brethren,' and Brethren from a 'Foreign Land'.

35
A Report by W H Medhurst and Lewin Bowring
FO 17/214, no. 85, enc. in Bowring to Clarendon, 14 July 1854

With reference to the present position and probable futurity of the T'ae ping wang movement and other matters which came under our observation, we beg to submit the following remarks.

Present position
The only places in the occupation of the insurgents between this and the furthest point we reached are Nanking, Kwachow and Chinkeangfoo. These are situated on the banks of the Yang-tszekeang, as are also Woohoo and other towns higher up regarding which we could only procure hearsay information. Chinkeangfoo is a formidable stronghold, commanding the whole navigation of the river, here not a mile wide. The garrison consists of about 10,000 men, commanded by a 'Military Governor', to whom are subordinate several Tseang-Keun or Generals, and a proportionate number of inferior officers. The heights are crowned by batteries, and the river bord is defended by stockades rudely but stoutly constructed, and lined with a great number of guns of small calibre. The fortifications are rough but in efficient order, and there are strong bastions in the direction of the Imperialist encampment. There is also a small outpost on Golden Island in the vicinity. Chingkeangfoo is besieged by an Imperialist fleet lying off Silver Island four miles from the city, but with little prospect of success, the Mandarins in command being unwilling to come to close quarters. A large Imperialist force aggregating nearly 50,000 men is encamped on the hills about two miles from Chinkeang, with which skirmishes frequently take place, but no decisive actions have been fought. All foreign ships proceeding up the river will be fired at from this insurgent post, and it is probable that the first collision will occur here. Woo Jooheaou the Military Governor is a young man of haughty and supercilious demeanour, and appears to possess influence over his followers, who are inspired with considerable enthusiasm and yield implicit obedience to their superiors, but are raw undisciplined vagabonds, badly armed and totally ignorant of European resources and power. The city was on its capture sacked and pillaged by the rebels and having been deserted by its former inhabitants presents a sad scene of desolation.

Kwachow, two or three miles up the river commands the entrance of the Grand Canal, and is therefore a place of considerable importance, giving the Insurgents an untoward influence over the trade of the interior. The batteries command both the canal and the main stream. The town is invested by an Imperialist force which however has made no decisive effort to capture the place. This city has likewise been much injured by the rebels, and is in a great measure deserted.

Between Kwachow and Nanking a distance of 45 miles, the insurgents hold no territory.

Nanking, the headquarters of the insurgents, is the centre of their strength and is consequently well defended by a strong garrison, whose numbers can scarcely be less than 50,000. The great extent of the circuit of the walls must render it difficult to defend against an enterprising and sudden attack by land, but the inner city is quite unapproachable from the river, being far beyond the range of the largest gun. A hill on which some guns are planted intervenes between the inner city and the suburb and is girt by the strong and lofty outer wall. The suburb, which is small and insignificant, is manned by a considerable force, and the whole river side is covered with stockades, masked batteries, bamboo barriers, and floating rafts to prevent approach, and all admittance into or exit from the city is rigidly prohibited. Two batteries, of 7 or 8 guns each, defend the approach to the suburb creek leading past the Efung Gate by which the city is entered, while another creek which debouches close by is protected by two strong stockades, a third being placed on a tongue of land between the creek and the main stream. Generals are stationed at the outposts, and great activity is shown in the construction of stockades and batteries, while a careful look out is kept in raised wooden towers which command a good view of the country around. The city is besieged by an Imperialist encampment to the west, but the insurgents do not show any alarm as to the result. A smaller Imperialist force occupies P'ookow, a town on the opposite bank of the Yang-tsze-Keang, but is too far off to be serviceable. The suburb and its fortifications could easily be destroyed by large guns in foreign ships lying on the farther side of the river, but the Imperialist vessels can make no impression. A considerable fleet of boats is in the hands of the insurgents, and is used for transporting troops in various directions, which they appeared to be busily occupied in doing during our stay. Communication with Kwachow and Chinkiang is difficult, owing to the intervening country being occupied by the Imperialists whose junks also scour the river constantly, and it is only effected by despatching armed boats or large bodies of men at a time.

Woohoo was not visited by us, but from all accounts it does not appear to be strongly garrisoned. We could not ascertain from the insurgents what other walled towns they occupy on the Yangtze-

Keang, but we do not believe that they possess any other cities of importance nor is the intermediate country occupied by them. In each case, of which we had cognizance, the insurgent post is invested by an Imperialist force, and the besieged, though confident as to the strength of their position, have not the power of collecting the land tax or levying imposts on the surrounding country. To the northward and westward, as far as we can judge from the imperfect information obtainable, their raid has not of late been attended with uniform success. On the contrary it would seem that recently they have met with a check, for during our stay at Nanking, a fleet of about 300 junks was despatched up the river with a reinforcement of 10,000 men for the purpose of retaking some place of importance wrested from them by the mandarins.

It is worthy of notice that they made no advance since last year in the immediate vicinity of the Yang-tsze-Keang, where they remain just as they were when visited by the 'Hermes' expedition.

Probability of ultimate success
The position of the insurgents north of the River Yangtsze-Keang appears to be unsettled, and their ultimate success and power of consolidating themselves are doubtful. Having for the most part been triumphant hitherto in the course of their aggressions upon the Imperial power, their victories having been many and their reverses few, they have been till lately flushed with success, and their zeal and fanaticism have carried them over all difficulties. It appears however, that their progress becomes more slow as they advance to the North and encounter in considerable bodies, and nearer his native country and climate, the more hardy Tartar, whom meeting in small numbers in the South they have found it easy to conquer and destroy. We believe that during the past year they have made little real progress in subjugating the country. They have occupied towns and proceeded onwards, it is true, but they have rarely retained what they have won, and consequently in case of defeat could have no stronghold north of the Yangtsze-keang to retire upon. At first when they gave out that their object was to relieve the people from the oppression of the Mandarins, to remit taxes and to re-establish in its purity the ancient Chinese Rule, it is not improbable that popular sympathy may have been on their side. But the blessings and advantages held out by them have not been realised. Their progress has been marked by devastation and desolation. Houses have been plundered and burnt, lives ruthlessly sacrificed, property confiscated, women ill-used, and the peaceable inhabitants of towns driven out or

forced to serve apart from their families as pressed soldiers. The towns of Kwachow and Chinkeang and the suburbs of Nanking present a lamentable scene of deserted homesteads and ruined trade. They have not been able moreover to reconstruct what they have destroyed. Instead of studiously courting the adherence of the literary classes, who constitute the bulwark of the whole Chinese social system and are the leaders of public opinion, round whom the people ever rally with delight and confidence, they have declared their honorary titles invalid and illegal, denounced their cherished ancient classics, burnt their public libraries, and made them enemies. Their proclamations, recently issued, inviting people to return to their homes have not been responded to. The wealthy, respectable, and educated citizens have betaken themselves elsewhere and the insurgent towns are mere military garrisons, strongholds without traffic, thinly populated and scantily supplied with the necessaries of life. Even the insurgents appear to feel the want of money, for although so long as the funds obtained by sack and pillage lasted, they were careless as to the future, now that their resources are considerably exhausted, it is by no means easy for them to procure a subsistence. Offers of service are held out to European adventurers, but the pay to be received is contingent on the ultimate success of the insurgents, so that it is not likely that this description of auxiliaries will ever join their standard. It seems evident that popular sympathy is not with them. They have done nothing to ameliorate the condition of the people, but on the contrary wherever they have been successful, they have been a curse and terror to the unfortunate, whose substance they have pillaged, whose gods they have insulted and destroyed, and whose houses they have burnt. In no instance are any of the towns they occupy, few though they be, in a flourishing condition. Trade is entirely extinct where their blighting influence has spread itself, and no measures have been taken to revive it, nor is it likely that the more wealthy merchants among the Chinese will voluntarily place themselves in the hands of people who have no resources but the ill gotten plunder obtained from peaceable and respectable members of society.

Disposition towards strangers
As regards their disposition towards strangers, it is incumbent on us to state that it is repellant in the extreme, and even surpasses in insolent pretension the hauteur and pride of the Mandarins of the present regime. No desire is shewn to court the advances of foreigners, save on conditions too degrading to be entertained,

they are looked upon with suspicion and distrust; and instead of being treated as equals by friends, they are considered to be inferiors and barbarians. It might be expected that a youthful power just struggling into existence would be only too anxious to receive aid and co-operation from Europeans, both from their power to assist and the fact of the insurgents having adopted the basis of their religious creed from the scriptures translated and distributed by foreigners. Such is not however the case, and the assumption of superiority religious, national, and social, which they at present affect will not be removed till a collision takes place which in its results shall demonstrate to them the superior power and resources of western nations. The greater part of the insurgents are natives of the inland Provinces of Hoonan and Hoopih and Kwangse whose inhabitants rarely if ever have come into contact with Europeans, while there is a large sprinkling of Cantonese among their prominent men, so that it is not at all extraordinary that they should feel a contempt and dislike for those whom they regard as 'outer barbarians'. The letter addressed to us by the Eastern King presents a curious mixture of insolence and fraternal feeling.[8]

Means of extending commercial relations
It has been supposed that further intercourse with the insurgents might lead to an extension of our commercial relations with the interior; but it must be borne in mind that their position is not that of a consolidated power, anxious to foster commerce, and bent upon the development of its resources, but simply that of a military organization at war with the existing Government striving to gain the ascendancy by declaring as its ultimatum the extermination of the Manchoo Dynasty. Trade properly so to speak is utterly non-existent, and although we have reason to believe that coal, the great instrument for the navigation of the Yangtszekeang, is to be found in considerable quantities in the Province of Keangse in the vicinity of the country which has been overrun by the insurgents, they show no disposition to dispose of it to foreigners—and indeed prohibit vessels from coming to carry it away. The development of commercial intercourse with the populous valley of the Yangtszekeang is more likely to take place through a collision with the insurgents, than through any friendly relations we may enter into with them.

8   For this letter and the complete version of the Medhurst-Bowring reports, with enclosures, see the Appendix to J. S. Gregory's *Great Britain and the Taipings* (London and New York, 1969).

Civil organization

Not having been admitted to an interview with the higher authorities at Nanking it became somewhat difficult to ascertain to what extent the insurgents have established an organized system of Government. The replies given to our queries on the subject by the Eastern King are very vague and unsatisfactory, but it would appear that they have not hitherto promulgated any code of laws. They profess to make the ten commandments the foundation of their polity, and their high officers are said severally to lay down laws in accordance with the decalogue; but it is obvious that there is no definite system to Civil Government. We know that certain offences such as opium and tobacco smoking, drinking, debauchery, etc., are nominally prohibited on pain of decapitation, but it is doubtful whether the leaders of the movement implicitly follow these tenets. We were told that they inflict five penalties for misconduct, namely the bamboo, the cangue, imprisonment for a period not exceeding two months, decapitation and tearing asunder by means of horses, but we could discover no law by which these penalties are regulated in relation to crime. It would appear that they have not hitherto issued any new coinage one of the chief emblems of Govt. among orientals, a defect which they excuse on the plea of being unable to force such coins upon the inhabitants of the districts in the vicinity of their posts of occupation; neither have they established any record of their rise and progress or official history of their proceedings. Nor have they commenced publishing their decrees in the shape of public Gazettes, a custom in China inseparable from established supremacy, the instructions of the leaders to the common people being as yet couched in the form of proclamations posted on the walls of their towns.

Military capabilities

The organization we found appeared to be an authority partly military and partly religious, grounded on assumptions of a most extraordinary character by the leaders, believed in and upheld by the enthusiasm and fanaticism of their followers. The obedience paid by the soldiery to the orders of their superiors is most implicit and is not a little remarkable. Though without discipline and imperfectly armed, their weapons being chiefly halberds, short swords, spears and inferior matchlocks, they are certainly imbued with considerable military ardour, and their activity and alertness present a curious contrast to the inertness and imbecility of the Imperial soldiers who look upon their opponents with awe and confess themselves by no means able to cope with them on equal terms. It was difficult to judge of the number of the insurgents but it is probable that they aggregate in the towns held by them on the Yang-tsze-Keang at the very least 100,000 fighting men to say nothing of their pressed adherents. Of guns they have a very large number, but they are utterly ignorant how to employ them with effect, though unlike their imperialist opponents they appear to be perfectly at home with the larger fire arms. We were unable to ascertain what leaders are in command of the forces at present in the North for the purpose of subjugating Peking, but it would seem that all the chief authorities are still at Nanking and have not themselves joined the expedition.

Religious creed
As regards the tenets adopted by the insurgents, which have excited so much interest in many quarters, we cannot do better than refer your Excellency to the extraordinary replies returned by the Eastern King to our queries, and to the no less eccentric questions put to us by him. It is a matter of grave doubt whether such a person as T'ae ping Wang alias Hung Seu Tseuen is in existence, for in all the correspondence we had with the Generals etc. the pleasure of the Eastern King, his power, his majesty, and his influence alone were brought prominently before us, while his reputed master received but a passing allusion, the Eastern King being evidently the prime mover in their political and spiritual system.

We cannot affirm that Taepingwang never did exist, but we cannot help conceiving it to be highly improbable that an individual possessed of the ability to organise and the energy to prosecute so remarkable a movement would permit a subordinate to appropriate so influential a post as the mouthpiece and oracle of God himself, the position which the Eastern King now most craftily arrogates to himself, and to make his master a mere puppet King, moved solely by *his* instigation. The reply given under this head to our enquiry was not such as in any way to resolve the doubt now prevalent as to the individual presence and identity of Taepingwang at Nanking. The assumption of Divinity by the Eastern King is so revolting and blasphemous as entirely to have shaken any belief we may have had as to the sincerity of the profession of Christianity made by the insurgents, nor can it be said that the title of the Holy Ghost taken by him was assumed in ignorance of its real meaning, for the questions of the Eastern King demonstrate that he has some acquaintance with the New Testament in reference to this very subject. The profanation is made worse by the assertion that the Father descends into the

Person of the Eastern King, and makes known his Divine Will through him to the People, our Saviour going through the same process with the Western King. The officers and soldiery generally appeared to us ignorant of this particular mode of manifestation, but to the fact of manifestation they give implicit credence. To our minds the Eastern King has assumed the title of 'Holy Spirit' as an engine of political power, and that his principal object has been to veil his pretensions under the false covering of heavenly commands, to surround with a myth all that appertains to the existence of the 'Celestial King', T'aeping-Wang, and to strengthen his authority by the doctrine that the Father has himself vouchsafed to invest him with Divine attributes. There can be no doubt that he has succeeded to a marvellous degree in imbuing his followers with these tenets, which they receive with the utmost faith, and regard as revealed truth. His ability must be remarkable, as evinced by the absolute dominion held by him over the minds of the insurgents, and the more so as it does not appear that he is a man of even moderate literary attainments, the mandate addressed to us being the composition of one quite unacquainted with classical Chinese. And here we take leave to remark that we observed no respectable nor educated men among either chiefs or followers; with very few exceptions they appeared to us uncouth and ill conditioned fellows evidently gathered from the lowest classes of the people. The pretentions put forth by Yang, coupled with the fanaticism displayed by the rebels generally, hold forth little hope that missionary labours among them will meet with success. Indeed we are of opinion that the experiment would be attended with considerable danger, unless, as is not probable, they should show more readiness to meet the advances of foreign nations than they at present evince. We felt ourselves compelled by our peculiar position to reply, however imperfectly, to the questions asked by the Eastern King, considering it to be a duty which we were bound to perform although at the risk of being taxed with presumption. In our answer we judged it best to tell the Eastern King in plain terms the simple truth, and to endeavour to disabuse his mind of the vain and ridiculous pretensions he has so unwarrantably assumed.

Dress and food
The dress worn by the rebels is somewhat peculiar. The chiefs wear a yellow robe with a yellow cap drooping behind, over which the generals and other high functionaries wear a very peculiar gaudy headdress, not unlike a fool's-cap, made of red cloth and covered with tinsel and embroidery. The soldiers wear

a yellow uniform edged with red or vice versa, but in other respects there is nothing remarkable in their costume. They all seem very partial to gay shewy colours which circumstance gives them in general a very motley appearance. They all allow the hair formerly shaven to grow luxuriantly and twist the tail round the head, and they do not shave either beard or moustache so that they look unkempt and farouche and very forbidding at first sight. Not having been admitted into the city, and having seen no women in consequence of their being kept in a particular quarter separate from the man, we are unable to offer any remarks upon their style of dress.

There is nothing peculiar about the rebel diet. They seem to indulge in and to enjoy all the good things of this life relished by other Chinese, with the exception of opium, tobacco and wine, which are strictly prohibited. Grace is said before meat in the form of a doxology to God the Father, Jesus the Son and the Eastern King, the Holy Ghost, the supplicants alternatively standing and kneeling with a great shew of devotion; and in the houses of the officials the ceremony is accompanied by the beating of gongs and other music. They appear to be very careful not to neglect this duty.

Religious publications
Among the publications procured by us were three books of the Old Testament, namely Leviticus, Deuteronomy and Joshua, together with the following treatises not hitherto obtained.
1 'Important Discourses on heavenly Principles.' A reprint of a Christian Tract on the attributes of God formerly written by Dr. Medhurst.
2 'Discourses upon branding the impish dens (Province of Chihle) with the name of Tsuyle.' Substituting in fact 'Tsuy' crime, for 'chih' integrity—as a component part of the name.
3 'Book of declarations of Divine Will' made during a late descent of the Father.
4 'Discourses upon the expediency of affixing the Imperial seal to the Imperial Proclamations.'
5 'Calendar of the Year 1854.'
6 'Treatise on Land tenure &c.'

These contain much new and curious information corroborative of what is already in our possession. Like the works procured by Sir Geo. Bonham, they are written in a diffuse ungainly style.[9]

9   These works are (1) *T'ien-li yao-lun* (2) *Pien yao-hsüeh wei Tsui-li lun* (3) *T'ien-fu hsia-fan chao-shu* (4) *Chao-shu kai-shi pan-hsing lun* (5) *Pan-hsing li-shu* (6) *T'ien-chao t'ien-mou chih-tu*. All are translated in Michael, op. cit., vol. II as Docs. 49, 44, 39, 45, 47 and 46 respectively.

36
An Account by Lewin Bowring
L. Bowring, *Eastern Experiences* (London, 1871), pp. 343–53

On nearing Nanking, we had a good view of the place, which was surrounded by a strong wall, the Porcelain Pagoda standing out conspicuously in the distance. The inner city, being no less than four miles from the river bank, could not be clearly discerned, while the frontage of the suburbs was very mean, giving no idea of the proximity of a large capital. The approaches to the suburbs were all stockaded, large stakes having been driven into the ground crosswise, and, between them, innumerable pieces of bamboo with sharp projecting points, so that no troops could possibly advance over them in line. Several batteries commanded the river, and high look-out towers had been erected to survey the surrounding country and watch the arrival of enemies.

We sent a boat on shore with our friend the Colonel[10] who, on landing, was immediately mobbed by numbers of the rebels anxious to know our errand. The next day, June 21, we moved across the stream, and anchored close to the suburb, and after waiting some time fruitlessly for the Colonel's return, took a ship's boat and went on shore. After vainly attempting to pass through the wickets of the stockade, we pulled a little way up the creek, and landed where there was a ferry. Close by, a triangular flag of yellow denoted the quarters of the Taiping General in command of the outpost, which was outside the north-east wall of the city towards the Hung Gate. We entered his house, and found him seated with two other officials, all three wearing the peculiar head-dress which we had seen at Chinkiangfu. Our reception was by no means civil, as they did not even rise to welcome us, a courtesy which Chinese politeness always dictates. On our seating ourselves, they enquired our object in coming to Nanking, and being informed that the British Government wished to cultivate friendly relations with them, and to receive information as to their power and resources, they told us to *petition* the Eastern King whose name and titles were furnished in the following curious address: 'The Comforter-The Holy Ghost-The Honai Teacher-the Eastern King-Yang, Commander-in-chief of the Celestial Forces.'

We promised to write to the Taiping Chief, to announce to this mighty potentate our arrival, and, having sipped some tea, took our leave. The Colonel never returned, and we shortly ascertained that the people had been forbidden to communicate with

10   A Taiping soldier brought with them from Chinkiang and so dubbed.

us, either on board the steamer or on shore, from which we concluded that something had gone wrong.

On examining one of the revelations which were presented to us at Chinkiangfu, we found out the origin of the blasphemous epithet applied to the Eastern King. The treatise stated that Yang, having given some excellent advice to Tai-ping-wang, the leader of the insurgents, the latter, being well pleased with his devotion, said, 'Our elder brother, Jesus, in leaving this world, promised to send after him a Comforter. You are this Comforter, and I give you henceforward the title of the Holy Ghost.' In the same revelation, it was alleged that the Heavenly Father came down from heaven, and ordered that Tai-ping-wang should receive forty strokes with a bamboo as a punishment for his misconduct in ill-treating various people, and his wives in particular, but Yang interceded for him, and he was let off with a severe reprimand.

On the 22nd, we passed through a part of the suburb, but were stopped at a wicket gate on our way to the city wall, and no persuasions would induce the rebels to admit us inside, so we entered the residence of a chief outside, who was very civil, but pleaded his positive instructions not to allow us to proceed beyond the gate. This man informed us that the 'second coming' had taken place the previous year at Nanking, and, in confirmation of the popular belief, we saw many people, when about to sit down to dinner, repeating, at their grace, a prayer 'in the name of God the Father, Jesus Christ the Son, and the Eastern King the Holy Ghost.' Some said this kneeling, others standing.

A great many junks were lying in the creek, full of fighting men, who, to the number of 10,000, were starting off on an expedition, in consequence of some news which they had received from the north, though of what nature they would not say.[11] All the boats had flags, chiefly triangular, and the soldiers wore a uniform of red and yellow, with the common fighting cap, each man having the number of his regiment stamped on his coat, or a piece of wood suspended in front. Their arms were rude and inferior, consisting mainly of long spears, short swords, and halberds, but musquets or fusils were rare. The rest of the population were poorly dressed, and their heads looked exceedingly grotesque, owing to their unkempt bristly hair, but they were tolerably civil and used no abusive language. The taboo was rigidly maintained, on the alleged ground that, on a previous visit from the American

11 This probably refers to the abortive second relief column under Ch'in Jih-kang which was sent to relieve the Taiping troops engaged in the northern expedition.

steamer 'Susquehanna', annoyance had been given by the rebels to the crew, but it is probable that they suspected our intentions. It was stated, however, that when the American minister was at Nanking, a middy who had wandered about the place in search of the Porcelain Pagoda, had climbed over the walls, and thereby created considerable sensation among the Taipings, who resolved from that time to keep all intruding foreigners aloof.

On the 23rd, while we were taking a walk in another direction, we were again stopped by a wicket. In reply to the request which we made for an interview, and for admission into the city, the General commanding the outpost wrote to say that he had received the 'golden commands' of the Eastern King, to the effect that he was too busy in sending off troops to see us, but he forwarded, for our initiation into Heavenly Precepts, sundry pamphlets similar to those we had received at Chinkiangfu. The following is a list of these productions.[12]

1 Leviticus
2 Deuteronomy
3 Joshua
4 Important discourses on Heavenly Principles
5 Discourse upon branding the impish den 'Chihli' (Pekin) with the name 'Tsuy le' (an opprobrious word)
6 Book of Declaration of the Divine Will, 2nd series
7 On affixing the Golden Seal to Royal Proclamations
8 Treatise on Land Tenures
9 Calendar for 1854

These pamphlets were all fairly printed, but were the oddest jumble of truth and falsehood, of sense and nonsense.

We then despatched a long letter to the Eastern King, putting a variety of questions as to the number of Taipings, the extent of country they had conquered, the number of their troops, their laws and usages, and so forth, while a request was made to be supplied with coal, of which in our walks we had seen great quantities.

On the 25th, crowds of a force just returned from some warlike expedition came on board the 'Rattler', and examined everything most curiously. Most of them were dressed as soldiers in yellow coats with a red border, having short swords swung on their backs. One of them, who said that he had been impressed into the service, stated that at Nanking provisions were scarce, and that the rebels had, latterly, been unsuccessful in the north. He further remarked that it was generally believed that we had come

12 See note 9 to Doc. 35 above.

to extort money, which had led to the refusal to see us. All our visitors had unkempt heads and a savage appearance, and, though sharp enough, they were a disreputable set. One small boy, ten or twelve years old only, bragged of having cut off the heads of five or six men, and inspected the ships guns in a most inquisitive way.

Having received verbal permission to take in coal from Kiahwan, in a creek close by, where there was an extensive coal-yard, we dropped down by what is called in the maps 'Theodolite Point', and anchored opposite the coal sheds. Soon after, a Colonel came on board to ask us to wait until the next day, to which the Captain of the 'Rattler' consented. In the afternoon a boat came off with a letter, written in the form of an order, telling us to go away, and demanding to know whether we wished to get into collision with the rebels. This letter, being offensively worded, was returned to the bearer. Two hours afterwards, a large gun was brought down by the rebels within a quarter mile of the 'Rattler', while several others which were in a masked battery on the river bank, were disclosed, bearing directly on the ship. The officers on board were indignant, one young middy stamping on the deck, furious with rage at the impudence of the Taipings; but the Captain, who had received orders to avoid, if possible, any conflict with them, thought it prudent to send a boat on shore to demand the meaning of this apparent act of hostility. The rascals who had dragged down the big gun swore it was only intended for the imperialists, but as it bore straight on the 'Rattler', and as, in the narrow creek on which we lay, we should have been exposed to the possible treachery of the 'Brethren', the Captain judged it advisable to shift his quarters, so we weighed anchor, and passing up the creek again, anchored in the main stream, near some mosquito-haunted marshes. These insects are most annoying at Nanking. They devoured us in swarms, and as we had no curtains, and the heat was great, we were obliged to submit to be stifled under a sheet, or to be bitten frightfully all over. The men rushed about the deck at night, angry and sleepless, pursued by their pertinacious tiny foes.

The Yang-tsze-Kiang river at Nanking, though 250 miles from the mouth, is a mile wide, and runs like a mill sluice, at the rate of five miles an hour.

On June 27, we received a letter from some minor official informing us that the Eastern King would answer our communication. This letter containing an offensive appellation, a remonstrance was sent in. The messenger was also told to acquaint his superior that a salute would be fired by the 'Rattler' the ensuing day in honour of the Queen's birthday, it being deemed prudent to mention this, lest the Taipings should suspect hostile intentions.

On the morrow, we received another letter to the effect that the word 'barbarian' had been used to distinguish between the Brethren and us, thus assuming all the offensive superiority to which we had objected. The letter also stated, with reference to our intimation, that a salute would be fired in honor of our Queen, that the Eastern King had been graciously pleased to accord his permission to us to do so, but desired at the same time that we should learn that the use of the word 'imperial', as applied to our Queen, was highly improper, it being employed solely to signify the Deity. No allusion was made to our application for coal, nor to the wish we had expressed to visit the far-famed pagoda. The letter was most offensively worded, and was accordingly returned by the bearer, while an answer was again requested to our previous communication.

In the evening, a boat came off, bearing a letter, or, so-called, 'order' from the Eastern King, enclosed in an immense yellow envelope, eighteen inches long and a foot wide. It was a great length, and contained answers to the questions put by us, while, at the same time, His Majesty, being greatly puzzled about the meaning of certain scriptural texts in his copy of the Pentateuch and the New Testament, put a great many questions to us in return, nearly all of them bearing on religious topics.[13]

The letter commenced with a prologue to the following effect: 'I am the Holy Ghost, appointed by special orders of the Heavenly Father, who personally took the trouble to come down on earth to instruct me', and a good deal more to the same effect. After this, our questions were answered, though, in most cases, very imperfectly and evasively.

The document asserted that the Heavenly Father, when about to enjoin His commands on mankind, came down personally on earth, taking the form of the Eastern King, and through his golden lips proclaimed his ordinances. Jesus Christ, it was said, similarly assumed the person of the 'Western King' the next dignitary, and the name of 'Tien-Kwoh' was given to the dynasty founded by the rebels. We were informed that they had not, up to that time, struck coin, nor issued Government Gazettes, while their army was vaguely stated to be innumerable, and their range of empire to include the whole earth. Their laws did not appear to be well defined, but drinking was denounced under severe penalties, and

13   See Gregory, op. cit., pp. 177–93.

many other crimes were apparently as severely punished as under ordinary Chinese law.

The theological questions put by Yang savored both of shrewdness and absurdity. For instance, he asked, 'What length and breadth has God?' 'What is the color of His beard?' 'What clothes does He wear?' The same queries were made regarding our Saviour, with additional questions as to the number of his daughters and grand-daughters. Then some pertinent enquiries were made as to the right interpretation of difficult texts, such as, 'Repent ye, for the Kingdom of Heaven is at hand.' Yang asked why Jesus was nailed to the Cross, and why he rose again on the third day?

It appeared from this strange communication that, though the rebels had procured copies of portions of the Bible, they had no one competent to interpret to them the meaning of Scripture. The last remark made by the Eastern King was amusing though. He enquired why we barbarians, who ought to bring tribute to the Celestial Kingdom, had the presumption to come to him and ask him for coal, thus showing our ignorance of heavenly precepts. In commenting upon our unenlightenment as to celestial doctrines, Yang compassionately observed that he was not much surprised at our ignorance, seeing whence we came.

The next day we formed a synod for the purpose of answering the questions put to us, by no means an easy matter, considering the absurdity of some of them. The rebels insisted that the Tartars must be the Satan mentioned in the bible, and Yang ingeniously tried to establish this by several quotations which he thought apposite.

On June 30 we left Nanking, and just before we got under weigh received a letter from one of the rebel Generals, requesting us to take to Chinkiangfu a brother of the Colonel whom we had brought up with us, and whom we had never set eyes on since we landed him. On the boat, which brought this missive, returning, we sent on shore our answers to the Eastern King's questions.

Section 2 Loss of contact (1855–8)

No Western government and very few individuals had any close contact with the Taiping between mid 1854 and the end of 1858. More by accident than design Roman Catholic missionaries stationed in the interior were from time to time forced to deal with them. The main concern of these missionaries was with the protection of their churches and converts, and they did not display any deep interest in, or attempt much analysis of, the

Taiping movement itself. For most of them the Taiping were both dangerous and Protestant though, as indicated in the report of the Jesuit Clavelin (Doc. 37), the imperial forces fighting against the rebellion were seen as hardly less dangerous. Also we learn from both Clavelin and the Lazarist Danicourt (Docs. 38, 42) that Western mercenaries were beginning to become involved in the struggle, and it is to two of these that we owe the only direct Western report of the leadership struggle in Nanking during 1856 (Doc. 41). The British consular intelligence service did its best, but had to rely either on such information, or misinformation, as could be gleaned from Peking Gazettes by the Chinese Secretary at Hong Kong, T. F. Wade (Docs. 39, 44), or on chance encounters, like those of the young customs service official H. N. Lay and the missionary R. S. Maclay (Docs. 40, 43).

A few individuals, such as the British Presbyterian Rev. W. C. Burns, still tried to reach the Taiping territory, but on the whole in this period the Western community in China did not go out of its way in search of new information about the movement, being preoccupied with other developments more promising to Western interests in China, taking place at Canton and elsewhere.

37
A Letter from Fr S Clavelin SJ
Annals of the Propagation of the Faith, vol. XVII (November 1856), pp. 310–15

Sir,

I avail myself of a few moments' leisure, for which I am indebted to the bad weather, to comply with my promise to satisfy your desire. The few details which I have to communicate will have no further interest than that which your friendship, as in former instances, will reflect upon them.

The journey which I undertook to visit the Christians dispersed in the neighbourhood of Nankin has hitherto been tolerably successful. On leaving you, two months ago, to return to my district, I went through Tsam-zo, seventy-five miles from Shanghai, and being night-time, went headlong into a troop of Imperialist soldiers, who had been stationed there for some days. All I could do was to produce my passport, and declare myself a Frenchman; but the officials were so slow, and reluctant to verify my papers, that I was not permitted to continue my journey till next day at noon. In this, as in a thousand other circumstances, the neophytes who came to my assistance had evident proof of the instinctively hostile disposition of the mandarins towards us, both as Christians and as foreigners. The favour which they grant us are always commensurate with the fear or the need which they have of the Europeans. The mandarin of Tsam-zo, finding that he could not discover in me a Shanghai rebel,[14] was obliged to raise the watchword and allow me to pass on. How proud he would have been to have given proof of his bravery and vigilance by seizing a poor fugitive. It appears pretty certain that the promise of a reward of from three to five sapees for every rebel's head produced, caused many an innocent traveller to lose his, when, like me, he happened to arrive at the wrong hour.

What a calamity the march of the Imperial troops has been for these districts! The monopolization of the barks and other means of transport, upon the whole line between Shanghai and Tchen-kiang, completely suspended commercial affairs for upwards of two months, entailing immense losses upon private individuals. On the approach of these troops, much less anxious to fight than to pillage, the towns closed their gates, like Rome in ancient times against the Gauls. The environs suffered so much the more. Amongst the generals commanding these troops, the most valiant appears to be Lieutenant-General Tcham-kie-siam, of whom I have spoken to you under other circumstances. He was one of the first promoters of the rebellion in Kouang-si, his native province. When the invading army arrived at Hou-Kouang, Tcham-kie-siam, in concert with the other rebel chiefs, entered the camp of the enemy, as if to propose a parley, but in reality to stir up the imperial troops to defection. The generalissimo, Hiam-ta-jen, more astute than he, received him very well, and, by his emissaries, managed to make the other insurgent chiefs believe that Tcham-kie-siam had abandoned their cause and adopted that of the emperor. Supposing this to be the case, the wife and children of the pretended deserter were brought upon an eminence, and decapitated in sight of the whole Imperial army. Tcham-kie-siam, exasperated at this barbarous act, joined a cause which had not been that of his choice; he vowed implacable hatred against his former companions in arms; and, at the head of a corps, principally composed of deserters, he so often made them feel its effects, that the rebels dreaded him in particular, and have surnamed him *Tcham-the-diabolical*. They have also attempted several times to seize his person. One day, a muscular Kouam-si-jen succeeded in taking and disarming him; then, mounting his

14 I.e. a member of the Small Sword Society, which occupied the Chinese city of Shanghai between September 1853 and February 1855.

horse, he conducted him towards the town. Tcham-kie-siam, whose hands had been left at liberty, recollected that he carried his dinner-knife in the mounting of his boot; he drew it out, and thrust it into the body of his conqueror, and thus regained his liberty.

Last year, about the month of October, Tchiam-kie-siam, now become the right arm of the generalissimo, and the only really remarkable man in his camp, was appointed by him to go and retake the town of Ta-pim-fou, situated about twenty or twenty-five miles from Nankin. By his directions, a flotilla was prepared and armed in secret; then, taking with him his best troops, he arrived in one day before Ta-pim-fou, took it at the first onset, massacred one or two thousand Koum-si-jen, and the King of the North,[15] by whom they were commanded. In the course of three or four days, he returned to join his chief, after having left a garrison in the town. Tcham-kie-siam presented himself at the camp, preceded by the spoils of his enemy; but the joy of his triumph was allayed, when, on the following day, it became known that the Kouam-si-jen, had suddenly returned, regained possession of Ta-pim-fou, and put all the garrison to the sword.

At Tchen-Kiang the operations of the siege were conducted with still less energy than at Nankin; but since the taking of Shanghai, the Kouam-si-jen, perceiving that they were about to be hard pushed, also decided on taking measures for their protection. And as the greatest danger they had to guard against was that of famine, they sent out foraging parties about the town to a distance of eight or ten miles, to seize all the money, clothes, and provisions they could lay their hands on. Another scourge, also, befel these desolated districts; I mean the Imperialists, who, under pretence of protecting them, seized upon everything the rebels had left; hence Imperialists and insurgents are included in one common malediction by these eighty or a hundred thousand victims of their rapacity. These events took place about a month ago. On my arrival at Tan-iam, everybody was under the impression of terror. A considerable number of the inhabitants, the Christians as well as the others, were flying in opposite directions to seek refuge, which compelled me to do duty in two different localities.

Judging from the reports that I heard on my road, it would appear that the position of the Imperialists is, in general, improved; and that the prestige of the Kouan-si-jen is con-

15   I.e. Wei Ch'ang-hui. However, Clavelin's report is mistaken. The Taiping were commanded by Shih Ta-ying, who was indeed killed—see Jen Yu-wen, op. cit., p. 207.

siderably reduced, at least on the south and east of Nankin. Moreover, they have gradually lost the bravest of their soldiers and officers. Their armed bands, which had advanced to the environs of Pekin, were compelled, at the beginning of the present year, to return towards the south, after the loss of the King of the West,[16] the principal chief of the expedition, who died on the field of honour. They consequently evacuated the position of Lei-tchen in Pe-tche-li, that of Kas-tam-tchen, in the north of Chang-tong, and formed their first line of defence on the southern bank of the Yellow river; the Imperialists, following in pursuit, occupy the opposite side.

But the principal and really important line of the Kowam-si-jen is that of Kiang; it is the basis of all their operations, and comprises an extent of from four hundred to four hundred and fifty miles. Its extreme right is at Tchen-Kiang-fou and Koua-tcheou, where it cuts the junction of the Imperial Canal, and its extreme left is at Han-iam-fou and Han-keou, positions equally commanding communications of the greatest importance to the interior. Meanwhile, the Kouam-si-jen are occupying Nankin, the general quarters, Tam-pim-fou, Lu-tcheu-fou, Ngan-kin-fou, the capital of Ngan-kouei, recently conquered, and Kiou-kiang, the key of Central China. These towns are on the Kiang, or at short distances from that river. The domination of the Kouam-si-jen also extends beyond this to several towns of the third class, dependent upon the preceding towns for their administration, and, like them, situated on a zone which passes along the Kiang.

The generalissimo, Hiam-ta-jen, in spite of his inaction, has managed, it appears, to preserve the goodwill of the emperor; he is in greater favour than ever at court. The troops under his immediate orders do not exceed twelve thousand men, and he finds it exceedingly difficult to replace by recruits those whom the numerous engagements, and especially disease, are daily carrying off. The Su-tchuen legion, amongst others, which, on its departure from Kouang-si, consisted of four thousand soldiers, now only numbers one thousand of the original corps. One of the officers assured me that, since the commencement of this war, he has seen at least forty generals die from one cause or another.

I recently heard that there were some Europeans amongst the Kouam-si-jen. They are supposed to have come from Canton, and accompanied the expedition as far as Nankin. According to these reports, which do not appear to me void of probability, these

16 Hsiao Ch'ao-kwei, who actually died in September 1852. This is presumably a mistake for Lin Feng-hsiang, a leader of the northern expedition who committed suicide on his capture in March 1855.

foreigners were principally instrusted with the keeping of the stores, the direction of the artillery and the mines. In reference to the principal chief of the insurrection, I obtained some few further details. I at length met with a person who has seen several times Hum-sieu-tsinen, called *Ta-pim-wam*, or the *Celestial King*. This person is a young captive, who, attached to the service of one of the wives of Ta-pim-wam, managed to escape from the palace together with those of her companions. The three latter were caught and decapitated. The other, having by accident found shelter amongst our Christians, remained concealed until she found the means of escaping from the town with all her family. That sojourn amongst the neophytes saved her life, and will also, I hope, save her soul; for she has already learned the Christian doctrine, and appears well disposed to put it into practice. This pagan woman affirms that, during the eight or ten months that she spent in the house of Ta-pim-wam, she saw him very often. This was, when followed by the queens of the first and second order, and the other women composing his household, he was going to preside at prayers, which are made with great regularity every Friday. Not content with directing these devotions, Ta-pim-wam, mounted on an estrade, commented upon and explained to his feminine hearers the tenets of his new religion. This woman says she should think he is a man of thirty-five or forty years of age, which corresponds with previous reports.

The five other kings have also built themselves palaces around that of Ta-pim-wam, but at respectful distances, and here they reside with their numerous retinues, except when performing tributary service. Ta-pim-wam is the only one who never goes out of his palace, from which he directs everything, giving his orders through the intermediary of the King of the East, his prime minister. The latter never leaves Nankin or the environs. From the top of a mountain, I saw his habitation, which, with its long yellow walls, resembles a citadel in the interior of the town. The Kouam-si-jen have also constructed a very lofty observatory, which, on account of the mountain serving as its base, is much higher than the famous porcelain tower. Hence all the environs of Nankin may be observed.

In the beginning of the present year, an extraordinary circumstance occurred in that capital. For several days an unusual noise was heard, as if all the petards, tomtoms, and Chinese cannons had been brought together at Nankin for the purpose. The occasion of this display was the celebration of the marriages which were taking place *en masse*. The rebel chiefs, it is said, with a view to attach their subordinates still more to their cause, wanted to fix them to the soil by marriage and the possession of property. They allotted the principal habitations of the town to the soldiers returned from Kouang-si and Hou-kouang, each according to his merit, and made them marry each one of the numerous young girls that had fallen into their power. The hilarity of these nuptials, however great or affected it may have been, must have been frequently clouded by the sight of the scenes of despair which they occasioned. Hundreds of women, unwilling to share the fate of these adventurers, preferred putting an end to their lives, as at the taking of Nankin, by hanging and drowning themselves or burying themselves under the ruins of the houses to which they had set fire.

38
A Letter from Mgr E Danicourt
E. J. Danicourt, *Vie de Mgr. Danicourt de la Congrégation de la Mission, évêque d'Antiphelles, vicaire apostolique de Tche-kiang et du Kiang-Sy* (Paris, 1889), pp. 322–4

What to tell you about the rebels? The whole episode is appalling, horrifying, frightful. Last June [1855], one of the savage hordes massacred at least one hundred thousand people in the town of Ning-Tcheou, situated at the northwest border of Kiang-sy: men, women, old people, children, all were killed with lance blows. They spared only about a thousand people. After the slaughter, they eat the human flesh, and they are frequently seen carrying human entrails on their shoulders, as if they were coming from the butcher's. Apart from several of our Christians, who were captured by them and who escaped from their clutches, telling us of these horrors, it is a fact that is well known by everyone.

There are certainly a few Europeans amongst them; for our Christians saw at Kiou-Kiang-fou four persons of whom two had fair hair and red beards, and two others had very swarthy complexions and hair like Indians. All of them had tight-fitting trousers and understraps. Everyone used to say that they were foreigners. This infamous breed nevertheless pray before and after meals; but they are obviously Protestant prayers, for the Catholics, even less so than the pagans, have never met with similar prayers before, where praises of the four Kings of the East, West, North and South are mingled with those of the three persons of the Holy Trinity. The biblical missionaries, who at first boasted so much of these new followers of their sect, must now blush for the abominations and cruelties committed by their proselytes: *A fructibus eorum cognoscetis eos.* The turncoat Gutzlaff, the hoarder of money, as the English call him, ... must be considered the principal author of the few Christian truths which one sees floating here and there upon the foul torrents of the rebels' morality; for he had in his service for several years some adherents from Canton, whom he sent into these various provinces, there to propagate *his doctrine*, for he also had his own doctrine, by means of copious salaries.

All the tea which the Europeans export from Shanghai comes from Ning-Tcheou, so that this town, which God's justice has just punished in such a terrible way, and which also had its corruptions, grew astonishingly in a few years. Four of our Christians from Kiou-Tou, who had gone there to get tea, could not escape when the rebels arrived. God delivered two of them from the slaughter, and after remaining for some time in the rebels' service, one as a doctor and the other as a transcriber, they were able to escape and return here. But we have reason to fear for the lives of the two others, the disappearance of one of whom, Laurent Yeou, an elder son, is causing his young wife and all his family bitter sorrow.

39
An Intelligence Report by T F Wade[17]
FO 17/246, no. 120, enc. in Bowring to Clarendon, 12 April 1856

The rebel front continues, therefore, nearly as it was, but in some sort insecure at both extremities. The increase of activity in its centre and supports is, on the other hand, so great as to afford no prospect of its immediate suppression. It is clearly more indebted to the imbecility of government for its continuance than to any compactness of plan or essential vigor of its own; and, that it is to the same cause that its origin is due, is attested by the very outspoken memorial of an ancient statesman (Tsang Wang-Yen)

17 While Chinese Secretary to the British Superintendency of Trade at Hong Kong T. F. Wade wrote regular reports on the rebellion and the general political condition of China which were enclosed in despatches from Bowring to Clarendon as follows:

10 September 1855	No. 296	FO 17/233
13 October 1855	No. 331	17/234
14 December 1855	No. 403	17/235
14 January 1856	No. 23	17/244
13 February 1856	No. 62	17/245
12 April 1856	No. 120	17/246
7 July 1856	No. 210	17/248
9 August 1856	No. 252	17/249
14 March 1857	No. 129	17/265
25 May 1857	No. 263	17/269
14 October 1857	No. 401	17/272
29 November 1857	No. 431	17/273

recently published, in which the lawless societies of Kwang Tung are emphatically declared to owe their existence to the faint-heartedness of the authorities, who have for years persisted in ignoring these seditious confederacies, and the crimes committed by members of them.

There is no incident in this wretched history that may enable one to name a term of years within which the struggle shall be concluded. The Emperor recovers ground lost in one province, only as it were to see rebellion condense itself in another; and the rebels, though stubborn and formidable, are still, considered as a whole, on the defensive, and have now to recommence, geographically speaking, from a point little in advance of where they were at the beginning of 1854. At Nanking and about it, large imperialist and insurgent armies have been engaged for nearly three years without effecting on either side any material change in the dispositions of each other. Communications throughout the land are embarrassed indeed, but their interruption is so manifestly imperfect, that it is hardly possible to pronounce any tract of the disturbed country positively in the possession of either party. The south of China is dotted like a chessboard with men of both, oftener, it would seem, intent on avoiding than seeking one another. Government, however, still maintains an official presence, civil and military, *in every province*, and if, as seems possible, it now recovers Chin-Kiang, little as that event may be due to the prowess of its arms, it will doubtless avail it something with the wavering and superstitious; that is to say, with the majority of inhabitants of the empire.

40
A Letter from H N Lay[18]
Bowring Papers in the John Rylands Library, Manchester, f 1228/163, in Sir John Bowring to Edgar Bowring, 21 November 1856

Of the rebellion we have heard almost nothing during the past month. The demand for Manchester goods has been active, which is a sign of the inactivity of the Belligerents.

While upon an excursion to the 'Hills' a fortnight ago, I met with a Nanking man who had recently escaped, as he said, with 'several thousands' prisoners like himself up to that time in the city, and was on his way to an adjacent village. He gave me a good

18   H. N. Lay had transferred from the British consular service to become Inspector of Customs at Shanghai for the Chinese government in May 1855—see J. Gerson, *Horatio Nelson Lay and Sino-British Relations 1854–64* (Harvard, 1972), ch. 4.

deal of information respecting the state of affairs at Nanking. Amongst other things he related the particulars, as far as he knew them, of the jealousy that existed between Yangsewts'ing and the Northern King—how Yang on a certain occasion closed the gates of the city against the latter, but at the end of ten days reopened them—that a conclave of the other chiefs was then held to decide between the two rivals, the result of which was a decision against Yang, whom they condemned to death—and he and all of the surname Yang were accordingly executed. He said that a large number, he called it Yih wan, of the rebels had 'grown tired of being Long haired men and talked of joining the Imperialists'! The rebels do not levy taxes, and do not as a general rule treat the people unkindly, though, added the man shaking his head, they have been guilty of horrible massacres. He related one from which he by an extraordinary chance escaped. His story was throughout straightforward, and given without any over eagerness to communicate—on some matters he was informed, of others he was ignorant, and he always gave an intelligible and simple reason why, so that on the whole I was inclined to believe his account.

41
A Narrative by 'two Europeans who for several months have been living at Nanking'[19]
Overland Friend of China, 15, 21 and 30 January 1857

15 January
Mr E. Reynolds, the gentleman mentioned by Mr T. T. Meadows in his last work on China in connection with the voyage of H.M.S.S. *Hermes* to Nanking and other matters,[20] has kindly placed at our disposal a narrative, as he wrote it, to the dictation of one of two Europeans, who, for several months have been living at Nanking, and who returned to Shanghae a few days ago. Having some knowledge of the party whose experience is recounted, we think we may safely indorse the story as truthful; and regret that in our present number we can furnish only one or two columns of it. There is no doubt of the massacre of the Eastern King and his party—of the destruction of the celebrated Porcelain tower, and of the rampant existence of much fanaticism where it was hoped better things would appear.

19 In this document the Taiping leaders are referred to by numbers thus: 1.—Hung Hsiu-ch'üan; 2.—Yang Hsiu-ch'ing; 5.—Wei Ch'ang-hui; 6.—Shih Ta-k'ai; 7.—Ch'in Jih-kang; 8.—Hu I-huang. C. A. Curwen's *Taiping Rebel* (Cambridge, 1977), pp. 198–208 also reprints a substantial portion of this account.
20 See Meadows, op. cit., p. 251.

CHINKEANG AND NANKING
Original Narrative

I left Shanghae in April 1856, and in four days reached the *Glenlyon*, at anchor off Silver Island. Not succeeding in my mission, I thought of taking a look at the Rebels, so, with a companion, we landed on the north side of the *Yang tse kiang*, and walked along the shore to the Rebel battery at Quachou. Entering it, they asked us where we were from; we told them Shanghae, upon which they tendered us a number of their books, thinking we were going back again. We told them we wished to stop with them—upon which they seemed much pleased. The commander of the battery then ordered us to go on our knees, which we did; he then went into a room and returned in full dress, and seated himself at a Table;—we then had to go upon our knees a second time;—not having any interpreter nothing further was said or done.—At supper time that evening they placed a small Table at the open door, upon which they put three bowls of rice, three cups of tea, and three pairs of chopsticks, and all, standing, sung a Hymn.—The Head man of the battery then kneeled at a Table in the middle of the room, all the people of the house kneeling behind him, said a few words, burnt some paper, and when it was partly burned threw the remainder into the air. They then arose, the servants removed the small table at the door, the meal was placed upon the centre table, and of it they all partook. If the members of the household are required to be at prayers, and if any are missing and do not give a satisfactory account of their absence, they are flogged—no thanks giving is offered after meals, but, as a rule, similar prayers are made before all the three meals.

Having been with the Rebels in the City of Shanghae we were already disappointed with our new position, and appeared, no doubt, somewhat sad; upon which the Commander of the battery, by signs, cheered us up telling us to walk about and go through the works where we pleased. It rained for the next two days, during which time we had no communication with Chinkeangfoo. On the third day a soldier came over with a large chop, which kneeling, he presented to the Commander of the battery. The latter said we were to go with this soldier to Chinkiang. Landing at Golden Island we walked thence to the Chief's house. He was not then at home. We were taken to an apartment where we were surprised to find five Manilamen, all dressed, 'a la Chinoise' with plaited tails, but long hair.—These men we soon learnt had deserted from Samqua's first fleet of Lorchas, and with an Italian and Negro had gone in together, and, up to that time had been three years in Chin-keang-foo. For the first five months they had been kept in prison. One of them was suspected of being a Cantonese, and was branded on the face and legs to make him speak Chinese.—They now were in high favor with the chief, and lived under the same roof with him. They followed the Chinese in their religious ceremonies and told us no one was allowed to marry, and that the women were shut up in houses, under the controul of an old woman, and guarded by boys. If any soldiers were discovered in any of the houses, the boys would immediately inform the chief, who had the guilty parties examined and beheaded. The Manilamen were the City executioners, and had knives given to them for that purpose. One in particular beheaded the women. They say that for two and a half years the whole garrison had nothing to eat but congee, and were about evacuating the place when *Lo-ta-kang* cut his way through from Nanking, with 30,000 men to their relief.—The whole garrison previous to this consisted of but 10,000 men. On one occasion they sent out 500 women at night, furnished with lanterns; the Imperialists opened fire upon them and killed several before they discovered who they were. While we were there several hundred women and boys were brought in from the Quachow side.

Prayers every seventh day, which appears to be our Wednesday at midnight: the head of the house or rather a petty officer, having a certain number of men under him, musters all his followers.—All these, kneeling, sing a hymn, after which the headman offers a prayer, occupying about ten minutes; when finished all rise and disperse for the night. In the morning, say Thursday, at daylight a white flag, quite the width of the street, having three large characters down the middle, is suspended; one across each main street of the City. Any officer or Soldier on Horseback passing under has to dismount and lead his Horse, not attempting to ride under it. Beyond this they did not in any way observe the sabbath—Mechanics never ceased to work on the seventh day—there was no meetings nor congregations. But to go on with my narrative, on being brought before the chief of Chin Keang foo, in whose presence we had to go on our knees, he, waving his hand for us to get up asked us where we came from, and wished to know if I would like to stop. To which we replied from Shanghae, and in the affirmative. He then asked the Manilamen whether they would be security against our running away. They nodded assent; upon which he seemed satisfied, and told us to live with the Manilamen.—On the second day we all went with a large force over to Yang-chow—had dinner and returned—all the soldiers and coolies, of which latter each soldier has three under him, were busily employed carrying Rice from thence to Qwachow, and Chinkeang. This occupied the space of one month, with about 30,000 men, women, and children. We remained in Chin keang five days longer, doing nothing, after which we went to a walled city inside from Qwachow taking 30,000 men a day's march. We fought for an hour against 10,000 Imps. Two or three of our men were wounded, and about thirty of the Imps. We took the city. The gates being open we entered at one side and the Imps went out at the other. Our men went round and cut off several of them. Searched the city for Imps, but did not molest any of the inhabitants. Found no provisions there, and that night retired about ten miles and threw up a mud fortification during the night. It is surprising how rapidly these men throw up a breastwork, or intrench themselves; they have regular sappers. Remained there for three days, until we had collected all the provisions in this neighbourhood, when we again retired about fifteen miles, threw up mud fortifications, stayed there some ten days, and burned nine large Junks found lying in a creek. Parties were sent out to protect the forageing parties from the inroads of the Imperial Horsemen who would attack them in large numbers, frequently driving our men within the intrenchments until we collected our forces and would drive them off again.

On one occasion they surprised and carried off twenty of our men who were out on a rice excursion. We also had about a hundred horsemen. Having now a sickness of these people, and wishing to escape while we were on the Quachow side, being dressed in Chinese clothing, I went over to Chinkeang to get our European clothes.—Next morning to my surprise two other Europeans were brought in.—I told them I was sorry to see them in there. However, having now an accession of two of our countrymen, I determined to remain. Taking my two comrades over with me, I went to the Chief, who, as with us, told them they could not expect any wages. We, all four Europeans, now agreed to remain with them, and next morning went in force to the north ward and east ward, to an Imperialist fortification which we found surrounded with water and unapproachable. We tried to entice them out, but they remained in their stronghold. We stayed there two hours, then the whole force returned to Chinkiang. During this foray we collected as much rice as would serve the City for two years. On our march we posted up chops, informing the people we only wanted them to pay duties, and all those who did so would not be molested. The next day 15,000 men of the

Nankin force left for Nankin. Marching for ten miles they encamped, having fallen in with an imposing force of the Imperialists. A body of 10,000 men of the Chingkiang force joined them, and were met by a large body of the Imperialists who had fortified themselves on the main road to Nankin, having thirty Canton Junks to support them; some of which had landed their guns.— We fought all that day, forcing the Imperialists within their batteries with the loss of about one hundred men. Ten of our men were blown up by their own powder bags through their own carelessness. We retired for the night to our encampments, where we threw up a breastwork. Next morning we advanced making a bridge of boats across the Creek on to an Island, one division of our force keeping the imperialists from observing us. About two hundred of our men crossed over and threw up a two gun battery to oppose a battery of six guns; they, however, had the advantage of us, and made it too warm work for us to remain, killed four of our men, and dismounted one of the guns. We deserted this battery and joined the main force who were attacking the imperialists on the opposite side.—After about three hours hard fighting we carried one of their batteries, driving them into the river, with their three remaining batteries. On the second day we took two more batteries, the imperialists, retreating into their middle battery—we then surrounded them, destroyed a few houses, collected the material and some straw, and placed fires all around this fort to prevent their escape.—Next morning before daylight we discovered the imperialists in great confusion, endeavouring to escape through our lines; the alarm was given, we arose in a body, and destroyed them singly.—The first day we lost 150 men, the imperialists 600; the next day in carrying the batteries we lost 400 men, and the Imperialists 500; the third day we lost none, but destroyed about 700 of the Imperials. We then took possession of all the batteries in which we found large quantities of ammunition—and turned the guns up on the Canton Junks who soon removed to the opposite side of the river.— Remained there one day and the next returned round back of Chinkiang.

The whole force attacked the Imperial batteries (which we have learned since our return here were commanded by Keih in person, and where he was killed, though no one either at Chinkeang or Nankin was aware of it). After considerable hard fighting the first day we took one battery; they retreating in to another. We here fought for three days and took in detail eight batteries. At last we drove them into their three remaining batteries, which we surrounded. Fought all this day without

effect.—Having got three small guns into position to play upon the batteries, about one o'clock five of the Imp. officers came out of their battery, and falling on their knees made signs to our people. We of Nankin and Chinkeang advanced. They had a parley for about an hour, but not coming to terms the imp. officers retired. Giving our Chiefs time to withdraw, the Imperialist recommenced firing which we returned. Fighting all that day at nightfall we surrounded them with fires during the night. They retreated from one of their batteries, which we immediately took possession of, killing a number of them who had not time to escape. We were so close upon them that some fifteen to twenty men were speared in one house. We found that they had been driven to great extremities, having neither meat nor drink. Their horses were half eaten. The next morning my comrade, Charles Thompson of Boston, while pointing a gingall, received a shot in his breast. Myself and two companions carried him back to Chinkeang where he was attended by three doctors. He lingered for ten days, fretting a good deal. Previous to his receiving the wound he would often say he would rather serve three years in the States prison then three months longer with these people. Having completely surrounded the Imperials, and finding they could not drive us away, they attempted to escape by running through our lines, but were completely destroyed: They lost about seven hundred men in the three batteries; our loss was none killed but about ten wounded.
—F. of C. Jany. 14

21 January
For about twenty days after this we were busily employed carrying guns and ammunition &c., in to Chinkeang. Although distant about three miles from the City, the rebels occupied these forts, and when we passed were still in position. About eight days after this the Nankin force of fifteen thousand men retired to the S.E. of Chinkeang about twenty five miles, and there built three or four batteries; remaining there a few days, till reinforced by the Chinkeang force. On the day of their joining, we were attacked by a body of Imp. foot and about seven hundred horsemen who drove us back several times. We then advanced in two divisions when the Imps retreated, the horsemen taking the country and the foot soldiers the hills. In going through the country we destroyed all the large buildings, but never disturbed those belonging to the poor. The villagers however would all flee on our approach.—We left the Chinkeang force in these batteries—the

other force leaving for Nankin, the Commander *Yeen ting yue*[21] asked us whether we would like to go to Nankin, saying he would give us horses, and we would be more comfortable in that place—so we agreed to go. On our march the second day we fell in with three batteries occupied by the Imps. which we avoided, not wishing to engage with them, our ammunitions being finished. We marched until ten at night they following us. We doubled up a hill and they approached us no further;—this was about twenty five miles from Nankin. We remained here for a few hours— when we proceeded into Nankin where we arrived on the third day—we (two Europeans) strayed from the main body, approached the City by the West about—the third gate from the Porcelain Tower—We were dressed as Chinese, got through the first gate, but were not allowed to pass through the second. We had dinner with the gateman, who kept us waiting for an order to allow us to enter. During our stay in the gateway we attracted great notice—the passage being jammed with gazers—we were taken to No. 8 who enquired if we knew *Lo-ta-kang*, an Italian named Antonie to whom they had given that title—he was in high favor with the Chiefs—he had been with them for about three and a half years—having joined them from some of the Portuguese Lorchas in the pay of Samqua. We did not know him—nor did we ever meet him, and we believe him dead. They say he was a very powerful man, carrying a sword fourteen catties weight. When the Imps. would fire at him he would fall down and fain dead—a number of them would then rush to cut his head off, when he would suddenly spring up and with his own hands slay two or three of them. He was a privileged man—was allowed money for his Opium pipe and Grog of which he seemed very fond—he could do almost as he pleased—No. 7 the Chief with whom we came from Chin-kiang hearing we were at No. 8's, sent for us; he immediately conducted us to the second King or No. 2, having previously searched us, no one being allowed to approach him with weapons on his person. All his officers, his brother in law, and ourselves went on our knees before him—the officers at the same time saying a short prayer. When either of his children, two boys of three and seven years of age made their appearance in the street, all the officers and soldiers would immediately fall on their knees, and we were compelled to remain so, as long as they

---

21   Ch'in Jih-kang, the Yen Wang; 'ting yue' is probably a partial rendering of his
     title Ting t'ien hou, 'Marquis to Support Heaven'.

were present. We have on some occasions, been kept in this position for ten minutes.

Not then having an interpreter the Number 2, *Toong Wang foo* said little to us—but gave us in charge of his brother in law—who conducted us to his house, where we were well cared for and furnished with a decent room. When our interpreter who was formerly a carpenter at Canton came before Number 2, he was continually falling on his knees, and would wish us to do so too, but when we remained standing the Chief did not take any offence—so we were under the impression we would have been better off had any other than a Canton man been the interpreter. The next morning about six we were brought up before No. 2, who enquired how we fought thinking we only used our fists. We shewed him, we could use both a sword and firearms, upon which he gave us a stick and we shewed him the cuts and guards as well as we knew. We told him we only used our fists when we were drunk, shewing our meaning by lifting a cup and motioning to be drunk. They made us go through a little pugilism, which amused the second King very much, he laughing heartily. They brought us an English pistol asking me to fire it off—placing a piece of paper against a wall some fifty yards distant. I put the ball into the centre—No. 2 standing behind me while taking aim appeared nervous while I was using the weapon.

Looking round and taking notice of his Palace which was very extensive, he asked us whether our Emperor had one similar to his, to which we, of course, answered—No! During our stay at Nankin previous to his death we noticed about five hundred ... cooking, making shoes &c. Every morning at 8 o'clock about eight hundred to one thousand respectably dressed women would come and kneel before No. 2's door, and remain there until they had received some orders from him. We learnt these women were the wives, relations and friends of those rebels who had been slain in battle, who came there for employment. After the interpreter came we told No. 2, that it was not the custom in our country to bend the knee to our officers—and so were only ten minutes before him on the second occasion. For the three months after this we did nothing but wander through the city, amusing ourselves as well as circumstances would allow us; we might be absent from our quarters for months without being suspected of being out of the city—so extensive is the place. On one occasion we saw three men and three women beheaded for fornication— and one young man was beheaded and then quartered for incest—the woman was only beheaded; and one man was beheaded for thieving.

We frequently saw the heads of those who had been found smoking opium. These are tied to a pole and carried between two men through the principal streets, one beating a gong, and the other proclaiming the crime—cautioning all to beware. Those who are found smoking tobacco and drinking are flogged, and any one found drunk or jolly is beheaded. We cannot say that No. 2 did smoke opium, and are inclined to the belief that he did not, but we do know that No. 2's brother in law both smoked opium and drank wine. After the death of No. 2 he was accused of having a great quantity of Opium and Tobacco in his place. There was a reward of five dollars offered for any of the articles belonging to the Opium pipe, such as the Lamp, Mudletray &c., but we did not hear that any had been discovered—and up to the time we left none had been found. These articles were wanted to prove that he indulged in the drug, and consequently was a bad man.

Getting tired of doing nothing, we sent the interpreter to the *Toong Wang foo* to tell him we wished to go out side to fight. He answered us not to be sad nor disheartened, as he wished to speak with us shortly. He however did not do so, and the last time we saw him he was lecturing in a public place to about three thousand Canton men, (short haired, a part of Hoe Aluk's men) who were all on their knees. We heard they had hesitated to go out to fight. We noticed in all parts of the City, and in all the streets that the women were distributed about; none were confined to live in any particular locality. All women with husbands were exempted from work, but all those who had no protectors were compelled to work at any manual labour such as carrying bricks, stones, wood, rice &c. The greater portion of the men in the City of Nankin are soldiers, who do not work nor carry burdens. No. 2's Palace was situated close to the West gate.—All the houses and a great part of the wall of the Tartar City are destroyed. Only the rebel officers are allowed to dress in yellow; the soldiers can dress in any colour they choose. Although the head is never shaved in front, they do not dispense with the tail, still keeping it plaited, sometimes with red and yellow silk. It is tied up behind and tucked under the cap. On two occasions we saw very long processions formed of Dragons, and representations of all sorts of animals made of paper. Our quarters were situated about fifty yards from No. 2's Palace, on the opposite side of the street.—We heard that No. 2 had ordered No. 5 division in a different direction from that they then occupied. No. 7 being at Tanyang was ordered to *N'ghan-whuie.*—On his way thither he met No. 5 who asked him where he was going, he replied to *N'ghan-whuie*, by the order of No. 2.—No. 5 said you must return with me to Nankin as I have letters from No. 1 of which you are not aware. No. 7 not knowing what was up until they reached Nankin—they halted outside, when No. 5 informed No. 7 that he was ordered by No. 1 to kill No. 2. At this time No. 2 had ordered all No. 1's men to go outside the City to fight, but they did not go. He also called his friend No. 6's men in. They however had not time to reach before Nos. 5 and 7 were in the City: this they effected unsuspected at midnight. The officers and men said that if Nos. 5 and 7 had not come in, it was the intention of No. 2 to have killed No. 1.

About 4 one morning we were awakened by the report of cannon, a shot falling near our residence. We immediately sprang up and attempted to gain the street, but were prevented doing so, the street being lined with soldiers who prevented any one leaving their houses. At daylight we got out, and to our surprise found the street covered with dead bodies.—These proved to be the body guard, officers, musicians, clerks and household servants of No. 2. We saw the body of one woman. There was at this time thousands of Nos. 5 and 7 and even No. 2's men plundering the Palace. We went in with the crowd and did not find the rooms extravagantly furnished. We heard his chopsticks, penholder, seal, and a few other small things were gold, his wash basin was silver. We saw two small gold Lions and a gold bell on his table. In the course of a few hours the Palace was completely gutted. During that day the whole city, was in the greatest state of excitement, the greater portion of the people not knowing what was the cause, the gates were all closed and the walls guarded. Hearing that any one could appropriate to themselves the property of No. 2's officers, and being in want of horses we seized two—which however the same night were claimed by one of No. 5's men to whom we gave them up—No. 2's brother in law through sickness removed from where we were living.—After No. 2's death we went to see him, we found his house was not disturbed, but was informed by his wife that he had been carried off with a chain round his neck. From thence we went to No. 7's and stopped there one day without seeing him, his forces being at No. 1's. Next day we went to No. 1's to look after him (No. 7) (as he was our only friend, he having brought us from Chinkeang). Our interpreter was there, and pointed out our friends to us, who to our surprise were with No. 5 kneeling at No. 1's door each with a chain around his neck and blue kerchiefs round their heads. They were not secured like criminals. One of No. 1's female messengers brought out a large piece of yellow silk about two and a half yards long and half a yard broad covered with red letters—

which was placed before these two, they reading it, and a great number of No. 2's officers were crowding in to read it also. Immediately it was read it was handed out and pasted on the wall opposite No. 1's palace. Nos. 5 and 7 sent in frequent messages by these female messengers, who are moderately good looking Canton women, and when delivering a verbal message do so with a clear firm voice, which could be heard at a distance of thirty yards. During the intervals of these messages Nos. 5 and 7 would retire to a small room and consult together.—Finally these two messengers proclaimed they were to receive each five hundred lashes or blows—upon which five sticks were handed out, No. 5's and 7's officers taking them.—No. 5 wishing a particular officer to flog him; upon his doing so and reaching the three hundredth blow, No. 5 drew a knife saying that if he did not lay it on harder, he would kill him, at the same time making pretence to cry.

During the time Nos. 5 and 7 were receiving this punishment their officers and men would rush forward and put their hands on their backs to receive the blows instead of them. Not knowing it was all mockery, I was fanning No. 7 at the time, and seeing the others put their hands on his back I did so also. After receiving a few blows on my hand the stick broke, and was replaced with another—they however did not receive more than three hundred and twenty lashes or blows each. One of No. 5's officers wishing to take the chain from off his neck—he prevented his doing so. During this mock punishment several hundred officers and men were seen crying—several of No. 2's officers and men were there also, but they were prisoners, having heavy chains and ropes around their necks. About six thousand of these were unsuspiciously taken prisoners and put into two large houses one on each side of No. 1's palace. As we were returning to No. 7's house, we met our officious interpreter with two soldiers bringing two of No. 2's officers prisoners—who had been caught concealing themselves. He told us No. 7 wanted to see us so soon as these two men were decapitated. On being presented to him we were pulled on our knees by the interpreter, through whom we explained to No. 7 we were very sorry he should have been flogged. Upon which he said no fear; and appointed a room for us to sleep in at the entrance to No. 1's, opposite which for a long time hung the head of No. 2 or the 2'd King. During the night we accompanied Nos. 5 and 7 who inspected the prison of these 6,000 men, listened at the windows, and planned their destruction. Next morning at daylight the doors and windows of these prisons were opened, and several powder bags thrown in on the prisoners, while the entrance was strongly guarded. In one house the soldiers entered with little resistance and massacred the whole, but in the other the prisoners fought with the bricks from the walls and partitions, most desperately for upwards of six hours before they were got under. In addition to musketry, a two pounder discharged grape at them. These poor devils then stripped themselves, and many were seen to fall from sheer exhaustion. At last Nos. 5 and 7 called upon their men to draw their right arms from their sleeves, so as to distinguish them from No. 2's men; they then rushed in and massacred the remainder. We shortly after entered, and, good heavens! such a scene, the dead bodies were in some places five and six deep; some had hung themselves and others were severely scorched from the explosions of the powder bags thrown in. These bodies were removed from this to a field and remained uncovered.—After this every master of a house in the city had to give an account of how many men and women and children were residing under his roof, to every one of whom was given a small chop which they wore on their breast, and if they found any of No. 2's men they were to secure them.—For several weeks these people were brought to the execution ground in parcels of fives, tens, hundreds, and thousands, who were all beheaded. All the women and children also, any one who had eaten of No. 2's rice suffered.

About six weeks after No. 2 was killed, No. 6 and a part of his force entered the City—and went to No. 1's where he met Nos. 5 and 7, who shewed him an account of their proceedings, upon which No. 6 said 'Why have you destroyed so many people who have all long hair and fought for us—would not the death of No. 2, and a few of the principal officers have satisfied you?'—to which No. 5 replies you are a thief—No. 6 in reply says you also are a thief, we both are fighting for one cause, consequently we must be both thieves. After this No. 6 said as you have gone so far yourselves, you can finish it, I will have nothing to do with it. That night he quietly collected his forces and came towards the west gate, but was refused to pass without permission from No. 5, upon which he slew the gate man and with the greater part of his force passed out. Had he not gone out that night he was to have been beheaded. A great number of the people availed themselves of the chance and went out. The next morning the City was in the greatest state of excitement, every one being under arms. They were about going out to apprehend No. 6, but were not certain which way he had gone. They plundered his house, killed his wife and children and also any of his followers who had not got away during the night. Early next morning we were sent for by No. 7, and were very much alarmed lest he would kill us, and had contemplated going over the walls and escaping rather than see him. We found our interpreter and got him to enquire of one of his officers what he wanted us for—he however only wanted to see we had not gone out. For three months the massacre of No. 2's adherents continued, and we estimated that forty thousand (more or less) men women and children must have perished. When they were satisfied, No. 7 took the fleet with about fifteen thousand men, us two following them up the Yang tse Kiang, this side of Wuhu to a place called *Sing ling shan*. At first we were prevented from entering the fort by the natives of the place (rebels in possession) the Chief, however, coming up with a small party was allowed to enter; we remaining outside about two hours when we all entered and plundered the place. We remained here for two days, then proceeded up a small creek about fifteen miles, to a fortification occupied by the rebels, where No. 7 went on shore and spoke for a short time to the Commander. We proceeded up the creek to a large village, where all our men landed and marched about twenty miles into the country, but we could not discover any Imps. We were here joined by about three thousand Canton Horsemen. No. 7 ordered all his musketeers to fire a volley, after which we returned to our boats for the night. Next morning we proceeded still farther up about forty miles where we landed all the force; the Horsemen following by land, they having already occupied a height near the Imperial army. We advanced and fought for several hours, losing five men killed, and several wounded, without driving the Imps. from their walled battery. We bivouacked for the night, and next morning found they had evacuated the place. We pursued them, but did not fall in with any of them. This was about one hundred miles up a creek west from the Yangtsekiang. We remained here for a few days—started farther into the interior and then encamped at a village, the headman of which went round sounding a gong, demanding all his villagers to prepare supper for us. Next morning we went still further about thirty miles—and crossed a creek on a bridge of boats which the people made for us, and approached to within three miles of a large walled city called [obscure] had dinner, received an unexpected order to retire to our boats. It raining heavily all the time, some reached the boats that night and some not for days after. We remained here for a few days inactive. One morning before daylight about one thousand Imperial horsemen made their appearance from the opposite side to where we had been. We landed all our men. At the same time the gun boats opened fire upon them, so soon as they saw this they retreated about two miles, and halted there until our men came up. After exchanging a few shots, we charged, they galloped off in great confusion leaving ten horses and their riders in our hands. We returned to our boats and stopt there for three days more. Next day great numbers of men, women, and children came to us, who had escaped from a city we had not reached—but which we learnt had been sold by the rebels to the Imperialists. A few days after this the imps. came down on both sides of the river in great force, both horse and foot. We landed our force on one side and drove up to a large creek. Those who reached the bridge first destroyed it so, we drove the remainder into the water by which numbers were slain and drowned. We then made a bridge and pursued them for a half a day.—That evening we retired to our boats which we found had been passing a large party of [obscure]—men at bay on the opposite side. Without resting we landed on the opposite side and drove them back also. That same night we left in some confusion, the Imperialists coming down by land in greater force. Bringing up at a village we stayed there for the remainder of the night. Next morning we reached sing ling-shan, remaining on board the boats for two days. We then landed all our force and remained there for three weeks. While there we received a supply of ammunition from Nankin. During our stay here we would frequently go out in large bodies to search for Imperialists, and had several severe engagements with them. On one occasion they drove us up to our forts, when our Chief No. 7, Teen-ting yue, rushed out heading his men crying 'On my brothers'. We took about six hundred prisoners which we killed. They formed themselves in two divisions and attempted to flank us, which movement was observed by one of our officers who gave us twenty musketeers and one hundred spikemen, with which we attacked one of their divisions so desperately that they went on their knees asking for mercy. They however were all killed. In the advance we killed about five hundred more, our loss was one man beheaded in a village. We stayed at a village all night, and the next morning the villagers brought us a number of Imperialist weapons and ten Imperialist soldiers. Not being further molested we retired to our boats, remaining here about a week.

At this time No. 7 received orders to return to Nankin. No. 2 of Chinkeang bringing a party of five hundred men with him, he taking command of the whole force, upon which seemed to cause very great disatisfaction, and considerable murmuring. During that night No. 7 left for Nankin. Previous to this we, the two foreigners and our boy who speaks Portuguese and English, had gone over the other side of the river to the encampments and fortifications of No. 6 from whose people we had learnt that No. 7

was shortly to be beheaded for his cruelties at Nankin, also telling us that No. 5 was already beheaded, and if we were in any danger to come over and quarter ourselves with them. No. 7 having left we joined No. 6's force, and found several of No. 7's men already gone over to him. Wishing to see No. 6 in person, chairs were procured for us, when we travelled about forty miles to Wuhu, where we found from sixty to eighty thousand men. We did not see the Chief, but he sent word to us we were all right, and gave us under the care of one of his officers. While there we noticed one of No. 5's officers with a chain round his neck, and also we saw No. 5's head stuck on a pole, which had been sent from Nankin preserved in salt. Previous to this and during our absence from Nanking No. 6 had sent to No. 1, that if he did not behead No. 5 he would come with his force and take the City. Upon which fearing he would approach in the direction of the Porcelain Tower, and make use of its elevation for throwing projectiles into the City, ordered it to be blown up. It was standing when we left, but we stood upon its ruins on our return. No. 6 not getting any answer took part of his force, and for three days stormed the city, killing five hundred of No. 5's officers and men. Not being able to take the City he retreated to his force at Wuhu. Shortly afterwards he received No. 5's head. On his second return when we accompanied him we found no opposition, the gates being opened as before No. 2 was killed. No. 6 was satisfied with the death of Nos. 5 7 and 8, but would not kill any of their officers or men—he only requested that any articles plundered from his residence (on the night of his sudden departure) might be restored to him, and he would not punish the party bringing it. Some days previous to our leaving Wuhu he sent forward six hundred men to prepare his house;—these men had however, before we reached the City, plundered the houses of No. 5, 7 and 8. We tried to see No. 6 to get some money and clothes—but we did not succeed, no one being allowed to see him. The officers on whom we were quartered sent a letter with our request to him, and in answer received as much clothes as we wanted and ten thousand cash. No. 6 being now next in rank to No. 1 has gone into seclusion, and all requests are sent to him in writing—replies to which are posted on the wall outside his dwelling, and all officers go next morning to see the result. We have seen fifty of these replies or notices at one time. No. 6 left his nephew, a young man of twenty—in charge of the forces at Wuhu, and Taipingfoo. We found Nankin, when we first entered it, very dreary, and it was exceedingly so on our return, and appearances seemed to argue for the worse. However the Chinese are so elastic, and so readily conform themselves to circumstances that in a few weeks we believe Nankin will pick up its former activity. It is one vast military camp. From some of No. 6's officers we learnt that it was his intention to behead No. 1. So finding matters at sixes and sevens, and beheading the order of the day, we thought it best to leave these rebels to themselves.

30 January
So, selling our surplus clothing and buying a Deane and Adam's revolver, and a sword, we started early on the morning of say the 12th December, and coming out at the West gate we walked about fifteen miles, coming to an island where the soldiers from the City make purchases, where we breakfasted. The inhabitants here are allowed to smoke tobacco and drink wine. We proceeded towards Chinkeang, walking all that day and part of the night—sleeping at the rebel consul's house who provided supper for us. Next morning after breakfast he furnished us with wheel barrows, upon which we travelled about forty miles, leaving us when we sighted Golden Island.—We refreshed ourselves this evening and continued on foot. Wishing to avoid Chinkeang, we departed from the main road, and went to the southward, but losing our way we sent the boy into a farmer's house to enquire it. They called us in to have some tea, and while there the boy got his head shaved for which we paid one dollar. Proceeding on the two farmers served us as guides. We had not gone far before they extorted two dollars more, and arriving in the vicinity of the Imperialist encampments, to which they were evidently taking us,—they told the boy that unless we gave them more money they would sell us to the Imperialists—upon which, for our own safety, we made them fast, and took our money from them.—We hastened on, reaching the bridge at Tamtoo, over which we passed, meeting two Imps soldiers on guard, who fortunately for us did not challenge. We hastened on reaching a small house where we slept for the remainder of that night.—Next morning we procured a boat, which took us to *Sung kung-yuen*.—Next day we reached Kiangyuen, here we separated, one walking down on the Shanghae side of the Yangtsekiang, and the other on the Tsungming side. One reached Shanghae on the 20th and the other on the 22nd December. After having come all the way from Nankin, dressed as Chinese, and having been away from Shanghae nearly nine months—so completely had we lost all dates, that we imagined that the year of 1857 had advanced to about February.

During the time of the slaughter of No. 2's adherents, occupying a space of three months—their religious observances were suspended.—Neither after it were they performed while we were on the march.—But on our return to Nankin they had recommenced, and were following their usual religious ceremony.—We saw all the five hundred women of No. 2's household beheaded.

We cannot say how many people are in Nankin, the streets are always crowded with soldiers, and the numbers killed were not missed—their name is legion.—Travelling from Nanking to Chinkeang, we saw the poor people carrying the blue clay, which the boy said they mixed with rice to eat, so scarce was the grain.—We saw them eating this mixture where the boy got his head shaved.—When about twenty miles distant from Nanking, we heard heavy firing, and from the direction of the sound we came to the conclusion it was in the city, (although at that distance we might be mistaken) and was caused by No. 6 beheading No. 1, which was on the day they had named to us it would probably take place. There is never any firing in the city except when there is a dissension.

In front of No. 1's house were two handsome brass 12 pdr. shell guns, marked Massachusetts 1855, with American oak carriages, painted lead colour, fitted with gutta percha buffers.—We were often called to explain the use of the hammer—which together with its other fittings were perfect.—The wad attached to the tomkin was quite new, and the guns appeared to have been seldom used by the Imps. These guns are quite familiar to many at Shanghae, from whom they were captured and presented to No. 2. When we first entered Nanking, and up to his death, No. 2 was the administrative officer of the city.—He supplied all the soldiers with provisions and clothing, directed all the military movements; he was up early and retired late—and appeared to get through a mass of business. In person he was a fine noble looking man, with a pleasant countenance and mild affable manner.* He appeared to be much respected and esteemed by all classes of the people. His children were also very much thought of. On one occasion while we were there, No. 1 came to No. 2's Palace to settle some dispute. He came in a closed chair and perceiving that some of No. 2's officers did not go on their knees at his approach, he complained of this want of respect to No. 2's who, forgetting his dignity, rushed out, and with his own hands cut off the heads of two or three of his officers—No. 8 being present was punished with one thousand blows for his remissness.

---

* His brother, who called on us last week, is of similar deportment. Ed.

196

The Manilamen at Chin keang told us that when the city was reduced to starvation, and the communication from Nankin cut off, they tried several means to send information of their situation to Nankin. They would seize a family of the villagers, and detain them, sending away one of its members with a letter, cautioning him and them that if they received no reply they would destroy the whole family.—This they did on two or three occasions.—These failing, they built two large floating batteries, which were sent away with three thousand men to protect them. No. 1 of Chinkeang and the five Manilamen embarked with them. On their way up they were met by the Canton flotilla, who burnt one, destroying one thousand men. The other was ran on shore, No. 1 and the five Manilamen with about two thousand men narrowly escaping back to Chinkeang. Finally they built a small boat, ten men volunteering to attempt to reach Nankin in her.—It was arranged if they succeeded, they were to throw large quantities of charcoal into the river. The men at Chinkeang keeping watch for its floating past* with the constant ebb, past Nankin and Chinkeang fu, which they noticed four days after the boat left. When about a week after this Lo-ta-kang cut his way through with thirty thousand men, bringing provisions and relief to the garrison. Since then they have had abundance of provisions. The morning we passed Tamtoo the rebels were engaging the Imperialists, and we were told they had been also engaged the day before. All the time we were at Ching keang and Nankin, we never heard any one speak about Shanghac, and they appeared quite ignorant of what had been going on here. At the time we left they had not heard of the movements at Canton.[22] A Cantonese woman mentioned something about Canton, which we did not understand. We were never asked anything about Loh-sean-sang.† We left at Chingkeang the five Manilamen and one Englishman—the Italian we could never ascertain what had become of, but supposed he was in Nganhuie. The rebels have gunboats and extensive fortifications on the opposite side of the river to Nankin, and have numerous fortifications on both sides of the river, as far as we went to Wuhu. A fleet of twenty Canton junks are stationed about twelve miles above Wuhu, and another fleet of sixty Canton junks are stationed about ten miles below Nankin on the opposite side of the river, where they have also extensive

---

* There is no flood in the Yang-tsi-kiang above Kiang Yiu, but the water constantly runs past Nankin and Chinkeang at the rate of three miles an hour.

† Revd. I. J. Roberts, Tai-ping-wang's preceptor—Ed.

22 I.e. the events following the *Arrow* affair at Canton in 1856.

forts. These junks never moved from their anchorage during our stay at Nankin, but the rebel gunboats would sometimes go down and exchange shots with them. No. 6 (E-Wang foo), is in great favour with his followers, and they expect great things from him.—Five days before we left Nankin, we heard that the Imperial General, Chang-kwok-leang, alias Ching-ka-cheang, who is a relative and a great friend of No. 6, had been in communication with No. 6, and was anxious to quit the Imperial service and join the rebels again. This was told us by our interpreter. We never noticed any of the rebels wearing mourning after the death of No. 2, and we are certain that if they had done so they would have been beheaded by Nos. 5 and 7's men. We found the weather at Nankin and inland about the same temperature as at Shanghae. We saw numbers of Locusts at Nankin, but the people did not exhibit any uneasiness about them. There is sufficient rice in the city of Nankin to last them for six or seven years. For several weeks after No. 2 (Toong wang foo) was killed, from eight to ten thousand people were employed carrying rice from his granary to other store rooms. At the time No. 7 was at Tanyang, it was intended after capturing that place, to have marched on and attempted Soochow, the farmers telling the rebel officers that if they would only stop the supplies that came to Tanyang every fortnight, they could easily starve them out, and so soon as they had taken that city, another city not far from it would open its gates to the rebels, and we are certain that at this juncture had not No. 7 been recalled, he would have taken Tan-yang and Soo-chow.

From the numbers of officers we frequently saw arrive at Nankin for orders from all directions, we believe the Rebels to be spread over a vast extent of the interior. The report about the Chief at Chinkeang having formerly been in Shanghae, and connected with the foreign hongs is not true;[23] he is totally ignorant of Shanghae; his name is *Woo-seen-sang*, and he has held command ever since Lotakang left; both at Nanking and Chinkeang they give him great credit for the able manner in which he has so long defended the City. In appearance and cleanliness the Yamuns of the Kings were on a par with the residences of Lew and Chun Aling when they held Shanghae. During all our travels we never met one man who had been in the City of Shanghae as a rebel. At No. 2's residence we observed a large silver fount, which our interpreter informed us was intended for baptizing. We however never saw it used. We never saw nor

23 This refers to a remark made by Lo Ta-kang in a letter to Bonham that he had worked with Europeans in Canton—see Michael, op. cit., vol. II, p. 513.

heard anything from which we could infer that either No. 1 or No. 2 had more than one wife. As customary, there was always numbers of women moving about their Palaces. No. 6 neither smokes nor drinks. Some of his officers, Canton men, drink a little at meals.

We frequently observed new accessions of several thousands of Canton and Fokien men. The majority of the fighting men outside are from the provinces of Canton, Kwangsi, and Fokien, and great numbers from Honam. The rebels have a penchant for all European articles, such as Musical Boxes, Gloves, Umbrellas, Watches and Pistols. We have frequently seen good foreign watches sold in the streets of Nankin for two and a half dollars. Almost every street has a Clock and Watchmaker's Shop. After the death of No. 2, No. 1 issued a proclamation that he would willingly accept any gifts of foreign make. This was looked upon by every one as a great condescension. They made no mention of the visits of the Foreign men of War, only the attempt of the sailors of the *Susquehanna* to take the Golden ball from off the once famed Porcelain Tower. They have abundance of Sulphur at Nanking, and they obtain Saltpetre by boiling the very old bricks. During our marches if we observed any Joshes the Rebels would immediately destroy them, and no one was allowed to have one in his house. Every house is furnished with their religious Books— which they do not appear to study much. They, however, are very careful of them, not allowing them to be torn or abused.

No. 2's brother in law was exceedingly amused at hearing us singing, and would, as encouragement, send out for wine for us. During our stay with them we never had any wages, but always had a few dollars given to us whenever we asked for them. They were very anxious to have foreigners in their service. Work is never suspended on their Sabbath.

42
A Letter from Mgr Danicourt
Annals of the Propagation of the Faith, vol. XIX
(March 1858), pp. 93–6

A LETTER FROM MGR. DANICOURT VICAR-APOSTOLIC OF KIANG-SI, TO M. SALVAYRE, PROCURATOR-GENERAL OF THE LAZARISTS, AT PARIS.

Kiang-si, February 17th, 1857

My Dear Confrere,

May the grace of our Lord Jesus Christ be with us for ever. During the last two or three months, our position at Kiang-si, as compared with the two preceding years, has wonderfully improved. After having been compelled to transfer the seminary of San-kia-gao to Kiou-tou, on account of the proximity of the rebels, we had been for a whole year prevented from communicating even by letter with our Confreres in the south-west of the province, after the sacking of Ki-ngan-fou,[24] which spread terror in every direction. Our movements were restricted to the district of Kouan-sin-fou, the only part that was not occupied by the insurgents and the imperialists—the former exterminating everyone that offered them resistance, and the latter pillaging everything that came in their way; the former requiring the people to wear long hair, the latter obliging them to shave their heads. For upwards of a month, we had witnessed the burning, first of a portion, and subsequently of the whole, of the suburbs of Kientchang, accompanied by the continual reports of cannons and guns; we had heard the lamentable accounts of the frightful devastations which have converted the flourishing town of Foutcheou-fou and Ya-tcheou-fou into piles of ruins, whilst, under our own observation, the open country of Kien-tchang-fou and the environs of Kien-tou were abandoned to pillage. We ourselves were obliged to ransom, at the cost of a hundred piastres, our Chinese master and one of our sick children, whom a *sipine* (rebel), of ferocious appearance, carried off from our chapel. For six months we were compelled to be constantly on the alert, for fear, on the one hand, of being killed or robbed by the imperialists, who often passed within a few hundred yards of Kiou-tou, and, on the other hand, in constant apprehension lest the rebels should pounce upon our seminary and seize our pupils to make soldiers of them. At length, after all our care and anxiety for the fate of our poor neophytes, who we knew were exposed, like the pagans, to the rapacity of the imperialists and the cruelty of the rebels, God, in His mercy, had pity on us, and through the medium of a Christian of Kien-tchang, who had been forcibly enlisted by the *sipines*, procured us an interview with the chief of the insurgents. Messrs. Amot and Montels[25] were well received by the principal officers, from whom they obtained for us permits of free circulation in all the district held by the rebels, that is, in the whole of Kiang-si; for there now only remain to complete their conquest the capital [Nanchang] and Kouang-sin-fou, two places against which an immense body of troops are now on their

24 Chi-an fu, which was captured by the Taiping early in 1856.
25 Antoine Amot was a Lazarist missionary who was stationed in Kiangsi from about 1843; Ferdinand-Felix Montels was another Lazarist stationed in Kiangsi from about 1850 and executed by Imperial authorities near Chi-an on 26 June 1857.

march, commanded by the King Y-ouang, who has left Nankin for the express purpose.

These insurgents come from Canton, and the other adjacent provinces. The chiefs are principally natives of Canton, and for the most part opium-smokers. As regards their religion, they acknowledge one God in three persons, and have some notion of the Old and New Testament, which they have obtained from the Protestants, or derived from their books. Perceiving that we are of the religion of Jesus, and that we are combating idolatry, they imagine that there is little difference between them and us. Hence, instead of molesting us, they appear favourably disposed towards us. Faithful to their oath to exterminate the worship of idols, with that of Confucius, they everywhere destroy the poussas[26] and the tablets of the national philosophy. I am induced to believe that, in the course of a few years, the religious opinions of the grandees and the people will undergo a radical transformation, because they are founded upon materialism and unrestrained cupidity, and because, on the other hand, misfortune is the great school of nations. Never was a country afflicted with greater calamities that those which have befallen China. To instance Kiang-si alone, there are, at the present day, in this province, upwards of fifteen millions of inhabitants reduced to the most abject misery.

In certain localities, the pagans, in hundreds, have undertaken to learn the catechism and the prayers,—the condition required by the faith to admit them to the grace of baptism. Since the last few years, the Europeans have met with great favour at Kiang-si; the Missioners have noticed the change of public opinion in this respect, as they pass along the roads, where they are saluted by the designation of *master* by the populace. The latter observe to them that they have seen Europeans in the free ports; that they are just, rich, and powerful men, which is the *ne plus ultra* of the title to esteem in the mind of the Chinese.

Although the revolution which China is now undergoing proceeds but slowly, in accordance with the characteristic habits of that empire,—although the revolutionary party is composed of wretches, thieves, and unprincipled vagabonds, brutalised by the use of opium, and having nothing to lose, it will be successful unless we are much deceived, because it has nothing more formidable to oppose it than a contemptible authority, detested by the people, and troops void of energy and incapable of resisting anything like a serious attack. I am convinced, like all others

26   I.e. pot bellied idols.

who are acquainted with the audacity and intrepidity of the insurgents, that in the course of two or three years, more than the half of China will be subject to their rule, unless the Europeans adopt the cause of the imperial party.

If it should please God to spare my life for a few more years, I hope to have the consolation of seeing our Sisters of S. Vincent of Paul established at Kiang-si. It appears to be the design of Providence to call them hither for the spiritual and physical salvation of the Chinese children, to act as mothers in grace to thousands of deserted children, born by their mothers according to nature. The gates of this immense empire will one day be opened to them; they will be established here, and extend and accomplish their angelic mission; they will be the support of the poor, the consolation of the dying, and the refuge of the orphan. After our long days of trial and tribulation, if Christianity, as we confidently hope, should at length obtain in China perfect liberty, so desirable a result can never by realized except by the active exercise of works of charity.

I am, &c.,
Fr X Danicourt,
Bishop of Antiphelles

43
A Letter from Rev R S McLay
Overland Register and Prices Current, Supplement 18,
15 October 1857

TO THE EDITOR OF THE 'HONGKONG REGISTER'

Fuh-chau, 9th October, 1857

Dear Sir,

The former troubles in the Western Department of this Province seem to be thoroughly settled. Trade has, apparently, resumed its usual course, and the general quiet that prevails must be most welcome to our Provincial Authorities.

It seems almost impossible to obtain reliable information with regard to the Rebels who disturbed the western portions of this Province, and threw our dignified Provincial Authorities into such a ferment of excitement and alarm. The general opinion, however, is that only a small portion of them were the Nankin, or Tai-Ping rebels: their number varying, according to report, from five hundred to five thousand. Among the Fuh-chau people they are designated Nankin rebels, Tai-Ping rebels, Long-haired rebels, or simply rebels. Either from ignorance or from fear of the present Authorities, the people of Fuh-chau appear averse to communicating definite information as to the character of these rebels. Recently I met a young man from the Department of Yenping, and from him I obtained some intelligence which, perhaps, may be reliable. He says the main body of the rebels numbered about ten thousand, of whom perhaps two thousand were the Long-haired rebels. The rest of the army was made up of natives of the Province, whom prospect of plunder, good pay, or fear had drawn to the rebel camp. Besides this main body, controlled by the Tai-Ping rebels, there were other marauding parties prowling about the country plundering and murdering ad libitum. The Tai-Ping rebels, he says, observe one day in seven as a day for worship and rest: they have portions of the Bible which they publish, read, and distribute: they destroy Budhist temples and kill Budhist priests; and proclaim as their religious faith a system which is evidently founded on the institutes of Moses. With regard to their treatment of the people, my informant said it was authoritative and severe but not wantonly cruel. He denounced, however, in the strongest terms the atrocities committed by the independent bands of plunderers who ravaged and desolated the country: and by portions even of the main army acting under the Tai-Ping leaders. In such a heterogeneous mass of Chinese it would, of course, be impossible to maintain strict military discipline, or prevent all acts of rapine and cruelty. It will not therefore be just, without clear evidence of their guilt, to charge upon these Tai-Ping rebels the violent outrages upon decency and the common instincts of humanity which their comrades are said to have perpetrated; at the same time it is somewhat difficult to conceive very highly of the mental or moral status of persons, in any way, connected with such atrocities . . .

Yours faithfully,

RSM

44
An Intelligence Report by T F Wade
FO 17/273, no. 431, enc. in Bowring to Clarendon,
29 November 1857

The period considered in the present summary of the *Peking Gazettes*, extends from the end of July to the middle of October. There is nothing to note to the advantage of the Imperial cause. The T'ai P'ing insurgents are immovable, still occupying, less exclusively perhaps on the south bank, an important section of the Yang-tsz' Kiang valley, viz., from Chin-kiang, in Kiang Su, up to Kiu-kiang, in Kiang Si. The chief places of the latter province are confessedly in the hands of rebels whom we may still hesitate to identify with the T'ai P'ing men. Fuh Kien and Cheh Kiang both speak, (though doubtfully) as if they were relieved from their invaders on the inland border; Ngan Hwui, which touches on the last, is evidently still disturbed on both sides of the Great River. In Ho Nan victories are still gained, which is not a favourable symptom; and in Shan Tung, and even in Chih Li, there is like evidence of the presence of an enemy. In Hu Peh there are still military movements. Hu Nan appears quiet. Kwang Tung and Kwang Si have too much active service on hand to admit of attention to the formality of the periodical inspections, and the "barbarian affair" figures as increasing Yeh's difficulties in politics and finance. Kwei Chau is still troubled by its Miau Tsz' aborigines, and Yun Nan by its Mahometan population. Lastly, the Mahometan Colonies in the farthest west of the empire, have been sufficiently disturbed to render necessary the movement of troops from different points, at great distance from the scene of operations . . .

In KIANG SU the great fact remains, that Nanking and Chin-kiang are in the hands of the rebels; but the recovery of Lih-shwui, noticed before was followed up, on the 15th July, by that of Ku-yung, which was carried in so brilliant a fashion by a night attack, that Hoch'un is made a Guardian of the Crown Prince, and the ex-rebel, Chang Kwoh-liang, presented with a yellow riding-jacket. The despatches of Ho Kwei-tsing, the new Governor General, which are numerous, tell us little else about the fighting; the Spirit of the District city of Kin-tan, in Chin-kiang Fu, he thinks deserves a title of honor, for personal intervention when the city was attacked some time ago. He also brings to notice a contribution of 10,000 taels by one officer, a native of the province, and another of 45,000 by the gentry of Shan-yang, in Hwai-ngan Fu: the last a truly patriotic and zealous act, which, he recommends, should be rewarded by an augmentation of the number of degrees, civil and military, to which the District is entitled . . .

In NGAN HWUI, there is not much detail of movements, but a pretty general admission of disquiet. Late in July, Shautsan, who commands in the north of the province, prays that six magistrates who should properly retire to mourn their parents may be required to postpone that filial duty until the war in Ngan Hwui is ended; some being engaged in defence and extermination, and others in the collection and disbursement of revenue: duties which it will not be well to commit to inexperienced hands. Across the Yang-tsz', late in October, Ho Kwei-tsing, Governor

General prefers a similar request in the case of a General, and later still, when the Commander-in-Chief of the Chinese provincial army and another General withdraw to mourn, he requests particular care in the selection of substitutes, as outlaws (or rebels) are to be found all over the south of the province. After applying for a seal for the General of a new Division lately added to the military establishment of the Province, he proceeds to observe, that although there is, *for the time being*, peace in the Prefectures of Hwui-chau and Ning-kwoh, the Prefectural city of Chi-chau-fu and Wu-hu, a District city in T'ai-p'ing Fu, are not yet retaken...

In KIANG SI, no victories are reported that affect the unhappy *status quo* of the Province. In the earliest memorial of our period, published in the beginning of September, Kiling highly commends two civilians belonging to the province for their activity at Hing-kwoh in the south. Two attacks on the city had been repulsed, and great exertions had been made to supply the army; but this seems an old affair. Presently we find him apologising for his inability to forward his autumn revenue; that of the spring was sent on in April, but 'the different prefectural cities taken this year by outlaws are not yet recovered, and the tribute cannot be forwarded by the time required by law'. Towards the end of the moon he has opened a sale of rank, and his levying a fractional 'benevolence' on trade, also called, like the purchase of rank, a 'subscription to meet military expenses,' which are heavy...

In FUH KIEN the story of the rebellion is retrospective. Rebels from Kiang Si crossed the border at the end of May, apparently invading Ting-kwoh Fu, Yen-ping Fu, and Shau Wu Fu, at the same time. Shun-chang, near the prefectural city of Yen-ping, was taken on the 26th May, but speedily recovered; the rebels, who had stormed the Imperialist camp, *sneaking* away. Kien-ning in Shau wu, fell on the 17th June, but was promptly reoccupied, the rebels moving north, and quitting the prefecture altogether. Still a Decree of the 16th August, acknowledging this intelligence, desires Wang I-teh, the Governor-General, to retake Siuen-hwa (? Kwei hwa) without delay. On the 20th September, another Decree of the 4th October, excuses the Commissioners of Finance and Justice from the penalties to which the fact of rebellion within the province should render them liable; the Governor General having represented that they had worked hard to put it down, when it did break out...

Section 3 Contact Renewed (1858–9)

A decisive new stage in the history of Western relations with the Taiping began with the end of the second Opium War. The Treaties of Tientsin which concluded that war in 1858, though not finally ratified until late in 1860, gave the Western powers the right to sail upon the Yangtze and to open three new treaty ports along its lower reaches—Hankow, Kiukiang and Chinkiang. Much of the river between the latter two cities was at that time still in Taiping hands, and the treaties therefore provided that the actual implementation of the new right for Westerners to sail upon and trade along the Yangtze should be delayed until such time as the rebellion was suppressed. However, Lord Elgin, who negotiated the British treaty, persuaded the Imperial authorities to allow him to make an exploratory voyage as far as Hankow, six hundred miles up river, in return for British concessions on the question of diplomatic representation and residence in Peking. Elgin's main object was to ensure that the newly won right to sail upon the great river was seen immediately to be a reality, despite a possibly long delay in its full enjoyment for Westerners. But a second consideration was, naturally, that such a voyage would provide an opportunity for the British to observe the Taiping once more at close quarters.

Elgin's expedition left Shanghai on 8 November 1858 and returned on New Year's day 1859, after traversing the whole length of the Yangtze held by the Taiping. Brief stops were made at several points within Taiping territory, including Nanking. There was some exchange of gunfire on the way up river, but not on the return voyage and Elgin, like all the high level Western officials who had preceded him, did not himself engage in talks with rebel leaders. He delegated this role to his chief interpreter, T. F. Wade, whose critical private account supplements Elgin's own coolly appraising official report (Docs. 45, 46). Unlike the earlier British expeditions, Elgin's did include a missionary representative, Alexander Wylie, of the London Missionary Society, who wrote reports decidedly pessimistic in tone both for his society and for the British Admiralty (Docs. 47, 48).

No immediate action or change in British policy resulted from Elgin's voyage. Events in central and north China during 1859 and 1860 were to lead Elgin subsequently to take, briefly, a more positive view of the Taiping than is apparent in the report given below. But this voyage, providing as it did an opportunity for a more extensive examination of Taiping territory than had been attempted previously, was pointing the way towards the much closer and more varied contacts with the Taiping that Westerners were to experience during 1860–2.

45
A Report by Lord Elgin
BPP, 1859, C.2571, no. 228, pp. 440–5, Elgin to the British Foreign Secretary, Earl of Malmesbury, 5 January 1859

My Lord,

IN my despatch of the 5th of November, 1858, adverting to certain objects beyond the express provisions of the Treaty of Tien-tsin, which I was desirous to obtain from the Chinese Imperial Commissioners, I took the liberty of making the following remark:—

'The Treaty-right to navigate the Yang-tze, and to resort to ports upon that river for purposes of trade, was also made contingent on the re-establishment of the Imperial authority in the ports in question; because, as we have seen fit to affect neutrality between the Emperor of China and the rebels, we could not, of course, without absurdity, require him to give us rights and protection in places actually occupied by a Power which we treat with the same respect as his own. Nevertheless, it is important that it should be known to Chinese and foreigners, that the Emperor has conceded, in principle, the opening up of the river; and I have long thought that if I could contrive to go up it in person, with the consent of the Imperial Government, under the plea of selecting the ports which would be most suitable for foreign trade, it would be a very effectual way of tendering to the public the required assurance on this point. It is only, however, by conciliating the goodwill of the Imperial Commissioners that this result can be brought about; for, until the Treaty of Tien-tsin is ratified, I have clearly no title to go up the river as a matter of right.'

In my further despatch of the same date, I inclosed the copy of a letter which I had addressed to the Imperial Commissioners, apprizing them of my intention to proceed up the River Yang-tze without delay, for the purpose of inspecting its ports, and determining which of them it will be most advisable to open to foreign trade, together with a copy of the reply made by them to that communication ... I have now the honour to submit, for your Lordship's information, a Report of the proceedings adopted by me in pursuance of the intention above stated ...

Having ... satisfied myself of the propriety of making an attempt to ascend the Yang-tze to Hankow, and having, moreover, as I reported in my despatch to your Lordship, of November 6th, succeeded in inducing the Chinese Imperial Commissioners to acquiesce in the proceeding, I addressed myself directly (there being no time for previous communication with Sir M. Seymour) to Captain Barker, of Her Majesty's steam-frigate 'Retribution,' requesting him to accompany me on my proposed expedition, with the vessels of war which the Admiral had placed under his command at the period of my voyage to Jeddo. It being, in my opinion, of the utmost importance that the expeditionary force should be sufficiently large to convey a suitable impression of British power to the inhabitants of the great centres of Chinese population, which were now, for the first time, about to be visited by foreigners, I also intimated to Commander Ward of Her Majesty's surveying-ship 'Actaeon,' that I thought the public service would be benefited if he were to avail himself of the opportunity to effect as accurate a survey as circumstances might permit of the River Yang-tze. ... I embarked on board Her Majesty's steam-frigate 'Furious,' at 1 p.m., on Monday, the 8th November, immediately after signing, at a formal interview with the Imperial Commissioners, the Tariff and Additional Articles transmitted in my despatch to your Lordship, of that day's date. At about the same hour on Monday, the 6th of December, after a voyage of four weeks, we anchored off Hankow, a commercial mart of great magnitude and importance, situated in the very heart of China, at a distance of some 600 miles from the sea. We left that place on our return voyage on the 12th of December, reaching Shanghae on the 1st of January.

This expedition, which has thus occupied, as your Lordship will gather from the foregoing statement, a period of nearly eight weeks' duration, proved to be even more instructive and fertile in incident than I anticipated at the time when I originally planned it. Much, however, of the valuable information obtained being of a professional character will, no doubt, reach the Lords Commissioners of the Admiralty through persons more competent than myself to do it justice.

Being conscious, therefore, that if I were to dwell on such details I should be trespassing needlessly on your Lordship's time, I shall confine myself in this communication to some observations of a more general character ...

The knowledge of the Chinese language possessed by Messrs. Wade and Lay enabled me to enter, without difficulty, into communication with the inhabitants of the towns and rural districts which we visited. At various points in our progress we wandered, unarmed and unattended, in parties of three or four, to a distance of several miles from the banks of the river, and we never experienced at the hands of the natives anything but courtesy, mingled with a certain amount of not very obtrusive curiosity. Notwithstanding, however, these favourable opportunities, the budget of statistical facts which I was able to collect was hardly as considerable as I could have desired. Chinamen of the humbler class are not much addicted to reflection, and when subjected to cross-examination by persons greedy of information, they are apt to consider the proceeding a strange one, and to suspect that it must be prompted by some exceedingly bad motive. Moreover, having been civilized for many generations, they carry politeness so far, that in answering a question it is always their chief endeavour to say what they suppose their questioner will be best pleased to hear. If, therefore, the knowledge of a fact is to be arrived at, it is, above all things, necessary that the inquiry bear a tint so neutral that the person to whom it is addressed shall find it impossible to reflect its colour in his reply. He will then sometimes, in his confusion, blunder into a truthful answer, but he does so generally with a bashful air, indicative of the painful consciousness that he has been reluctantly violating the rules of good breeding. A search after accurate statistics, under such conditions, is not unattended with difficulty.

Nevertheless, the inquiries made in various quarters by myself and my companions, have led me to some general conclusions, in which I am disposed to place a certain amount of confidence. In the first place, I am inclined to believe that there is little or nothing of popular sympathy with the rebel movement, in the sense which we give to that phrase in Europe. It is no doubt true that the general attitude of the population does not argue much enthusiasm on either side of the dynastic controversy; and it is also certain that we saw more of the districts in Imperialist, than of those in rebel occupation. But the tone of the natives with whom I conversed, certainly left on my mind the impression that they viewed the rebellion with feelings akin to those with which they would have regarded earthquake, or pestilence, or any other providential scourge. When I come to describe the state of the towns which I visited, your Lordship will probably see grounds for the opinion that it is not so very surprising that the peaceful inhabitants of China should form this estimate of their interest in these revolutionary proceedings, from which some of their enthusiastic friends among foreigners at one time expected such great results.

Secondly, I am also disposed to think that the people in the districts in question anticipate generally, rather with favour than otherwise, the prospect of the resort of foreigners to their neighbourhoods for purposes of trade. When a Chinaman says that he is delighted to see one, it does not of course always answer to interpret his sentiments by the letter. But the great majority are desirous of peace and commerce, and they suppose that the presence of foreign merchants will contribute to the restoration of these blessings. It is to be hoped that we shall not disappoint these expectations, by pouring into the districts already agitated by civil dissension, the additional ingredient of foreign adventurers and foreign munitions of war.

Thirdly, I am confirmed, by what I have witnessed on this expedition, in the doubts which I have long entertained, as to the accuracy of the popular estimates of the amount of the town population of China. The cities which I have visited are, no doubt, suffering at present from the effects of the rebellion, but I cannot bring myself to believe that, at the best of times, they can have contained the number of inhabitants usually imputed to them. M. Huc puts the population of the three cities of Woo-chang-foo, Han-yang-foo, and Hankow, at 8,000,000. I doubt much whether it now amounts, in the aggregate, to 1,000,000, and even when they were flourishing, I cannot conceive where 3,000,000 of human beings could have been stowed away in them.

And, fourthly, what I have seen leads me to think that the rural population of China is, generally speaking, well-doing and contented. I worked very hard, though with only indifferent success, to obtain from them accurate information respecting the extent of their holdings, the nature of their tenure, the taxation which they have to pay, and other kindred matters. I arrived at the conclusion that, for the most part, they hold their lands, which are of very limited extent, in full property from the Crown, subject to certain annual charges of no very exorbitant amount; and that these advantages, improved by assiduous industry, supply abundantly their simple wants, whether in respect of food or clothing. In the streets of cities in China some deplorable objects are to be met with, as must always be the case where mendicity is a legalised institution; but I am inclined to think that the rigour with which the duties of relationship are enforced, operates as a powerful check on pauperism. A few days ago a lady here informed me that her nurse had bought a little girl from a mother who had a surplus of this description of commodity on hand. I asked why she had done so, and was told, that the little girl's husband, when she married, would be bound to support the adopting mother. By the judicious investment of a dollar in this timely purchase, the worthy woman thus secured for herself a provision for old age, and a security, which she probably appreciates yet more highly, for decent burial when she dies.

During the period of my detention at Silver Island, I walked over Chin-kiang-foo, where I had an opportunity of witnessing for the first time the fruits of the rebellion. This wretched city has been taken and retaken, and has experienced therefore the tender mercies both of rebels and Imperialists. I never before saw such a scene of desolation. A wall of considerable circumference surrounding heaps of ruins, intersected by a few straggling streets, is all that remains of a town which was supposed to contain, in 1842, 300,000 inhabitants. In order to save repetition I may here observe, once for all, that, with certain differences of degree, this was the condition of every city which I visited on my voyage up and down the Yang-tze.

In one of my rambles in the vicinity of Silver Island, I found in a cottage which I entered, two men smoking opium. They told me that it was of foreign growth, the native article being inferior in quality; that they smoked at the rate of 80 cash (4d.) worth a-piece per day; 120 cash, or 6d., being the ordinary amount of the daily earnings of each. I asked them how they could support their families if they spent so much in smoking. They shrugged their shoulders, and said that when times were bad they were obliged to reduce their allowance. I may observe, however, that at Hankow I saw shops where native opium was openly advertised for sale.

Soon after leaving Silver Island, we passed the mouth of the Great Canal, which we found to be entirely deserted, save by a few Imperialist war-vessels. Captain Osborn[27] informed me that, when he was at the same place in 1842, the grain-junks were so numerous that it was difficult to force a way through them. Your Lordship may perhaps remember that when, in April last, I resolved to bring pressure to bear on the Emperor by ascending the Peiho river to Tien-tsin, it was remarked in some quarters that we ought rather to have followed the precedent of the former war, and to have instituted blockade in the River Yang-tze. I thought at the time that this suggestion was an anachronism, and what I have seen on this trip confirms that opinion. We could hardly have done more than the rebels have done to inflict suffering on the population, and render these districts unproductive to the Government, and yet no effect has been produced by these proceedings on the Court of Pekin.

27 Capt. Sherard Osborn was at this time the Commander of Elgin's flagship HMS *Furious*. He was later to be involved with H. N. Lay in the Anglo-Chinese flotilla scheme—see Gerson, op. cit., chs. 7–8.

On the evening of the same day we passed the city of Nankin, and as the occurrences which took place there were of a somewhat critical character, I consider it my duty to narrate them in detail.

When, at the commencement of November, I satisfied myself that it was proper that I should endeavour to ascend the River Yang-tze to Hankow, and obtained the assent of the Imperial Commissioners to the proceeding, I, of course, resolved that no human power, and no physical obstacle which could be surmounted, should arrest my progress. It was obviously essential to the prestige of England, that a measure of this description, if undertaken at all, should be carried out; I could not, therefore, recognize in the rebels a right to stop me, nor could I take any step which they might construe into such an admission. Subject to this limitation, I was ready to give them every assurance that our movement was of a peaceful character, and that we did not intend to take part, one way or another, in the civil war to which they were parties.

The naval officers by whom I was accompanied were fully cognizant of these views. In order, however, to prevent misapprehension in a matter of so much delicacy, I addressed, on the 20th of November, a short Memorandum to Captain Barker, a copy of which, together with the copy of a letter from him to me, inclosing his instructions to Lieutenant Jones of the 'Lee', are inclosed in my subsequent despatch.[28]

At about 4 o'clock in the afternoon of that day, the gun-boat 'Lee' steamed under the forts which protect the river-front of the city of Nankin; she was about a mile and a-half in advance of the other ships of the squadron, having on board of her Mr. Wade, who had instructions from me as to the language which he was to hold to the rebel chiefs, in case an opportunity for conferring with them should present itself. Her orders were: if a boat came off, to communicate with it; if a shot were fired, to hoist a white flag; and if the white flag were fired on, to await futher directions before replying to it. These orders were carried out by Lieutenant Jones with the fidelity and good judgment which has characterized, throughout, his proceedings on this expedition. . . .

It was a lovely evening, and I was on the paddle-box of the 'Furious,' anxiously watching the progress of the gun-boat, as it was my earnest wish to avoid, if possible, a collision with the rebels. She had already passed several of the forts unmolested, and I was beginning to think that my wishes on this point were

28   For the text of this memorandum see the source of this document, p. 452.

about to be realized, when a puff of smoke, followed by the boom-ing of a cannon, undeceived me. Seven additional shots were fired on the flag of truce before the British ships proceeded to reply.

By this time the other vessels of the squadron were within range of the nearest forts, which opened upon them with all the vigour of which they are capable. They steamed slowly by, return-ing, with considerable effect, the fire directed against them. Most of the vessels were repeatedly struck; but the only casualties which occurred were on board of the 'Retribution,' where one midshipman, a gallant youth of the name of Birch, received a wound, which has necessitated the amputation of his arm; one seaman was killed, and another badly injured.

We anchored for the night immediately above the city; but the naval officers accompanying me held the opinion, which I entirely shared, that it would not do to leave this matter where it then stood. Although the rebels had had a good deal the worst of it in the transactions of the afternoon, it was impossible to say what view they might take of the result, if, without further notice of their conduct to us, we were to proceed quietly on our voyage. Besides, as we were about to grope our way in the dark for some hundreds of miles through unknown perils, both of navigation and politics, it was equally impossible to say in what guise we might present ourselves on our return, or what inconveniences might arise if the rebels had any doubt as to whether we or they were the stronger party. It was therefore determined that we should re-descend the river in the morning, and punish severely some of the forts which had fired upon us. This measure was successfully carried out. The rebels, exhausted, apparently, by their exertions of the previous night, hardly ventured a reply. After about an hour and a-half, enough having been done to effect the object desired, Captain Barker, with, I think, excellent judgment, gave orders that the firing should cease, and that the force should proceed on its way.

On the evening of the same day, a trifling affair took place at an isolated fort a few miles below the city of Tai-ping, near which we anchored for the night. It had the effect of inducing the rebel authorities to make a communication to me, and enabled me to hand to them, in return, a notification which I had prepared in the morning for delivery on the first occasion that should offer itself. Translations of both documents are inclosed in my despatch of the 6th instant.

On the following day I received from them a verbal message, of an informal character, expressing contrition for what had happened, and adding the assurance that we should not be again molested. The assurance in question was, I am disposed to believe, given in sincerity; for, although we afterwards passed several rebel forts and stations, we were not again meddled with, until we reached Ngan-ching, between which point and Nankin it is probable that the communications are uncertain and slow.

Finding them in these improved dispositions, we anchored for the night on the afternoon of the 23rd of November, off Woo-hoo, a town in their occupation, at a distance of about 250 miles from the sea. Mr. Wade, by my desire, went on shore at this place, in order to put himself into communication with the authorities. They were civil, but, as your Lordship will gather from his Report forming Inclosure No. 1 of this despatch, not, to all appearance, in a very flourishing condition.

The town of Kieu-hien, at which the "Retribution" remained when we left her on our way up the river, is at no great distance from Woo-hoo, which enabled Captain Barker to receive from the rebels, during my absence, certain communications, of which more will be said hereafter.

At about noon on the 26th of November, we reached Ngan-ching, the town furthest up the river, which is now in possession of the rebels. As we were passing it, several shots were fired at us. We adopted, in this instance, a policy precisely similar to that followed by us at Nankin. The provocation being less grave, the chastisement was proportionately less severe. The whole affair did not last above half-an-hour. As the result has since proved, it was, however, sufficient for the purpose.

Between this point and Hankow our voyage was not marked by any very striking incident, although at all times, the novelty, and at some the grandeur, of the scenes through which we were passing, coupled with the uncertainties attending the navigation of an unknown river, maintained those concerned in a constant state of more or less pleasurable excitement.

When we had advanced beyond the rebel lines, greater signs of commercial activity displayed themselves on the river, although I should observe that the rebels do not appear in any part to command it beyond the range of their guns. Nowhere did we see any rebel junks, and both Nankin and Ngan-ching were closely beleaguered by Imperial fleets. . . .

46
An Account by T F Wade
FO 17/371, no. 29, enc. in Bruce to Russell, 10 April 1862[29]

News from Nan-king, and possibly the ten-inch admonitions of the 26th Nov., had changed the mood of the insurgents. They were all apology and civility. Their firing before was all a mistake, which would never be repeated. So the gunboats passed down without noticeable incident, until the 27th, when they learned at Kiu Hien that the *Retribution*, finding the water fallen to the tenth foot below its earlier level, had run down to Wu-hu. Below this it will be remembered she had touched on the 22nd Nov., but she now crossed the flat under guidance of the gunboats, and descended with them past Tai-ping and the presumptuous little batteries in its vicinity, to the neighbourhood of Nan-king. As gunboats would have to communicate with the *Furious* and *Cruiser* throughout the winter, Lord Elgin deemed it advisable that there should be no farther question about the flag. Four gentlemen accordingly landed, and after a weary ride in the snow, entered the ancient capital by one of the gates on its western face. Nothing could present a more forlorn appearance than the interior of this city, which in its better days must have been fair to see. The streets are broad and sightly; comparatively few houses in ruins; but the population was elsewhere, and a mournful stillness and absence of life was everywhere remarkable. A chief named Li,[30] of high rank in the Tai-ping establishment, received the party, who pronounced him a constrained, uninteresting personage. From him they learned that Hung Siu-tsiuen still reigned as T'ai P'ing Wang; that Yang Siu-tsing, the King of the East, was *in heaven*; that his, Li's force, was some millions strong; that trade was interdicted in Nan-king, the heavenly capital; that no new books, the calendar excepted, were obtainable; that the brethren celebrated worship in their houses every day, and once a week at the place of worship in T'ai P'ing's heavenly court; that they, the party, might visit the court if they would stay the night, but that unless invited, he could not himself repair thither. The firing on the 20th Nov. had been the mistake of ignorant men and would never be repeated. A Cantonese he sent to reconduct his visitors, who were obliged to leave him after but a short inter-

29 This unofficial account was privately printed as a broadsheet by Wade soon after the return of the expedition; a copy is to be found in the source as indicated. For Wade's official report see *BPP*, 1859, C.2571, pp. 450–2.
30 Presumably Li Ch'un-fa. L. Oliphant in his *Narrative of the Earl of Elgin's Mission to China and Japan* (Edinburgh, 1859), vol. II, p. 548 gives the title of this official as Yih-tien-fuh, a title given to Li Ch'un-fa in 1858.

view, was more intelligent and communicative. He begged a passage on board the ships-of-war; this being impossible, he was ready to buy revolvers or opium, which he smoked himself, as did one-third of the inhabitants of Nan-king. He admitted the death by violence of Yang, and the badness of the T'ai P'ing Wang case, but seemed not cast down; confident that the war would last long, each side being in the habit of running away when the other attacked. The great head of insurrection he put in Ngan Hwui. It was dark before the north gate was gained. This was closed, but the state of the watch was such there and throughout, that it would be hard to say how small a body of resolute men would suffice to surprise the city. It is remarkable, that amongst the many proclamations posted on the walls, one issued by Li himself enjoined the inhabitants to trade, as their poverty was great.

This rambling narrative has already far exceeded its proposed dimensions. It is enough to add, that the *Lee* quitting the rest, ran safely on and landed her live freight at Shanghai, upon the 1st January, 1859, and so the tour was ended, which most people interested in China were agreed it was a duty to make, and of which the same holders of opinions will not fail to admit the importance.

That which seemed most untoward was to no slight extent of advantage. The period of the year may be pronounced ill-chosen, but had the fleet reached Han-k'au a fortnight earlier, it would have returned with a very false impression of the navigability of the river above Wu-hu, up to which point the influence of tide is certainly felt. As it is, there can be no doubt that while nothing but steamers will ever profitably navigate a current so strong in a bed so tortuous, no steamer drawing more than nine or ten feet will be able to run the whole year.

None will run at all, it is to be presumed, till the valley is cleared of rebels; an awkward condition truly. These gentry, it may be thought, have been very flippantly treated in this paper, and the writer is compelled to own that, without any strong prejudice originally against the T'ai P'ing movement, nothing that has been written about them, had satisfied him of the probability that they were to supply a better order of things than what it is the manifest tendency of this insurrection to overthrow. Its mongrel Christianity appears less intent on emancipating itself from, than compounding itself with, the mixture of superstitions of which the popular religion of modern China is composed, and to her political condition, to judge from our experience of this new regime, it offers even less of hope than the elder Confucian teaching with which it cannot co-exist. The half fanatical vigour that at first seemed to animate the great rebellion, is, to all appearance, extinct at its head quarters. It may be premature to declare that it has degenerated into pure and simple brigandism, but its leaders have so far established their incompetence to govern a country like China, that to her well-wishers the decline of their power must be matter of satisfaction. And it is undoubtedly on the wane. The almost perfect freedom of the river from junks bearing the rebel flag, confirms the report of the Chin-kiang officials, that all the rebel fleets had been recently destroyed by the renegade Chang Kwoh-liang, an insurgent chief who deserted to the Imperialists three or four years ago. On the waters not traversed by Imperial war-junks, there are not either any merchant junks of more than a peddling character, and very few of these. In Wu-hu few shops were open, and only such as supplied the necessaries of life, opium included. The drug was openly sold. The people, whether in town or country, shewed nowhere any sympathy with the insurgents; the few questioned in their own jurisdiction, shrugged their shoulders and pleaded their helplessness. It was difficult in the places burned west of Nan-king, to get the inhabitants to say who were the authors of the destruction: you know very well, a man would answer, and then, if pressed, the long-haired men of course. It might not be safe to infer too much from this, and certainly there is proof enough that recapture by the Government is at least for the time an equal occasion of ruin with capture by the rebels. Still there is ground for the impression, that the last five years have taught the population of the Yang-tsz' Kiang valley, that there can be no trade without peace, and no hope of peace from the T'ai P'ing insurrection. The chiefs again in all the chief positions are Cantonese, and *soi-disant* Kwang Si men. The former especially have maintained their unpopular character among the people of other provinces, to whom one of the chief horrors of the war, on the other side, is the presence of the Canton war-junk men in pay of the government; most of them, doubtless, as at Shanghai in 1853-5, triads and pirates. Territorially, the T'ai P'ing dominions are now little more than one-third of the region originally overrun by them. We hear, it is true, of formidable raids made eastward, and the Cantonese *cicerone* at Nan-king, spoke specially of the expedition of the chief Shih Ta-k'ai, though he seemed not quite clear whether he was just now in Cheh Kiang or Fuh Kien; but we do not hear of the occupation of the great centres of government, and since December 1856, the rebels have lost along the Yang-tsz' alone the prefectural cities of Chin-kiang, Hwang-chau, Han-yang, and Wu-ch'ang, the two last with Han-k'au under their lee, most important as a focus of commerce, and the first of great political value as the official capital of Hu Kwang. At Nan-king, and Ngan-king, they are unable apparently to force back the Imperialist lines, which are pushed to within gun-shot of their walls. On the other hand, as they seem to exist everywhere rather by the sluggishness of their unenergetic foe, than by any inherent ability of their own, it is melancholy to reflect that, however shorn of dynastic pretension, the motley, planless, insurrection may be long protracted, and without a vestige of capability to reconstruct the edifice it has done something to undermine, may with other troubles, owing birth like itself to the supineness of the authority it opposes, accomplish at last the total subversion of the present government, the torpor of which is at least to be preferred to the anarchy which would follow its dissolution.

T F Wade
Chinese Secretary

47
A Report by Rev A Wylie
FO 17/322, ff.198-200, enc. in Admiralty to Foreign Office,
2 March 1859

We hear little now of their pretensions to supreme sovereignty; their aim seems more like a struggle for existence and a savage determination to retaliate on the Imperial forces.

Much has been said about the religious character of the movement, and several circumstances in their history forbid the charge that it has all originated in imposture. The books they have published, although they indicate little in the way of literary ability, and a number of them contain a large admixture of error and fanaticism, yet seem to point to some originating motive more pure than other circumstances would imply...

It is very evident that there is little feeling of security among the people in the territories under their control, for it is a necessity with them to victimize every man of opulence who comes within their reach; hence we find nothing worth the name of commerce in their neighbourhood, and the few unfortunate shopkeepers who remain in their limits seem to be merely eking out a miserable existence. The leaders are tolerably well supplied with money and can thus induce many of the country people in the vicinity to bring them in supplies from day to day. The conscripts who are pressed into the service are frequently drawn from the peasantry, who hold aloof from all dealings with them. These require to be more strictly guarded than the original body, to whom are committed all positions of confidence . . .

They seem to be very poorly supplied with arms and ammunition, and it is a great desideratum with them to obtain a stock of foreign musketry.

There is very little discipline apparent in their camps, though there is a degree of stringency in some of their regulations. Opium and tobacco smoking, although not now pursued with the vigour that it was formerly, is yet a very common practice among them. Spirits also may be obtained in small quantities in their territory. Prostitution is said to be very uncommon. . . .

48
A Report by Rev A Wylie
Missionary Magazine and Chronicle, vol. XXIII (July 1859), pp. 179–81

From the large and formerly important city of Chin-keang-foo, at the mouth of the Grand Canal as far as Kew-heen (and I believe the description will apply for several hundred miles higher up), the banks of the river present a most complete scene of desolation—flourishing cities turned into literal masses of ruins, peasantry forced from their humble tenements, all trade at a stand, and scarcely a vessel, with the exception of war junks, to be seen on the mighty stream. This is no doubt a natural consequence of civil war, but it is lamentable to see one of the fairest portions of the country, abandoned to such a state of strife as it has been for this past six years, and with no prospect of a settlement of the impending contention. In estimating the comparative strength of contending parties, I would say the superiority of the insurgents is rather due to the imbecility of the imperialists than to anything really super-Chinese in the Tae-ping force. As matters now stand, there is little appearance of either party gaining the complete ascendancy, while the great bulk of the people, who wish to stand aloof from the contest, are the victims of the continued disorders. From Nanking, as far up as Ganking, the country on both sides of the river may be said to be almost entirely in the hands of the insurgents, the imperialist forces being stationed intermediately at various small towns and villages. Such was the town of Keu-heen, where we stayed, a general with two or three thousand men under him being located there. Like every other town along the banks, it has been visited by the rebels, who have left a token of the fact in a considerable proportion of the houses being laid in ruins. The temples have been especially marked out for destruction, and I find that is an invariable practice with them, for there is not a single temple for idol worship to be seen anywhere within their reach. In the temple of the god of War, nothing remains but a semi-calcined marble tablet, and a pivot of clay seated on a pedestal, which formed the nucleus of the grim idol—apparently reproaching his besotted worshippers for their folly. While thus unsparing in their iconoclastic zeal, however, they have habitually respected the ancestral halls, implying at least the toleration, if not the practice, of this deep-rooted form of Chinese worship. The destruction of the temples seems to be very little heeded generally by the people, who are very willing to leave them in their present dilapidated condition, till more pressing wants are first attended to. The usual indifference prevails on religious subjects, but I did not find any special aversion to Christianity in consequence of the name of Jesus being adopted by the insurgents, nor are the people indisposed to listen to the exposition of the Christian truth. Beyond that, I cannot state any further encouragement. Christian books were gladly received, but the number of readers in the region to which I had access was exceedingly limited. There was no appearance of the existence of Roman Catholicism, but I found Mohammedan mosques still standing among the ruins at Chin-keang and Nanking, and one demolished at Teih-keang.

Having spent a week, on our homeward journey, at the insurgent city of Woo-hoo, I had some opportunity of acquiring information regarding that party. The early history of at least an influential section of that body, as it has been given to the public, is sufficient to enlist our sympathy in their progress; but there is doubtless much yet remains undeveloped, which might account for the incongruities that strike an observer. The fact is indisputable that the Christian religion, in some form, must have exercised a powerful influence at the origin of the movement, but their present position is, I think, a very questionable attitude for the disciples of Christ.

While at Woo-hoo, I learned from some of them that they attributed their initiation into the doctrine to the late Dr Gutzlaff, a fact which I had not heard before, although I think it extremely probable that that most energetic man, through the native agency of his Christian Union, may have had a very important share in the establishment of the Society of *God worshippers*. The fact that they have adopted, and still continued to publish, his translations of the Bible (a part of which I procured from them at Nanking), is also evidence in favour of this view. As they still publish books and issue manifestoes explicitly acknowledging one supreme God and Jesus as the Saviour of the world, we may suppose that the Christian element, as it exists among them, is countenanced in influential quarters. As it extends to the multitude, I am led to believe that its influence must be very feeble indeed. The monstrous doctrine they have adopted of Hung-seu-tseuen being the second son of God, and on a par with Jesus Christ, however it may be excused by reference to historical parallels, is, I fear, a most serious obstacle to their humble reception of the truth as it is in Jesus, as they have put forward this claim not only as a great theological but as a political truth, on which they have staked the success of their cause; and in the late despatch for Lord Elgin, which I received from a relative of Hung's, there is almost as high a claim put forward for Yang-seu-tsing. They say that as Jesus is the Saviour of the world from sin, Yang-seu-tsing, is the saviour of the world from sickness—the one the physician of the soul, the other of the body. Yang has been dead, we know, for several years; there is great reason to believe that the demise of Hung is of still earlier date. These pretensions do not seem to excite any degree of enthusiasm among the numerous followers, among whom there is little in their conduct to distinguish them from other Chinese, further than they are bound by certain stringent disciplinary regulations. They are, indeed, free from every vestige of idol worship, which is an important step, and will, I believe, tell powerfully on the future history of China. Opium-smoking, the bane of China, although severely prohibited by their laws, is not entirely suppressed, as some of the officers acknowledged to me that they smoked it; but the practice is very much less common than among other Chinese, and is not done openly at all. Neither did I see tobacco-smoking among them, although it is almost universal among other Chinese. The more particular practice of Christianity seems to be left very much to the chief officers, whom I found to be invariably men from the west and south, who had come up at the original irruption. These are also the preachers to the people; but I fancy their expositions must be very infrequent. Some of them I spoke with laid great stress on their observations of the Sabbath every seventh day, which is carefully marked in their almanacs on the same day as ours, but I found the great bulk of the people had no knowledge of which was the Sabbath day. There is no public acknowledgement made of it in Woo-hoo, nor indeed have they public worship of any kind. This was explained to me by the fact of Woo-hoo being a camp, and they refer to Nanking as the place for public preaching. As I was anxious to visit their chapel when at Nanking we made particular inquiries for it, but were informed that it was in the palace of the prince, which we could not visit without sending in a communication previously, which would have detained us another day, and was consequently impracticable. As far as I could learn, the only form of worship common among them is a grace said by the officers at meals. The circulation of the Scriptures by them in an uncorrupted form is a redeeming feature in their practice, and is calculated to induce the hope that, under judicious instruction, they might be led to abandon their errors and submit to the precepts of the Great Teacher. Is their present standing, however, consistent with such a hope? I confess I see a great difficulty in the way, and I fear that difficulty will apply in some measure to any Mission undertaken in their favour. Not that I think such a Mission altogether impracticable, but it will require extreme prudence on the part of any who should undertake it; for if we admit the fact that the conduct of the body is inconsistent with the principles of Christian doctrine—and I do not see how it can be denied—no Christian man will feel justified in sympathising to that extent in their cause; hence arises the difficulty.

3
The Later Years 1860–4

In 1859–60, under capable new military leaders, the Taiping movement erupted for the second time on a grand scale, breaking completely out of the loose Imperial encirclement of Nanking and launching a series of wide ranging campaigns through the provinces of central China. Now at last they drove towards the coast, capturing great cities such as Soochow and attacking, in August 1860, the treaty port of Shanghai. This resurgence, coming as it did when the Ch'ing dynasty was suffering defeat and humiliation at the hands of the British and French in the last phases of the second Opium War, seemed once again to presage a change of dynasty.

The Ch'ing dynasty in fact survived, mainly through the determined efforts of provincial Chinese gentry and officials who, with some Western assistance, were able to turn the tide decisively against the Taiping by 1862, and to besiege them once more, this time ever more closely, in their capital. By mid 1864 Nanking was recaptured and the main force of the Taiping at last destroyed. A few remnants fought on in other places for some time, but by the end of 1864 the Taiping Tienkuo no longer posed a major threat to the Ch'ing, or a problem for the West.

Western contact with the movement during these last years once again fluctuated considerably. The Taiping victories of 1859–61 brought them very close to what was now the main Western base in China at Shanghai, which they would almost certainly have captured but for Western intervention. But even short of the actual occupation of Shanghai their presence in the countryside around it, plus their capture of nearby Soochow and, in December 1861, of the lesser treaty port of Ningpo, made inevitable much more frequent, varied and sustained contacts for many more Westerners than had been possible hitherto. There were many close encounters between Westerners and the Taiping for over two years before the rebels were forced to fall back to their last, desperate defence of Nanking during 1863 and 1864.

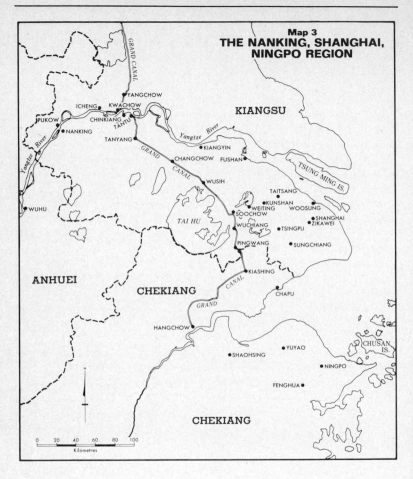

Map 3
THE NANKING, SHANGHAI, NINGPO REGION

Missionaries now constituted the main, but by no means the only, group of Westerners observing the movement at close quarters. But by the end of 1861 even those missionaries most sympathetically disposed toward it, and there were always many who could never be counted sympathetic, became fully convinced that a Taiping victory was neither likely nor desirable. As did other Westerners in China they turned their energies, and a great part of their faith, toward exploiting the gains made under the new treaties. Save for a handful of committed sympathisers, such as the military adventurer A. F. Lindley and the consul T. T. Meadows, now stationed in Newchwang, far from the Taiping, hardly any Westerners mourned the end of this great revolt. Its last years were observed by them, as its beginning had been, from a distance.

Section 1 The Missionaries Make Close Contact (1860–1)

The Protestant missionaries provided the eager vanguard of Western contact with the Taiping during 1860–1. Within a few weeks of the rebel capture of Soochow, early in June 1860, missionaries were reporting their impressions and the results of their interviews with Taiping leaders such as the Kan Wang and the Chung Wang. The prevailing tone of many of these early reports is one of hope, sometimes of almost exuberant hope as in those of the LMS representatives Griffith John and Joseph Edkins (Docs. 50, 52, 59). More qualified, even hostile, reports came from the American Baptist J. L. Holmes, the Anglican J. S. Burdon and from another representative of the LMS at Shanghai, W. Muirhead (Docs. 49, 51, 53, 57). Roman Catholic missionaries were also less disposed to view the Taiping sympathetically, especially after their mission at Zikawei, near Shanghai, was overrun (Doc. 54). On the other hand the Western missionary most favoured by the Taiping, the American Baptist I. J. Roberts, felt it worthwhile to take up residence in Nanking, where he was accorded official status and received in audience by the Tien Wang, the only Westerner ever so honoured. Though he was to leave in disgust after little more than a year in the Taiping capital, his reports during late 1860 and early 1861 indicate a kind of quizzical hope and approval (Docs. 55, 56, 58).

Until the British expedition up the Yangtze led by Rear-Admiral Sir James Hope in February–March 1861, the missionaries were almost the sole direct Western observers of the movement. Their reactions, although mixed, were on the whole more positive and committed to the Taiping cause than those any Westerners had shown since the heady days of 1853, or were to show again after the early part of 1861.

49
A Letter from Rev J L Holmes
The Commission, vol. 5 (November 1860), pp. 144–7

Thursday, 21st—We reached Qungsau about noon. Gliding through the silent suburbs of the forsaken city, we reached the gate of the city wall, on which a flag was flying. We were immediately hailed by the guard, and having assured them that our visit was a friendly one, we were visited by one of their officers and after some delay invited into the city to see the Military Mandarin in charge of the place. We were led for a long distance through streets inhabited only by the soldiers, and here and there an old woman who had braved the storm when all the rest had fled, and still clung to their homes, uninterrupted by the soldiery. The empty houses were open, and the furniture with various articles of value, which the people had left in their haste, still remained as they left them, or were tossed carelessly about. Rich garments, and thousands of their copper money, were trampled in the street, only the silver and the rarest articles of value having been taken by the victors. We at length entered the presence of a man clothed in ornamented yellow habit. He was the commanding officer of the place. We stated to him the object of our visit and inquired if we would be allowed to proceed to Suchau. He expressed himself gratified at seeing us, and assured us that he would not only not prevent our proceeding to Suchau, but would send an escort with us if we desired it, or give us a letter to the authorities at that place. After some conversation about their religious belief and the ends which they have in view, we returned to our boat. We waited till near night for the letter or the escort to come, when at last an officer came and informed us that the commander having heard that there was a band of armed villagers and country people obstructing the road, advised us to wait till he should clear the way for us. Either wait till we shall send out and have them all 'killed off', said he and then proceed, or else wait till morning and follow in the rear of the soldiers who go out. Both of these propositions we of course declined.

We had almost come to the conclusion to return to Shanghai the next day. Providentially, however, it rained very hard during the night, and the military excursion was delayed, giving us an opportunity to go on at our own risk. After the rebel chief had been informed of our willingness to proceed alone, he sent us a letter directed to the 'Middle King'[1] at Suchau. We had scarce left the city when our boatmen were hailed from the shore, and such an exaggerated account given them of the dangers of the way that they refused to proceed. They were finally induced to go a little further, and doing so we met some country people who told us that the bands of whom we had heard such formidable accounts were only armed country people who had come together to prevent the rebels from destroying their property. About ten miles farther we came upon one of these bands; at our approach they began to beat gongs and make very furious demonstrations; mistaking us for the 'long-haired' as they called the rebels. We went ashore as we neared them and taking some books in our hands walked forward to meet them. As soon as they recognized us they earnestly begged our pardon, and let us pass without further difficulty. We passed the large town of Eding, thirteen miles from Qungsau, which we found in a great measure deserted of its population of fifty or sixty thousand. All the way along from Qungsau we had seen many bodies floating in the canal and lying upon the shore; here they began to be more numerous still. Proceeding a short distance we turned aside into a small lake to spend the night. A number of fugitive people have already resorted to the same place. They were frightened and began to hurry away at our approach, but when assured of our true character came and gathered around us. So here we are already to spend the night in the midst of twenty-two families of our new made friends who hover near us as if they felt more secure for our presence.

JOURNEY TO SUCHAU, &C.

Saturday Morning, 23—Started at an early hour for Suchau. Met another armed party of men at a bridge, three miles from the city, numbering over two hundred, and in a furious state of excitement. Poor, deluded people, they had learned from the Imperial proclamations and from their proceedings, in case of such rebels as were taken, that they were only robbers of a most murderous character, and thus deceived, were taking the step that was sure to secure their own destruction. The policy of the rebels is not to harm those who quietly submit, but to destroy the lives and burn

---

1 Li Hsiu-ch-eng, the Loyal King. Holmes has misinterpreted 'Chung' as meaning middle instead of loyal.

the houses of those who take up arms against them. A cruel policy it is true, but reasonable compared with that of the Imperialists, who will kill every one of the rebel party that comes into their power—sparing neither male nor female, old nor young. We appeased them as we did the party previously met with, and passed on. Scarcely had we left them, when we saw a short distance ahead a band of rebels coming out to fight with them. We narrowly escaped being between the two parties in their battle, by turning aside into a small canal which led into a lake near at hand, and hurrying away as fast as we could. We had not proceeded far when we heard the din and saw the smoke of the battle. We crossed the lake and reached the mouth of a canal about two miles from the city. Here the boatmen obstinately refused to proceed, and leaving brother Crawford in the boat, Bro. Hartwell and myself proceeded on foot towards the city. We walked for about a mile and a half along a shady path on the bank of the canal, when we at length entered the suburbs, which had in vain been destroyed by fire to prevent the rebels from taking refuge in it, and besieging the city from this vantage ground. We walked on amid the blackened ruins, till within a short distance of the city gate.

Here an incident occurred, which we feared would lead to our being fired on from the city wall. A young rebel soldier who was walking outside the city was the first to descry us. At first seeing only myself, brother Hartwell being concealed by my person and the umbrella I carried in my hand, as he walked behind in the narrow pathway, he strutted boldly towards me with the evident design of taking me prisoner, and making a display of his valor by marching me into the city, and delivering up his prize. He carried a short sword at his side, and a very bold look upon his face. Brother Hartwell observing his approach, stepped to my side, carrying in his hand a bottle of water, which he had brought to quench our thirst, by the way; upon seeing this he turned and displayed, notwithstanding our endeavors to call him back, such a degree of fleetness as we have rarely had occasion to give a Chinaman credit for. We feared that the imagination which had transformed our innocent bottle into a revolver, would likewise transform ourselves into the advance of an army, and we should be fired upon before we could explain who we were. We providentially met, however, with a small band a few steps further on, and putting ourselves under their protection, proceeded to the city gate.

Here we had to wait till our arrival was announced. In course of time, officers were sent out to receive the letter which we had brought, a part of whom staid with us while the rest carried the letter in. We waited but a short time longer, and horses were sent, on which we were escorted into the city and carried to the house of an official, whom we afterwards ascertained was the Prime Minister of the Middle King. Here we were treated with the greatest kindness and hospitality. We were shortly visited by a mandarin, who came in and shook hands with us familiarly, and expressed himself delighted to see us in Suchau. He had found an opportunity to know something of foreigners having lived for several years in Shanghai, which accounted for his familiar mode of receiving us. He had learned that pomp and ceremony made no such impression upon us as it does upon his country-men. We informed him that we had no civil authority, and that we had no mercantile objects in view—that we were simply preachers of the gospel, and had come to preach to them and to ascertain whether they would prevent our going to preach among the people whom they governed. 'Assure your hearts', said he, 'we shall be glad to have you come, we shall be glad also to have merchants come; we have no enmity against foreigners, but are anxious to secure their friendship.' We took occasion to ask him many questions about their religious belief, civil policy, &c. We deprecated the cruelty which they had in some instances practised upon the people, to which he replied, that it was not the policy of the government to be cruel, their enmity was not against the people but against the Manchu dynasty; when such cruelties were practised it was not done with their approval, but contrary to their orders, by small bands, whom in the present disordered state of things they could neither supervise nor control.

We remained all night in the city, and spent the next day, which was the Sabbath, there also. We went to our boat in the morning, and brought a lot of Testaments and other books, a part of which we gave to them to be handed to the Middle King, and a part of which we requested should be sent to the rebel Emperor. We had no opportunity to preach publicly, but spent considerable time in talking to them of their religious belief and enquiring as to the facilities which would be enjoyed for preaching the gospel among them. In the evening we repaired to our boats, and at an early hour next morning we were on our way to Shanghai, which we reached three days afterwards without any extraordinary incidents.

We came back with much more favorable impressions of the rebels than we had carried with us, judging them by the only standard which is justly applicable to them—the Chinese one— they seem to be far in advance of the Imperialists—more liberal in their views, less selfish in their purpose, and less cruel in carrying them out. That any of them are converted men, we are not prepared to say; but that many of them have a tolerably correct idea of the leading truths of the Bible, we know from our own observation. Portions of Christian books, Scripture truths and Christian hymns were repeated to us by them. A soldier who came on board our boat at Qungsau, surprised us by repeating a doxology which was written years ago by Rev. J. L. Shuck[2]. Their soldiery is composed of a much more vigorous and healthy looking set of men than the Imperial army, and will doubtless prove their superiority in the field, if the English and French governments will only let them alone. They have possession already, as nearly as we can learn, of about one-third of China, and were foreign interference discontinued for one month, they would probably have two-thirds, if not all.

The desolate tracks of war were visible in many places that we passed, and especially in and between the two cities of Qungsau and Suchau. As we passed through the suburbs of the former, we saw not a single human being, where thousands once had their busy abodes; only the dogs sat in the doors of the deserted houses, grotesquely personating the proprietors; but even they had forgotten their usual noisy habits, and not one moved his tongue as we passed through the silent scene. Hundreds of bodies were exposed to view on the way in and about Suchau; a part of them were soldiers who had been killed, but a large portion— perhaps the larger portion—had in their infatuation drowned themselves, as the Chinese frequently do in time of a panic. But of all the heart-rending sights that met my eye, and one that will perhaps haunt my memory longest, was that of a little child which had been starved to death, as it sat propped up in a kind of chair or crib, such as the Chinese use for children who are unable to walk. Forsaken by all amid the din and confusion it had lain there and wept and moaned its little life away, and the little wasted form still reclined where it had once received the caresses of those who are now, no one knows where. I had seen floating on the stream, in distorted forms, and lying ghastly on the shore, human bodies, till my heart was sick; but the sight of none moved me as did this.

We cannot look upon this great revolution as other than a judgment of God upon this idolatrous people. Idolatry is one of

2   John Lewis Shuck was an American Baptist missionary who resided variously at Hong Kong, Canton and Shanghai between 1842 and 1852. In 1850–1 in Shanghai he was on a Committee of Protestant missionaries for translating the Old Testament into Chinese.

230

the direct occasions of the rebellion. They claim that they are appointed of God to put it down, and though we think that their zeal is 'not according to knowledge', we also think ourselves justified in the conclusion that like Cyrus of old, they are the appointed instruments of His wrath. The demolished idols were to be seen floating along the sluggish stream with those who died in their defence. That God is here making the wrath of man to praise Him, we think is very evident.

We are in suspense as to the next movement of the rebels. They are now besieging the great city of Hang Chau, and it will probably be in their possession. Suchau, which they now hold, is probably next to London, the most populous city in the world. We are all quite secure in Shanghai, inasmuch as neither rebels nor Imperialists have any designs against foreigners here, and there is so large a force here that they could not harm us if they wished.

Yours fraternally,

J L Holmes.

50
A Letter from Rev. Griffith John
Missionary Magazine and Chronicle, vol. XXIV (October 1860), pp. 270–5

In my last communication, I stated that I had some intention of visiting the Insurgents' camp, for the purpose of ascertaining for myself, the character of the movement. This intention has since been put into execution, in company with our brethren, Edkins, Macgowan, and Hall, and the result is given in letters which have appeared in the North China Herald of which I send you a copy.[3]

The week we spent in the Insurgents' territory is by far the most eventful in my history. In fact, it is the experience of a twelve-month, condensed into that of a week. We passed through many a scene of danger and trial. The second night we were in danger of being set upon by enraged and suspicious villagers. We were told, on the next day, that at one time they were on the point of beating the gongs, to summon all the villagers to action. After matters had been explained, they dispersed. The third night our boats were anchored between two fires—that of the villagers on the one hand, and the Insurgents on the other. We found afterwards however, what we did not know at the time, that the villagers were firing at a distance, so that we were in no real danger. The fourth night (and this was by far the most trying of all) we spent among dead bodies that were floating in the canal. For two or

3   See letters by 'G.J.' in the *North China Herald*, 14 and 28 July 1860.

three hundred yards our boats had actually to push through heaps of bodies, in an advanced state of decomposition. Many of these had been killed by the insurgents, but, by far, the majority were cases of suicide. In returning, also, we had many an anxious moment. But our Heavenly Father, in whom we trusted, and in whose service we were employed, was near unto us, not only to shield us from harm, but also to fill our hearts with the most implicit confidence in His presence and watchfulness. We reached Shanghae at the end of the week, and found our families in health and peace. Our object was strictly Missionary, which was not lost sight of for a moment. You will rejoice to learn of Hung Jin's advent in the insurgents' camp. I trust that this man will be the means, in the hand of God, of enlightening the chief on some very important points. He certainly deserves our warmest sympathy, and a deep interest in our prayers.

EXTRACTS FROM THE NARRATIVE OF THE TRAVELLERS
RECEPTION OF THE MISSIONARIES BY AN INSURGENT CHIEF

A party of five, consisting principally of English Missionaries, returned yesterday morning from Suchow. They went with the desire of gaining information respecting the opinions and feelings of the Insurgents, now in possession of that city, and also of communicating, as occasion should arise, information on Christianity.

The reception they met with was remarkably friendly. Proceeding towards Bing bong (Ping wang), they reached the territory now under the insurgents, at a village three miles to the southward, called Wang kia chi. A body of about a hundred horse and foot were proceeding in single file towards Bing bong, on their way from Kiahing. They stopped on seeing foreigners, and entered into friendly conversation, showing their confidence by freely partaking of cake and tea. They are many of them strong in muscle, free and bold in manner, and open in countenance, and appear to communicate their thoughts unreservedly.

Bing bong, an unwalled town, is defended by several thousand long-haired people (Insurgents), and is strongly defended by earthworks and small bamboo stakes. The officers at this place supplied their foreign visitors with passports to Suchow, and also to Wukiang, a city on the way to it. Provided with these, they went forward along the Grand Canal, noticing in many parts that the people were in the fields working, although this is one of the lines by which the Tai pings (Insurgents) pass in large and small bodies between Suchow and Kiahing. When they appear, the villagers withdraw.

At Wukiang, more state was observed in the appearance of the chief in command, it being a walled city, and the rank of chief being that of i, *right*, in the rebel nobility. This title stands immediately after that of wang (king). But the gay show here made of yellow and red banners before the residence of the chief, and his stately robe and turban of yellow, were far surpassed by the display witnessed at Suchow in the palace of the Chung wang. This chief is the conqueror of Chang kwoh liang at Tan yang, and the subjugator of Ch'ang chow, Soochow, and Kiahing. In addition to his remarkable military successes, he has the character of a good man, opposing the excesses of the troops, and protecting the suffering people, who are the victims of this civil war, from injury and insult. To his English visitors he behaved in the most friendly manner. They were allowed, on stating their objection to kneeling, to dispense with that ceremony, and appear with simply a bow, and uncovered. They had however to wait an hour and a half for the interview. This was accounted for by a visit the same evening, while they were waiting in another apartment, from the Ying wang (flourishing king), who arrived from Nanking two days before. When he was gone it was about eight P.M. The foreign party of four were then conducted to the entrance hall, where they stood for some minutes at the end of the long train of officers and servants, nearly a hundred in number, who stood facing each other in two rows. In the far interior was the Chung wang himself. After a salute of six, fired with Chinese petards, with music and gong-beating to a most deafening extent, the visitors were marshalled up the long and gorgeous vista, through which they had stolen a few glances of curiosity. After bowing, and standing before the chief for a minute, they were conducted to his right, where they stood during the interview. The hall of audience was carpeted with red. Large lanterns were held between the officers who stood on each side. They all wore robes and caps of red and yellow silk. The only person seated was the Chung wang himself. He is a man of small keen features, wears spectacles, and appears in a rich yellow robe and gold-embroidered hat after some ancient model.

Conversation then commenced. The king was informed, in answer to his inquiries, that his visitors had asked an interview as followers of the religion of Jesus, and worshippers of God the heavenly Father. The king then enumerated several leading points in Christian doctrine, and was satisfied to find that they are believed also by foreign nations. He asked what days in the cycle of twenty-eight we keep for worship, and when told that they are Fang, Hü, Mau, Sing, he observed that they are the same with theirs.[4]

When he asked if the foreign visitors had any other subject to bring forward, he was informed that they had friends and countrymen engaged in trade. It would be highly satisfactory if the silk trade should not be altogether obstructed by the presence of the Insurgents at Kiahing and Nantsin. If by some arrangement it could continue, both natives and foreigners would find it beneficial. He replied that the celestial dynasty desires this, and if trade continue, the celestial king will levy customs accordingly.

He willingly accepted an offered present of Bibles and other books, and invited the party to remain for two or three days in quarters to be provided for them. They were then, after the same salute as on entrance, conducted on horses to the residence of Lieu, a high officer of amiable disposition, who entertained them hospitably enough for the rest of the evening. On their expressing a wish to return at once to Shanghae, they were escorted on horses to their boats.

DETERMINED OPPOSITION OF THE INSURGENTS TO THE POPULAR IDOLATRY

The iconoclastic tendencies of the Tai Pings are still in full vigour. Nowhere, apparently, do they leave the idols untouched. At Bing bong, near the residence of the chief in command, a temple was noticed which has been entirely cleared of its images. A table is placed instead of the incense stand, and on it are three tea cups covered. The insurgents said that they were intended for use in offerings to the Heavenly Father.

In other temples the idols are simply mutilated or destroyed, without being removed. It is common to see the nose, chin, and hands cut off. The floors of these buildings are bestrewn with relics of helpless gods, Buddhist and Tauist, male and female. Some are cast into the canals, and are found floating down the stream mingled with the débris of rifled houses and the remains of the dead.

At Pa-ch'ih to the north of Bingbong, the temple only has been attacked. The houses on the other side have not been touched. On the walls of the temple was a proclamation exhorting the inhabitants to desert bad superstition, and worship the Heavenly Father; also to bring tribute to the ruler of the new dynasty. If they act in this way they will be well treated, otherwise they must expect punishment.

4   Fang, hsü, mao and hsing are four of the twenty-eight zodiacal signs—see Table V in *Mathews Chinese-English Dictionary* (Harvard 1952 edn.), p.1177.

THE RELIGIOUS VIEWS AND PRACTICES OF THE INSURGENTS

From the information acquired it is evident that the religious element enters very powerfully into this great revolutionary movement. Nothing can be more erroneous than the supposition that it is a purely political one, and that religion occupies but a subordinate place in it. So far is this from being the case, that, on the contrary, it is the basis upon which the former rests, and is its life-perpetuating source. The downfall of idolatry, and the establishment of the worship of the true God, are objects aimed at by them, with as much sincerity and devotion as the expulsion of the Manchus, and the conquest of the empire. In opposition to the pantheistic notions of the philosophers of the Sung dynasty, they hold the doctrine of the personality of the Deity; in opposition to the popular polytheistic notions, they have the clearest conception of the unity of God; and in opposition to the fatalism of philosophical Buddhism, they believe in and teach the doctrine of an all-superintending Providence. This appears on the very surface, and no one can be among them for any length of time without being impressed with it. They feel that they have a work to accomplish, and the deep conviction that they are guided by an unerring finger, and supported by an omnipotent arm in its execution, is their inspiration. Success they ascribe to the goodness of the Heavenly Father, and defeat to his chastisements. The Deity is with them, not an abstract notion, nor a stern implacable sovereign, but a loving father, who watches tenderly over their affairs, and leads them by the hand. The Scriptures of the Old and New Testament are their proposed standard of faith now, as they were at the commencement of the movement. This is a very important fact. As long as they receive them as the Word of God, we have reasonable grounds to hope that their errors will gradually be corrected. The Missionary can always refer to these, and they cannot consistently object. They often speak of the death of Christ as atoning for the sins of the whole world, though they do not seem to have a clear notion of the *divinity* of his person. They regard him as the greatest human being that has ever appeared in this world, and as *specially* the God-sent; and this will account for the revolutionary chief styling himself the *brother* of Christ. He does not suppose that he himself is divine; his idea, probably, is that the Saviour is the greatest of God's messengers, and he himself the second. On this point, as well as on the doctrine of the Holy Spirit, he needs enlightenment. Could he be convinced that Christ is divine as well as human, he would immediately see, and perhaps renounce, his error. That errors

235

have crept in, is not surprising; on the contrary, it would be one of the greatest miracles on record were it otherwise. The amount of religious knowledge diffused among the people is necessarily limited; that of the chiefs, though not very profound, is more extensive.

Among their adherents, perhaps the Canton men are the most sensible of the value of foreign trade, but they are less impregnated with the religious views of Tien-wang. Both the religious earnestness of the Kwang-si men, and the instinct for commerce of their companions from Canton, will, it is to be hoped, promote friendliness to foreign nations.

Comparing the present religious state of the revolutionists with what they were at Nanking and Chen-kiang eight years ago, there appears to be little difference. They have free prayer on week days, and they burn a written prayer on the Sabbath, something after the mode adopted by the Confucianists at the spring and autumn sacrifices. They have a solemn act of worship at midnight, when offerings are presented to the Heavenly Father. The subjects of their prayers are, in the case of those who possess a coarser mould of mind, victory in battle, and a speedy subjugation of 'the hills and rivers'. The more thoughtful pray for forgiveness of sin and the salvation of the soul.

Sympathy with the religious views of the Insurgents, so far as they agree with Scripture, does not involve an approval of plunder and bloodshed. There are doubtless many among them who are no better than robbers. Their actions prove them to be so. But such an appellation ought not to be applied to the leading men and the better class among them. The people make a clear distinction between the 'true long-haired men' and those who have joined them to enrich themselves by rapine. They are often heard saying to one another that the true long-haired men would not be guilty of such and such crimes which have occurred within their knowledge. Too many gross crimes have in all ages been committed by those who made profession of virtue and piety, for us to wonder that when the Kwangsi men had embarked in this struggle, a crowd of hypocritical and unprincipled men should soon have joined their ranks. These men will oppress the people whenever they have opportunity. It is they, we believe, that kill well-dressed persons, who plead that they have no silver, and ill-treat the women of the towns they take. The impression among the people is, that when leaders of rank arrive at newly-captured places these outrages are prevented, and their commission is punished with death.

Should they establish their dynasty there can be no doubt that they would set on foot a far more rigid and vigorous morality than that to which the Chinese have long been accustomed. Our knowledge of their past history, and of their books, required that we should expect this. But at present they are encumbered with a motley multitude of men, who have nothing better than the common Chinese conscience, with the slightest possible knowledge of the T'ai P'ing religious system. A large number of these have joined them by compulsion, and are therefore destitute of the principles which animate those who compose the original nucleus of the movement.

51
A Letter by Rev. J S Burdon
The Church Missionary Intelligencer, vol. XI (December 1860), pp. 284–6

NARRATIVE OF AN INTERVIEW WITH THE KAN WANG

July 30—After a hard and hot day's work of preparation, I started in company with Messrs. Edkins, John, Innocent, and Rau, the latter a French Protestant Missionary.[5] Between nine and ten P.M. all had arrived at the boats, and we divided ourselves into two parties, Messrs Edkins, John, and Innocent, occupying one boat, and Mr Rau and myself the other. As reports have been rife for some time of the intended advance of the rebels on Shanghae, and the foreign authorities have determined to keep them away, guards of English and French soldiers have been for some weeks posted in different parts both in and outside the city.

July 31—Made rather slow progress. Anchored for the night just outside a floating bridge constructed by the rebels near Luh-kia-pang, some forty English miles from Shanghae, which marks the commencement of the rebel territory so far as hitherto acquired.

Aug. 1—Early in the morning we moved up to the bridge, and asked to be allowed to pass. The poor country-people opened the bridge most readily. It consisted principally of the doors of the cottages seized for the purpose, which were placed on bamboos fastened across the river. The houses thus stripped of their doors

---

5   Joseph Edkins and Griffith John were both London Missionary Society representatives stationed at Shanghai at this time; Burdon had been a Church Missionary Society representative there since 1853; John Innocent was a newly arrived representative of the English Methodist New Connexion; Oscar Rau had also arrived in 1860 representing the Société des missions évangeliques of Paris. See also a letter from Griffith John, 16 August, in the *Missionary Magazine & Chronicle*, vol. XXV (November 1860).

and windows presented a most miserable appearance. The place of these, which the poor rustics dared not to take back, was supplied by pieces of matting, to shelter the residents from the sun and rain. It was heartbreaking to see the misery of the people. They spoke very earnestly against being thus treated. They said it did not matter to them who held the empire, but the struggle for it should surely be confined to the contending parties, and not be made the means of bringing such miseries on the people. All they wanted was to till their land and eat their rice in peace, and, for all they cared, anyone might be Emperor. They complained bitterly of the excesses committed by the soldiers, both of the Imperialists and the rebels. A rebel proclamation was posted up at this place, requiring all to submit to the 'heavenly dynasty', and to render tribute. The fate of these poor people is sealed, should ever the Imperialists be able to muster men or courage enough to make their appearance near them; and thus the people, in their present struggle, are the great sufferers. The rebels come down upon them for plunder, and kill indiscriminately where there is any opposition.

In the afternoon we passed Kwun-shan, a perfect scene of desolation. We did not think it advisable to leave our boats. A few rebels were posted about one of the bridges as a guard; and their mirth contrasted painfully with the miserably dejected looks of the few natives that we saw. The whole sight was sickening.

At dusk, I-ting was passed; and the desolation surpassed any thing that I had before imagined. Here was a large town, containing, when I last visited it, some twenty or thirty thousand inhabitants, made a heap of ruins, without one sound of life, save that of the authors of the ruin. They were stationed at one end of the town, barricaded off from the ruins, from which, however, they had nothing to fear, but from the ghosts of the injured people that might, in indignation, be hovering amidst them. These representatives of the 'great peaceful' dynasty had the wicked desperado looks of a band of robbers who had glutted their appetites upon victims powerless to resist them, and were living on the destruction which they had effected. After passing their noisy camp, the silence that reigned in the once busy market-town, the ruins of the burnt houses, joined with the dusk of the evening, produced the most melancholy feelings in our minds. A solitary cat, peering out from among a heap of bricks and broken furniture—a few dogs keeping watch over property that lay in terrible confusion all around them, or prowling about to find some food, either from dead bodies or from the filth that Chinese dogs mostly live upon—were about the only signs of life visible in this once thriving mart of trade. One single human being—an old man tottering on the brink of the grave—was seen wending his way over the rubbish. We accosted him with a kindly word of greeting; but he merely lifted his vacant eyes, shook his aged head, and resumed his melancholy and lonely walk. Our hearts bled as we passed this scene; and I cannot say that I wished success to the rebel movement. We anchored for the night a little beyond I-ting, but we were soon ordered off by some voice from the opposite shore.

Aug. 2—Very early we were on the move, and by seven o'clock we had arrived at Soo-chow, just outside the gate called Leu-mun. Here again ruins met our eyes on every side, and the stench from dead bodies was almost insufferable. We anchored near to some foreign boats which had come from Shanghae, and were engaged in trading with the rebels in articles of all kinds, lawful and unlawful. Amongst these, opium, which is prohibited by the Tai-ping chief under the penalty of death, was by no means the least esteemed by the rebel soldiers. Immediately after breakfast, we started to pay a visit to the Kan wang; but on reaching the gate we were most unceremoniously treated, and flatly denied admission. Mr Edkins showed the gatekeeper the letter written on yellow silk received from the Kan wang, but it produced no effect on the mind or countenance of the relentless Cerberus. He was the very personification of wickedness and insolence, and his conduct made it evident that if combination does not exist among the insurgents, inferiors did not think it inconsistent with such combination to manifest disrespect to superiors. Mr Edkins, however, made one other attempt, and was admitted just inside the outer gate; on which we all followed. Some one with a little more politeness—a native of Soo-chow, who was stationed with the Kwangsi keepers of the gate—spoke with us; and after finding that some of us were acquainted with Lieu, the officer in command of that part of the city, at once offered us a guide to that gentleman's residence. This we gratefully accepted; and we were soon on our way to Lieu ta-jin.

My walk through the city did not tend to produce any better impressions in favour of the Christian insurgents of China. The desertion of the streets, except by the rebels who were located in the houses that had been spared from violence—the desolation, almost as great in some quarters as that at I-ting—a dead body of a child here and there seen lying on some door-step—the thorough upturning of every article of furniture in the search for treasure—the opening of the very coffins with, no doubt, the same object—and the desperado looks of those who had caused all this evil—all deeply pained me . . .

The Kan wang was sitting on a sofa, dressed in a long yellow damask robe, embroidered all over with that invariable mark of Chinese royalty—the dragon. On his head was a high pasteboard hat, completely gilt, in which were set, in different places, a few precious stones. It is the revival of the crown of the Ming, or last Chinese dynasty, which, in A.D. 1644, was displaced by the Manchoo Tartars, who have held possession of China till the present day. From head to foot but one colour—the Imperial yellow—predominated in the dress of the Kan wang, his wide pantaloons and his very boots, which had soles twice the ordinary thickness of even Chinese boots, being of the same material with his robe. Behind him stood a few boys, whose business was to fan him by turns; and on each side of him, ranging themselves in two rows in front, stood his ministers, dressed in long green or yellow silk robes, many of them having their hair completely enveloped in a yellow handkerchief. On our entrance, the Kan wang rose; and the manner in which he was dressed gave, as may be imagined, no little appearance of dignity to his person. He bore it, however, with great natural ease; and without insisting on any ceremonial, such as is required among themselves, he stretched out his hand in the most frank manner possible, and gave us a true English reception. He immediately after beckoned to us to be seated on the chairs which were placed in the usual Chinese style on each side of his sofa, motioning to Mr Edkins to take the seat of honour.

Conversation immediately began; but after the complimentary and some other general remarks had passed, it flagged, in consequence of the number of listeners. This was soon perceived by the Kan wang, and a word from him at once halved the waiting company. Those who still hung behind were, in a like unceremonious manner, again ordered to withdraw; and, with the exception of his personal servants, we were, to our great relief, left to as unrestrained a *tête-à-tête* with our host as we desired. The conversation lasted for three or four hours; and he most willingly, and apparently with no desire to conceal even the defects and evils of the Tai-ping Christianity, answered our numerous questions. Before going to him we had already determined on the leading questions to be asked, and these we put to him just as they occurred to us.

52
A Report by Rev. Joseph Edkins
North China Herald, 11 August 1860

QUESTIONS RECENTLY ADDRESSED TO THE KAN WANG, WITH THE ANSWERS

Q 1 The visions of the Chief: When? How many? In what light does he regard them? What do you think of them?

A His visions are two. In the year 1837 he imagined that his soul was taken up into heaven, and that the affairs of the celestial world were clearly pointed out to him. God, he says, conferred upon him a sword and a seal, with a commission to conquer and subdue all the imps (evil spirits, idols, and the Tartars); for the accomplishment of which task he granted him the co-operation of Jesus and the aid of the angelic host. In 1848 he himself was much distressed, when the Great God, bringing his son Jesus with him, appeared on his behalf to instruct him (the Chief) how to sustain the weight of government. The Chief makes no pretensions to any other visions. He believes in them as revelations from God to him. The Kan-wang (Hung Jen kan) believes them to be real, though he is doubtful as to how they should be understood.

2 The visions of the Eastern King: in what light does the Chief regard them? What do you think of them?

The Chief will not allow them to be questioned, and was displeased when the Kan-wang presented objections to them. The Kan-wang does not believe in them.

3 Is Yang, the Eastern King, now called the Holy Spirit and the Comforter when written or spoken of?

Yes. The Chief has no adequate conception of the Scriptural import of these terms.

4 What does the Chief mean by calling himself the natural brother of Christ, (Tung-pau-ti-hiung)?

His views of the divine nature of Christ are imperfect. (We were not told that he disbelieved in this truth. His error is of a negative rather than of a positive nature.) He regards Christ as the greatest of God's messengers, and himself as second only to him; and it is in this light that he believes himself to be brother of Christ and God's son. He calls all the ten Kings his natural brothers.

5 What are your own views of the Trinity?

The Kan-wang's views of this doctrine coincide with those which are generally held by orthodox Christians.

6 What is the precise idea attached to the practice of presenting meats, tea, &c., as offerings?

They are merely thank-offerings, not propitiatory. The Chief is fully aware of their uselessness as a part of divine service. Neither he nor the Kan-wang make use of them themselves. He appointed them in accommodation to the crude notions of a people just emerging out of heathenism.

7 What is the precise idea attached to the practice of burning written prayers? Is the practice to be continued?

This practice is explained in the same way as the above. The practice is disapproved of, and will, in the course of time, be given up. At the end of a prayer prepared by the Kan-wang for general distribution among the soldiers, he says, 'Let each man have a copy of this prayer; after using, it should not be burnt.'

8 Polygamy?

Polygamy is practised. The Chief is aware that it is anti-Christian. The Eastern King had the principal hand in introducing it. The Kan-wang himself has been obliged to give up his scruples on this point, and has become a polygamist.

9 Is the separation of the sexes still continued?

It was a temporary expedient and has been given up.

10 The sabbath: is it observed? How?

The sabbath is observed by assembling at midnight for prayer and praise. When peace is restored, the sabbath is to be observed strictly. It is kept on Saturday.*

11 Is the ordinance of the Lord's supper observed? How? Is wine used?

It is not observed, and is not known among them. Wine is not used in any of their religious observances, and the private use of it is strictly forbidden by law.

---

* ('The Chinese reckon twenty-eight constellations in their Zodiac, one of which is attached to each day throughout the year. Four of these, namely, the 4th, 11th, 18th, and 25th regularly occur on the Christian Sabbath, and are used by the Christian Chinese to specify that day. It is worthy of observation that the insurgents in their Calendar have always made the Sabbath to fall on the above-mentioned days; but by some strange mistake, they have made all the days of the twenty-eight constellations and of the sixty horary characters to fall one day earlier than that specified in the Imperial Calendar and observed by the other Chinese. The consequence is, that the rebels actually keep their Sabbath on Saturday. On this being pointed out to them by Mr. Meadows, they said it was a mistake.'—Dr. Medhurst.

The Kan-wang stated the very same thing, and that they do not designedly keep the *seventh* day.)

12 Baptism: How administered? Is it repeated? By whom administered?

It is administered by sprinkling, which is followed by washing the chest. Not rigidly observed at present, though such was the case at the commencement of the movement. It cannot be repeated. Any one may baptize.

13 The Scriptures: What parts have you printed and published? In what light are they regarded?

The whole Bible was been printed and published. They are regarded as of supreme authority. The Chief reads them diligently, and has committed large portions to memory. He also enjoys reading the Rev. Mr. Burns' translation of the 'Pilgrim's Progress.'

14 Among the six Festivals that which occurs on the 21st of the second month is commemorative of the accession to the throne of the Heavenly Brother and of the Tien-wang. What does this mean?

It is an attempt to make the time of the Saviour's crucifixion agree with that of the Tien-wang's accession to his dignity. The Kan-wang stated to his relative that he had formerly heard from Mr. Hamberg that the Jewish passover occurred on the 24th. The Tien-wang insisted on adopting the 21st, because the Chinese characters for two, ten, and one together make up the character 'chu', lord.

15 What do you mean by the expression 'Kiang-fan' ('descend into the world') as applied to the Tien-wang?

It means nothing more than natural birth, with a divine commission. The Chief uses the same phrase in speaking of the birth of our Saviour. He was not aware till recently of the pre-existence or of the proper deity of our Lord.

16 Do you desire to have missionaries to teach your people? Would you like to have some elementary work prepared by missionaries?

We desire to have missionaries, and would be thankful for a small collection of prayers for the use of the soldiers. Should missionaries come to Nanking chapels will be built for them, and they will be allowed to teach and carry on their work in their own way, and according to their own views.

17 Is your book 'Tsi-cheng-sin-pien',[6] of which we have received manuscript copies, approved by the Tien-wang? Is it to be printed?

6 The 'Tsi-cheng sin pien' was the Kan Wang's *New Treatise on Aids to Administration*, a full translation of which is in Michael, op. cit., vol. III, pp. 748–76.

It has been corrected by the Tien-wang himself, and he approves of its being printed. The passages which he has altered are chiefly those which speak of God as immaterial. The words which represent God as not material have been erased by the Tien-wang. The Chung-wang has promised to print the book at Soochow.

18 Is the phraseology employed by you in the above-mentioned work to be henceforth adopted by the Tae-ping Dynasty?

The Tien-wang has not consented to change the phraseology to which he has been accustomed, and which has been hitherto employed in the books and documents of the Dynasty. The Tien-wang uses 'Chen-shen', 'Shang-ti', and 'Tien-fu' for 'God', while the Kan-wang objects to the first of these terms, on the ground that the words 'chen' ('true'), and 'kia' ('false'), cannot be affirmed of 'shen'. The Tien-wang, said his cousin, is unwilling to abandon terms the use of which he learned from Mr. Roberts.

19 What is the state of religion at present among the adherents of the Tae-ping party?

It has deteriorated considerably. The Kan-wang observed this on arriving at Nanking. Even among the Kwangsi men there is less religious warmth than there was at the beginning of the movement. The Kan-wang has printed a prayer for distribution among his men.

20 Have any new books been recently published?

The Kan-wang gave the missionaries who visited him copies of (1) 'Hing-kiün-tsung-yau', a military work, published in 1855; (2) 'Sing-shï-wen', published in 1858, urging the Chinese nation to accept the religion and politics of the Tae-ping Dynasty; (3) 'Calendar of 1860', prepared by seven Kings, and prefaced by two Edicts of the Tien-wang; (4) 'Tsi-cheng-sin-pien', by the Kan-wang; and (5) 'Tien-ma Tien-sau-pien-cheng', an apology, in manuscript, by the same author, for a part of the 'Visions' of the Tien-wang.[7]

Between the years 1855 and 1858 three other authorized books are mentioned in the most recent list, of which copies were not obtained.

---

7   Of the documents mentioned in this paragraph (1) is Hsing-chün tsung-yao, *The Elements of Military Tactics for Troop Operations*, translated in Michael, op. cit., vol. II, pp. 445–39, and (5) is Tzu-cheng hsien-p'ien for which see the preceding note. The others have not been identified, though for (3) note Doc. 204 in Michael, op. cit., which is the Calendar for 1861. For the Kan Wang's writings generally see Michael, op. cit., vol. III, pp. 729–76, 799–897 and Jen Yu-wen, op. cit., pp. 362–9.

21 Is there any regulation requiring Confucian and other books to be destroyed?

No.

22 Is the Tien-wang preparing a new history of China?

He is correcting the history of the country according to his own views, for the use of the Princes and the Court.

23 What is the present extent of your territory, and the position of your Kings?

The Assistant King, Shih-ta-kai, has taken Cheng-tu, the capital of Sï-chwen, and resides there at present. He is also subjugating Kwangsi and Yünnan. Several myriads of Kwangsi men have recently joined him. He has also 40,000 or 50,000 Miau-tsï in his army.

The Ying-wang ('flourishing King') has gone to Hwei-cheu, to conquer that part of Ngan-hwei Province.

The Chung-wang has recently acquired great influence through his success in conquering the Province of Kiangsu (to be called, in future, 'Su-fuh').

There is to be a new division of the country into twenty-one provinces. The word 'fu' in the names of cities is to be replaced by 'kiun'.

The Kings are eleven in all, including the Tien-wang and two of his nephews (Nos. 2 and 3):

1 Tien-wang.
2 Successor of the Western King, Siau-yeu-ho.
3 Successor of Eastern King, Siau-yeu-fuh.
4 Kan-wang (Hung-jen-kan).
5 Yih-wang (Shïh-tah-kai).
6 Ying-wang (Chen-yuh-cheng).
7 Chung-wang (Li-sieu-cheng).
8 Tsan-wang (Mung-teh-ngen).
9 Shï-wang (Li-shï-hien).
10 Fu-wang (Yang-fu-tsing).
11 Chang-wang (Lin-shau-chang).

The following are the names of official ranks under that of Wang, King or Prince: Chang-shuh, Chu-tsiang, I, Ngan, Fuh, Yen, Yü, Heu, Siang, Kien-tien, Chi-hwei, Tsiang-kiün, Tsung-chi, Kien-kiün.

24 Do the other Kings, and especially the Tien-wang, accept your views of social and political improvements?

They are at one on this point. The proposition to introduce European improvements—railroads, steam-power, and the like—is looked on with great favour by the Tien-wang in particular. He was highly pleased with the Memorials, on these and similar subjects, presented by his cousin on his arrival at Nanking in 1859, and insisted, in consequence, on his accepting the duties of Chief in the Administration, the post formerly filled by the Eastern King.

25 Did you meet with difficulties in reaching Nanking?

He was, he said, in all about a year on the way. On arriving at King-teh-chen, in Kiangsi, he was not allowed to pass. He then went to Kieu-kiang, and from that city ascended the Kiang to Hupeh, where he spent four months with a friend. He then came down the river to Nanking in a trading-boat. He went on board one of the vessels in Lord Elgin's expedition, hoping to meet Mr. Wade, with whom he was formerly acquainted; failing in this, he entrusted to a Chinese letters to foreign friends at Shanghae and Hong Kong, which were duly received.

26 Does the Tien-wang determine all State matters?

Yes; but on most affairs not connected with religion he looks with contempt, remarking that they are 'things of this world', and not 'heavenly things' ('tsien-tsing'). He often approves of memorials and propositions of a 'worldly' kind at a glance, and without careful examination.

27 Is ancestral worship abolished?

Yes, among those who form the nucleus of the movement—the old Kwangsi adherents. The 'new brethren' are not particularly informed of the prohibition of ancestral worship, for the present.

28 Does the Tien-wang hold materialistic views of God?

Yes, and does not brook contradiction on this point.

29 In the thank-offerings, what ideas are attached to the three tea-cups placed on the table which serves as an altar?

They refer to the persons in the Trinity. So thought the Kan-wang. He had not inquired. The sacrifices were nothing but a temporary substitute for idolatry. He did not make use of them himself. There was much in the Tai-ping books which he had not read. He did not feel pleasure in doing so.

30 What is the meaning of the second public festival (2nd month, 2nd day),—thanksgiving to the Father?

It is to commemorate the commission of the Tien-wang to destroy the imps and the serpent.

53
A Letter from Rev J L Holmes
North China Herald, 1 September 1860

... We ran all night, and next morning August 8th, at about 9 o'clock, anchored in the mouth of the creek which leads from the river up to the city of Nanking, and abreast the fort or rather walled village situated there. On enquiring for some one with whom we could communicate, I was invited to enter the fort, and on doing so was received by a tall Quangsi officer, clothed in a gaudy robe and wearing a brassy looking hat or helmet. He greeted me as his 'ocean brother', and drawing me down to a seat beside him in the place of honor, entered at once into conversation. On being informed who I was, and for what I came, he immediately sent a messenger into the city to announce my arrival to the higher authorities. At $3\frac{1}{2}$ o'clock p.m., horses were sent by the Chang Wong and an officer to escort us to his house. We found the gates near the river on the northern side of the city all closed, and were obliged to ride outside for about three miles till we reached one of the West gates where we entered, and after passing about half a mile through the half ruined streets reached the Chang Wong's dwelling—a building distinguished from ordinary Chinese establishments only by the large number of his apartments—altogether covering with intervening courts, near an acre of ground. We were received by a venerable looking and very polite old man whom we learned to call Pung ta jun (his excellency Mr Pung). He had been requested by the Chang Wong to entertain us with supper, he said, after which that dignitary would see us. Said Pung was dressed in a long blue robe, and wore a sort of hood with a cape. He was, we learned, an adherent of the Tien Wang's and was merely present on this occasion as a sort of representative of his master. His office was something like that of Chaplain, according to the account we had of its functions. We found him extremely polite and affable, and I thought I could discern some appearance of real religious character, which is more than I can say of any other man I met, for in general it did not appear to me that their religious motives were nearly so strong as those suggested by a rich city to be opened, or dignity to be obtained, which would give to them in turn an establishment like those they now helped to grace. This man however spoke freely of his religious faith, and though his ideas were exceedingly crude and mingled with superstition, he appeared to be in earnest. He remarked in course of conversation that we had long had the Gospel, whereas they had had it but a short time, and acknowledged our ability to instruct them in religious matters.

After supper we were led into the presence of the king. We found him seated in a raised recess behind a long table, on which were placed burning candles (it being after dark) and various ornamental articles. He was dressed in a richly embroidered robe and had on his head a sort of gilded mitre or crown. His officers formed an avenue before him through which we were led up to a seat in the recess in which he sat himself, while a series of discordances of a most excruciating character were produced by fire crackers, gongs, and drums outside. On our being seated he began the conversation as follows,

'Wah Seen Sang,[8] be assured, Foreigners and men of the Heavenly kingdom are all brethren. We all believe in the Heavenly Father and Son, and are therefore brethren. Is it not so?' I assented, when he proceeded! 'The tree has its root, the stream has its fountain, and man has his origin. He is a very wicked man who is unfilial to his earthly parents; how much more that he neglects the Heavenly Father the giver of all good. He is the Creator of Heaven and Earth and all things, and yet this Manchu Dynasty with its adherents persist in worshipping wooden and stone idols. Are we not right in styling them imps?' I replied that such conduct was no doubt very wicked, and yet I questioned the propriety of calling them imps, as they were still living men and might still repent.—We too were once unbelievers. He then said something about the people of this world having much intercourse with the spriitual world, the bearing of which I did not see, and after a few passing remarks and questions, he added, 'We could not in three days and nights finish talking about religious matters. Have you other matters to speak of?' I then mentioned the object for which I had come, speaking of the deep interest which had long been felt in their cause by Foreign Christians.—How we had hoped and feared as to the purity of their doctrines, and as to their success if they were indeed Christians. After receiving from him assurances of their gratification at my arrival, we retired . . .

10th August. Spent the day mostly in conversation with visitors among whom a brother of the Chang Wong and one of the Chung Wong whose royal curiosity was excited by the visit of the 'Ocean brother'. We are attended by a number of boys, all of whom had, as we learned, been carried away from their parents; some had been in their present situation a number of years, some but a short time. It appears to be their policy to take all the boys they can get, and they use them for servants while they are small, and

8 Hua Hsien-sheng, i.e. Mr Holmes.

for soldiers when they are large enough to fight. I asked one of them if he would like to return to his parents again. He replied that he would, but if he tried to escape the consequences would be what he indicated by drawing his hand across his neck—his head would be taken off . . .

At night (Aug. 10th) we witnessed their worship. It occurred at the beginning of their Sabbath, midnight of Friday. The place of worship was the Chang Wong's private audience room. He was himself seated in the midst of his attendants—no females were present. They first sung, or rather chanted, after which a written prayer was read and burned by an officer, upon which they rose and sang again, and then separated. The Chang Wong sent for me again before he left his seat, and asked me if I understood their mode of worship. I replied that I had just seen it for the first time. He asked what our mode was. I replied that we endeavored to follow the rules laid down in the Scriptures, and thought all departure therefrom to be erroneous. He then proceeded to explain the ground upon which they departed from this rule. The Tien Wong had been to Heaven, he said, and had seen the Heavenly Father. Our revelation had been handed down for 1800 years; they had received a new, additional revelation, and upon this, they could adopt a different mode of worship . . .

11th August. At day-light we started for the Tien Wong's palace. The procession was headed by a number of brilliantly colored banners, after which followed a troop of armed soldiers; then came the Chang Wong in a large sedan covered with yellow satin and embroidery and borne by eight coolies, next came the foreigner on horseback, in company with the Chang Wong's chief officer followed by a number of other officers on horse-back. On our way several of the other Kings who were in the city fell in ahead of us with similar retinues. Music added discord to the scene, and curious gazers lined the streets, who had no doubt seen kings before, but probably never witnessed such an apparition as that which accompanied him. Reaching at last the palace of the Tien Wong, a large building resembling very much the best of the Confucian temples though of much greater size than these generally are. We entered the outer gate and proceeded to a large building on the eastward of the palace proper, and called the 'Morning Palace'. Here we were presented to the Tsan Wong and his son, with several others. After resting a little while during which two of the attendants testified their familiarity with, and consequent irreverence for, the royal palace by concluding a misunderstanding in fisticuffs, we proceeded to the audience hall of the Tien Wong. I was here presented to the Tien Wong's two brothers,[9] two nephews and son-in-law, in addition to those whom I had before met at the 'Morning Palace'. They were seated at the entrance to a deep recess over the entrance of which was written, 'Illustrious Heavenly door'. At the end of this recess, far within, was pointed out to us His Majesty Tien Wong's seat, which was as yet vacant. The company awaited for some time the arrival of the Western King, whose presence seemed to be necessary before they could proceed with their ceremonies. That dignitary, a boy of 12 or 14, directly made his appearance and entering at the 'Holy Heavenly Gate', took his place with the royal group. They then proceeded with the ceremonies as follows: First they kneeled with their faces to the Tien Wong's seat and uttered a prayer to the Heavenly Brother, then kneeling with their faces in the opposite direction, they prayed to the Heavenly Father, after which they again kneeled with their faces to the Tien Wong's seat, and in like manner repeated a prayer to him. They then concluded by singing in a standing position. A roast pig and the body of a goat were lying with other articles on tables in the outer court, and a fire was kept burning on a stone altar in front of the Tien Wong's seat, in a sort of court which intervened between it and the termination of the recess leading to it. He had not yet appeared, and though all waited for him for some time after the conclusion of the ceremonies, he did not appear at all. He had probably changed his mind, concluding that it would be a bad precedent to allow a foreigner to see him without first signifying submission to him, or it may be that he did not mean to see me after learning the stubborn nature of our principles, but anxious to have us carry away some account of the grandeur and magnificence of his court, had taken this mode of making an appropriate impression, leaving the imagination to supply the vacant chair which his ample dimension should have filled . . .

I went to Nanking predisposed to receive a favorable impression. I came away with my views very materially changed. I had hoped that their doctrines, though crude and erroneous, might notwithstanding embrace some of the elements of Christianity. I found, to my sorrow, nothing of Christianity but its names, falsely applied—applied to a system of revolting idolatry—whatever there may be in their books, and whatever they may have believed in times past, I could not escape the conclusion that such is the system which they now promulgate, and by which the character of their people is being moulded . . .

9 Hung Hsiu-ch'üan's two brothers were Hung Jen-fa, the Hsin Wang, and Hung Jen-ta, the Yung-Wang—see Jen Yu-wen, op. cit., pp. 302–3, 409 etc.

The city of Nanking is in a ruinous condition. It would be no exaggeration to say that half the houses have been destroyed. The country around is not half cultivated. Provisions are very scarce and expensive. Their trade is very limited. We observed instances in which workmen were compelled to labor without compensation. All indicates a policy which has little regard to the welfare of the people, or to any interests other than those immediately connected with the war, and with the indulgence of their rulers.

The present state of their political affairs would indicate that Hung Siu Tsuen's career must close before the present dynasty can be supplanted. His horrible doctrines, which have served to break down every distinction between right and wrong in the minds of his soldiers and send them forth to perform every enormity without remorse, have secured him the lasting hatred of the masses of the people.

54
A Letter from Fr M Lemaitre SJ
Annals of the Propagation of the Faith, vol. XXII (January 1861), pp. 45–7

On the 17th August, 1860, bands of rebels approached like a torrent, and the population were driven back upon Shanghai in an alarming manner. Father Louis Massa[10] was upon the road of the rebels, thirteen miles from Shanghai, at the orphanage of Tsa-ka-wei. About four o'clock in the evening, he perceived innumerable pavilions blazing in all directions; and, in proportion as they advanced, the farms and villages were enveloped in clouds of dust and flames. There was no longer time to escape with his hundred and odd orphans. He sent away two bands, however, in charge of two safe men. Whilst he was praying with the others and the Christians of the village, the rebels approached with ferocious shouts; the Father presented himself at the door, and entreated them to spare his innocent little flock. This request was met by several thrusts with sabres and pikes. The rebels demanded money; he gave them all that there was in the house; they struck him to make him give them more; they sought everywhere, and as there was none, he was still further maltreated, and at length dragged out of the orphanage, and thrown into an adjacent rice-field, where he soon after died.

He had, however, occupied the rebels, and in the mean time many of the children and Christians effected their escape. Twenty-seven were killed, together with their beloved Father;

10 Fr Louis Massa was a Jesuit missionary in Shanghai from 1848.

three or four were found left alive. The others were received first into the college of Tzi-ka-wei, and thence transferred to Shanghai. The house would have been entirely burnt down but for a catechist and six children left with him, who extinguished the flames, and thus saved one half of the establishment.

On the following day, 18th August, Tzi-ka-wei and the neighbouring villages shared the same fate. We had fortunately been enabled to send away all the Religious and the pupils of the college, together with the children who escaped from the orphanage of Tsa-ka-wei. The servants' lives were spared, but almost everything in the college was carried off or broken; the house itself would doubtless have been burnt, if the chiefs had not made it their general quarters. The congregations of the neighbourhood have suffered much from pillage, massacre, and fire.

On the 19th and 20th, the rebels advanced upon Shanghai, committing several atrocities in the environs; they even ventured to attack the European posts, but were vigorously repulsed and compelled to retreat into the country. The following days were days of terror; one portion of the environs was committed to the flames. The large Seminary of the Cathedral was in danger, and, had it not been for the energy of ten French soldiers and the activity of some Christian volunteers, everything would have been destroyed: we were called upon rather to moderate than to stimulate their courage.

Thanks to God, matters are assuming a better aspect; the rebels, alarmed at the victorious advance of the Europeans, have retired to a distance of fifteen or eighteen miles from Shanghai, and it is expected that the troops who are victorious from the north will pursue them and drive them out of the country. These insurgents have a great number of partisans at Shanghai; since they have become better known, they have only excited contempt and horror.

For our part, anxious to avoid all interference in matters that do not concern us, our only desire is for peace. We have had many losses which will not be easily repaired; our Christians are ruined in half of the province; we shall therefore have to labour and wait with patience, and also to afford consolations to many afflictions. The prosecution of the war would throw us back very much; but with peace and the aid of your exhaustless charity, we will try to retrieve our position, and I have great hope of being able to save the souls of an immense number of honest Pagans.
. . .

M Lemaître, SJ

55
A Letter from Rev I J Roberts
Overland China Mail, 29 November 1860

Chung Wang, the faithful king, as commander-in-chief of his army, arrived at this place [Tanyang] on the 7th instant, took his quarters in the best house in the place, and immediately sent for me by a messenger and horse to come and share his house while here; rose up and met me without any ceremony as an intimate friend, shook my hand cordially as a hearty welcome, and insisted on my eating dinner with him again, though I had eaten with Chong Wang only an hour or two before, having arrived here a few hours before he did. This evening he sent for me into his room, and told me that he was going from here to Chin-kong, i.e. Chin-kiang-foo; but that I would be forwarded on my way to Nanking on the 10th instant with a conductor, passport, and every needed requisite for my journey. In fact, the conductor has told me all the way along that whatever I wanted, eatables, money, or any thing else, that Chung Wang had put money in his hands with which to supply me fully; so that my expenses have not cost me a penny from Shanghae to this place. He farther remarked that my passport would let me immediately into the city without stopping me at the gate; for want of such I had consider-able trouble at Soo-chow. But what would become of me when I got into the city, would have been a serious question, had it not been for his generous hospitality. He invited me to go directly to his house; though *he* should not be there so soon, yet the persons there would receive me, and I should be welcome to make that my home until better suited. I have travelled a great deal as a stranger among strangers, and have often met with much kind hospitality; but never such as this before, so kind, so generous, and so timely—I can't help but love the man; he is one of a thousand! He is not only a man of learning, affable and amiable, but a king, and a general of no ordinary abilities, commanding more than a hundred thousand troops, a large portion of whom are now at his heels in line of march for the battlefield. But he feels the way he was treated at Shanghae last month, much more than he expressed in his letter to Lord Elgin, which I translated for him the other day. He generously passed it by for Love's sake, on account of the anxious desire he has to maintain the goodwill of foreigners, without upbraiding them of killing two hundred of his men and several of his officers! without his having killed one foreigner or having intended to do so! If this was not a flagrant shame I am utterly at a loss to know what could be reckoned as such! Is not this the only apology that can be conceived for such an egregious mistake, that the officers, soldiers, community and all, took a panic, and was thereby precipitated into a course of action that sober reason never would have dictated!

But Chung Wang has requested me this evening to reiterate his earnest desire for intercourse and commerce with foreigners. He is quite at a loss to understand why foreigners would prefer trading with the Imperialists, who are idolaters, than with the revolutionists, who have cast away idols and worship the same God, and are willing to trade on at least as good if not better terms! They have the means of commerce, teas and silks, within their territory.

They expect to retake Ching-kiang-foo in a few days, and if so, he is willing to open it as a port of entry which was manifestly desired according to the last English treaty; and so as soon as the foreign protection is withdrawn from the native part of Shanghae, he will be most happy to take that place too, and continue it open to foreign commerce as hitherto, on at least as good if not better terms than heretofore under the Imperialists. Then why not approve and practice this course! Simply because there is no treaty yet with Tae-peng Wang. Then why not make a treaty? Echo responds in England and France—Why not make a treaty? Reverberation answers in the United States—Why not make a treaty? Tae-peng Wang has held on his way ten years, seven since he took Nanking. He and his generals have fought noble battles, perhaps none braver or more successful with such accoutrements as were within their reach; they have thrashed out their idolatrous enemies, and have chased them off the field, and now, when they are ready to reap the fruits of their toil, why not make a generous treaty with them at once, giving them the due advantages which they have so worthily won by their sword, and their people the Christian religion?

*IJR*11

56
A Letter from Rev I J Roberts
Overland China Mail, 15 December 1860

Nov. 12th—Today I was conducted to Teen Wang's presence. He is a much finer-looking man than I thought he was. Large, well-made, well-featured, with fine black moustaches which set off considerably, and a fine voice. His mind seemed to be taken up

11 Another letter of this kind by Roberts, written from Soochow and dated 2 October 1860, is in the *Overland China Mail*, 16 November 1860.

with the subject of religion; not like Chung Wang, who talked with me most on politics, he scarcely introduced that subject. His theology, I must acknowledge, was not very correct, but so far as time and opportunity offered I endeavoured to improve it. I let him know that I had come to preach the gospel according to the scriptures, and should acknowledge them as my only rule of faith and practice. At this he somewhat demurred but did not interdict. At interludes in our conversation he had his Kings and high officers about twenty before him to kneel down and chant his praises two or three times, during our conversation of about an hour. In this I took no part. None of us sat but himself, and his own little son, heir apparent. He invited me to dine, but not with him—with the other Kings elsewhere; none dine with him. He also ordered me to be supplied with every thing I needed from his bounty; signified his good pleasure at having seen me; and charged his kings and officers as they retired to pay due respect to Lo How-chuen,[12] as the heavenly Father said he was a good man!

57

A Letter from Rev W Muirhead

Missionary Magazine and Chronicle, vol. XXV (July 1861), pp. 202–8[13]

ARRIVAL AT NANKING AND CONFERENCE WITH THE KAN-WANG

During the following two days we had snowy and bitterly cold weather, and the accommodation by the way at towns nearly destroyed, was not inviting. However, we reached Nanking on the evening of the second day, when I was received into the house of Mr. Roberts, the American, the first instructor of Tae-ping-wang, who is residing here. Shortly after I saw the Kan-wang, and had a cordial welcome from him. I remained with him about an hour. He seemed glad to renew an old friendship, and talked in a pleasant manner about himself, and the work of christianizing the people under him. I stated that my single intention in coming was to preach in the country round about, and that I would have been satisfied to do so in other parts of the territory if I could have had the opportunity. I wished, therefore, to know where I

12 I.e. Roberts—Lo Hsiao-ch'üan. For another account of this interview see Doc. 73.

13 Compare Muirhead's other report written for British officials, which is reprinted in *BPP*, 1862, C. 2976, pp. 18–21 and is rather more consistently critical than this report, written for his religious associates. Muirhead was probably genuinely in two minds about the movement, but it would seem also that the audience for which he was writing affected his conclusions.

might conveniently go to for a week or ten days, and by what means. He approved of the object as such, but reserved it for after consideration. The next day he called on me, and said that the state of things at present in the city and the neighbourhood, rendered it scarcely suitable for foreigners to engage in public preaching. It would require him to issue proclamations informing the people, calming their apprehensions, and prohibiting them saying improper things. Were it a time of peace, he would also order his under-officers to use their influence in promotion of the object; but he was just now busy in preparing to lead out an army, and he was not sure that the king would consent to the requisite arrangements. Altogether, he advised delay, and specially that preaching might not be carried on in the capital. At subsequent interviews the matter was brought fully up. He then stated that the desire of his royal master was to evangelize the country; and when I asked if that was their mutual intention, he at once replied, most certainly it was; the thing had been contemplated from the first, and would be strenuously followed out. But it was necessary to observe, he added, that the king intended to prosecute this object in his own way. 'In what way?' I asked. 'By native means,' he said. Examinations would be held annually, at which all the public officers would be present. The text-book, on such occasions, would be chiefly the Bible; and according to the attainments of the writers in Scriptural knowledge would their respective positions in the empire be determined. The successful essayists would be appointed to certain offices, and in each, large and small, would regular instruction be communicated to all around. I observed that something more than that was required, in view of ascertaining the religious character of the candidates, and for promoting the ends and objects of a spiritual kingdom. He replied that such was the scheme contemplated by the 'heavenly king', and that it was supposed by him to be a complete one. 'Well, then,' it was asked, 'what position would foreign teachers have in the case?' He stated that, at first they would be useful in diffusing among the scholars and people a general knowledge of Christianity; but the fact was, that the king did not like the idea of depending on foreign aid in the matter. He thought that the thing could be done by the Chinese themselves, who were naturally proud, and not disposed to accept the Gospel at the hands of foreigners. He was desirous of being friendly with us; but there was such a variety of sentiment among us, and the simple fact of our being what we are, determined him to follow his own course.

I spoke further to the Kan-wang on the subject of Missionaries coming to reside at the capital. He answered, in a very friendly way, that he would not advise it, at least in the meantime. The place was nothing else than a camp. Though he would be glad to see a few of his special friends now and then, yet he could not encourage the idea of the metropolis being made the centre of Missionary operations, at all events at present. It was impossible to provide houses here, and it were better, in his view, to work our way gradually from Su-chow upwards. However, he said, 'If any one feels himself imperatively called upon by God to under-take a mission to this place, let him come by all means, but do not ask *me* in the matter.' He repeated these words in an emphatic manner, on the understanding that they should be told abroad.

ORIGIN AND EARLY HISTORY OF THE INSURGENT MOVEMENT

I was introduced to many persons that had long been connected with the movement, and particularly to one who was the keeper of the palace gate. His position and the title belonging to it, were in consequence of the high idea entertained of his religious senti-ments. I had many pleasing interviews with this man. Though illiterate, he is well instructed in the religious principles of the insurgents, and believes them in a spirit bordering on credulity. Still, he listened to my representations of the truth with respect, and appeared to have formed a special attachment to me as a servant of Christ. I asked him to tell me how it was he became connected with the 'heavenly dynasty'. He said that one day he was labouring in his field in Kwangsi, when the 'heavenly king' came up and told him that he was commissioned by the Heavenly Father to preach the Gospel, and to command him no longer to worship wicked spirits, such as he had been accustomed to do, but to worship the true God and the Heavenly Brother. My friend inquired how this was to be done, when the matters of sacrifice and prayer were pointed out to him. 'At once,' he said, 'I resolved to act on the advice, and follow my new preceptor.' He destroyed his idols, and became an adherent of the religion of the Heavenly Father. His story as to the origin of the rebellion corresponded entirely with Kan-wang's previous account, as detailed in the work entitled 'The Visions of Tae-ping-wang.' He thoroughly believes in all these, and as carried out at subsequent times, both in the case of the chief and his subordinate kings. To these visions and revelations, as coming from the Heavenly Father, and as clothed with His authority, he ascribes all their proceedings. When I spoke to him about the extreme use of fire and sword, in the course of their career, he told me that at the outset of their history, there was no such plundering and burning as afterwards. But, on one occasion, when in great straits, the boys connected with them said they had received a mandate from a heavenly angel, to act as they were now doing, and, under the inspiration, even youths like these were led to achieve wonders. At the same time, he laments, in common with many others, the barbarities and cruelties perpetrated by recent conscripts, and earnestly desires a reformation in their character and conduct. While believing in his own view of things, he appears to court religious conversation, and takes great pleasure when the providence of the Heavenly Father and Heavenly Brother is acknowledged. . . .

CELEBRATION OF THE NEW YEAR

Two days ago was the first of the rebel new year, and there was much in the ceremonies connected with it to interest a stranger. In one part of the city there is the palace of the 'Heavenly King'. It is a new erection, and is yet far from finished; however, it is in imitation of the imperial as much as possible. At first sight it is very imposing. Over the outer gate there is this inscription, 'The sacred heavenly gate of the true God', and over the second, 'The royal heavenly gate.' All around these is a profusion of strange figures, dragons, phoenixes, &c. On the above day the kings, chief men, and under officers went to pay their respects to his majesty. The assemblage was large. Every one of these had a number of civilians and soldiers in attendance, conveying him to the palace. The kings came in yellow coloured chairs borne by sixteen men, and those next in authority in chairs of different colours, carried by eight bearers, while before and after them there was an immense variety of silken flags and streamers, covered with strange devices, or recording the name and titles of their respective owners, and headed by the inscription, 'The peaceful heavenly kingdom.' The kings and chief men went into the inner court, where the 'celestial king' was seated, while the others, in number at least 300, remained in the outer court. I was amongst the latter, and witnessed their proceedings, which corresponded with those going on inside, though imperfectly seen from my position. At twelve o'clock all in the outer circle fell on their knees, after a given signal, in a direction towards Tae-ping-Wang. They then sang his praises, or wished him a long life in imperial style, of 'ten thousand years, ten thousand years, ten thousand times ten thousand years.' Turning in a different direction, they were told to worship the Heavenly Father, when they knelt again in front of a table, on which were several basins of food and two lamps, that were intended for sacrifice. At the head of the worshippers was a man with a paper containing a prayer to God, which he read and then burned. The assembly rose up, but very soon were summoned to fall down in the direction of the king once more, and in that attitude remained a considerable time. Nothing was said, yet, with few exceptions, much decorum was observed during the service. At about half-past twelve o'clock the whole was over, and the chief men returned into the outer court. Their appearance in dress and manner, was certainly much superior to the class of outside worshippers, and the prevailing colour of the long robes worn on the occasion was yellow, while the caps worn by all were different from those of the reigning dynasty. The assembly dispersed in a very quiet manner. . . .

DEPARTURE OF THE KANG-WANG FROM NANKING

12th. Last Sabbath morning the Kang-Wang left the city to take command of an army. It is the first time he has done so, and the proceedings on the occasion were rather splendid. A large retinue assembled outside his palace, while a number of his chief men went in to pay their respects to him. Just as he was starting, and as the end of the affair, they all knelt before him and sang the doxology: 'May Kang-Wang live a thousand years, a thousand years, a thousand times a thousand years.' He then came down from his throne, and entered his chair of eight bearers. He was dressed in a gorgeous yellow robe, with a golden crown on his head. My reflections at the time were rather strange, in view of his antecedents and Christian profession. The above anthem is a daily song in his ears, and when being raised by any coming to visit him, in presence of those he was formerly acquainted with, he appears, in a religious point of view, ashamed of it, I believe. But such is the order of things in China. In prospect of his going out, I had occasion some time ago to allude to his constant dependence on God, and to urge upon him the duty of earnest prayer. But in this I was anticipated by a previous request of his own, when, after describing the trials and difficulties of his situation, he said to me, in a rather impressive manner, 'Mr. Muirhead, pray for me.' He has need of our prayers, and I trust, his request will be attended to by many friends at home.

CHINESE WOMEN IN NANKING

While walking along the streets, the number of females that are seen on the way is rather a novelty. They are in general well dressed, and of very respectable appearance. Many are riding on horseback, others are walking, and most of them have large feet. Not a few stop to hear our preaching, and always conduct themselves with perfect propriety. This is new, as compared with the former course of things, and the whole reminds one partly of home life. It will be a blessing if the revolution should tend to break up the system of female exclusion, hitherto practised.

CHARACTER AND PROSPECTS OF THE INSURGENTS

And now a word or two, with regard to the character and prospects of the movement. Those engaged in it speak not boastfully, but calmly and confidently of its sucess. They acknowledge the difficulties in the way, yet believe in the Lord God that they shall be established. They do not apprehend it will be an easy thing to overcome their enemies; but fighting, as they think, under the banners of the Heavenly Father and Heavenly Brother, they contemplate a happy issue as a matter of course. As Kan Wang's followers were assembling in front of his palace, a young man came upstairs. I asked him if he was going out to join the army. He said yes. 'Was he not afraid of being wounded or killed?' 'Oh, no,' he replied, 'the Heavenly Father will befriend me.' 'Well, but suppose you should be killed, what then?' 'Why, my soul will go to heaven.' 'How can you expect to go to heaven? What merit have you, to get there?' 'None, none in myself. It is entirely through the merits of the Heavenly Brother that this is to be done.' 'Who is the Heavenly Brother?' 'I am not very learned,' he said, 'and request instruction.' I then began to tell him that He was the Son of the Heavenly Father; but before I had finished the sentence, he replied correctly. 'What great work did Christ do?' I asked. The young man gave an explicit statement of the Saviour's work for sinners, of his coming into the world, suffering and dying in the room of sinful man, in order to redeem us from sin and misery. I inquired if he believed all this. 'Assuredly,' was his reply. 'When did you join the dynasty?' 'Last year.' 'Can you read?' 'No.' 'Who instructed you in these things?' 'The Tsan Wang.' 'What does he in the way of instructing his people?' 'He has daily service in his palace, and often preaches to them alike at home and when engaged in the field.' 'What book does he use?' 'He has a number belonging to the dynasty.' 'Do you know the New Testament?' 'Yes, but cannot read it.' 'Can you repeat the doxology of the Heavenly Father?' He went over it correctly. It contains in simple language the fundamental tenets of Christianity. 'Are there any special laws or commands connected with the dynasty?' 'There are the ten commandments.' 'Repeat them.' He went over a number of them, till he came to the sixth. 'Now,' I said, 'how is this command observed by you, seeing that so much cruelty and wickedness are practised by your brethren all around?' 'Oh!' he replied, 'in so far as fighting in the open field is concerned, that is all fair play and cannot be helped. It is not intended in the command.' 'No,' I remarked, 'that is not my meaning; but look at your brethren going privately into the country and robbing and killing the innocent people: what of that?' 'It is very bad, and such will only go to hell.' 'What, notwithstanding their adherence to the dynasty, and fighting under the same banners as yourself?' 'Yes, that is no matter; when the laws of Christ and the Heavenly Father are not attended to, these guilty individuals ought to die and go to hell.' 'But is not this the case with a great number of your adherents?' 'Alas! it is especially among our new recruits, whose hearts are not impressed with the true doctrine.' 'In all the public offices is care taken to instruct the soldiers and civilians connected with them?' 'Yes, every man, woman and child of reasonable age in the capital, can repeat the doxology of the Heavenly Father.' 'And what about those in the country?' 'Those who have short hair are not yet sufficiently taught, but books are being distributed among them, in order that they may learn those things.'

Such, in brief, is a faithful transcript of what I have seen and heard in the course of my ten days' visit to this place. When I began to write, it seemed impossible to record a tithe of all that had transpired. Incidents without number appeared to crowd upon my mind, so as to debar all idea of entering into details. The whole may be regarded by you as rather prolix, but you have it such as it is, and I close with a few thoughts in the way of

GENERAL CONCLUSIONS

I   We cannot but acknowledge that by means of the Tae-Ping chiefs, a gratifying amount of Bible truth has been diffused among their numerous adherents. True, it is limited, and mingled with much that is erroneous and blasphemous; still, the continued and extensive employment of the same means would tend much to spread a knowledge of the cardinal truths of Christianity.

II   We cannot but believe that the rebellion, even if ultimately unsuccessful, has inflicted a death-blow on idolatry and superstition in many parts of the country, which will be of service when other means are employed, in the providence of God, for the overthrow of 'Satan's seat' in this land. Such indignation has been shown to the idols, that the reverence of fear once entertained in regard to them can never be revived in the minds of their former worshippers.

III   But notwithstanding this favourable aspect of things, I cannot but regard this city and its neighbourhood, and the rebel territory generally, as an *unsuitable* sphere for the establishment of a Mission at present. It is not desired by such as are at the head of affairs, and their unwillingness is different from that of mere heathen rulers in respect to the same thing. The grounds of their dissent I have already alluded to.

IV I would, however, recommend that in the meanwhile Nanking be occasionally visited by our Missionaries. This will be especially useful as being best acquainted with the Mandarin dialect spoken here, and will serve to show Kan-Wang and others the lively interest we have in the place. When peace is restored, or when war has been removed from the immediate vicinity, and when a settled population is being gathered, arrangements may be made for a permanent stay. At that time, too, international treaties will be formed, on the basis of which open and public labour will be carried on.

V There is every prospect of the new dynasty making great progress in the course of this year. The insurgents are resolved and preparing to do so, while the imperial forces are greatly reduced. The conquest of these in a few more instances will utterly rout their strength in several surrounding provinces. Altogether, in the present aspect of affairs, it would be well for your Missionaries, in so far as the banks of the Yang-tsze-Kiang are concerned, to settle down where they can most usefully labour, and without incurring a heavy expense until matters assume a more definite shape, and the balance of power on either side, in the providence of God, points the way.

I am dear Brother,
Yours very sincerely,
Wm Muirhead.

58
A Letter from Rev I J Roberts
North China Herald, 30 March 1861

To the Editor of the North China Herald

Sir,

I have the pleasure of acknowledging a number of the copies of your paper this day received, and as a return of thanks for these, I propose now making you a short communication, with the double object of answering some enquiries compounded by * * *, one of your correspondents. I have but little time for writing private letters.

'1 What is their (the revolutionists') government?'
Answer—Martial Law, as far as I have yet been able to discover

from common observation. They have lately issued a Law Book, but I am sorry to say I have not had time to read it. I am studying the Nanking dialect, and that keeps me rather busy.

'2   Have they any regular organization?'
Answer—The have the six boards, in imitation of the Peking government. Farther than these I am not aware of any, only such as appertains to an army. And these Six Boards, which have their offices below the room in which I live, are broken up for the time being and gone out on a campaign with Kan Wang.

'3   Do the people, the better classes, accept their rule?'
Answer—They simply have the choice between doing so, or yielding up their heads. And of the two evils (should they think their rule such) of course they would choose the least; and without venturing to grumble submit to their rule.

'4   Are Church and State separate?'
Answer—I have constituted no Church yet and of course there was none before I came, for I suppose there is not another ordained minister located within Teen Wang's territory. But I think Teen Wang has as yet only a very indistinct idea of the true difference between Church and State, and their distinct duties and prerogatives.

'5   Do they follow the rules of faith and practice laid down in the New Testament?'
Answer—How would that be possible without a preacher? They certainly do not.

'6   What are their prospects of securing the peace of the country?'
Answer—This is not the time to talk about peace. It is Jehu's time, when he asked. 'What I have to do with peace?' One king went out with an army on a fighting campaign two days ago; Kan Wang went out about two weeks since; and Teen Wang's brother also goes out in a few days with an army: and four or five kings were out before. So that there will be in all seven or eight kings out with main armies, besides many lesser officers, in every direction, fighting to the uttermost. Talk about peace to them before "the devilish imps" are exterminated,—you might as well have talked to Jehu about peace before the house of Ahaz was exterminated. But they seem pretty determined now to do up their work as fast as possible. I presume they never had so many troops, and so many royal commanders, in the field at any one time before.

'7   What books have they published, and can you send me a complete set of them and of their proclamations?'
Answer—Kan Wang has ordered you a set at my request, but they have not come in yet. Their titles and subject matter you will please examine when you get them.

'8   Will you please state what seems to you their present position?'
Answer—This is rather an intangible question to work out. It seems to me—1. That Nanking is secure against imperial attack, without foreign assistance: this is the first and foundation position. 2. That they are yet in a revolutionary state without any treaty relations with foreign nations, or other government than comes under martial Law. This is their political position. 3. They worship God daily under the name of Heavenly Father Shangti, and heavenly elder brother, Christ. But not according to New Testament usages. They have no regular immersion or Lord's Supper; and the Doxology and Hymn which I taught Hung Siu-tsiuen when he was with me at Canton in 1847, I fear they are using (some of them at least) as the Jews did Moses' serpent, worshipping them formally instead of the God whom they praise. They are at any rate now sung I presume by millions every day. This is their religious position. And now, our position is to stand still and see the glory of God. We cannot control this matter. We can only pray that God will overrule it for good.

IJR

59
A Pamphlet by Rev. Griffith John
The Chinese Rebellion (Canton, 1861)

A MONTH AMONG THE INSURGENTS
GENERAL CONCLUSIONS

The preceding [*Referring to the paper in the 'Friend of China' of the 9th February,*] is an outline of the experiences of nearly a month, in the Insurgents' territory. The reader is now in a position to judge for himself on various points of interest. Perhaps, however, it would be well to sum up the result in as short a space as possible, by answering the questions that are generally proposed in reference to the movement.

First: What is the nature of their government?

It seems to me to be *professedly* a 'theocracy'. According to their own representations, the subjects of the Celestial dynasty are the chosen people. God is their king, the Chief is His Viceregent, and Nanking is the holy city—the modern Jerusalem. The Celestial King says, that he has received his authority from God, that he is supported in it by God, and that he holds the kingdom in subjection to God. The distinction of Church and State is wholly ignored. The one is cöextensive with the other. Until the death of the Eastern king—the evil-genius of the movement in a religious point of view—the theocratic idea was carried out to its fullest extent. From one of their published works, which pretends to give a full account of the descent of the 'Heavenly Father', on various occasions, we learn that, from the beginning, nothing was done without an express declaration of the divine will through the Eastern and Western kings. Not the minutest improvement could be effected, nor the slightest change introduced, before the oracle had spoken. When narrowly watched by spies, and oppressed by enemies on account of their profession of Christianity, whilst yet in Kwangsi, the 'Heavenly Father' commands them to hold their meetings of prayer and praise in the night. The change has been perpetuated. The Chief was not to declare his mission, nor publish his religious works, before the divinely appointed time. The 'Heavenly Father' commands them to pitch their tents, and they pitch them; he commands them to march on, and they obey. A spy is in their midst, and he is pointed out by the 'Heavenly Father'. The officers and people have the most implicit confidence in these pretended visions of the Eastern and Western kings. 'The Heavenly Father', they say, 'has taken the trouble to come down, times without number, and spoken by the mouth of the Eastern and Western kings. At the commencement of the movement when our brethren were but few, and the cause but feeble, His descent was frequent; now that we are numerous, and our cause is strong, there is not 'the same necessity for it'. In a very remarkable communication from the Chiefs to the Rev. Mr Roberts, the descent of the 'Heavenly Father' is mentioned as a fact, not to be called in question.

The object of the Eastern king was simply to establish the throne of the new dynasty on a firm basis. This, he supposed, he could not do by speaking in his own name; and hence, he blasphemously feigned to speak in the name of God. Whether the Chief had a hand in introducing this species of fraud, or whether he regarded it in this light, we have not the means of knowing. One thing is certain, that, in whatever light these visions were received by the principal men in the transaction, the mass of converts believed them to be none other than authentic revelations. This may seem strange to *us*. But we must remember that the Chinese are firm believers in an intimate connexion between the spiritual world and this, and in the possibility of carrying on a constant intercommunication between both. Spirit writing, and something akin to spirit rapping, they have had from time immemorial. Nothing is more common, if the Chinese are to be believed, than for a spirit, or even a god, to take possession of a man and convert him into a mouthpiece. In these things they believe, as strongly as our forefathers did in ghosts, hobgoblins, and witchcraft; or, as not a few of our contemporaries do in table turning and spirit rapping. Though these men have renounced their former gods as vile and false, still from the want of Christian teachers, they have not divested themselves of all their superstitious notions. As a wicked man might, according to their notions, become the mouthpiece of an evil spirit or a false god, why might not a good man become the mouthpiece of a good spirit, or even of the true God. Whether they have reasoned thus, or no, I am not prepared to say. I simply affirm, that nothing could be more natural, than for a Chinaman to do so, if left to himself. Now, it is difficult for us to say, how far a designing man might, by taking advantage of this general credulity, succeed in deluding the mass; or how far the actor himself might fall a victim to self delusion. Though the visions are closed, the form of government still remains professedly theocratic. The chief still speaks of his throne as the throne of the Heavenly Father and the Heavenly Elder Brother; of his kingdom as the kingdom of heaven; and of the angelic hosts as his guardians.

The real form of government, I was told by Chun at Tan Yang, is monarchical. The rank of kings is a temporary expediency. They are mere generalissimos. When peace is restored, they will become governors, and governors-general, and Hung Siu tsüen *alone* will be acknowledged king. Though each of the kings governs the territory which he himself has conquered, and has his civil and military officers, over whom he exercises the sole jurisdiction, still they are all amenable to the Celestial king. He scrutinises their actions, and watches over their movements, with great care and vigilance, and keeps them completely under his power and control. He raises up the one, and pulls down the other, according to the council of his own will.

At Nanking there are the six boards corresponding with those of Peking. The Kan Wang is president. Some of the members are very respectable scholars. They have civil as well as military officers in the cities, who watch over the interests of the country people. As the cities are, *pro tem*, mere garrisons, and therefore under strict martial law, there is not the scope for the exercise of civil government, as there would be in times of peace. For the same reason, the civil department is, for the time, inferior and subservient to the military. When peace is restored, this order will be reversed. At present the gentry, and the people, through the gentry, may petition the civil Magistrate for redress of grievances; and, from what the people themselves say, this is not done in vain. The whole of the Insurgents' country is under a regular system of taxation, which is somewhat more moderate than the old.

The system of community of goods still continues. At Nanking it is carried out to its fullest extent. Every thing is in common. They have no salary. The Celestial king supplies all the chiefs, kings, and soldiers, with their respective portions of food, money, and clothing. He is the father of the family. Of course, the kings and officers, who go out to fight, do not depend solely on the allowances assigned to them by the Chief. The Chung-wang is probably richer than the Celestial king himself. The Ananiases and Sapphiras are doubtless many.

Second: Why do not the people return into the cities?
Does not this prove that the Insurgents fail to win their confidence?

From the Chiefs Liu and Chun, I learnt what I did not know before, namely, that the people are *not permitted* to live in the cities at present. They say that, whilst the dynastic change is going on, the cities must for the most part belong to the soldiers, and the country to the people; and that in this they do not deviate from the policy adopted by every other dynasty, the Manchu not excepted. To throw open the gates of the captured cities to the people, whilst surrounded by the enemy, would, they say, be a most suicidal course. They would soon be filled with Imperialist soldiers in the shape of shopkeepers and coolies, who would render their case desperate in the event of an attack. As soon as a definite portion of the territory is thoroughly subjugated, and all the strongholds of the enemy within the same taken, the people will be admitted into the cities, and order will be restored.

But, it is often asked, how is it that the people are not permitted to live in cities which have been held by them for years? Those who ask this question forget that, until very recently, nearly all the cities in possession of the Insurgents were actually besieged, or in danger of speedily being so. In April of last year, even Nanking itself was surrounded by 100,000 men. At one time the city was, to all human appearance, within ten days of falling into the hands of the Imperialists. We would do well to remember, also, that the English and the French have done much towards delaying the important work of reorganization. What can be done at Tsing pu, Kwun shan, Su cheu, and other cities in the vicinity of Shanghai, whilst this city is in the hands of the Imperialists, and rendered impregnable by the presence of English and French soldiers within its walls? Out of it they may sally forth to harass the Insurgents in their movements, and into it they may return, when defeated, to rally their forces. In it they are beyond the reach of harm. Our shot and shell are a wall of fire round about them. Were Shanghai in the possession of the Insurgents, the work of reorganization might commence at once in the southern part of Kiang su province. But this day has been indefinitely deferred by our shortsighted policy.

Third: Can these men be regarded in any other light than that of lawless marauders?

There are not a few who think and speak of them as such. The Magistrate of the town in which I am now writing, does not view them in this light. 'Thieves', said he, the other day, when I called upon him, 'seek nothing but plunder, and are satisfied with it; but the Long haired rebels are aiming at the throne.' The facts, that they have a regular system of government; that the persons and property of their subjects are protected and respected; that the people open markets for them, and are paid the full value for all they sell; that foreigners can travel (as we did) night and day through their territory without molestation from either the soldiers or the people; and that they aim at nothing less than the subversion of the Manchu, and the establishment of a native dynasty—these facts, and such as these, are a conclusive answer to the above question.

The chief, kings, and the officers, discountenance the burning of houses, and the plundering and murdering of the people. On these points the Chung-wang's orders are very strict. At Su cheu and other cities, proclamations are posted up on the walls and the city gates, forbidding all these, under the penalty of decapitation. These atrocities are not essential, but accidental, to the movement. It is true that the state of the towns and cities, from Su cheu to Nanking, proves that the work of destruction has been carried on to a fearful extent. Houses in heaps, widows and orphans in mourning, old men and women with broken hearts and downcast looks moving slowly and timidly among the ruins, and dead bodies in various stages of decomposition, are objects which continually meet the eye and sicken the heart. I have no desire whatever to exculpate the Insurgents by becoming their special pleader. They are guilty of having brought a vast amount of misery upon this people, which might have been avoided. Still, it is but simple justice to them to ascertain candidly the nature and the amount of their crime, before pronouncing a judgment. Much of the burning, as well as other works of destruction is done by the Imperialists themselves, before the arrival of the Insurgents. Such was the case at Su cheu. The king Chung found the city and the suburbs in a blaze; and he offered a large reward to anyone who would undertake to quench the devouring element.

The extremities to which the Insurgents had been reduced, in the city of Nanking, and the suddenness, completeness, and greatness of their subsequent victory, must be taken into consideration. Cut off from all supplies by the besieging army of Chang-koh-liang, the kings, officers, and soldiers were reduced to congee and roots. Starvation stared them in the face. Just at this time deliverance came. The King Ying came from the North, and the King Chung from the South, and surrounded the Imperialist host, with 200,000 men. On the second day of the fourth moon, the Imperialist army was put to flight, and a most brilliant victory was won by the Insurgents. The barrier having been removed, this huge mass, like a mighty cataract rolling down with an irresistible impetuosity, and sweeping everything before it, pursued the enemy from city to city, and from town to town, till, on the thirteenth day of the fourth moon, only eleven days after the first victory, Su cheu was entered triumphantly. Is it to be wondered at, that such a body of men, burning with a spirit of revenge, and elated with such a series of triumphs, should commit many atrocious deeds? They regarded the people as guilty in their opposition to them, and, as such, deserving a severe chastisement.

In the vicinity of Shanghae, we witness the very worst feature in their character. Had the Shanghae district been in their possession from the time they paid us a visit, looting and impressment would have died away long ago. In the Insurgent territory there is no looting. The people are protected, and private property is respected. The Shanghae district, and parts of the neighbouring districts, are in the Imperialist territory. The people have refused to yield allegiance. On these grounds, the Insurgents believe that they have a right to plunder them to the utmost. They are enemies, and are to be treated as such.

Again, it should not be forgotten that tens of thousands of the very vilest characters, from the Imperialist army, and of the Honan filchers,[14] have recently joined them. These are very different from the 'old Rebels'. They know absolutely nothing of religion. The people generally speak of the latter as kind and

14   Presumably a reference to the Nien rebels.

conciliatory, whilst they represent the former as everything that is bad and hateful.

We would do well to remember, also, that the Insurgents are not alone in this respect. Even Christian nations are capable of deeds of cruelty and rapine, equal to anything recorded of the Insurgents. Follow the bloody track of the British conqueror in India. Behold towns in flames, fields strewn with the bodies of the slain and the murdered, rivers crimsoned with blood, homes rifled, and the quivering lips and uplifted hands of thousands muttering curses and calling down vengeance. Listen to the frantic cries of the broken hearted widow, the sighs of the orphan, and the tales of woe which the aged are wont to tell. But we need not go to India. If report be true, a faithful history of the war which has just been brought to a close with this empire, would reveal deeds of spoliation and cruelty, which, even the Insurgents would find it hard to contemplate without a blush for our common humanity. The burning of the suburbs of the city of Shanghae, and the reckless destruction of property at the Emperor's palace, equal, if they do not surpass, anything perpetrated by the Insurgents. And the conduct of the English and French, at Shanghae, towards the 'Rebels' far exceeds, in point of atrocity the most infamous deed of the perfidious Tartars in the North. We mention these things, not to excuse the real crimes of the Insurgents, but to show that they are crimes which accompany war in every age, and in every country, whether waged by Christians or pagans.

Compared with the Imperialist army, they shine. The crimes of the one are the wild freaks of a wayward boy, whilst those of the other are the inveterate, ingrained, incorrigible habits of an abandoned old man.

Fourth: What portion of the country do they possess?

They claim the best portions of six provinces, namely Kiang Su, Kiang Si, Ngan Hwei, Kwang Si, Sü Chwan, and Honam. I find that they are now pushing their way into the very heart of the province of Shan Tung. Chang Loh Hing, the head of the Honam filchers, has sworn allegiance to the Celestial King, and has been promoted to the rank of Chu Tsiang, which stands next to that of King. He is now with a large army only sixty miles from the capital of the province. His army is much larger than that of the Imperialists. We must wait and see what the spring will bring forth.

Fifth: What is their numerical strength?

Though I have made repeated inquiries on this point, I have not been able to obtain any definite information. They are far stronger than they have ever been. Within the last two years, they have had large accessions to their number. All the Honam filchers have been incorporated in the Insurgent army. Tens of thousands of Chang Koh-liang's soldiers were taken prisoners of war at Nanking and Tan Yang; they also are scattered among the army. Besides the above, thousands of people have been impressed.

Sixth: What are their prospects? Are they likely to succeed?

If left alone to fight their own battle, without the interference of foreign nations, they have every prospect of a signal and speedy (Chinese speed of course) success. Whatever may become of the Celestial king, the Kwangsi Insurrection must triumph. There is no power in China to put it down. All minor insurrections have been lost in it. The Tartars, unaided, might as well attempt to blow the sun out of the heavens, as to attempt to quench this flame. They did their utmost, when far stronger than they are now, or ever will be hereafter, but in vain. The Tartar power is a myth, a phantom, at which the Insurgents can afford to laugh.

Unintentionally, we have done much to hasten the downfall of the existing dynasty. The series of defeats which they have sustained, has given the people of China an insight into the weakness of their masters, such as they never had before. The spell has been broken for ever. They believe in their invincibility no longer. 'Every dynasty', remarked a very superior scholar, and, formerly, a very devoted Imperialist, not many days since,— 'Every dynasty has its four seasons. The existing one has passed through its first three, and is now far advanced in its fourth. The next must be either English, French, or Russian.' Such is the general sentiment touching the speedy downfall of the tottering Manchu dynasty.

Intentionally, however, we have done our best to breath a new life into this dead carcass, and to quench the youthful ardour of the rising giant. In holding Shanghae for the Imperialists, the Insurgents have received a very severe check in their onward march, and their fair prospects have been considerably overcast. With Shanghae in their hands the work of conquering and reorganizing, would move apace. As it is, the former must progress more slowly, and the latter be postponed indefinitely.

We must not expect the work to be accomplished in China, with the same rapidity as it would be accomplished in the West, where everything moves on at railway speed. Almost every dynastic change in China has been preceded by twenty, thirty, and forty, years of contest and anarchy. The Kwangsi Insurrection is still in its decade. A Chinaman would think this nothing.

Seventh: May they in any sense of the term be called Christians?

They hate idolatry with perfect hatred. The Chief regards it as the great curse of China, and is determined to sweep every vestige of it from the land. 'Let the foreign brethren know,' says the King Chung, 'that we are determined to uproot idolatry out of the land, and to plant Christianity in its stead.' They believe in, and worship, *one* God, the creator and preserver of all things. They believe in Jesus Christ as the saviour of the world from sin and hell. They believe in the Holy spirit as the regenerator and sancti-fier. They believe in the doctrine of providence. In opposition to the pantheistic notions of the philosophers of the Sung dynasty, they hold the doctrine of the personality of the deity; in opposi-tion to the popular polytheistic notions, they have the clearest conceptions of the unity of God; and in opposition to the fatalism of philosophical Buddhism, they believe in and teach the doctrine of an all superintending providence. The Deity is not, in their opinion, an abstract notion, nor a stern, implacable sovereign, but a loving father who watches tenderly over their interests, and leads them by the hand. It is from a profound conviction of the fact itself, and of the *practical* importance of the fact, that the Chief teaches his people that the Supreme Lord is Tien Fu, 'Heavenly Father'.

They receive the scriptures of the old and new Testaments as the infallible word of God; and as such, they have printed the whole of the New, and the old to the Book of Judges. They believe in a future state of rewards and punishments.

There can be no doubt of their belief in the above doctrines; and if this creed was not mixed up with many errors, none would hesitate to pronounce them Christians. But, unfortunately, the enemy has been active in sowing tares among the wheat. Their errors and defects are neither few nor insignificant.

One of the worst features in the movement was the pretensions of the Eastern and Western Kings to divine revelations and heavenly visions. Nothing can be more disgusting than the length-ened accounts given of the descent of the Heavenly Father on various occasions. The abominable twaddle that is put in the mouth of the infinite God, sounds blasphemous. In this we discover not only ignorance, but the very blackest passions of our corrupt nature manifesting themselves. Strange though it may seem to us, still it is a fact, that these pretended visions are solemnly believed in by the kings, officers, and soldiers. The throne of the chief is partially built upon them.

272

Polygamy is another dark spot on the movement. The chief kings—the Kan Wang not excepted—have all a plurality of wives. The custom was introduced by the Eastern King. It has taken a deep root by this time.

They entertain notions touching the Supreme, which are not quite free from error. They teach that he is not a *pure* Spirit. The chief maintains that he has form. This error is one into which the human mind may easily fall, from its impotence to grasp the idea of a pure Spirit. Some of the Fathers ascribed corporeality to God. Tertulian asks, *quis negabit Deum corpus esse, etsi Deus Spiritus est.* One who had been listening to the instructions of one who spake as no man spake, made the request—*Show us the Father.* On the nature of Christ and the doctrine of the Trinity, the views of the chief are positively wrong; those of the Kan Wang are strictly scriptural; and those of the other Kings, officers, and soldiers are defective. The nature of Christ, the personal distinction and essential unity of the three persons in the Godhead, and such questions, are points to which the latter have given but little, if any, attention. They simply believe in the Father the creator, in Christ the saviour, and in the Holy Spirit the regenerator and sanctifier. Of the influence of this belief on their moral character, I can say nothing. The amount of Christian knowledge they possess varies considerably. That of the Kwangsi and Canton men, who have been taught by the chief himself, is more extensive. With some of these I have had delightful conversations on religious subjects. That of the soldiers is limited to two or three elementary truths. They can nearly all repeat the doxology and their daily prayers. The Sabbath is regarded by them as a day for spiritual worship. They do not keep it strictly. They intend doing so, they say, when peace is restored.

Such is their religious belief, theological errors, and the extent of their religious knowledge. Every one must judge for himself how far they may be called Christians.

Eighth: Does the Chief receive the scriptures of the old and new Testaments as the *word* of God?

Yes, decidedly. (See Journal, Nov. 19th.)

Ninth: Does he receive divine honours?

This has been erroneously affirmed concerning him. From the testimony of the soldiers, officers, kings, and his own, it is evident that he does not. They seem shocked with an instinctive sense of impropriety whenever the question was put to them. All the worship they pay to him is to repeat the 'Wan swei—May the King live for ever.' They say that they worship Christ as God, and not as the Celestial King. They understand the distinction perfectly well between divine worship and a mere court etiquette.

Tenth: Do they grant full permission to Missionaries to preach the gospel in their territory?

They do this. I have brought with me an edict to this effect, written by the young prince on satin with the vermillion pencil, and stamped with the Imperial seal. This edict has already appeared.[15] They have given this permission not in ignorance of, but with their eyes quite open to, the difference which exists between us, and the possible consequences which may spring from a collision of sentiment. They are quite willing and *anxious* that Missionaries should go at once among the people to propagate Christianity. So far as the *people* are concerned, they throw the door wide open at once and for ever. I cannot say that they are *anxious* that Missionaries should go among the soldiers at *present*. They fear two things, namely, the *possibility* of the Missionaries being accidentally injured, and the probability that the detection of error would shake the confidence of the army in the Celestial King, and thereby undermine his throne. This apprehension, however, is temporary. It will pass away when the throne is firmly established. Many of the chiefs seem to entertain no fears whatever on this score. This edict opens, not only the country, but also the cities. 'Let any of the Missionaries come among us,' said the chiefs Liu, Hiung, and Chun, at Su Cheu, 'and it will be all right. We will furnish them with houses and chapels.' 'Though', said the Kan Wang, 'I should be very sorry for an injudicious man to come among us, still should any Missionary come even to Nanking, the edict binds us to receive him.' As to the propriety, safety, and utility of going among them at present, each Missionary must judge for himself.

Eleventh: What are the pretensions of the Chief?

This man is a great puzzle. In many respects, he is a man of very great power. His whole history proves this. All his subjects are under his complete control. He pulls down one, and sets up another according to the counsel of his own will. They all look up to him with something like superstitious reverence. He writes all his own edicts. For some years he has been busily engaged in correcting the classics, and rewriting a history of China, with additions and corrections. His favourite books are the Bible and the Pilgrim's Progress. He is intimately acquainted with the scriptures, and quotes them readily on all occasions. He has read the

15   For a translation of this Edict see Michael, op. cit., vol. III, pp. 926–8.

Shanghai Serial[16] carefully, and refers to the theological articles contained therein on controversial points. He is now devouring with avidity the scientific books which have been presented to him. The Kan Wang believes him to be a devout worshipper of the true God. He smokes neither opium nor common tobacco, nor drinks intoxicating drinks. All these are prohibited under the severest penalties. Such a character contrasts very favourably with the imbecile monarch who sits on the throne of China at present. All this speaks well for him, and were there no drawbacks, would make him an object of universal admiration.

He sets up certain pretensions, which, to our ears, sound very much like blasphemy. What these pretensions precisely are, it is very difficult for us to determine. My own impressions are the following. Others must judge for themselves.

He calls himself 'son of God', Heavenly ruler 'Tien Chiu', the *natural* and *second* brother of Christ. He says that, in the year 1837, his soul ascended to heaven when he saw God and Christ, conversed with them, and received powers from them to exterminate the idols, propagate the true religion, and expel the Tartars. He often speaks and writes of himself as the Lord of all nations and peoples under heaven. Before passing a judgment on this man, let us remember that he is a Chinaman, and by no means exempt from the common infirmities of his race—that he has had to struggle almost single-handed out of the darkness of heathenism, and to work out his own theological creed—that the wonderful success which has followed his path, and the almost miraculous deliverances which have been wrought in his behalf from time to time, must have worked very powerfully on his imagination. The first title Shangte tsi, 'son of God', corresponds with that of the Emperor of China, Tien tsi, 'son of Heaven'. Every Emperor is supposed to be divinely appointed by Heaven to rule. The Celestial king believes this of himself, and as such, appropriates the above title.

The second Tien Chiu, 'Heavenly ruler', has this meaning and something more. Besides the idea that he is the heavenly appointed ruler, there is another, derived from the *supposed* theocratic constitution of his government. God is the King; and hence the kingdom is called the Kingdom of *Heaven*. Being the appointed viceregent in this kingdom, he calls himself the 'Heavenly ruler', that is, the *visible* hand of the kingdom of heaven. For the same reason, the dynasty is called the *Celestial*

16 The *Shanghai Serial* (Liu-ho ts'ung-t'an) was a monthly published by Alexander Wylie in 1857–8 which consisted of articles on religion, science and literature, as well as general news.

dynasty, the capital the Celestial *capital*, and the soldiers *Celestial* soldiers.

To understand the precise idea he attaches to the expressions, Tung pau it hiung[17] and ih hiung, 'natural brother' and 'second brother of Christ', it is necessary to inquire into the views which he entertains concerning the person of Christ, the Trinity, and the origin of the human soul. Of the doctrine of the Trinity, as understood by orthodox Christians I believe, he has not the slightest conception. According to this doctrine, there are *three inseparably connected* with one another possessing equal glory, but making unitedly only one God. He *denies* the equality of the persons; and says that Christ can not be called God. He does not recognize a distinction of persons in the Godhead. The 'Heavenly Father' is God alone; Christ is altogether a distinct being. He sees nothing in Jesus but a human soul united to a human body—a man. Of the union of the *divine* nature with the human, so as to constitute one person—'*God* with us', he is utterly in the dark. One of the oldest of the Kwang-si disciples told me, that the Celestial King taught them that the souls of both Christ and himself were *created* before the world. The 'Heavenly Father' is alone uncreated and self-existent. All souls have been created by Him, and are variously appointed for the accomplishment of various purposes. By nature they are all the sons of God, and in their pre-existent state are perfectly pure and happy. But, though *all* souls are the creation of God, and as such, his sons, still there is the important distinction of time, greatness, and dignity. Christ is the first and greatest begotten son of God, vastly superior to all other, whether men or angels. His mission also was far more important than that of any other son of God. He came to redeem the world from sin and hell. All human spirits being created by God, are in this pristine state intimately related to Christ; and men can only forfeit their claim to this relationship by sin and unbelief. 'All who worship and believe in the Heavenly Father', said the chief Lin, 'are sons of God in the *same* sense as the Celestial king is.' All believers, then, are, both in relation to Christ and to each other, *Tung pau ti hiung* 'natural brothers'. There is, however, a distinction of nearness and remoteness in the order of creation and of dignity in rank. The Chief says that, as Christ is the first, so he is the second begotten or created son. Hence the reason why he calls himself the *second* brother of Christ. His mission also is only second in importance to that of Christ. He does not make himself God. On the contrary, God

17   The text reads thus; 'it' is presumably a misprint for ti—younger brother.

276

according to his teachings is alone, and infinitely above all creatures—Christ not excepted. When he speaks of God, Christ, and himself, as one family and one person, he simply means to say that they are one in sympathy, interest, and aim. Such is the metaphorical sense of the term, and is often used by them when speaking of the whole body of believers. Such, doubtless, is the sense attached to the expression *Ih kia ih ti* 'one family one person', in the case before us.

We must remember that this man has had to form his theological theories independent of foreign aid. The *scriptural* doctrine of the Trinity has, probably, never been presented to his mind in such a way as he could understand it. He is a thinking man, and won't take the mere *ipse dixit* of any one for proof and demonstration. I believe that, if it were proved to him that his views do not harmonize with the word of God, he would renounce them. With the renunciation of his errors, he would, it is to be hoped, cease to assume some of these high sounding titles, and to arrogate to himself such extravagant pretensions.

As to the vision of 1837, both he and his followers seem to have the most implicit confidence in it as a revelation of the divine will and purpose concerning himself. Even the Kan wang is a firm believer in it. That he had some sort of a vision or a dream, corresponding with the description, is probable; that he, being an oriental, (and the majority of occidentals are not much more sane on this point) should believe in it as a revelation from heaven is very natural; that his wonderful success should deepen his own convictions, as well as those of his followers, on this point, is exactly what we might have expected.

Touching the strong and, to us, offensive language which he employs to express the extent of his dominion and the greatness of his power, the Kan wang says that it is hyperbolical, and simply intended to inspire all around him with confidence and courage. The kings and chiefs with whom I have had any intercourse, so far from looking with contempt upon western nations as petty states, seem to regard them as great, wealthy, and prosperous. Not a few of them know and confess that they have much to learn from them, politically, socially, and religiously.

Twelfth: What is our duty in reference to them?

The duty of missionaries is very plain. They ought, by prayer and effort, to do all that lieth in their power to correct their errors, and to promote pure Christianity among them. They are determined to uproot idolatry, and plant Christianity in its stead. Whatever the missionaries may do, they will go on demolishing the idols. The first part of the task they are performing themselves in a most masterly manner, the second part they will attempt, but cannot accomplish alone. Notwithstanding all their errors, which are neither few nor insignificant, I firmly believe that they are the chosen instruments to relieve China from the darkness and thraldom of idolatry, and, in connexion with foreign Missionaries, to bless her with the light and liberty of the gospel. Were the Insurgents nominally Roman Catholics, instead of being what they are, professedly Protestants, the Church of Rome would not abandon them on account of their errors. In the midst of the rubbish, she would detect the stones of a magnificent building; and in the midst of the confusion and discord she would not fail to discover the elements of an order and an harmony that might ravish a gazing world some day.

Protestant Missionaries in China! This Insurrection is your offspring. From the want of your parental care, it has grown deformed, and wayward; it still possesses the elements of a perfect man. It depends upon yourselves whether it will prove a blessing or a curse to this Nation. If you do your duty, it will be the former; if you abandon it to itself, it probably will be the latter. As Christian, and especially Protestant Missionaries in the land, it is your duty to watch this struggle intelligently, and with parental solicitude to wait patiently the evolution of events, and to pray that He, who is the God of battle, as well as the God of peace, would graciously bring harmony out of the present discord, and order out of the present confusion.

The policy which western nations should adopt in reference to the movement, is that of strict neutrality. To oppose it would be censurable in principle, subversive of the kindly feeling which the leaders of it cherish towards foreigners, and pernicious to the best interests of trade. They only want to be left alone to fight their own battle; and to grant them this is the least thing we can do. They don't seek our assistance. They feel perfect confidence in themselves, and the justice of their cause. The demolition of idolatry, and the downfall of the Tartar dynasty, they regard as unalterably fixed by an inviolable decree. And further they have a deep and unmistakable conviction, that they are the instruments divinely appointed to secure this end; and that time is all they need to accomplish their task, *single-handed*. They are now in possession of some of the fairest portions of the Empire; and are looking forward, with glowing anticipation to many a speedy and brilliant victory. Ere long our safety in travelling for missionary and commercial purposes, together with the very existence of one of the most important branches of trade, will depend upon them. Whatever we may say to the contrary, they have it in their power to convert this great fertile commercial field into a barren heath. They are our friends; and nothing could justify the step that would convert them into our foes. Moreover, there is only one course left open to us, if we wish to avoid territorial aggression. These men must be treated as *open* foes, or else left to themselves. There is no middle ground. If we don't give them fair play to fight their own battle, we must drive them out of the field entirely, and take possession of the Empire ourselves. We have nothing to do with the question, whether the movement is right or wrong. The Chinese must decide this for themselves. Revolutions have been common in China, and more than one of the revolutionary chiefs have been canonized as *saints*. Should the present Chief succeed to establish a native dynasty, based upon righteous principles, his name, though now greatly maligned, will be transmitted to posterity with applause, and he himself will be ranked among the greatest of China's sons. The interests of religion, commerce, and civilization, point out *neutrality* as the only legitimate ground for Western nations to take.

To attempt to uphold a dynasty, which is doomed speedily to fall, is folly; to perpetuate the vitality of a dynasty, which does not deserve to live, is sin; and to retard the onward march of a power, which must wax stronger in spite of us, is infatuation. Should we be able to put down this insurrection, what advantage would accrue to either the people of China or ourselves? Another would immediately break forth, which would run precisely the same course. A dynastic change must be effected. The Tartar yoke must be shaken off as an intolerable incubus on the nation. Let no one suppose that another race of Insurgents would do the work better than the present. The mere tyro in Chinese history must know that the Kwangsi insurrection would suffer nothing by comparison with most of the past. It is generally by a slow process of exhaustion that the old dynasty is consumed. In China, the new dynasty, phoenixlike, rises out of the ashes of the effete one. If England does not wish to assume the reins of government herself, she had better keep aloof from this contest, and have nothing to say to either of the contending parties. Let her stand on neutral ground, and she will command the respect of both parties; let her step aside, and she will be hated by the one, and despised by the other. This principle has been grossly violated at Shanghae. In holding the city for the Imperialists, we have committed a great political blunder; and in firing on the Insurgents, and murdering 200 of their men, without having given the slightest *official* intimation of our intention to do so, and without their having given us the the faintest provocation, we have perpetrated a horrible crime. No right thinking and right feeling Englishman can look back upon this perverse and mean display of brute force without a blush. It is to be sincerely hoped, that such a blunder will never be committed again, and that our civilization and national character be never tarnished with such another foul blot.

Griffith John.

Section 2 The Missionaries Withdraw (1861–2)

The surge of hope apparent in the missionary reports of late 1860 and early 1861 was not long sustained. By the latter half of 1861 practically all the missionaries, even the most sympathetic among them, had turned away, convinced that effective work with the Taiping was, for the foreseeable future, not practicable. Indeed most came to see the rebel movement as hopeless in a political as well as a religious sense, even when they were critical of the developing policy of Western intervention against the rebellion. Some, such as the LMS representatives and the American Methodist Young J. Allen, turned away in sorrow and uncertainty (Docs. 61, 63, 65); others, including Roberts, did so in evident anger and irritation, feeling cheated and deceived (Docs. 60, 62, 64, 67, 68, 69). A new arrival, meeting the Chung Wang in Soochow and there seeing the best of the movement in its last years, might still maintain some hope (Doc. 66), but for the most part this had ebbed completely by the beginning of 1862.

60
A Letter from Rev. W N Hall
Missionary Herald, n.s., vol. LVII (September 1861), pp. 137–8

Nankin is a ruin, except a few palaces. Outside and in you walk over broken bricks. All trade in the city is prohibited (except the sale of drugs) *on pain of death*; and outside there is very little doing. It may generally be said, that the citizens of Nankin are all in Government employ, and are provided for by rations; all the boats are in the same way in connection with Government; the presence of one or two vessels was sufficient cause to make the suburb nearest to them the busiest part of Nankin, and straw hovels for shops sprung up like mushrooms. . . . I saw no indication at Nankin that the Teen-Wang's government cared one jot for the public weal in this particular; all is in a state of desolation. *Loot* is the staff of life; and the Chang-Wang was not ashamed to confess, when spoken to on the subject of the utter destruction of property, &c. which marks the course of their armies, and that the time must come when loot will fail, 'Ah, well, we may as well have a clean sweep out, and begin again'. *At present*, as far as I can learn, their policy is nothing but to destroy. . . .

Whatever the Teen-Wang may have been when he started, I cannot now but look upon him as an imposter, in the same category with Mohammed, and as very Anti-christ. Without disputing about language and terms, my own investigations led me to the following conclusions concerning him and his doctrine:

I   That he claims equality with Jesus.
II That he has added to 'the things which are written in *the book*'.
III That he is worshipped by his followers as equal to Christ; and
IV I cannot but believe that this he has done, and is doing, *knowingly*, to answer his own ends.

With regard to his followers, *some may have* some better ideas of divine truth; the great bulk, however, I think, know no more than the use of a few terms; and, as Mr Roberts remarks, he thinks the 'Shangti' worshipped by the masses is the *Chinese* 'Shangti', and not the 'Shangti' of the 'Delegates version'.

61
Narrative of a Visit to Nanking by Rev. Joseph Edkins
From Jane Edkins, *Chinese Scenes and People* (London, 1863), pp. 247–81

The next sun saw us early in the city, where we were courteously received by the second insurgent chief. He was a man of easy manners, intelligent, and devoid of all desire for pomp and parade in dress, or in the mode of receiving his visitors. He at once granted us a passport to Nanking, given in the name of the *great peaceful heavenly dynasty*. This document was perfectly effective in securing us from all trouble on the part of customs' collectors, and intrusive rebel subordinates, for the whole distance to Nanking. Taiping flags wave on all city gates along this route, and the unhappy people, submitting without resistance to the sway of their new rulers, respect all their documents and regulations.

A celebrated temple in the midst of Sucheu gave clear witness to the uncompromising iconoclasm of these singular revolutionists. It is called Hiuen-miau-kwan,—'The temple of the dark and wonderful'. All the host of Tauist divinities used to appear seated in pride and splendour in the niches and galleries of this building. The trinity of the pure ones, the highest of all in rank, occupied a central position. Then there was the jadestone god, the god of the black north, and the god of thunder. There were the gods of time, who preside in succession over each year in the cycle of sixty, the gods of the stars, fixed and planetary, tabulated and not tabulated, the gods of the metals, elements, and essences, and so forth. This temple is the highest structure in Sucheu, except the pagodas. Gallery rises above gallery so high as to give a commanding view of the whole city and the neighbouring hills. The idols presented a sorry appearance. The larger were well battered and much defaced, and the smaller ones strewed the floors. The priests' books were lying neglected on the ground, forming, with other debris, heaps of rubbish. The rebels have shown their scorn of the idols, by chopping off their noses, and placing them in ridiculous attitudes. A blow has been inflicted on Chinese idolatry, by the actors in this movement, such as it never before received. Whatever mischiefs accompany this civil war, the onslaught on the senseless images of clay, which have sat in triumphant dignity in the temples of Buddha and Tau for fifteen hundred years, cannot but effect good on behalf of right reason and true religion.

From the upper gallery of this temple, vast masses of houses are seen stretching in every direction. A million of people used to reside in them, and another half million outside the walls, in habitations now almost entirely destroyed. Only a few of the occupants now remain, some of whom have entered the rebel service, and others wander sadly in and out of their once happy homes with a poverty-stricken expression on their countenances, harmonizing too well with the silence and solitude around them. Instead of busy commerce and pleasant domestic life prevailing through these vast lines of houses, bands of military chiefs, with their followers, and their horses, are quartered in the best locations, while all the poorer dwellings are deserted.

For the better defence of the city, the people are not allowed to return to their homes, nor are shops permitted within the walls except here and there for the sale of medicines. The medicine-vendors and gate-keepers are chiefly natives. At the gates it is necessary to employ natives, on account of their local knowledge and *patois*, by means of which the entrance of dangerous persons can be checked.

We met a crier, with a gong, going through the streets, whose duty was to publish a new order from the chiefs, prohibiting the wanton destruction of houses. There were proclamations posted at the gates, forbidding exorbitant charges for articles brought to the morning market by the country people. The surrounding country is under the control of the third chief in Sucheu. Head-men are appointed by him in all the towns and villages, who are responsible for collecting taxes and preserving order, and are periodically visited by detachments from the garrison in the city, called by its present possessors Su-fuh, instead of Sucheu, its old and best-known name. The distribution of responsible officers among the natives, and the regular system of taxation now intro-duced, have very much restored confidence in the neighbourhood of this important city, and trade is beginning to revive.

Another measure recently carried into effect by the insurgent leaders here, is the institution of literary examinations. Very few of the educated class will attend such examinations. Years must elapse before they could be prevailed on to do so. Only sixty attended the late examination. The theme was 'Uniting to elevate the heavenly father and heavenly brother to the headship over all duty and morality'. It is painful to find these men, who are prosecuting their enterprise with so much misery to the people, making a parade of Christianity. Those who perceive the nature of that religion, who are convinced of its truth, and sincerely try to obey its requirements, are at best but a small minority among them. Few or none of such are to be found among the chiefs who adopted the theme just mentioned—professing faith in God and in Jesus Christ—and who were nominally the examiners of the papers written upon it. Besides, they can lay just as little claim to the character of literary men. Did they not take the precaution to associate with them the best scholar they could find, to perform the task of reading the papers, the whole affair would be nothing better than a farce. These examinations cannot be respectably conducted, unless the party should gain more power in the country, and attract to itself good scholars and men of ability, who may assist in reconstructing the ruined fabric of the political institutions of the nation ...

Emerging from the immense western suburb, we found the banks on each side almost uncultivated. The grass grows thick and high, affording cover for numberless pheasants, quails, and other wild birds. A few poor people were gathering herbs for the Sucheu market. The little hill called Hu-chieu, crowned with an old crumbling pagoda, is passed on the right. Another canal leads from it to the city. The 'hill canal' used to be the favourite resort of fashion and pleasure, when this great provincial capital was still unvisited by the ruthless scourge of war. Now the silent waters no longer bear on their glassy surface the too celebrated 'flower boats', gaily and luxuriously fitted up, where the youth of Sucheu learned vice in forms elaborately fascinating. No longer now do sounds of revelry, coming from large junks hung with painted lanterns by night, disturb the bats and owls which make their home in the upper stories of the pagoda. Footsteps are seldom heard now in the once busy street, with its incense shops, tea taverns, and restaurants, which leads from the water-side to the temple on the hill. Scholars from a distance, and students aspiring for a master's degree, have ceased to visit the monumental edifices where poets and philosophers, who once resided at Sucheu, are worshipped and kept in remembrance by pictures and personal relics. There is a plot of ground here which belonged to Peh-hiang-shan, a famous poet of the olden time; and it was in a building on this spot that he entertained Li, Tu, and Su, contemporary versifiers, and all of them first-class names in the annals of Chinese poetry. Years must pass away before this and other literary antiquities in the neighbourhood can be restored, and become the resort of educated travellers from far and near. But all this is nothing in view of the misery of the people, which must continue more or less till the present revolutionary time is gone by, and a peaceful government established.

On the left many hills are passed, dotting the plain at intervals. Beyond them lies the great lake Tai-hu, thirty miles in length and breadth. We passed very near to some of these hills, and stopped for the night at the custom-house. This is ten miles from Sucheu. At the commencement of the town which surrounds it, is a little hill, and temple to the god of literature. A crowd of rebels, large and small, now appear on the banks of the canal, shouting violently to us that we should stop to be registered at the custom's office. We showed our pass, and went on to the other end of the town.

The road to Wusih wears the same desolate appearance. Lands lie untilled for half-a-mile on each side, and long grass has taken the place of rice and other crops. No one gathers up the human bones, which here and there are scattered on the roadside. They have been bleaching in the sun for months, and as many more will pass before some charitable person will bury them. Wusih is garrisoned by two thousand rebels. The chief in command is reported to be a man kindly disposed, just, and considerate.

Proceeding onwards we reach Changcheu. Posted at the gates we observed several proclamations from high chiefs and low. They forbade the destruction of houses, robbery, burning and the abduction of women. The chiefs desire to establish social order, and to restrain the excesses of their troops. But it is a hard thing to effect this. They set a bad example to their followers, by taking several wives from among their captives; and even if they were strictly moral in their own life, their followers are too undisciplined and lawless in their dispositions to obey the proclamations. Yet a large number of women from the distant provinces of Kwangsi and Hunan accompanied their husbands, and are now living with them at Nanking and other cities. An active trade in provisions was proceeding in the market, and moderate prices were required.

The most of the insurgents met here were from the provinces of Hupeh and Hunan, in the interior of the country. When, ten years ago, the rebellion extended north from its cradle in Kwangsi the insurgent troops swept these provinces like a whirlwind, and added immensely to their numbers by forced and voluntary recruits. Many of these, by length of service, have been promoted to important posts, and are only second in influence to the original rebels, who accepted Hung-sieu-tsiuen as their religious teacher, and then fought for him as their king.

At the insurgent custom-house here our boats were challenged but permission was at once given us to proceed when it was known who we were. Young rebels in their teens were very noisy and peremptory in their demands for us to remain for examination. As soon as we had given satisfaction to the clerks, whose duty it is to register and inspect boats as they pass, these juvenile adherents of the Taiping movement returned to a congenial occupation. It was their appointed task to pull down a temple. Strong ropes were placed over a high wall with its remainder of roof. About fifty young men and boys applied their strength to pull these ropes. They did so with the most lusty shouts. After a few minutes the old pile of bricks and timber began to totter. Then still louder vociferations were heard, and above them the crash of the falling ruin. Truly these young rebels have their amusements, a pleasant change from the war of Cannon and the brunt of battle.

The canal near Tanyang pursues a course straight as an arrow. A high pagoda, visible from a great distance, marks the city. Some hillocks and entrenchments near the south gate indicated a deserted camp. Entering the gates, we introduced ourselves to one of the chiefs in charge, a brother of Ying-wang, a young and successful rebel leader, who suddenly rose into notoriety during the last three or four years, and as suddenly has recently been captured and beheaded.

Chen, the younger chief, brother of his well-known leader, received us in his hall for visitors, in a yellow robe and cap. He was very willing to assist us in our object, and promised us a letter to the chief in the next town, requesting him to facilitate our arrival at Nanking. In reply to questions respecting the battle at Tanyang, when the great Imperialist commander, Chang-kweh-liang was killed, he told us that he came with his troops to this place after a hasty flight. His men had been too severely defeated at Nanking to recover their courage. They had no power to fight. He refused to enter the walls, and encamped in a bad position, with a river behind him. The Taipings, flushed with their victory, attacked him in his position. His soldiers thought of nothing but flight. Having the river to cross, they were slaughtered in immense numbers, and their chief himself died on the field, as our informant supposed. No one, he said, noticed what became of him. A soldier, who bore a banner before the general, himself afterwards told us that he was shot with a musket-ball fired by his own hand, within the city of Tanyang. This was probably the real end of the once trusted and dreaded Chang-kweh-liang. He was one of those characters who often appear in a revolutionary period. A pirate in early life, he became a Taiping, and fought in this cause for several years. He afterwards joined the Imperialists, it is said, hypocritically, to serve the interests of his old party. But he was so loaded with honours, so trusted and rewarded, that he became an Imperialist at heart. While besieging Nanking at the head of an immense army, his old associates, to pierce his soul with bitterness, brought out his wives and children, and put them to death with tortures before the walls, thus for ever rendering a reconciliation impossible.

The young chief with whom we were conversing, when the subject of religion was introduced, wore a serious, convinced air. Their victories were gained, he said, not by the merit of this or that general, but by the favour of the heavenly Father. He had no opinion as to the time that would elapse before the establishment of peace. The issue of the present struggle depended entirely on the will of God. It might be decided tomorrow, and it might require several years. It is this serious mode of speaking that has impressed so many foreign visitors, at Nanking and elsewhere, with the belief that there is much religious earnestness among the Taiping chiefs. So long ago as Sir George Bonham's expedition in 1853 to their capital, then recently captured, intelligent observers who conversed with them were persuaded that there was reality in their religious faith. Less was known of them then. Since that time, civil war and a life of plunder have done much to demoralize them. Their religious character, as it then was, has suffered. It is less now in extent and depth, but the impression on many of those who have conversed with the chiefs during this and the last year still is, that there is a large amount of religious earnestness in not a few of these men.

Beyond Tanyang, the stream winds tediously on its way to Pau-yen, where we were to leave our boats, after travelling in them two hundred English miles. We came into the society of country people on our way to this place. Leaving the boats, we walked along the high bank of the stream, at an elevation of twelve or fifteen feet above the sluggish waters, a height caused by the annual throwing up of the river's sediment by artificial means. The flat plain on each side was only broken by those immemorial funeral mounds—some of vast size and some small—which everywhere dot the surface of time-honoured China, by shrubberies of trees, a few bramble copses, and blue hills in the distance. At the foot of a bridge we stood for a while watching a boat drawn off a mud bed in the river. A knot of villagers collected round us from an adjoining hamlet, and communication commenced by some inquiries addressed to one of them.

'Are you happy here under the government of the "long hairs?"'

'Far from it. We are very wretched. We are called on for contributions of rice or money once a month.'

'How many men in a hundred have you lost in these parts?'

'Fifteen or twenty have been killed, and thirty or forty have been carried away to join the rebel army.'

'Where are the recruits taken to?'

'To places at a distance. To Sucheu or Kiahing, or some other province.'

'Are your women also taken away?'

'Yes. The older and plainer among them are sent back, but the young and good-looking do not return.'

'If you are wronged, can you not appeal to the nearest magistrates for redress?'

'Yes; we are told that we can do so; but we dare not.'. . .

It was not safe for our boats to remain at Pau-yen. They must return to Tanyang, where the chiefs, being higher in rank, could undertake the responsibility of protecting them. Li wrote a letter for us, which was intrusted to the boatmen. They received it with trembling hearts, and under protest. How could they return twenty miles without an Englishman to accompany them? The first party of the rebel brethren they met would seize the boats and dismiss them penniless. With a little pressure they consented, and on our return, sixteen days after, we found them at Tanyang, in good spirits, with placards forbidding to meddle, under the seal of several high rebel officials, pasted on the boat doors and windows. The despatch of our friend Li to those in command at Tanyang, said that it was not safe for the boats of the 'ocean brethren' to remain at a place like Pau-yen, where large numbers of the 'brethren' were constantly passing and repassing. He had therefore advised their return, requesting the chiefs to whom he wrote to protect them. Not only, he added, would the three foreign brethren be very grateful for this, but he would esteem it as a mark of particular kindness to himself.

This document did not seek to conceal, or blush to acknowledge, that strangers' property was unsafe in the vicinity of the 'brethren', unless under special protection. We were told that the seal of a king would alone be a sufficient guarantee. On arriving at Nanking, the necessary seals were granted on application, and forwarded to the boats, where we afterwards found them. . . .

The chief at Ku-yung gave us a hospitable entertainment, and lodging for the night. He inquired much more about muskets and cannon than respecting religion, of which he professed to know little, being, he said, a fighting-man.

Setting out again, with a retinue of twenty-five coolies, whose number was increased by the want of wheelbarrows for our luggage, we passed over the same kind of rolling surface as the day before. The country was in most parts a waste, as that we had traversed the previous day. On the tops of the rising grounds the land had never indeed been cultivated. It would not repay labour. But what we noticed with pain was that fields of productive soil were lying untilled for want of cultivators.

Women on the road, engaged in selling refreshments, gave us distressing accounts of the fate of the male members of their families. In many instances *all* had been taken away to serve as soldiers. The number of deserted towns we passed gave us a vivid impression of the terrors of a civil war in China,—in the border land between the territories of the contending parties. In some towns the inhabitants, returning from their temporary exile, were re-commencing trade. They left their homes in the spring of 1860, when the insurgents drove the Imperialists from their camp, and overran the country in their rear—that through which we were travelling. They fled to the north of the Great River, and stayed till the end of the year, when the strong desire to go home and till their land prevailed over their fear of their new masters.

It is not without reason that the country-people fear the insurgents. They are obliged, without pay, to work for them as carriers of burdens, returning when their tasks are done to their own employments, till it is their turn again to labour for these hard masters. Head-men were appointed by the insurgents to superintend this system of forced labour. A ticket is given to men while employed, which protects them from liability to be impressed as soldiers.

We found on the second day that our own coolies were compelled, like others, to work without pay, and we therefore from that time took care that they should not do so, although we were still indebted to insurgent chiefs for obtaining their services.

At a town twelve miles from Nanking, called Shun-hwa, we were very hospitably received by the chief in command, a native of Chang-sha, the capital of Hunan province. Finding it too late to proceed, we remained here for the night. The chief has prayers daily in the hall of his residence, at morning and evening meals. Rice is brought into the hall, and placed in three bowls on the centre-table, as an offering to the Trinity, before the family meal commences. After prayer, these bowls are again taken away, and the implements for writing and other moveables replaced. The chief told us, that on the Sabbath he assembles all his family, but on other days does not deem it essential for them to be present. Pasted on the walls of this hall we noticed a proclamation from the son of Hung-sieu-tsiuen, commanding the soldiers of the celestial dynasty everywhere to preserve discipline, and requiring the officers in all parts to protect in their rights the cultivators of the ground, the traders, and all the people.

The chief has his family with him from his distant home. He brought in his son, a boy of eleven, of a pleasant manner. He reads the religious books published by the Tien-wang, with the assistance of a tutor. I asked him to bring the book he was now reading. He disappeared, and returned from the schoolroom almost immediately with the Three Character Classic, and the Book of the Commandments. He then read part of the one, and his father, the chief, turned over the pages of the other to show me the prayers and doxologies addressed to the Heavenly Father, constantly used by them.

That the publications of Hung-sieu-tsiuen are used extensively as reading-books in the families of his followers, is unquestionable. They are employed both for educational purposes and as guide-books in conducting religious services, and in communicating religious instruction. But, in general education, they can never supply the place of the Chinese classics, or be anything more than first reading-books. Supposing that he conquer the country and establish peace, of which the prospect at present is extremely slight, these works can only be employed as books of instruction in the system of religion professed by the Taipings. They cannot form the basis of a national education, not being suited for it. It would appear, indeed, that the chief himself has views not yet developed publicly on the subject of a new system of universal education. He is said to be engaged in revising the national classics. If so, he will doubtless conform them to his own religious opinions, and leave them in other respects much as they are . . .

The front of the *fu* was very gay with gilt coloured paper, and paint. Passing through it, we arrived at the quarters occupied by Lo-hiau-tsiuen (Mr Roberts). He resided in two rooms upstairs. Here he had been placed on his arrival a few months before, when conducted with great show of respect from Sucheu to the rebel capital by a well-known rebel chieftain styled the 'Faithful King'.

We heard from Mr Roberts that he had recently received a letter from Tien-wang, his former pupil, the head of the movement, in which, speaking like one raised to the position of universal sovereignty, he appointed Lo-hiau-tsiuen to be his minister for foreign affairs, and judge of all criminals belonging to the 'outside countries'. Matters of more serious difficulty were to be referred to the young prince for decision.

This document is a good example of the rebel chief's unfortunate habit of acting in political matters. Everything political he regards as subordinate in importance to that which concerns religion and his own inspiration. He had been divinely informed, so he believed, that Lo-hiau-tsiuen was a good man. He therefore concluded that he was the fittest person to conduct negotiations with foreign countries, and to act as judge in all foreign criminal cases. He ordered it to be notified to the various foreign ambassadors and consuls that this appointment had been made, and that all trade carried on by the merchants of their respective countries was to be under the superintendence of Mr Roberts.

Mr Roberts very properly represented in reply that he was a minister of religion, and could undertake no other office. The nomination was repeated by the rebel chief, and was persistently declined by the missionary. Doubtless he desired to honour his former friend, at whose table he had eaten, and whose instructions he had received in years past at Canton, but he should have paid more respect than he did to Mr Roberts' repeated refusals.

The reason why the young prince was appointed to be arbiter in all matters of difficulty, lay in the fact, that Tai-ping-wang wished to restrict his own duties as far as possible to the sphere of religion, while his son and intended successor controlled the ordinary affairs of government. It was to a boy of thirteen that he attempted to intrust the reins of the Taiping administration.

When this fanatical chief professed, at the time of introducing this change, that 'heavenly things' are more important than those which belong to this world, and selected for himself the religious duties of his position, by so doing he indicated the true character of his pretensions. He claims to be a religious teacher. Believing himself to be in some high sense a son of God, he considers it his duty and destiny to destroy idolatry, and restore the worship of God among mankind.

For more than a decade of years he has held consistently to this belief, and the scenes of death and wide-spread carnage in which his enterprise has resulted, have never been able to relax the maniacal sternness of his resolution.

The secular administration of his son is of necessity more a form than a fact, but it is unfortunate that the chief, though still governing in reality, should believe the direction of public affairs to be so unimportant as to be, if only in name, intrusted to the tender years of youth. This, with the fanatic perversity of the father, and the want of administrative talent among the subordinate chiefs, prevents the establishment of peace and order in the broad tracts of country controlled by the Taipings. . . .

The residence of the chiefs are painted and ornamented in as lively a mode as the circumstances will admit. Immense birds and other animals are painted on the centre of the inner walls. Bright-coloured flower-patterns wind round ceilings and panels. Scroll sentences are inscribed on pillars, or upon broad pieces of cloth, partly expressive of the religious opinions of the insurgents, and partly of their political position as the would-be founders of a new dynasty. Some rooms we saw had in front of them small pools of water, square in form, and surrounded by high stone balustrades. While, from Nanking, commerce is excluded, and with it the innumerable artisans of a Chinese city, little can be accomplished in the way of art according to the established national ideas. These homes of the chiefs must have been erected with great difficulty from the debris of ruined houses, and ornamented by a limited number of skilled workmen accidentally included in the Taiping fighting host.

In the afternoon of our first day in the rebel capital, we walked with Mr Roberts for a mile through the broad and sad-looking streets, to call on the chief denominated Tsan-wang. He was an old man then, and an invalid, unable to transact business. Since that time he has taken his farewell of the world altogether, and done so more peacefully than a multitude of his former associates, who have bravely fallen in battle, or been caputured and ignobly beheaded. We did not see him. In his place we saw his son, a young man, 'the heir of Tsan', about thirty years of age. Mr Roberts sat on his left—the place of honour—robed in Taiping costume, a blue satin fur gown, and yellow embroidered jacket over it, with red hood, and satin boots. The young chief and the grey-haired missionary held a conversation in the Canton dialect, a lingo to which ears accustomed only to northern dialects listen with slight chance of catching what is said. But 'the heir of the Tsan nobility' could also speak in mandarin, and held a conversation with me in that dialect. He asked our names and titles, and politely received my papers on the Divinity of Christ. He commenced reading them, but after a page or two returned to conversation, and volunteered a long statement of the principal chief's ascent to heaven. This foolish story, which describes a sort of trance into which he fell many years ago, is found in the rebel books, and has been translated into English, and published in the newspapers. The young chief also related the descent of the Holy Spirit into the person of Yang-sieu-tsing, the once notorious 'Eastern King'. This person the Taipings believed to be the subject of a divine possession, the spirit that descended on him being, in their view, the Heavenly Father in the form of the Holy Ghost. Among the utterances of the 'Eastern King', while in a state of possession, was a command to Hung-sieu-tsiuen to exterminate the Tartars, with the help of the eastern and western kings, and establish the Christian religion in China.

These things were told us by the narrator with the air of one who thought them true, and very important, and, as in the case of other chiefs that I met before and after, there seemed no reason to doubt his sincere faith in them. The delusion which has seized on these men has been very extensive and enduring. It is this that has added vigour to their movement, and kept alive their fighting power. They believe Hung-sieu-tsiuen to be divinely commissioned, and he believes it himself. They also believe that his first great helper, the 'Eastern King', was divinely possessed, and he probably believed so himself. If so, the Taiping enterprise has originated not in imposture, but in fanatic delusion. This, in fact, is the key to the right understanding of it. It is this that explains the first successes of these men, their perseverance under discouragement, their boldness, their contempt of death, and their unwavering confidence in the ultimate success of the movement.

The position the Taipings assume is, that they have a new revelation; and we of the west, among others, ought to give it credence. But whether we do so or not, they regard it as authoritative upon them, and will adhere to it in the face of our scepticism. . . .

During the next two days some of the notable spots in this vast and ancient city were visited. Where the porcelain tower once stood, there is now a mass of glazed bricks, whole and broken, white and coloured. The Taiping people, had they the power, would destroy all the idol temples and pagodas in China. Their religious fanaticism is too essential a part of the movement to allow of any change in this point. If they are to be exterminated by their opponents, they will continue to be iconoclasts, as they will continue to call themselves Christians till their power is broken. To abandon their religious creed and customs, would be to weaken their system to a fatal extent. Nanking was famed for the grandeur of its monasteries, and the number of its priests. They have all disappeared.

Hung-sieu-tsiuen lives within a double yellow wall, with imperial dragons painted on the gates. Every morning a few scribes may be seen copying new edicts, written on yellow satin, and pasted on boards near the palace entrance. They are in red ink in the chief's own handwriting, and consist in great part of statements on the subject of the Taiping religion. In some I read he attempted to define the relation of our Saviour to the Father in regard to his divine nature, and in doing so, expressed Arian views. The door of the palace is called 'The holy heavenly gate of the true God'.

A walk in the Manchu city helped us to appreciate the intense hatred of the Tartar rulers felt by the Taipings. Only one house was left standing in a city of 25,000 inhabitants. The city walls and gates, too massive to be thrown down, are overgrown with wild flowers and weeds. All ornamental structures of coloured bricks which once stood upon them have been carefully destroyed. Broken bricks and porcelain of many colours lie along the wall and near it.

On one day this week, Mang, the young chief, invited us to join him at the mid-day meal. There was no wine, or any fermented drink. One Chinese guest was present, beside the host and our party. The chief asked a rather long blessing in a somewhat low tone. The sentiments of his prayer were, so far as I could catch them, correct and Christian. The conversation turned upon the productions of foreign countries, the prices of Chinese produce abroad, the price of steamers, and so forth.

28th—The chief styled Kan-wang is anxious to introduce among the Taipings a taste for European improvements. Near his residence we saw his printing-office, where he has a staff of printers engaged in carrying through the press, with moveable types, works prepared by himself. These books are partly explanatory of the religion of the Bible, and partly political. They recommend various improvements in the constitution of the state, the institutions of social life, and in the arts. They describe the advantage of railways, of the electric telegraph, of a post-office, of newspapers, and of steam machinery. These he would have set on foot in China upon the re-establishment of peace. Unfortunately these visions of future prosperity, indulged by some of the Taiping chiefs, are not accompanied by the genius for conquest and for government, which alone could afford the opportunity of realizing them. They live upon the plunder of the people, and therefore the country is against them. They have no friends among peaceable citizens; and without extraordinary victories, and unexpected turns of good fortune, they cannot drive out the Tartars, or even reduce to an orderly state a single province. They would do better to busy themselves in forming an efficient government for the territory now under their power, than to be dreaming of possible improvements when the present era of anarchy shall close.

But the Taipings are not statesmen. They have a certain system, and strong convictions regarding some great religious truths. They have entered upon a political enterprise too great for them. Under the influence of those convictions, and undaunted by difficulties which they cannot surmount, they are careless of the future, and indulge in imaginary creations of a re-constituted China, modelled by themselves, or rather by some force of fate, which is to work the change for them.

Be this as it may, Kan-wang amuses his leisure with literary occupations, in pursuing which he hopes to pave the way for beneficial changes in public education, and in the diffusion of knowledge. His moveable types were captured by the Taipings at Yangcheu, which was taken by them when they first came to Nanking, ten years ago. They were made some years since at Canton for a native of Yangchau, then residing there as a high official. The compositors were some engravers of wooden blocks for printing, who had learned to 'compose' the (to them) new-fashioned moveable metal types.

Another house we visited, at the distance of a few streets, proved to be a warehouse for the publications of the Taiping dynasty. Here we found arranged on shelves the complete New Testament, as printed by the insurgent chief, and the Old, as far as Joshua. His own compositions, religious, fanatical, and political, were all here, including those written by the Eastern King, and by Kan-wang.

62
Letters from Rev. S J Schereschewsky
Spirit of Missions, vol. V (July 1861), pp. 211, 213

(9 March) I have now a decidedly bad opinion of the Tai-ping insurgents. Since I have come in contact with them, and seen with my own eyes what they really are, I have come to the conclusion that they are utterly unworthy of any Christian sympathy. The spurious Christianity which they pretend to profess, besides its horrid blasphemies, does not seem to have produced in them the slightest moral effect for the better. On the contrary, if it has effected any thing, it appears that it consists in rendering them by far worse than other Chinese. All the regions they have overrun are perfect deserts. It is impossible to form an idea of the ruinous condition of the places held by them, if not personally seen. No trade, no agriculture, nor any other element of even well-organized heathen society, are to be met with in the places occupied by these pseudo-Christian insurgents. It is positively preposterous to call them, as some do, 'the regenerators of China'. But more of them in my next . . .

(16 March) Throughout the whole rebel territory, as may naturally be supposed, provisions are very dear and scarce, and in some places not to be had at all. It has been the constant wonder of many: Whence do the rebels get their provisions, seeing that neither commerce nor agriculture is carried on among them?

As to establishing a missionary station in any part occupied by the rebels, so far as my judgment goes, it would be very impracticable, and of no use. The rebels, in spite of what has been asserted to the contrary, are very unfavorable to missionaries settling among them. They seem to be very suspicious of foreigners. They would prefer to have nothing to do with them. Besides, they believe that missionaries have nothing to teach them; on the contrary that the former ought to be instructed by them. This much I have learned during my stay at Nanking. Even Mr Roberts, the quasi 'Minister of Foreign Affairs' among them, is barely tolerated at Nanking, simply on account of Hang-Kow Tsuen's personal regard toward him. They would like to get rid of his presence—the sooner the better.

63
A Letter from Rev Griffith John
Archives of the London Missionary Society Central China
Letters, Box 2, Folder 3, Jacket D

My dear Brother,

Having but just returned from another visit to the Celestial Capital, I beg leave to trouble you with a few lines more on the Kwangsi insurrection.

I left Shanghai on the evening of the 9th inst., and reached Nanking on the morning of the 14th [April].

On my arrival, I was much disappointed with the general aspect of things. When I visited the city in Nov., there were thousands of the *people* in it, and *hundreds of shops* opened. A brisk trade was carried on, and considerable life seemed to pervade the whole place. I regarded this as the commencement of good things; and hoped that before the end of the twelve months something like a civil government would be reestablished in Nanking at least. On this occasion, I found that all the *people* had been excluded from the city, and that none are permitted to live *within* the walls except the soldiers and their families. All the shops shut and no trade is carried on in the city. Seven or eight made the attempt to remain behind and to carry on trade quietly. They were discovered and reported to the Tien wang, who ordered them to be decapitated at once.

One of the results of this measure, is the increase of poverty and destitution. The beggars, and those that perish from cold and starvation, on the road side, are far more numerous now than they were then. The people, having been driven out, have been building themselves small huts at the gates. At one of the gates, a suburb is springing up rapidly.

The principal cause of this 'Imperial Mandate' is fear. They were afraid that the city would be filled with Imperialist emissaries in the shape of coolies and tradesmen. A great many of the country people from different parts of the country supply both parties with provisions. Today they are Imperialists, tomorrow they will be Insurgents. This class, being a necessity to the Insurgents is exempted from certain liabilities which are imposed on all other natives who approach the Capital. They are allowed to wear the tail and shave the head. But it would be very easy for these men, or for others in connexion with them, if freely permitted to enter the city, to do great mischief to the Insurgent cause. In the event of an attack, they might render their cause desperate. Again all the kings, except one, are absent on duty. The soldiers in the city are comparatively few, so they have to adopt more restrictive measures with the people. Though the case as stated by themselves seems plausible enough, still it is to be greatly regretted that they do not devote more of their time and energies to the work of reorganization, and to social improvements; with a view to promote the interests of the *people*.

Whilst at Nanking, an instance occurred which shows how lightly they hold human life.

A countrywoman was brought to the banks of the river with her hands tied behind her back. At the appointed place she was thrown down on her face. Chop, Chop, Chop went the Short Sword, and in a moment her head was held up to public gaze. I was amazed to learn subsequently that her only crime had been *accidentally* to set an insignificant hut on fire. Capital punishment seems to be the order of the day for almost every crime.

The work of rebuilding is still going on slowly. They employ all the artisans that they can procure for this purpose. They have day schools both in the city and suburbs. I visited one which had fourteen boys. The text books are those of the Tien Wang. Among others, I observed the Trimetrical Classic which begins with the important declaration, In the beginning God created Heaven, earth, man, and all things. This contrasts well with the first sentence in the Old Chinese one—'Man at his birth, his nature is perfectly good.' This little book contains a brief account of the Creation of the World, the fall, deluge, the history of the Children of Israel, the Incarnation and Crucifiction of Christ, and many other important particulars. In most of these books, unfortunately, these truths are mixed up with a great deal of error.

I was happy to find that they seem quite willing to have missionaries amongst them. The Chief himself says that preaching the gospel is a good and an important work, and that he is quite willing for missionaries to come to the 'Celestial Capital' for this purpose. Both Mr Edkins and myself would like to go, but there are certain obstacles on the way which, I fear, will prevent our going for the time being.

As to the Chief himself, we have learnt more of him within the last four of five weeks than we ever did before. We have his answers to and remarks upon communications which have been addressed to him personally. By the time Mr Edkins reached Nanking, Mr Roberts had commenced a correspondence with the Celestial King. His answer to the first throws considerable light on his peculiar views. It is one of the most important documents in our possession. It seems that he found it rather difficult to read my letter, and treatise on the doctrine of the Trinity, on account of the smallness of the writing. He read a *part* of it however and made his corrections. Mr Edkins will write you about his corrections.

64
A Letter from Rev John Hobson
Archives of the Church Missionary Society China Letters (Box H-R); copy also in Letter Book CH/M3 1859–62, pp. 141–3

I have just returned from a three week trip up the Yangtse. I visited Chin Kiang, Nankin, Woo Hoo, Kew Kiang, and stayed a week at Hankow the great central emporium of China. At Nankin I saw the Rebels. Nearer view does not remove any of my unfavourable impressions, rather increases and multiplies them.

Tae Ping Wang & his son are in a spacious palace—the king has 104 wives—& is waited upon by 1000 women. No other male is allowed within the walls of his palace. I believe everything else is just in accordance with the beginning. The religious men amongst them I am persuaded are but a very small fraction of the whole & the religion of the religious is but a sort of cross between Mahometanism & Mormonism. Tae Ping Wang professes to be the *uterine* brother of Jesus Xt——& of course a son of God just in the same sense as Jesus Christ is—his views of the Divine being are gross & blasphemous in the extreme. The non fighting people at Nankin had just the air of slaves—I saw Roberts—dressed in his dirty yellow Chinese robe—a miserable spectacle of dirt & slovenliness—a reproach to Western civilisation—& I very much fear of our religion likewise.

In steaming up the river there was no need to be told where the rebels were. Towns and villages are in ruins—vast tracts of country silent as the grave—rich lands all uncultivated & rapidly falling into a wilderness state, these were every where the outward signs of the Rebel rule. Call the Rebels 'The National Party' as I see Col. Sykes did in the House of Commons! Why the people loathe them—the very land abhors them, and I would engage to empty any city or town in the whole land in two days by simply raising the cry 'The Rebels are coming'. And yet the Imperialists with immense bodies of men & large supplies of the material of war (as we ourselves saw) are unable to drive these rascals out. What is to be the end of things who can tell? Our one only comfort is 'The Lord reigneth'....

65
A Letter from Rev Young J Allen
W. A. Candler, *Young J. Allen; 'The Man who seeded China'*
(Nashville, 1931), pp. 72–9

The latter part of November last, the rebels abandoned Hangchow, and as it was deemed a favorable time for visiting and ascertaining its true condition, etc., by the consent of the Mission, Brother Lambuth and myself made a visit to it.[18]

We did not succeed in entering the city, as it was strictly guarded and the gatekeepers had orders not to let any strangers enter without special permit from the chief. They proposed to present our case to him, but we declined to wait on them, as it did not materially interfere with our object not to enter. We conferred with some military chiefs outside, and from a mountain near the west gate we could ascertain not only the condition of the city within, but also without for miles around.

We found it both inside and outside a most melancholy ruin. The rebels have been there several times. The first time they succeeded in entering the city, held it seven days, and did the work of destruction by fire most thoroughly while inside.

They were not forced to leave it, but went away of their own accord to succor another place, where one of their armies was in imminent peril. While gone, it was repossessed by the imperialists and has since, so far, proved impregnable.

It is one of the most important cities in all China, and the rebels have determined on its entire destruction. It was once a beautiful, populous, and flourishing city, but now in ruins. Its location is beautiful, and from external appearances a desirable place at which to live; but we had to leave it under most deep and decided convictions that it would not soon be practicable or prudent to attempt missionary labor there.

On our return to Shanghai, via the Grand Canal, suddenly and unexpectedly we met a rebel army on a forced march to Hangchow. It was really a magnificent spectacle. There were not less than twelve thousand boats and sixty thousand soldiers. The rebels say there were one hundred thousand, but our estimate of boats and the average number on each places the number at not more than sixty thousand.

18   Rev. J. W. Lambuth was an American Methodist missionary who had been at Shanghai since 1854; Allen himself had arrived in July 1860. The withdrawal to which Allen refers was presumably that by the forces of Ch'en Yü-ch'eng, the Ying Wang. For details of the Taiping campaigns around Hangchow, which was first captured briefly by the Chung Wang in March 1860 and re-taken by him in December 1861, see Jen Yu-wen, op. cit., pp. 371, 400, 435–7, 440–2 etc.

The canal averages, perhaps, more than one hundred feet broad, and the line of boats extended along it, densely crowded and rapidly moving, for at least twenty miles. We were both in motion, and it took us very nearly five hours to pass each other by. We were neither insulted nor molested by them. On first coming in sight of them, they began to make preparations to capture us and our boat, but on a nearer approach they saw that we were foreigners. Some cried out *foreign devils*, others *foreign brethren*—had a hearty laugh, and passed on.

It seems like a wonder—yea, it is truly wonderful—that we should be able to pass among so many boats and so many men, and especially such an army as that was, and yet be not in the least interfered with. I was heartily glad when I could see the end of the rear line. I had enough of the rebels for once. We passed through many miles of their territory, visited many cities and towns held by them, and were treated with the greatest kindness and respect. Every place, however, with scarcely an exception, has shared a most doleful, ruinous fate. We saw many sights and scenes to make one shudder and recoil.

On our return to Shanghai, we stated to the Mission our observations and convictions in reference to Hang-chow. It was abandoned for the present and other places were taken under consideration. In accordance, therefore, with the wishes of the Mission and by its sanction, Brother Lambuth and I, with my teacher and our native preacher, Lieu, set forth on a trip to Nanking and the large cities situated intermediately around it and held by rebels. We visited Soo-Chou-fu, Vu-sih, Tsang-Tsen-fu, Tang-Yang, besides many other large walled towns, and lastly Nanking, the capital of the insurgents.

This trip was rich in incidents, scenes, observations, etc., which would doubtless be interesting to you in detail, but I forbear to enter upon such an undertaking in the limits of this letter. Our native preacher kept a journal of the trip, which has been translated by Brother Cunnyngham, and will be forwarded by this mail to the Board. It was read last night before the Branch of the Royal Asiatic Society, and was highly complimented as a Chinese production and much credit given to the views he expressed of the rebels and their affairs. I hope the Board will in due time publish it. If they do, you will see it. I refer you, therefore, to that for all the details and particulars.

In advance of that, I will simply state that, so far as I could discern or learn, there was no disposition on the part of any of the chiefs and kings to oppose our coming among them and introducing Christianity. They seem earnestly to covet communication, commercial and friendly relations with foreigners. The only difficulties they mentioned were those arising from the present condition of the country, the depopulation and desolation of almost every city, town, and village.

In reference to their present movements and purposes, I discovered a bold, vigilant, and active spirit. Their conduct and actions impress you that when [sic] they have undertaken they are determined and brave to accomplish. I am most thoroughly convinced that, unless foreign resistance be provoked, they will speedily reduce the whole of China to their sway. They believe, like Napoleon Bonaparte, in destiny, and they have sworn eternal vengeance against their twofold enemy, idolatry and the Tartars.

Their success has been wonderful hitherto, even in their own eyes. The Kang Wong (*king*) in Nanking, with whom we had the pleasure of dining and spending two or more hours, said to us, in reference to their success—that it was not by their might nor by their power, but in answer *to prayers of the people of God*, that it was to be accounted for. Many of the subordinate chiefs think the same.

Now, in view of the above facts, my conviction is that the best thing we can do is to go directly into their midst and set up the standard of the cross. The longer we shun them the worse it will be for the cause of God. They proclaim toleration, and with it the downfall of every place that tolerates idolatry. If we remain outside of their territory, we will be liable any time to their approaches, and, though they would not harm us, yet the people would all flee from the place and leave us in a much worse condition than if in the first place we had gone among them and settled where reaction had begun among people and business. These views were gathered and impressed very deeply upon my mind during our recent visit among them. In conclusion, I must say that we had all our wants and wishes readily and kindly met by them. Both king and coolie waited on us, and we moved among them as honored brethren. Thus much for the rebels, to the great disparagement of the opposition, imperialists. *I am most decidedly rebel* notwithstanding all their errors, cruelties, etc. But after all I am reduced yet a while to the alternative of learning over again my first lesson, 'wait, wait'.

66
A Letter from Rev Robert Dawson
Archives of the London Missionary Society Central China
Letters, Box 2, Folder 3, Jacket D

The day after I reached Sucheu I repaired to the Yamun of Li who had assumed the chief command of the city. After waiting in the assembly hall for half an hour, where I was served with tea and cakes, meantime undergoing a minute inspection from a crowd of Rebels of all descriptions, I was ushered into the private room of the Governor. I found him over head and ears in business which he seemed to be dispatching with a promptitude that spoke well for the prosperity of his Government. Almost as soon as I entered, he came forward and greeted me in true English style, for which I was scarcely prepared. I then made known the business which had brought me to Sucheu—and wished to know from his Excellency whether there would be any obstacle in the way of my repairing at once to Sucheu in order to prosecute missionary labour. I further asked whether I could have a house in the city. He enquired whether any house would do—and on being told that any house would answer my purpose for the present, but that afterwards I should want a new one, he said he should be most happy to give me a building—any I liked to choose—but that in reference to a chapel, he thought he must first consult with the Tien-wong. I put these questions to test the continued sincerity of the Governor and from this and other interviews I have not the slightest doubt that their professions are thoroughly honest—and that while there are great difficulties in the way of preaching the Gospel at present—to which they are by no means blind—they are still very anxious that the second article of their mission should be accomplished—viz. the establishment of the worship of the Heavenly Father. With the Governor of Vusih I had also an hour's conference. Vusih is an important town 30 miles N.W. of Sucheu. Like all other places in the hands of the insurgents, it is desolate, a mere garrison—my objective seeing the Governor was to get a passport to other places. He received me very cordially. A quiet thoughtful man—a native of Canton, about 46 years of age—anxious to hear and understand the doctrine of Jesus—and devoutly believing it so far as he knows it, he expressed himself as much gratified that it was my intention to come among them, and hoped that I would come to reside in Vusih, promising me a house and chapel, if I wished it so; and to shew that his word was not empty sounds he begged me, before leaving, to accept 50 dollars to prove his good will—a sum equal to about 15£, which I shall find no difficulty in usefully applying. I suppose I might have lived a hundred years among the mandarins before even one of these dollars had crossed my hand; Fancy a Chinese mandarin becoming a Subscriber to the L.M.S. But I have little doubt you will reckon many of these men among your supporters, if this great movement succeeds.

The immediate suburbs of Sucheu are still unpeopled, but at the distance of, perhaps, a couple of miles the houses are occupied with a busy population, engaged in their former business. The suburb of Hukiu is crowded, and here we had no difficulty in securing large audiences, who for the most part were attentive listeners to the word of life. There is here a romantic hill of some elevation, once crowned with a pagoda and temple— the latter is in utter ruins; and here beyond doubt is the place for a missionary Colony. I apprehend there would be no difficulty in securing almost any tract of ground for building purposes, and a more admirable spot could be found nowhere in the neighbourhood. Were there any likelihood of Sucheu being rapidly repeopled I should ask the Directors to allow me to commence operations there at once, so that no time would be lost.

67
A Letter from Dr D B McCartee
Home and Foreign Record, vol. XII (November 1861), pp. 335–8

The city of Chinkiang, which we[19] first visited, was in the hands of the Imperialists, who were then besieged by the insurgents. Ruined houses and heaps of rubbish remaining to mark the sites of former mansions and temples; miserable hovels, filled with squalid people, whose lives were all that remained to them for a prey after the devastation wrought first by insurgents, and then repeated by the Imperialist forces in their turn; coarse and brutal-looking soldiers passing to and fro; an occasional headless trunk, and anon a trunkless head, carried in the hands of the executioner, or hanging against a wall, with the fresh blood still dripping from it, and a label placarded beside it, to say that the

19 McCartee was an American Presbyterian medical missionary stationed at Ningpo who was asked to act as interpreter for an American naval expedition up the Yangtze in May 1861. Two US vessels, the *Hartford* and the *Saginaw* sailed to Hankow and back, calling at Nanking on the way. Part of the object of the voyage was to gain Taiping co-operation for the passage of American merchant vessels through their territory, as Admiral Hope had done for British traders in February–March 1861. For Taiping communications to the Americans and indications of American sources on this voyage see Michael, op. cit., vol. III, pp. 1136–9 (where McCartee's name is mis-spelled as 'Carter').

303

poor wretch to whom it had belonged was executed as being (or suspected of being, which is the same) a spy; and the whole view of the desolation and misery inflicted by civil war soon satisfied us with Chinkiang, and caused some of us, in heaviness of heart, to pray, God save *our* native land from such scenes as this.

NANKING VISITED—DREADFUL DESTRUCTION OF LIFE— A PASSPORT OBTAINED

Nanking, once a palatial city, a residence of mighty kings, but now looking like a desolation of many generations, was the next city we visited. If I should attempt to compare the situations of the people at these two places, I should say that those at Chinkiang were like persons in all the agonies of a shipwreck; whilst those at Nanking were like those left floating in silent despair upon the surface of the ocean, after the ship has gone down—even when the excitement of despair is past. Just opposite to Nanking, across the Yangtsze, was once a large and populous city called Kiang-yiu. We saw the city walls still standing, but perfect solitude reigns within. The inhabitants submitted to the insurgents after they took Nanking. They were compelled to deliver up their crops to the insurgents, and were put upon rations. These were served out scantily, and in insufficient quantities to support life. They murmured, and threatened to apply to the Imperialists. The insurgents heard of it, and one day the sun went down upon the corpses of seventeen thousand people, who the day before were in the midst of life. Some fifteen thousand escaped to the Imperialist camp, but the city has lain desolate ever since.

Nanking is situated upon a rising ground, a short distance from the bank of the river. A small low island lies off the city, and is separated from it by a narrow channel, with which is connected a creek running up toward the city, and joining the city moat. On the island, and at the mouth of the creek, fortifications have been erected to defend the city from any attack from the river. In one of these forts is the 'Heavenly Custom House', where 'His Excellency' Liang (with a long title and a military command of one hundred and seventy thousand troops, as they told me) resides, although in not much state. I went on shore and asked Mr Liang to grant a passport, and provide horses and a sedan for a party of five officers, who wished to go to the 'Heavenly City', to the palace of King Tsan upon public business. 'His Excellency' was not visible, but the man who seemed to act as his secretary promised that all should be in readiness as desired, at eight o'clock, A.M., on the morrow.

A WALK AND WHAT WAS SEEN IN IT

In the afternoon, I accompanied a party of officers on shore, and we strolled into the fort, and walked about to see what was to be seen. We had not gone far, when a man came from Liang's quarters, objecting to our going further. I asked 'Why?' He said, 'Because there were a great many of the brethren about'. I replied, 'We certainly ought to have nothing to fear from *brethren*'. This answer seemed to non-plus him; but soon after another man came with a similar message, and finding that there was really nothing worth seeing, we retraced our steps. Passing Liang's quarters, we were invited to go in and take a cup of tea, and accepted the invitation. 'His Excellency's' palace was quite destitute of anything like splendour or even of neatness or comfort. He received us, dressed in a yellow crape robe, and wearing on his head a sort of crown made of gilt paper, and resembling those that we see upon the heads of the Chinese god of wealth. His principal attendants were a crowd of dirty boys from eleven to eighteen years of age, and the *tout ensemble* was anything but 'heavenly', malgre the style and title assumed by these insurgents. Crossing the creek by a sort of floating drawbridge, we walked through a suburb consisting of one-story houses, occupied by persons connected with the army, or by small shopkeepers, among whose wares silver and jade ornaments, embroidered satin and silk dresses, and other articles of 'loot' or plunder, were prominently displayed. From inquiries I learned that there were in Nanking and its suburbs some four hundred and thirty thousand persons of all descriptions, ages, and sexes, all upon an allowance of one quart of rice, eight ounces of oil, and two ounces of salt per diem for each adult, and a proportionate quantitiy for children. No *pay* is given to the soldiers, and they are expected to make it up in the plunder of the towns and villages which they captured. It had been their custom, whenever the least resistance was opposed to them, to put to death all the adults, and spare only the children, whom they carried off. This would account for the large number of little boys we met in every direction. I believe that orders have been issued latterly by the 'Heavenly King' to his generals, to pursue a less sanguinary policy, and I have heard that at Kin-hwa, in our province, which has lately been captured by Chung-Wang, or King Chung, one of their generals, there was much less slaughter . . .

THE PALACE; OFFICIAL INTERVIEW—FEW SIGNS OF CHRISTIANITY

The palace of Tsan Wang is about a mile and a quarter from the western Han gate. It is new, and highly varnished and ornamented. A few straggling soldiers, not in uniform, carrying vermilion coloured muskets, were around the gate. We were ushered into the council chamber, where the councillors were in session and arose to receive us. Our mission was a delicate one, namely, to obtain a formal document under seal, guarantying to our citizens and their property security from molestation or loss, without formally recognising the insurgents or giving them an official document in return. Yet, by the favour of God, we succeeded so well that if the insurgents perform what they have promised, the expedition will not prove to have been a fruitless one, either to our merchants or our missionaries.

We were courteously treated, accepted an invitation to dine with these kings, or *princes* as Wang might be more properly translated, one of whom afterwards came down and visited us on board the 'Hartford' on Monday following. Saving and excepting that a blessing was asked by the young prince who sat at the head of our table, and the inscriptions on the houses, I saw no signs of anything resembling Christianity in or near Nanking, although the young prince told me it was their Sabbath. I saw and heard no religious worship, save the firing of some fire-crackers, which I was told was done in worshipping the Heavenly Father. The shop-keepers, boatmen, and labourers seemed to know no Sabbath, nor had the council of state ceased from business on the day they call by that name. The Cantonese in the junks lying off the city went through apparently the same kind of gong-beating and burning of papers and fire-crackers as in the other parts of China.

WINE NOT OFFERED, BUT USED—OPIUM USED—THE LANGUAGE SPOKEN—THE COUNCILLORS

No wine was offered us at Tsan Wang's palace, and we were told they did not think it right to drink it. Yet a gentleman who passed some time in the palace of Kan Wang told me that dignitary drank it habitually; and Moh Wang, during his visit on board the 'Hartford', drank a sufficient quantity of sherry and champaigne, and with sufficient imperturbility, to show that he was either no stranger to the habit, or that he possessed remarkable natural powers in that line at least. Boats came alongside the 'Saginaw' at night, wishing to buy opium, and many countenances among the insurgents indicated that they were no strangers to that drug. Three of the council spoke the Mandarin dialect passably well, as also did Mr Liang. The rest spoke together in the patois of their native province, (Kwang-si) which was to me almost wholly unintelligible, All along the banks of the Yang-tse, and in the Tongting lake I found no difficulty in understanding and being understood by the people and officers. As to the literary acquirements of the councillors, I saw sufficient to convince me that they were of very moderate pretentions, and they themselves, when in session, had the air of a group of village tavern politicians. When Moh Wang and Liang visited the Hartford, the theatrical airs assumed by them, particularly by the latter, were exceedingly ridiculous and absurd.

RELIGIOUS VIEWS AND PRACTICES—KAN WANG— MISSIONARIES NOT WANTED

I could not find that they were publishing the sacred Scriptures at present. I got a copy from the young prince Tsau-tsz-kiun, but it proved an old edition and imperfect. I distributed among the insurgents, as well as among the imperialists, Christian almanacs, tracts, and copies of the Gospels, and to the higher officers I gave a few copies of my Diatessaron, or Harmony of the Gospels in the Mandarin colloquial. A large number of tracts, &c., were distributed also at Wis-wei-chau, Kiu-kiang, Hankow, Wu-chang, and Yoh-chau, in which good work Chaplain Bartow and other officers helped.

I was sorry that we did not meet Kan Wang, who is properly the minister for Foreign Affairs, and who was absent from Nanking on a fighting expedition. Kan Wang was instructed at Hong-kong, and is better informed on general subjects than most of his colleagues. Yet he practices polygamy, and falls in with most of their errors. From a gentleman who resided some time in Nanking, I learned that the 'Heavenly King' Hung Siu-tsiuen asserts that 'No man hath seen God at any time, *save Hung Siu-tsiuen.*' 'Jesus is said to be the *express image of the Father's person*, and a spirit cannot have an image or likeness, consequently it is not true that *God is a Spirit*, Hung *has seen Him*. He is just like one of us; the passage referred to, was probably written to keep the Western brethren from making an image of God.' Kan Wang distinctly said that they 'did not wish missionaries to come to Nanking'—that it was well enough for them to preach through the country now, as a preparatory work, but when the empire is subjugated by the Tai-pings, the missionaries will be *in the way*, and will not be wanted. The insurgents in their theology give a wife to God the Father!—make the Elder Brother (Jesus) inferior to the Father, and give him a wife also!

UNFAVOURABLE IMPRESSIONS OF THE INSURGENTS

Where the imperialists have recovered possession for a few years, people and things begin to look natural and flourishing, but where the insurgents hold sway, desolation reigns, at least wherever I have seen. For more than 400 miles not a comfortable house was left standing—empty blackened walls, mud hovels, or burning villages, with hundreds upon hundreds of wretched people in the open fields, trying in vain to shelter themselves from the heavy rains—all these left but an unfavourable impression of the insurgents and of their work upon my mind; and I believe the same impression now almost universally prevails, even among those who a short time ago were enthusiastic in their hopes relative to these so-called 'Christian patriots of Nanking.' I had intended to write somewhat relative to the other ports on the Yang-tsze visited by the United States squadron, but my letter is already so long that I must defer stating my views particularly relative to their adaptation and desirability as locations for missionary labour until some future opportunity.

Respectfully and affectionately yours,
D B McCartee

68
Journal of Rev Josiah Cox
Wesleyan Missionary Notices, 3rd series, vol. IX, 25 April 1862, pp. 69–72

21st (December 1861): After a wet and stormy passage, I arrived at Shanghai. I thought it seemly to go first to the Missionaries of the American Methodist Church, and ask their hospitality for a few days; and was kindly passed on to Mr. C. . . ., who bade me a Christian welcome. As it was too late to bring off my luggage, I returned to sleep on board the 'Pekin.'

Sunday, 22nd: At dinner I discovered that my kind host and hostess are of the American Baptist, and not the Methodist, Church, as I supposed yesterday. I unexpectedly met H. S. Parkes, Esq., after the afternoon service, who told me he was about to accompany Admiral Hope to Nanking,[20] and intimated that I should find it a good opportunity of travelling there. I was favoured with an interesting account of three weeks spent at Nanking by a Missionary of the London Missionary Society. He (Mr Edkins) and another gentleman journeyed there overland from Shanghai. There appeared but little encouragement for Missionary labour in Nanking. Permission was obtained by Mr

20 Cox went on Hope's second voyage to Nanking, which took place between 28 December 1861 and 2 January 1862. The American missionary to whom Cox refers was probably Rev. Solomon Carpenter, of the American Seventh Day Baptist Missionary Society.

Edkins to rent a house there; but such were the difficulties and delays interposed when a house had been selected, and the prospect there was altogether so unpromising, that he abandoned the purpose of labouring among the rebels, and removed to Tin-tsin. The Heavenly King assumed the position of instructor to the Missionaries, and corrected the communications addressed to him. The officers and followers were generally found to be ignorant of Gospel truth, and utterly indifferent to it. Only a few of the oldest adherents, with one setting himself up as an inspired man, cared to discuss Christian doctrines. A ceremonial of worship they witnessed displayed several of the features of an idolatrous feast; and an address they heard from one of the officers imparted no religious instruction; but exhorted them to be loyal, vigilant, and bold in fighting for the Heavenly Dynasty.

CHARACTER OF THE REBELS

In the evening I had a long conversation with Mr C ... on the insurgents. His opinions were at first strongly in their favour, and he earnestly wished to establish himself as a Missionary amongst them. He has twice visited Nanking, also Shu-chau, Wu-hu, and scores of towns and cities under their sway. His conclusion is, that the time has not yet arrived for the establishment of Missionaries amongst them. The observation and practice of nearly every Missionary in Shanghai has confirmed this conclusion; for they have sought to establish themselves among the rebels, and in every case have either failed or chosen other fields as more inviting. He believes that the first visits of Missionaries were encouraged in the hope of making useful tools of them for political ends; failing which, their visits were encouraged no longer. He found their soldiers quite indifferent to Christian doctrines. His heart is still sick and sore at the recollection of the scenes of desolation and death he has witnessed. When approaching Su-chau, himself and three others found the canal covered with dead bodies at some distance from the city; after two of them were completely overcome by the stench, they pushed on until their boat could no longer make way through the thickening pack of human bodies, and they were compelled to reach the city by another route. He still thinks, however, that more good is to be hoped from the Tai-pings than from the Government, or any other political party which at present appears in China.

KINDNESS OF ADMIRAL HOPE

23rd: I called on Admiral Sir James Hope, and accepted his courteous offer of a passage to Nanking in the 'Coromandel'. I packed a trunk, and came on board in the evening to be ready for starting at daylight. The officers are ready with every assistance to make me comfortable.

VISIT TO NANKING

25th: I started for Nanking at four a.m. Weather extremely cold. 26th: We cast anchor off Nanking at about three p.m. We have passed five trading steamers, which shows that this noble river is rapidly becoming a great highway of traffic to foreigners. With the exception of some bold peaks at Chin-keang, the country is a level tract until we approach Nanking; showing now, under its winter garb, it offers little of the picturesque in its landscapes. Here and there, we noticed clusters of mat-shedding, affording frail and cheerless shelter to crowds of distressed refugees. At the city of Kwa-chau a scene of busy commerce has been changed into an unsightly spread of ruin. I was a little excited when the 'Coromandel', after threading her way through a narrow channel, came suddenly under the walls of Nanking. There was little to betoken the vicinity of the once grand capital; only an angle of its wall, with some small boats carrying rice, and others carrying brown reed up a narrow creek to its Western Gate. The wall stretches far away to the east, until it is lost in climbing over a spur of a mountain-range, which forms a background to the scene, and is in admirable contrast to the broad river flowing in front. In the external aspect of the great city there was quiet; although a handsome gunboat sat in conscious strength upon the stream, and looked very bold. 27th: Chan, S.S., and myself, accompanied Mr Parkes to the city. We walked almost four miles parallel with the wall to the Western Gate. There are but few houses remaining of the populous suburb that lay along this route in former years. We had an altercation with the guard at the gate, which ended in our obtaining a guide to the palace of the Chang-Wang. The distance was a mile, and the intervening space has been the scene of wide-spread conflagrations. The palace is an unfinished building of great architectural pretensions, conspicuous with its red and yellow paint, and abounding in lofty folding-doors, pictured over with dragons. The Chang-Wang is a rather short, sharp, common-looking man; he was gaily bedecked in yellow satin and costly furs; but evidently not yet trained in the etiquette of his country, and not at ease with his foreign visitors. Before business had commenced, I requested a guide to the residence of the Kan-Wang, and went away immediately. In palace, person, and dress, the Shield King is not unlike the Chang-Wang. He has become fat, and looks more coarse than when he was associated with me in Canton and was a thin, hard-worn, active Native Helper. I had a full three hours' interview with him, and passed the remainder of the day and night in his palace. (As I have written a detailed account of this visit to the 'Watchman', it need not be repeated here.)21 My visit enabled me to offer a few words of earnest counsel to my former friend, to express the solicitude with which this revolution of the Tai-pings is watched in England, and to ascertain, with the deepest regret, that the faithful preaching of Christ by myself, or by any other Missionary our church would send, would not be tolerated in Nanking.

28th: I left the palace of the Shield King soon after one p.m. and, after a walk with Mr Roberts, repaired to that of the Chang-Wang, to await Mr Parkes, and with him return to the ship, as I had been obliged to promise. I could converse with some of the Kwang-se, retainers of the Chang-Wang, and took occasion to inform them of my previous acquaintance with their Kan-Wang, and of the purport of my present visit, knowing that what I said would be repeated to the Chang-Wang, and hoping it might obviate that mistrust, of which the Kan-Wang appeared so much afraid when I first saw him yesterday. I had the opportunity of seeing two other of their Kings (brothers, I believe, from the description of Mr Roberts, of Kan-Wang himself), and thought them more vulgar and fierce-looking men than the Chang-Wang. Those of the retainers whom I saw knew little and cared less about the religious dogmas of their party, or of Christianity. I endeavoured to converse with sundry parties in the streets; but as they were natives of a different province, they could not understand my Canton dialect. There is quite a Babel jargon of dialects among the followers of the Tai-ping flag, because they have been impressed from every district traversed by their victorious bands. I picked up many scraps of information about this movement, which it would be tedious to detail here. The impression produced on my mind by this first visit has been very unfavourable, of the political rule established, and of the prospects of Christianity in Nanking. Idols are certainly swept away; and as fortune-telling, opium smoking, and gambling are prohibited under their common penalty of decapitation, such vices and practices nowhere appear in the streets of Nanking; notwithstanding, my guide, pointing out two streets, said, 'Canton men live here, they all smoke opium', in which habit they are joined by some of the Kings. The Heavenly King sets up himself, and is

21   For this account see the source of this document, 25 March 1862, pp. 61–6.

worshipped as Divine. He has refused instruction at the hands of Missionaries, and will not tolerate other teaching than his own dogmas, the presence of Mr Roberts in Nanking notwithstanding. The Heavenly King (lucus a non) is of imperious and cruel temper, and reigns supreme, with despot power, and without respect to law, or the liberty of the individual. In like manner each King is a feudal Lord over his retainers. It is difficult to ascertain the relation between the King in chief and these subordinate Kings; but the people with whom I conversed appeared to be enslaved by a dire reign of terror. An offence which would not fine a man sixpence in our courts, or even a trivial mistake, may cost a man his head. Life is sacrificed on the whim or bad temper of the petty officers, even of their people.

Sunday 29th: I conducted Divine service on Board the 'Coromandel', and did not go ashore.

30th: Two officers, Mr Parkes, and myself, took a long stroll through Nanking. Going upon the wall, we started from the West Gate, southwards, and then along the south face of the wall. A noisy crowd kept up busy market outside the South Gate, just beyond the site of the porcelain tower, now only a mound of the debris of that famous structure. One becomes accustomed to look on ruin when revolution reigns. In the south portion of Nanking, the streets and houses have not been much injured. In the east and central quarters the eye roams over vast plains of desolation. The latter are relieved by the palace of the Tien-Wang, conspicuous in the distance from its yellow colour and the extent of its walls, and by the glitter of three or four gilded cupolas or small towers which mark the sites of the King's palaces. There is no trade in the city, and it is forbidden to open shops except for the sale of medicines. The stillness of the great city is melancholy. The aspect of the citizens is worse; for we saw none but the abject poor slaving as helots at the public works, and the coarse-looking, well-fed soldiery. As we pursued our way along the eastern wall, an old man would have turned us back; we possessed a passport, however, and continued on our way. From the east side we turned across the city to a tower which supplied a good look-out over the northern quarter. As we quietly gazed around, a company of about fifty armed men came up, and ordered us to accompany them to Chang-Wang. We showed our passport, and reasoned with them in vain. They laid arrest upon us under threat of violence if we attempted to escape. On our demand, the officer ordered his rough-looking fellows away; but they returned to surround us, and marched in company a disorderly rabble to the designated palace. The Chang-Wang offered explanation and apology, followed by an invitation to dinner, which it was too late to accept. A meeting was arranged for the following day on business, to which the Wang invited our presence. Hoping for a chat with him, and a pass for an overland trip to Su-chau, which the Kan-Wang refused, I intended to go.

31st: We arrived at the palace of the Tsan-Wang about eleven o'clock, a.m. Two 'Kings' were present whom I had not seen before. They bear the same stamp of vulgarity I have noticed in others. I am surprised at the absence they manifest of the mien and manners of the Chinese gentleman. It corroborates the statement of Kan-Wang, that, besides himself, they are all illiterate men. Their origin and manners are of little consequence, perhaps, provided they possessed the wisdom and power to establish a Government. Power to fight and destroy are the only power I yet discover among their qualifications. How these unlettered who gain not the confidence of any among the educated or influential classes of the people, and who are indifferent to civil laws, and the interest of the populations of the territory they win, can succeed in establishing a dynasty, I am at a loss to conceive. That by the way.

When business commenced, I went away to visit Mr Roberts once more. He had seen the Kan-Wang since my call, who had ordered him (Mr Roberts) not to invite a foreigner to spend a night in his (Mr Roberts') quarters, and had repeated that he was unwilling to give me a pass to Su-chau. I returned to the palace of the Tsan-Wang before the negotiations pending there terminated. They were conducted in the Mandarin dialect which I do not understand. I obtained conversation with one of the retainers, who readily gave me a few of their books, though he himself knew little of the religious doctrines of the Tai-ping chief. At the conclusion of their business, I mentioned my wish to proceed to Su-chau overland, to the Chang-Wang, but found him in no temper to forward my project. He began to complain of the unfairness of the proposals made to him, speaking a Canton dialect. Whereon I told him I was quite ignorant of the business, and being a Missionary, did not understand political affairs.

January 1st, 1862: I strolled about the shopping which lines the banks where we landed, and on to some forts, but found neither shopkeepers nor soldiers who can speak Cantonese. The shops are small and slightly built. They have been run up for the sake of supply of the commonest articles of food; both supplies and dealers appear to be increasing.

RETURN TO SHANGHAI

2d.—We started for Shanghai in a dense fog at daylight, and came to anchor within two miles of the foreign settlement on the evening of the third. We passed two Imperialist fleets, fully manned and equipped, and accompanied by three foreign vessels they have purchased, all lying idle in the river. At Chin-keang, the bank of the river, just outside the city, was lined with a forest of their flags, fluttering in the wind. Were there any pluck or power left to the Imperialists, they could soon crush the Tai-ping rebellion; but their dynasty seems destined to fall.[22]

69
A Letter from Rev. I J Roberts
North China Herald, 4 February 1862;
also in *BPP*, 1862, C. 2976, pp. 142–3

From having been the religious teacher of Hung Sow-chuen in 1847, and hoping that good—religious, commercial, and political—would result to the nation from his elevation, I have hitherto been a friend to his revolutionary movement, sustaining it by word and deed, as far as a missionary consistently could, without vitiating his higher character as an ambassador of Christ. But after living among them fifteen months, and closely observing their proceedings—political, commercial, and religious—I have turned over entirely a new leaf, and am now as much opposed to them, for good reasons I think, as I ever was in favour of them. Not that I have aught personally against Hung Sow-chuen; he has been exceedingly kind to me. But I believe him to be a crazy man, entirely unfit to rule without any organized government; nor is he, with his coolie Kings, capable of organizing a government, of equal benefit to the people, of even the old Imperial government. He is violent in his temper, and lets his wrath fall heavily upon his people, making a man or woman 'an offender for a word', and ordering such instantly to be murdered without 'judge or jury'. He is opposed to commerce, having had more than a dozen of his own people murdered since I have been here, for no other crime than trading in the city, and has promptly repelled every foreign effort to establish lawful commerce here among them, whether inside of the city or out. His religious toleration and multiplicity of chapels turn out to be a farce—of no avail in the spread of Christianity—worse than useless. It only amounts to a machinery for the promotion and spread of his own political religion, making himself equal with Jesus Christ, who, with God the Father, himself, and his own son, constitute one Lord over all! Nor is any missionary who will not believe in his divine appointment to this

22   For the continuation of this journal, where Cox recounts a visit to Ningpo, see Doc. 85.

high equality, and promulgate his political religion accordingly, safe among these rebels, in life, servants, or property. He told me soon after I arrived that if I did not believe in him I would perish, like the Jews did for not believing in the Saviour. But little did I then think that I should ever come so near it, by the sword of one of his own miscreants, in his own capital, as I did the other day.

Kan Wang, moved by his coolie elder brother (literally a coolie at Hong Kong) and the devil, without the fear of God before his eyes, did, on Monday the 13th instant, come into the house in which I was living, then and there most wilfully, maliciously, and with malice aforethought, murder one of my servants with a large sword in his own hand in my presence, without a moment's warning or any just cause. And after having slain my poor harmless, helpless boy, he jumped on his head most fiend-like, and stamped it with his foot; notwithstanding I besought him most entreatingly from the commencement of his murderous attack to spare my poor boy's life.

And not only so, but he insulted me myself in every possible way he could think of, to provoke me to do or say something which would give him an apology, as I then thought and think yet, to kill me, as well as my dear boy, whom I loved like a son. He stormed at me, seized the bench on which I sat with the violence of a madman, threw the dregs of a cup of tea in my face, seized hold of me personally and shook me violently, struck me on my right cheek with his open hand; then, according to the instruction of my King for whom I am ambassador, I turned the other, and he struck me quite a sounder blow on my left cheek with his right hand, making my ear ring again; and then perceiving that he could not provoke me to offend him in word or deed, he seemed to get more outrageous, and stormed at me like a dog, to be gone out of his presence. 'If they do these things in the green tree, what will they do in the dry?'—to a favourite of Tien Wang's, who can trust himself among them, either as a missionary or a merchant? I then despaired of missionary success among them, or any good coming out of the movement—religious, commercial, or political—and determined to leave them, which I did on Monday, January 20, 1862.

IJR

P.S.—Kan Wang seems disposed not only to be a murderer, but a robber also. He refuses to give up my goods, clothes, books, and journals. And though I have waited ten days, and he and others have been corresponded with on the subject, yet he retains all; sending me off so destitute that I have not sufficient clothing to

keep me warm from the chilling blasts of a cold winter. What is still worse he refuses my two servants and assistant preacher the privilege of coming out of the city and returning with me to their families. And he and others inside have been trying every device to get me back into the city, in all probability with the design of either making me a prisoner or a corpse—and that without any just cause of offence on my part, and none whatever on the part of the assistant and servants. The most sotted heathen cannibals could not act with more cruelty and impropriety.
'Renard' Steamer, January 30, 1862.

Section 3 Other Close Encounters (1861–2)

In the early part of 1861, after the conclusion of the second Opium War and the ratification of the Treaty of Tientsin, other Westerners, mainly British, followed the missionaries. The expedition to Nanking and beyond led by Rear-Admiral Sir James Hope during February and March was of major importance in expanding Western contact with the Taiping. It was a kind of delayed follow up to Elgin's 1858 voyage, with the object this time of actually opening the Yangtze river to British trade despite the continuance of the rebellion along much of its length. This required, as Hope put it, 'that in the districts of which they hold possession, the Taiping authorities must be regarded as those of a *de facto* government, and must be dealt with accordingly.'[23] It was as near as the West was ever to come to recognising the legitimacy of the rebellion.

Hope took with him the soon to be knighted Harry Parkes as his chief interpreter, plus a number of other unofficial observers, including the entrepreneur Alexander Michie and the missionary William Muirhead. Also in the group were the military men Lt Col. G. J. Wolseley, later to become Commander in Chief of the British army and the model for W. S. Gilbert's modern major-general, and Capt. T. Blakiston, intent on exploring the Yangtze. As well, other missionaries and two French representatives were in the party. It was the largest mixed party of Westerners ever to visit Taiping territory at the one time.

Naturally a number of reports resulted, official and otherwise, all of them critical in one way or another of Taiping practice and

23   Hope to the Admiralty, 7 March 1861 in *BPP*, 1861, C. 2840, p. 7.

potential (Docs. 70–3).[24] At this point in time an acceptable alternative to the highly suspect Ch'ing dynasty might have won Western support, but neither in a political, commercial or religious sense did the Taiping attract the sympathy of these influential observers. Others followed, sometimes giving, like the sharp eyed consular official R. J. Forrest, mixed messages, indicating some reasonable possibilities but on the whole confirming the critical views reported from the Hope expedition (Docs. 74–9). The official British policy of neutrality limped along for a year or so yet, but the trend of opinion was clearly increasingly hostile.

Most of the reports in this section date from the first half of 1861. By late 1861, save for the special case of Ningpo, direct contact between Westerners and the Taiping once again lessened sharply. Admiral Hope returned briefly and aggressively to Nanking in December to attempt to force an agreement not to attack Shanghai upon the rebels, but by this time there was no attempt at wider observation or reassessment of the movement.[25] The refusal of the Taiping then to give any guarantees about Shanghai, plus their occupation of Ningpo also in December, was the prelude to a policy of active, though limited, intervention against the rebellion which both the British and French followed during 1862–3. A few Westerners still made contact during the last years of the movement, but for the most part Westerners, including the missionaries, turned decisively away, intent upon exploiting the concessions wrung from the Ch'ing between 1858 and 1860.

70

A Report by H S Parkes

BPP, 1862, C. 2976, pp. 25–7, 35

Sir James Hope having given me the option of waiting his return from the mouth of the river either at Chin-kiang or Nanking, I proceeded on to the latter place on the 24th instant [February][26] in her Majesty's ship 'Attalante', in the hope of gaining time for

24 Apart from the four reports printed here note that one of the French representatives on the voyage, Capt. M. Chanoine, wrote a general article entitled 'Les Taipings à Nankin' to be found in *Société de Geographie Bulletin*, vol. 9.1 (1865), pp. 413–22. There are also some letters on the voyage in issues of the *North China Herald* during March and April 1861.

25 For reports relating to this visit see *BPP*, 1862, C. 2976, pp. 97–104.

26 Parkes' report is dated 10 May 1862, but the reference here is clearly to February. It was addressed to Frederick Bruce, who had recently taken up residence in Peking as the first British Minister to China. None of the enclosures referred to by Parkes are reprinted here—for them see the source of the document, pp. 35–7 and *BPP*, 1861, C. 2840, pp. 32–3.

observing the condition of the insurgents in this, their principal position. As the Admiral did not arrive until the 28th, I had three days for this purpose, and with the assistance of the Rev. Mr. Muirhead, who had been paying a visit of some weeks in Nanking, I visited as a private individual nearly every point of interest in the city and suburbs.

The inhabited part of the city is soon seen. Even when in the possession of the Imperialists, it covered only about a fifth part of the vast area inclosed within the walls, which are eighteen miles in circumference, and now several long straggling streets in the southern quarter supply all the accommodation that is required for the present occupants. The north-west angle is the only point of the city wall that approaches the river side, and it is sheltered by a portion of the old suburb inclosed by rude outworks of mud or uncemented stones and brick, and defended by some very indifferent artillery. A creek leads from this point along the west face of the city. It is the seat of the trifling trade that reaches Nanking from the river, consisting, as far as our observation extended, of little else than salt, reeds used as fuel, and fresh supplies in limited quantities. A few boats laden with these articles are to be seen at the mouth of the creek, and the rebel fleet, which numbered only eight West Coast boats, occupies the same position. Most of the city gates remain closed, and only those Chinese who are specially authorized by badge or pass can enter within the walls. The streets inside the city wear a desolate appearance in consequence of all trade being strictly forbidden, and so rigidly is this interdict carried out that, with the exception of a few druggist establishments, not a shop or stall is to be seen within the gates. The object of the rule is to secure the exclusion of a mixed population, and, indeed, every other class than that which is under strict military governance. In adopting it, the rebels could not have given greater proof of their inability to govern, and if they have to resort to the extirpation of the people as the means of preserving order and their own safety in their capital, the circumstance affords but faint hope that their rule is attended with better results in places where they have fewer resources and smaller means of control.

The long hair worn by the men, although all of them are careful to retain their tails, and their fondness for clothes of the most gaudy colours, give them a motley and slovenly appearance; but with the exception of extravagancies in taste, and the bag or hand-kerchief which replaces the ordinary cap, their dress is the same as that of other Chinese. The officials, however, have a costume of their own, which professedly resembles that worn prior to the time of the present dynasty. The women attract attention from their numbers, comely appearance, and rich attire; circumstances which may be explained by the recent sack of Soo-chow and other large cities, as well as by the absence of many of the men with the armies now in the field. I noticed that the Tien Wang had recently attempted to regulate the division of this portion of the plunder by a Decree, in the name of his son, apportioning the number of women to the rank and merit of the men, and forbidding marriage (if it may be so called) until a certain amount of service has been rendered. The rule is provisional, however, until larger captures admit of a wider scheme of distribution. Frequent notices of young women lost or strayed, and offering rewards for their recovery, were observed posted in the streets.

The large number of young boys is also a remarkable feature in the rebel population. Many of these are of course carried off in the same way as the females, and although they may soon become reconciled to the change of home or of masters, they are not allowed any option on the point; and an instance came to my knowledge of three little fellows who had been seized by the Chung Wang (or 'Faithful Prince'), being killed by his orders in consequence of their having attempted to rejoin their parents.

It was difficult to obtain any information in respect to their tribunals or administration of justice, for the reason that they can scarcely yet be said to have any settled system; and constituted as their society at present is, their procedure must necessarily be of a summary and arbitrary nature. The power of life and death seems vested in, or to be assumed by, a large number of persons; and Mr Roberts, who has lived for some time at Nanking, attests the frequency of capital punishments, and the light grounds on which they are inflicted.

Few of the rebels visited the 'Attalante'. Those that did so, came only to ask us for opium or arms, and occasionally they inquired after a few minor articles, such as umbrellas, spy-glasses, and lucifer matches. Opium-smoking appears now to be only excluded from the city, as it is freely indulged in outside the walls, and the old rules against the use of spirituous liquors and tobacco appear to have been rescinded in practice to the same extent.

The Insurgent Government, as far as they have yet formed one, appears to be a pure military despotism. Their officers or chiefs seem to owe their advancement not more to their ability or services than to the number of their slaves or retainers, and as there appears to be no limit set to the trains of followers they thus collect round them, a leader may return to Nanking from a successful raid with no small rise in rank, wealth, and influence. I was told by one of their principal men that when a chief has

100,000 men under his protection, he may put in his claim for the title of Wang, or Prince. The distribution of honours and position must already be a source of embarrassment to the leader of the movement, and a recent Proclamation complains of the number of claims to place and rank, and the difficulty of meeting them. The number of Wangs or Princes already amount to sixteen, there are six orders of nobility, and a long list of high-sounding titles have been created, answering in their signification to Generalissimos, Commanders-in-Chief, Captain-Generals, &c., whilst almost every mud-house in the place is styled a yamun, the name given on the Imperial side to official residences. The Wangs appear to be in the position of feudatories of the Tien Wang, whose personal revenues are stated to be limited to the tribute which they send him. Such a position, and his complete seclusion within the walls of his palace, which he never leaves, and into which females alone are admitted, are not favourable to the exercise of a vigorous control over the actions of these Wangs; and from remarks let fall by some of their number, it appears already to be a question how far they really respect his supremacy, or are led to support him in it as a safeguard against dissension among themselves. Statements from the same source show that the cohesion of the movement depends upon his existence, and that this may at any time be placed in jeopardy is proved by the revolt, several years ago, of the Eastern Prince. Dissatisfied with his title of 'Nine Thousand Years', which was only one degree below the Imperial title of 'Ten Thousand Years', (the equivalent of 'may the King live for ever'), the Eastern Prince aspired to the latter distinction, and the Tien Wang, in order to maintain his own position, had to authorize the massacre of the Eastern Prince and 12,000 of his adherents by the Western Prince. The affair did not end until the last-mentioned Chief was also put out of the way in a similar manner; but in order to allay resentment and divert unpleasant recollections, all public allusion to the violent death of these Chiefs was supressed, and the Eastern Prince was speedily elevated to a place in the Godhead, where the highest spiritual honours could be freely ascribed to him by his worshippers without injury to the temporal interests of the Tien Wang. Since that date, however, the Wangs are not allowed to take a higher title than 'One Thousand Years'.

Soldiers and slaves form the only two classes of the rebel population within Nanking; many of the latter are branded with the four characters 'Tae ping teen kwoh', or 'Tae-ping heavenly kingdom'. They have been brought from all the provinces that the rebels have overrun, receive no pecuniary remuneration, and are fed twice a day in the palace or yamun of the Wang or Chief to whom they belong. Their countenances reveal very clearly the degrading character of their servitude, and the remarks made by a few who could speak without being overheard, betrayed their anxiety to escape from it. Many of them, again, who found their former mode of life a hard struggle, or who belonged to that deserted class which is now so numerous in China, would probably care little to regain their liberty, and are satisfied with a sufficiency of food and shelter in exchange for their labour, which, though forced, does not appear to be severe. The soldiers appear well satisfied with their circumstances, for although they also receive no pay except in the occasional instances in which they are placed in permanent garrisons, the degree of liberty and power which they enjoy, and oportunities they have of paying themselves, naturally attach them to their adventurous and easy mode of life.

It is clear that the behaviour of men of this stamp towards foreigners cannot always be counted on, and the rebel Chiefs expressed themselves anxious that foreigners should not walk about Nanking or the country round it without being accompanied by officers to guard against rudeness on the part of their people. Their manners are of course much at fault, and their advances, even when meant to be friendly, are often marked by an unpleasant degree of familiarity. The boys are the most troublesome class, and I noticed that the cry of 'kwei-tsz' (devil) came oftener from them than the grown-up men, who not unfrequently salute the foreigner as 'yang-heung-te', or foreign brother, and tell him in the patronizing manner that is common to them, that they look upon him as one of themselves.

I shall avoid the vexed question of the religion of these men, except to invite your Excellency's attention at the close of this report to some papers which bear upon the subject. I may remark, however, that on one occasion I saw a figure of the Dragon paraded in the streets of Nanking, and the parties engaged in this idolatrous observance remarked in my hearing that they considered themselves free to combine the worship of this idol with that of the ideal Being to whom they give the same name as our Saviour.

As soon as it was known that the Admiral had arrived at Nanking, two of the rebel authorities having the titles of Mung, Prince of Tzan, and Lin, Prince of Chang, sent to the ship a letter, translation of which I inclose, requesting that all parties visiting the city should first obtain a guide from an office on the river-side called the Customs. The address of this letter to the 'Great Officer deputed by the Admiral of Great Britain, the Consul, and the Reverend Teacher', has reference to the three gentlemen (Mr Ashby, Secretary to the Commander-in-Chief, Mr Vice-Consul Hughes, and Mr Muirhead) who had landed with the first message sent by the Admiral a week before. On this occasion Sir James Hope determined to announce in a formal manner to the rebel authorities, that Her Majesty's ship 'Centaur' would be stationed at Nanking to protect British interests; that our right to navigate the river must not be interfered with, but that we should continue neutral in the struggle between them and the Imperial Government; and that the naval authorities would recognize with certain limitations the authority of the Tae-ping authorities at places in their possession. Captain Aplin, of Her Majesty's ship 'Centaur', the senior naval officer in the river, was directed to make this communication in his own name, and to deliver it personally to the principal Tae-ping authorities, and by desire of the Admiral, I accompanied him on the occasion as interpreter. To aid your Excellency in judging of the character of the rebel authorities, I inclose copy of a Minute of this interview and of Captain Aplin's communication. The singular style of their correspondence, and the extent of their attainments and information, is also illustrated in the inclosed letter to the Commander-in-Chief from an officer charged with the collection of imposts on the few boats that enter the creek at Nanking, written for the purpose of proposing a meeting between himself and the Admiral to arrange the mode in which general relations should be conducted.

On the 2nd March, the fleet, consisting of five small vessels, proceeded up the river, and on the evening of the 6th anchored at Hukow, at the entrance of the Poyang Lake, distant 236 miles from Nanking. We found that the rebels held no part of the river above Woo-hoo (54 miles from Nanking), and thus, with the exception of about 70 miles of its course, the Yang-tze, when we ascended it, was in Imperial possession. Ten miles above Woo-hoo, we passed Imperial posts, and at almost every town on the banks we noticed small gun-boat flotillas, although at a very short distance inland the country on both banks continues in the possession or at the mercy of the rebels. The degree of protection thus secured to the river converts it into a sort of general asylum for the refugees from the cities and villages in the interior, and we saw many instances in which numbers of these poor people had provided themselves with temporary shelter in small reed huts which they had constructed on the banks at those points where gun-boats are stationed. Near Ngan-king (the capital of

Ngan-hwuy) there is a very considerable Imperial fleet co-operating with the land force that is engaged in the siege of that place. Skirmishing was going on between the Imperialists and rebels at the time we passed the city, and the position of the contending parties appeared to have undergone no change since Lord Elgin's expedition passed the same spot twenty-seven months before. Beyond Ngan-king (170 miles above Nanking) the Imperialists have the country entirely in their own hands, the effect of which is seen in the increase of population and trade; so that by the time we had arrived at Hukow the character of the river had changed, and life and activity had taken the place of stillness and desolation . . .

The friendly interest taken in the Nanking insurgents by the Rev. J. Edkins and the Rev. G. John, both of the London Missionary Society, is well known. The former was at Nanking as I passed down, engaged in a further correspondence with the Tien Wang, the result of which, as I have since learned, is to induce both Mr. Edkins and Mr. John to abandon the idea of taking up their residence among the insurgents. In the straight-forward language of Mr. Holmes, 'it is easy to see how long they (the insurgents) would be willing to tolerate men who would preach doctrines radically opposed to those they themselves promulgate, and upon which they found their claim to the obedience of China and the rest of the world. Their willingness, if indeed they are willing, to receive Christian missionaries among them, is doubtless founded upon a misapprehension of their true character. They suppose that the missionary will prove an instrument which they can bend to suit their own purposes.'

The Rev. Issachar Roberts, another American Baptist missionary, to whom the Tien Wang, at a date prior to the outbreak of the insurrection, had applied for baptism and pecuniary support, and who went to Nanking last year at the Tien Wang's request, remains there still; but he entertains doubts, I have been told by those who have visited him, as to whether his duty requires him to continue in, or to leave, that sphere of labour. His missionary teachings are not received as he would desire, and he has no inclination for the temporal honours and employment which the Tien Wang wishes to confer on him. He is justly offended at having had to kneel before the Tien Wang on the only occasion on which he was admitted to an audience, and disappointed at finding that the 'eighteen churches' that he was assured would be opened at Nanking prove only to be rebel designations for so many of their public offices.

I have, &c.
(Signed) Harry S Parkes.

71
An Account by Capt. T W Blakiston
Five Months on the Yang-tze (London, 1862), pp. 11–15, 58–60

. . . On the morning the 24th of February the anchor was weighed, and at half-past eight the 'Attalante' left Chin-kiang under steam. Mr. Parkes was on board. The distance to Nanking is forty-five miles, but to which, in estimating the voyage, has to be added the force of a strong current. Immediately after starting we passed the principal mouth of the northern section of the Grand Canal, where a large fleet of Imperial junks was collected, besides a brig and schooner in the same employ. The southern entrance to the Canal is about eight miles below Chin-kiang, whence it passes through a gap in the range of hills between that place and Kiunshan. It was said to be filled up in many places and altogether useless.

Above Chin-kiang the hills, trending to the westward some three or four miles from the river, are from 500 to 800 feet high, and connected with those in the neighbourhood of Nanking. On the north bank the first high land is met half way between the two places, and a pagoda or two serve as landmarks. Hitherto the country on both banks of the river had been in the hands of the Imperialists, but now we passed their land outpost, where a few war-junks, displaying numerous variegated banners and standards, lay in a small creek on the north bank. A short distance above, we found a similar position held by the Rebels, and on the point where the river makes a bend before forming the last curved reach below Nanking, and opposite a line of red sandstone cliffs, a large number of people were employed throwing up a heavy earthen battery. The position had been well selected for commanding the passage of the river, and the work itself would have done credit to other than Celestial engineers.

After stemming the yet pea-soup-like current for over ten hours, we arrived near the Heavenly city just at dark, and anchored for the night as best we could in the stream. On the following morning we shifted and took up a position out of the strength of the current, off Theodolite Point, the upper end of an island formed by a loop of the river, cutting off a considerable round; having plenty of water, though narrow, it will doubtless, notwithstanding the edict of the 'Great Wang' to the contrary, be used by most vessels on the upward voyage.

Our stay at Nanking embraced the rest of the month of February; and, as the weather was fine, the Taipings not quite so bad as they had been represented, and the country well stocked with game, we made daily excursions either within or without the walls, passing the time very pleasantly. The nearest point of the city is about a quarter of a mile from the river, the intervening space being occupied by moats, ruined temples, and the remains of a suburb. Under the Taiping rule part of this has been walled in, and some batteries thrown up on the river bank. An officer of rank, formerly a common coolie, acts as Chief of the Customs, and all trade is supposed to be carried on here, as no mercantile transactions are allowed within the city.

The first day we were ashore a large party of us made our way, through this stinking suburb, to the city. What struck every one most at first was of course the tremendous heads of hair, when we had been accustomed to see clearly shaven pates. But next to that were the gaudy colours of the dresses of both men and women; being a striking contrast to the sombre blue and grey of the inhabitants of the settled districts. These colours, and the textures of the silks and satins from which they shone, told tales of plunder and robbery—of fire and the sword—of Soo-chow and Hang-chow; they showed why the waters of the Grand Canal cease to be ploughed by deep-laden craft; why China requires to be fed with the rice of Siam; and they scented of a government become rotten.

Proceeding towards the north-west gate of the city, we obtained admission only by making a rush just as the keepers were in the act of closing the doors against us, and by forcing them back. The consequence of which was, as we were officially informed from head-quarters, that these poor people were beheaded the same day. This we considered such summary justice, that we resolved to find out their widows, and do what we could in providing for the fatherless children. With these best of intentions, and resolving in our minds how they could be most satisfactorily carried out without the knowledge of the authorities, imagine our surprise on meeting these very same guards two or three days after, alive and kicking. Being ignorant of the language, we could not gain from them any knowledge of this miraculous mode of curing decapitation. Truly, we thought, wonderful things may be done in these heavenly regions! but on reflection we fancied it might be possible for a Wang to tell a lie.

On ascending a hill, just inside the gate already mentioned, a view is obtained of a considerable portion of the space enclosed by the twenty miles of wall, but no description that I know of gives any just idea of it. The extent is enormous, but, instead of being, as one would have supposed, covered with houses, Nanking in its best days must have been for a great part fields and gardens under cultivation, and now there is even wood and waste land.

Hills of some elevation exist, particularly on the west side, where the scarped sides of the crooked line of heights form a natural wall of red sandstone. The height of the wall varies from fifty to seventy feet. Outside the north and west walls, an extensive moat, or rather series of ponds, extends; but farther on, its place is taken by a creek, which approaches the city at the west gate, and then continues round the south-west angle, towards the site of the famed Porcelain Pagoda. To the east is the Taiping Gate, where a large sheet of water is banked in with masonry. Thence towards the Yang-tsze the walls are regular, but the ditches are choked up with reeds, affording cover to immense numbers of pheasants. Beyond the Taiping Gate, and at the foot of a mountain which overlooks the city from the east, are the sepulchres of the Ming dynasty. Several of the other gates are now bricked up.

Within the city, the inhabited part of which is some miles from the river, there is much desolation, ruin, and filth. There are some palaces, if such they deserve to be called, in a state more or less advanced towards completion, the residences of 'Wangs,' or kings. The walls are dotted with proclamations on imperial yellow paper, and the proportion of women is large, many being captives, and proving that the Taipings act on the adage that 'All's fair in love and war.' . . .

Wu-hoo is situated at the mouth of a tributary stream of clear water falling in on the right bank of the pea-soup-coloured Yang-tsze, fifty-six geographical miles above Nanking; or, rather, a suburb with an old pagoda stands at the mouth of the creek, and the walled town itself is about a mile inland. The day following the evening of our arrival was Sunday, consequently the squadron remained at anchor, the Admiral being always careful that there should be no work on that day. It rained the whole day; but from necessity some of us were obliged to put on our oilskin coats and go ashore in search of provisions. The scene of desolation was as complete as at Nanking or Chin-kiang, and the whole distance from the suburb to the town was one heap of ruins. We walked around looking for provisions; but fish was the only thing to be found, and the population appeared to be in a starving condition. One square place—I think, the ruins of a temple—was literally filled with beggars lying in filth, and but partly covered by some cotton rags alive with vermin. One or two were lifeless, others breathing their last gasps of the noisome stench that pervaded the den. Most were affected with virulent skin disease, and all had the verdict stamped unmistakeably on their countenances, 'Died from starvation.'

After searching in vain for some time, we arrived at the Custom-house, where the people seemed inclined to be civil. But at no reasonable price could we obtain either eggs, fowls, or a goat; seven dollars were asked for a wretched apology for the last; and as for fowls, we offered ten dollars (about forty-two shillings) for a couple of dozen, and were refused. The only chance was one bullock known to be in existence in some part of Wu-hoo, and he was sent for accordingly for our inspection. I forget what we paid for this last of the Wu-hoo bullocks; but we ultimately succeeded, thanks to the Celestial distaste for beef, in striking a tolerably satisfactory bargain. We had a great job to get our purchase to the river, and harder work still to get him on board our vessel, which lay half a mile distant. We first put him in a sampan; but this craft, being unseaworthy, sank under him, which forced us to tow him the whole way astern of the cutter. The blue-jackets enjoyed the fun greatly, and the animal was at last hoisted on board by his horns, after being half-drowned on the passage. So ended our Sunday afternoon's foraging excursion; certainly not a right proceeding, but pardonable under the existing circumstances.

In the neighbourhood of Wu-hoo the country retained the same desolate appearance as we had observed below; the hilly ground on the right, or southern shore of the river, being equally devoid of trees with the low land which stretches away towards the distant hills to the northward. It seems to be a distinctive mark on all districts which have been overrun by the locust-like hordes of the belligerents.

Leaving Wu-hoo and its possessors on the 4th of March, sixty miles in a W.S.W. direction, and then fifty more on various courses, brought us on the day following to An-king, the capital of the province, which had for some time been in the hands of the Taipings, but closely besieged by the Imperial forces under Chin-koo-fang, one of the ablest generals left to the Emperor. The state of siege appeared to be pretty much as it was when the squadron of 1858 gave the batteries a dose of iron in return for a similar compliment. The lines of circumvallation were distinctly visible, and those of contravallation showed that the besiegers were apprehensive of danger from the field as well as the fortress. In fact, when we were at Nanking the 'Coolie Kings' accounted for the smallness of their force at their capital by saying that an army had just left for the relief of this place; but, if I mistake not, the same story was told two years before, which we may charitably put down as a Celestial mistake, otherwise, were we accustomed to use unparliamentary language, a harder word would be substituted.

A considerable fleet of war-junks lay below, and another above the city, quite blockading the river against native craft, while the Rebels were devoid of any naval force. A few desultory shots at long range, and some rockets thrown towards the town by the Imperialists, showed us that the game was still being carried on. The walls, as we passed, were crowded with spectators, but the garrison was said to be in a very forlorn state. This place has since been captured.

72
A Letter from Alexander Michie
BPP, 1862, C. 2976, pp. 7–8

> *'Couper'*, at Kiu-kiang,
> March 8, 1861.

My dear Antrobus,[27]

My last was from Nanking, and would reach you by the 'Waterman'.

We stayed a week in Nanking, called by the present occupants Tien-king, or 'Heavenly Capital'. We occupied the palace that is being got up for the Chung wang, who commanded the forces at Soo-chow last summer. The rebel chiefs put themselves to a great deal of trouble to make us as comfortable as they could, and showed great anxiety to cultivate our friendship. Fortunately for us Muirhead, hearing a steamer had arrived, returned and remained with us, an arrangement which tended greatly to our comfort with the rebels, and enabled us to obtain much more information than we could have done as strangers. We had interviews with several of the Wangs. We spent a week in Nanking before the Admiral returned with the other ships, and I will now give you in as few words as I can, my general conclusions respecting the Tae-ping rebellion, leaving details for another opportunity.

They don't in any way encourage trade, excepting in fire-arms and gunpowder. These, as well as steamers, they are anxious to buy. They pretended a willingness to facilitate trade, and even transit from Imperial territory through their own, but I am persuaded these soft speeches were merely to gain our goodwill. I tried to prove to them the folly of burning and destroying towns

27 Alexander Michie was one of a delegation of three representatives from the Shanghai Chamber of Commerce, of which R. C. Antrobus was the chairman. The two other members of the delegation on the voyage were R. Hamilton and T. F. Ballance. For their joint report entitled 'The Commercial Capabilities of Ports on the Yangtze' see *BPP*, 1861, C. 2840, pp. 11–16.

and villages, and stopping trade at its fountainhead, as without trade they could never prosper. They assented, but said it was difficult, and that their whole attention was now devoted to subduing the 'hills and rivers', as they call it. After peace was established they would then look after trade, as well as schools and other peaceful institutions. The fact is they live on loot, and so long as they can loot they will neither work nor trade.

I found the internal condition of the rebels much better than I expected. They are extremely well dressed and well fed. The population of Nanking, entirely official, no ships or anything unconnected with the army or Administration being admitted within the gates, I estimate at under 20,000. Of this number very few are soldiers, the greater part are captives and slaves from all parts of the country. These are the hewers of wood and drawers of water, and able-bodied men are looked to as valuable prizes. They are either pressed into the army or kept as coolies in Nanking. They get no pay at all, only their food. There is a wonderful number of good-looking young women in the place, all exceedingly well-dressed in Soo-chow silks; these are also captives of war from Soo-chow and other places, and amusing advertisements are met with on the subject of stray women. The city of Nanking, as well as the suburbs, the fine old tombs of the Ming Emperors, and the famous porcelain pagoda, are utterly destroyed. The walls are very high, twenty miles in circuit; but the once wide and well-paved streets are merely roads leading through heaps of bricks. The palaces of the Wangs stands conspicuous among the ruins. These are new; the old yamuns and temples, and the whole Tartar city, having been destroyed. A few houses line the road here and there; but not in my opinion supplying accommodation for more than 20,000 people.

The Tien-Wang has a large palace. His attendants are females, 300 in number, besides 68 wives allowed to his rank. He is never seen by any but the Kings, and his person is held sacred. He is, however, by no means a puppet, for it is he alone who keeps the movement together. There are ten or eleven Kings in all; but only two or three in Nanking. Kan-Wang and Si-Wang are leading troops into Anwhuy. Chung-Wang is about Soo-chow, and there is one they say in Sze-chuen. The discipline is as good as that of the Imperialists, perhaps better, and the juniors have a dashing rollicking manner that is rather taking. The Wangs that I have seen, on the contrary, have a drowsy dissipated appearance, while their mountebank yellow dresses and tinsel crowns, with their theatrical efforts at dignity of deportment, render them quite ridiculous. Not one of these Kings can speak the mandarin dialect, and none of them have had education above that of a coolie, excepting Tien-Wang, who was two months with Mr. Roberts, and Kan-Wang, who was under Dr. Legge in Hong Kong for a time; they have linguists attached to them who read and write for them. Their armament is of the most contemptible kind, and the fact of their dominating over the Imperial troops merely demonstrates the utter and hopeless prostration of the Government. The rebels hold all the country round Nanking. It is scoured by their foraging parties. No Imperialists force comes above Kea-chow. Nanking could be taken as easily as possible if the Imperialists had an atom of pluck. Nganking is also held by the rebels; but they are so beleaguered by the besiegers that they are in great straits for food. We passed close under the walls of Nganking. The outer defences and the wall itself are in first-rate order. Fortunately they did not molest us. The wall was crowded with people as we passed. It must be more populous than Nanking, and no women were to be seen. In fighting men it must be far stronger. The Imperialists are also in great force. They are strongly entrenched in a semi-circle round the city, at an average distance of at least two miles. The rebels have no fleet, while a well-armed Imperial fleet blockades the river, about three miles below the city, and another the same distance above it. The Imperialists also hold two fortified positions on the opposite side of the river. The rebels are, therefore, completely invested, and must either be starved out soon or make a sally, as they did at Nanking last year. Meantime a large rebel army is advancing for the relief of the garrison, and the Imperialists are also advancing reinforcements to Anwhuy. A pitched battle is expected soon, the result of which will be interesting.

I have no hope of any good ever coming of the rebel movement. No decent Chinaman will have anything to do with it. They do nothing but burn, murder, and destroy. They hardly profess anything beyond that. They are detested by all the country people, and even those in the city who are not of the 'brethren' hate them. They have held Nanking eight years, and there is not a symptom of rebuilding it. Trade and industry are prohibited; their land-taxes are three times heavier than those of the Imperialists; they adopt no measures to soothe and conciliate the people, nor do they act in any way as if they had a permanent interest in the soil. They don't care about the ordinary slow and sure sources of revenue; they look to plunder, and plunder alone, for subsistence, and I must say, I cannot see any elements of stability about them, nor anything which can claim our sympathy. . . .

330

73
An Account by Lt Col. G J Wolseley
G J Wolseley, *Narrative of the War with China in 1860*
(London, 1862), ch. XIV

Being neither a missionary nor a merchant, I was most anxious to visit the rebel headquarters, and, if possible, by a stay there to judge for myself of their merits or demerits. Having had some little experience of the imbecility and rottenness of the Imperialist Government, I went to Nankin strongly prejudiced against it, and only anxious to recognise any good which we might discover in its rival for supreme power. We were accommodated in a palace belonging to the Chung-wan or Faithful King, and received daily a supply of fowl, eggs, &c. &c., for which no money would be received. It would appear almost as if they wished to abolish altogether the use of coin, and reduce society to that patriarchal state in which the people receive their daily food, clothing, &c., and have all the ordinary wants of nature supplied by the master under whose banner they served. Such, at least, is the system now in practice within Nankin. There are eleven kings, to one or other of whom every man is attached, the name of each man being duly registered at the public office, over which his king presides, and from which he receives a daily allowance of food. At present eatables are scarce, but all sorts of wearing apparel are to be had in abundance, having been obtained in immense quantities upon the capture of Soochow, the great Chinese emporium of all such articles. Upon several occasions we endeavoured to pay the poor, wretched, half-starved looking coolies who carried our traps, but although sometimes the money was offered to them when none of their superiors were present, they almost always refused, fearing lest it might be discovered, and so bring down the vengeance of the executioner's sword upon them. No shops of any sort whatever are permitted within the walls of Nankin. There are, however, one or two insignificant markets in the ruined suburbs, where a small quantity of vegetables and fish are daily exposed for sale. For a considerable time it has been a contested point, whether Hung-seu-tsuen, the originator of the movement, whose pretended visions first gave rise to the crusade against idolatry, is really still living or not. But that he still lives is now ascertained beyond doubt. Mr. Roberts, a Baptist American missionary, at whose school in Canton the Tien-wan, or Heavenly King, as he calls himself, first received any biblical knowledge, is now a resident in Nankin. We saw him during our stay there frequently, and from him I learnt a great deal of the information now given here.

He reached Nankin last October, after experiencing much difficulty in getting through the rebel forces stationed in the neighbourhood of Soochow. Shortly after his arrival, the Tien-wan sent to him, saying, he wished to have an interview with him. This was a most marked favour, as none but the other kings are allowed into his 'sacred presence', and then only upon matters of state business, when they kneel before him. Some difficulty occurred about the etiquette necessary at the presentation, as Mr. Roberts most properly refused to kneel down on both knees to any man; but this was at last got over; and those who were arranging the interview, promised him that he should not be obliged to do so. However, as Mr. Roberts said, 'they did him', for as soon as he entered the hall of audience, Tien-wan exclaimed, 'Let us worship the Heavenly Father;' so, as Mr. Roberts could not refuse to join in praising God, he knelt, whilst all present repeated a doxology, which was originally composed by him for the use of his scholars at Canton. The difficulty thus overcome, they had a long conversation, chiefly upon religious subjects, in which Tien-wan reversed their former relative positions, and sought to convert his quondam teacher to the new light of religion, not as laid down in the Holy Scriptures, but as it has been, he says, revealed to him directly from the 'Heavenly Father'. . .

Tien-wan now lives thoroughly secluded from all male society, within the recesses of his palace, surrounded by his host of wives and swarms of concubines, or female attendants, whichever he may choose to term them, no male servant being under any pretext whatever permitted with the sacred precincts of his residence. His palace is quite new, and forms with one or two others and some very badly constructed fortifications, the only monuments of the new dynasty. In appearance it has nothing peculiar about it, being built according to the general design of all public buildings in the 'flowery land'. In its decoration, however, it copies most accurately the imperial yellow tiling and unmeaning-looking royal dragon. As on the day we visited this palace an edict was issued by the Heavenly King, we had an opportunity of witnessing the ceremonies usual upon such occasions.

A long, covered porch leads up to the gate of the private residence, and on this a red carpet was spread. All the officials of the guard, and those apparently belonging to the public offices in the immediate neighbourhood, came forward in their state dresses, and kneeling in rows facing the gate, waited in that position until it should be opened. After a little time the lofty yellow doors were thrown open, and a woman appeared, carrying a highly ornamented tray, upon which was a sort of despatch-box, painted a bright, canary colour, and having pictures of dragons on each side. It was sealed up, and contained within the sacred edict. Upon seeing the box, all present, immediately bent their heads, and the great crowd which had assembled, partly to witness the ceremony, and partly to stare at the *'foreign devils'*, fell down upon their knees, all repeating, with a regular cadence, 'Ten thousand years, ten thousand years, ten thousand times ten thousand years', which, although as it were analogous to our loyal exclamation of 'God save the Queen', is with them repeated with all the fervour of adoration. A sort of yellow-coloured sedan-chair, with glass sides, was then brought forward, in which the previous mandate was placed, and then borne away on the shoulders of eight coolies, amidst a loud salvo of guns, a band of music playing in front and a swarm of attendants following. It was being taken to the Tsan-wan's palace. All the edicts and letters coming from the Tien-wan are written either by his own hand or that of his son, a child of twelve years old, who professes to have direct revelations from God, and whose name is now associated in all public documents with that of his father. The 'sacred' epistles are always upon yellow satin or silk, and written with red ink. I saw one which had been sent to Mr. Roberts. The style in which they are worded would be blasphemous in the extreme if it were not so essentially ludicrous . . . Tien-wan himself makes use of numerous quotations from the sacred writings; but they are mostly from the Pentateuch, which appears to have had great weight with him in his system of absolute government and in many of his customs. He keeps the Jewish Sabbath, although most certainly not after the Hebrew manner. On Friday evenings you see flags hung out in many of the principal streets, announcing that 'To-morrow will be the Sabbath and all are commanded to reverence and keep it'. I could not, however, discover in what manner they kept it; for they refrained in no way whatever from any of their ordinary amusements or occupations, and, as they have not attempted to construct any churches, no semblance even of public worship is gone through. I was told by a zealous advocate of theirs, that at a certain hour in the day I should hear a gun fired, when all the inhabitants would kneel down and worship God; but although I carefully watched for the signal during the Saturday which we spent there, I never heard it; nor did I in any place see any number of people praying, although I was wandering about the city all day. I am quite sure that the Chinese servants who attended upon us never adhered to this admirable plan. . . .

The escape of women from their domineering lords and masters does not seem to be very uncommon, as more than once we came across advertisements placarded upon the walls, offering rewards varying from fifteen to two dollars to any one who would bring them back. These bills entered into the most minute particulars, reminding one of the notices one sees in England regarding 'dogs lost, stolen, or strayed'. The power of punishing with death is given to almost the meanest officials. Men whose rank corresponds with that of a constable with us, possess and use it most freely. The man who on the day of our landing was sent with us from the customhouse to show the road into the city had this power. All who have it carry a little three-cornered flag, with the character 'Ling' in its centre. Such is their 'attribute of awe and majesty'. This guide was a very common-looking fellow indeed; dressed little better than a coolie, and holding such an inferior position, that the gatekeeper of the city refused to let us enter at his request. Mr. Roberts told us that when he was leaving Soochow *en route* for Nankin, a petty officer of this sort was sent with him to obtain chairmen for him at the different stages; and that upon one occasion some poor person having annoyed him (the official) he said he would behead him, and was only prevented by Mr. Roberts from actually carrying his threat into execution. Mr. Roberts also informed us, that he passed on the road, during his journey, numbers of human bodies from which the heads had been but lately severed. The men who were sent by the Tsan-wan to attend upon us during our stay, said they had been in former times silk weavers at Soochow, but were then slaves, having been captured at the taking of that city. Their lives were spared, because they could be made useful in carrying away the loot from thence. These poor wretches were in the most abject misery, but did not dare to express their feelings when any other Chinamen were present. They were really grateful when we gave them a cheroot to smoke, the use of tobacco being nominally prohibited, but like opium still much indulged in by those who can obtain it. Although smoking is said to be punishable by death, all the officials who visited us were delighted to get cigars; indeed at last they became rather importunate in their applications for the fragrant weed. Wherever we went the same question was universally asked us, 'What have you got for sale?' 'Have you any opium?' 'Have you any firearms?' A man went on board one of our ships lying off Nankin, and asked for a hundred chests of opium. Some of our party had once to pay the Tsan-wan a visit late in the evening, when that royal personage was quite stupid, and most unmistakeably under the influence of the above narcotic. To say that the Tien-wanists deserve any praise for their proclaimed laws prohibiting the use of opium is absurd; and although it may serve as a good missionary cry, to create sympathy for the cause in England, it will be laughed at by every man who has lately paid the Yang-tse-kiang a visit at any point where the rebel territories touch upon it. We visited many such places, and at all, as at Nankin, the great cry was for opium and arms. . . . . All the rebel soldiers that we saw were badly armed, the universal weapon being a long bamboo with a pike on the top—a very small proportion having old muskets, matchlocks, or pistols; a few, fowling-pieces and rifles. Every second man carried a huge flag, and some carried swords—altogether it is impossible to imagine a more undisciplined or inefficient mob. Wherever they go they plunder and destroy. Civilisation and even animal life seems to disappear before them, and their march may be tracked by the bodies of murdered peasants and the ruined habitations which they leave behind them. The country people, far and wide, fly from contact with them, transporting their little all to some place which they deem safer. On the banks of the river, beyond the territories thus laid waste, numbers of large, strawbuilt villages are now to be seen, hastily thrown up by the unfortunate refugees, who endeavour to support life by fishing, or by any other local employment which they can obtain. In all such places as we had an opportunity of visiting, the distress and misery of the inhabitants were beyond description. Large families were crowded together into low, small, tent-shaped wigwams, constructed of reeds, through the thin sides of which the cold wind whistled at every blast from the biting north. The denizens were clothed in rags of the most loathsome kind, and huddled together for the sake of warmth. The old looked cast down and unable to work from weakness, whilst that eager expression peculiar to starvation, never to be forgotten by those who have once witnessed it, was visible upon the emaciated features of the little children. With most it was a mere question of how many days longer they might drag on their weary lives; whilst even the very moments of many seemed already numbered. The rebel ranks are swelled in two ways: first, by the capture of unwilling men; and, secondly, by those who, being deprived of all they have in this world by the invading marauders, have, as their only alternative, either to starve, or join their spoilers and thus obtain a subsistence by becoming spoilers themselves. The destructive policy of the rebels in this way serves them well. As we steamed from Nankin up the river, how we desired that all those good people at home, who wish the Tien-wanists well and pray daily for their success, could but make a similar voyage, and thus have an opportunity of judging for themselves regarding the two rival powers who are now struggling for mastery. When once you have passed clear from the last rebel outpost, and got some distance within the still Imperial territory, the contrast around could scarcely be believed without seeing it. The river which near the rebels is a great deserted highway, is there to be seen well covered with trading craft; highly cultivated farms stretch down to the water's edge, whilst neatly-built and snug-looking villages and hamlets are scattered along both banks.

74
A Report by H S Parkes
BPP, 1861, C.2840, pp. 22–5; also 1862, C.2976, pp. 53–6

Report by Mr. Parkes of Visit to the Ying-wang, at Hwang-chow, 50 miles from Hankow, March 22, 1861.[28]
Her Majesty's gun-boat 'Bouncer' anchored at Hwang-chow at 11.15 a.m., and I landed with Messrs. Hamilton and Ballance. An officer dressed in a long red silk gown, and accompanied by an attendant, who held a light blue satin umbrella of foreign shape over his master's head, received us on the beach, where we were soon surrounded by a crowd of rebels, who came running from the suburbs and the entrenchments at which they were at work to look at us. On mentioning to the officer that I wished to see their principal leader, and should enter the city for that purpose, he simply stated that the leader's name was Chin, and thought that he was absent in a camp outside the city. This officer was not very communicative, but gave the number of the rebels in Hwang-chow at 20,000 or 30,000, and stated that they had taken the city on the 18th instant without fighting; the suburb through which we passed was full of rebels who were busy foraging in the houses, which already bore the appearance of having been gutted, and were entirely deserted by the people, while other parties were engaged in demolishing all the buildings near the city wall, in order to clear the approach to the latter, and to obtain timber for a triple barricade which they were throwing up around the walls. At the gate by which we entered I observed a Proclamation in the name of the Ying-wang assuring the people of protection, and inviting them to come and trade freely with the troops. Another Proclamation addressed to the latter prohibited them from that date from wandering into the villages and plundering

28 For other reports by Parkes of interviews with Taiping chiefs at various places along the Yangtze see *BPP*, 1861, C. 2840, pp. 25–7, 30–2 and *BPP*, 1862, C. 2976, pp. 35–7.

the people. A third notice, appended to the heads of two rebels, made known that these men had been executed for robbing the people of their clothes while engaged in collecting grain for the troops. The very motley garb of those rebels who surrounded us suggested the idea that many among them must have shared in the same offence; few of them wore any distinguishing dress, and while most of them had allowed their hair to grow, they all appeared to have preserved their tails. In reply to the inquiries I put them, I found them to be men collected from at least six or eight provinces; those from Hoonan and Hoopeh probably predominated, and the large proportion of young lads attracted our attention.

Following the main street we soon came to the building which had been the yamun of the Prefect, where we found preparations being made to give us a formal reception. We were saluted with music and three guns, and were received by several officers dressed in yellow gowns, who conducted us through two large courts lined with troops, armed for the most part with spears or halberds and carrying a large number of very gaudy flags without any definite emblem. The doors of the principal hall, which usually stand open, were kept closed until we put foot upon the steps, when they were suddenly thrown back, and we saw seated in state, in the middle of the hall, a young looking man, robed in a yellow satin gown and hood embroidered with dragons. A number of officers dressed in long yellow gowns with yellow handkerchiefs on their heads stood by him, but the crowd of men in coolie or menial garb who pressed into the hall interfered somewhat with the theatrical effect that it appeared intended these arrangements should produce. The principal personage seemed at a loss to know how to receive his visitors, and was evidently relieved when I drew a chair from a somewhat distant point to the table at which he was seated, and broke the silence by entering into conversation with him.

He informed me that he was the leader known as the Ying-wang (or heroic Prince); that he was charged from Nanking to relieve Nganking, and had undertaken a westward movement with the view of gaining the rear of the Imperial force besieging that city on the western side. So far he had been completely successful.

Leaving Tung-ching, a city forty miles to the north of Nanking, on the 6th instant, he marched in a north-westerly direction upon the district city of Hoh-shan, thus avoiding all the Imperialists' posts in the districts of Yung-chung, Tseen-shan and Tai-hoo. On the 10th he took Hoh-shan, where there was no considerable head of force opposed to him, and then turning to the south-west, reached Yung-shan on the 14th, which fell in the same way.

Hastily securing the munitions of these two places, of which he stood in need, he pressed on to Hwang-chow, and succeeded in surprising a camp of the Amoor Tartars, killing, as the Ying-wang said, all the men, and capturing all their horses. This, and a small affair at Paho, placed him in possession of Hwang-chow, which he entered without opposition on the 17th instant.[29]

He had thus taken three cities, and had accomplished a march of 600 *li* (say 200 miles) in eleven days, and was now in a position either to attack in rear the Imperial force which he had just turned, and draw them off from Nanking, or, postponing that operation, to occupy Han-kow, from which he was distant only fifty miles. He added, however, that he felt some hesitation in marching upon the latter place, as he had heard that the English had already established themselves at that port.

I commended his caution in this respect, and advised him not to think of moving upon Han-kow, as it was impossible for the insurgents to occupy any emporium at which we were established, without seriously interfering with our commerce, and it was necessary that their movements should be so ordered as not to clash with ours. In this principle he readily acquiesced, and said that two of his leaders who had pushed on beyond Hwang-chow should be directed to take a northerly or north-westerly course, and go towards Ma-ching or Tih-ngan, instead of towards Han-kow.

Having put several inquiries to him as to the future plans of the insurgents, he readily entered into the following particulars relative to the campaign, in which he said they were then engaged, and to which his information appeared to be limited.

Four rebel columns are in the field, his own and three others, severally commanded by the Chang-wang, Shi-wang, and Ho-wang. These three Wangs (or Princes) were to leave Hwang-chow in the middle of the 1st month (February), and marching in different directions on the south of the Yang-tze, while he, the Ying-wang, moves through the country on the north bank, they propose to rendezvous at Woo-chang in the 3rd month (April). The Chung-wang is to cross Kiang-si below Nan-chang (the capital of that province), and to march by Suy-chow to Yoh-chow on the Tung-tsing lake, and thus reach a position to the west of Woo-chang. The Shi-wang is to cross the Poyang Lake, and visiting or passing by Nan-chang is to enter Hoo-peh by Ning-chow, and thus approach Woo-chang on the south face. The Foo-wang is to make

29 For accounts of the Ying Wang's Western campaign at this time see Jen Yu-wen, op. cit., ch. 18, esp. pp. 409–13, 572 (map) and Michael, op. cit., vol. I, pp. 153–7 and map 11.

for Hoo-kow and Kiụ-kiang, and embarking his force if he is able
to do so, is to ascend the Yang-tze and attack Woo-chang on the
east side, while, as already pointed out, Ying-wang's force is to
close in upon the north side. Returning to the subject of Hankow,
he observed that although he might desist from occupying that
place, the other Wangs being uninformed of our position there,
might still continue to carry out the above plan, and he suggested
that both the English and insurgent interest might be accommodated by our taking Hankow and Woo-chang, and allowing him
to occupy Han-yang.

I explained to the Ying-wang that our objects in coming up the
Yang-tze were strictly commercial; that our recent Treaty with
the Imperial Government, with whom we were now at peace, gave
us the right of trade upon the Yang-tze, but as the insurgents
utterly destroyed trade wherever they went, they would render
this right nugatory if they occupied those ports that had been
expressly opened to our commerce. Han-yang was one of three
cities connected with each other, and forming one great mart,
commonly called Hankow. The rebels could not take any of these
cities without destroying the trade of the whole emporium, and
hence the necessity of their keeping away altogether.

These subjects, however, I added, are in the hands of the
Admiral who commands the English expedition in the river. He is
now on his way back, and as he passes Nanking will, doubtless,
come to a distinct understanding on the above points with the
insurgent authorities there; the latter, it may be presumed, will
then forward instructions to the Ying-wang for his guidance, and
until the receipt of these instructions he should refrain from
making any further movement upon Hankow. That as nothing had
been heard at Kiu-kiang of the advance of Chung-wang or the
other leaders up to the 9th instant, it might be presumed that at
that date they had not yet crossed into Kiang-si. He would not,
therefore, have the advantage of their support if he moved at once
upon Hankow, and would have to contend alone with the
Imperial force assembling for the defence of Woo-chang, as well
as with the Nganhwuy force, which would then form in his rear.

The Ying-wang seemed to concur entirely in what I urged. He
computed his own following at 100,000 men, but considered that
scarcely half of them had reached Hwang-chow. He should first
fortify his position, he said, at Hwang-chow, and then be guided
by circumstances as to his next operations. Perhaps he might
attack the Imperialists between him and Ngan-king, or perhaps
make an incursion into the North of Hoopeh. He had only a few of
the Nienfei (or Northern insurgents) with him, but these roving

bodies of marauders, as he himself called them, are always ready to join the Tae-ping standard when wanted. They had just had certain operations against them in the North of Ngan-hwuy, which were to be conducted under the joint direction of a Tae-ping and Nienfei leader. They are to move from Leu-chow near the centre of Ngan-hwuy, first North and then East, taking the cities of Luhgan-chow, Show-chow, and Fung-yang-foo, or passing through the departments named after these cities, and then, turning South, they are to fall upon the important commercial city of Yang-chow, opposite Chin-kiang. The Ying-wang also repeated the report common in other quarters, that Shih-ta-kai has undertaken a movement in Sze-chuen, his force for this purpose being principally composed of the banditti of Yoo-nan and Kwei-chow.

I was favourably impressed with the modest manners and the intelligence of the Ying-wang, and he appeared to be respected by those around him. His literary attainments are probably limited, though his pronunciation of Mandarin is better than that I have hitherto heard spoken by Tae-ping leaders. He gave his age at 20 only, but this is probably five or six years under the mark.[30]

After leaving him we walked round the city. This has long been in a decayed state, and when we visited it on the 10th instant, might have contained, in the small portion of its large area that is built over, including also the suburbs, a population of about 40,000. The whole of these had fled from the place, but every house was now filled with rebels, of whom we saw in all, probably from 20,000 to 30,000. Working-parties swarmed outside the walls, engaged in the construction of the triple row of stakes above mentioned, and in which they had already made considerable progress. Other parties, whom we saw arriving, seemed greatly fatigued with their march, and many of the men threw themselves down in the streets and slept without taking the trouble to remove their burdens. These consisted chiefly of clothes and provisions of all kinds, as rice, pork, poultry, &c., obtained on the line of march. Many of them seemed also in a sickly and diseased state, and appeared to be of the mendicant class. Their strength may have been tried by their long and hurried march, or the force may have been joined by the poor and destitute of the country through which they passed. We saw few weapons but knives and spears upon them, and these only on the persons of the parties just arriving. Those who had already been quartered, or were at work on the defences, had already returned

30   Ch'en Yu-cheng, the Ying Wang, was in fact 25 at this time.

their arms (as we were told) into store. They did not seem to possess a single piece of artillery, but had a considerable number of ponies, those in best condition having belonged to the Tartar camp they recently surprised, and they stabled these animals in the houses they themselves occupied. They had no females with them, and stated that they had left all their women at Nanking.

The general appearance of the whole force was that of a mob, or probably that of a Pindaree host; but while no discernible steps were taken for preserving order among them, they all appeared on the best terms with each other; and although engaged in the exciting work of the division of plunder, or of accommodation, no instance of fighting, dispute, or drunkenness came under our observation, nor did we see any of them indulging either in gambling or in smoking tobacco.

(Signed)
Harry S Parkes

75
A Report by R J Forrest
BPP, 1862, C. 2840, pp. 27–30

We passed the rebel outposts without molestation, but were compelled by an excessively dirty man to pay a tax of 5 taels for each of our boats on entering the moat at Soo-chow. Several soldiers visited us, from whom but little information was to be gained; most of them had been pressed into service, and not a few had the Chinese characters for the dynasty pricked into their cheeks. Some had been present at the repulse from Shanghae, but none seemed to think that the Imperial authorities could ever get hold of them. They knew nothing of their future movements, but answered inquiries with the remark that they had rice enough every day, and that to-morrow might take care of itself. The Kings take care to send the men captured in a new district to the other extreme of their territory and we found that men from Hoonan, Hoopeh, and the Two Kiang formed the garrison of all towns along the Grand Canal. The soldiers stated that about a hundred foreigners were employed by the insurgents; they are living in Ching-poo and Soo-chow, and get 30 taels per month. With the exception of one man with blue eyes and flaxen hair, I saw nothing like a foreigner during the whole journey.

We were well received by Lin, second in command at Soo-chow, who at once gave us a passport, and entered into a long conversation with us. He has a strong objection to any show or state, and lives in a very quiet manner.

Words cannot convey any idea of the utter ruin and desolation which mark the line of Tae-ping march from Nanking to Soo-chow. The country around the last unfortunate city will soon be covered with jungle, while the vast suburbs, once the wonder of even foreigners, are utterly destroyed; a few miserable beings are met with outside the gates selling bean curd and herbs, but with these exceptions none of the original inhabitants are to be found, and we actually flushed teal in the city moat, where only a year ago it was barely possible to find a passage from the immense number of boats actively engaged in commerce and traffic. The interior of the city is equally desolate, the whole of the house-fronts have been torn down, and the numerous water-courses are filled with broken furniture, rotten boats, and ruin. The same may be said for all cities on the canal, and as for the villages and places unprotected by walls, they have been burned so effectually and carefully that nothing but the blackened walls remain.

A very large body of rebels was engaged in the erection of defences outside the Chang gate of Soo-Chow. The forts have for object the protection of the entrance to the Grand Canal, which was crowded with boats laden with foreign arms, furniture, and goods of all sorts. Great preparations, we were informed were being made for the storming of Hang-chow, against which place the Kan-wang and 70,000 newly arrived Cantonese insurgents had proceeded. The mass of boats, with the utmost civility and with infinite trouble, made a passage for our boats, and we entered on the Grand Canal.

The same sad story everywhere suggested itself. Devastation marked our journey. The land on either bank was waste to the distance of a mile from the bank, while the towing-path, which is also the grand rebel highway, was like an upturned churchyard. Human remains were lying about in all directions. During the retreat of the Imperialists after the fall of Woo-si, the rebels followed them on horseback; no quarter was given to the fugitive troops, whose ranks were augmented by the frightened peasantry; they were slain as overtaken, and if the towing-path yet shows the signs of slaughter, the waters of the canal conceal the remains of by far the greater numbers of the victims.

Large numbers of Tae-ping soldiers were passed every day, in fact there was one continuous stream of them going from Nanking to Soo-chow and Chin-keang-foo, against which last place the insurgents are making great efforts. We heard the roar of the guns at and near Tam-yang, and the Chief at that town told us that they should undoubtedly take the city very soon.[31] We could see

31 The Imperialists had recaptured Chinkiang in December 1857 and held it thereafter—see Jen Yu-wen, op. cit., p. 338.

by the smoke of burning houses in which direction Chin-kiang lay, and remarked at the same time that the rebels had in no way changed their usual destructive habits.

I had heard, and believe it to be true, that the Tae-pings are making such efforts to take the Yang-tze ports in consequence of an idea that if a foreign Consul once is established in any of them, the same protection will be given to the place as is given to Shanghae.

I took some trouble to examine the foreign arms carried by the insurgents, and find that the purchasers have been, in almost every instance, the victims of foreign fraud. Most of the guns and all the pistols I looked at were very old, and badly made, useless weapons, with the detonating apparatus broken. A number of muskets that I saw at Soo-chow, recently bought (the soldier said) from American strangers, were of such a description that half-a-dozen shots will certainly destroy them, and probably their owners too. On the whole I am convinced that the foreign arms, of which they have a very large quantity, are far more dangerous to the insurgents themselves than to their enemies.

One characteristic of the Tae-ping movement is the employment of a vast number of boys in the army. Every Chief has several, and although I never saw a rebel soldier who could be called old, where there is one grown-up man there are two or three boys of from twelve to eighteen years of age. They have all been kidnapped at various places, but appear quite delighted with their profession, giving themselves the most insolent swagger and airs. These youths always saluted us as 'devils', while their superiors and Chiefs were very particular in calling us foreign brothers when they had occasion to talk to us.

On leaving our boats at Pao-ying, we had more opportunity of getting among the people, who were not alarmed at the sight of strangers as were the few wretched people along the canal. In fact, much more confidence and safety was apparent around us. A large number of people had returned to their homes and former occupations. The proclamations, not few in number, of Tien-wang's son and Chung-wang, prohibited the soldiers from carrying off men or women on pain of death.

The people gave us a melancholy history of the Tae-ping outbreak, and the treatment accorded to the newly conquered districts. A great deal of indiscriminate slaughter at first took place; the young men and women were carried off; all portable valuable property became the prize of the conquerors, and only the old men and women left behind. Crowds of fugitives crossed the Great River to await better times; they are, I am glad to say, fast returning to their homes. The insurgents do not molest them much: a certain number are compelled to attend on the Chief to do the coolie work of the public service; when their turn is finished, others take their place, and they themselves are permitted to return home; of this class of men were those who carried our baggage and chairs, they worked cheerfully and well, asked for no gratuity, and were very grateful for the little present we gave them when they left us.

The rebel authorities pay a visit to the rural districts once a month, and exact a tribute of cash or rice from the inhabitants of the villages. Regularly-appointed officers are stationed in all important places, in whom the people seem to have confidence, and unless some new military operations disturb Nanking, the villages around will soon become peopled, and the land resume its wonted fertile appearance.

We arrived at Nanking soon after an Edict had been passed prohibiting trade in the city. The reason given was, that as Tien-kiang (Nanking) was the Imperial residence, it should not be disturbed by the clamour of the tradesfolk, and that bad characters had come in as traders. Fourteen unfortunates, who tried to make a little gain in spite of the Edict, were at once executed; a brisk trade has consequently sprung up outside the several gates. The market at the south gate is particularly busy and crowded, nor are there houses enough in the suburbs to meet the demand. I should estimate the population of the city and suburbs at about 70,000 men, against the 200,000 spoken of by the authorities.

Building is going on in the city, and people who have known the place before say that marked improvement is taking place. A good deal of wealth exists among the people, and it is not a little curious that the Tae-pings have a silver currency of very convenient size and value. The common coin is of the size of a shilling, but worth rather more; it is exactly like a copper cash, and has an inscription engraved on it. A large silver coin of the value of a sovereign exists, but I have seen none. Imperial cash is used in preference to their own Tae-ping copper coins, and, of course, sycee is readily taken.

The authorities assert, and with some show of truth, that the rulers are now giving their attention to the formation of a fixed order of government, and to the improvement of the condition of the people; measures impossible before, because of the Imperialist army. Only one King, the Chan-wang, is in the city at present, to wait upon Tien-wang, and all his work is done by his son. I saw this son twice, once in his palace, when he volunteered an

344

account of Tien-wang's visions, and once when he was preaching to the public with his robe and crown on. This sermon had but little to do with religion, and was merely a collection of orders to the people.

I enclose a translation of an interesting Edict of Tien-wang, in which his intentions with regard to foreigners are made known.[32] Mr. Roberts, the gentleman mentioned therein, has refused for the sixth time the honour conferred, and is, in fact, without any influence in Nanking.

I cannot conclude without mentioning the obligation I am under to my travelling companion, the Rev. J. Edkins, who was indefatigable in assisting me to get any information during our journey.

I have, &c.

(Signed) R J Forrest

76
The Diary of John Heard
The Archives of Augustus Heard & Co., vol. FP.3

Saturday April 20 (1861)

We left Chinkiang at 7 a.m. of the 19' and anchored at Nankin at a little before 4. It rained a little when we started but soon cleared up fine. Scenery interesting but as we were now in the rebel districts—the fields seemed deserted and we missed the fine cultivation which we had previously remarked. When near enough to the banks we could see that the men there were Changmaous. We found the Centaur and Bouncer at Nankin. A boat from the former boarded us at once, and we found that the gun boat was to leave for Shanghae this morning. Wrote A.F.H., E.F.P., G.W.H., & E.A.G. After finishing our letters went ashore for a walk and make our first acquaintance with the long haired race—and a nice acquaintance we made of it. After strolling about for some time, and coming to the conclusion that they were the most infernal scoundrels on the face of the earth, we walked to the end of the beach opposite the anchorage. We soon came to the dead body of a person for whom they were digging a grave— and as soon as we got a good look at it, we saw the trunk was headless! A little farther on was a pool of blood quite fresh showing where the execution had just taken place! Again a little farther was the head on a pole and we saw that it was a woman! A pleasant sight and a pleasant introduction to Nankin and our friends the Rebels!

32   For a translation of this edict see Michael, op. cit., vol. III, pp. 1129–31.

The Interpreter, Mr. Forrest, from the Centaur, who boarded us yesterday, very kindly offered to go with us today to the city. So this morning at 10 Meredith [?] and I went on board to call on Capt. Aplin. We found, however, that Mr. Forrest was ill and could not go, so Aquan having obtained for us a pass from the official at the point, we started off by ourselves accompanied only by two or three of our Chinese satellites. We must have had a pace of 6 or 7 miles up the creek before coming to a gate, where we attempted to enter, although we had a rebel guide with us, they refused to allow us to pass, alleging that the paper we had was no use and that it must be exchanged for another from a higher official. Our young rebel was sent for this, and we went into the guard house to escape the horrible crowd that surrounded us. They followed us in however, and such a vile set of wretches it would be difficult to find elsewhere. Mr. Cox and Yungchang's brother were in an awful funk—Akang seemed pretty plucky. There were some Keangshan and Kwangsi fellows among them with whom our men had a talk. The Centurion at the gate, an old chap, was as dignified an old ruffian as we would wish to see. After waiting an hour we could stand it no longer and came away—losing the day as far as sight seeing is concerned but having had a pleasant enough excursion.

Mr. Bryant, the 2nd Officer, was named to stop up the creek for the Chinese of our staff, who, I forgot to mention, had started from the ship an hour or two before us. To our great surprise we saw them come aboard about 5 in a native boat having seen nothing of Mr. B. We started off late in another boat to look for him, and at $\frac{1}{2}$ past 8 had the satisfaction of seeing both boats safely back again. Mr. B. had remained at his post all day until 7, when seeing nothing of the Chinese—and one or two stones having been thrown at the boat he thought it best to come away. He seems a very good man, Mr. B.

The Chinese Seotong [?], Aquan, Endicott's boy and one or two others were detained at the same guard house as ourselves for about an hour, when Mr. Roberts came to their relief and accompanied them to the office of some man whom they called the Secretary of State—where they were kept a long time, but did not get the pass after all. They, however, seem to have gone about the city a little—but to have gained little or no information. The prospects of trade here seem to be very slim, and I suspect the Granada has forestalled the small demand which existed. Some vague promises were made about Woohoo, but I have little confidence in them and suspect we shall have to lug our Drug and

346

Rebel Stuff about with us wherever we go as it will not be saleable above Woohoo. What D. meant by his large vague talk, I can't imagine.

Monday April 22nd.

Yesterday morning Aquan went again to his friend at the point for a pass and came back swearing that this time it was all right. The morning was bright giving promise of a very hot day which was not afterwards belied. We started immediately after breakfast, with two rebel guides and Aquan,—pulled up past the gate where we were refused the day before about two miles, until we came to a third bridge where we stopped and walked through a dirty and crowded suburb to the porcelain tower, or rather to the site of it, in fact is ruthlessly and utterly destroyed. The Goths! It must have been very large as the area of the base is still plainly seen and is of considerable extent. I am a bad hand at guessing distances, but I should call it more than 100 ft. square. It is now nothing but a confused pile of bricks—among which we groped for specimens, as long as we could stand the sun and brought away all we could carry. One of our rebel guides left us when we landed here. We reembarked and went to the gate at which we had spent a great 'heure de Rabelais'. This time we were admitted without difficulty—and proceeded at once to Mr. Roberts' place. This gave us a walk of about a mile and a half through streets nearly deserted. We saw no shops and few people—but much destruction—further evidences in fact of Rebel rule. Mr. Roberts was out preaching so we did not see him, and as it was evident that a longer walk through the streets would be simply a repetition of what we had seen, and as it was very hot, we decided to return—Had a hot pull back and reached the ship about 5 and found that they had sold half a chest of opium at about Ts.870— and a few pieces of shirtings for which, however, the man never came back. We left Aquan in the city as he wished to see another man in the hope of making arrangements to sell more cargo. He came aboard however shortly after us saying it was of no use and we made up our mind to be off in the morning for Woohoo.

Mr. Forrest spent the evening with us and told us a deal about Rebel matters. He said our Chinese had been in considerable danger and might have had their heads taken off at any moment. This was confirmed by what Mr. Roberts said to Cole.

We did not get off until 9 this morning, having lost some time in arranging with Mr. Puison [?] to take 3 chests of merchandise for sale on our app. The rebel mandarin at the point came aboard to look at the steamer—son nomme Aleong.

I don't know that I can say much of Nanking—It is a deserted city—and another proof of the infernal scoundrelism of the Rebels. The number of inhabitants is said to be about 70,000 all of whom are soldiers—when needed to serve. It formerly was a city of a million. It is the Capital of the Heavenly Kingdom of the Taepings—and the residence of the great Teen Wang, who is Hung tsow tsuen—old Roberts' quandom pupil.

Am now underway for Woohoo.

Some pages back I spoke of the execution of a woman on the beach opposite our ship. It seems, from what we heard afterwards, to have been the most horrible and cold blooded murder that was ever perpetrated. The order was given by a small mandarin at the point, not our friend Aleong, whom we saw the same afternoon and who had a very bad look, as it struck us at the time. She, with her husband, had only come over from the other side of the River within a few days. One cause of the execution was alleged to be that she spoke a little different dialect from the villains around, and was therefore supposed to be a spy, another was that she had fired her house—but the real cause no doubt was that she objected to yield to the advances of some of the rebel crew.

Tuesday April 23rd

Had a delightful run of 8 hours yesterday from Nankin to Woohoo—weather hot and clear—passed the Teen mun—a Heavenly Gate formed by two bluffs—280ft. high. They are also called the Se-liang-shan, and Tung-liang-shan a Eastern and Western pillar hill. Mr. Olyphant goes into raptures about them—but we thought them only pretty. Just above them saw a village in flames.

Anchored just below Woohoo off a parade ground—across which rebels in gay raiment were galloping furiously on little ponies. The scene was very animated and pretty. It was too late to go on shore but Aquan went to Dent's boat and learned there that there had been fighting here lately—or rather a few li up the river, and that the Rebels had sent large reinforcements to relieve Nganking, which they regard as the key to their position.

Most unfortunately it is raining steadily this morning which I fear will interfere with our obtaining information and doing [?]. Aquan is off, however, to see what he can learn.

Wednesday 24 April

Rained all day yesterday—but notwithstanding this there was a good attendance of Rebels and two or three bales of shirtings and about 3 cases Mdze [?] were sold. To this there was more row

348

made than would suffice to build a church and we were overrun
with dirty brutes all day. The head man came aboard, a sulky
looking brute who looked as though he could snap off heads with
great gusto.

Towards evening, my fellow passengers went ashore for a walk
on the parade ground as we call it. I did not go as it was only plod-
ding through a swamp. They came upon a headless trunk on
which execution had been done but a few moments, or say half an
hour before—the body was still warm, and the Capt. of Dent's
boat who was just ahead of them had met the head being carried
into the city. There was no attempt to bury the body—indeed it
would seem that they were in the habit of cutting off heads at this
place (the parade ground) and leaving them for the dogs to
devour.

We decided last night to remain until 12 today but Aquan went
ashore this morning and says more fighting has been going on,
and he thinks few buyers will come today so we are now (7 A.M.)
getting underway.

Yun wing came aboard from Dent's boat yesterday—says nothing can be done in Teas—this is the Taeping Country, and we
have had an idea of being able to get hold of a lot which the Rebels
had prevented from coming down.

Aquan says—two heads over the city gates this morning!

77
A Report by R J Forrest
BPP, 1862, C. 2976,pp. 43–4

I have the honour to report that no trade whatever is doing at
Nanking; the people themselves are too poor, and the Government trade is a monopoly in the hands of a person styled 'Tien mai
pwan' (Heavenly Compradore) who alone is allowed to trade in
the city; this man is also Commissary-General for the army, and
is, I believe, Inspector of the public store-houses. A similar state
of things existed at Soo-chow, where Chung Wang's compradore,
by the sale of luxuries and provisions, brought into his master's
coffers no small portion of the plunder of the city.

Provisions are given from the public stores to the people once
in each month; the number of names of men, women, and children on the supply-roll is upwards of 400,000. The distributors are
changed every two months in order to prevent peculation.

No attempt has as yet been made here to collect duties, nor
have I been able to find any tariff, although I saw one at Soo-
chow, and I have been informed that at Woo-hoo the import

duties are collected according to a regular scale. The Tien Wang hints at duties in a proclamation which was sent to Mr. Roberts with the wish that all foreigners should see it. I have the honour to inclose translation of this document, and also of a most curious one with regard to marriage.[33]

The general bearing of the Tae-ping officials with regard to foreigners is much improved. Captain Aplin has been invited to a visit of ceremony in the city, horses being sent for him. Chung Wang's brother has also been off to the 'Centaur', and the Commandant of the Hai-kuan forts received a reprimand for not treating us with proper courtesy. A plot of land has been given to us for the purpose of building a coal-store, but in a situation that makes it useless; the Tsan-szu-kueun is now consulting about another plot in a good situation. While on a visit to this official a few days since, he confessed that Tien Wang never interfered with the existing order of things without consulting the other Wangs, and never commands, but 'requests', them to take his wishes into consideration; the wishes so coming from the capital are only carried out as far as convenient, and very often not at all.

The insurgents report some success at Ngan-king; they say that they defeated the Imperialists in nine sorties. Chung Wang is on his way to Fo-kien province, where he intends to wait for Kan Wang, who is now before Hang-chow. Ying Wang is very slow in his movements, being much in want of provisions. A large body of Cantonese have joined the Taepings at Soo-chow, and are to hold that city. Large quantities of rice and other plunder are continually arriving at the capital.

I have, &c.

(Signed) R Forrest

78
An Account by R J Forrest
From T. W. Blakiston's *Five Months on the Yang-tze* (London, 1862), chs. 2, 3; first published in *North China Herald*, 29 June 1861

Every one who has a little time to spare at Nanking should go and see the ruins of the Ming tombs . . .

After South Gate Bridge the moat goes on winding and twisting through utter desolation and the abomination thereof. The huge walls rise at its side solid, strong, and lofty, but no soldiers or flags or sign of life can be observed. A couple of minas are

---

33 For these documents see Michael, op. cit., vol. III, pp. 1127–8 and pp. 984–5 respectively.

inspecting a hole in the battlements for the purpose of therein building their nest, and so great is the stillness that their chatter sounds harsh and disagreeable to the ear, although they are a hundred yards from you; no wind disturbs the broad clear water, and a little swallow is fluttering tamely enough about the oars trying to pick up a large insect before a fish can get at it. There is a corner of the moat that I should much like to make a sketch of. It is where the wall shoots out a long stretch almost due east. In former days a gate existed here and a fine broad bridge. Here, too, are the remains of a large granite wharf and dock with water-gate leading into the city canal. The whole was magnificently made, but neglect soon ruins even granite walls. Roots of trees have raised the stone slabs from their places, Taiping rapacity has rudely forced away the iron rings and bolts, the bridge has been partially destroyed, the gate built up, and the entrance to the canal in the city choked up with stones, furniture, and mud, 'lest imps' should force their way into the Heavenly capital by that entrance. Not long ago—only twelve years—that particular corner was teeming with life. You can see the remains of what must have been a fine suburb; and the marks where large merchants' houses and temples were erected against the city wall are most plainly distinguishable. The high road to Tan-yang, Soo-chow, and the cities on the Grand Canal ran across that bridge, and across it were conveyed the silk to feed the city looms and the provisions for its inhabitants. Across it came and went the inhabitants, old and venerable, young and pretty, of fifty cities that have since melted before the horrors of war. Now a man on the wall stares with a weary look at a couple of foreign devils going by in one of their own boats. It is just the place to see when you are going to visit a tomb; it cannot fail to strike you and make you feel sad. Observe, gentle reader, if ever you go by that place, although you have a dozen friends in the boat, not a word will be spoken by any of you while passing it, nor for five minutes afterwards. You get out of your boat about a mile from the place and walk towards the Taiping Gate, having a series of large ponds between you and the city wall. A few country people, perhaps a dozen, are hanging about, but they are silent and sorrowful.

There is a little watch station a few yards in the country, where soldiers are lolling about, smoking, gambling and drinking samshoo in utter defiance of the commands of the Heavenly king whose cause they are defending. They laugh violently at the foreigners and frown at the timid peasantry as they go by. I fancy the few miserable beings who are compelled to live outside the east side of Nanking must suffer considerably from the depredations of the insolent troops constantly coming and going along the way to the canal. Anon comes a file of labourers who have been to some ruins for the purpose of extracting tiles to build a house for some city magnate. A man accompanies them with a draw sword to see that they are not lazy or mutinous, so they walk along sulkily and silent, having no hope of better days, getting no money and but indifferent rice. Speak to some of them, and you will perceive they are utterly cowed, scarcely daring to draw breath, and talking in a low suspicious tone of voice like people whose *lives* are in constant danger. All the chatter and laugh that so eminently distinguishes the coolie in other parts of China is wanting under the Taiping rule. The unhappy folk are compelled to work almost gratuitously for very hard taskmasters. Their homes are wretched to a degree. There is nothing anywhere to make them laugh at life, and their appearance can hardly fail to excite the sympathy of passing foreigners . . .

You are walking along a country that was once smiling with happy villages and cultivated fields. See how the rice-grounds were terraced up to the hill-side that not a yard of ground should be lost, and behold how ruin on ruin encumbers the ground below us in the valley where once stood a village of three thousand inhabitants. But the inhabitants, houses, rice, and cultivation have left the place for a while, the black duck is preparing to nestle in that fish-stew, where ducks of a tamer nature once sported. Aim low at the roebuck standing in the ruins of that farmhouse, and try and hit him in the fore legs, or he will get away from you, oh dog-less one! although severely wounded. There, I told you so! Now go and ask that old man, who has been looking on, which way the 'Changtsze' has run. He will crouch and chin-chin, ay and kowtow too, if you will let him, when you stand before him, and stammer something out and call you 'Foreign Excellency,' and know nothing at all. The man is frightened, heartbroken, demented. The deer was standing on the ruins of what was once his homestead. He is labouring for others now, his sons have gone to war for a cause they little love, his daughters are in the city where he cannot see them, the spoil of masters they love even less, and all his life is a blank. He will be down in the ditch there before long, and his troubles will be over. I hate the stillness of the country near the Ming tombs, it is so utterly unnatural. Everything seems sleeping or going to decay. The half-dozen people one sees only make it worse. The crow of the pheasant is loud enough, and the petards resound from the distant palace of the Heavenly king, but the merry sounds of human happiness and comfort and business which ought to enliven that spot are missing, perhaps for ever . . .

In returning, you may make a detour and strike into the road from the Grand Canal. The country all the way from Paoying to Nanking is in a wretched condition. Ruined villages and burned houses mark the fury of last year's war. A small crowd of old women are generally to be met with at the entrance of each village, trying to eke out a living by the sale of tea and congee to the passers-by. All the able-bodied men are gone—some were killed, but more enlisted in the Taiping army, from whose ranks death alone will relieve them. They will never return to the home of their fathers, and their possessions are in the hands of new masters. All the old women we saw were left in contempt by the Taipings to till the fields; all had lost some relations, and two of them sat down on a bank and cried sadly, one for the loss of her husband and two sons, the other for her husband and father. 'They killed my husband,' said an old women 'because he was not strong enough to do their coolie work.' 'They carried off my daughter because she was pretty,' said another to me beyond the Great River. It is all one story—girls carried off, useful men compelled to go to the camps, old ones who perhaps might excite commiseration ruthlessly murdered! One great story of violence and wrong carried with a mighty hand throughout the land in the name of the Christian faith, by men as merciless as the stones they tread on! When and where it will stop Providence alone can tell; the land is threatened with depopulation; trade, industry, and manufacture are at an end, wherever Tien-wang's commands extend. The Tien-hai-kuan said to me, by way of a joke, that, when all were slain, then truly the reign of 'Great Peace' would have arrived. A ghastly joke truly; but I hope, before such a state of things is brought about, 13-inch shells will be exploding in the palace of the blasphemous imposter ruling at Nanking. . . .

The South Gate is pierced in a straight line through the enormous wall. A large crowd is always assembled here, for no trade is allowed in the city. Women's clothes, ornaments of all sorts, pistols, caps, and small tins of powder, marked Curtis and Harvey, but made at Ningpo, are exposed for sale. The loot of Soo-chow might some time ago have been bought here for a song. Vendors of fish, women on horseback, soldiers, flags, and chow-chow apparatus were crowded together in this motley scene. A man is lying with the cangue round his neck, on which is stated that he did not obey the celestial commands, and the head of another is hanging up in a basket. You pass under the walls through a long dark tunnel, then through three more gates and three more small tunnels, where brass guns are placed, and Nanking, the Heavenly Capital, stands revealed to your mortal

eyes. But let us pause ere we describe it. On the gate is a proclamation from the Heavenly King, on which is written—'The
Heavenly Father, Christ, Myself, and my Son are Lords for ever.
The Heavenly Kingdom is established everywhere, and the effulgence of the Father, Brother, Myself, and the Young Lord is
spread upon the earth for a myriad myriad autumns.' Let us pause
before attempting to describe the heavenly effulgence, lest the
description might dazzle mankind . . .

Allons! Entering the South Gate, a dirty man asks for the pass of
His Foreign Excellency, while an admiring boy claws hold of your
umbrella or coat-tails; and, having inspected you to his satisfaction, screams out that the Foreign Devil has arrived. Having
satisfied the janitor, you must look sharp to get out of the way of
two faggots of enormous reeds which are approaching you,
apparently of their own accord, for no motive agency is visible.
When alongside you find that a little donkey is propelling the
bundles, or perhaps a little girl—boys do not seem to like the
work. If you watch the donkey you will see that in China he loses
nothing of his proverbial obstinacy. He will lie down in the
middle of the gate with his bundle on the top of him, and defy all
the powers that be to move him, until it is his good will and
pleasure to resume his journey. All the passengers have little
wooden billets tied round their waists, with a Heavenly seal
impressed thereon. Did a Chinaman venture into Nanking without this badge, his head would be in the greatest danger. The
street from the South Gate toward the North is fine and broad. In
its happier days great attention was evidently paid to the pave-
ment thereof; in some places the stones were even fantastically
carved; but now there are holes and gaps, little ponds and gutters
reeking with filth, and on a wet day lakes impassable to any but
the bare-legged inhabitants wandering about on their proper
occasions. A man comes riding along dressed in scarlet or parti-
coloured garments, with a yellow cap on his head; in his hand he
holds a bright red umbrella of foreign make; two little boys run
after him—one with a big rusty gun, holding on to the tail of the
pony (who does not resent the insult as other ponies would), the
other with a flag on a bamboo pole. The horseman scowls on you
as he passes, but he is a chief. Those little slaves following were
kidnapped by him during an expedition, and will never see home
or parents more; but they call him 'Tajên' (Excellency), and
follow him everywhere. He has a dozen more boys at home, likewise kidnapped; he can kill them if they run away or disobey him.
It is a hard life, although they are well fed; but brighter days are
in store for the urchins—they will grow old and strong, will

themselves go to the war, and murder, kill, and destroy, until they in their turn are Ta-jêns, and can ride in the streets of the Heavenly City with slaves at their heels. But there is another side to this: you see a little boy throwing stones and calling you a devil, laughing with all his might; he has forgotten all about home, and is beginning to enjoy Taiping life and laziness; although only twelve years old he has got an ugly knife, and would fain run it into a Yao (foreigner) or anybody else, if only let loose to do so; but he has got an incipient skin disease, and will be a frightful object in a week or so; his master will kick him out into the street, and he will lie in a corner with a little bowl in his hand, begging for rice or cash to try and keep his life's lamp a little longer alight. Let us leave the city for a moment to follow this story to an end, and walk through the T'ien-hai-kwan village, where the starvelings have flocked together in hundreds; for there is the port, and foreign brethren are wont to give cash away, and eke rice from the neighbouring cookshop. There they lie or crawl; this one with his toes off from frostbite, that one too weak to speak. What! not take money when it is given to you? shut your hand on it, or it will be stolen. Alas! the hand can move no longer; not even a dollar would make a muscle start. The beggar is dead at his bowl, and the flaunting proclamation of the Heavenly King on the wall over his head tells us that Great Peace has gone out over the whole earth!

We are in the city again, going along the street where the Tien-wang's brothers live. A large wall in a curved shape is erected opposite to a house redolent of red paint and gold. About three-fourths of the road passes between the wall and the house—I beg pardon, palace. People on horseback, nay even pedestrians, must go behind the wall *en passant*, or lictors will rush from the gilded doors and beat them. The guardians of the gate are however good-natured, and very lazy. People do go by in front, but no horsemen. Of course foreigners are exempted from all such nonsense, and pass by with much greeting from the soldiers at the gate. Two small cannon are placed at the door, pointed across the street; they are of course useless as a defence, but it looks something, and that is all a Chinaman cares about. . . .

We will now take a stroll towards the Celestial residence of his very Celestial Majesty Hung-tsiu-tsuen. We cannot get in, but can see a good deal outside. This palace is of great size, enclosed in a yellow wall forty feet high, and very thick. Within you can see yellow and green roofs and a couple of not unhandsome minarets, but the mass of buildings is hidden from the curiosity of visitors by the wall aforesaid. The palace is only half completed, and is intended to cover twice its present area; but when His Majesty's devoted and loving subjects will have completed this project Heaven only knows; for only a dozen workmen or so are loitering about; hardly enough to keep the place clean. Near the palace in a ruined shed is a curious boat formed like a dragon with an immense head; it is fast going to decay, but was once evidently most gorgeous with paint and gilt. That is the Sacred Dragon Boat in which His Majesty descended the Great River from Han-yang to the siege and capture of Nanking. It was once kept inside the walls, but has now been turned out, and nobody takes much notice of it. There is a huge yellow wall about three hundred yards from the first gateway, whereon are painted the most ferocious-looking dragons possible. It is on this wall that Tien-wang posts his own peculiar proclamations. See, there they are, all on yellow satin, written in vermilion ink, in the straggling ill-looking handwriting of the King himself. He is most indefatigable in getting up these documents, and in them are to be found the most startling and infamous blasphemy the human mind can imagine. I have seen the wall half covered with yellow satin, and often wondered whence it all came from. In your front is a tall curious gateway, very handsome in its way, and, although un-finished, gilded with great taste. It is built on columns, painted in red and gold, and the top is formed of that curious combination of woodwork so familiar to us in the Yamên at Canton. Passing through this gateway and the outer door, you approach the grand door of the palace by a covered way supported by gilded columns. The roof is covered with dragons of all sizes and sorts doing all kinds of things, from eating the sun to pursuing a gigantic shrimp. Over the door, which is as gaudy as paint and gold can make it, is an inscription 'of the True Shên, the Sacred Heavenly Door.' On either side are two gigantic drums, which were you to beat you would create intense alarm. In the inner chambers gilded lan-terns suspended on silken cords and ornamented with rich tassels are hung about in every direction; a very large and hand-some glass one suspended in the centre once graced the Yamên of Ho-quei-ching at Soo-chow. To the right of the Sacred Heavenly Door is a space containing chairs and tables, where Heavenly soldiers are lying about in easy but not graceful positions. The arrival of foreigners does not create much sensation; and the old janitor, who told me that his age was great when he nursed Tien-wang, then a coolie child in a village near Canton, asks you to take a seat and cup of tea politely enough; and, as you cannot get any farther into the palace, you had better accept his invitation and rest after your long walk. There is a map called the 'Map of the

Entire Territory of the Heavenly Taiping Dynasty to endure for a myriad myriad years.' It is an amusing document, or whatever you like to call it. A vast space of ground, almost square, and surrounded by seas, is China; a great square place, surrounded by apparently four walls, is the Heavenly Capital; Hongkong is nowhere, Japan a small speck; nor could I detect Peking in the part of the map where I should have supposed it to exist. Two little islands in the north-west are called England and France. Other European nations are, I suppose, suppressed by Heavenly command; and the whole of Asia, with the exception of China, is swallowed up, probably by a dragon. Now you would fancy that so much gold and red paint, lamps and flags, would make a very grand sight. Nothing of the sort; everything is dirty to a degree. The gilding is fast sinking beneath a brown coating put upon it by dirty hot hands, dust, and rain; the red and the blue, the white and green are badly laid on, and seem inclined to run together; the dragons on the ceiling will not be visible much longer unless repainted; the floor is covered with saliva and filth; the Heavenly troops lolling about are dirty, unkempt, and ragged; ruins that can be seen all round you look like misery in spite of Tien-wang; and you cannot help feeling that you are sitting in the centre of a vast system of human degradation and imposture.

Presently there is a dreadful noise of drums, cymbals, and gongs, mingling with the roar of petards and the shrill notes of the wry-necked but celestial fife—Tien-wang is going to dinner, and that noise will continue until repletion comes to His Majesty. For some time previously the Sacred Gate has been partially open, and seedy-looking women have been entering and coming out with the plates, chopsticks, and other articles about to be used in the royal repast. Most of the articles are of gold. From the appearance of the chow-chow which was conveyed into the interior, I should opine that the celestial taste had a leaning towards cabbage. Although we cannot put our legs under the royal mahogany, we can listen to what the fellows outside tell us of the glories of the interior. His Sacred Majesty the Heavenly King is fifty-one years of age, tall, strong, and healthy. He will never die; but when tired of sublunar affairs, a dragon-car will descend, and he becomes a guest on high. He has had many interviews with the Almighty, and according to his own proclamations this favour has lately been extended to his wife—I cannot tell you which out of the hundred and eight, but probably the mother of the Junior Lord. None but women are allowed in the interior of the palace; and I have been told there are about a thousand of them. How they must talk! His Majesty has a crown of gold that weighs eight catties, a necklace of golden bosses of like weight; and his gold-embroidered dress is thickly studded with lumps of gold, something like and probably an imitation of foreign buttons. He is drawn from his distant apartments to the Audience Chamber in a gilded affair, called the Sacred Dragon Car, by his ladies, and is there seated on a throne to receive the prayers and flattery of his high officers. His son usually attends, but is rather a sickly youth by all accounts. He is very industrious, writes dozens of proclamations, receives and answers the letters from the Kings, and has a keen eye for business. I am not a missionary, and can consequently give only a lay opinion, which, however, is strong and well-founded, that Tien-wang's Christianity is nothing but the rank blasphemy of a lunatic, and the profession of religion by his followers a laughable mockery and farce. . . .

Having, on my arrival at Nanking, resolved to see as much as possible of the chiefs and people, without becoming exactly familiar with them, I was very glad when a civil letter came one morning from the Chung-wung-tsun, the brother of the redoubtable conqueror of Soo-chow, inviting myself and my friends to come and take dinner with him. He sent ponies and an escort; and in a couple of hours we arrived at Chung-wang's palace, and were duly ushered in by crowds of fantastically dressed youths. Chung-wang's brother, by name Le (*anglicé*, Jones or Smith), is the exact counterpart of the great fighting king, who is at present away spreading Great Peace in Hupeh. About five feet four high, with a good-looking cunning countenance, always laughing, he is not at all a disagreeable man to spend a day with. His dress was of bright scarlet satin, with a yellow cap, to which is fixed a fine pearl as large as a hazel-nut. He led us through a good many rooms to a pretty little pavilion looking out on a miniature garden of rockwork and trees, where he gave us a very good Chinese dinner, keeping up a merry chat the whole time. The food came to his table in a series of nine porcelain dishes shaped like the petals of a rose, and all fitting into one another on the table. He said that Heaven had been kind enough to give this equipage to his brother at Soo-chow. The chopsticks, forks, and spoons were of silver, the knives English plated ware, and his wine-cups of gold fitting into cases of enamelled silver. After a couple of visits, I made a practice of going and talking to this man whenever I had time; and he has shown me some very curious things belonging to Chung-wang. This potentate is the only one after His Celestial Majesty who has a crown of real gold. It is to my idea a really pretty affair. The gold is beaten out thin enough, and then formed into leaves and filigree work like a tiger,—enormous as to tail in front and behind. On either side is a bird of what species you please, and on the top a phoenix. It is covered from top to bottom with pendent pearls and other gems. I put it on my head, and should guess the weight to be about three pounds . . .

Being one day very late in the city, and a storm coming on, I resolved to accept Le's invitation to stay a night at his palace. He did his utmost to make me comfortable, and I certainly have been compelled to put up at worse places than Chung-wang's abode. A very nice supper was prepared at eight o'clock, consisting of fowls, mutton, and other such viands delightful to Western tastes. Two bottles of sherry—with paper rolls, however, instead of corks to stop them—and a large silver pot of hot Celestial wine, were passed round very briskly among the Ta-jêns who had been invited by Le to meet me. It was very evident that the more important chiefs pay but little attention to the absurd mandates of the Heavenly one who rules over them, for every one of my friends certainly appreciated sherry, and the Celestial winepot was replenished more than once during the evening. Nor was tobacco-smoke strange to the lips of these Maos, who have nevertheless strictly prohibited its use. I slept in Chung-wang's state bed, with a beautifully soft mat and with scarlet silk curtains all round. While dozing off, I was somewhat startled by the sound of Chinese boots in the room, and put my head through the curtains to see what was moving. Judge of my astonishment at seeing a couple of Celestial girls crossing the place with lanterns in their hands, and an old attendant with another. The moment they caught sight of my ugly foreign head, they screamed and made a most precipitate retreat, although I assured them that I was not in the least alarmed. They got to their quarters by another way, leaving a horrid dog snarling and barking about the door all night. I found in the morning that I had cut off the retreat of their Majesties the two Mrs. Chung-wangs, who had been out visiting the ladies of the double-eyed dog Ying-wang. They, little dreaming that a foreign devil was lying in state in the palace, had taken the usual road to the harem through the room in which I slept,— hence the adventure.

These Celestials rise at most unconscionable hours. At dawn a deputation waited on me to know whether I would have a hot bath. Seeing that it was intensely hot already, I asked for a cold one, upon which much alarm was expressed, and the writer or secretary assured me that the use of cold water would certainly produce some malady or other. On my persisting, another Ta-jên came and remonstrated with me, but without effect. At last H.E. Le came himself, but left me despairing of prevailing against foreign obstinacy. So I had my bath, and was looked on during the day as a kind of wonder.

After breakfast Le took me to see the new palace his brother was building, on a spot about a quarter of a mile from his old one. It is certainly going to be a vast affair, little less than the Yamên at Canton. Upwards of a thousand workmen were engaged—some building, some carving stone and wood, and not a few standing with a bundle of rattans in their hands ready to inflict blows on any one shirking his work. A great portion of the building is already completed, and the whole will be a good specimen of a Chinese Yamên of the old style, with its network of beams at the gables, its large wooden columns, and fantastic carvings. Asking what the workmen were paid, Le laughingly replied,—'You English pay for work; we Taipings know better. Is not ours a truly great empire?' About 11 o'clock Le told me that he, in common with every other chief, was going to sleep until about one; and to sleep he went, leaving me a pony, on which I rode round to such other friends of mine as could be found awake. I returned to dinner and found his Excellency learning to write, for, although brother to Chung-wang, and styled 'Heaven's Righteousness,' his fist cannot be called pretty. He soon gave up the work, and, curling himself up in a chair, ordered a couple of boys to fan him; and in this position he remained until dinner, after which I left him.

And now we will go and have some chow-chow with perhaps the most eminent man connected with the Taiping movement—I mean Hung, the Kan-wang. I frequently pitied this man before I knew him, as from his knowledge of foreigners he has always been put prominently forward in everything connected with them, and has suffered not a little from the absurd way in which his Western friends have talked about him. I have seen a good deal of Kan-wang, and will proceed to give my lay opinion about him. Kan-wang told me some months ago that he was going to spread Great Peace towards Gan-hui. He did so, and the foreign ships saw the smoking and flaming villages that marked his course. Can we not therefore call him 'a burning and a shining light'? . . .

But now the great gates open, and inside, seated in his Yamên, dressed in full robes, is the Kan-wang. His attendants finely dressed stand at his side. He will shake hands with you when you have advanced, and say in English, 'How do you do?' and bid you to be seated. Kan-wang is, I should say, about 45 years old, rather fat than otherwise, and has an open and very pleasing countenance. He is an extremely pleasant companion, can drink a glass of port wine, and, if necessary, make a dinner of *bifstek à l'Anglais*, with a knife and fork. I must confess that he is the most enlightened Chinaman I ever saw. He is perfectly acquainted with geography, moderately so with mechanics, acknowledges the superiority of Western civilization, has books of reference with plates on all imaginable subjects, is generous, and very desirous of doing good. *Per contra*, he is indolent, and consequently takes but little trouble to see his theories put into practice. He is not a soldier, and the fighting kings are therefore very jealous of his perpetual stay at the capital. He was even compelled to go to the wars, but made a mess of it, and returned on being informed that certain foreign devils were making extravagant and insolent demands in Nanking. He told me that he hated war, and tried on his excursions to make it as little terrible as possible. 'But', said he (and Kan-wang has some appreciation of truth), 'it is impossible to deny that this is a war of extermination: quarter or mercy is never shown to our men by Hsien Fêng's soldiers, and in revenge our people never give any. But men under my command never unnecessarily slay country people.' He also hinted at what I know to be a fact, that if the Taoutai at Shanghai would take it into his head to show mercy on runaway Taipings, instead of immediately ordering their execution, it would be a most difficult matter to keep the frontier Rebel armies together ...

I could tell much more concerning the Taipings individually and collectively, but will now only add that it is impossible to live a long time among a set of people and not take an interest in them, and in a certain way to like them. I have met with not only civility, but actual courtesy from them, and shall never regret the time I have spent among them. Not being a clergyman, I have not looked at Taipingdom from its weakest side—its Christianity; but I must state that I see no hope of the Taipings becoming the dominant power in China, because they are simply unable to govern themselves, except by a species of most objectionable terrorism. But neither do I see any prospect of the Manchoos reinstating themselves in their former position. There is more or less rebellion (not always Taiping) in every province except one in China. Something will spring from this state of disorder to restore order, as has been the case a dozen times before in the empire. The greatest cause of the frightful disorder into which the nation has been plunged is the want of a sufficiency of civil officers—one man ruling over a place as big as Yorkshire, and knowing nothing of his district during his reign. The Taipings might remedy this, inasmuch as every other man is an officer of some kind or other, at all events a Ta-jên. As yet it is but the beginning of a chaos in which trade and commerce, prosperity and happiness, must for a time sink, but only to rise again more flourishing and glorious than ever. Heaven forbid that England, or France, should ever make confusion worse confounded by interfering in the internal struggle now raging! Things are governed in China by rules that we don't understand. The springs of vitality which have enabled China to trace her way through political convulsions as bad as the present, and to exist as a powerful empire through such a series of years as makes our European dynasties look small enough, are not yet exhausted. It will be well to look at the present crisis in a broader light than we are inclined to at present, and see in it merely Chinese fighting Chinese, righting, or attempting to right, their injuries in their own peculiar way. ... The disease is at present very intermittent, but by-and-by the patient will need repose, and will most indubitably find it without calling in to its aid Western soporifics—opium perhaps excepted. I pray my readers, when perusing of Chapoo failings and other dismal records, to consider that the dreadful cruelty therein enacted is hardly a counterpart of Tsing atrocities. But the other day, at Ngan-king, the Imperialists enjoyed a three days' slaughter, and left neither man, woman, nor child in that unfortunate city. The Great River is crowded now with their headless victims. I have always had my opinion as to the brigand-like character of the Taipings, but after seeing a good deal of both I must confess that I have no better opinion of the other party. But I know this, that there is much hope; that order is doing valiant battle with disorder, and is conquering; that English prosperity and rule, manifested in many mercantile houses in Hankow, Kiukiang, Shanghai, and elsewhere, are silently becoming the umpires in the Celestial struggle; for round such beacons the tired Chinese will cluster and reform their strength. But this restoration will be fatal to both the Manchoo and Taiping dynasties sooner or later. In the mean time, looking on the mighty highway—the silvery track of the Great River, where the forerunners and pioneers of coming peace are going and returning—I anxiously await the time when the tide of disorder shall have flowed by. And now good-bye to Nanking, the city of the Coolie Kings.

79
Diary of a Traveller between Ningpo and Shanghai
W. H. Sykes, *The Taiping Rebellion in China* (London, 1863),
pp. 49–53

THE DIARY OF TRAVELS IN THE SILK DISTRICTS

To the Editor of the *Daily Press*, Hong-Kong

Ningpo, June 20 (1862)

Dear Sir,

Inclosed we have the pleasure of handing you copy of a diary kept by a man who was some months employed by us in the country between Ningpo and Shanghai. We also inclose a Chinese paper issued by the Taoutai of Ningpo, containing the rate of taxes now levied on the people, which we consider amounts to almost a prohibition of trade.[34]

Trade quite at a stand, with no prospects of its again recovering.

From the country we hear of no definite movements of the rebels. The piratical fleet are still blockading the river, and preventing any produce being brought to this place.

Yours faithfully,

W and G M Hart

1862
TRAVELS IN CHINA FROM NINGPO THROUGH THE SILK COUNTRY
INTO THE FAI CHOW TEA DISTRICT AND ON TO SHANGHAI

Tuesday, March 18—Left Ningpo.

Wednesday, 19—Arrived at Yow-yow; at this place was treated respectfully by the rebels.

Thursday, 20—Proceeded to Pockwan; arrived there at 2 p.m., and remained for the night; the rebels quiet and friendly, and the country people quite happy, the country all round looking beautiful.

Friday, 21—Paid duty on our cargo, and proceeded towards Show Shing, the country all around looking very nice and the crops healthy.

Saturday, 22—Arrived at Sah-Kee. This place is small; the country all round looks well as regards cultivation; remained at this place up to the 26th, during which time all was quiet; had an offer of several small parcels of tea; price rather high.

Thursday, 27—Left Sah-Kee for Ping-Suey at 4 p.m. Having proceeded as far as we could with the boat, landed, and walked about

---

34   Not reprinted by Sykes and not included here.

six miles to a Hong in the country; arrived there about 7 p.m., found all quiet; remained there for the night.

Friday, 28—Took all we had from the boat to the Hong, and made preparations for business; all quiet here.

Saturday, 29—Received several samples of tea, but did not purchase.

30 and 31—Still at this place; all quiet, and lots of teas.

Tuesday, April 1—This day received samples of silk.

Wednesday, 2—A rumour that a party of rebels are coming to rob this place; natives making preparations to leave. Sunset, no further news.

Thursday, 3—People leaving for the mountains, at 6 p.m. no rebels, they are expected tomorrow.

Friday, 4—At 9 a.m. a small party of rebels came to the Hong, but did not touch anything; at 10 a.m. left the Hong for the head-quarters of the Wong; as the rebels had commenced to plunder the village, he advised us to bring all our things to his place for safety; returned to the Hong, took all our things to the boat, and proceeded to Soth King, where we arrived at 6 p.m.

Saturday, 5—The Wong or chief paid us a visit and offered to send one of his men to accompany us; he informed us that the rebels did not wish to interfere with any foreigners trading. Remained here for the night.

Sunday, 6—Started for Sah-Kee.

Monday, 7—Arrived at Sah-Kee; found everything quiet; much the same as when we left.

From 7th to 13th—Remained at Sah-Kee.

Monday, 14—At 9 a.m. left Sah-Kee for Ningpo with a boat load of silk; at 5 p.m. arrived at Le-Tze-howe, and remained there for the night.

Tuesday, 15—Was not allowed to pass until duties were paid, 200 dols. They refused to take our dollars on account of their not being No. 1, but allowed us to pass on leaving 255 dols.—deposit to be redeemed on our return from Ningpo; at 3 p.m. reached Lot-Sing-poo and paid 240 dols. duty on silk; proceeded without any further trouble.

Wednesday, 16—Arrived at Ningpo.

17th and 18th—At Ningpo.

Saturday, 19—Left Ningpo for Sah-Kee with dollars for the purpose of purchasing silk; nothing of importance occurred this day.

Sunday, 20—Passed at Yow-Yow; all quiet.

Monday, 21—Arrived at Lot-Sing-poo; redeemed our dollars there; at 10 p.m. arrived at Sah-Kee, found everything quiet—much the same as when we left.

Tuesday, 22—At Sah-Kee took all our dollars to the Hong; everything quiet.

Wednesday, 23—Purchased a large quantity of silk, and more expected. The country about here looks most beautiful, and the crops in a very flourishing condition. There are a few rebels stationed here; they have visited us and are very friendly, offering us assistance if required.

Thursday, 24—Made more purchases of silk; no news of importance, all remains perfectly quiet.

Friday, 25—Wednesday, 30—At Sah-Kee.

Thursday, May 1—Received orders from Ningpo to return, as there was expected some trouble there; made preparations for leaving; all quiet here.

Friday, 2—At 10 a.m. just on the point of starting, when a Shroff arrives from Se-Tze-howe, informing us that they were not allowed to pass or return until the rebels had heard from Ningpo; everything quiet here; wait until we receive further news.

Saturday, 3—Shroff returns to Se-Tze-howe, having left two Europeans there in charge of silk and dollars.

Sunday, 4 and Monday, 5—Still at Sah-Kee; all quiet here.

Tuesday, 6—Received information from the Chinese of expected troubles at Ningpo. We are also informed that the Wong of Sooh-Hing, with 4,000 men, was on his way to Ningpo; this caused us to feel rather uncomfortable. Everything here quiet.

Wednesday, 7—No further news of trouble.

Thursday, 8 and Friday, 9—All quiet with us.

Saturday, 10—Received a letter from Ningpo informing us that all was quiet, but to come down as soon as possible, and that the Shroff, with the two Europeans from Se-Tze-howe, had arrived all safe at Ningpo.

Sunday, 11—Settled accounts, and made preparations to leave.

Monday, 12—Left Sah-Kee at 9 a.m.—at 4 p.m. arrived at Tung-Vien; here they wanted additional duties; thought we could go a cheaper route; left during the night and proceeded to Poquan; found it the same; was advised not to go to Ningpo.

Tuesday, 13—At Poquan, at 2 p.m., received news that the Imperial soldiers were at Tze-Chee, and on the river; sent a despatch boat to see if true. Everything quiet here, and no appearance of trouble.

Wednesday, 14—A Poquan boat returns, and informs us that what we heard yesterday was quite true; all quiet here.

Thursday, 15—Left Poquan and returned to Sah-Kee, being afraid now to take our silk on to Ningpo; at 4 p.m. met a boat three days from Ningpo; informed us that the city had been attacked by the

English and French, and nearly destroyed; the rebels had all gone to Yow-yow, and from what we now learn we have determined on going to Shanghai, as we consider it quiet unsafe to proceed to Ningpo through the pirate fleet, though we shall be quite safe in going to Shanghai, although it will be a long and tedious journey.

Friday, 16—Left Quan-ding-quan in Hankow Bay; had to change boats; engaged a junk, put all our things on board, and at 3 p.m. left for Kew Chong; the rebels very friendly to foreigners; they treated us well.

Saturday, 17—At Kew Chong we hear that an European had been killed at Su Moon, about five miles from Sah-kee; we are now in sight of the city of Hanchow.

Sunday, 18—At Kew Chong no news.

Monday, 19—At 3 a.m. a heavy blow from the S.E. with a very heavy sea. Junk and cargo in much danger. Three junks foundered near us. At 8 p.m. the weather clears up; no news.

Tuesday, 20—Landed all our cargo at the custom-house, the rebels took possession of everything; engaged a chop, and after settling our duties put all our goods on board. The rebels made no attempt whatever to molest us, but wished us to return again as soon as possible, promising us assistance and protection.

Wednesday, 21—At 3 p.m. left this place for Shanghai. The country here rich with vegetation, and the people all busily employed. Passed a great number of rice boats from Shanghai.

Thursday, 22—Arrived at Sing-song at 6 p.m. A great number of rice-boats arrive in charge of Europeans; all quiet here.

Friday, 23—Remained all day at Sing-song.

Saturday, 26—At 6 a.m. left Sing-song; at 4 p.m. arrived at Wug-ho-kow, found several Europeans here in charge of boats waiting the arrival of silk to take it on to Shanghai; trade very brisk here, and the rebels quite friendly.

Sunday, 25—At 5 p.m. leave Wug-ho-kow, and at 6 p.m. come to for the night.

Monday, 26—At 5 a.m. started on our way towards Shanghai; at 7 passed a custom-house, a second at noon, and at 4 p.m. the third; paid fees to have our duty chops stamped, had no detention at either of these places, these are the last of the rebel custom-houses; at 6 p.m. came to for the night amongst a fleet of rice-boats bound up; several Europeans in charge; all quiet here.

Tuesday, 27—At 5 a.m. got under weigh; at 7 a.m. passed two Chinese steamers and one English lying at anchor about thirty miles from Shanghai; at 7 p.m. came to anchor at Ming Hong; one French steamer and one gun-boat at anchor here.

Wednesday, 28—At 6 a.m. weighed and proceeded towards Shanghai; at 10 a.m. anchored, the tide against us. Shipping at Shanghai in sight.

Thursday, 29—Arrived opposite the French cathedral; we are stopped here by the custom-house, and not allowed to pass until duty has been paid on the whole of our cargo; went on to Shanghai for funds.

30th and 31st, and June 1—Duties not yet paid.

Monday, June 2—Duties paid, are allowed to proceed.

Tuesday, 3—Arrived at Shanghai.

Wednesday, 4—Discharge our cargo.

AZ

P.S.—Through the whole of the country which we travelled—viz., from Ningpo to Wug-ho-kow, the people all wear long hair, and all appear quite contented and happy; the only place that we found at all unsettled was at a village near Soth King at the foot of the hills on which the Ping Suey tea grows, but their difficulties here were soon amicably settled, and all was quiet before we left; the country from Ningpo to Wug-ho-kow was all in a most flourishing condition, and the crops promising well.

After leaving Wug-ho-kow the country wears a different aspect every mile it becomes more barren and wretched, the people poor, and appear to be suffering much; the villages dirty, and many of the people attributing their present wants to foreign soldiers coming to fight the rebels, as before the fighting commenced last year, they knew not what it was to want for anything.

AZ

Section 4 The Ningpo Encounter (1861–2)

The five month occupation of Ningpo between December 1861 and May 1862 provided the only opportunity for any sustained contact with the Taiping by a European community on the China coast. Practically all other direct contact was occasioned by Westerners travelling into Taiping held territory, sometimes as individuals but more often in small parties or as members of a ship's company, and staying rarely for more than a few weeks, usually much less.

In August 1860 and again during 1862 the Taiping did attempt to occupy Shanghai, but on both occasions were repulsed by the intervention of Western forces. Hankow, opened to foreign trade and settlement only during 1861, was also threatened with a Taiping occupation, but Ningpo was the only treaty port ever actually occupied. The European community there at the time was not large—probably less than one hundred all told—but it included the usual mix of consular officials, merchants, missionaries and their families, and the port was within easy reach of visitors from the larger settlement at Shanghai. The Taiping occupation of Ningpo therefore seemed to provide a useful testing ground for working, day to day relations between Westerners and the Taiping movement.

It was quickly judged by Westerners as confirming their already prevailing judgment that neither in a political nor an economic sense, not to mention a religious, were satisfactory relations with the rebel movement possible. The historian may reasonably question whether it was ever really a very satisfactory test. The Taiping forces which occupied the Chinese city, though by several accounts not totally undisciplined, were certainly not the most impressive, nor under the command of the best of the Taiping leaders. Although they captured the city easily they were never secure against an Imperialist counter attack and, worse, Western intervention such as had occurred at Shanghai in 1860. Fear of this had delayed their capture of Ningpo (Docs. 80, 81), and they were in fact driven from the city in May 1862 by the action of British naval forces. A campaign against them in the interior of Chekiang was subsequently carried on by French led forces. In such circumstances 'normal' commercial or diplomatic relations could hardly be expected to develop.

Nor is there evidence of much open mindedness on the part of the Westerners observing and reporting on the occupation from the safety of the Ningpo foreign settlement area across the river and outside the walls. The least judgmental was the Jardine Matheson agent, Capt. F. S. Green (Doc. 84), but all the reports from missionaries on the scene were strongly hostile, revealing none of the qualified hopes and reserved judgments which had marked at least some of the missionary reports of visits to Soochow and Nanking (Docs. 83, 85). Finally the British Consul at the port, Frederick Harvey (who had visited Nanking with Bonham in 1853), for all his protestations of objectivity, ended by writing the most highly charged and emotively hostile report against the movement in the British consular archive (Docs. 82, 86).[35]

The Taiping occupation of Ningpo came too late to do either the Taiping cause or their relations with the West much good. By December of 1861 nearly all Westerners, including their erstwhile sympathisers, had become fully convinced of the hopelessness of the movement as offering an alternative government for China. Had it come about earlier, or under the command of leaders of the calibre of the Chung Wang or the Ying Wang, it is just possible that the Western view of the movement in its last years might have become a little less stark. Instead it served only to reinforce the prevailing harsh judgment.

80
A Memorandum by C Alabaster
BPP, 1862, C 2976, pp. 61-2

CAPTAIN DEW[36] having applied for my services as interpreter, I accompanied the expedition to Chapoo, with a letter from Admiral Hope requesting the rebels to abstain from any attack on Ningpo.

On arrival, the gunboat anchored about 1,400 yards from the hill, on which there was a rebel encampment, and Captain Dew and I, with a Chinese servant of mine, landed with a flag of truce.

We were warned back, and subsequently discovered that the matchlocks had been re-primed; but rapidly advancing, and showing the letter, some of the more courageous came to meet us, and on being assured that our ships were not going to fire on them, treated us very civilly, sending off messengers for the Chief. On his arrival, in the person of one Ko-chên-ching (a subordinate, it appeared subsequently), we delivered the letter which was handed to a secretary, and answered verbally by protestation of friendship and earnest asseverations of the absence of all intention of attacking Ningpo; the Chief winding up by taking off his

35 See comments and references in Gregory, op. cit., pp. 107-8, 230-1. Karl Marx, in an article in *Die Presse*, 7 July 1862, quoted Harvey's despatch at length, commenting that 'What is original in this Chinese revolution are only its bearers. They are not conscious of any task, except the change of dynasty. They have no slogans. They are an even greater scourge to the population than the old rulers'. See S. Avineri (ed.), *Karl Marx on Colonialism and Modernization* (Doubleday, New York, 1969), pp. 442-4. For some pertinent comments on the attitude of Marx to the Taiping see Perry Anderson, *Lineages of the Absolutist State* (London, 1974), pp. 493-4.

36 Capt. Roderick Dew, commander of HMS *Encounter*, was sent to Ningpo in May 1861 to advise the Imperial authorities on the defence of the port. One year later he was to take the initiative in its re-capture.

yellow, and exceedingly dirty, turban, and begging Captain Dew to wear it for his sake.

We then returned to the ship, having given notice of our intention of landing in greater force in the afternoon, and promising, on their appearing somewhat alarmed, to come as we were then, quite unarmed. Accordingly we landed about 2, and were met on the hill by the bearer of the answer to our morning's despatch, which proved quite satisfactory, and a Chief was sent to guide us into the real head-man's yamun. On arrival there, we were ushered into the reception room, tea was handed round, and the Chief, a dirty, red-clothed, ordinary looking man, who seemed greatly at a loss how to receive us, begged us, finally, to be seated.

We mentioned the object of our visit, stated our desire to maintain friendly relations, and hoped there was not, as we feared, a chance of these being broken off; and having thus broken the ice, his Excellency, as his attendants called him, clearing the room of the people crowding in by a few words decidedly uttered and immediately obeyed, addressed us, expatiating on the absence of all difference between foreigners and Tae-pings, declaring they had no intention of attacking Ningpo or Shanghae, saying he had received orders from Ching [Chung?] Wang to treat foreigners with courtesy, and begging to be provided with arms and ammunition: 'Tell your countrymen to come here with arms, and I will take care they are not cheated.' And what, we asked, will you give us in return? Bricks, wood, old nails, the debris of the city he had destroyed; he wanted the means to destroy more, and would give us the remains of what he had already destroyed. Opium he was willing to take, but, before all else, guns, powder, and shot. We asked him how he had taken the city. He said some of his best men had got upon a house, and some on the wall, and had opened the gates to his army; he had lost but three men killed, but could not tell the loss of the Imperialists: they had killed every Manchoo they found and there were two days before the slaughter came to an end. We asked where were the people; the town was deserted, and save some evidently pressed men engaged in repairing the wall, we had seen none but soldiers in the city. Oh! he replied, I let them go, I did not kill them. We asked how they would do for supplies if the people went; three shops only being then open in the city, one stocked with a pound of tobacco, another with three salt fish, the third with half a leg of pork. He was in no fear; they would take another city. They had no objection to the people cultivating their fields, but the people would not stop, and it was not his business to prevent their leaving. Trade, in so far as it comprised the exchange of arms for old bricks, was advantageous; he saw the necessity, and wished he could impress us with equal desire for it: but it was a hard task to govern the people.

He told us he was expecting Chung Wang down with reinforcements from Cha-hsing, but he did not appear to fear the Imperialists much. He had 5,000 troops, and though three-fifths of these were little boys, and did the things pertaining to little boys, his men were equal to the lying imps who had deluded us and told he was going to attack Ningpo.

He was anxious to know whether we should defend Hang-chow, and was relieved when he heard not. We were, he said, but one family; foreigners had no reason to interfere with him nor he with foreigners; there were many at Soo-chow, Tsing-poo, and Kia-hsing not soldiers but selling guns.

As we sat talking, various Chiefs lounged in, all dressed gorgeously in the brightest coloured silks and all dirty and diseased, their arms covered with gold bangles and scabs, a gay but unpleasant-looking crowd. This man, a fine tall fellow, second in command; another was a Civil mandarin. The table behind which the Chief sat was covered with red cloth embroidered with golden dragons. They we addressed 'ta jen' and 'ta lao yeh'. In a courtyard two rebels were seated in the cangue; a new crucifix was leaning against the wall. There was an evident attempt to inspire awe and respect on all beholders; but the universal coolie-look, the want of intelligence even in the higher, and the utter inability of the highest to write more than (and that with great difficulty) his name, must have utterly failed to excite any feeling unless fear, and, as it did with us, disgust.

We were impressed with the energy with which a portion of the wall was being repaired, and the manner in which they had staked the ground surrounding the wall; but the long walk through the burnt and plundered suburbs, where fearful dogs and gaunt cats stalked about, frightened from the bodies still lying here and there by our approach, the utter desertion of the country as far as we could see, the contrast between what the place had been and what it was then, made every one echo heartily the answer of our greatest rebel admirer, when asked, on returning, whether he was disenchanted, 'Quite'. He could no longer admire the horde of savages who seemed ruining the country that they might prey on its destruction.

During the day an Imperialist fleet of sixteen lorchas, junks, &c., came up to inquire whether we proposed to attack the place, but readily retired when we said no, seeming to think it scarcely worth risking life or limb for uncertain pay against men who had a certainty of plunder in success, and nothing but death to look for should they lose.

81
A Report by A R Hewlett
BPP, 1862, C 2976, pp. 108–9

Sir,

HAVING, in obedience to your orders, accompanied Her Majesty's ship 'Kestrel' in her late visits to the rebel headquarters at Yu-yaou and Fung-hwa, I have now the honour to present you with details and results of said visits.

We left Ningpo at noon on Thursday the 28th ultimo, and having arrived at Yu-yaou at 9 a.m. on the following morning, rode into the city at noon to have an interview with Hwang, a Ta-jen, and Commander-in-chief of the forces stationed at that place.

He received us attired in a yellow silk robe richly embroidered, with a hood of the same material and colour sitting uneasily on his head; contrary to Chinese etiquette, and probably with a view of impressing us with a sense of his dignity, he presided, rather than sat, at a table at the head of the room occasionally diverting himself by sipping almond tea and chewing the areca nut.

He is a native of Kwang-se, nearly 40 years of age, and, to judge from his appearance and demeanour, has evidently risen from a very low walk of life to his present high position and command. We found him almost incapable of understanding Mandarin, and unable to read several of the characters in the letter we handed to him. Hence conversation was conducted mainly through his Secretary Pwan, or Liaou-chin-tsz (Goldbeater Junior), who informed us that he had distinguished himself at the capture by the rebels of Shanghae in 1853, and who seemed somewhat surprised and hurt because we had never heard of him before. This man had met us on our first arrival at Hwang's residence, asked us in broken English to sit down, and inquired whether we were the 'barbarian officers' ('E kwan') from Ningpo. Being informed that such expressions, as applied to foreign officials, were wholly inadmissible, he then began in a somewhat humbler tone to request that we would communicate to him the purport of our visit, as he was the confidant and principal adviser of Hwang. This we refused to do, and after some little delay were received by Hwang as detailed above.

We at once informed Hwang of the object of our visit, and explained to him fully, and sentence by sentence, the four requisitions contained in, and forming the principal subject of, the communication to his address, drawn up in the names of the Representatives of England, France, and America, stationed at Ningpo. To every one of these he gave his unqualified assent, 'although', he added, 'in the event of the mandarins resisting, and of my having to attack Ningpo, I cannot be responsible for the lives of any of your countrymen who may remain inside the city. Otherwise I will do all I can to prevent their being molested, and will at once behead any of my followers who dares to offer them any annoyance.'

He assured us that his desire was to keep well with foreigners, with whom he was anxious to open trade; spoke of us as worshippers of the same God and the same Jesus as themselves, and denominated us 'Wai-hsiung-te'—their foreign brothers. His mission, he said, was to overthrow the Tartar Dynasty, and this mission had been put into the hands of their Ruler, Tien Wang, by God himself.

He seemed to entertain no doubt whatever of being successful in his attack on Ningpo (on which place he intended to advance in a week's time at the latest); indeed, he appeared to think that the mandarins would offer no resistance, though he begged us to urge on them the advisability of surrendering the city without a struggle, should they be inclined to attempt to hold it.

Eager inquiries were made on all sides for foreign fire-arms, of which they seem to have but a few—a want that would be sufficiently felt were they ever to come in contact with troops courageous enough to stand against them.

As far as human life is concerned, the rebels, at the capture of Yü-yaou, appear to have used their opportunity with forbearance; we saw but few dead bodies, and of those some, as we were informed, were their own men who had been caught plundering and burning.

There had been a large fire just outside the South Gate of the old city, a considerable portion of the town there being in ruins.

On questioning them about Hang-chow, we were told that it was now being closely invested by the Chung Wang (the Faithful Prince), and that they looked forward to its falling at the close of the year.[37]

Yen-chow-foo was in the hands of another of their Princes, She Wang, (the Attendant Prince), under whose orders they were now

37   Hangchow was taken by the Chung Wang 29–31 December 1861.

acting. They informed us that it was their intention to take Shanghae at no very distant date.

We then left, and returned on board, the conviction on the minds of every one of our party being that, however much they might promise us immunity from annoyance, they would not themselves be able to secure it to us, or to control the lawless bands of ruffians and desperadoes who form too large a portion of their numbers.

We weighed anchor at Yu-yaou at 3 p.m. on Friday afternoon, bringing away with us twenty-one rebel Proclamations for posting on foreign houses, as well as a reply from Hwang to the official communication presented to him in the morning, and reached Ningpo the same night.

Of the villages which line the river banks at intervals many were entirely deserted, while at others an anxious and panic-stricken crowd were collected to watch our return; in the fields crops of rice were still standing ungathered in, as if, at the dreaded approach of the insurgents, all had fled indiscriminately. Those who remain behind are, without distinction of age or station, pressed into the rebel service.

Hwang having informed us that another body of troops, also under the She Wang's orders, and commanded by one Fang, a General of equal rank with himself, were advancing on Ningpo from the Fung-hwa or south-west side, we proceeded up that branch of the river early on Monday morning the 2nd instant, and found the said insurgents encamped at a place called Pih-too, but ten miles from Ningpo.

We at once went ashore, and put ourselves in communication with the leader Fang, a man of only 25 years of age, and a native of Kwang-se. We hastened to represent to him the serious injury to trade that must ensue on the capture of Ningpo by his forces, and the consequent loss that would accrue to foreign interests, besides the danger, in reality no slight one, to foreign life and property, to be apprehended both from lawless characters in his own ranks, and equally so from the bands of unruly Cantonese and Chin-chew men at Ningpo, ever on the lookout for an opportunity of indiscriminate plunder. We ended by eagerly dissuading him from advancing on Ningpo.

To our two objections Fang replied by assuring us that his party were most anxious to keep well with foreigners, who, indeed, were no other than their brothers, inasmuch as we both worshipped one God and one Jesus, and that as for trade, that would be allowed to go on as formerly, while he begged us to feel quite at ease as to the persons and property of our countrymen, any molestation shown to whom would be followed by instant decapitation. The object being the overthrow of the present dynasty, they could not allow Ningpo to remain in the hands of the imperialists.

It was with difficulty that we succeeded in persuading Fang to delay his attack on Ningpo for one week; another day was to have seen him there, he said, had we not interposed.

One could not help feeling struck with the earnestness and apparent sincerity of this young leader. Whilst alive to the dangers attending the cause in which he was engaged, he seemed to be confident that the support of Heaven would carry them through all their difficulties, and that, so aided, they must prevail. He told us that nearly the whole Province was in their hands, or would be before long, and that Hang-chow, the provincial capital, would fall, 'as soon as Heaven should see fit to give it into their hands.'

We had no means of judging of the numbers of their forces, though Fang informed us that they amounted to some 100,000, besides a Division left in charge at Fung-hwa . . .

82
A Despatch from the British Consul F W Harvey
BPP, 1862, C. 2976, pp. 107–8

The insurgents continue to conduct themselves with moderation towards the Chinese, evincing at the same time a strong desire, based on fear and the want of money, to cultivate a good understanding with us. They would wish it to appear that they are not the scourge so often depicted, and in respect to Ningpo at all events they would claim to be considered as the faithful keepers of the promises made at Yu-yaou and Fung-hwa, to respect life and property on their arrival here. In support of these pretensions they have issued Proclamations in all directions, calling on the people to return, to re-open their shops, and to live in peace and security under their rule. They have even established a native Custom-house, wherein duties will be levied on the Chinese after ten days' grace. But all these placards, appeals, and measures have hitherto met with just the amount of success that they deserved, a natural mixture of dread and suspicion being the only response given by the half-dozen respectable Chinese who are still here, living on our side.

As to inducing the richer classes, and indeed the city population, who fled some time ago from Ningpo, to return, and live under the present anarchical regime, much as we are accustomed to witness strange events in China, I should think this return a very improbable contingency. The insurgents have deep stains on their cause, which years of moderation and good government could alone tend to wash off, and they will find, to their cost, that the confidence of the people having once been lost, cannot be regained by issuing placards, and by undergoing a few weeks' probation in a port open to foreigners. The inhabitants of these and other districts entertain too lively a recollection of past treachery to entrust their lives, families, and property in the hands of the Tae-pings, without some better guarantee than promises, and, for my part, I can well understand this natural mistrust.

With regard to such public intercourse as necessity compels me to hold with the Chiefs in the city (in the present extraordinary state of things, and without a single Imperial Authority within a radius of 100 miles), so far all our demands have been satisfied and our complaints listened to. The Tae-pings have kept all the promises made to the requests conveyed to them at Yu-yaou and Fung-hwa, by committing few excesses on arriving here, by avoiding the foreign side of Ningpo, except as quiet citizens, and by exhibiting other proofs of their desire to live at peace with us; that desire being founded solely on their dread of our power. They continue to declare that they propose keeping Ningpo, which, being the seaport of Hang-chow, or rather the channel by which Hang-chow (now closely besieged by one of their so-called Princes) is fed by the sea route, the provincial capital will be under the necessity of capitulating at an early date. From late accounts, however, it would seem that the Imperialists have obtained successes over the rebels in the vicinity of Hang-chow, so that the fall of that large city is not altogether a decided matter. We shall doubtless learn something more definite on this subject in a few days.

It has been reported to me that the insurgents propose establishing a foreign Custom-house at this port, such being, it is said, one of their favourite ideas, and forming part of their programme (if, indeed, such hordes have any settled scheme or plan of action) in the capture of Ningpo; for the same reason that the foreign duties of Shanghae tempt and prompt them to the seizure of that important mart.

Should the report prove correct, and I find that they really intend establishing a foreign Custom-house here, it will, of course, become my duty, pending instructions from your Excellency, to see that no higher rates are fixed than those now in operation under our Tariff with the Imperial Government. But I doubt whether there will be much necessity for vigilance, as I do not apprehend that any extensive or legitimate trade can be carried on under their blighting rule; the total want of confidence on the part of the entire population of Chinese acting as an insuperable obstacle to that which we all understand by the words 'commercial intercourse.'

Respecting Shanghae, to which allusion is made above, I understand that the insurgents here are reported to have declared, probably at the suggestion of certain unprincipled foreigners, that if they are not allowed to seize that city, they will stop all supplies of tea and silk reaching it; and these rich products finding, necessarily, their way to Ningpo, will bring in their rear the natural accompaniments of large sums of money, in the shape of Customs duties and other charges. I do not, personally, believe that it is the intention or in the power of the Tae-pings to carry out, even under foreign advice, so difficult and complicated an undertaking as the entire stoppage of produce reaching the port of Shanghae; but the point is, nevertheless, of sufficient importance to deserve serious consideration, and, as such, I submit it to your Excellency's superior judgment. Against the probability of this gigantic blockade being determined upon, I deem it right to inform your Excellency that I have ascertained, from a hitherto very reliable native source, that the question of abandoning Ningpo altogether, and retiring towards Hang-chow, has been seriously discussed in the Councils of the Chiefs in this city. The opinions on the point being conflicting, no decision has been arrived at, and the matter has been referred, for final instructions, to the Tien Wang at Nanking, to whom the leader's despatch on the subject was forwarded in the course of last week.

The Tae-pings here are aware of Admiral Hope's proposed visit to Nanking, and are very anxious as to its purport and issue.[38] They must feel, and indeed say, amongst themselves, that, though on good terms with us, the fact of their having destroyed one of our Consular trading stations, to which they were invited by foreigners on the assurance of entire immunity from British interference, cannot be a pleasing object of consideration to the British authorities and Government. For these and other reasons, therefore, nothing would surprise me less than to see them evacuate Ningpo; the capture of this city having proved so far, viewed in a business and commercial sense, a bad speculation, a source of endless political embarrassments with foreign functionaries, and, in short, more of a deception than a realization of their hopes and great expectations.

38   See above, note 25.

83
A Letter from Rev. W H Russell
Archives of the Church Missionary Society,
Letter Book CH/M3, 1859–62, pp. 182–91

On Monday morning [December 9] about 8 o'clock the Rebel force made a bold and simultaneous attack on the south and west gates, scaled the walls in both places with considerable agility and bravery, dislodged the Imperialists from their positions and threw open the gates to their own people, who entered in considerable force, probably not less than from eighty to a hundred thousand men. In a few minutes after this several bodies of the Rebels were to be seen running to and fro in all directions on the walls and in the streets, some hunting up Imperialist soldiers, who had already thrown off the garb of their profession and tried to assume the appearance of the common people, and some in search of plunder. From our own veranda we observed several parties of the latter catching geese, ducks and fowls in our neighbourhood, and taking off every particle of food they could find in the houses of the poor people who live near us.

On seeing the Rebels in the city I ordered a British flag, which I had obtained for the purpose, to be hoisted up on a long bamboo pole close by our front entrance, hoping it might be recognized by them and prevent them from entering our premises. Though it seemed to have the effect of preventing them from entering by the front door, yet several rebels during the day did come into our compound, some by scaling the wall on the rear of the house, and some by forcing open a door leading to our little family chapel, still from none of them did either we ourselves or the converts and others who had fled to us for refuge receive the least injury. The only thing on which any of them ventured to lay violent hands was our little pony. To one of the rebels, who visited us, it proved too strong a temptation. After several remonstrances on our part, and a struggle between him and me of undefined earnestness, neither of us quite understanding how far it might be prudent to venture, he carried off his prize, followed by Mr Burdon to some distance, who threatened to bring the matter before his chief. Mr B. however thought it better to leave the affair for the present and attend to other things more important. In a short time the rebel himself returned bringing with him $30—to pay for the pony. This I declined taking, telling him in a half earnest, half laughing manner, that as he had forcibly carried off my pony I should not consent to take in exchange for it all the wealth of the Taiping Tai-Koh (The Heavenly peaceful Dynasty) that he must either restore my pony to me, or that I should be under the necessity of bringing the matter to the notice of his chief. Subsequently Mr Parkes did very kindly speak to the chief about it and in a very short time the pony was sent back to me by the very individual who took it away. This great desire to secure my pony, arose I believe from the fact that those amongst the Taiping soldiers who are able by fair or foul means to secure horses are promoted at once to the rank of officers, for which my friend was doubtless a very eager aspirant.

During the first day, which was indeed a very anxious one to us all, my dear wife very bravely kept guard on the veranda, calling out, when necessary, to those who passed by the front door that ours was a foreign entrance. Mr Burdon and I kept moving about other parts of the premises, requesting those who came in to leave, which they did with a little expostulation on our part. In the evening we called on the chief, who had by that time taken up his quarters in a large house belonging to a wealthy native, to request him to send one of his trustworthy adherents to assist us in keeping watch during the night, fearing that we could not so easily check his people then as during the day-time, should they think of entering our house. To this the chief readily assented and ordered one of his men to accompany us for this purpose. The night passed quietly, though it proved a very anxious one to us all under our very strange and peculiar circumstances, with bodies of these unknown men passing backwards and forwards by our door the whole time. Still then and all through these very trying events, Our Father's protection which we had earnestly sought for ourselves and our people was graciously vouchsafed in our hour of need. He indeed has proved abundantly better to us than all our fears.

The next few days were occupied by us, and indeed by all the missionaries at Ningpo, in hunting up some of our converts and others connected with us who had not taken refuge in our houses and who consequently had been impressed by the rebels into their service. In this we were altogether successful even beyond our expectations, as we were enabled to find out and get possession of every individual whom we had a right to claim, who as a general rule were freely surrendered by their captors at our request on the plea of their belonging to us. Hundreds of others also who did not belong to us escaped under our shelter from the deserted city, by joining the processions of our people, who from time to time passed through the city gates with us. To prevent this, had we been disposed, would have been a difficult matter, as the poor creatures regarded it as an escape from slavery, captivity, or death, if they were men, and from what was worse, if they were women. To openly claim them as our own people would be a violation of truth, which we could not be guilty of, and so we determined to connive at it, if the rebels did not interfere, not feeling called upon, under the circumstances to become informants against those, who were flying for their lives and liberties and whose only offence, if it was one, was an unwillingness to submit to slavery or captivity under the Taiping yoke.

Several of the scenes witnessed by us during these days were of the most heartrending character. Of the comparative few inhabitants who remained in the city until its capture, perhaps not more than thirty thousand souls, probably none were left untouched by the hands of these wicked men, whether in their own persons or their nearest relatives. All the strong-bodied men, Fathers, husbands, brothers, sons were forcibly dragged from their families and in most instances compelled to act as coolies with chains about their necks, while all the young women were carried off to a still more deplorable fate. The few that remained, old people and children of both sexes, were left to starve in the streets, without food, clothing, or a home to live in, having death in one form or other continually before them. In addition to this the houses of the poor people were rifled of every valuable they possessed, and in thousands of cases levelled with the ground to supply firewood for their conquerors. In a word the descent of those followers of the so-called 'Heavenly King of Peace' to the city of Ningpo has caused, as everywhere else they have come, universal and untold misery to its inhabitants and reduced its once flourishing and busy streets to a camp for the most depraved of soldiery, who have no fear of God or man before their eyes, and who consequently perpetrate enormities in the face of day which my pen should be ashamed to describe.

Still all this, and even worse, might be tolerated, did this strange movement seem to indicate the least gleam of hope for the future to this miserable country which I confess I feel utterly unable to discern. My views of the whole movement in a political and religious aspect, which hitherto have been constantly oscillating between hope and fear, though the latter was generally in the ascendant, have now assumed a very decided character that its mission under God is one of *Judgment* alone, sent on this miserable land for her long night of gross idolatry and fearful iniquity, and that when this object is accomplished the movement itself will probably be overwhelmed in the very desolations it has caused. This conclusion I have arrived at principally from my observation of the strange character and doings of these Taipingites, who have now visited this Port, and who, I understand from those who have seen them elsewhere, are a fair specimen of what they are and do everywhere.

1. The leading men in this movement who have come to Ningpo, as almost all their followers, personally considered, are the most illiterate, and most depraved, the most barbarous Chinese in every sense with whom I have had the misfortune to be brought into contact. As far as I can ascertain, and already I have had considerable intercourse with representatives of all classes from amongst them, there seems to be no redeeming feature in their character, not even the outward politeness and external grace which so generally characterize the most abandoned of ordinary Chinese.

2. The character and conduct of these men is such, their notions and modes of procedure so contrary to all recognized standards of right and wrong that amalgamation with others in business or otherwise seems not only never designed by them, but also utterly impracticable. A training of several years in the practice of living altogether on plunder, accustomed during this time to overlook the rights of others, has so seared their consciences, that the principle of *meum and tuum*, seems now completely forgotten. Consequently as there is no security under their rule for life and property the people fly from them whenever they can, so that even in those places longest occupied by them there is not the slightest appearance of the resumption of trade or of any confidence in them on the part of the people generally.

3. They seem to be utterly unconscious of the work they are commissioned to perform. Carried along by a blind impulse no one appears to comprehend or care what he does or in what his work may terminate. Desolation and destruction on as large a scale as possible seem to be the only object they have in view. True it is that their war-cry 'Down with the Tartars' 'Down with the idols' might be regarded as a sufficiently intelligible motive to urge them forward and doubtless it would be had they any distinct apprehension of its meaning, but while this is the cry continually on their lips and the work it indicates is strangely but effectively executed by them, they themselves seem utterly unconscious agents in the hands of Him Who doubtless is using them for His own wise though mysterious purposes.

4. As to the Christian element supposed to pervade the movement I have been unable to discern any whatever except the negative one of 'Down with the idols' referred to above. In their hymns of praise to the Heavenly Father, Heavenly Elder Brother, and Heavenly King, the trinity of the Taipingites, there might seem at first sight to be some approximation at least in phrase-

ology to Christian truth, but a closer investigation of their views, so far as they may be regarded to possess any, with reference to God, seems clearly to shew that they are as far from orthodoxy on this point as the idolators they so affect to despise. The terms referred to above would appear to be taken up by the majority in a sense scarcely more intelligible than *oh-mi-do-fah* as employed by ordinary Buddhists. So far as any do possess distinct notions about what they say, these notions are perfectly blasphemous, terribly repulsive to the mind and heart of a Christian. To them the Heavenly Father and Heavenly Elder brother are absorbed in the person of the Heavenly King, whose dictum is law, whose fancies and hallucinations are superior to the Scriptures of Truth, which notwithstanding they in some sense profess to reverence.

From the above therefore, and from many other things which might be added, had I time, I am compelled to believe that the Mission of the Taipingites is one of Judgment alone and that when this strange work of the Almighty and Allwise Judge and Ruler of all is accomplished they themselves will perish with a terrible destruction. I cannot persuade myself to think that they will ever be employed as instruments for the work of reconstruction and for the dissemination of pure Christianity in China. Yet for this it is doubtless our duty to pray and hope, though it may be to hope against hope.

Should these men ever attain to the Government of the whole country and be permitted to establish a national religion I am strongly inclined to apprehend that they will become a terribly persecuting power, who will brook no interference with their religious views but who will everywhere enforce them at the edge of the sword. When reasoning with one of their head-men the other day about the blasphemy of putting the Heavenly King on a level with Jesus he replied that he was not responsible for the tenets he held, that the Heavenly King propounded these to his followers and that all must receive them at the risk of their lives.

Still however gloomy the present aspect of things looks as to these Taipingites, we know that the Lord reigneth, we know that He will give His son the ends of the earth for a possession and that China emancipated from all error and thraldom will be part of that inheritance, and it strikes me at times in the midst of all these terrible desolations that we may look up with encouragement and hope that the redemption even now draweth nigh. . . .

84
Reports by Capt. F S Green
Archives of Jardine Matheson & Co.,
Local Correspondence, Ningpo 1858–62

1 *29 November, 1861*
I am sorry to say that the Rebels are still advancing towards this city and are today only 12 miles distant on the main branch of this River, and it is reported they intend to take Ningpo tomorrow or Sunday. Several foreigners have been amongst the Rebels who report that they are friendly with all Foreigners and say they only want to take Ningpo city and do not wish to trouble the Foreign Settlement ... It is not yet known if the Toutai of this city will defend the place or will give it up to the Rebels on their appearing before the city. The latter would be best as there are very few soldiers here and they are now threatening to join the Rebels if they do not get their pay in a few days. All the cities that the Rebels have lately taken have not been defended by the Imperialists so they have not been burnt or destroyed, the Rebels only pulling down the joss houses and Mandarins Yamuns ... Mr Consul Harvey is of opinion that the Rebels will not interfere with Foreigners but all business will be stopped for some time to come.

2 *17 December, 1861*
I have to advise you that the city of Ningpo is now occupied by the Taeping Rebels. It was taken on the morning of the 8th inst. without any fighting and the Rebels did not slaughter anyone on their entrance into the city. They attacked the city at 7 a.m. and at 8 they were in full possession of the place. The same evening HMS Scout arrived having Sir Harry Parkes on board, also the Keelong (?) under the French Admiral Protet. On the following day the English and French authorities went into the city and had an interview with the Rebel chiefs but what transpired has not been made public but it is rumoured that the Rebels will be allowed to hold the city for a space of time to see if they can form any kind of Government or induce the Chinese Bankers and Merchants to return to their business as these people had all left and either gone to Shanghai and Chusan or fled into the country. But by what I can judge these Rebels will not be able to do any business as the people here are so much afraid of them they will not return. The Rebels are now destroying all the joss houses in the city and plundering all that is left of any value they are also strengthening the defences of the city and building small Forts and Redoubts outside the Walls, and to do this they force all

Chinese they can catch and to prevent them running away they have them chained together in couples . . .

3 *29 January, 1862*

I hope to see an improvement in our Drug Market after the Chinese Holidays if the Rebels will allow the Inland trade to be resumed. I hear from a seaman that many Tea and Silk Merchants from the Interior had memorialized the Rebel chief of this city to be allowed to bring their goods to this place for exportation, but as yet these people have not received an answer to their memorial. The Merchants (Chinese) are willing to pay the same duties as heretofore . . . The Rebels still remain in charge of this city and some apprehension is felt that they are not now so civil to Foreigners as they were at first—the disturbances at Shanghai may account for this.

4 *7 February, 1862*

I have still to advise you of the very dull state of Trade at this Port nor do I see any chance of improvement whilst the Rebels hold this City. There has not been a chest of opium sold here during the past fortnight, consequently I can give no quotations. It is now said amongst the Chinese that the Rebel chiefs will not allow Opium to be carried into the Interior, although they allow their own people to use it here . . . The Rebels still continue quiet and are very civil to all Foreigners.

5 *21 April, 1862*

The Rebels up to the present time are quiet and seem favourably inclined to Foreigners but I doubt if they will ever be able to do any trade in the Country, and they are establishing Customs houses and levy a small duty on any goods passing, and the further you go into the Interior the more numerous these Custom Houses are and greater the duty demanded.

85
Journal of Rev. Josiah Cox
Wesleyan Missionary Notices, 3rd series, vol. IX, 25 April 1862, pp. 72–6

VISIT TO NINGPO

9th.—At the suggestion of friend I resolve to run down to Ningpo, where I shall see more of this rebel party, and ascertain the opportunities of preaching Christ they offer the Ningpo Missionaries. I went on board a small trading-boat, and we began to drop down the Woosung river about ten P.M. The boat made rapid passage, and arrived in Ningpo early on Saturday, 11th.

11th.—I took a walk in the morning through a piece of ground on which the foreigners are located, and which has therefore been placed under American, French, and English protection. The foreign residents are few. It is now crowded with Chinese refugees, who throng the streets, and are rapidly increasing the houses and shopping. Amongst the crowd we noticed several batches of the 'long-haired' people, selling their spoils, and purchasing firearms and provisions. Messrs. Russell and Burdon, of the Church Missionary Society, though driven from their own premises, offered me a cordial welcome to their hospitality.

At about one P.M., under Mr. Russell's guidance, two or three of us went out to visit the Custom-house and the city. The Custom-house is opened to-day. We found it profusely decorated with flags, in which these rebels, like other Chinamen, do greatly delight; and the people were keeping festivities within. Twan, the 'great man,' appointed to be Commissioner of customs at Ningpo, is a sharp fellow, who has dealt with foreigners in Shanghai, and, doubtless, wishes to keep up friendly relations with them. He received us pleasantly, and conversed freely with Mr. Russell. He informed us that as their arrangements were imperfect, it was proposed to make Ningpo a free port during three months; afterwards to collect duties according to our present tariff with the Imperialists and by foreign agents. He complained that difficulties arose by giving the foreign flag to Chinese boats. For a short time we witnessed a theatrical performance in an adjoining hall. Everything was coarse, but coarsest of all the audience; for I never saw so low and wicked-looking a set of men in my life. Many of them are young, well-fed, and well-clothed, yet they wear a look of cruelty and vice, which is to me very repulsive. It is the impress of a lawless and ferocious life.

From the Custom-house we crossed the river, and after walking for half a mile through the scene of a frightful conflagration, we entered the city by a gate from the north-east. The afternoon was wearing away, and we could only make a rapid passage across the city. Through the influence of the foreigners, Ningpo and its inhabitants have suffered less from the incursions of the rebels than any other city captured by them. House-property has not been destroyed, though the houses have been plundered and are now been stripped of their woodwork for firewood. The Missionary houses and chapels, and the houses of foreigners, remain uninjured. The idols have been upset, maimed, and broken to pieces with an unsparing hand. The whole population has fled from the city; and as one walks these silent, deserted streets, the thoughts of the myriads of homeless refugees, who have lost their goods and their employment, and are exposed to the cold of this severe winter, makes one sad.

I had a long conversation with Messrs. Russell and Burdon, on the party now at Ningpo. For a time they feared the English and French would defend the place, and it was not until they were informed to the contrary that they advanced here. One of our Captains had improved the defences, and drilled some Imperialists in gunnery. Messrs. Russell and Burdon were the first who from the city walls descried the rebel flags. Preparations were useless; not a gun was fired. The Imperialists fled, and the rebels climbed the walls, meeting none to repel them. As they rushed through the city, pillaging from house to house, parties of them entered touses of the Missionaries, and began to despoil them; but the leaders readily granted a guard to defend them. The Missionary families deemed it prudent to move out of the city a few days after it was captured. They were permitted to take out hundreds of people for whom they interceded; and rescued many poor creatures from the rude hands of the soldiery. The leaders paid marked attention to the representations of the Missionaries, and there was evidently a fear of foreigners generally among their followers. Here, also, the leaders are illiterate men, and formerly of the Coolie or labouring classes. They pay no heed to the organization of civil government, nor have they yet displayed any capacity for administration. They are possessed with two objects,—to destroy the stupid idols, and exterminate the Tartar rulers; and beyond this, they appear to be void of definite design, and are ignorant of the religious doctrines of their leader, though familiar with the titles he assumes himself, and ascribed to God and Jesus Christ. Most of the Missionaries have been busy in conversing with them about Christianity, and have employed their native assistant in the same work; and the common opinion is, that such efforts find little to encourage them in the character of the Tai-ping people at Ningpo. They are sensual, cruel, and very indifferent to such truths.

Sunday, 12th.—I attended two of the special services of the week of prayer. All the Missionaries present. An Episcopalian preached us an earnest and instructive sermon; after which the sacrament was administered by a Presbyterian, to which all remained except the Baptist brethren. After the service, I accompanied Mr. Burdon on a preaching tour among the rebels of the city. I met with none who spoke the Canton dialect. Mr. Burdon addressed one company in the street, at the entrance of the residence of an officer, and entered the *kung-kwans*, to talk and read with them there. The common soldiers live together in companies of from twenty to forty or fifty in a mess: their place is called a *kung-kwan*. We saw two of the headmen of one *kung-kwan*, who could not read: nor did I observe more than one man in each place who knew the characters. The men were ignorant of the teaching of the Heavenly King, and indifferent to religious truth of every kind. I have rarely known a company of Chinese listeners exhibit so little curiosity when the Missionary has been preaching. In the afternoon the converts of all the Mission churches assembled and filled the small Presbyterian chapel, (which is built on the ground, protected by foreigners,) to hear Mr. Russell, of the Church Missionary Society, preach. There were present a larger proportion and a more respectable-looking class of women than I have ever before seen in a gathering of native Christians, which is one happy result of Miss Aldersey's girls' schools.[39] The members are sadly scattered by the present turmoils. It is a day of calamity to the Ningpo churches, as it is to the Chinese populations. It is touching to hear the fervent prayers offered on behalf of the poor, and that this commotion may be over-ruled of God for good.

13th.—I made another interesting tour through the city under the escort of Mr. Burdon. We had first to obtain a passport from one of the Chiefs to protect Mr. Burdon and myself, in a projected visit to Chan-King. We saw three of their *ta-jin*, or 'great men.' Suh-sin-lan was the first. Suh was formerly a trader with foreign merchants; after amassing considerable wealth, he retired to occupy the declining years of his life, in enjoying the fruit of his toils in his native town, Tsz-ki in this province. When the rebels captured a neighbouring city, Tsz-ki was evacuated by the Imperialists. The inhabitants entreated Suh to assist them. After due consideration, it was resolved to forward the allegiance of the town to the Tai-ping authorities. Suh prepared a feast, and sent messengers to invite them to take peaceable possession of the place. A Chieftain arrived, enjoyed their spread, and occupied the town, but committed fearful butcheries amongst the unresisting people. They impressed Suh into their service, appointing him first to the charge of Tsz-ki; when they moved forwards in Ningpo, supposing him to be acquainted with foreign affairs, they brought Suh with them, and have nominated him a kind of prefect of Ningpo. I think this shows a desire on their part to avoid difficulties with foreign powers. Suh is now enfeebled by age, and unfortunately possesses only the name, unaccompanied with the necessary power, of office; nor is his counsel regarded by Wong

39 Probably a reference to one of the 'missionary ladies' attached to the Church Missionary Society station in Ningpo.

and Tan, the military leaders in Ningpo. Suh received us courteously, and is by far the most gentlemanly Chinaman I have yet seen amongst them. He advised us, however, to obtain a pass from Pwan or Wong. Pwan is the Custom-house officer. Being friendly with Mr. Russell, Pwan accompanied us to Wong, one of the two principal military leaders. Wong was born in Kwang-Si, and has been an adherent of his party for eleven years. Like the other leaders, he is an uneducated man; he is reputed to be a daring soldier, and carries a look of energy and honesty, such as I have not seen in the fraternity of Kings at Nanking. He was despatching two boxes of foreign muskets to a distant party of his force. Our passport was readily granted.

In the temples we entered, the destruction of idols has been unsparing. The god of war and his satillites lay in scattered fragments about their former shrines; here lay a dishonoured image prostrate on its nose. Another had lost its head. Others stood with bruised eyes and mouths, and ears and noses missing. Some lay about in dismembered heaps. One of the Confucian halls and some ancestral halls we saw this morning have also been defaced. We saw two or three groups of gamblers; and in one place we entered, there was opium smoking. We passed several corpses, one of them at the gate, which had been beheaded since we entered the city. Decapitation seems to be the only punishment they inflict, and they pay little heed to the value of a human head. An excellent native Catechist, who is shortly to be ordained by the Bishop of Victoria, and has been left within the city to preach among the people, was bewailing their ignorance and indifference to religious truth. He finds those who have been to Nanking and know anything of the assumptions and dogmas of the Heavenly King, are the most unwilling to receive the Gospel doctrines of the Saviour of the world. 'Ours is not the religion of Jesus; the doctrines are different; we must believe the Heavenly King.'

14th.—I joined Mr. and Mrs. Russell, who were leading a troop of Coolies to fetch some of their goods from their deserted residences. I went on with Mr. Russell, who was taking three or four men to rescue some articles of a native member from a house near the South-Gate. Mr. Russell is a noble-hearted man, and has spared himself no risk nor labour to befriend the poor in their present afflictions. I never enter the city with him without some one crying to him for deliverance from this melancholy place.

Whilst the Coolies were collecting their goods, three rebels came up, and, whispering, asked Mr. Burdon to aid their escape. They were Ningpo men, and had been impressed. Though well

388

clothed and fed, they are miserable, and under terror of decapitation on the slightest offence.

SHAON-KING

We started in the evening in company with Mr. Burdon, of the Church Missionary Society, on a trip to Shaon-king. It is a prefectural city, within about a dozen miles of Hang-chan, and formerly contained upwards of 300,000 persons. It was celebrated for its production of silk for the foreign market. Tea is also one of its products; and, being situated in a fertile district, it was the seat of great wealth and commercial influence. Mr. Burdon was commencing a Mission at Shaon-king; he succeeded in renting a house, and had occupied it six months, when the place was emptied of its inhabitants, and captured by the rebels, in October last. Mr. Burdon sought to rescue a Chinese friend from rebel servitude in Shaon-king, and recover portions of his library and furniture. I gladly joined him for the sake of seeing a district overrun by rebels, and thus making up in part for my failure to journey overland from Nanking.

15th.—Our two boatmen were alternatively sculling us along through a good part of the night. The weather is cold and wet, and our rough strong boat is only covered with loose matting, open at the ends. The boats in the south are much more comfortable; but they could not climb the sluices we shall meet. In passing the village of Chang-tung, about noon, we were called up to a custom-house and required to show our passport, which was at once satisfactory. The petty officer here showed little sign of friendliness; but all were civil, and examined the pass and dismissed us in as prompt and business-like a manner as one could meet anywhere. It was the same, also, at Yu-Yan, where our pass was again demanded in the evening, and where we cast anchor for the night, in consequence of the strong tide against us. It is a walled district city, of perhaps 70,000 people. Mr. Burdon once occupied a house here, and on our return journey we must look at the place. Its extreme suburb is a scene of ruin. We have passed some burned villages today.

SUNG-HA

16th.—Most of the villages passed today appear to be deserted by all but the poor. At the market-town of Sung-ha, however, provision-shops are open, and there are many people moving about. I observed the fields dotted over with busy labourers, and extensive tracts covered with winter vegetables. Our passport was examined at a third custom-house, and in an equally business-like manner. Two hundred cash, value 1s.9d., were demanded for the *visé*; but the demand was immediately withdrawn when we informed them that we were not traders making profit, but Missionaries. Our clumsy, heavy boat, was hauled by Coolies over two sluice-banks today; the last one slipped us into the Tsung-po river about seven P.M. The full moon shed her rays on the stream, and revealed some noble mountains, making a lovely nightscene; but the wintry temperature, below freezing point, drove us quickly to the shelter of our blankets.

APPROACH TO SHAON-KING

17th.—Our clumsy boat was carried up the bank of the river by a stalwart shouting company, and shot into the canal before daylight. This locality is thickly covered over with towns and villages, and the goodly sight of farms and farming lay on either side of our not quite deserted watercourse. We approached Shaon-king through wide sheets of water, on which were fishermen busy, some with small nets, others with cormorants; and in one sheet we saw a fleet of over twenty boats dashing quickly to and fro in the excitement of pulling home their wide cast and heavily burdened netting. The water, the long, striking and hill-climbing wall, and three or four peaks crowned with beautiful pagodas, make a very pretty approach to the city. The suburbs are in some parts in ruins, and in others filled with noisy and numerous inhabitants. At the gate we came upon five British flags covering as many trading-boats from Ningpo. The crack and ring of pistols and muskets proved that their trade, in part, at least, was contraband; and we were therefore sorry to appear amongst them. These boats, and every part of the landing-place, were thickly packed with the long-haired soldiery. They all continue to wear the tail, which, with the long hair that occupies the once-shaven part, is twisted round the back part of the head. I observed here a great quantity of red silk braid mingled with their hair, being plaited into the tail. These red colours first caught my eye as I came up to the city gate, and looked on the busy eager market scene. The ordinary rebel soldier is a young man with fat cheeks, indulging in as many vestments of silk and fur as his person can well carry, and glaring in his favourite colours of red, blue, and green. Yellow belongs to their ta-jin. To add to our bewilderment, in coming suddenly on the motley scene, a couple of the guard came rushing among the crowd, and belabouring the shoulders of a poor offender with a cane, and his ears with heavier curses. We passed on to the city gate at once, and were conducted by one of the guard to the residence of Fu, one of the two leaders in charge of Shaon-king. Fu is another coarse fellow, and has the appearance of an opium-sot; as also a young Kwangsi man who lives with him. Their gaily-bedecked women were peering at us from one side-room; and in the other, into which—a private side-room—I had occasion to follow Fu, I saw he must have risen from the opium-pipe to meet us. He was just civil, and ordered a man to go guide us to Mr. Burdon's old house. It was distant nearly two miles, and our way led through the ruins of a vast conflagration, which had devoured the shopping of the wealthiest street in the city. One Lun, the fellow-officer of Fu, had occupied the house we sought. No opposition was offered to the removal of Mr. Burdon's library and furniture, of which he has saved the greater portion. Thence we traversed many streets, and entered several kung-kwans, but could hear nothing of the Mr. Ching whom he sought to rescue. We returned to represent the case to Fu, who coolly observed, 'He is probably beheaded;' and then took down his name, promising to look for him. In one house we entered, the head man was half-drunk, and gave other evidence that his house was an abode of vice. Every house has been ruthlessly plundered, the canals within the city are covered over with broken furniture, and here and there lay an unburied corpse. The desolation and ruin of this fine city are indescribable. In consequence of our Coolies having left part of the goods behind, we had to return to Mr. Burdon's home, and walk through a portion of the city after the gates were closed. In nearly every *kung-kwan* we heard sounds of carousal. From one of these a man staggered upon us, asking 'his foreign brethren to sell him a musket.'

We started to return so as to reach the first sluice before daybreak. One of the traders overtook us here with three boats: he was bringing thirteen bales of silk. He had not sold all his piece goods.

YU-YAN

19th.—We went into Yü-yan, and brought away a few books from the house Mr. Burdon once occupied here. The scene of desolation equals that of Shaon-king, and the unburied corpses are more numerous. I saw dogs and birds feeding on them in two or three places. We stood on the bridge for upwards of half an hour to watch a large company of rebels, probably between three or four thousand, marching forth on an expedition. Two-thirds of the force were impressed villagers, who were evidently under great terror of their new masters. A large proportion of the genuine rebels are mere boys of fourteen or sixteen years old, to whom it seems rare fun to brandish an ugly knife, or carry a matchlock. We were again required to show our pass at the custom-houses. A man had been executed, and his head hung up as a terror to others at the landing-place of the Chang-teng custom-house. The people said he had been an impressed man, and was beheaded for attempting to return home.

RETURN TO NINGPO

20th.—Under the good care of God we arrived safely at Ningpo this morning. Rumours of a collision with the rebels at Shanghai had created some uneasiness during our absence, and our return allayed some friendly fears on our account. This day being the birthday of the Heavenly King, is kept as a festival by his followers within the city. Guns are fired, and the walls are gaily decked with flags. We went across to witness the ceremonial, but were too late. We heard the officers had all assembled, and that Wong, the Chieftain, had chaunted them an address of one hundred sentences respecting the Heavenly Dynasty; but all we saw was a spread of fruits, cakes, and roasted pig, very similar to the offerings laid out on a festive day to idols.

21st.—I went again into the city, and called on the Missionaries, with whom, in this day of discomfort, anxiety, and sorrow, I deeply sympathize. They are performing many works of charity to the afflicted Chinese. Some cases of barbarous cruelty to women, and crushing calamity to families, have come under my notice.

22nd.—Under guidance of Mr. Russell, I made another long tour through the city. Mr. Russell called on and held long conversations with Suh and Pwan. From the former he gathered that their affairs in Ningpo are conducted with great irregularity and difficulty; and from the latter that they fear a rupture with foreigners at Shanghai. There is a more suspicious bearing towards foreigners than was exhibited when they captured the city. In one place I saw nine unburied skeletons that had been picked clean by dogs and vultures.

26th.—I took passage from Ningpo in a small steam-boat on the 24th, and was very thankful to land again this morning at Shanghai.

86
A Report from F W Harvey
BPP, 1862, C. 2992, pp.13–16

Being desirous not to be considered too hasty in any judgment which I might pass upon the Tae-pings at this port, I have purposely abstained, until the present time, from expressing any decided opinion in regard to their occupation of Ningpo, and their promise of organization; and I have been the more guarded in this respect as I am aware that there are people amongst us who, from the first, augured well of the Tae-pings, and thought it was only right they should have every chance afforded them of showing what they could accomplish in the shape of a 'good government.' Perhaps I may now be deemed more competent to speak on the subject, and I accordingly submit with deference, the following report to your Excellency, as the result of close observation and matured consideration.

Three months have elapsed since Ningpo fell into the hands of the insurgents; and from the hour of its capture to the moment when I am penning these lines, not one single step in the direction of a 'good government' has been taken by the Tae-pings; not any attempt made to organize a political body or commercial institutions; not a vestige not a trace of anything approaching to order, or regularity of action, or consistency of purpose, can be found in any one of their public acts; the words 'governmental machinery', as applied to Tae-ping rule, have no possible meaning here; and, in short, desolation is the only end obtained, as it has always been, wherever the sway of the marauders has had its full scope, and their power the liberty of unchecked excesses. I feel that this is but a melancholy result to have to report; and this sad account may, probably, not prove satisfactory to, or be concurred in by, those whose minds have been deceived, and their ardent imaginations carried away by exaggerated expectations, such as 'regeneration of the Empire', 'redemption of China', 'introduction of Christianity', and 'salvation of the people'. But to those who, like myself, were not influenced by these imaginary hopes, and who judged of Tae-pingdom in sober sense and dispassionately, the last three months' probation is by no means startling, the experiment having produced exactly what was expected—ruin, desolation, and the annihilation of every vital principle, in all that surrounds the presence, or lies under the bane, of the Tae-pings.

Your Excellency will doubtless have been prepared for this fruit, for the tree has never yielded many promises; still, painful as the experiment has proved so far, it will be a source of satisfaction at a future date to feel that at one of our Treaty ports the fullest freedom of action had been allowed to the Tae-pings in order to try the range of their mental powers, and the means of organization, and that in both those spheres their capacity failed signally. This result will be the best answer to those who now support the movement, and who will perhaps then admit their error. For my part, unlike many foreigners in China, I am far from condemning this party because most of its chiefs are not of high birth, and their education not on a level with Chinese literati generally. The history of the world's past ages shows that polities of durability have been founded by men not superior to the Tae-ping leaders in learning and acquirements; but I am forced to turn my face away from them simply because they must represent, to well-balanced minds, anarchy, confusion, and unproductiveness, the latter in its most comprehensive acceptation. It is palpable that a Party which, after ten years' full trial, is found to produce nothing, and to destroy everything, cannot pretend to last, or be admitted, even indirectly, into the comity of nations; and that, on the contrary, it deserves to bring upon itself the well-merited opprobrium of all the enlightened classes of society.

These may appear strong expressions, but it seems to me that the time has at length arrived when, to speak of the Tae-pings and to judge of their acts, the utmost freedom of opinion and of expression should be exercised by public functionaries in China; on that account, therefore, I consider I am only fulfilling a duty in passing my judgment, such as it is and whatever may be its worth, upon this extraordinary movement. I repeat I have no bias one way or another, and indeed I should state that personally I have received every mark of courtesy and proper regard from the Tae-ping Chiefs; and further, I have found in official dealings with them a rough and blunt sort of honesty quite unexpected and surprising, after years of public intercourse with the Imperial mandarins. Nevertheless, the Tae-pings with their frank demeanour and bluff energy have a fume of blood and a look of carnage about them, from which I, for one, recoil with horror.

With these prefatory remarks, I shall now reply, as well as I am able, to the several points mooted in your Excellency's despatch, and respecting which your Excellency is desirious of having my opinion. In doing so, I would respectfully remind your Excellency that the information required has been obtained with difficulty from the naturally-suspicious Tae-pings, who amongst other peculiarities possess a power of concealment and general secrecy quite wonderful to meet in China. I think, however, I may well rely on the correctness of the following statement:

The first point has reference to the payment of the Tae-ping troops. The insurgent soldiery do not, as an established rule, receive pay; they live, like pirates, on whatever they can obtain in the shape of booty, either in kind or specie. If the capture of a city has produced a rich harvest of plunder, the men benefit generally in the prize; if, on the contrary the town has yielded little profit, the Tae-pings wait for better days with exemplary patience. The neighbouring districts are then (and indeed in almost all instances) made to contribute to the support of the army. The country about Ningpo, for example, was compelled to remit its quota of tribute in the shape of rice, pigs, fowls, vegetables, and the like farm produce, to feed the troops. The peasants, forced to send in these supplies, were seen, by me, bringing provisions, &c., into the city, with chains and ropes round their necks, in token of servitude. That the Tae-ping soldiers live upon what they can get may be inferred clearly from the invariable answer made to me a dozen times, and which I remember was likewise given to Mr Consul Parkes in my presence. On questioning decently-dressed Tae-ping soldiers as to how they liked their profession, the reply has ever been the following: 'Why should I not like it? I help myself to everything I choose to lay my hands upon; and if interfered with, I just cut the man's head off who so interferes;' at the same time making a motion with his hand as if he were sawing off a head. This being an answer often heard, and the motion being a notorious one with the chiefs in the city, I submit both as apt illustrations of Tae-ping institutions, and of their reckless contempt for human life.

The Tae-pings possess a regular embodied force, a draft from which forms the nucleus of the body of men sent upon any special service or expedition, such nucleus being composed of old and well-tried rebels of several years' standing; and the remainder of the armed force in each case, being younger recruits, or peasants pressed into their service. The corps which attacked and captured Ningpo might have had one old rebel in ten in its formation, the veterans serving principally to keep in a proper state of submission the younger volunteers or pressed men, as well as to inspire courage to those who might recoil from their duty, such inspiration being particularly Tae-ping in its nature. Another peculiarity of the rebels is their habit of drafting from one province to another the inhabitants of conquered districts, the policy of which course being self-evident I need not enlarge upon it. I should imagine that at the present hour, in the city of Ningpo, more than twenty different dialects are spoken amongst the rebels—dialects pertaining to distant provinces and districts: in the same manner that I suppose the Ningpo dialect is now becoming familiar, hundreds of miles from this port, to ears that were never intended or expected to receive it. What prosperity can the most sanguine expect under such rule, when the men of the soil are driven into exile and misery, leaving behind them their homes in ruins, and their wretched families to die of starvation?

It is notorious that their forces are swelled considerably by all the bad characters of the districts they pass through, and who, being under no possible moral control (except so far as military obedience and a *pseudo* discipline are concerned), commit every excess known, and let me add, almost unknown to the human mind. These are delicate matters to allude to in a public despatch, but my meaning will be sufficiently clear when I state that the conduct of some of these monsters to women and young girls is such that no pen, however guarded, could convey an idea. In regard, therefore, to your Excellency's query as to their behaviour to the young women who fall in their hands, I have too good cause to know that it is horrible beyond belief or description. Your Excellency is doubtless aware that marriage is strictly forbidden amongst the Tae-pings, and forms, with opium-smoking, a capital offence; and if the latter habit or vice is often winked at, it would be next to impossible for an ordinary rebel to live with a wife, or a concubine. The standing orders are, that marriage will only be allowed when the Empire has been conquered; until which time, the penalty for marrying or cohabiting with a woman is death. As a compensation, however, and, I presume, as a reward for valour, it appears that in captured towns and cities, where the population have not had time to resort to flight, three whole days are given to the Tae-ping soldiers to do whatever they please—to commit every excess, and to perpetrate every abomination under the sun, after which not a single woman is permitted to remain in the city. I think these statements will suffice, and I need proceed no further upon this distressing topic.

Their great aim—I should say their chief condition of success—is to strike terror; first, by numbers, and secondly, by the tawdry harlequin garb worn by them, and which (however incredible it may seem) has such a strange effect on the minds of all classes of people in this country. Your Excellency will perceive, in this unaccountable effect, another instance of the perversion of thought, and of the opposite mode of analysing and accounting for causes and effects ruling the Chinese race, in contradistinction to Europeans. With us, the burlesque costume, and other ridiculous devices of the Tae-pings, would only tend to raise a smile; but I firmly believe that this dress, *per se*, has an effect the very reverse on the ignorant and somewhat primitive inhabitants of this country, and is half the battle with the rebels, as they well know. Their long, shaggy black hair again adds to the wildness of their look; and when this fantastical appearance is accompanied by a certain show of fury and madness, it is really little to be wondered at if the mild Chinese, constituted as we know them to be, either take to flight or submit tamely.

Able-bodied men, as stated above, are compelled to serve in their ranks, whatever may have been their previous calling in life; for after the loss of their property, some of them have no option left but to fight or starve. Sometimes, also, respectable denizens are under the absolute necessity of joining the Tae-ping flag; solely because they find that in conquered districts such a compromise is unavoidable, in order to save remnants of property, and very frequently to place their necks out of jeopardy. It is simply, in all instances, a forced subjection. I do not myself believe that the insurgents have had the voluntary allegiance of half-a-dozen respectable Chinese, since they first appeared at Nanking in 1853; I will even go further and express my conviction that not one single respectable Chinaman has ever gone over to the Tae-pings of his own free will and accord. How could this be possible? The respectable Chinese are an orderly, shrewd race of men, and they must feel, and are convinced, that prosperity, confidence, and a good name can never follow in the footsteps of brigandage, however extensive a scale upon which it may be carried on.

The military tactics of the Tae-pings are of the simplest, and the most primitive in their action; indeed, I doubt whether the word 'tactics' can in any way be applied to their uniform mode of warfare. Numbers, as I already remarked, are the first consideration with them; and these they pour into any given place, or upon any spot selected as a prize. Before the main bodies appear, however, spies and emissaries are sent secretly to feel the way, and to spread false reports; and in the midst of the panic and alarm caused by these reports and intrigues, the spies set fire, if they are able, to detached buildings, and often to entire streets, in and out of the city. Should these emissaries be seized and beheaded by the mandarins, others are deputed by the rebels to take their place, without delay, when similar manoeuvres are again commenced, until either the mandarins or the city population take to flight, or, as in the case of Ningpo, such thorough demoralization is created that the place falls an easy prey to the insurgents. Meanwhile, runaway villagers have not failed to rush in breathless, with exaggerated reports of the numbers and doings of the Tae-ping forces seen by them. In the confusion, a few rebels appear in the distance, their gaudy multi-coloured dress having its usual strange effect, and their melancholy shouts and yells striking terror in the hearts of the timid Chinese. If, then, the game has been so far successfully played out, and the coast appears pretty clear, very little remains to be done; hundreds and thousands of insurgents rush wildly on to the goal, armed with knives, spears, and fowling-pieces, carrying, of course, everything before them. It is then, and then only, that the Chiefs, or leaders, or Princes appear for the first time; for these are seldom or never heard of, nor is their immediate action seen, until the high road has been opened by the skirmishers, called in Shanghae marauders. The late events of that port show, I think, the correctness of the above account. In the repeated attacks upon Shanghae, the supposed marauders were, in accordance with the universal usage of the Taepings, thrown in detachments in advance, burning villages and creating panic, the Chiefs of course remaining behind, watching the result of the game; which there, I am happy to say, turned out, as we know, to have been a losing one, thanks to Sir James Hope and our volunteers. I think the Shanghae lesson will have a salutary effect on the Tae-pings, for they are in painful dread of hard blows, notwithstanding their spiritual origin and pretensions.

This despatch has already assumed such a length that I will not add to it accounts from Hang-chow, which I propose sending in a separate communication. Your Excellency's belief in the sufferings of the people in that city are fully borne out by facts. All the details which have reached me represent the misery experienced as truly heart-rending.

I would now, with due deference, close this despatch with a few observations on Tae-pingdom; and in so doing I feel that perhaps I am travelling beyond my legitimate functions as Consul, as your Excellency is alone, from your high position and experience, competent to deal with so grave and important a question. But the subject of the Tae-ping rebellion is now so much discussed, and lies under such serious consideration in London, Paris, and Peking, that I have, like other people, ventured to give my evidence in this case. I therefore rely on your Excellency's indulgence in excusing this intrusion, on the grounds of the peculiarly favourable position in which I have been placed during the last three months for arriving at not incorrect conclusions, and also because I was one of the first Europeans at Nanking in 1853, on board Her Majesty's ship 'Hermes', to come in contact with the Tae-pings, and to become acquainted with this extraordinary rebellion. These circumstances may perhaps be deemed by your Excellency to be sufficient titles to my free speaking.

I now, therefore, take the liberty of declaring, once for all (and for ten years I have firmly adhered to and been consistent in this opinion) that the Tae-ping rebellion is the greatest delusion as a political or popular movement, and the Tae-ping doctrines the most gigantic and blasphemous imposition as a creed, or ethics, that the world ever witnessed. I can find no parallels in past history to match the spiritual doctrines, and certainly no standard of comparison by which to measure the political aspect, of the rebellion. I look in vain in the darkest ages for a similar faction and upheaving of men: but there is nothing in past records so dark or so bad; such abominations committed under the name of religion; such mock-heroic buffoonery; such horrors accompanied by pantaloonery; and so much flimsy web worked in the midst of blood and highly tragical events. The ravings of John of Leyden and his impious Munster adventurers in 1534–36 are left far behind in the race of folly by the Tae-ping madmen.

The first impression of a sensible and reasoning Englishman, on coming in contact with Tae-pingdom, is one of horror, then of amazement, with contempt and disgust following each other in succession. Tae-pingdom is a huge mass of 'nothingness' (I can find no other word to express my meaning); there is nothing to lay hold of in it. It is a gigantic bubble, that collapses on being touched, but leaves a mark of blood on the finger. In its ten years rampant carousing, what has it ever accomplished? Nothing. Has it obtained the least respect or popular sympathy, or even the apathetic toleration of the people? Who will presume to reply in the affirmative? Is it a popular movement for the purpose of shaking off a heavy yoke, or is it a sanguinary raid, and an extended brigandage over the country, burning, destroying, and killing everything that has life in it? The answer, alas! is but too obvious. Does it foster or even encourage commerce, or are its declared principles inimical to trading in any shape? Let the published experiences of the Rev. Mr Roberts, and of others upon this point, serve as a guide to merchants in England. And further, it must not be supposed that there is any peculiar gallantry in the Tae-pings: They are decidedly cowards, and I would not have them enlist unjustly the sympathies of the people at home, on the false assumption of bravery; for it is no proof of courage to strike an enemy when he is down, to torture women and children to death (such tortures!), and to burn alive poor creatures who refused to submit, as I have myself witnessed. The Tae-pings, I venture to affirm, have never been known to face a well-determined resistance, either native or foreign; and I say so, in spite of the objection which might be made, as evidenced by the hordes that the rebel Chiefs near Shanghae lately threw upon us, those hordes being compelled, on pain of death, so to advance.

To conclude, Tae-pingdom is a scourge; and if it has travelled unchecked through provinces and districts, both plague and pestilence have often done as much. Not unlike those dire visitations, the Tae-pings traverse the country. They come, and the helpless inhabitants crouch down and submit. They go, and the people breathe again and rejoice, making good the havoc and losses caused by the visit of this terrible enemy.

Your Excellency may rest assured that we shall only arrive at a correct appreciation of this movement, and do it thorough justice, when it is treated by us as land piracy on an extensive scale—piracy odious in the eyes of all men—and, as such, to be swept off the face of the earth by every means within the power of the Christian and civilized nations trading with this vast Empire.

Section 5 The Mercenary Experience (1861–4)

The involvement of some individual Westerners in the actual fighting between Taiping and Imperialists began at least as early as the mid fifties (Docs. 25, 38, 41), but it was only after the opening of the Yangtze to foreign trade in 1861 that this became a marked feature of the struggle. Westerners fought on both sides. One of the most important mercenaries was the American Frederick Townsend Ward, who created the mixed Sino-European force known as the Ever Victorious Army which fought against the Taiping in campaigns around Shanghai. The command of this force was to pass, in March 1863, to Major Charles Gordon, released temporarily from the British army for the purpose. Whether or not Gordon and the few other British officers who joined him should be classified as mercenaries in quite the same sense as Ward may be left an open question, but it seems appropriate to include at least one document representative of the Western experience of fighting against the Taiping (Doc. 88).

On the Taiping side many of the Western mercenaries were not very articulate nor particularly concerned to assess the movement for which they fought. The minutiae of their personal campaign experience is what comes through strongest in such records as they left behind (Docs. 91, 92), and their conditions were clearly sometimes very miserable (Doc. 87). Some, like the American adventurer Burgevine, might defect in classic mercenary style from one side to the other (Doc. 89), but others appear to have become involved as much by mischance as by deliberate choice (Doc. 92). Either way some of them clearly became attached to the Taiping and were ready to speak out in their defence (Doc. 90), and, in many cases, to die fighting for their cause.

The most committed and articulate mercenary on the Taiping side—so committed in fact that it seems inappropriate to classify him in this way—was of course A. F. Lindley, who published in 1866 a long and passionate account of his experiences, which was at the same time a defence of the movement and a critique of British policy toward it. (Doc. 93). He was associated mainly if not exclusively with the forces of the Chung Wang, probably the most generally capable of the Taiping leaders, and this helps explain the glowing terms in which Lindley wrote of the movement as a whole. His account must be taken seriously, but whether it counterbalances convincingly the weight of the other Western accounts and opinion represented in this collection is for the reader to judge.

87
A Report by R J Forrest
BPP, C 2976, pp. 41–2

Centaur, Nanking, April 20, 1861

Sir,

I HAVE the honour to report the capture of twenty-six foreigners, supposed to be British subjects, five of them deserters from Her Majesty's ships, outside the city of Nanking on the 18th instant. These men formed portion of a body of 104 foreigners of all nations engaged by the Tae-ping chiefs for warlike purposes.

The circumstances of the capture are as follows: Captain Aplin, R.N., senior naval officer, having received instructions from Admiral Hope to demand from the Tae-pings the surrender of all British subjects in their employ, requested me to wait on the chiefs and demand of them that proper measures should at once be taken to effect the object.

It was Captain Aplin's intention to have gone to Soo-chow, where he believed the men to be living, and he had been promised an escort, and proper orders to the officials to parade all foreigners before him, and hand over such as he should demand. It was quite by accident that the discovery was made of the existence, outside the city, of the very men we wanted. The authorities had most carefully concealed the fact, intending, no doubt, to send them away while we were at Soo-chow. Time after time the assurance was given that the authorities were entirely ignorant of such a practice as foreign enlistment, and did not know that any foreigners had been hired to fight for them.

On the urgent demand of Captain Aplin the whole of the men were collected in one large house, and the supposed British subjects formally handed over by an official of rank to an armed party from Her Majesty's ship, 'Centaur' on the 18th instant.

I am happy to inform your Excellency that the measures taken by Captain Aplin this matter have destroyed the foreign corps in the service of the Tae-pings, for such is the fear among them that each country will take similar steps, that the whole of the mercenaries are to be sent at once to Shanghae, and the Chiefs ordered to discontinue the practice of hiring them.

The men were in a most miserable condition, getting no pay, but plenty of rice and spirits. They were allowed to plunder wherever they went, but seem to have had little success. They made no secret of such crimes as rape and robbery, and even hinted at darker deeds. Most of them had been present at a fight near Sung-keang, where their leader, named Savage, was wounded, and an Italian killed. An American named Peacock, at present living in Soo-chow, is Captain over all; he is of high rank among the Tae-pings, and has the power of life and death. The men say they were on their way to Hankow, under what commander they knew not. One is dying of dysentery on board the 'Centaur', and another was murdered by an Italian and thrown into the city moat. The gun-boat 'Bouncer' takes the men to Shanghae to-day for trial.[40]

I have, &c.

(Signed) R J Forrest.

88
Letters from Lt T Lyster
T. Lyster, *With Gordon in China* (London, 1891),
pp. 84–5, 103–6, 114–16

1   SHANGHAI.

My dearest Mother,

I arrived here all right on the 25th inst., [August 1862] after a pleasant passage from Hong Kong . . . If I had been here a week sooner I should have been sent 700 miles further north, to

40 The men were sent to Hong Kong for trial but the Attorney General there ruled that there was no case for them to answer under the British Foreign Enlistment Act. Nine men subsequently sentenced to nine months imprisonment under a Hong Kong Neutrality Ordinance of 1855 for fighting on the side of the Imperialists claimed remission of sentence on the grounds that these men had been released—see Bruce to Russell, 1 October 1861 in FO 17/355, no. 133.

Tientsin, to look after important work there; but as it was urgent, another fellow has been sent. There is another Engineer Officer here, Captain Gordon; he is a first-rate fellow, and a very good officer. He and I live together. I was very lucky in getting such good quarters, and, as the house has been given to Gordon by some civilians (he has done so much for the settlement), there is nothing to pay.

This is an immense place. There is a Chinese town surrounded by a large ditch and high wall, and then there are the European settlements. We had no troops here a short time ago, but the Taipings came down in such numbers, the authorities were obliged to send a military force to protect the inhabitants.

I suppose you know all about the Taipings. They number about 100,000, and are nothing but a band of marauders. They come down on a village, rob it, slay all the inhabitants they can lay hold of, and then burn the place. We could see the smoke from the burning villages as soon as we got into the harbour on Sunday. When I got on shore I heard that the rebels were close to an advanced post of two companies of the 31st Regiment, stationed at Fah-wa, about five miles from here. They sent out a reinforcement of one hundred men in case the post should be attacked. I borrowed a horse and went with them. I never saw, or could have imagined, such a sight as I saw on the way. The road was covered with unfortunate creatures, who had been driven out of their homes by the Taipings. The poor women were in a most fearful state; there were numbers of them lying by the side of the road, some dead, and others dying from starvation and exhaustion. I was horrified then, but have become used to it now, as it is an every-day occurrence. I scarcely ever go into the country without seeing some poor people dead or dying.

When I got out to the post the rebels had retreated about four miles, and were amusing themselves burning villages in their usual style.

On the morning of the 27th, as the rebels were coming quite close to the town, another expedition went out to meet them. Gordon and I went with twenty-five sappers up a creek, in the hope of gaining possession of a bridge six miles off, in order to cut off their retreat. The remainder of the troops went by a different route to try to take them by surprise, but the expedition was a failure, as it is impossible to get near the rebels unless you surround them.

2   SHANGHAI, October 25, 1862.
My Dearest Mother,

I write you a line to say that I have just returned from Kahding, and am all right, wind and limb.

I left here on Tuesday, 22nd of October, to repair bridges, &c., along the route the troops would take the following day. I arrived in Naitzean, a town half way between Shanghai and Kahding, at 3 a.m. (Naitzean was for some time in the possession of the rebels, and is now in ruins).

I started on Wednesday morning at five o'clock, and prepared the remainder of the bridges. On Tuesday, 23rd inst., the troops moved from Naitzean to a village about a mile from Kahding. We then got our boats with the scaling ladders and bridges up to within 200 yards of the wall. The rebels fired a good deal that day; they wounded an officer of the 31st Regiment and some Chinese soldiers.

On Thursday night we got the guns into position; there were about twenty-seven guns, including French and Ward's Chinese troops. We returned no shots on Thursday, but on Friday morning we opened fire from all the batteries at daylight. It was a grand sight to see the shells breaking down the wall and look-out places. I, with a naval officer, had charge of the boats in which were the ladders and bridges. When the cannonading had gone on for about an hour and a half, we got the boats up the creek which ran towards the wall, dividing to the right and left of it. We went down about 250 yards to the right, to where we thought there was a good place to make the bridge. We formed the bridge in a very short space of time, and then the storming party, got across, and had no trouble in getting into the town, there being only a palisading to clear away. The rebels fired only two or three shots at us as we brought up the boats. I got two men to hand me rifles, and the moment I saw a fellow looking over, or through the wall, in order to fire, I let fly at him. You must not think it boasting if I say I was well up to the front; but these Taipings are such a despicable lot, there is no credit in beating them. They made no resistance after we got in; we might shoot them like dogs. When I got over the wall I found a lot of them within a few yards of me; I sent a shot amongst them, and told them to 'wilo,'[41] which means 'hook it.' They all took to their heels, and I bolted after them as hard as I could go, but I had to wait in the middle of the place till a soldier of the 67th and two of Ward's officers came up. We then went on together and took about twenty prisoners. We were very near being cut off and surrounded, but we hooked behind a house and waited till the main body came up. I saved as many poor wretches as I could. Ward's men wanted to shoot them right and left, but I objected. I was obliged to hit a couple of fellows; one had a spear,

41   Possibly *hui-lo*—come back!

and, as I wanted to pass him to get to another—a swell in a green jacket (the mandarins wear green), who was running like fury—I was obliged to pepper him in the hams before he dropped the weapon. I am happy to say I did not kill one of them, and tried to save a good many. I told them to 'hook it,' as I knew the Chinese troops which were coming after us would kill them without mercy. I pitied the poor women toddling away on their little feet. A soldier near me fired into a crowd of men, women, and children, and killed a nicely-dressed woman. I would not let him fire again, except at single individuals.

When I got to the other side of the town I found a great number jumping over the wall and swimming across the creek; many of them had their legs broken, and some women were drowning. The beasts never help each other. I met the Chinese troops coming in as I went out, looting the place all over. I did not go into a house to get anything, and the only memento I possess of the place is a pony, whose owner I put to flight. I got pony, saddle, sword, and pipe complete. He is a very fine pony; I rode him into Shanghai today. I might have taken five or six ponies, and no end of donkeys, but I only wanted one. The French, as usual, took everything they could get. People at home think looting is wrong, but, though I did not loot myself, I do not consider it wrong with these people. They run away, leaving everything they possess; they are rebels; and why should not we have their goods as well as the French or Chinese? I saw some of them even take off their clothes in order to swim the creek and get quickly away.

The mail closes at once—so good-bye.

3   December 20, 1862.
To his brother P.

I was staying in a Chinese city a week ago, and inside the wall (four miles in circumference) there were pheasants, wild duck, and snipe! It is the grandest shooting country I know. You can get to any place in boats, and make yourself quite comfortable, shoot all day, and sleep in the boat at night. The merchants here do not shoot much, as they are not sportsmen, and are only keen on the dollar!

Just now we are driving the rebels outside the bounds, namely, thirty miles round Shanghai. There is talk of taking Nankin from the rebels. The English troops will not be allowed to go against it, but some English officers may be allowed to direct the operations. If so, the place will probably be taken; if not, there is not much chance of it, as the drilled Chinese are officered by civilians, sailors, and private soldiers discharged from our service, *not one* of whom could direct any operations. I will do my best to go. It would be a grand thing if I were the only English officer, and we succeeded. But I think it is very likely that Captain Gordon, R.E., will go. If he does, they have the best man in China to show them the way.

4   27 December 1862.
To his mother,
. . . Our operations against the rebels are over for some time, at least. We have cleared the country for the specified distance round Shanghai (thirty miles). I am still employed surveying it. There was nothing known of it before, not even the existence of large towns. The rebels can return at any time, as the towns are only garrisoned by Imperial troops; but I expect when they find we do not interfere with them as long as they keep clear of the thirty miles radius, they will have sense enough not to come closer . . .

89
A Letter from H A Burgevine
Gordon Papers, British Museum MS 52386, Fols. 83–6

Thanks for your kind letter and expressions of regard. The step I have taken was after due deliberation, and was *not* to avenge any injuries inflicted upon me by the Imperialists. I have the same object in view now that I have had for the last three years, and I assure you that no selfish considerations have induced me into the serious step I have taken . . .[42]

I am perfectly aware from nearly four years of service in this country that both sides are equally rotten. But you must confess that on the Taeping side there is at least innovation, and a disregard for many of the frivolous and idolatrous customs of the Manchus. While my eyes are fully open to the defects of Taeping character, from a close observation of three months I find many promising traits never yet displayed by the Imperialists. The rebel mandarins are *without* exception brave and gallant men, and could you see Chung Wang, who is now here, you would immediately say that such a man deserved to succeed. Between him and the Footai,[43] or Prince Kung, or any other Manchu officer, there is no comparison. . . .

42   For another statement by Burgevine on his defection see *North China Herald*, 24 October 1863.
43   I.e. Li Hung-chang, Governor of Kiangsu.

90
Draft of a Letter to *The Friend of China* by George Smith
In the Taiping Museum, Nanking

Sir,

We, the undersigned Twenty Europeans, real (though perhaps personally unkown) Friends of China, request you to publish this communication from true friends of China—twenty Europeans who are at present in Soo Chow and fully determined to defend to the uttermost the cause we have espoused. We came here under the command of Gen. Burgevine, and when and wherever we have met the Imperials we have beaten them which publish what they may they well know. Moreton betrayed us and took half our men over to the Imperials leaving the sick and wounded in Suchow. Had Mo Wang the Governor of Su Chow been a vindictive man he would no doubt (which he easily could) use all his vengeance on the remainder of us. But mark his action in this matter. He assembled the Europeans, asked if any more wished to go to Shanghai, if so he would readily give them a pass—and said he was glad that that Moreton, the infamous traitor had left and taken all the disaffected with him.[44] Even then he insisted that the severely wounded men should get European medical attendance and sent them where it could be obtained, Gen. Burgevine giving security for their proper reception. The wounded accordingly left in two boats which M. Wang passported and we hope the poor fellows are convalescent if not well by this time. We who remain are under the command of a certain Captain of whose ability Gordon and the Hyson can give the best account.

On our Captain assuring M. Wang that we remained voluntarily to fight for the Rebels and dethrone the Mantchou [illegible—Emperor?] he gave some order to one of his boys and told us he was glad to prove that so many of us were faithful in the midst of such base desertion.

We have just heard that Waters the traitor and Dominick Lynch a true man with many others have been beheaded by the Futai. Now for a contrast. Three Frenchmen joined us from Gordon's army. M. Wong recd. them kindly, brought them to Gen. Burgevine who enrolled with his command and treated them well.

These Sir are indisputable facts and surely facts will outweigh vague assertions.

---

44 For statements by these defectors from the Taiping cause see *North China Herald*, 24 October 1863.

M. Wong appreciates Europeans and shows his good sense by adopting their suggestions whenever their intelligence is brought in play.

We hope that this our statement will controvert the base slander of the Footai's sycophants. Yesterday we the Europeans made a rush on the r.f. of the imperial force and after *a few vollies* and *a little firefiring* we secured 6 prisoners and found 4, 1 wounded besides, all Chinese. The Imperials however managed to carry off the remainder of their wounded.

The boy he had just sent away returned with two carts loaded which he divided among us as cumsha.[45]

91
Diary of George Smith at Soochow
In the Taiping Museum, Nanking

Oct. 16	I I agree with Mou Wong to remain having under my command Europeans II He agrees to pay $40 per month III The sick and wounded leave (also the well men who are disaffected) IV Recd. $400 for distribution to the men V Burgevine is recalled by order of M. Wong
Oct. 17	Nothing of importance
Oct. 18	General Burgevine leaves for Shanghai
Oct. 19	Went out to the East Gate Stockade with Lee Wong and fired three shells. Only one exploded.
Oct. 20	Attacked by Diarrhoea
Oct. 21	Still the Diarrhoea
Oct. 22	Nothing of importance
Oct. 23	Nothing important
Oct. 24	Firing at the South Gate
Oct. 25	Captain Smith issues orders and arms and ammunition to each man II Chon Wong arrives and we have lost 3 stockades today

45 This is the end of the draft, which has no date nor any signatures on it, but Smith's Diary (Doc. 91) indicates that he wrote it on 4 November 1863. The Diary consists of fourteen small sheets of grubby white paper roughly pasted and sewn together and the draft of the letter of two separate sheets. We are indebted to Dr C. Curwen for drawing our attention to these documents which, he advises us, are now in the Taiping Museum, Nanking. Smith was apparently a deserter from the Royal Navy who had commanded Burgevine's artillery and took over command of the European force in Soochow after the American's departure. He was killed in fighting elsewhere in February 1864.

Oct. 26   Monday. M. Wong goes out, and my men are making cartridges and filling shells.

Oct. 27   M. Wong out again. The imperialists retire. Europeans making cartridges. Speak to M. Wong about allowing Louis to leave on acct. of his sickness. He consents and Louis and the Interpreter leave for the enemies' lines with the understanding that Porter returns tomorrow.

Oct. 28   M. Wong outside and Interpreter has not returned.

29   Went to see M. Wong at the South Gate. Had some Rifle and Revolver target practice with him.

Oct. 30   Walked to the East Gate and Stockade to see M. Wong. He agrees to mount a 24 pdr. and take the Imperial Stockade across the Creek.

31   Went out to the East Stockade taking 6 men along and fired 4 shells—2 burst splendidly among the hostile boats and 2 burst short owing to the shells being flawed.

1 November   Went to the South Gate to see M. Wong and advised him to look out that Gordon did not cut off our communication between Nanshing and Yuza. From Gordon's demonstrations I suspect and have suspected for the last fortnight that the interception of our communication is his primary object. However M. Wong appeared to be satisfied with strengthening the S. and E. gate.

2nd   Called out by M. Wong as the Imperials are advancing. Arrive at the E. gate and find they are extending their right flank and threatening the Nanshing route. Cross the Creek and under cover of some old walls picked off 10 or 12 youpings.[46] By this time our ammunition was nearly exhausted and we had to retire and ford the creek the sampam having left. Started immediately to assist M. Wong but met him retreating as some of the Imperials were threatening to intercept him. Just as well. We had only two rounds per man and could not hold our ground long. M. Wong promises to have one 32 and one 24 pdrs. guns ready for us in the morning to drive them back. The enemy has luted [sic] the village above the N.

46   Probably yu-ping, meaning straggler, an unattached or roaming soldier.

stockade in the direction of the lake. We entered the city for the night. Eleven shells were picked up outside today. We shall return them to Gordon with interest.

Nov. 4   Mo Wong sent for me and informed me that from one of his Shanghai spies who was present he ascertained that the Gen. (Burgevine) Maj. Waters, D. Lynch, Porter Ah Sing and five others were docked by the Footai. He asked me to write to Shanghai and I accordingly wrote to the 'Friend of China' stating facts and also to Butler requesting him to renew his intercourse with us. In the evening I had the letter interpreted to M. Wong and he was very well pleased with its contents.

Nov. 5   Can hear the heavy guns to the Northward. They appear to be very far off.

Nov. 6   Nothing important

Nov. 7   do

Nov. 8 9   do

Nov. 10   Alick and Williams start for Shanghai at 9 pm.

Nov. 11   Nothing important

Nov. 12   do

Nov. 13   Received 18 coats and issued them to the men.

Nov. 14   Nothing important outside. Labourix arrives with 5 more men increasing our force to 25.

Nov. 15   We have received $340 to pay up the men.

Nov. 16   Paid the men

Nov. 17   Nothing important

Nov. 18   do

Nov. 19   do

Nov. 20   Radinov and his party go outside to have a look around. They have returned and ne plus [?]

Nov. 21   I go with all the Europeans sending Radinov [?] in advance with 12 men. We arrive. The boat (gun) is not ready. Rad. proposes to advance with his party and take Firefly Steamer and all the Chinese around her. I object and Mo Wong wont hear of the affair. We return and Mo Wong also for the night.

Nov. 22	Go out at 11 Pm East gate.
Nov. 23	Return at 12 m.
Nov. 24	Went out joined Mo Wong'g bodyguard, took two stockades and beat both the Imperial steamer leaving our 24 Pounder ashore as we could not pass up the Creek owing to its being blocked. The axle bands broke and we had to return. Mo Wong is highly pleased.
Nov. 25	Making cartridges etc.
Nov. 26	Presented a plan of a side paddle Boat, worked by Chinamen, for the 32 Pdr. Mo Wong likes the idea much and orders it be made.
Nov. 27	The Boat is measured and the arrangement under weigh. At 11½ PM we are summoned by M. Wong to the East Gate and find a steamer and 6 G. Boats assailing our stockades. As we advance Labourix is mortally wounded and taken to Soochow. We arrive at the Stockade and find Rocket, Mortar, Shell Round + Rifle & musketry pouring fast upon us. We beat back the boats which were outflanking our stockades abreast the Embankment and hold them with little loss to us till morning of the [?]
Nov. 28	(Peter wounded in the face). When the fog cleared away we expected an advance on the part of the Imperials. However our steady fire scared them and they retired in a body. We re-entered Soo Chow. Alick and Williams return without being able to reach Shanghai owing to want of funds at 1 P.M. We start to assist in defence of the South Gate Breast work but finally from the continuous fire of the last business and the large number of gun boats assailing us we are obliged to abandon the embankment under heavy fire and reach the city with no loss to Europeans.
Nov. 29	Leave for the S.W. Gate but are kept inactive by M. Wong who wishes us near his own person. Chon Wong charges the Imperials who are in immense force and is repulsed. He returns for his Body guard and beats back the Imperials. We return to the city at 6 P.M.

92
Statement of Patrick Nellis
FO17/411, enc. in Bruce to Russell 9 December 1864; also in
North China Herald, 12 November 1864[47]

Patrick Nellis was 12 years in the Royal Engineers, and came to
this country with Captain Osborne. He served after the break up
of that Flotilla with Quinsan Artillery, but was not required after
the fall of Soochow. Whilst in the Army, his character was good,
and he was well conducted whilst in the Quinsan Force; his statement is as follows:
I left Shanghai, 25 February, 1864, with a Cantonese going up to
buy silk, being engaged at $200 a trip as a guard to the Boat. The
destination was Chanza, a village on the canal leading from
Pingwang to Wu-chow-foo. We found that the Rebels had moved
out and surprised the place two days previously. The Cantonese
went on shore to make enquiries, and never came back. Soon
after, the Rebels came down and took me and the crew prisoners.
They placed a chain round my neck and threatened to cut my
head. I was brought before the chief. A Ningpo man who could
speak English told me to say that I knew how to fire guns, which,
being translated to the Chief, he asked me to stay with him. I,
having no alternative, said yes. I was then sent on to Wu-chow-foo
and well treated on the way, provisions being plenty from the loot
of Chanza. At Woo-chow-foo I was brought before the Tow Wang
(the Yellow Tiger), commander of the city, who was much pleased
at my capture. He laughingly asked me what I had been doing at
Chanza. I told him I had come up to buy silk. He looked as if he
disbelieved it, and said, 'You all say that'. A rifle was produced
and I was asked if I understood it. I said yes and was taken out to
fire at a magpie; having struck the tile the bird was on, Tow Wong
told me that if I liked to stop, I should command all the foreigners
in the place, whom I heard of now for the first time. These having
accepted me as their commander, the chain was taken off my neck
and I was given quarters with them, near the Tow Wong's
quarters, at the North Gate.
The names of the men were:
English: Conroy Dillon
Austrian: Raffaelli, Giovan
French: Pasquali
Greeks & Ionians: Demetrius Anasthasius Palasiostrolis
Demetrius Crolis Antonio Veanisius

47 There is a similar statement by Mark Conroy in the same issue of the *North
China Herald* and E. A. Wilson, *The Ever Victorious Army* (London, 1868), pp.
393–4, also prints a statement by Baffey.

They were seafaring men, and were glad to get a soldier to command them. They had come from Ningpo and Soochow and from the silk boats. Tow Wong asked me if there were any Yang Quitzers fighting with the Imperialists against them. I say no, that they had been withdrawn. He agreed to give me 4000 cash a day for the men. He gave me a mule and we were used as a sort of body guard. I had to drill the foreigners. The Imperialists began to advance in July against the city from Chang shing. I went out with Tow Wong against them. We met them 40 li from the city, and Tow Wong divided his men into two bodies. The right body under a Kim Wong was to outflank the Imperialists, whilst Tow Wong retired in front of them. The manoeuvre succeeded; the Imperialists rushed on after Tow Wong who retired and then turned at them while Kim Wong took them in flank and drove them back. About 150 Imperialists were killed; no quarter being given. Tow Wong pushed on till he came in sight of the Imperialist stockades, situated on small hills. We got round them, and being out of fire from the stockades under the brows of the hills, threatened their rear, which, being seen by the Imperialists, made them run, leaving everything standing in their camps, five of which were taken with some boats. Tow Wong afterwards went back to the city. He dressed in very common clothes when going out to fight. His body guards of young men were all armed with revolvers and breech loading rifles, and in fact there were plenty of arms of all sorts with the Rebels, some of evidently recent purchase. Tow Wong was very daring. He led his men himself, and made them fight desperately. He was a tall fine-looking man, at first inclined to be corpulent, but after a time, thro' excessive fatigue and exertion, he became thin. He scarcely slept 2 hours in the 24; was always about and very much feared by the Rebels. Death was the punishment of any who shewed cowardice when he commanded. The garrison may have been 50,000 or more.

On our return to Wu-chow-foo, Kang Wong arrived from Nankin with an escort. Great ceremony was shewn at his reception; he did not look as if he had suffered any hardship. The Rebels said nothing about Nankin, and in fact all conversation of that sort was most dangerous, for the small boys in the service of the Wong's, were nothing but spies, and any talk of this sort was certain death. The villages in the immediate neighbourhood of Wu-chow, and the suburbs, were mostly in ruins, and existed in a starving half-squalid state. Within the city there were provision shops up to the last, which received a sort of protection, but there was no other kind of business carried on. The city was in a state of filth, no measures being taken to cleanse it. Bodies were never burnt. Houses were pulled down for firewood; the place was very unhealthy from all these causes. Itch, sores and ulcers were common to everyone. All offences received one punishment—death. I saw 160 men beheaded for absence from duty. 2 boys were beheaded for smoking, there being orders against use of opium and tobacco. All prisoners of war were beheaded. Spies or people accused of being such were tied with their hands behind their backs to a stake and brushwood being put around them, they were burnt to death. I saw six such cases at different times so treated. In spite of the orders against smoking, the chiefs were inveterate smokers.

About a week after our return to the city, Tow Wong ordered us to accompany him to the east of the city. We went in small quick boats. We drove back the Imperialists who were attacking the Stockades at Suizu with a large number of gunboats and a steamer, when Tow Wong saw the steamer, he said I had deceived him, and that Foreigners were fighting against them, and instead of 4000 cash a day, we should only have 1000. From Suizu we went down to Tungpoo [?], where an Imperial Force had advanced. We had a great deal of fighting here. The Rebels had got a Force of Imperialists surrounded and were keeping the others from helping them. Tow Wong had not many gunboats and the Imperialists had plenty. He drilled his small boats in the lake and taught them when to advance and retire. He then sent one of them to go and fire at the Imperial gunboats, while he landed some Rebels on a bank in secret. The Imperial gunboats came out against the small boat which retired. The gunboats pursued when Tow Wong ordered the other small boats to advance. They dashed forward and the party on the bank fired on the gunboats, whose crews deserted them. We pushed on, and came close up to the Stockades, capturing a boat with a 12 pr. English Howitzer V.R. and some six boxes of shell, etc. The Frenchman whom I have seen before, fired two rounds and then jumped overboard. Tow Wong gave the gun over to me with another 12 pr. iron gun. Some 30 or 40 gunboats were taken from the Imperialists. We had many rencontres with them and with the French Force with varied success. The Imperialists had their breastworks on the opposite side of the creek to ours; they tried to cross but were driven back. All the Imperial soldiers belonging to the Mandarin who was surrounded, were beheaded, cut down, and driven into the creeks. One of the men, Demetrius, was killed in a fight, and the Frenchman, Pasquali, died of sunstroke. Two other Frenchmen, came up with arms. They had been told that if they did not bring better arms they would lose their heads next time. They did not bring better arms, but were allowed to go back. I heard that they were waylaid and killed afterwards. When we went back to the city, Tow Wong and Kan Wong assembled all the men in a square, mounted a sort of scaffold made of tables. Tow Wong addressed them first. He mentioned the words, Soochow, Quinsan, Kashingfoo, Hangchow, Kiangsi, and Yang Quitzer very frequently. I understood enough of what he said to make out that he was mentioning the places the Rebels had lost, and in alluding to the Yang Quitzers, referred to their present situation. Kang Wong then addressed them in the same strain. This lasted 2 or 3 hours. While it was going on, some of the soldiers commenced firing off their muskets. Tow Wong ordered silence, but another report was heard. He ordered up the offender, who was a clean looking boy, 15 years old. He was made to kneel down, but Kan Wang begged his life. Tow Wong, however, saw 2 or 3 rebels playing with their spears at some distance, and saying it was no use, ordered his officer to go down and 'cut'. The officer returned in a very short time with two heads which were laid down in front of the Wongs. Kan Wong, in coming down from the tables, spoke to me in English, very slow. He asked me what I was. I said, an Englishman. He said he had never met a good foreigner and asked me if I would go with him to Kiangsi. I said I should be very glad if Tow Wong would let me. He said he would see about it. I did not see him again. I think he left with some men soon after. Shortly after, I was ordered to go to the N.W. side of the city against the Imperialists who were advancing. I went out and found they had placed one of their stockades within 200 yds of the Rebel Stockades. I was ordered with my men, to put my gun in the Rebel Stockade, which I did after making good the parapet. I fired on the Imperialists, but they opened such a fire of shell on my gun, as to cause great loss to the Rebels, who were butted in rear of the gun. About a day or two after, the Imperialists assaulted at 4 p.m. They were bothered with the ditches, and were repulsed. Several Rebels were beheaded for running away. A shot struck my gun on the trunnion and disabled it and one of my men Demetrius Coolis was wounded severely. The Chief of the Stockade told me that I had better go away, as he was afraid that they would lose the stockades, and that if they did and the gun was taken, they would get into trouble with Tow Wong. I therefore went back to Wu-chow-foo with the boat and gun. The 1000 cash per diem had been discontinued and we were told to subsist ourselves. There was now some distress in the city, and we saw signs of evacuation. Rice being sent out to a place 40 li off towards the north. On the 24th August, a Rebel chief came to me and said it was likely that they would move and that we had better get ready. I asked him what he would do about the wounded man. He said he could do nothing, but that he must go with us. We had several meetings on this subject. I feared that one or two of the men would escape and sacrifice us. They all agreed not to attempt it, except in a body. It was now evident the city was to be vacated, as the shops were shut, and the shopkeepers and their goods embarked and shut into a small lake 50 li to the N.W. of the city. On the night of the 26th August, the headman came and told us that the start would be made at daylight the next day. Our idea was to escape during the confusion, but the wounded man was our drawback. At 12 midnight we tried to get him into the boat, but were met by Tow Wong himself at the N. Gate, who was furious and ordered us back at the peril of our lives. We went back and waited until 2 a.m. 28th Augt: When we were ordered to take down the wounded man to the boat. At this time signal lights were hoisted to the outposts to retire. Men were patrolling the streets to cut down any who might try to escape. That evening we saw fearful sights. The Rebels were embarking their wounded and could not take all. The women were crowding down into their boats, but were cut at and driven back by the Rebels. We left the city which was empty at 3 a.m. and soon saw it in a blaze. It rained however, heavily. We pushed on, and passing through the lake came to the entrance of the creek. Here the most fearful confusion existed. All the boats were yulowing [?] on and jamming one another. The rebels were marching along the bank. Here we halted the night. The next day the confusion still continued, and we could not advance. Six of the men, viz. the two Englishmen, the two Austrians, two of the Greeks here left me for the ostensible purpose of getting firewood. They never came back. With me were the two remaining Greeks, the interpreter and the wounded man. The Rebels resumed their march at daybreak, but they soon began to be apparently hurried, and one of them called out that the Imperialists were advancing. The wounded man was our great trouble. Nothing further could be done for him, and it was certain death to remain. I took leave of him and told him I could do no more, as we could not carry him. He begged me to shoot him, and offered his ring and money. I said I could not do it, but that he could ask his own two countrymen. They refused and we left him in the boat. The Rebels were now in confusion, running everywhere. The Imperialists were close at hand. We landed and took to the Hills, and after wandering about two or three days got a boat, and with some difficulty got down to Shanghai. Tien Wong's son was not in the city and I never heard of him.

93
Observations by A F Lindley
A F Lindley (Lin-le), *The Ti-Ping Tien-Kwoh: a History of the Tiping Revolution* (London, 1866), pp. 248–51, 300–3, 306–9, 317–18, 362–3

Much has been stated about the desolating and ruthless character of the Ti-pings, but I entirely deny the accusation. I have been on many a long march with them and have never found them act with the barbarity that marked the late American war, or commit the atrocities perpetrated in Poland and Circassia, or act as Englishmen have done to the unfortunate natives of New Zealand. The Ti-pings never committed wanton devastation, never destroyed crops of standing corn, as has been done by civilized troops in New Zealand, in Algeria, and in the Shenandoah Valley.

The perfect organization of the Ti-ping armies contrasted favourably with that of the Imperialists. The former, unpaid and voluntary, observed strict discipline; the latter, receiving hire, constantly mutinied; all military crimes, especially those of ill-using the villagers and opium-smoking, were promptly and severely punished. Outrages, no doubt, were committed by the Ti-ping forces, but, if so, it was by those raw recruits who neither understood nor cared for the Ti-ping cause. The great body of the army observed a moderation unknown to the Imperialists; were it otherwise, instant execution was sure to follow. If a village was invested, its inhabitants might command security by tendering allegiance and conforming to the customs of the conquerors. If a village was merely passed by, a moderate contribution was required. There may have been, particularly in latter years, exceptions to this course, but it was none the less the fundamental rule which guided the operations of the Ti-ping armies. If they occupied a district for any length of time, peace and contentment reigned there; it was only when they rested but for a short period, and were followed by the Imperialists, or, perhaps by hordes of local banditti and straggling bands of camp followers, that the country was desolated. Such was my experience. Each Ti-ping Wang or Prince has under his special control 100,000 people, including one army. Between the Wangs and generals of armies come nine descriptions of officers, ranking as ministers, and other great officers in charge of civil and military departments of state. The military organization and all the titles, are those used previous to the conquest of China by the Manchoo Tartars. Each Ti-ping army, or keun, is composed of 13,125 officers and men, under the command of a general (keun-shwae), and is divided into five divisions (ying), front, rear, right, left, and centre . . .

... Attached to each division of guards (or the first class of the three brigade divisions) is one large black flag, and when this is advanced, the division is compelled to follow it upon pain of death, the rear rank men carrying drawn swords to decapitate any who might attempt to run. This flag possesses not only the signification the "black flag" does with Europeans, but must never be carried in retreat before an enemy, nothing but death being permitted to arrest its progress. This was well known to the Imperialists, and, until assisted by British troops, officers, and supplies of shell, artillery, &c., they rarely, if ever, awaited this terrible attack, and even if courageous enough to do so, their chance of success was but small indeed.

The absence of all mercenary attraction to their ranks arose from the wish of the Ti-ping Government to have no adherents who could possibly join them from other than religious or patriotic motives, these being recognized as the element that contributed so largely to success. The appearance of the men is quite a sufficient guarantee of the beneficial effects of the system, for, instead of being taken from the very lowest dregs of the people, as with the Imperialists, it is nearly always the case that they are men of respectability, from either the working, servant, or trading class; frequently they are of much higher social position, and this is generally the case with the Kwang-tung and Kwang-si men, whose superiority is such that it is mostly from their ranks the officers are selected.

One of the wisest and most advantageous regulations of the Ti-ping army is, that officers of every grade can rise by merit alone; a regulation highly beneficial, most of their leaders having proved very superior men; among others the Chung-wang, who, unaided, rose by his brilliant attainments alone to the highest military rank.

The total inability of the Manchoos to alone meet the Ti-pings with any chance of success, is easily to be understood when the different military constitutions of the two powers are made known; for how is it possible that armies entirely composed of the very lowest and most degraded of the people, and whose officers obtain their rank by corruption and bribery, can be able to compete with the patriotism of the Ti-pings, or the superior talent of their chiefs? ...

... During my intercourse with the Ti-pings, if one part of their system and organization appeared more admirable than another, it was the improved position of their women, whose status, raised from the degrading Asiatic *regime*, approached that of civilized nations. This improvement upon the ignorant and sensual treatment of 2,000 years affords strong evidence of the advancement of their moral character. Although the practice of polygamy has by some warlike Christians been used as an argument to justify murdering the Ti-pings, I do not remember an instance in which those ultra-moral personages have endeavoured to teach the Ti-pings the difference between the law of well-beloved Abraham's time, upon which many of their religious rules are framed, and the later dispensation of the Gospel. It is, however, a great mistake to imagine that the Ti-pings are either confirmed or universal polygamists. In the first place, as they have thrown off *all* the other heathen practices of their countrymen, there is no reason to suppose they would make this an exception. In the second place, I know that many who have become enlightened by the New Testament, have abandoned polygamy; while a vast number of the rest, only partially instructed, are either averse to it, or simply maintain the establishment of one principal and several inferior wives, or concubines, according to ancient custom, and as a mark of high rank. It is also a fact that in some countries a plurality of wives is rather beneficial than otherwise; and it may be that China is one of these. But above all, however detestable we may consider polygamy, where is the *Divine* command against it?

The Ti-pings have abolished the horrible custom of cramping and deforming the feet of their women. But although, under their improved system, no female child is so tortured, many of their wives have the frightful "small feet;" having, with the exception of the natives of Kwang-se, some parts of Kwang-tung, and the Miau-tze, originally conformed to the crippling custom. All children born since the earliest commencement of the Ti-ping rebellion have the natural foot. This great benefit to the women, their consequent improved appearance, and the release of the men from the tail-wearing shaven-headed badge of former slavery, form the two most conspicuous of their distinguishing habits, and cause the greatest difference and improvement in the personal appearance of the Ti-pings as compared with that of their Tartar-governed countrymen. The much higher social position of the Ti-ping ladies over that of their unfortunate sisters included within the Manchoo domestic *regime*, has long been one of the brightest ornaments of their government. A plebeian Ti-ping is allowed but one wife, and to her he must be regularly married by one of the ministers. Amongst the Chiefs, marriage is a ceremony celebrated with much pomp and festivity; the poorer classes can only marry when considered worthy, and when permitted to do so by their immediate rulers. In contradistinction

419

to the Manchoos, the marriage knot when once tied can never be unloosed; therefore, the custom of putting away a wife at pleasure, or selling her—as in vogue among the Chinese—or the proceedings of the British Court of Divorce, has not found favour in their sight.

Every woman in Ti-pingdom must either be married, the member of a family, or an inmate of one of the larger institutions for unprotected females, existing in most of their principal cities, and superintended by proper officials; no single woman being allowed in their territory otherwise. This law is to prevent prostitution, which is punishable with death, and is one which has certainly proved very effective, for such a thing is unknown in any of the Ti-ping cities. The stringent execution of the law has, in fact, been rather too severe, for I have seen cases where women have rushed about the streets to find new husbands directly they have received the melancholy tidings of their late beloved's decapitation by the 'demon imps.' It is possible these bereaved ladies may not have been on the strength of the regiment; but at all events this acting of the law was rather too exaggerated. The conduct of the Chinese lady who fanned her husband's grave to dry it previous to her early acceptance of a new lord, and so preserve a correct propriety, is more excusable than this. Woman is by the Ti-pings recognized in her proper sphere as the companion of man; the education and development of her mind is equally well attended to; her duty to God is diligently taught, and in ordinary worship she takes her proper place; many of the women are zealous and popular teachers and expounders of the Bible; in fact, everything is done to make her worthy of the improved position she has attained by reason of the Ti-ping movement.

The institutions for unprotected women are presided over by duly appointed matrons, and are particularly organized and designed to educate and protect those young girls who lose their natural guardians, or those married women whose husbands are away upon public duty, and who have no relations to protect and support them. Very many of the women accompany their husbands upon military expeditions; inspired with enthusiasm to share the dangers and severe hardships of the battle-field. In such cases they are generally mounted upon the Chinese ponies, donkeys, or mules, which they ride a la Duchesse de Berri. In former years they were wont to fight bravely, and could ably discharge the duties of officers, being however formed into a separate camp and only joining the men in religious observances. The greatest physical comfort to the women is their enjoyment of natural feet and the ability to move about as they wish; though, unfortunately, it is only amongst the youngest that this prevails entirely...

...I have probably had a much greater experience of the Ti-ping religious practices than any other European, and as a Protestant Christian I have never yet found occasion to condemn their form of worship. In the first place, the principal and most important article of their faith is the Holy Bible in all its integrity—Old and New Testaments entire. These have always been circulated through the whole population of the Ti-ping jurisdiction, and printed and distributed to the people gratuitously by their Government. Besides the Bible, numerous religious works by the Tien-wang (the Taiping king), and Kan-wang (his prime minister), have been commonly circulated among their followers; but I entirely deny that these, or any single one of them, tend to alter, modify, or supersede any part of the Word of God, as some persons have taken upon themselves to intimate. These works have been issued as the individual explanations and opinions of the two authors, but never as any essential article of belief. Had such not been the case, is it likely the Bible would have been given in a complete form, by which any peculiar and erroneous teaching of the Tien-wang would have become exposed? And is not this free and unlimited circulation of the Scriptures the very best and most certain prospect of improvement? So anti-Christian, however, have been the arguments of nearly all opposed to the Ti-pings, that it is even possible some of their sect may dispute this truth... It may be urged by some that the sanguinary war maintained by the revolutionists can be held as a proof of their un-Christian character, and that they are endeavouring to propagate their faith by the sword. The simple reply to this is, that the Ti-pings have proved themselves to be far more merciful than their enemies. Oppressed and persecuted, their patriotism became aroused; they sought not to establish their faith by the sword; they sought to recover their patrimony from the usurping Tartar. They fought to uphold Christianity, not to crush it. Far from being incited by fanaticism to deeds of blood, it is a well-known fact—particularly stated by the Revs. Griffith John, Joseph Edkins, Lobschied, Muirhead, and others—that the Ti-ping chiefs have always deplored the great loss of life consequent upon their struggle for liberty. In the tenth century, Christianity was introduced into Denmark by the sword, in the thirteenth into Prussia, and became established throughout Europe by religious wars. All Christianity has been compelled frequently to maintain itself by force of arms....

... When the statements of the various missionaries are perused, it must be wondered how it is that those who have been sent to China through the Christian generosity of the British public, have never yet attempted to succour or guide aright the great Christian revolution. The Bishop of Victoria, the Revs. Griffith John, Muirhead, Edkins, Mills, Milne, Lobschied, Lambath, and many others too numerous to mention, have rejoiced in the most eloquent terms about the Ti-pings, have particularly approved, and criticised their acts, when sending *their reports* to England. What have they *done* to assist those who have "entreated" them, as Mr. Holmes, the Baptist missionary, was entreated, to come and teach the Word of God? Absolutely nothing! . . .

Marriage among the Ti-pings is solemnized with remarkable strictness, and the ceremony is performed by an officiating priest, or rather presbyter. All the heathen and superstitious customs of the Chinese are completely relinquished. The ancient customs by which marriages were celebrated—the semi-civilized espousal of persons who had never previously seen each other; the choice of a lucky day; the present of purchase-money, and many others— are abolished. Those only that seem to be retained are the tying up of the bride's long black tresses, hitherto worn hanging down, and the bridegroom's procession at night, with music, lanterns, sedan-chairs, and a cavalcade of friends (and in the case of chiefs, banners and military honours), to fetch home his spouse. As a natural consequence of the absence of restraint in the enjoyment of female society, marriages amongst the Ti-pings are generally love matches. Even in cases where a chief's daughter is given in alliance to some powerful leader, compulsion is *never* used, and the affianced are given every opportunity to become acquainted with each other.

I have frequently seen the marriage ceremony performed, and I can only say that, excepting the absence of the ring, it forms as close and veritable an imitation of that practised by the Church of England as it is possible to imagine. When the bridal party are all met together, they proceed to the church (i.e. 'the Heavenly Hall,' within the official dwelling of each mayor of a village or circle of twenty-five families, excepting in the case of chiefs, who are married in their own hall), and after many prayers and a severe examination of the bride and bridegroom's theological tenets, the minister joins their right hands together, and when each have accepted the other, pronounces a concluding benediction in the name of the Father, Son, and Holy Spirit. To the best of my belief divorce is not only not permitted, but actually unknown or thought of. Adultery is punishable with death; and it may be that this is the only case in which the Ti-pings consider a complete release a *vinculo matrimonii* justifiable. All their rules upon the subject, and in fact their entire penal code, I once possessed; unfortunately I have no translations, and none are to be obtained outside their ranks . . .

I frequently visited the Minister of the Interior, the Chang-wang (Accomplished Prince), and other chiefs, with my two companions, and we were always received with such kindness and hospitality that every house in Nankin became our home. We usually employed a part of each day instructing the Ti-ping soldiers in gunnery or drilling them upon a plan combining the line and column formation of European tactics with their own more undisciplined manoeuvres. The Chinese are well known for their imitative ingenuity; but we found these *free* Chinamen still more easily taught, their quick acquirement of English words and extraordinary aptitude for every kind of instruction being really marvellous.

When I look back upon the unchangeable and universal kindness I have always met with from the Ti-pings, even while their dearest relatives were being slaughtered by my countrymen, or captured by the Manchoos to be tortured to death and their wives and daughters when not killed infamously outraged and passed from hand to hand by the rabble Imperialist soldiery, it almost seems to be a dream, so difficult is it to comprehend their magnanimous forbearance, when, according to the *lex talinois* in vogue among civilized nations, they should have executed every Englishman they met with similar barbarities to those practised upon the unfortunate Ti-ping prisoners given up by British officers (during the years 1862–3–4) to the Manchoo authorities.

During all my intercourse with the Ti-pings I can recollect nothing *more* unpleasant than being made 'bogie' to frighten unruly children; and even this was of rare occurrence, so great a feeling of respect for Englishmen did their parents entertain. Sometimes, while strolling through a city, I have been pointed out as a white man bogie to little yellow-skinned Ti-pings by their black-haired pretty mother, qualified, however, in most cases by a polite invitation to enter and partake of a cup of tea; and so the only offence that could be taken at becoming 'bogie' would be from the unflattering opinion one's appearance caused in the juvenile imagination. How different are the scowling looks and the epithet 'Yang-quitzo' applied to us with the aspiration of hate by our Manchoo allies!

4
The Aftermath

The recapture of Nanking by Imperialist forces in May 1864 marked the effective end of the Taiping Tienkuo, although it was not the end of the fighting. Sizeable forces escaped from Nanking and other Taiping held centres and fought their way southward, back towards their original base area, occupying other cities for a time on the way (Doc. 94). Central China was, however, soon cleared of organised Taiping resistance and the long process of rehabilitation began. Certain cities and areas recovered fairly quickly (Doc. 95), but others had been so devastated and depopulated that it took them many years to do so (Doc. 97).

The orthodox Western view of the Taiping movement after its final defeat remained for long that it was totally destructive and unproductive—a disaster. Not until the twentieth century was serious Western—and Chinese—historical reassessment of the movement attempted. But apart from the deeply committed Lindley at least one contemporary Western observer, who had seen much of the Taiping, questioned the validity of the predominantly negative Western view that had come to prevail by the time of their final defeat (Doc. 96). The problem of assessing the Taiping movement accurately was raised by at least a few Western observers even at the time of its final defeat.

94
A Letter from Rev. Carstairs Douglas
English Presbyterian Messenger, vol. XVI, May 1865

My Dear Mr Matheson,—In the beginning of last week I had the privilege of visiting Chang-chew city,[1] along with Mr. Pedder, the British consul.

Many of the streets within the city have been destroyed, but a great many (I should think the greater part) are still uninjured Among the uninjured streets are those in which our chapel and

1　Changchou in Fukien was occupied by Taiping remnants under Li Shih-hsien, the Shih Wang, in October 1864 and held until May 1865—see Jen Yu-wen, op. cit., pp. 538–40 and Michael, op. cit., vol. I, p. 178 and map 13.

the chapel of the London Missionary Society stand. I visited both of them, and found them entire, even some of the inscriptions still remaining. They are occupied, like the adjoining houses, by the Taiping soldiers. I made many inquiries about the Christians, both at the chapels and at other places, both from the Taipings and from the Chang-chew people, who are still in the city, but could obtain no information.

As we were but a short time in the city, I was not able to make any special inquiries as to the present religious views of the Taipings. The idols and temples are, as usual, destroyed. We heard incidental allusions to the worship of the 'Heavenly Father', and the 'Heavenly Elder Brother', but we met with no allusion to the *dead* Thien Wang (Hung-sew-tsieuen), who killed himself at the fall of Nankin, nor to any living person bearing his title of 'Heavenly King'.

Since we returned to Amoy, the city of Chang-poo (due south of Chang-chew) has been taken by the Taipings; but there is a rumour that it has been retaken, and the principal chief in this neighbourhood severely wounded or killed. There is no doubt that four days ago a large Taiping force from Chang-poo re-entered Chang-chew, carrying some chief, dead or severely wounded, on a board covered over with flags, but it is not certain who that chief was. Many say that it was the Shi-Wang, who has chief command in all this region, and who is a half-brother of the famous Chung-Wang [Li Hsiu-ch'eng]. Many, however, say that Chang-poo is not retaken, but that a sufficient garrison being left there, the rest of the army which captured it has been recalled to Chang-chew, and that the chief who is wounded is not the Shi-Wang. You will recollect what I mentioned lately, that it is extremely difficult to get correct information. Yesterday morning it was said (and generally believed by the Chinese at Amoy) that Chang-chew itself has been retaken, but when the passage boats arrived in the evening, it was found that the story was a mere groundless rumour.

95
A Letter from Rev. W Muirhead
Archives of the London Missionary Society, China Central Letters, 1862–71, Folder 2 (May, 1866)

I returned a few days ago from a missionary tour of 200 miles into the interior. My object was to see the state of the country formerly occupied by the rebels and to judge of its adaptation for missionary work. My course lay in the way of Soochow and the imperial canal as far as the treaty port of Chinkiang. The country on this side of Soochow is slowly recovering from its recent desolation, and the cities are beginning to be occupied with people. The proportion of the inhabitants however is very small as compared with former times, and by means of our native assistants the Word is being preached in different places. I had considerable audiences in most of the towns, cities and villages that I visited, and there was a general readiness to hear on the part of the people. Advantage was everywhere taken of alluding to their circumstances and the widespread desolation all around, the lessons connected with their suffering were enforced upon them, and their attention was earnestly drawn to the things of God and Salvation. They acknowledged at all hands the folly of idolatry and many appeared familiar with Christian truth from having heard it in our City chapel here.

On arriving at Soochow I was agreeably surprised at the vast progress that has been made in building and repeopling the city. Crowds were met in all directions, and the principal streets were in good order and condition. Though greatly inferior to what it once was, I was reminded of Woochang opposite Hankow as by no means in advance of it. As I stayed there several days I talked with numbers of people from different and distant places, and the whole aspect of things gave promise of a speedy revival of olden times. The authorities are doing their utmost for the replenishing of the city and suburbs, and it is fast becoming a centre of influence for the country at large. There was life, real Chinese life, all around, and in this respect it presents a striking contrast to our neighbourhood here ...

After leaving Soochow I went on towards Woosih, Changchow, Tan-yang and Chin-Keang. The country in this direction presents a varied aspect. Where fertility and abundance once reigned poverty and wretchedness now exist. Large tracts of land are lying untilled from there being no one to own or attend them, and the cities, towns and villages intervening are in strange contrast to what they once were. I preached in many places, and often had encouraging congregations ...

... The city and suburbs are somewhat more prosperous than they were lately and the Mandarins are endeavouring to draw back the former citizens now scattered in different directions. As an avenue to the surrounding country, and especially to the work of the Yangtsze Kiang, Chin Kiang is an excellent place, and very valuable Medical Missionary work might be done there.

96
Comment by R J Forrest
Journal of the North China Branch of the Royal Asiatic Society,
n.s., vol. IV (December, 1867), pp. 187–8

So if I were to tell what order did really reign at Nanking—very much like the Warsaw article it is true, but still order—that there were some uncommonly clever generals among the T'ien Wang's officers, notably the Chung, Ying and Mo Wangs—that in places not actually the seat of war the ground was well cultivated—that the conduct of the Taiping troops was not one bit worse than that of the Imperialists—and that the inhabitants of such towns as Shaoshing and Hangchow have asserted that their lot under Ch'angmao rule was infinitely better than their unhappy fate when those cities were recovered and fell for a time into the hands of barbarian officers;—and if I stated these things, with every proof, I should be reviled as a rebel and a speaker of blasphemy against the brilliant political dawn now spreading over the empire. I never saw a foreigner return from Soochow (his excellent sport the result of the late troubles) who did not indulge in strong invective against the rebels for the destruction of the enormous suburbs of that city. And yet the rebels burnt neither Soochow nor its suburbs. The imperialist soldiery did it seven days before Chung Wang left Wusi! But facts, no matter how recorded, never overthrew prejudice. The suburbs of Soochow will always rise in judgment against the Ch'angmao though they were innocent of their destruction; and my experience of Taiping rule, although the result of a long residence at the Capital, will never be favourably regarded if in any way opposed to existing ideas.

97
Letters from Baron Richtofen
Baron Richtofen, *Letters 1870–72* (2nd ed., Shanghai, 1903),
pp. 74–6, 85–6

1 *25 July 1871*: (Letter on the Provinces of Chekiang and Anhwei)

The valley of Lan-ki, although a beautiful and fertile country, with many a hundred square miles of alluvial soil, is at present of little commercial importance, because it has not yet recovered from the devastation it suffered from the Taipings. The cities and villages are demolished, the inhabitants decimated. Large tracts of ground are uncultivated. Yet a considerable population is left.[2] At Kin-hwa-fu a beautiful arched stone bridge and a fine city wall, built of large square blocks of red sandstone, are monuments of a better time. A few streets only in the city have been rebuilt; they are merely lines of shops where the necessaries of life are sold. Lan-ki-hien is the commercial centre of the valley, and a tolerably busy place. The articles of commerce are, however, few and of little value. The imports are chiefly: salt, sugar, fish, and cotton: the exports: tea, paper, vegetable tallow, some tung-oil, and a few small articles. Pottery, lime, and building material are the rest of the bulky articles of boat traffic. I omitted, however, the hams of Tung-yang-hien, which enjoy a Westphalian fame with Chinese gourmands, and are a considerable article of export to the remotest portions of the Empire. The consumption of foreign goods is small, a great deal of the clothing being provided for by importing raw cotton. Opium is little used by the country people; but those living in cities are considerably addicted to it.

The Fan-sui valley is, as regards scenery, among the finest pieces of ground that I have seen in China. The hills are covered with vegetation, partly forest-trees, and partly a dense jungle of shrubbery, among which are the most exquisite flowering plants that adorn the gardens of Europe. A luxurious semi-tropical vegetation fills the gorges and recesses in the hillsides with indescribably rich and varied foliage. The branches and twigs are intertwisted with creepers, so as to baffle all attempts at ingress. Shade, after which the traveller in China so often longs in vain, is afforded in abundance by numerous groves of lofty trees, none of which, however, can rival those on the southern slopes of the Tien-mu-shan, as regards beauty and extent. A trip through these regions in the summer season is a source of incessant enjoyment, and repays amply the hardship of walking under a burning sun. There is, however, one drawback. While Nature is usually divested of its finest charms in China, too free action has been left to it here, of late years. The valleys, notwithstanding the fertility of their soil, are a complete wilderness. In approaching the groups of stately white-washed houses that lurk at some distance from underneath a grove of trees, you get aware that they are ruins. Eloquent witnesses of the wealth of which this valley was formerly the seat, they are now desolation itself. Here and there a house is barely fitted up and serves as a lodging to some wretched people, the poverty of whom is in striking contrast with the rich

2   For a general analysis of the effects of the Taiping struggle on population see Ho Ping-ti, *Studies on the Population of China 1368–1953* (Harvard, 1959), pp. 236–48.

land on which they live. The cities which I have mentioned, Tung-lu, Chang-hwa, Yu-tsien, Ning-kwo-hien are extensive heaps of ruins, about a dozen houses being inhabited in each of them. Such is the devastation wrought by the Taiping rebels, thirteen years ago. The roads connecting the district cities are now narrow foot-paths, completely overgrown in many places with grasses fifteen feet high, or with shrubs through which it is difficult to penetrate. Formerly the valley teemed with population. The great number and size of the villages is evidence thereof, while the fine style of the houses, all of which were built of cut stone and brick and had two storeys, gives proof of the more than usual comfort and wealth that reigned here. The fields in the valley, as well as the terraced rice ground on the hillsides, are covered with a wild growth of grass, no other plants being apparently able to thrive on the exhausted soil. Plantations of old mulberry trees, half of them decayed from want of care, tell of one of the chief industries of the former inhabitants; in other places the ground is covered with perfect forests of old chestnut trees.

It is difficult to conceive of a more horrid destruction of life and property than has been perpetrated in these districts, and yet they are only a very small proportion of the great area of country that has shared a similar fate. One must have seen places such as these to value at their full extent the ravages which the races of eastern Asia are capable of performing when full sway is left to their excited passions. There can be little doubt that the destruc-tion of life, of which the province of Chekiang was repeatedly the theatre during its history, was not less fearful than it has been in the last instance. I used to enquire in different places into the percentage of population that had escaped death by the Taiping rebels. It was generally rated at three in every hundred. Of four hundred monks who lived before in the temple of Si-tien-mu-shan, only thirty survived after the rebellion; but the ration is less in the villages and cities. Most people died from starvation, in the recesses of the mountains to which they fled, but still the numbers of men, women and children killed by the hand of the rebels is excessively great.

The decrease of the productive power of the ransacked pro-vinces, and the amount of taxes by which their exchequer is diminished, must be very large; and surprising figures would be arrived at, if it were at all possible to compute the damage which the reduction of the number of consumers in the provinces con-tiguous to Shanghai has caused to foreign commerce.

There is reason to expect that these regions will revive. The course of immigration has set in. In the Fan-sui valley I found quite a number of new settlers, mostly from Ningpo and Shao-hsing in Chekiang, but also a few from other provinces. They are less numerous than in Nganhwei, but the influx of people will probably increase.

2 *August 31 1871* (Letter on the Region of Nanking and Chinkiang)

The Nanking hills cannot compare with the mountainous regions in Chekiang and Nganhwei as regards beauty of scenery, although they are not devoid of picturesque sights. The views from the high summits are perhaps their greatest charm. The valley of the Yangtse is spread out below, with its majestic river, its labyrinth of canals and creeks, its numerous villages and cities, and the varied crops due to the fertility of the soil. And beyond, the volcanoes form an interesting and beautiful frame of the panorama, some of them being but dimly recognisable on the horizon. Rarely does a view from a high summit convey so perfectly the image of a map, owing to the many straight lines in creeks, fieldmarks and footpaths, which touch each other at all angles. The whole country suffers still heavily from the fearful devastation wrought by the Taiping rebels, and it will take a long time before it shall have fully revived. Of the alluvial lands, a good portion is again under cultivation, chiefly by the labour of immigrants. But all rising ground, a considerable area of which was formerly terraced and well-cultivated, is still a wilderness.

Glossary

Terms and Titles

Document Form	Meaning	Pinyin Form	Wade-Giles Form
Book of Commandments		Tiantiao shu	T'ien-t'iao shu
Book of Declarations of Divine Will		Tianfu xiafan zhaoshu	T'ien-fu hsia-fan chao-shu
Calendar		Banxing lishu	Pan-hsing li-shu
chan-ti	god	shangdi	shang-ti
chang-fah	long-hair, i.e.	changfa	ch'ang-fa
ch'ang-mao chang-maou	Taiping		
chang-ti	god	shangdi	shang-ti
shau	sub-prefecture	zhou	chou
chee-heen chi-hien	district magistrate	zhixian	chih-hsien
chin-chü	true lord	zhenzhu	chen-chu
Ching-seang	prime minister	Chengxiang	Ch'eng-hsiang
chou chow	sub-prefecture	zhou	chou
chu-tsiang	commanding general	zhujiang	chu-chiang
chun-sun	god	zhenshen	chen-shen
Chung Yung	The Doctrine of the Mean	Zhong Yong	Chung Yung
coum-tou	governor-general	zongdu	tsung-tu
Discourse on Building the Heavenly Capital at the Golden Mound	Taiping document	Jian Tianjing yu Jinling lun	Chien T'ien-ching yü Chin-ling lun
Discourses on Heavenly Principles	Taiping document	Tianli yaolun	T'ien-li yao-lun
Discourse upon branding the impish den 'Chihli' with the name 'Tsuy le'	Taiping document	Bian Yaoxue wei Zuili lun	Pien Yao-hsüeh wei Tsui-li lun

431

Document Form	Meaning	Pinyin Form	Wade-Giles Form
Discourse upon the expediency of affixing the Imperial Seal to the Imperial proclamations	Taiping document	Zhaoshu gaixi banxing lun	Chao-shu kai-hsi pan-hsing lun
e-kwan	barbarian officers	yiguan	i-kuan
foo-tai foo-t'ai	governor	futai	fu-t'ai
foo fou fu	prefecture; palace	fu	fu
fung-shwui	wind and water	fengshui	feng-shui
Hau King	Classic or Filial Piety	Xiao Jing	Hsiao Ching
hien	district	xian	hsien
ho-nai-sz	the 'ho-nai' teacher; one of Yang Xiuqing's titles	henaishi	ho-nai-shih
Hung-kia	Hung family, i.e. the Triad Society	Hongjia	Hung-chia
ih hiung	second brother	er xiong	erh hsiung
kwang-tee	emperor	huangdi	huang-ti
Keuen-shi leang-yen	Good Words to Exhort the Age—Christian pamphlet	Quanshi liangyan	Ch'üan-shih liang-yen
keun	army	jun	chün
keun-shwae	general	junshuai	chün-shuai
kieuen-wei-sz	the comforter	quanweishi	ch'üan-wei-shih
Kouam-si-jen Kuan-si-jen	men from Guangxi, i.e. Taiping	Guangxi ren	Kuang-hsi jen
kwei-tsz	foreign devil	guizi	kuei-tzu
leang-sze-ma	lieutenant	liangsima	liang-ssu-ma
leu	regiment	lü	lü
leu-shwae	colonel	lüshuai	lü-shuai
mai-pwan	comprador	maiban	mai-pan
Meaou-tsze Miao-tse Miao-tsz Miau-tsz	the Miao people	Miaozi	Miao-tzu
Nieh fi	Nian rebels	Nian fei	Nien fei
Ode to Youth		Youxueshi	Yu-hsüeh-shih

Document Form	Meaning	Pinyin Form	Wade-Giles Form
Pih-lien kiau	White Lotus Society	Bailian jiao	Pai-lien chiao
San-ho hwuy San-hoh hwui	Triad Society	Sanhe hui	San-ho hui
Seaou-taou hwuy	Small Sword Society	Xiaodao hui	Hsiao-tao hui
Seen-sang	title of address	xiansheng	shien-sheng
seong-ti shang-de shang-te shang-ti	god	shangdi	shang-ti
shang-te hwuy shang-ti hwui	God Worshipper's Society—Bai shangdi hui	shangdi hui	shang-ti hui
shang-te tsi	son of god	shangdi zi	shang-ti tzu
shing-ling	holy spirit	shengling	sheng-ling
shing-shin-fung	wind of the holy spirit	shengshenfeng	sheng-shen-feng
sie-shin	false god	xieshen	hsieh-shen
siu-tshai	first degree	xiucai	hsiu-ts'ai
sze-shwae	general of division	shishuai	shih-shuai
Ta Hëoh	The Great Learning	Da Xue	Ta Hsüeh
ta-jen ta-jin ta-jun	title of respect	daren	ta-jen
Ta Tsing Tai Tsing	Qing dynasty	Da Qing	Ta Ch'ing
Ta-pim Ta-ping Tae-peng Tae-ping T'ae-ping Tai-ping T'ai-p'ing Taie-ping T'hae-ping Ti-ping	Great Peace	Taiping	T'ai-p'ing
taou-tae	intendant	daotai	tao-t'ai
tcheou	sub-prefecture	zhou	chou
teen-foo	heavenly father, god	tianfu	t'ien-fu
teen-keo teen-kwoh	heavenly kingdom	tianguo	t'ien-kuo
Teen-te hwuy	Triad Society	Tiandi hui	T'ien-ti hui
Teen-teaon	heavenly commandments	tiantiao	t'ien-t'iao
t'ien-chiu	heavenly dynasty	tianchao	t'ien-ch'ao
tien-chiu tien-chou tien-chu	heavenly ruler, god	tianzhu	t'ien-chu

Document Form	Meaning	Pinyin Form	Wade-Giles Form
tien-fou	heavenly father,	tianfu	t'ien-fu
tien-fu	god		
t'ien-fu			
tien-kwoh	heavenly kingdom	tianguo	t'ien-kuo
tien-kwok			
T'ien-ti hui	Triad Society	Tiandi hui	T'ien-ti hui
tien-tsi	son of god	tianzi	t'ien-tzu
tou-tai	intendant	daotai	tao-t'ai
Treatise on Land	Taiping document	Tianchao tianmu	T'ien-ch'ao t'ien-
Tenure		zhidu	mu chih-tu
tsan-szu-kueun	secretary	can si guan	ts'an ssu kuan
tseang-keuen	commander	jiangjun	chiang-chün
tseang-keun			
tsi-cheng sin-pien	New Treatise on	zi-zheng xin-pian	tzu-cheng hsin-
	Aid to		p'ien
	Administration		
tsin-kung	to bring tribute	jingong	chin-kung
tsin-tzu	the highest degree	jinshi	chin-shih
Tsing	dynasty	Qing	Ch'ing
tsuh	military company	zu	tsu
tsuh-chang	captain	zuzhang	tsu-chang
tung-pau ti-hiung	natural brother	tongbao dixiong	t'ung-pao ti-hsiung
urh-hiung	second brother	erxiong	erh-hsiung
ih hiung			
wa-choong-te	foreign brother	waixiongdi	wai-hsiung-ti
wae-heung-ti			
wai-hsiung-te			
wam	king	wang	wang
wang			
wong			
wan-swei	'long live!'	wansui	wan-sui
woo-chang	sergeant	wuzhang	wu-chang
woo-tsuh	private	wuzu	wu-tsu
xam-ti	god	shangdi	shang-ti
yang quitzer	foreign devil	yang guizi	yang kuei-tzu
yang-heung-te	foreign brother	yangxiongdi	yang-hsiung-ti
yang-hsiung-ti			
yang-shoong-dee			
yen-lo wang	king of Hades	yanluo wang	yen-lo wang
Yik King	The Book of	Yi Jing	I Ching
	Changes		
ying	army division	ying	ying

Personal Titles and Names

Document Form	Identification	Pinyin Form	Wade-Giles Form
A-lih-tsung-a	Imperial Commissioner	Saishanga	Sai-shang-a
Ah-ling	Small Sword Society leader	Jin Alin	Chin A-lin
Assistant King	Yi Wang	[Shi Dakai]	[Shih Ta-k'ai]
Attendant King	Shi Wang	[Li Shixian]	[Li Shih-hsien]
Brave King	Ying Wang	[Chen Yucheng]	[Ch'en Yü-ch'eng]
Celestial King	Tian Wang	Hong Xiuquan	Hung Hsiu-ch'üan
Chan Wang	Lin Shaozhang	Zhang Wang	Chang Wang
Chang Koh-liang	Imperial commander,	Zhang Guoliang	Chang Kuo-liang
Chang Kweh-liang	ex-rebel		
Chang Kwoh-liang			
Chang Kwok-leang			
Chang Loh-hing	Nien leader	Zhang Luoxing	Chang Lo-hsing
Chang Wang	Lin Shaozhang	Zhang Wang	Chang Wang
Chang Wong			
Chau Tien-tsioh	Lt governor, then governor of Guangzi, 1851	Zhou Tianjue	Chou T'ien-chüeh
Chin	Governor of Guangxi, 1850	Zheng Zuchen	Cheng Tsu-ch'en
Chin-koo-fang	Imperial Commander	Zeng Guofan	Tseng Kuo-fan
Ching-seang	'prime minister'	Chengxiang	Ch'eng-hsiang
Ching Wang	Chen Bingwen (?)	Tin Wang	T'ing Wang
Chong Wang	Lin Shaozhang or Li Xiucheng	Zhang Wang or Zhong Wang	Chang Wang or Chung Wang
Chun	Taiping leader at Dunyang, 1860	Jun	Chün
Chun	Small Sword Society	Jin Alin	Chin A-lin
Chun A-ling	leader		
Chung Wang	Li Xiucheng	Zhong Wang	Chung Wang
E-wang	Shi Dakai	Yi Wang	I Wang
Eastern King	Dong Wang	[Yang Xiuqing]	[Yang Hsiu-ch'ing]
Faithful King	Zhong Wang	[Li Xiucheng]	[Li Hsiu-ch'eng]
Fan	Shou Wang, Taiping	Fan Ruzeng	Fan Ju-tseng
Fang	leader at Ningbo		
'Feudal' King			
Foung Hien-san	Nan Wang	Feng Yunshan	Feng Yün-shan
Foung Je-tchang	early Taiping prime minister	Qin Rigang	Ch'in Jih-kang
Fung	son of Feng Yünshan	Feng Ayang	Feng A-yang
Fung Shau-tsun	father of Fen Yünshan	Feng Shoucun	Feng Shou-ts'un
Fung Yun-san	Nan Wang	Feng Yunshan	Feng Yün-shan
Fung Yun-shan			

Document Form	Identification	Pinyin Form	Wade-Giles Form
Heavenly King	Tian Wang	[Hong Xiuquan]	[Hung Hsiu-chüan]
Heang	Imperial commander,	Xiang Rong	Hsiang Jung
Heang Jung	1850–6		
Heang Yung			
Hiam-ta-jen			
Hiang Tsiou-tsing	Dong Wang	Yang Xiuqing	Yang Hsiu-ch'ing
Hien-feng	Qing Emperor,	Xianfeng	Hsien-feng
Hien-fong	1851–61		
Hien-fung			
Hiung	Taiping leader at Suzhou (?)	Xiong Wanquan (?)	Hsiung Wan-ch'üan
Ho A-luh	Taiping commander, 1856 (?)	He Lu (?)	Ho Lu
Ho-ch'un	Imperial commander, 1856–60	Hechun	Ho-ch'un
Ho	Governor-general of	He Guiqing	Ho Kuei-ch'ing
Ho Kwei-tsing	Jiangnan, 1857–62		
Ho Kwi-tsing			
Ho quei-ching			
Hoe A-luk	Taiping commander (?) 1856	He Lu	Ho Lu
Hong Sow-tsei	Tian Wang	Hong Xiuquan	Hung Hsiu-ch'üan
Hoo E-kwang	early Taiping leader	Hu Yihuang	Hu I-huang
Houan	father-in-law of Shi Dakai	Huang Yukun	Huang Yü-k'un
Houng Sieou-tsiuen	Tian Wang	Hong Ziuquan	Hung Hsiu-ch'üan
Hu	early Taiping leader	Hu Yihuang	Hu I-huang
Huang Jung	Imperial commander	Xiang Rong	Hsiang Jung
Hum Sieu-tsinen	Tian Wang	Hong Xiuquan	Hung Hsiu-ch'üan
Hung Jin	Gan Wang	Hong Rengan	Hung Jen-kan
Hung Kow-tsuen	Tian Wang	Hong Xiuquan	Hung Hsiu-ch'üan
Hung Saw-chuen			
Hung Seu-tseuen			
Hung Sew-tsieuen			
Hung Sieu-tsiuen			
Hung Siu-tseuen			
Hung Siu-tshuen			
Hung Siu-tsiuen			
Hung Siu-tsiun			
Hung Siu-tsuen			
Hung Sow-chuen			
Hung Sü-chuen			
Hung Sui-tshuen			
Hung Tsow-tsuen			
Hung-wu	Ming Emperor 1368–98	Hongwu	Hung-wu
Hwang	Taiping commander at Ningbo	Huang Chengzhong	Huang Ch'eng-chung
Kan Wang	Hong Rengan	Gan Wang	Kan Wang
Kang-hi	Emperor 1662–1727	Kangxi	K'ang-hsi

Document Form	Identification	Pinyin Form	Wade-Giles Form
Kang Wang	Hong Rengan	Gan Wang	Kan Wang
Ke-shen	Imperial Commissioner 1853–4	Qishan	Ch'i-shan
Keih	Manchu general to 1856	Jierhanga	Chi-er-hang-a
Ki-ling	Governor of Jiangxi, 1857	Qiling	Ch'i-ling
Kien-lung	Qing Emperor, 1736–96	Qianlong	Ch'ien-lung
Kim Wang	Taiping leader at Huzhou, 1864	?	
Ko-chen-ching	Taiping subordinate at Chapu	?	
Prince Kung	Manchu court official	Gong	Kung
Kwan-wan	Governor-general of Huguang, 1855–66	Guanwen	Kuan-wen
Lae	brother-in-law of Hong	Lai Hanying	Lai Han-ying
Lai	Xiuquan		
Le	Zhong Wang	Li Xiucheng	Li Hsiu-ch'eng
Leang	Taiping officer (?)	Liang Litai (?)	Liang Li-t'ai
Leo, General	Taiping general	Liu Zhaojun	Liu Chao-chün
Lew	Small Sword society leader	Liu Lichuan	Liu Li-ch'uan
Li	Shun Wang	Li Chunfa	Li Ch'un-fa
Li	Zhong Wang	Li Xiucheng	Li Hsiu-ch'eng
Li	Imperial Commissioner, 1850–1.	Li Xingyuan	Li Hsing-yuan
Li Sing-yuen			
Li	Peasant leader	Li Zicheng	Li Tzu-ch'eng
Li Tsing	1605–45		
Liang	Qi Wang	Liang Chengfu (probably)	Liang Ch'eng-fu
Liau Ch'an-kwei	Xi Wang	Xiao Chaogui	Hsiao Ch'ao-kuei
Lieu	Small Sword society leader	Liu Lichuan	Liu Li-ch'uan
Lieu [ta-jin]	Taiping commander	Liu Zhaojun	Liu Chao-chün
Lin	Zhang Wang	Lin Shaozhang	Lin Shao-chang
Lin	Imperial Commissioner, 1850	Lin Zexu	Lin Tse-hsü
Lin Tseh-seu			
Liu	magistrate at Nanjing, 1853	Liu Tongying	Liu T'ung-ying
Liu	Taiping commander	Liu Zhaojun	Liu Chao-chün
Lo Hiao-tsiuen	I. J. Roberts	Luo Xiaoquan	Lo Hsiao-ch'üan
Lo Ho-sun			
Lo How-chuen			
Lo	Taiping commander to	Luo Dagang	Lo Ta-kang
Lo Ta-kang	1855		
Lo Ta-yun			
Lo Tsun-tien	Justice in Hubei, 1857	Luo Zundian	Lo Tsun-tien
Loh Ping-chang	Governor of Hunan, 1850–60	Luo Bingzhang	Lo Ping-chang

Document Form	Identification	Pinyin Form	Wade-Giles Form
Loyal King	Zhong Wang	[Li Xiucheng]	[Li Hsiu-ch'eng]
Lu Luh	early adherent to God Worshipper's society	Lu Liu	Lu Liu
Luh Kien-ying	Governor-general of Jiangnan to 1853	Lu Jianying	Lu Chien-ying
Mang	son of Meng Deen, the Zan Wang	Meng Shiyong	Meng Shih-yung
Mo Wang	Tan Shaoguang	Mu Wang	Mu Wang
Moh Wang			
Mung	Zan Wang	Meng Deen	Meng Te-en
Nan Wang	Feng Yunshan	Nan Wang	Nan Wang
Northern King	Bei Wang	[Wei Changhui]	[Wei Ch'ang-hui]
Ou-lan-tai	Assistant Imperial Commissioner to 1852	Wulantai	Wu-lan-t'ai
Ou San-kouei	Ming-Qing general and official (1612–78)	Wu Sangui	Wu San-kuei
Pe Wang	Wei Changhui	Bei Wang	Pei Wang
Pih Wang			
Pung ta-jun	Taiping official	?	
Sae-shang-ah	Imperial Commissioner, 1851	Saishanga	Sai-shang-a
Samqua	Daotai at Shanghai, 1853	Wu Jianzhang	Wu Chien-chang
Se Wang	Xiao Chaogui	Xi Wang	Hsi Wang
Seaou	Xi Wang	Xiao Chaogui	Hsiao Ch'ao-kuei
Seu	Governor-general of Liang Guang, 1848–52	Xu Cuangjin	Hsü Kuang-chin
Seu Kwang-tsin			
Sew Chaou-kwei	Xi Wang	Xiao Chaogui	Hsiao Ch'ao-kuei
Shau-tsan	Imperial commander in Anhui	?	
She Wang	Li Shixian	Shi Wang	Shih Wang
Shi Wang			
Shield King	Gan Wang	[Hong Rengan]	[Hung Jen-kan]
Shih Ta-k'ai	Yi Wang	Shi Dakai	Shih Ta-k'ai
Shih Tah-kai			
Shing-pau	Manchu general to 1863	Shengbao	Sheng-pao
Si Wang	Xiao Chaogui	Xi Wang	Hsi Wang
Siao Tcha-kouei	Xi Wang	Xiao Chaogui	Hsiao Ch'ao-kuei
Siau Chau-kwei			
Siu	Governor-general of Liang Guang, 1848–52	Xu Guangjin	Hsü Kuang-chin

438

Document Form	Identification	Pinyin Form	Wade-Giles Form
Toong Wang	Yang Xiuqing	Dong Wang	Tung Wang
Toung Wang			
Tow Wang	Huang Wenjin	Du Wang	Tu Wang
Tsan Wang	Meng Deen	Zan Wang	Tsan Wang
Tsang A-sun	early adherent of the God Worshipper's society·	Zeng Ashun	Tseng A-shun
Tsang Chu	magistrate at Jiangkou	Zeng Zhu	Tseng Chu
Tsang Tsu-kwang	early adherent of the God Worshipper's society	Zeng Zuguang	Tseng Tso-kuang
Tsang Wang-yen	Governor-general of Sichuan to 1860	Zeng Wangyan	Tseng Wang-yen
Tsang Yuh-chin	early adherent of the God Worshipper's society	Zeng Yuzhen	Tseng yü-chen
Tscham Kie-siam	Imperial commander, ex-Taiping	Zhang Guoliang	Chang Kuo-liang
Tseng Kuo-fan	Imperial commander	Zeng Guofan	Tseng Kuo-fan
Tseou	Lt governor of Guangxi, 1851	Zhou Tianjue	Chou T'ien-chüeh
Tsoung-tching	Emperor, 1611–44	Chongzhen	Ch'ung-chen
Tsu-tse	Sung Confucian philosopher, 1139–1200	Zhu Xi	Chu Hsi
Tu-hing-ah	Garrison general in Hubei	Duxinga	Tu-hsing-a
Tung Wang	Yang Xiuqing	Dong Wang	Tung Wang
Wang I-teh	Governor-general of Fujian and Zhejiang, 1857		
Wang Ki	Justice at Jiangkou	Wang Ji	Wang Chi
Wang K'ing-yun	Governor-general of Sichuan, 1857–9	Wang Qingyun	Wang Ch'ing-yün
Wang Lieh	magistrate at Jiangkou	Wang Lie	Wang Lieh
Wang Tso-hsin	graduate from Guangxi	Wang Zouxin	Wang Tso-hsin
Wei Ching	Bei Wang	Wei Changhui	Wang Ch'ang-hui
Wei Tching			
Western King	Xi Wang	[Xiao Chaogui]	[Hsiao Ch'ao-kuei]
Woo	Taiping commander at Zhenjiang, the Gu Wang	Wu Ruxiao	Wu Ju-hsiao
Woo Joo-heaou			
Woo-lan-tai	assistant Imperial Commissioner to 1852	Wulantai	Wu-lan-t'ai
Wu	Taiping commander at Zhenjiang	Wu Ruxiao	Wu Ju-hsiao
Wu-ran-tai	Assistant Imperial Commissioner to 1852	Wulantai	Wu-lan-t'ai

439

Document Form	Identification	Pinyin Form	Wade-Giles Form
Y-ouang	Shi Dakai	Yi Wang	I Wang
Yang	Dong Wang	Yang Xiuqing	Yang Hsiu-ch'ing
Yang Seu-tsing			
Yang Sew-ts'ing			
Yang Shau-tsing			
Yang Sieu-tsing			
Yang Siu-tsing			
Yeen-ting-yue	Qin Rigang	Yan [Wang], Ding[tian] hou	Yen [Wang], Ting-[t'ien] hou
Yeh	Governor-general of	Ye Mingchen	Yeh Ming-ch'en
Yeh Ming	Liang Guang, 1852–8		
Yeong Sew-tsing	Dong Wang	Yang Xiuqing	Yang Hsiu-ch'ing
Yih	Governor-general of Liang Guang, 1852–8	Ye Mingchen	Yeh Ming-ch'en
Yih Wang	Shi Dakai	Yi Wang	I Wang
Ying-kwei	Governor of Henan, 1857	Yinggui	Ying-keui
Ying Wang	Chen Yucheng	Ying Wang	Ying Wang
Yugung	Commander at Chengdu	?	
Yun Wing	returned student	Rong Hong	Jung Hung

440

Place Names

Note: Since the spelling in the documents is in very many cases fairly close to, if not identical with, later Wade-Giles and Post Office spellings no attempt has been made to list all the places mentioned. Only spellings which may lead to some uncertainty are given. Some identifications are uncertain.

Document Form	Province	Pinyin Form	Wade-Giles or Post Office Form
Bing-bong	Jiangsu	Pingwang	P'ing-wang
Cassia River	Guangxi	Gui Jiang	Kuei Chiang
Cham-cha	Hunan	Changsha	Changsha
Cham-xa			
Chang-tong		Shandong	Shantung
Chaon-ping	Guangxi	Zhaoping	Chao-p'ing
Chi-chau	Anhui	Chizhou	Chihchow
Chiang-kiang	Jiangsu	Zhenjiang	Chinkiang
Chin-keang			
Chin-kiang			
Chin-kong			
Ching-kiang			
Chin-tu	Sichuan	Chengdu	Chengtu
Choui-tcheou	Jiangxi	Ruizhou	Juichou
Dziau-hing	Jiangsu	Shaoxing	Shaoshing
E-ching	Jiangsu	Yizheng	I-cheng
E-ding	Jiangsu	Weiting (?)	Wei-t'ing (?)
Elephant Trunk Hill	Guangxi	Xiangbishan	Hsiang-pi-shan
Gan-king	Anhui	Anqing	Anking
Gnan-hwuy		Anhui	Anhwei
Golden Field	Guangxi	Jintian	Chin-t'ien
Han-iam	Hubei	Hanyang	Hanyang
Han-pe		Hubei	Hupei
Hing-kwoh	Jiangxi	Xingguo	Hsing-kuo
Hwa hien	Guangxi	Hua Xian	Huahsien
Hwai-ngan	Jiangsu	Huai'an	Huai-an
I-ting	Jiangsu	Weiting (?)	Wei-t'ing (?)
Jouo-chou	Hunan	Yuezhou	Yochow
Ka-shing-poo	Zhejiang	Jiaxing	Chiashing
Kau-chau-fu	Guangdong	Gaozhou	Kaochow
Keu-heen	Anhui	Jiuxian	Chiu-hsien
Kew-heen			
Ki-ngan	Jiangxi	Ji'an	Chi-an
Kien-tou	Jiangxi	Jiandou (?)	Ch'ien-tou (?)

441

Document Form	Province	Pinyin Form	Wade-Giles or Post Office Form
Kieu-hien	Anhui	Jiuxian	Chiu-hsien
Kiou-kiang	Jiangxi	Jiujiang	Kiukiang
Kiu-kiang			
Koua-tcheou	Jiangsu	Guazhou	Kwachow
Kouang-toung		Guangdong	Kwangtung
Kouei-lin	Guangxi	Guilin	Kweilin
Ku-yung	Jiangsu	Jurong	Chü-jung
Kwang-chow	Hubei	Huangzhou	Hwangchow
Kwun-shan	Jiangsu	Kunshan	K'un-shan
Lie-tchen	Zhili	Lianzhen	Lien-chen
Lo-fau mountains	Guangdon	Luofushan	Lo-fu-shan
Nan-tsin	Zhejiang	Anji (?)	An-chi (?)
Ngan-ching	Anhui	Anqing	Anking
Ngan-kin			
Ngan-king			
Ngan-hoey		Anhui	Anhwei
Ngan-huie			
Ngan-hwei			
Ngan-hwui			
Ngan-hwuy			
Ngan-kouei			
Ng'han-whuie			
Ning-tcheou	Jiangxi	Ningzhou, or Ningdu	Ning-chou Ning-tu
Non-ning	Guangxi	Nanning	Nan-ning
Ou-cham	Hubei	Wuchang	Wuchang
Pe-tche-li		Zhili	Chih-li
Pearl River	Guangdong	Zhu Jiang	Chu Chiang
Po-kwan	Zhejiang	Baiguan	Pai-kuan
Po-quan			
Quin-san	Jiangsu	Kunshan	K'un-shan
Qung-sau			
San-kia-gao	Jiangxi	Shangrao (?)	Shang-jao (?)
Seang	Guangxi	Xiang	Hsiang
Seaou-jin	Guangxi	Xiuren	Hsiu-jen
Si-ka-wei	Jiangsu	Xujiahui	Zikawei
Siam-tan	Hunan	Xiangtan	Hsiang-t'an
Sinchau	Guangxi	Xingiao	Hsin-ch'iao
Siuen-hwa	Fujian	Guihua	Kuei-hua
Su-moon	Zhejiang	Simen (?)	Ssu-men (?)
Su-tchuen		Sichuan	Szechuan
Sze Hwuy	Guangdong	Sihui	Ssu-hui

Document Form	Province	Pinyin Form	Wade-Giles or Post Office Form
Tamtoo	Jiangsu	Dantu	Tan-t'u
Tchao-tcheou	Guangdong	Chaozhou	Ch'ao-chou
Teih-kiang	Anhui	Dijiang	Ti-chiang
Ting-kwoh	Fujian	Tingzhou	T'ing-chou
Tsa-ka-wei	Jiangsu	Xujiahui	Zikawei
Tse-hing	Guangxi	Zijingshan	Tzu-ching-shan
Tsin-chow	Guangxi	Xunzhou	Hsün-chou
Tsiuen-chau	Guangxi	Quanzhou	Chuanchow
Tsuei-ti-tchen	(Taiping name for Beijing)	Zuidi cheng	Tsui-ti ch'eng (i.e. Peking)
Ung-yuen	Guangdong	Wengyuan	Weng-jüan
Vu-sih	Jiangsu	Wuxi	Wusih
Wing-on	Guangxi	Yongan	Yungan
Wong-poo River	Jiangsu	Huangpu	Huangpu
Wu-siuen	Guangxi	Wuxuan	Wuhsüan
Y-tchin	Jiangsu	Zizheng	Icheng
Ya-tcheou	Jiangxi	Raozhou (?)	Jao-chou
Yu-yaou			
Yow-yow	Zhejiang	Yuyao	Yü-yao
Zikawei	Jiangsu	Xujiahui	Hsu-chia-hui

443

Bibliography

Before his death Prescott Clarke had compiled an extensive bibliography, listing approximately one thousand titles, of Western language materials concerning the Taiping Tienkuo and the Christian missions in China between 1800 and 1865. The titles given here are taken from this larger bibliography which it is hoped may be published separately. The selection here is of books, pamphlets and a few journal articles published either during the Taiping period or not long afterwards.

[ALCOCK, R.] 'The Chinese Empire and its Destinies', *Bombay Quarterly Review*, October 1855.

ANON. *The Chinese Revolution, the causes which led to it*, London, 1853.

ANON. *Christianity in China. The History of Christian Missions and of the Present Insurrection*, London, 1853.

ANON. *A History of China to the Present Time, including an account of the rise and progress of the present religious insurrection in that empire*, London, 1854.

ANON. *Memorials of James Henderson, M.D., Medical Missionary to China*, London, 1870.

ANON. *Notice sur monseigneur François-Adrien Rouger, évêque titulaire de Cissame, vicaire apostolique du Kiang-si méridional*, Paris, 1888.

ANON. *Rebellion and Recent Events in China*, 1853.

ANON. *Suppression of the Taiping Rebellion in the Departments around Shanghai*, Shanghai, 1871.

ANON. 'Ein Besuch bei den Tchangmaos, die chinesischen Rebellen', *Das Ausland*, 1861, pp. 83–6, 112–15.

BAULMONT, CAP. 'Le corps franco-chinois et la révolte des T'aiping 1861/5', *Revue Indo-chinoise*, Hanoi, 1907, vol. 1.

BEARDSLEE, L. A. 'Episodes of the Taiping Rebellion', *Harper's Magazine*, August 1899.

BEAUVAIS, M. J. 'Livres Chinois à Angoulême', *T'oung Pao*, vol. 3, May 1892.

BLAKISTON, THOMAS W. *Five Months on the Yangtze, with a narrative of the exploration of its upper waters, and notices of the present rebellion in China*, London, 1862.

BONNEY, CATHERINE V. R. *A Legacy of Historical Gleanings*, Albany, New York, 1875.

BOWRING, LEWIN. *Eastern Experiences*, London, 1871.

BRINE, COMMANDER L., RN, FRGS, *The Taeping Rebellion in China, a narrative of its rise and progress*, London, 1862.

BROULLION, LE P. NICHOLAS. *Mémoire sur l'état actuel de la mission de Kiangnan, 1842–1855. Suivi de lettres relatives à l'insurrection 1851–55*, Paris, 1855.

BRYSON, REV. THOMAS. *A Week in Nanking, the old Metropolis of China*, London, 1872.

The Calcutta Review, 'Recent Events in China', 1854, vol. 22, no. 43.

CALLERY, JOSEPH G.P.M.M. AND YVAN, DR MELCHIOR. *History of the Insurrection in China, with notices of the Christianity, creed, and proclamations of the insurgents*, London, 1853.

Calwer Missionsblatt (Tubingen), 1847, vol. 20.

CLAVELIN, STANISLAS AND CANDLER, WARREN A. 'Un missionaire au milieux des Taipings', *Etudes Religieuses, Historiques et Littéraires*, 1863, 3rd ser., vol. 2, no. 7.

CONROY, MARK. 'Narrative of a Captivity among the Taipings', *Chinese and Japanese Repository*, 1865.

COOKE, GEORGE W. *China: being 'the Times' Special Correspondent from China in the years 1857–1858*, London, 1858.

COURCY, R. DE. 'L'Insurrection chinoise, son origine et ses progrés', *Revue des Deux Mondes*, vol. 34, July 1864.

[CULBERTSON, M. S.] *Essay on the bearing of the publication of the Tai-ping Insurgents on the controversy respecting the proper term for translating the Words Elohim and Theos in the Chinese Version of the Scriptures*, Shanghai, 1853.

CULBERTSON, M. S. *The Religious Condition of the Chinese and Their Claims on the Church: A Sermon*, New York, 1857.

DANICOURT, E.-J. *Vie de Mgr. Danicourt de la Congrégation de la Mission, évêque d'Antiphelles, vicaire apostolique du Tché-kiang et du Kiang-sy (Chine)*, Paris, 1889.

EDKINS, JANE R. *Chinese Scenes and People, with notices of Christian missions. With a narrative of a visit to Nanking by Joseph Edkins, B.A.*, London, 1863.

EDKINS, J. *The Religious Condition of the Chinese; with observations on the prospects of Christian conversion among that people*, London, 1859.

ESCAYRAC DE LAUTURE, LE COMTE PIERRE-H.S.D'. *Considérations sur le passé et l'avenir de la Chine, examen de la rebellion actuelle*, Paris, 1863.

Evangelischer Reichsbote (Missionsblatt des Berliner Hauptvereins für die evangelische Mission in China), vol. 1, 1851.

FERRIÈRE LE VAYER, TH. DE. *Une ambassade française en Chine. Journal de voyage*, Paris, 1854.

FISHBOURNE, CAPT. EDMUND GARDINER. *Impressions of China, and the present revolution; its progress and prospects*, London, 1855.

FISHER, LT COL. ARTHUR A'COURT, CB, RE. *Personal Narrative of Three Years' Service in China*, London, 1863.

FORESTER, GEN. EDWARD. 'Personal Recollections of the Tai-Ping Rebellion', *The Cosmopolitan*, New York, vols. 21–2 (Oct.-Dec. 1896).

FORREST, ROBERT J. 'The Christianity of Hung Tsiu Tsuen, a review of Taiping books', *JNCBRAS*, Dec. 1867, n.s., vol. 4.

FORTUNE, ROBERT. *A Residence among the Chinese from 1853 to 1856. With suggestions on the present war*, London, 1857.

FOSTER, REV. LOVELACE S. *Fifty Years in China*, Nashville, Tenn., 1909.

[G.B.] 'The Last Months of the Taiping War', *Harper's Magazine*, vol. 32, April 1866.

GIQUEL, PROSPER. 'La France en Chine. Le Commerce français dans le Céléste-Empire, les opérations du corps franco-chinois et les missions en 1863', *Revue des Deux Mondes*, vol. 51, June 1864.

GONCHAROV, I. A. *Fregat Pallada*, Moscow, 1957 (1st edn. 1858).

GORDON, CHARLES G. *The Journals of Major-Gen. C. G. Gordon*, London, 1885.

GRIMMER, JAMES. 'Some Personal Recollections of the Taipings', *North China Herald*, 7 Aug. 1891.

HAKE, ALFRED EGMONT. *Events in the Taeping Rebellion. Being a reprint of Mss. copies by General Gordon*, London, 1891.

HAMBERG, THEODORE. *The Chinese Rebel Chief, Hung-Siu-Tsuen, and the origin of the insurrection in China*, London, 1855.

HAMBERG, T. *The Visions of Hung-siu-tshuen and the origin of the Kwang-Si Insurrection*, Hongkong, 1854.

HAUSSMANN, J.-M. AUGUSTE. *La Chine, résumé historique de l'insurrection et des événements qui ont eu lieu dans ce pays, depuis le commencement de la guerre de l'opium jusqu'en 1857*, Paris, 1864.

HÉRISSON, MAURICE-D'I., CONTE D'. *Etudes sur la Chine contemporaine*, Paris, 1866.

IMBAULT-HUART, CAMILLE. 'Le siège et la prise du Sou Tcheou par les imperiaux en 1863' in 'Miscélanées Chinoises', *Journal Asiatique*, April-June 1882.

J., T. M. 'The Taeping Rebellion—Its Rise and Fall', *Hunt's Merchants' Magazine*, 1865.

JOHN, GRIFFITH. *The Chinese Rebellion*, Canton, 1861 (from the *Friend of China*).

JOHN, G. AND EDKINS, JOSEPH. *A Visit to the Insurgent Chief at Soochow*, Shanghai, 1861 (from the *NCH*).

KESSON, JOHN. *The Cross and the Dragon or, the fortunes of Christianity in China with some notices of the Christian missions and missionaries, and some account of the Chinese secret societies*, London, 1854.

LA SERVIÈRE, LE P. JOSEPH DE. *Histoire de la mission du Kiangnan. Jésuites de la province de France* (1840–1899), Zikawei, 1914.

LAVOLLÉE, C.-H. *La Chine contemporaine*, Paris, 1860.

LAY, WALTER THURLOW. *The Autobiography of the Chung Wang*, Shanghai, 1865.

LINDLEY, A. F. *The Taeping as they are, by one of them*, London, 1864.

LIN-LE [LINDLEY, A. F.] *Ti-Ping Tien-Kwoh; The History of the Ti-Ping Revolution, including a narrative of the author's personal adventures*, London, 1866.

LOCKHART, W. *The Yang-tse-keang and the Hwang-ho or Yellow River*, London, 1858.

MACFARLANE, CHARLES. *The Chinese Revolution with details of the habits, manners, and customs of China and the Chinese*, London, 1853.

MACKIE, JOHN MILTON. *Life of Tai-ping-wang, Chief of the Chinese Insurrection*, New York, 1857.

MACLAY, ROBERT S. *Life Among the Chinese*, New York, 1861.

MAROLLES, JULES DE. 'Souvenirs de la revolte des T'ai P'ing 1862–1863', *T'oung Pao*, ser. 2, vols. 3, 4 (Oct. 1902; March 1903).

MARTIN, WILLIAM A. P. *A Cycle of Cathay; or China, South and North. With personal reminiscences*, New York, 1896.

MATHESON, DONALD. *Narrative of the Mission to China of the English Presbyterian Church. With remarks on the social life and religious ideas of the Chinese by J. MacGowan and notes on climate, health, and outfit by J. Carnegie*, London, 1866.

MAYERS, W. F. 'Col. Gordon's Exploits in China', *Cornhill Magazine*, vol. 10, November 1864.

MEADOWS, THOMAS T. *The Chinese and their Rebellions, viewed in connection with their national philosopy, ethics, legislation, and administration to which is added an essay on civilization and its present state in east and west*, London, 1856.

MEDHURST, WALTER H., DD. *Books of the Tae-Ping-Wang Dynasty. Pamphlets issued by the Chinese insurgents at Nanking; to which is added a history of the Kwang-se rebellion; concluding with a critical review of the above pamphlets*, Shanghae, 1853 (from the *NCH*).

MERCIER, R. P. VICTOR. *Campagne du 'Cassini' dans les mers de Chine 1851–1854, d'après les rapports, lettres et notes de Commandant de Plas*, Paris, 1889.

MERCIER, V. *Marin et jésuite: vie et voyage de François de Plas ancien capitaine de vaisseau, prêtre de la Compagnie de Jésus, 1809–1888*, Paris, 1890.

MILNE, W. C. *Political Disturbances in China*, London, 1855 (also in *Edinburgh Review*, October 1855).

MOULE, A. E. 'Ningpo under the Tai-p'ings', *The East of Asia Magazine*, Mar.-June 1906.

MOULE, A. E. *Personal Recollections of the T'aiping Rebellion 1861–1863*, Shanghai, 1884.

NEUMANN, KARL F. *Ostasiatische Geshichte vom ersten chinesischen Krieg bis zu den Vertragen in Peking (1840–1860)*, Leipzig, 1861.

NEWMARK, J. (ed.) *Die Revolution in China in ihrer Enstehung, ihrer politischen und religiösen Bedeutung und ihrem bisherigen Verlauf, nebst Darstellung des auf christicher Grundlage beruhenden Religionssystems der Insurgenten.* n.d.

NEVIUS, HELEN S. COAN. *The Life of John Livingston Nevius, for forty years a missionary in China*, New York, 1895.

NEVIUS, REV. JOHN L. *China and the Chinese: a general description of the country and its inhabitants; its civilization and form of government; its religious and social institutions; and its present condition and prospects*, Philadelphia, 1882; 1st edn. New York, 1869.

NYE, G. (JR) *The Rationale of the China Question: Comprising an inquiry into the repressive policy of the Imperial Government with considerations of the three Treaty Powers England, France, and America, in regard to it: and a glance at the origins of the First and Second Wars with China, with incidental notices of the rebellion, by 'An American'*, Macao, 1857.

OLIPHANT, LAURENCE. *Narrative of the Earl of Elgin's Mission to China and Japan in the years 1857, '58, '59*, Edinburgh, 1859.

OLIPHANT, L. 'The Taiping Rebellion in China', *Good Words*, vol. 4, 1863.

OPPENHEIM, H.-B. 'La Chine contemporaine', *Revue de Paris*, vol. 6, July 1857.

OSBORN, S. *The Past and Future of British Relations with China*, London, 1860.

RAU, OSCAR. 'Une visite au T'ae-p'ing, ou révoltes chinoises. Souvenirs de la vie missionaire', *La Famille, Journal pour Tous*, Lausanne, 1868.

RENARD, LEON. 'L'insurrection chinoise: Les Tai-pings', *Le Correspondant*, n.s., vol. 23, June 1863.

RENNIE, D. F. *Peking and the Pekingese. During the first years of the British embassy at Peking*, London, 1865.

RICHTOFEN, BARON FERDINAND VON. *Baron Richtofen's Letters, 1870–1872*, Shanghai, 1903.

ROBERTS, ISSACHAR J. 'Tae Ping Wang', *Putnam's Monthly*, vol. 8, Oct. 1856.

RULE, WILLIAM H. *The Religious Aspect of the Civil War in China*, London, 1853.

SCARTH, JOHN. *British Policy in China. Is our war with the Tartars or the Chinese?* London, 1860.

SCARTH, J. *Twelve Years in China. The people, the rebels, and the mandarins. By a British resident*, Edinburgh, 1860.

SICA, R. P. LOUIS-MARIE. *Une famille napolitaine, notice historique sur les cinqs frères Massa, de la Compagnie de Jesus, missionaires en Chine, et leur famille*, Paris, 1892.

SMITH, G. *Religious Movement in China, a letter to the Archbishop of Canterbury dated Hongkong May 23, 1853*, London, 1854.

[SPRATT, LT] *The Chinese Revolution: the causes which led to it, its rapid progress, and anticipated result; with abstracts of all the known publications emanating from the insurgents* (H. Vizetelly), London, 1853.

SYKES, COL. WILLIAM H., FRS, MP. *The Taeping Rebellion in China, Its origin, progress, and present condition in a series of letters addressed to the 'Aberdeen Free Press' and the London 'Daily News'*, 1857.

TAYLOR, CHARLES, MD *Five Years in China with some account of the Great Rebellion*, Nashville, Tenn., 1860.

THE-RULE, ARMAND. *Les Tai-pings*, Rouen, 1869.

VARANNES, A. DES. 'La Chine depuis le traité de Peking. Les Anglo-français, les Impériaux, et les Tai-pings', *Revue des Deux Mondes*, 1863.

WILSON, A. *The 'Ever-Victorious Army'. A History of the Chinese campaign under Lt. Col. C. G. Gordon, C.B., R.E., and the suppression of the Tai-ping Rebellion*, Edinburgh, 1868.

WOLSELEY, LT COL. GARNET J. *Narrative of the War with China in 1860. To which is added the account of a short residence with the Tai-Ping rebels at Nanking and a voyage from thence to Hankow*, London, 1862.

WYLIE, ALEX. *Memorials of Protestant Missionaries to the Chinese*, Shanghai, 1867.

YATES, MATTHEW T., *The T'ai-ping Rebellion*, Shanghai, 1876.

Index

Subject Index

Personal and Place Name Index

(With a few exceptions only personalities and places referred to fairly frequently are listed, plus most authors.)

Prescott Clarke was a graduate of Harvard and of London Universities. His M.A. thesis, done at the London School of Oriental and African Studies (SOAS), was a study of English language newspapers on the China coast. He became deeply interested in the Taiping movement, especially in its connections with Western missionaries, and completed an extensive bibliography of Western works dealing with it. He came to Australia in 1967 to teach Chinese history at Monash University in Melbourne, where he died in March 1980. He visited China several times, the last being in May–June 1979, when he presented a paper at the Nanjing conference on the Taiping.

J. S. Gregory is a graduate of Melbourne and London Universities. After completing his Ph.D. at SOAS in 1957 he taught for ten years at Melbourne University, before moving to La Trobe University, where he is now a professor. His study of British policy and attitudes towards the Taiping was published in 1969. He has also worked on Church–State relations in Australia, and has recently completed a short biography of Chiang Kai-shek to be published by the University of Queensland Press.

Text photocomposed in 10 point Media, 11 point leaded and printed on 85 gsm Semi Matt Coated at Griffin Press Limited, Netley, South Australia.